SINCERITY
AND OTHER WORKS

SINCERITY
AND OTHER WORKS

Collected Papers of
Donald Meltzer

edited by

Alberto Hahn

Routledge
Taylor & Francis Group
LONDON AND NEW YORK

First published 1994 by Karnac Books Ltd.

2 Park Square, Milton Park, Abingdon, Oxfordshire OX14 4RN
52 Vanderbilt Avenue, New York, NY 10017

Routledge is an imprint of the Taylor & Francis Group, an informa business

First issued in hardback 2019

British Library Cataloguing in Publication Data

Meltzer, Donald
Sincerity and Other Works: Collected
Papers of Donald Meltzer
I. Title II. Hahn, Alberto
150

ISBN: 978-1-85575-084-5 (pbk)
ISBN: 978-0-367-32695-1 (hbk)

ACKNOWLEDGEMENTS

Permission to reprint or translate the following chapters is gratefully acknowledged:

Chapter 1, from: *Psychiatry: Journal for the Study of Interpersonal Processes, 18* (February, 1955), No. 1. Copyright 1955 by The William Alanson White Psychiatric Foundation, Inc.

Chapters 2, 6, 7, 8, 11, 21 first published in Italian in: *La comprensione della bellezza* (Loescher Editore).

Chapter 4, from: *International Journal of Psycho-Analysis, 44* (1963), Part 1: 83–96.

Chapter 5, from: *International Journal of Psycho-Analysis, 45* (1964): 246–250.

Chapter 9, first published in French in: *Revue Française de Psychanalyse, 34* (1970).

Chapter 10, from: *Journal of Child Psychotherapy, 11* (3) (1969): pp. 57–61.

Chapter 14, from: *Contemporary Psychoanalysis, 14* (2) (1978): 210–225.

Chapter 16, from: *Contemporary Psychoanalysis, 10* (3) (1974).

Chapter 18, from: *Contemporary Psychoanalysis, 11* (3) (1975): 289–310.

Chapter 19, from: *Contemporary Psychoanalysis, 11* (2) (1975).

Chapter 20, from: *Schizophrenia 75* (Jarl Jorstad & Endre Ugelstad, Eds.). Scandinavian University Press.

Chapter 26, from: *Contemporary Psychoanalysis, 17* (2) (1981): 232–238.

Chapter 27, from: *International Journal of Psycho-Analysis, 62* (1981): 243–249. © Mauro Mancia and Donald Meltzer.

Chapter 31, first published in French in: *Journal de la Psychanalyse de l'Enfant* (1988).

CONTENTS

EDITOR'S INTRODUCTION

Most of the papers included in this volume were produced in the last 35 years and have appeared in various journals of psychoanalysis in this country and abroad. Others are published here for the first time.

The range of themes and the breadth of interest in Donald Meltzer's work will no doubt give the reader a good idea of the stature of his pioneering contribution to the Kleinian psychoanalytic development. The author's acute observational skills, subtle sensitivity, clinical discipline, fertile imagination, erudition, and honesty are brought together in the depth and freshness of his ideas as reflected in the quality of his outstanding writings. This places him among the thinkers in this country who have done the most to push forward the boundaries of psychoanalytic thinking. Among the subjects this volume touches on are adult psychopathology (narcissism, borderline states, obsessional neurosis, psychosis), psychoanalytic technique, developmental theory, the training of psychoanalysts, child and adolescent psychopathology, and the appraisal and application of the work of W. Bion and of R. Money-Kyrle. The editor's task was not made easy by having to select a limited number of papers from the author's massive output—the wealth of material that remains warrants the production of further volumes of collected papers. The difficulty in selection comes from not wanting to leave out papers that provide the basis for understanding the evolution of the author's thinking—and every paper seems to do so. This difficulty is offset by being able to re-read these papers, and in particular the work on Sincerity—a book in itself—and to discover how new readings yield new clinical and theoretical insights. It is a characteristic of Dr Meltzer's work—as that of Dr Bion's—that further readings bring out new shades of meaning that enrich in depth and texture the understanding gained in previous readings.

The papers in this volume will be accessible to most readers; it will be a good introduction to Dr Meltzer's work and will provide the guidelines for approaching other publications. His books—*The Psycho-analytical Process* (1967), *Sexual States of Mind* (1973), *Explorations in Autism* (1975), *The Kleinian Development* (1978), *Dream Life* (1984), *Studies in Extended Metapsychology* (1986), *The Apprehension of Beauty* (1988) (with Meg Harris Williams), and *The Claustrum* (1992)—develop many ideas that appear in these papers and are the inspiring source of others. But it is those readers with clinical psychoanalytic experience and a working acquaintance with Dr Meltzer's neo-Kleinian contributions who will enjoy this book the most.

SINCERITY
AND OTHER WORKS

Author's Preface

As I used to run through the teeming corridors of Blackwell's to deliver books to the philosophy and psychology section, I was often reminded of Leonard Wolf, at the celebration of the completion of the *Standard Edition* of Freud's works, talking about the Greek who stood on his head on the table at his marriage feast. "Hippolites, you are making a fool of yourself!" the King said, to which he replied, "Hippolites doesn't care." As I looked about this great book shop, I didn't care. To write without being a writer is a foolish thing, but a lover must express himself.

These papers are a record of vanity, certainly, but its evacuation is a necessity of development. Every book and paper is a record of impact, by persons, books, paintings, the crowd in the underground, the majesty of the landscape. A person without artistic talent and training, particularly without music, must do something to unburden himself. Writing is the last resort of the incapable. So long as it is not hopelessly agrammatical, poorly punctuated, or misspelt, it will pass for writing. What, then, can be its claim to interest, that an editor should collect it and a publisher spend his money and time on it?

To call these papers an evacuation is not to call them rubbish. The book shops are not filled with rubbish, any more than the galleries. That they will be forgotten is beyond a doubt, but that they are part of a cultural process, an industry, is equally true, as our bread is made of grains of wheat and the beach of grains of sand. Culture is formed of individual lives, and there operates over all a law of the conservation of experience, a cycle, a life-cycle.

These papers, embarrassing as they may be, testify. They testify to the life-experiences and the modes of thought that have enabled a relatively sane development in a relatively mad world. They are a tribute to the efficacy of a system of thought that starts with "constant conjunction", finds expression in symbols, and produces dreams. The dreams of individuals, if they are at all autonomous rather than received in their symbolism, cannot be identical but only congruent, cannot be communicated but only suggested, cannot be uniform but only having a family resemblance. If all the members of this family represented here look alike, like a Gainsborough family, it is to be attributed not to genetics but to the mysteries of the individual mentality and character, which is, after all, the sum of individual history painted on the background of the history of the species. And every grain of sand counts.

Donald Meltzer

CHAPTER ONE

Towards a structural concept of anxiety

(1955)

The author formulates here the existence of an anxiety apparatus whose functioning is a part of the ego and the personality structure and illustrates how in attacking this apparatus the ego is attacking itself. An example is given of the workings of the death instinct, and a differentiation is made between the ego's defence mechanisms and other pathological character devices.

The concept of anxiety has long held a central position in the psychoanalytic theory of personality functioning and disorders. And yet, much as it is talked of and written about, there is no consensus about it, and it is variously considered an affect, an ego state, transformed id energy, or a

Since this paper is a restatement and re-synthesis of existing concepts in psychoanalysis, I would like to identify my sources of background theory: (1) An over-all view of the central nervous system as a servo-mechanism has been utilized (see Wiener, 1948). (2) Dualistic dynamism. This vagueness and fluidity of concept seems to have an adverse effect on communication among workers in the field. This paper represents an experiment in thinking about anxiety as a structural entity and attempts to follow up the implications of such a point of view. First I shall try to outline a broad concept of a way of life to which anxiety is essential, viewing it as an apparatus available to the ego. A structural concept of anxiety will be offered, and the functioning of this so-called anxiety apparatus, with its two-fold implication for the ego, will be examined. Next, two sources will be defined, followed by a discussion of their relative importance for psychic health and disease. This finally will lead to a discussion of the mechanisms of defence and an attempt to distinguish them from various character processes.

Anxiety viewed as an apparatus available to the ego

For the purpose of exposition here, one might consider the term ego as a rather broad one—a term referring to all central nervous system processes that regulate the interaction be-

---

Instinct theory has been used, as formulated by Freud (1920g, 1933a). (3) The concept of unconscious and conscious phantasy, which I have referred to in the paper, has been most beautifully elaborated by Susan Isaacs (1952). (4) The important function of the unconscious body image has been described in terms of Paul Schilder's (1950) formulation. (5) Perceptual processes are considered in the constructive sense of Paul Schilder's (1942) theories. (6) The theory of personality development used in this paper follows that developed by Erik H. Erikson (1950), with emphasis on the concepts of infantile life described by Melanie Klein (1932a, 1948). (7) The relationship of the ego to the forces arising from inside and outside the organism has been conceptualized from the point of view of field theory (see Lewin, 1935), and the transactional concepts of Harry Stack Sullivan (1953). (8) The concept of anxiety used in this paper is, I believe, that of Freud (1933a) and later amplified, with emphasis on prospective phantasy, by Sullivan (1953, 1963).

tween organism and environment. For example, even the nerve net of a jellyfish can be said to perform ego functions in that the nerve net deals with problems of disturbed homeostasis by commencing, at the moment of threshold stimulation, a process of hunting through its meagre bag of adaptive tricks until the stimulation ceases; after that, total relaxation may be permitted again until further stimulation.

Although such a simple organism needs no insight into causality and no awareness of time and sequence, the possible patterns of adaptive behaviour in more complex animals are so abundant that hunting through the bag of tricks at the time of stimulation becomes hopelessly uneconomical. Consequently a very different way of life has been developed in more complex animals, which operates by processes of vigilance for minimal stimulation, followed by prediction and planning for the re-establishment of homeostasis. To accomplish this, an awareness of time continuum must be maintained in the organism, so that sequence of events may be noted and theories of causality derived.

In the ego operations that accomplish this way of life, the segmentation of time into past, present, and future finds representation as memory, perception, and prospective phantasy (prediction). The functional design of what I call the anxiety apparatus stands in intimate relation to those ego-processes that elaborate prospective phantasies. These phantasies are apparently created by bringing the continuously constructed percepts into association with memories of past events. The anxiety apparatus is viewed as carrying the predictions forward in time, awaiting the moment when it can test their validity against the percepts of the ego, which it constantly monitors. The degree of matching between prediction and subsequent percept is then signalled to the ego, which reacts with certain phantasies and affects.

In this paper, I shall speak of the apparatus as separate from the ego—a tool rather than a part—in order to stress that the functioning of the anxiety apparatus is quite mechanical and is free from involvement in the conflicts that confront the ego. Thus, the apparatus merely collects and transmits data of a specific sort which the ego may use or abuse as it sees fit.

The two-fold origins of anxiety

But such a broad description of ego functioning is not particularly useful to clinical thinking. It may be true that each prediction–validation cycle involves potential anxiety, but clinical interest must be focused on particular events of real economic importance to the ego. Since the making of predictions must depend on knowledge of both external and internal realities, the question arises as to whether faulty predictions that result from misunderstanding of external realities produce anxieties with different clinical implications from those arising from the misunderstanding of internal realities. And a question also arises as to when the anxiety apparatus begins to function. To answer both of these questions, it is necessary to examine the psychoanalytic view of infantile psychic life in respect to this concept of an anxiety apparatus.

Psychoanalytic investigators have long assumed that the capacity for anxiety is innate in the mental apparatus. Much ado has been made over the assumption that birth produces extreme anxiety, a prototype for all later anxieties. Observers of infant behaviour have interpreted many infantile reactions as indicative of anxiety. The concept presented here of an anxiety apparatus cannot be reconciled with such a view. And in fact it is likely, in my estimation, that the infant knows nothing but vague organ distress and organ-tension relief prior to the time that his perceptual capacities mature and allow the beginning delimitation of body-boundaries; without being able to distinguish body from external object, the infant cannot, I believe, experience yearning-towards or frustration-by, but only distress.

Probably toward the end of the first month of life the distinguishing of fragmentary external objects by the infant has become consistent enough to allow their cathexis as objects of libido and aggression. The infant will only then be in a position to experience the rhythmical interplay of his tensions and the appearing–disappearing objects from which the ego-awareness of sequence develops. Without this rudiment of time-awareness, I would assume that the anxiety apparatus is not functioning.

How then does one account for the many instances of neonatal behaviour in which being comforted by the voice of the nearby mother, for example, seems to suggest that some interpersonal process is relieving anxiety? It is my opinion that these are instances of hallucinatory gratification, in which minimal cues have touched off plastic phantasies and have temporarily diminished the excitation in the ego or even caused some organ relaxation.

If one proceeds then with the concept that prospective phantasies cannot be elaborated until objects are discerned as external to the body limits, one is in a position to investigate the infant's psychic life in a way that may clarify the distinction between anxiety from the two different sources. Some realization has begun to form in the infant of about one month of age to the effect that his tensions are relieved only by making and breaking relationships with certain objects. The earliest objects, and the prototype for all later objects, are the breast and the faeces. Making contact and interacting with the breast relieves many tensions, especially those of the upper gastro-intestinal tract. Disrupting contact with the faecal mass relieves many muscular and lower gastro-intestinal tensions.

The experiences with these two objects and the impulses to make and disrupt relationships with them helps the ego to form its first primordial distinction between libido and aggression (*destrudo*). This duality of instinct in its earliest form has no implication of good and bad, life and death, love and hate. Only later does this simple duality become contaminated, when the impulses have begun to look dangerous as viewed through the lenses of megalomania and the still weak ego is trying to control them. When the valences of good and bad do appear, they are at first attached only to objects. Any object that serves the ego in relieving tensions is experienced as good, and only when it is expected to serve and fails to do so does it become bad.

In the earliest object-relation phantasies, the breast and faeces are not seen as the cause of tension but only as the implement of their relief. But at moments of painful yearning or intense frustration, when breast will not appear or faeces will not leave, the instincts become intensified to the point of greed and sadism, and the bad object is blamed for the distress. When the objects are not performing in the expected way—that is, when they have become bad and persecuting—the infant is unable to form a prospective phantasy of relief. Therefore the current percept which includes the distressed organ extends itself as prospective phantasy to eternity.

Thus I have defined the first form of anxiety, object (or objective) anxiety, and found that in severe form it carries the implication of a persecutory origin. It is apparent that this earliest of anxieties produces phantasy in the ego far more germane to hell than to death.

What of the second form of anxiety, that arising from the ego's difficulty in predicting and controlling the internal world of organ tensions and their psychic representation (id)? Do valences of good and bad become involved here too? To answer this, one must look at the infant of approximately four months of age. At this point, objects have begun to be discriminated in less fragmentary fashion. The good mother begins to become a fused object, taking on meanings originally attributed to breast and faeces. The good mother brings relief and takes away distress. In other words, there is nascent the capacity for a single ambivalent object, the object of both libido and aggression.

Yet the fusion probably does not usually proceed as smoothly as this suggests, because of certain other processes that have gone on earlier in the infant's efforts to deal with the persecutory anxieties. I am referring to the processes of internalization (introjection) and externalization (projection) of objects in relation to the body image. The earlier use of these mental processes had unfortunately placed the infant in a position to formulate a new theory of the origin of his current deprivations and frustrations. That is, he may "say" to himself, in effect: "If I had not gobbled up all of mother in my greed (or destroyed her in my sadism), she would still be available to feed me (or relieve my pain)."

Thus the intensified forms of libido and aggression (*destrudo*) take on the valence of bad, and the ego's feeling of weakness toward them threatens to make the future uncertain as far as the relief of tensions is concerned. This, then, is the source and configuration of instinctual anxieties, which in their earliest form are most accurately called depressive anxieties. Since the development of the capacity to recognize the fused object must be quite gradual, one can well imagine that the frequency and intensity of persecutory and depressive anxieties will have an important bearing on the attainment of this synthesis. To attribute the existence of non-fused objects to a mechanism of "splitting" seems to me to be putting the cart before the horse. What is involved is a hindrance of maturation rather than any specific defence against anxiety.

These two forms of anxiety, persecutory and depressive, are the primitive forms and the prototypes for later objective and instinctual anxieties. The distinction between the primitive and mature forms is founded on the degree of reality underlying them, which in turn is based on the degree of megalomania within the ego and the extent to which processes of introjection and projection underlie the perceptual organization of the life-space.

The two-fold orientation of the ego towards the anxiety apparatus

I have already outlined the broad perspective of ego functioning which emphasizes a way of life in which adaptation is regulated by planning within a time continuum. I have pictured an anxiety apparatus as a specific tool of the ego, available for testing the validity of predictions and therefore the efficacy of plans. In so doing, I have placed anxiety in a nuclear position with respect to learning, and thus with respect to ego maturation.

I am assuming that this anxiety apparatus is quite free of involvement in the conflicts of the ego and that—with the possible exception of instances of brain damage—its performance of its task is faultless. This implies that one must turn to an examination of ego-processes to understand defects in learning and distortions in personality maturation. The fault must lie in the ego's way of using its tool, not in the tool itself. This is not to deny that the signalling by this apparatus of a faulty prediction is unpleasant. As I have said, when a prediction that is of importance with regard to plans for relief of tension fails, the phantasy that results is of the current tension extended in time. The content of this phantasy will extend to eternity until a new prediction is formulated. These anxiety phantasies are accompanied in the ego by affects of varying shades and intensities, depending on the problem being dealt with and its background. They range from uncertainty to terror, and shade through guilt, shame, remorse, and despair under certain circumstances. Conversely, one can envision the signal of a successful prediction as exciting phantasies of eternal gratification, accompanied by affects ranging from pleasure to elation.

One further question may be useful to deal with before passing on. When I speak of the ego's experiencing anxiety in terms of certain phantasies and accompanying affects, does this mean that these frighten the ego? My interpretation of psychic phenomena would suggest a negative answer. The ego, when unable to formulate a new adaptive plan or to defend against the anxiety, experiences a perpetuation of its distress and a feeling of helplessness about ever recapturing a comfortable equilibrium. Anxiety phantasies and affects express this position in plastic fashion; they do not cause it. In other words, an ego that cannot work out a comfortable solution *is* weak in that area of life-space, and the configuration of its anxiety-phantasy is *a result* of the poor organization in the ego—and therefore a reliable indicator of ego organization, as the clinician knows. Perhaps this is a fundamental implication of the term *psychic reality*, that the ego *really is* only as strong as it behaves, since it can deal only with the life-space that it constructs in its own perceptual activities.

Thus in the physiological state, when the ego is making appropriate use of the anxiety apparatus, a certain degree of tolerance to distress is required. Moments of unpleasant signalling, and the phantasies and affects excited, will continue until a new prediction and plan to relieve the tensions are formulated. But there are times when the ego finds itself unable to do this. It cannot reorganize its perceptual field, or it cannot associate to more pertinent memories; fatigue may lower its tolerance to the signalling, or noxious agents may disorganize its processes. At any event, there are moments when the ego fails at the crucial issue of adaptation and turns against the anxiety apparatus as if its signalling were the cause, rather than merely the result, of the ego's dilemma.

Later I shall examine the techniques, or mechanisms of defence, by which the ego sabotages the anxiety apparatus. At this point, before going on to examine the role of anxiety in character formation and character pathology, I wish to distinguish between warding off anxiety and shutting it off. Operations of the ego that terminate an anxiety reaction, once it has started, are best thought of as involving some technique of shutting off the apparatus. One might call them expedients of the ego, and, as I shall explain shortly, they play an important part in healthy as well as disordered functioning.

But the warding off of anxiety is quite another matter. Here the ego, for reasons that I shall not examine in this paper, adopts a policy never again to experience some specific anxiety phantasy and its affect. This is quite a serious determination, for such a policy implies the abandonment of maturation within the life-space compartment involved. The result is a functional disease.

Anxiety as related to character formation and character pathology

As I have indicated, the anxiety apparatus is a vital tool in the hands of the ego for the achievement of learning and the accomplishment of maturation. The apparatus is principally used for predictive validation of tentative hypotheses concerning the origins of deprivations and frustrations. The ego's task in maturation is to develop an accurate knowledge of both the internal and external worlds over whose interaction it must preside. From such knowledge it must crystallize the broad strategy and finer tactics through which this interaction may be regulated. In the accomplishment of this monumental task, the ego goes through a sequence of developmental stages. In each of these stages the ego characteristically prefers a given theory of the origin of its difficulties; in each stage there is a body zone of most intense interpersonal involvement; and in each stage there are favourite interactional stratagems, or modes. These three form the superstructure of character at each stage, filled out by character tactics of varying colour, texture, and rigidity.

But the various elements of this structure that are unsuccessful or are noxious to others have come to be called *character symptoms* and are customarily regarded as being derived or preserved because they serve some function of defence against anxiety. They are labelled pathological largely because of this assumption. Is this in harmony with the concept of an anxiety apparatus as formulated here?

In order to answer this, one must ask the more specific question: do these character facets derive from ego operations in which the physiological orientation towards the anxiety apparatus has been sacrificed? If one examines more closely the processes of prediction and validation, one will find that certain errors in judgement can easily be made by the ego. For instance, the validity of a prediction may be taken as proof of the effectiveness of the strategic plan that was involved. Or again it may be taken as proof of the accuracy of the underlying causal theory. If all the objects in the life-space behaved with scrupulous respect for reality, these conclusions might be correct. But this is not the case.

So one might conclude that somebody somewhere is defending against anxiety. But this was not the question. The character facets are derived from repetitive transactional experiences in which there has been success at adaptation, meaning that defence against anxiety has not been a primary factor. But what of the people who find it necessary to constrict their life processes to a relatively meagre set of interactional patterns with highly selected objects? Has not this constriction been necessitated by a determination to ward off anxiety?

This can best be answered by again going back to the concepts of infantile psychic life. Young children clothe their parents in omnipotence and mistake their parental responsiveness for obedience to the child's will. This delusion of mastery of the parents forms an important part of the infant megalomania which must be tediously and painfully replaced by a feeling of self-mastery during the maturation process. Parental behaviour that continues to dramatize for the child his infantile desire to control the grown-ups will serve to perpetuate this megalomania.

The so-called defence of ego-restriction is really not a defensive operation at all, but an inevitable part of character immaturity. I shall touch again on this problem of differentiation between character and symptom when I discuss rituals and repetition compulsion.

Anxiety as related to functional disease and symptom formation

As already indicated, the ego is not always able to sustain the position of tolerating anxiety signals for the sake of their valuable information. Occasionally, out of confusion or a feeling of helplessness, it turns against the anxiety apparatus as if it were really the source of the ego's trouble. The various devices used by the ego for shutting off or warding off anxiety are called the mechanisms of defence, and the alterations in personality functioning that result from their use are called diseases and symptoms, depending on certain dynamic factors.

But before investigating these factors, it may be useful to clarify the mental processes that I envision as making up the cooperation between ego and anxiety apparatus. If one thinks of these two structures related as in a wiring diagram, a feedback mechanism, the ego may be said to feed its predictions to the apparatus at an Instant A. The anxiety apparatus will carry this prediction through a period of Intervening Time, as it monitors the continual perceptual processes of the ego, awaiting the arrival of the Instant B whose configuration has been predicted. It will then test the validity of the prediction and signal its findings to the ego.

These two psychological instants, together with the intervening ones that are germane, will compose a complete psychological event—one prediction-validation cycle. The amount of actual chronological time involved will, of course, vary from seconds to decades. In the hope of finding some reasonable basis for classifying defence mechanisms, I shall try to outline in crude form the sequence of mental operations that I envision.

Instant A

Ego (1) constructs current percept of the life-space (internal world ↔ body image ↔ external world);

(2) associates (1) with memories of related configuration;

(3) formulates prospective phantasy or prediction (with necessary adaptive plan) of Instant B.

Anxiety apparatus picks up (3).

INTERVENING TIME

Ego carries out adaptive plan from (3) which is aimed at bringing about the predicted configuration.

Anxiety apparatus monitors the continual perceptual processes of ego, awaiting arrival of Instant B.

INSTANT B

Anxiety apparatus signals arrival of Instant B and validity of the prediction.

Ego (1) recalls life-space percept of Instant A, the prediction, and the adaptive plan;

(2) recalls relevant aspects of Intervening Time;

(3) reconstructs percept of Instant B with focus and emphasis germane to the prediction.

I have indicated my assumption that the ego, if it chooses to sabotage the anxiety apparatus, must do so by some omission or distortion of its own functions. I suggest that objective anxieties are largely dealt with by expedients that result in temporary (if ever so often repeated) alterations in personality functioning called psychogenic symptoms. On the other hand, occasionally instinctual anxieties (and rarely severe objective anxieties) are so catastrophic that the ego adopts a policy of determination never again to experience them. These policies result in the alterations in personality structure that are called functional disease. In the following section, I shall investigate the mechanisms underlying these two outcomes, naming them, respectively, *symptomatic mechanisms* and *disease manoeuvres.* By adherence to my classification of psychic events, a subdivision of each will be derived.

Disease manoeuvres

At this point I shall begin to investigate the relationship, which is important for clinical psychiatry, between anxiety and functional disease. I have already indicated that the basic dynamic originates in an ego policy never again to experience some specific anxiety, usually an instinctual one. The problem now is to understand the ego techniques for carrying out this policy and the clinical manifestations that result.

I should like to consider for a moment the position of an ego that has invoked such a policy. In order to avoid being surprised by similar experiences, it must sabotage the pertinent cycles at their very inception, some time during Instant A. In my outline of the ego operations of this instant, I indicated three processes, all essential to setting a prediction cycle in motion. By omitting or distorting any one of them, the ego can break the awareness of time continuum and depart from a planned way of life—that is, it can depart from it within the specific compartment of the life-space that embraces a certain relationship and the id constellation involved.

A relationship to the basic classification of functional disease is suggested as follows: (1) distortion of the current life-space percept by a *psychotic manoeuvre;* (2) distortion of the processes of association with past events by a *psychoneurotic manoeuvre;* (3) distortion of the processes of prospective phantasy by a *psychopathic manoeuvre.* By each of these three manoeuvres the way of life that permits maturation has been sacrificed within a life-space area, be it large or small in the total economy. The primary cost of each to the ego is the same, although the environment may react in ways that provide secondary gains or penalties.

Of course, this organization of disease provides very little information about the dynamics of the manoeuvres themselves. Nor is it within the scope of this paper to go very far in investigating them. But for the sake of clarifying my meaning in the above classification, I might mention some of my suspicions about the ways in which the disease manoeuvres work.

The psychotic manoeuvre. I suspect that this defence against anxiety involves a severe contamination of the perceptual processes by psychotic transference phenomena, in which archaic internalized objects are externalized and juxtaposed with a correspondingly archaic body image.

The psychoneurotic manoeuvre. The production of amnesias is, of course, due to the working of repression, which I feel is initiated by omission of organs of conflict from the unconscious body image. By so doing, the ego in effect screens out associations, including memories, in whose configuration the conflictual organ holds a central position.

The psychopathic manoeuvre. My formulation of this technique of defence indicates that the basic device is making object relations within the particular life-space area *futureless*. This is perhaps accomplished by intensifying the narcissistic cathexes of body parts at the expense of object cathexis. By so doing, the ego is left free to change objects frequently, thus avoiding reaction from other people to its exploitative and corrupt character tactics, as well as retaliation from others. Again I must mention that these formulations are put forth hesitantly, and only for the purpose of clarifying my classification of defence mechanisms and the processes by which the disruption of time-continuum awareness can be accomplished.

Symptomatic mechanisms

The next problem that arises relates to the mental mechanisms by which the signalling of the anxiety apparatus may be shut off. I have called these symptomatic mechanisms. My chief reason for thus naming them stems from the analogy to the place of somatic symptoms in the economy of the body. Training in medicine teaches one to distinguish between disease and symptom; yet this fundamental concept has not been consistently applied in psychiatry. No better testimony to this fact can be found than that offered by the mixed nomenclature of psychiatry: obsessive–compulsive psychoneurosis, paranoid schizophrenia, conversion hysteria, and so on.

The distinction between disease and symptom is too real and too useful to be lost sight of. In medicine, disease means substantial alteration in function or structure of tissues or organs, while symptoms are merely manifestations of those organismal processes that are aimed at stabilizing some imbalance of the body economy. The same differentiation applies in psychiatry, which I have expressed in terms of the distinction between ego expedients and ego policies. Just as well-stabilized somatic disease is symptomatically silent (for instance, a well walled-off abscess), so a "successful" psychic disease is silent. Its existence is really suspected by lacunae in the life functioning, being analogous, for instance, to sterility due to a fibroid. It is only at times of flux in the disease process that the symptoms erupt, regardless of the nature of the flux. Whether the flux represents progression or resolution of the disease, it may produce identical symptoms.

And again, analogous to somatic symptoms, psychic ones are not found exclusively in relation to underlying disease by any means. Just as the impinging on the body of any object that cannot be integrated into the body's economy will be dealt with by symptom-provoking processes of extrusion or containment, so will circumstances that cannot be dealt with in an integrated way be handled by the ego with symptomatic mechanisms. This amounts to assigning to symptomatic mechanisms the task of regulating anxiety, a service essential to the preservation of the broad cooperation between ego and anxiety apparatus. It should be mentioned that I do not intend to include under psychogenic symptoms the so-called psychosomatic disturbances. Their eruption seems to be derived from an absence of ego efforts to deal with tensions until their accumulated excitation spills over into vegetative pathways.

What then are the symptomatic mechanisms of the ego and how do they work? As was done in the case of disease manoeuvres, an attempt will be made to present these devices in relation to my organization of Instant B, in the hope of evolving a reasonable classification. Instant B, as previously outlined, is envisioned as embracing three essential ego-processes, all of which are necessary for consummation of the act of accepting the anxiety: (1) recall of Instant A; (2) recall of the relevant aspects of Intervening Time; and (3) reconstruction of the percept of Instant B with focus pertinent to the prediction.

I assume that the ego may shut off the apparatus by certain distortions of these three processes. Distortion of Process (1) constitutes the defence of *denial*, in my opinion. That is, the ego retrospectively denies that a prediction was made, or that it was of any economic importance. Distortion of Process (2) makes up the defence of *dissociation*. That is, the ego dissociates, from an integrated place in the cycle, certain events or activities of the Intervening Time. Of greatest importance, of course, is the dissociation of certain behavioural items which derived from the original adaptive plan. Distortion of Process (3) produces the defence of *negation*. That is, the findings of the anxiety apparatus are thrown out by negation of the percept on which they were based. The many gimmicks that may implement this defence are familiar to psychiatrists and have been given names reflecting their part in dream distortion and the psychopathology of everyday life.

I would like to pay some special attention here to phenomena related to the defence of dissociation. The part that it plays in the working out of the repetition compulsion, the fate neurosis, and accident-proneness is well known. It is perhaps less clearly recognized as having an important role in determining the timing, although not the structure, of such phenomena as obsessions, compulsions, tics, and autoerotisms. The timing of the outbreaks of such behavioural items often depends on their unconsciously determined interpolation into some prediction-validation cycle as magical devices for influencing the outcome.

Thus it will be understood that I have not included as mechanisms of defence the ego-activities that give form and substance to these phenomena. From my point of view it is only the act of dissociation that constitutes an act of defence against anxiety, for only it embraces an antagonistic orientation of the ego towards the anxiety apparatus. While these forms of behaviour are truly symptoms of some sort, they are best viewed as symptoms of character immaturity or regression. They are essentially various sorts of rituals. It is no doubt true that rituals themselves, be they interpersonal or autistic, involve little prediction–validation cycles. But here anxiety is only played with as part of the character processes for working through to a mastery of some problem in adaptation. At least that is their original function in the personality, although, as mentioned earlier, their use in later life may be necessary for the preservation of megalomania in the ego.

CONCLUSION

The reader may feel that my investigation of anxiety and the mechanisms of defence is somewhat incomplete. Where are the well-known defences of reaction-formation, regression, undoing, and turning against the self, as well as others, which are less well known? I feel quite strongly that, in the sense in which anxiety has been construed here, these cannot be called defences against anxiety. They are primarily character stratagems or tactics. True regression is an exception to this, but it is not an ego mechanism at all. Rather, it is a process that occurs *to* the ego, when methods of adaptation as well as defence against anxiety fail. It is no more truly an operation than is the "withdrawal to a more strategic position" of war communiqué fame. I shall not deny that regressive movements, like orderly withdrawals, are often used to bait an interpersonal trap, but this is not true regression.

After all, to call every ego operation that is either unsuccessful or unrealistic a defence against anxiety is to lose sight of the issue. Avoidance of anxiety is not the great motive of life nor the impetus to maturation. It is an error to mistake a dynamism for a motive, a tool for a goal.

Before summarizing some of my main points, I would like to comment on the fundamental concepts that form the background of this paper. First of all, with rare exception, no distinction has been made between conscious and unconscious processes because I feel that the distinction is not germane to this discussion. I assume that the great bulk of the ego processes discussed are generally unconscious, although not necessarily repressed. Second, I must beg indulgence for the inadequacy of words in describing processes that are largely non-verbal. These proceed by plastic phantasy which defies all but the poet to put into words. Third, I have stressed the economic point of view, in the sense that life-space-time is regarded as compartmentalized, with varying degrees of integration among the different compartments, depending largely on the stability and integrity of the body image. I think it unlikely that any person could be truly innocent of poorly integrated and diseased compartments. Each of us must be psychotic, neurotic, psychopath, and—in the Shavian sense—

saint. The important question for clinical evaluation is a relative one, resting on economic factors: how large is a diseased compartment in the total life space? Does a poorly integrated compartment cause reverberations that interfere with the harmonious interaction within other compartments?

The concept of anxiety that I have used is that of Freud, which has been clarified and extended by Sullivan in his emphasis on prospective phantasy. But this debt to Sullivan should be delimited by some statement of a fundamental difference also. This difference is not, I believe, referable to conceptualization of the dynamic role of anxiety in personality development and functioning, but, rather, to a more subtle distinction. This I would describe as a difference in attitude towards anxiety as intrapsychic experience. Sullivan has taken the attitude that severe anxiety exerts a disorganizing influence on the ego, "like a blow on the head". In so depicting anxiety, he has limited himself to those internal events that I have described as the momentary (or longer) state between failure of one prediction and formulation of a new one. I can view the "blow on the head" phenomenon as attributable only to weakness and impoverishment of the ego with respect to the particular problem at hand.

By such an attitude towards anxiety I have removed from it qualitative variations and returned these to the realm of ego-structure, the realm in which they are best investigated. The "blow on the head" idea lends itself to variations of the quality of usefulness to the ego that I prefer to view not as inherent in anxiety itself, but, rather, as a quality varying according to the ego's attitude toward the anxiety apparatus.

I should draw attention to the fact that in describing the anxiety apparatus as separate from the ego I have used a structural allegory that is not exactly accurate.[1] The apparatus is part of the ego and, in attacking the apparatus, the ego does in fact attack itself. This, I feel, must involve a use of destrudinal cathexis, thus being an important example of the working of the death instinct.

* * *

This paper has been an attempt to present an experiment in thinking about anxiety as a personality structure. It is felt that the implications drawn with regard to personality dynamics and genetics, although often apparently at variance with psychoanalytic thought, are in harmony with the fundamental concepts of this science. The emphasis has been on the way of life in which awareness of time, and therefore of sequence and implied causality, makes possible a planned adaptation as well as a process of maturation of adaptive capacities. This latter I have viewed as accomplished by learning through predictive validation. The anxiety apparatus has been described as an essential tool of the ego in this way of life, although its appropriate use is not consistently maintained. I have given some scrutiny to the origins of the two forms of anxiety and have tried to describe the effects of each on the ego. While I have hinted at the causes of failure in the ego's orientation towards the anxiety apparatus, chief attention has been given to describing the mechanisms of defence against anxiety, distinguishing them from pathological character devices.

NOTE

1. The importance of this has been pointed out by Dr Hanna Segal, to whom I am grateful for having reviewed this paper.

CHAPTER TWO

Note on a transient inhibition of chewing

(1959)

This analysis of a borderline case in the threshold of the depressive position was written one year after the publication of Melanie Klein's "Envy and Gratitude" (1957) and is an application of the theory of envy and a study of splitting processes through projective identification. With clinical material from one week of a young man's analysis, the author shows how the reconstruction of good internal objects and a surge towards the integration of the ego is intimately linked to the danger of fragmentation of the ego and objects.

This brief clinical paper sets out to demonstrate a critical week in the third year of the analysis of a borderline schizoid case. The material represents the culmination of certain lines of work during the previous year aimed at demonstrating psychic reality to the patient but also stands as

Read before the British Psycho-Analytical Society, 20 May 1959.

the beginning of a period of six months characterized by marked clinical improvement outside the analysis and the most dogged resistance to any further advance within the consulting-room.

This 23-year-old single man had been continuously under psychotherapeutic care since the age of 13, following a breakdown at boarding-school characterized by insomnia, paranoid attitudes towards other students, ruminative concern and periodic panics about his mother's safety, and complete inability to do his studies. His developmental history, though still only partly known to me, was markedly schizoid from early on, shown by such items as indifference to parents following a two-week separation at the age of 3, withdrawal into intense megalomanic identifications, fear and dislike of other children, compulsive masturbation, and eating difficulties. At the time of starting the analysis, he presented a very flaccid demeanour, leptosomic body configuration, stereotypy in speech and gesture, and extreme secretiveness about his way of life and about his reasons for seeking analysis. It has been gradually revealed that he has had no sexual contacts, he views his body as horribly deformed and practises both anal and genital masturbation along with a sado-masochistic perversion in relation to his own body and occasionally with animals. Although his somatic delusions, still incompletely known to me, seem to centre around the feeling that his body parts are repulsive and dare not be shown to others, impaired functioning also plays a role, as it also does in his complaints about his inability to make constructive use of his excellent mind. But what I wish to stress is the intactness of his ego and his body image, albeit deformed and useless. His parents are alive and well, and he makes his home with them still, as do an older sister and a younger brother.

The first 18 months of the analysis, much to the patient's surprise, produced significant improvement in his ability to work and a lessening of the compulsion to masturbate or practise sado-masochistic perversions. To his horror he found himself coming across evidence in dreams and in the occasional hallucination of a connection between his relation to the analyst and early positive feelings towards the mother and her breast. He promptly acted out at his new job, was sacked, and entered upon a period of rather psychotic dilapidation and semi-vagrancy for the next four months. As the analysis brought him out of this, through work on his dreams and acting out, I was able to show him the fundamentals of psychic reality—the relation of his ego-state and body image to that of his internal objects, the connection between his instinctual life and the state of preservation of his internal object, and the connection between his relationships to internal and external objects. During this last period he twice had nocturnal psychotic experiences, which, he hinted, were linked with events of his breakdown at the age of 13 and with recurrent dreams from earlier on. On one occasion he lay awake all night fully clothed and armed with a knife for fear his parents would enter his bedroom and murder him. On a second occasion he hallucinated his mother, eyes blazing, holding a knife to his belly. During this period, as the positive maternal transference pressed into consciousness again and again, a typical configuration in his acting out appeared. The moment positive feelings were aroused toward the analyst, they would be split off into an external person, generally at home or at work. The patient would then provoke this person into disappointing or hurting him, with the result of spoiling his internal and subsequently his external relationship to the analyst. These two nocturnal experiences mentioned were the sequelae of such acting out with the parents. This, in outline, is the background of the events revealed and analysed during the three days, Tuesday, Wednesday, and Thursday, to be reported. Before going into detail, I wish to direct the reader's attention to the main sequence.

On the Thursday, the patient reported that he had eaten no solid food since the evening meal following the Tuesday session. That session had been devoted largely to the analysis of a dream—the "First-Lady" dream, which followed a bit of acting out on his motor-bike. The Wednesday session was given over to intense resistance growing out of a hallucinatory experience of the previous evening. This resistance also involved the withholding of a dream that followed the hallucination, the "Delicious Jaw" dream, which emerged on the Thursday. Thus Monday—positive feelings and acting out; Tuesday session—analysis of "First-Lady" dream, ate dinner, hallucinatory experience in bed, dreamed of the "Delicious Jaw", but withheld the dream from analysis on the Wednesday and was unable to eat solids until after it was analysed on the Thursday. The inhibition of eating solid foods was presented in the Thursday session, characteristically for the patient, as a voluntary act under the aegis of an elaborate phantasy about his body physiology.

These three sessions represent the convergence of several threads of analytic work that were aimed at demonstrating to the patient that the defects in his body image and related impairment in mental and somatic functioning were the result of identification with mutilated internal objects, and that this identification was a defence against internal persecution, which, in turn, was the result of a strong tendency to regress to part-object relationships as a defence against overwhelming depressive anxiety composed of grief, guilt and despair.

Thus we will try to demonstrate in the following material that the analysis of the "First-Lady" dream, by partially restoring the internal object as a whole object, enabled the patient to diminish his identification with it and to experience some of the despair and grief of the depressive position in the internal object relationship—*the hallucinatory experience.* The recognition that this improved relationship to his internal object had been brought about by the analyst (external object) resulted in the greedy yearning to complete the restoration by stealing from the analyst—"Delicious Jaw" dream. But this dream implied very clearly that the origin of the mutilation of his good internal object lay in his own greedy stealing introjection. This so threatened to confront him with the *guilt* of the depressive situation that identification with the mutilated object was invoked again, resulting in the inhibition in chewing solid food and associated resistance in the analytic situation.

With this route map in hand, we may now proceed with the details of the clinical material. The analysis of the Monday hour brought the patient into an unusually strong contact with feelings of admiration and envy for the fertility of the analyst's mind and the richness of the analytic process. Immediately on leaving the session, acting out took place in which he went quite far out of his way on his motor-bike to pass by the house of his previous therapist, who appears in the manifest content of the "First-Lady" dream that night. The great urgency to destroy these positive feelings through immediate acting out was a function of the unusual intensity of the admiration.

> *Tuesday session.* The patient reported driving past the house of his previous therapist, and associations included an incident in which he felt she had once "*sniggered*" at his jokingly calling a small church a cathedral. He dreamed last night that
>
> *. . . she had come to visit him at his home, but it was like the present consulting-room. Her husband was with her, but the patient was not sure if he entered. The patient did not notice her deformities until he put his arm around her shoulder, then noticed that her back was hunched, one foot was huge and mutilated, and she was blind. He was horrified and recalled that he had just seen a press clipping in which she was referred to as the "First Lady of the Land" and wondered if it was an obituary. He was then with his father and siblings, being taught the art of killing in self-defence. The patient was crying about his therapist, but his father said to stop "snivelling", whereupon he began a tirade against the father's callousness.*
>
> His association to the dream was only that he felt depressed last night after his father had *failed* to laugh at a joke he had made. The session, including another dream, centred around the analysis of the depressive feelings connected with differentiating between internal and external objects and confrontation with the contrast between the "First Lady of the Land" analytic mother outside and the horrifying object he gets inside himself as a result of splitting and projecting the "sniggering" envious part of himself into her. I also showed him how he projected the guilt into the analyst father, who is held responsible for preventing rather than fostering reparation of the mother. The detailed linking of this with the transference, the acting out, and the content of the previous session brought a tirade of self-pity and accusations against the analyst of callousness towards *his* suffering. This outburst of "snivelling" through identification with the mutilated internal object did not

seem to be significantly lessened by interpretation at the time. So, up to this point the patient had split off his positive maternal transference onto the previous therapist (a woman), degraded her by projecting the "sniggering" envious part of himself into her as shown by his association about the church he called a cathedral. Thus she became, internally, a hideous object, while the guilt for this attack was laid at the feet of the analyst, now in the role of father who strengthens, not his capacity for love but for "self-defence"—that is, defending the intactness of his ego against the guilt connected with his envy of the good mother. This left him "snivelling", or, in other words, filled with self-pity.

Wednesday session. This hour was given over to intense resistance, composed of unusually overt hostility for this patient. There was at first a barrage of belittling attacks on the analyst, ridiculing the previous session and the theories of psychoanalysis, denying the existence of psychic reality, asserting the accuracy of his perceptual apparatus ("even babies can see"), and defending the rational nature of all anxiety ("babies are not afraid of cats unless they have previously had bad experience with cats"). Buried in this avalanche of words was a brief mention that he'd had a "vision" of his mother looking old and tired, her face lined and eyes hollow, looking at him without hatred but clearly unable to give him the comfort for which he was yearning. A terrible dread came over him. There was a strong opposition to acknowledging the vision as a hallucination. The interpretation of it in the transference, linking it with the "First-Lady" dream, and the fear of the analysis dying slowly as he felt his previous therapy had brought a renewed and prolonged tirade of abuse and ridicule. He was "tired of having to correct the (analyst's) mistakes", he "could do the analysis better by himself", the analyst was seeking to destroy his self-confidence and independence. We can see that the transference had shifted back to the maternal, but the external analyst-mother was now experienced as being just as disappointing as the lined-cheeked, hollow-eyed internal mother—not a source of nourishment, but useful only as an object for projection of bad feelings and impulses.

Thursday session. This hour I wish to present in some detail as the main body of the paper, giving in substance both the patient's material and the interpretations. Although it will easily be seen that the interpretations are in many ways incomplete and inadequate, it can be recognized that the patient showed unusual responsiveness to them. This can be taken as good testimony that the integrative capacities of his ego were joining in the analysis to a degree extraordinary for him. The patient was on time, assumed his usual motionless position on the couch, and immediately reported that he had not taken any solid food since the Tuesday session. However, it was deliberate abstinence based on scientific theories concerning his body, though the analyst would probably not agree. He was too heavy, which placed a strain on his body. Since it took more work to digest solid food than liquids because of the chewing and grinding inside, he was giving his digestive organs a rest by a liquid diet; and it was quite good fun.

Interpretation. That the patient was claiming that he was deliberately controlling his greed towards the analyst, out of concern over the very rapid increase in his mental capabilities, which he felt to have been the result of causing the analyst to work too hard inside him, digesting the material that he supplied. By this he was denying what had happened, which the analyst had repeatedly shown him was the reverse—that in his digesting of the analytic food, he mutilated it until the sound and meaning became separated so that he was taking in the form without the substance, out of envy towards the object that fed him. He felt hopeless about being able to take inside a real mother with her breasts, but only the milk alone from a bottle devoid of human relationship. By splitting off this incapacity to feed properly into the realm of actual food, he was able to deny both the seriousness of it—since he can get adequate nourishment from liquids—and the fact that his incapacity was also the result of an identification with an internal object (inside) whose capacity to digest difficult material had been in some way impaired—namely, the analyst. Therefore he could only use the analyst on the previous day as a receptacle for his own horror about the dream and hopelessness connected with the vision, not as a source of good analytic food.

PATIENT: He does not think yesterday was a waste of time. He had a dream on Tuesday night, but the post-mortem on the "First Lady" dream had been much more pressing in his opinion.

Interpretation: He had felt yesterday that he was pushing into me the responsibility for the mutilation of the first lady and forcing me to further dismember her, until her identity was unrecognizable and could be fed back to him as a formless substance.

PATIENT: That is not what a post-mortem is for—it's to determine the cause of death. Anyhow, in the dream:

> *. . . a gaunt middle-aged man, a pleasant chap really, was holding another man down while someone, perhaps himself, was removing the man's jaw very carefully, painlessly—it seemed to be attached by a sling-like arrangement—like two strips of bacon rind. The man offered no resistance, perhaps he was dead. Then the patient ate the jaw—probably cooked it first; it was absolutely delicious* [with genuine feeling].

Perhaps it satisfied him so that he had had no need for solid food since.

Interpretation: Here we could see the answer to his defence in the Wednesday hour that in the analysis of the "First Lady" dream the cause of mutilation had not been revealed. The bacon rind linked this dream to the "Masturbating-pig" dream and the "Coitus" dream, in both of which he had felt a horror of what was being done, both as regards spoiling and greed.

Much of the clinical improvement prior to the summer holiday had stemmed from a detailed analysis of his compulsive anal and genital masturbation and its effect on his relation to internal objects. These advances had been epitomized in the analysis of two dreams eight months apart. The first dream was of:

> *. . . a "rosy little pig" masturbating on some fresh pork, while in the background a cow was being milked by a machine.*

In the second dream,

> *. . . an unrecognized couple were embracing in the nude, and the patient was both masturbating between the woman's buttocks and grasping her breast with the other hand.*

PATIENT: Oh, there was no horror in this dream; it was painless—not gentlemanly perhaps, but done with consideration.

Interpretation: In order to protect against the longing and hunger for the analyst-mother outside, he had stolen his jaw to eat it at leisure, to get the meat of the analysis in order to complete by himself the restoration of his internal mother. By that act he got inside himself again another mutilated object, a jawless analyst, like a nipple-less mother, with which, if he cannot bear to look at the object to recognize who had caused the damage and perhaps to repair it, he must become identified—jawless, and unable to use his own jaw in a constructive way, as in the previous day's hour and in his inability to chew solids.

[In this interpretation, in comparing the jaw of the analyst with the nipple of the mother, a reference to symbol formation was not meant. The patient knew from previous material how concretely the analyst's jaw was taken as a part object containing the analysis. This has been most clearly seen in a dream, following a session in which admiration had been aroused, of *Frank Sinatra opening his mouth extremely wide and shouting very loud.* The patient had admired, in the dream, Sinatra's ability to dislocate his jaw, as a snake does in swallowing its victim.]

PATIENT: Oh, that's quite neat. A very possible interpretation, but it does not take into account all the facts—*he was* terrified of that vision of his mother and he hated her for disappointing him.

Interpretation: That was a distortion of what he had reported yesterday, that the vision, unlike the blazing-eyed one reported earlier, knife to belly, had not been of a frightening object but only inspired a dread that comfort would never come. His hopelessness was derived from the conviction that he could never keep that internal mother from being harmed by the envious part of himself, from his own cruelty. He was closer to acknowledging that it was the injuries to *her* inside that condemned *him* to a mutilated body and defective mind, regardless of the "First-Lady" goodness of what the analyst-mother could offer him outside.

This precipitated attacks of ridicule and contempt for the analyst and psychoanalysis and a re-assertion that the patient's difficulties were all due to fear, not cruelty. The only way to stop being afraid of someone was to be exactly like them, to yield to everything. In the past few weeks he had begun to free himself from this, to feel better, to be better—so of course the fear had returned, and he could not bear it any longer.

Interpretation: But he was forgetting that his ability to free himself from his identification with this mutilated persecutor was the result of the analysis having first rehabilitated her from the blazing-eyed mother with a knife at his belly of two years ago, to the "neurotic invalid" of two months ago, and then to the hollow-eyed mother of two days ago.

Two months previously, there began to appear the first evidence of acknowledgement of the relation between the analyst's efforts, the improved state of his internal objects, and his own clinical improvement, along with feelings of admiration for the analytic process and the analyst's manner of carrying it out. This had all come together with greatest clarity in a dream in which the patient:

> . . . *was concerned with trying to extinguish a smouldering fire under the floor in his room, but without success, using a hose borrowed from his father. In the meantime the analyst had entered the room and was leading to safety a "neurotic old invalid" woman whom the patient had not noticed before. He admired the analyst's calm and*

business-like manner and thought he meant to rehabilitate the woman.

What had occurred was a *renewed* mutilation, a consequence of yielding to a cruel greed in an attempt to protect himself from being hungry when alone and jealous in isolation. In the Friday session he was depressed, but this was quickly split off from the week-end separation onto the departure of a girl from his office. A hastily improvised and frantic sequence of sallies against the analyst, aimed at destroying all positive feeling prior to the week-end, dissolved fairly easily in the face of interpretation. The week-end was characterized by intense hunger, jealousy of siblings, and anxiety dreams showing his improved capacity to respect and protect the good food. In one dream he:

> . . . *rode out into the desert on his motor-bike to round up some dirty little Arab boys who had put dirt on some eggs. He made them clean up the mess. Rain immediately began to fall in the desert, and he ran out to enjoy it in the nude.*

It is of special interest to note that the motor-bike used for splitting on Monday in his ride past the previous therapist's home is now used for diminishing splitting and taking responsibility for the envious "dirty little Arab boys" part of himself.

DISCUSSION

In the foregoing material I have presented a week of analytic work in the third year of the analysis of a severely schizoid young man—a week that shows him on the threshold of the depressive position, in contact for the first time with psychic reality and its implications, and experiencing for the first time in his analysis strong admiration and real hopefulness. But I wish to draw attention to the great danger that he is also confronting at this time: the danger of fragmentation of his ego and his objects, as against previous mutilation—i.e. the danger of psychosis as opposed to character disorder—as the reconstruction of his good object brings in its wake a surge towards integration in his ego, linked to greed.

Melanie Klein writes, in her paper "On the Development of Mental Functioning" (1958):

> Among the hated and threatening objects which the early ego tries to ward off, are those which are felt to have been injured or killed and which thereby turn into dangerous persecutors. With the strengthening of the ego and its growing capacity for integration and synthesis, the stage of the depressive position is reached. At this stage the injured object is no longer predominantly felt as a persecutor but as a loved object toward whom feelings of guilt and the urge to make reparation are experienced. [p. 241]

In this material we witness the patient's encounter with the problem of introjecting his good object, first of all spoiled by immediate destructive envious projective identification and jealous *isolation* of it—the "First Lady" dream, although it was not possible to demonstrate it to the patient at the time other than through the sniggering-snivelling material, subsequent material has shown clearly that the deformities-enlargements were the consequence of violent penetration into the object by the envious part of himself. The analysis of this dream corrected to some extent the damage done by projective identification but left the patient with an object only partially restored—the hallucination of the mother. The consequence was a greedy yearning to steal a part of the analyst to complete this restoration—the "Delicious Jaw" dream.

Melanie Klein, in her book, *Envy and Gratitude*, stresses the fragmenting effect of greedy introjection. She writes:

> . . . I found that concurrently with the greedy and devouring internalization of the object—first of all the breast—the ego in varying degrees fragments itself and its object, and in this way achieves a dispersal of the destructive impulses and of the internal persecutory anxiety. [p. 191]

The patient's reaction to the failure of this greedy introjection and to the renewed internal persecution was one of despair and resulted in a temporary weakening of his drive toward integration and a very intense strengthening of his drive towards fragmentation, manifest in relinquishing his own jaw and the related functions of his ego, as well as a strong tendency to do the "post-mortem"—that is, a complete fragmentation of his object and his ego.

The subsequent six months of analysis, made up of a nearly unremitting continuation of the type of resistance manifest on the Wednesday, has finally brought a clarification of his dread of a total psychotic collapse. Only through recent analysis of the mechanisms potentially responsible for this—namely the oral sadism and the omnipotent expulsive power of his eyes—has it been possible for a renewed approach to the depressive position to be made, which I hope to be able to report in a subsequent paper.

CHAPTER THREE

Lectures and seminars in Kleinian child psychiatry

in collaboration with Esther Bick

(1960)

These previously unpublished transcripts of impromptu lectures, given at the Tavistock Clinic to Tavistock-trained child psychotherapists—John Bremner, Edna O'Shaughnessy, Dina Rosenbluth, Isca Salzberger, and Frances Tustin—follow the original format. Each theoretical introduction is followed by the discussion of clinical material of early analytic sessions. The colloquial style with some repetitions was left unchanged and gives a flavour of those early teaching seminars. They also illustrate a novel way of presenting clinical material with careful monitoring of psychic changes in the patient and in the transference, recorded in parallel to the clinical descriptions. The heading of the lectures on elementary Kleinian nosology of childhood disturbances are: (1) the technical basis of psychoanalytic observation and the theoretical basis of classification of psychological disorders; (2) psychosis: domination by psychotic anxieties; split-off

---

Lectures and seminars given at the Tavistock Clinic in 1960; with the cooperation of John Bremner, Edna O'Shaughnessy, Dina Rosenbluth, Isca Salzberger, and Frances Tustin.

psychotic parts; (3) mutilations of the ego; (4) the unifying concept of hypochondria; (5) infantile autism, and (6) adolescence. One can see many ideas put forward in these lectures that appear later in The Psycho-analytical Process *(1967a) and other works—in particular, the notions of the aesthetic appreciation of the object, the intrusive attack through projective identification into the internal object, autism, and differential diagnosis.*

INTRODUCTION

The following material, consisting of six lectures and five related seminars, is derived from a series sponsored by The Study Group of The Tavistock-Trained Child Psychotherapists in the autumn of 1960. The lectures were given extempore, recorded and edited; they cannot therefore be taken as complete or systematic. The seminars were presented by the psychotherapists, in five out of six cases on patients known to the lecturer from supervision. The material consists of the therapists' summary of the session and the lecturer's summary of the ensuing discussion in the form of notes on the session and evaluation of the dynamic and therapeutic implications that could be culled from the case material.

The aim of this series was to make an attempt at a nosology of childhood psychological disturbances from the Kleinian viewpoint, with an emphasis on diagnosis and prognostic evaluation from early therapeutic sessions. It will be seen from the first lecture that it is assumed that occasionally full-blown psychoneuroses and psychoses of the type described in the nomenclature of adult psychoanalytic psychiatry do appear in childhood. These cases have been passed over in subsequent lecture–seminars as presenting relatively little difficulty diagnostically or prognostically. The vast and relatively uncharted field of nomenclature in childhood disturbances we have tried to chart in a conceptual framework of three dimensions: (1) the nature of object relations, especially internally; (2) the nature of the defences, particularly splitting, projective identification, and the manic defences; (3) the predominant anxieties, with special reference to the progression from the paranoid-schizoid into the depressive position.

1
The technical basis of psychoanalytic observation and the theoretical basis of classification of psychological disorders

Before going into the two main areas of discussion tonight, I would like to refer you to two publications that will help you to understand the hopeless difficulties faced by classifiers of childhood disturbances, either on a descriptive basis or a dynamic one, which does not reach into the depths for its material. In the former instance I would suggest you look at Leo Kanner's *Textbook of Child Psychiatry* (1948) as the best on its category; and for the second, I would recommend Nathan Ackerman's article in Hoch and Zubin's (1954) *Child and Family Psychotherapy*.

I would also like you all, in preparation for the following lecture-seminars, to read Edward Glover's article, "A Psychoanalytic Approach to the Classification of Mental Disorders" (1933) as the best example of the Kleinian view of the classification of adult disorders—one that I think would give relatively little ground for alternation at least in the arrangement of disorders in relation to one another and to the differentiation of nervous (neurotic) from mental (psychotic) illness. He also distinguishes between the diseases and the character disorders corresponding to them on the basis of internalization ("introjective") as against externalization ("projective") of the infantile relationships that are at the foundations of personality structure.

Psychiatric diagnosis with children as carried out in most hospitals or child guidance clinics is a rather elaborate and unstandardized process in which history-taking, psychological testing, and play interviews with the child play a variable part in different centres. But the basic method is to amass data and, in conference, to reach a group impression by reviewing the data. My own experience in running a large child guidance clinic as against an extensive experience in private psychiatric consultation convinces me that the psychoanalytic method of observation is far more accurate, both diagnostically and prognostically, if psychotherapy or child analysis is a real possibility. Of course, where educational or environmental methods are all that can be made available, the more detailed environmental study would serve better.

I want to emphasize tonight and in ensuing lectures the evaluation of the psychoanalytic interview with the child, keeping in mind that these are cases where the continuation of the contact as psychotherapy or analysis is a great probability. The interpretation of the transference cannot otherwise be used as a diagnostic tool, for it has a precipitously deepening effect on the relationship, which would make discontinuance of contact a trauma.

As you know, Freud first discovered the unconscious and later the structure of the mental apparatus. His first theories dealt largely with psychic energy, leading up to the libido theory. Later the theories of metapsychology based on structure, dynamics, genetics, and the economy of the mental apparatus were developed.

Abraham in particular added to this a clarification of the early stages of development and began to broaden the concepts of narcissism and the concept of the superego in the direction that Melanie Klein has followed in her work. Psychic reality and the internal relationships were brought into very great prominence by her. The processes of introjection and projection as they inter-relate from the very beginning of life were likewise emphasized in Klein's work and she showed how these contribute to the evolution of ego structure and the internal object relationships that we conceptualize as superego. As the central role of these mechanisms began to emerge, a certain reformulation of the Freudian conception of the genesis of personality structure resulted. First of all, there had been Freud's description of the progression from multiple erogenous zones to erogenous primacy, starting with orality, to which Abraham added some clarification by subdividing the oral and the anal phases each into two relatively distinct phases. What Klein had described as "positions" is not to be understood as replacing the concepts of erogenous primacies. The concept of position is primarily a concept having to do with the organization of object relationships. These positions exist throughout life. A person does not leave the paranoid–schizoid position ever entirely, nor does he ever entirely work his way through the depressive position. The positions describe organization of object relationships, and their fundamentals have to do with the progression from part-object relationship to whole-object relationship, with the emergence of love for a unique object. In this progression the defensive use of mechanisms of splitting and projection and particularly projective identification, gradually diminishes and is replaced by introjective mechanisms and the processes of reparation, modulated by the safety valve of the manic defences. This is also part of the concept of "position".

In this theoretical framework, when examining children we evaluate the transference situation from the point of view of (1) the level of object relationships, (2) the extent to which particular defence mechanisms are being utilized and, (3) the predominant anxieties. We try also to evaluate their impulses, particularly the balance between the life and death instincts, as they are manifest in the material. By linking these observations with the history and assessment of the environment, we try to estimate whether the child's pathology is in conflict with or is being fostered by the environment, particularly the major figures in the environment. Later, in the clinical material, we will also see the importance of another aspect of the child's unconscious mental life—what you might call the geography of its object relationships. We have to try to understand *where* the object-relation is going on. The geography of the life-space of the child and the unconscious is really in four layers. There is (1) the outside world, (2) the inside of his objects in the outside world, (3) the inside world, and (4) the inside of his objects in the inside world. In order to understand the child's material thoroughly, we must particularly distinguish whether the object relationship we are seeing is going on inside an object or outside it, and whether that field of action is in the inner or outer world.

When we are trying to evaluate the transference situation, we have a particular tool in psychoanalysis whereby we introduce something into this situation that is, fundamentally, from the point of view of scientific method, no different from what any scientist does when he has a situation and introduces a variable. This is what a physicist does when he sends a charged particle into a cloud chamber and sees what kind of splitting goes on when it hits another particle and fragments in different directions. We have the interpretation that we introduce into the situation, and we then observe what happens as a result of this intervention in the patient's mental processes. What we do after we have made an interpretation is to follow the shift in the transference situation and try to understand how they are specifically related to the correctness or incorrectness of the interpretation we have given and how they are related to the specific content of the interpretation. By this method of introducing this interpretation, which causes a flux in the transference situation, we are also able to gain some idea of the mobility of the object relationships—that is, some idea of the flexibility in the ego for utilizing different mechanisms in dealing with its objects, impulses, and anxieties.

You will notice that I have left for this point a discussion of the question of anxiety. Freud, as you know, described anxiety in his first theories as primarily and fundamentally castration anxiety. Then, in the paper on "Mourning and Melancholia" (Freud, 1917e [1915]) he related the affects of depression to mourning in the same way as he had related castration anxiety—as the prototype anxiety—to the general category of fear. In Melanie Klein's hands this has turned into the two general categories of depressive and persecutory anxiety, each of which is a term including a whole spectrum of affects and affective experiences, with an almost infinite shading not only in intensity but also in quality. In our conception of the genesis of personality, the concepts of anxiety and the painfulness of anxiety are absolutely central. We consider anxiety and the need to deal with it as one of the great factors driving the organism towards growth and integration, while excesses of it or specific intolerances to it are the great factors driving it in a direction of various disintegrative mechanisms. These two broad categories of anxiety—or, rather, categories of emotional pain—seem to be dealt with preferentially by the mental apparatus by different mechanisms. Melanie Klein has described the schizoid mechanisms as being preferentially employed for dealing with excesses of, or intolerance to persecutory anxieties, while manic defences and various mechanisms of reparation and sublimation are the ones preferred for dealing with the various aspects of depressive anxiety. In our attempts to evaluate transference situations, we try to understand what are the dominant anxieties and what are the particular mechanisms that are in force for dealing with them. It is particularly the shift between depressive and persecutory anxieties that we are most concerned with in evaluating shifts in the transferences.

The ways in which we do this evaluating are the primary points of attack on our method by people who do not really understand psychoanalysis. Our source of information is our own relatively analysed mental apparatus by means of which we can experience a degree of identification with the patient and to follow the affective and phantasy processes in ourselves resulting from partial identification. This is not understood, yet it is no different methodologically from the calibration of any scientific instrument as an extension of the human sensorium. And of course it is to the extent to which we have succeeded in what other scientists call standardizing the apparatus that we become accurate psychoanalytic observers.

The accuracy of our penetrations into the patient's experiences depends on one other thing: the differentiation between understanding on the basis of introjective and not projective identification. It is particularly when the mechanism of projective identification is dominant, that what we call countertransference *disturbances* occur. Countertransference is not in itself a disturbance, as it is the emotional and phantasy experiences that accompany the identification with the patient and with his objects, both external and internal. We seek to identify countertransference *disturbances* through insight, but also through watching for breaches in technique and by recognizing interpretive constellations that are too forced or too theoretical and not in keeping with the patient's material. Finally, of course, we correct such disturbance through supervision.

In closing, I want to emphasize that the method of psychoanalytic observation is a method that particularly utilizes the tool of introducing interpretations and following the resulting shifts in the transference. The structure of the transference consists of (1) the geography of the situation (2) the nature of the object relationship, (3) the dominant impulses and the erogenous zones that are involved in the object relationship, (4) the specific nature of the anxiety, (5) the mechanisms of defence that are being utilized, and (6) the consequences, when we can see them, of the utilization of these mechanisms. Put down intellectually like that, it seems like a terrible amount to figure out, as it were. But we do not "figure it out", we observe it in ourselves through our introjective processes and we understand it by recognizing the phantasy pattern aroused, having seen similar patterns over and over again in our own analysis, and in our previous clinical work. Deep and thorough training analysis and clinical experience potentiate one another to increase the richness and accuracy of the analyst's work.

2
Psychosis; domination by psychotic anxieties; split-off psychotic parts

The subject I plan to discuss tonight represents a point in theory where people who have not studied Melanie Klein's work thoroughly have come to grief, thinking that she has not made a clear distinction between infancy and psychosis, or coming to the conclusion that she thinks that every disturbance is really a psychosis, or underneath it is a psychosis, or something of that sort. Actually, what Klein did was to differentiate more clearly than had been done before between the two general categories of anxiety: the persecutory anxieties and the depressive group of anxieties. She also has given us a much firmer conception of the development of object relationships, and this gives us a basis for more sharply differentiating between psychotic types of anxieties and neurotic types of anxieties, both in the depressive and persecutory types. That is, her work has shown us how to distinguish more clearly between part-object and whole-object relationships and to recognize the mechanisms that dominate the paranoid–schizoid position, particularly projective identification, as differentiated from the various mechanisms that dominate the depressive position, the mechanism of internalization, reparation, and the manic group of defences. In helping us to differentiate between psychotic anxieties and neurotic anxieties on the basis of the object-relationship involved, Melanie Klein's work has added a qualitative perspective. There used to be a category that psychiatrists talked about as "catastrophic anxieties" as against phobic anxiety, paranoid anxiety, or neurotic free-floating anxiety, and so on. It is true that there is this other category of catastrophic anxieties, which is related specifically to what has been called "minute splitting" of schizophrenia as against the ordinary splitting processes that are so manifest in relation to the paranoid–schizoid position. If we take three-fold differentiation between catastrophic anxiety, psychotic anxiety, and neurotic anxiety, I think that we can make a little headway in trying to understand the distinction when we meet it in our patients between (1) psychosis, (2) domination by psychotic anxieties, and (3) a split-off psychotic part of the personality.

To start with, when I say psychosis, I mean primarily a schizophrenic psychosis. To differentiate a schizophrenic psychosis from the position where a personality is dominated by psychotic anxieties, and one sees all sorts of fragmentation and a terrible degree of flux in the ego structure and in the object relationships: I think it can be stated definitely that a schizophrenic psychosis is not really a state of lack of integration dominated by psychotic anxiety. The schizophrenic process is a very different process, which first of all starts with a catastrophe, as Bion has said very clearly. It starts with a catastrophe in which the objects and the ego are fragmented minutely. What Freud calls the "reconstructive phase" or "restitutive phase" of the disease is a process by which the minutely split fragments are variously agglomerated—fitted together in all sorts of non-anatomical and non-physiological ways, you might say, to form again what Bion has called *bizarre* objects. This is the picture of schizophrenic psychosis; the object relationships are *bizarre* because both ego-parts and the seemingly "whole" as well as part-objects are *bizarre* agglomerations of what had been at the catastrophic phases in the disease, minute bits of the objects and ego. One sees either the very fleeting and ever-changing ego states of the early schizophrenic or the rigidification into delusional constructions in later phases.

In contrast to this, when one sees a child or adult patient who is being dominated by psychotic anxieties, one sees a patient with a great deal of splitting existing in the ego, with a tendency for integration but not with the formation of really sound bonds between various parts of the ego, so that the integrated states quickly fall to pieces under the pressure of anxiety. Thus one sees a very migrating kind of object relationship and rather fleeting ego states and fleeting symptom formation, and this presents a picture of a very turbulent state, in terrible flux, which can at first glance be very difficult to distinguish from the early schizophrenic process, which also often presents a very turbulent fluctuating state as far as its surface manifestations are concerned.

In the third instance when we are dealing with, a split-off psychotic part of the personality, what we meet is a much more stable structure—in fact, a structure that is often appalling in its stability. I say "appalling" stability because what is presented most obviously is a structure that is grimly determined to resist any kind of influence in the direction of great integration. What we conceive of and what we generally discover in such patients is that a very early splitting process has gone on in which most of the destructive impulses that had not been projected into objects to make bad objects have been segregated into a particular portion of the self usually linked to one specific aspect of the bisexuality that had then been very deeply as well as widely split off. I say "deeply" and "widely" because these are two very different kinds of processes, although I do not think we really know in detail very much about them yet, except that you see them manifest differently in dreams. The patient dreams that something is across the channel as against something being down deep in a chasm, for example.

What we see in these split-off psychotic parts is that they are both widely and deeply split off, so that their content is very inaccessible both to consciousness and to recognition as part of the self. The resistances against integration with other parts of the ego and being brought into consciousness are immense. The content of this particular bit is *not* a schizophrenic illness, but during the process of integration, as I understand it, there is certainly the danger of a schizophrenic break-down. Although we speak of it as a psychotic bit, it is not schizophrenic in the sense of minute splitting and agglomeration of bizarre objects, and so on. It is psychotic in the sense of being extremely primitive and extremely sadistic, so that often during the processes of integration it is first represented as a kind of ruthless machine, later represented as a kind of cold-blooded animal, and so on. When we finally do get a clearer picture of it, it often seems more correct to call it the criminal part of the personality, and my experience thus far is that when it begins to be represented in human form in dreams it is usually represented first as a criminal, dominated by absolute hopelessness about ever being admitted to the good family of relationships.

In adult psychiatry and psychoanalysis one must make a differentiation that probably does not become pertinent with children until adolescence—namely, between a split-off psychotic part of the personality and a hidden-from-view, but quite conscious, late-phase schizophrenic illness with crystallized delusions, etc.

CASE MATERIAL

Domination by psychotic anxieties Metaphysical and prognostic significance

Eight-year-old girl

Third session, Friday, with second analyst. Pleased at therapist's appearance. In

This material shows that the patient is able to feel a good object internally only in the play-room, holds paper to light to reveal water marks, saying it is magic, making it disappear by placing on the table. She then draws around the water-mark, saying this is "Aladdin's Lamp", rubbing it and then holding the paper to the light, recognizing that there are two water marks.

Interpretation: Waiting for the therapist in the waiting-room or over the week-end caused her to assert that she need not worry as she had a magic by which she could make the therapist appear, like a genie of the lamp, denying that she could leave her as her first analyst had had to do.

presence of her good external object. Through the omnipotence of her masturbation an internal object is enslaved as an ally against persecutory figures in the internal darkness. This "genie" figure is a different object from the good object.

The patient noisily jammed the end of this interpretation, getting a bottle, which she rubbed.

Interpretation: Repeated the end of previous interpretation, emphasizing the dread of losing the therapist.

The patient became wild, and said she would do tricks, wrapping a pencil in a paper and hiding it behind her for the therapist to guess which hand, triumphantly crowing over the therapist's being wrong each time, stirring some feeling of irritation in the therapist.

A very strong tendency to identify with persecutory internal figures and act out so as to project her anxieties.

The triumphing and ridiculing shows strong envy at work, here being projected into the therapist.

Interpretation: She felt that the therapist went away just to puzzle and frighten her and that the interpretations of her anxiety were made cruelly, ridiculing her for her fears.

Because the therapist has not taken up the interplay of internal and external, the patient here abandons the interaction and represents the renewed splitting of her "fierce" envy, utilizing obsessional mechanisms to reinforce the splitting in herself.

She then took animals from the box, putting tame ones inside the "encampment" and the "fierce" monkey outside.

Interpretation. She felt the therapist went away to get away from the patient's fierceness, which she feels is made worse if she is puzzled or bewildered.

This interpretation has brought renewed comfort with the split-off envy. Pressed on by the approaching end of the session, a greed-game is established, which suddenly breaks off to dramatize her identification with the old and ridiculous internal mother (or, more accurately, breasts) resulting from this greedy introjection.

She started a game that was intended to be a mutual snatching of objects from one another, then left the room and returned with her glasses on the tip of her nose, looking old and ridiculous.

Interpretation. She felt a battle to be going on for control over one another.

Summary

The patient reveals her inability to introject and preserve a good object and her reliance on omnipotent control over an enslaved, dangerous, probably phallic object to protect her from the internal persecution at the hands of an internal mother (more likely on a part-object level, the breast) derived from both the projection of envy and greedy exploitation in relation to the external mother (and breasts).

Dynamic implications: Domination by severe persecutory anxieties, very little capacity to bear depressive anxieties, primarily part-object relationships. *Potential paranoid personality.* Strong capacity to transfer, strong wish for a good object, some drive towards integration, strong and immediate response to interpretation.

Therapeutic implications: Unusually good assets for treatment, considering the severity of the pathology.

History: Illegitimate, mother a minor. Breast-fed some time; 18 months with mother, who lost interest in baby. Foster home at 2½ years. Extremely destructive with teeth and hands. Enuretic. Unable to learn or to make friends, a nuisance at school.

Therapy: Two and one-half years with two therapists. A severe technical problem of containing her and resisting her aggression. Overcome by interpretation on the basis of the aggression in identification with insane internal objects, particularly the damaged breasts. Considerable headway into the depressive position made, with resulting gains in all areas of behaviour and learning capacity. Termination forced by move of foster parents. Will require further therapy in adolescence.

3
Mutilations in the ego

In this particular category of psychopathology that I have called for you "mutilations in the ego" we have a process that is in many ways similar to what I discussed with you last time under the heading of "split-off psychotic parts of the personality". But under the heading of "mutilations of the ego" rather than the splitting-off of bad and ill parts of the personality, what we are dealing with fundamentally is the splitting-off or leaving behind in the developmental process of very valuable parts of the self. The most extreme form of this, you may know, is what is called the *idiot savant*. Such a person leaves behind and leaves undeveloped in itself everything except one particular ego faculty, which is then developed, if there is encouragement, to a point of extraordinary hypertrophy, often seen in mathematics or in bodily movements in dance: Nijinsky was something of an *idiot savant* in the dance; there are musical prodigies, chess-playing prodigies. (Stefan Zweig's little novel, "The Royal Game", was about a chess-playing *idiot savant*—a very interesting little story.) That is the most extreme form of it.

Generally, we can divide these patients into several categories. The most predominant of these, of course, are the children who have lost something of their intellectual capacities. These children are usually called inhibited; in fact, I suppose the term "inhibition" really has been used rather widely for describing all of these types of difficulties, but in the Kleinian understanding we recognize that these are not inhibitions. These are really manifestations of splitting processes in the ego, and they are not to be overcome by any kind of education or reassurance or training or anything of the sort, as simple inhibitions due to social anxieties very often can be. The biggest category you come across in your clinical practice is, of course, the children with intellectual inhibitions. These are not necessarily children who are ineducable in the sense of being incorrigible in the class setting. I think you have to differentiate them from the children who are dominated by psychotic anxieties in the school environment and are completely unable to adapt to this situation. Generally what one finds in treatment is that such children are so dominated by the school situation representing the inside of the mother's body that they are overwhelmed both with sexual excitement and with claustrophobic anxieties of one sort or another, and they are completely unable to attend to the learning function. These children cannot learn and, depending on the severity of this problem, they are brought to you as children of very low intellect, borderline or sometimes considered frankly mentally defective; less severe cases are brought as children who could do better. You hear that they could do better if they would try, or sometimes they do well and then they do not. There is a category of children who seem to learn, but then they cannot use their learning, and their teachers never really know whether they have learned something or not.

Then there is a category of children—a very large category of children—who are, I think, relatively seldom brought for treatment; these are the children who have lost something of their neuro-muscular capacity. These are the terribly clumsy—children who cannot do athletics, who cannot learn to dance, who are always falling, and who always look a mess because the loss of the neuro-muscular capacity is often accompanied by the loss of the capacity for beauty and for achieving any kind of pleasing cosmetic result in their dress, the fixing of their hair, staying clean, and so on—children who just look a mess and act a mess, too.

Then there are the children who are sexually incapacitated, who have lost their capacity for sexual responsiveness. This is not, of course, noticed in childhood, and they are seldom brought to you except in the case of very effeminate little boys, who seem to lack all boyishness and all the vigour and vitality that usually goes along with boyish sexuality. This becomes very noticeable in the adolescent who simply does not develop an adolescence from the sexual point of view. The whole period of transition seems to be absolutely muted in them.

Another category is the loss of aesthetic capacity. These children cannot see or appreciate the beauty of anything about them; everything is very matter of fact, not in the sense of uninteresting, but in the sense of completely lacking in beauty. I am sure that you can think of other examples. These are just the ones that have come particularly to mind from my own clinical experience.

If we try to look at the underlying pathology in this, of course we recognize that a splitting process is involved and that a portion of the ego has been widely and generally deeply split off and left behind in the development and remains quite unintegrated with the rest of the development of the ego. In the diagnostic approach to this problem the most fundamental thing is to distinguish, as always, between manifestations of difficulty within the depressive position and manifestation of difficulty in the paranoid-schizoid position or in the early approaches to the depressive position. In this particular type of psychopathology the difficulties fall into two very clearly distinct groups that you should be able to recognize clinically from clinical material. The one belongs to the psychopathology of the paranoid-schizoid position and consists of a sacrifice of a portion of the ego as a placation of a persecutor—a persecutor that has been erected by the splitting-off and projection of the envy into an internal or external object. This envious persecutor is continually being placated by the manifest incapacity of the ego, in that particular area where the persecutor is felt to be most envious.

The second category that I think is very clear is the splitting-off of a portion of the ego that contains capacities that are felt to be linked to aggression towards the good object. That is, it is in the nature of a depressive sacrifice, where there is a certain hopelessness about the integration of a particular striving and the capacities in the ego to fulfil this striving. The hopelessness about being able to integrate it is because of the amount of aggression towards the good object that is felt to be linked to it; that for the sake of the preservation of a good object this particular capacity in the ego—the particular impulse and the ego capacities for implementing it—have been split off and, as it were, sacrificed for the sake of the good object. These two categories are very distinct, and they show up quite clearly in early clinical material when you are examining this sort of a situation.

Sexual development is commonly sacrificed for the sake of preserving peace with the good object, particularly in the female child. To a great extent the frequency of the frigid development in the female is a manifestation of this kind of splitting off and sacrificing the whole capacity for sexual appreciation and sexual responsiveness to the male in order to bypass the oedipal conflict with the mother as a loved but usually very fragile object. In that particular category the fragility of the good object may contribute to the hopelessness; in other cases this hopelessness may be due to the virulence of the aggression.

CASE MATERIAL
Splitting off of valuable parts of the self

An 8-year-old girl, looking messy, with slurry speech, open sores on face where she had scratched, heavy inner canthi folds, and general appearance of mental deficiency.

Eight-year-old girl

Fourth session, Thursday, first week

Renewed previous day's demand for red nail-varnish as got paper and pencil; manner overbearing, saying that mother suggested the therapist did this.

Interpretation: Linked this with jealousy of therapist, having shown mother where magazines were in waiting-room, and envy of therapist having grown-up things.

The material shows an inability to differentiate the therapy from the home and school situations. Her role-playing does not involve genuine identification but a very superficial mimicry and ineffectual attempt to control the therapist.

"Come on, writing today." But very uncertain demeanour, sideways glances at therapist.

Interpretation: The anxious glances connected with fear therapist had discussed with mother the "secrets" she had revealed last session about her masturbation.

Began banging table with ruler, telling therapist she must not be naughty today, as the teacher had a bad cold.

Interpretation: She is now the mother who knows all the child's secrets and is very harsh with the child, whose masturbation makes her an ill teacher-mother.

This interpretation brings a somewhat deeper contact and a genuine identification with a damaged and harsh internal mother. But the therapist's failure to interpret the internal situation causes the patient to move into a paternal persecutory transference. This also is not adequately interpreted, and the contact is lost, ending in the imitation.

Patient said she felt afraid the therapist would hurt her, as a certain boy at school always does. But continued her lecturing teacher-role, suddenly broken by asking therapist to come to a party at her house on Sunday.

Interpretation: The wish to have a different relationship than in the analysis, which frightened her. Indicated she could not come to parties while patient in analysis with her.

Contact with the infantile transference is renewed by the indication of the incompatibility of an analytic and social relationship, bringing out a naive and explosive revelation of infantile undifferentiated excretory attack on the internal parents in masturbation and the external mother–therapist.

Patient asked directly what therapist does during weekend, writing the question out and demanding that the therapist copy it, being cruel and uncompromisingly critical.

Interpretation: She feels it cruel of the therapist not to answer her questions and not to come to her party and is showing her how it feels to be in that position of a deprived and criticized child.

Wrote "wee–wee" and "big jobs", and giggled, showing the paper to the therapist.

Interpretation: Pushing her urine and faeces into the therapist to punish her for the weekend.

Got out paints and plasticine, demanded therapist make a fish and became enraged at her refusal, threatening to leave.

Interpretation: The envy of the mother and father therapist at

Interpretation brings forth a seduction to placate the angry baby by conniving in its denial of the differences between babies and adults. The threat to leave is not a transference activity but a threat to withdraw the infantile transference.

the week-end, demanding that she be given a fish-penis like the father and a grown-up nail-varnish body like the mother.

When stopped from leaving, she attempted to alter the hands of the clock, which the therapist stopped, indicating it was not part of the things for her to play with. She then started singing "Mulberry Bush", gradually adding "wee-wee", and "big-jobs" and her word for masturbation, ending in sitting and beginning to masturbate using thighs and pressure against the chair.

Interpretation: The urinary and faecal attacks during the masturbation, on the therapist-parents at the week-end.

Again firmness of technique brings back the explosive attacks.

The patient said it was her sister who masturbates, but the therapist must not tell mother, who always sends her to the toilet when she does it. After termination of the session she said it was really herself who masturbates and, in mother's presence, again cautioned the therapist not to tell mother.

But again the internal situation not clarified, with another withdrawal of transference and loss of differentation between the levels of relationship to mother and therapist.

Summary

A little girl functioning on a feeble-minded level shows the shallowness of her superficial dependent relationships at home, at school, and in the treatment situation, with a variety of coercive, seductive, and shallow imitative devices for dealing with the anxieties involved—anxieties that also seem shallow and colourless. But those elements of the technique and the interpretive process that both resist her manipulation and give evidence of intent to penetrate into her inner life rather than simply to placate her and keep her from being a nuisance bring little rushes of infantile transference, internal anxieties, and intense emotion. It is clearly difficult for her to preserve and maintain the contact and extreme dependence on the therapist.

Dynamic implications: There has been a severe splitting-off of the capacity for intense infantile attachment, leaving a greatly impoverished façade. Little can be gathered about the structure of the split-off part except for the evidence of critical and cruel sadism, of oedipal conflict at a part-object level. The striking phenomenon is the lack of integrative drive shown in the tenuous transference contact and the readiness to continue at a defective, valueless, placated level, as seen at termination. A potential schizoid psychopath and pseudo-mental defective.

History: Eldest by three years of four girls. Breast-fed only one week and cared for by mother only for nine months before being turned over to nanny so that mother could return to work in father's business. Baby cried every morning when mother left with father. Did not walk until two years nor talk until four years. Next two siblings ill, one with eczema and the other with coeliac syndrome, both requiring a great deal of mother's time, for which purpose she stopped work.

Symptoms: Intellectual retardation at all levels. Neuromuscular incoordination in all movements, large and small. Bites and tears her clothes, scratches face, scalp sore and even bleeding. Noisy, infantile, slurred, and manneristic speech. Greedy, outgoing to adults.

4
The unifying concept of hypochondria

Before discussing hypochondria, I would like to go into a brief discussion of the whole concept of introjection and internalized objects.

Hypochondriasis is really a descriptive term including various disturbances in the relationship to the body, and it is quite correct to speak of hypochondriacal anxieties themselves and to speak of hypochondriacal symptomatology. Hypochondriacal anxieties may also be said to exist without hypochondriacal symptomatology, as an aspect of the phantasies and anxieties stirred by disturbances of non-psychogenic origin in the body, or the anxieties centring around any kind of manipulation or care that has to be extended to the body by doctors, and so on. But hypochondriacal symptomatology refers to those psychogenic disturbances of the relationship to the body that range—speaking in terms of developmental strata, as it were—from the highest levels of loving concern about the body or parts of the body, down to the most pathological formation of somatic delusion and hatred of the body. It seems to me that, going down in this stratification, first you have symptoms that manifest concern about the body: (1) *hypochondriacal concern* about the body or a proportion of it. This is usually very obsessional in its structure. The next type of more severe hypochondriacal symptom is somatic disturbances of sensation in the body: (2) *disturbing body sensations*, ranging all the way from tickling to intense pain. At a deeper and more primitive level of disturbance you have (3) *persecutory hypochondriacal anxieties*, which are disturbances of somatic sensation accompanied by feeling of persecution and intense anxiety. At a deeper level you have the beginning of the (4) *psychosomatic disturbances*, which are disturbances in the actual functioning of the organs, i.e. a disturbance of motility and secretory functions. At the deepest levels of infantile anxiety we find actual tissue pathology, bleeding, tissue damage, the formation of irreversible changes in the tissues, which are present in the genuine

(5) *psychosomatic diseases*. At a somewhat different level, but properly considered in the category of hypochondriasis, are the symptoms that are called (6) *somatic delusions*. These I will discuss later.

Now to the concept of introjection and internalized objects. Freud's earlier descriptions dealt with the superego as a very unified structure, although there is reason to think that originally he thought of it as divided in two, into the *ego-ideal*, which is a very good portion, encouraging, exhorting, and setting ideals for the ego, and a more chastising, punishing, scolding *superego* portion. I do not think this is too clearly differentiated in his writings, for sometimes he talks about one or the other interchangeably. But through Abraham's work and later Melanie Klein's, the superego has been dissected into its various components of internalized objects, whole and part-objects, good and bad.

In order to understand something about the way in which internalized objects have access, as it were, to the organs and tissues of the body so that they can cause hypochondriacal symptoms, it is necessary to conceptualize internalization, the *introjection process*, in a way that goes far beyond concepts that are embraced in terms such as imago, phantasy, memory, and faces, object-representation, and so on. It is true that all of this is carried on in phantasy, but it is something much more than that. When an object is internalized—and you must realize that every time you look at an object you do not internalize it—it is internalized by a process of phantasy in which it is really taken inside, but not necessarily in the sense of removing it from the outside world. There is a spectrum again of modes of introjection, ranging from extremely sadistic and cannibalistic to very loving and cooperative. The cannibalistic ones do have the aim of removing the object from the outside world and taking possession. In addition to the introjective origins, internalized objects can also be established as a result of phantasy processes in which external objects are felt to project into one—that is, of other people's projective identifications. These, again, range from being penetrated by projections really violently and sadistically to being penetrated by very loving, benign, and helpful projections.

In the relationship to the breast in its most loving and cooperative form, the introjective process is really a cooperative process of projection and introjection, the baby introjecting and the breast projecting. The result of this good sucking and relationship to the breast is the establishment inside of a very loving and good object. I think what needs to be understood in order to conceptualize this correctly is that the internalization of an object involves the ceding to it of territory in the mental apparatus. It does not float around in empty space or around inside your tummy. It involves yielding to it a precious portion of the mental apparatus, giving it the equipment and territory to live inside you. Of course in the unconscious phantasy life this is experienced primarily as giving it a room and furniture and allowing it freedom to come and go and do as it pleases within the internal world. When possessive jealousy dominates the introjection, a "dog in the manger" domination of the object without making use of it exists, as seen in autistic children. Less loving introjection means imprisoning the object, keeping it locked up and making it do this and that, and projection means being invaded, partitioned, and occupied. It is only when you understand this particular aspect, that an internalized object is in possession of a part of the mental apparatus, that you can understand that the degree of love with which an apparatus is internalized determines whether it is given a very choice bit of apparatus, or whether it is given a desultory bit with which it can hardly do anything worth while. It just has to try to scrape up a living, as it were, in this way. The reason I make this point is because it is only by understanding this that you can understand how by having a portion of the mental apparatus at its disposal, and being really ensconced in this portion of the real-estate of one's mind, an internalized object really has access—direct access—to the tissues and the organs of the body for the expression of its life processes within the individual. It is only by understanding this that you can come to understand hypochondriacal symptoms and overcome the mind–body schism.

As always when it comes to understanding psychopathology in the Kleinian framework, we have to make the primary distinction between persecutory and depressive relationships to objects. If you go back to the original little classification of hypochondriacal disturbances mentioned above, you can easily draw a line there. The more developmentally advanced disturbances manifest themselves as solicitude and concern about an organ that is felt to be unhappy. At a deeper level it is an organ that is in pain, that is felt to be damaged, and so on down into the more severe forms of depressive disturbance. When you cross this very wiggly line between the depressive position and the paranoid–schizoid position, you get into areas where the concern about the object becomes so painful and looking at its damages becomes so excruciating that the whole situation begins to be experienced as being very persecutory. That is when you cross into the area where the patient's desire is not to have the organ healed but to have something taken away—either taken away in the sense of surgically removed, or taken away in the sense of being smothered, as it were, with medication, so that it stops screaming. Deeper into the schizoid position, these objects are not only persecutory because of the amount and intensity of painful guilt and anxiety that they cause, but they become persecutory because they become malevolent. Then, depending on how primitive they are, they are in the position to cause varying kinds of disturbance of a persecutory nature to the functioning of the organ. They can cause pain; at a deeper level they can cause tissue damage. These tissue-damaging objects, of course, are very primitive fragmented bits of part-objects of an intensely oral sadistic nature that really bite to pieces the tissues. They cause bleeding and ischemic damage, and this is the basis of the real psychosomatic illnesses. They strangle the asthmatic, they bite the stomach of the ulcer patient, they squeeze vessels of the hypertensive, and so on.

The category of somatic delusion is another matter, and it is not really well understood yet. Somatic delusions are structured in this way—they are delusions of malfunction or malformation of the body, accompanied by the feeling that the relationships to other people in the outside world are being very severely adversely affected by this malfunction or malformation. The ordinary hypochondriacal symptom is not felt to affect other people or to affect one's good relationship to them; it is not accompanied by ideas of reference, you might say. But the somatic delusion is accompanied very intensely by ideas of reference.

In order to make this clear, let me give a little clinical example. After some years of analysis, a patient finally made it clear to me without actually telling me that people stayed away from him because he smelled bad. After some months it became clear that he smelled bad because flatus was felt to be continually escaping from his anus. He could never hear it, he could never feel it; he could not even really smell it, but he could tell from other people's reactions about him that he really stank. These reactions consisted of people avoiding him. After another year of analytic work it became clarified that this was going on in the analytic room, and my life in the analytic room was felt to be unbearable; that when he left, he was quite sure I throw the window open and just hang out of it gasping for air. After about four or five more months of analysing, it had become more and more clear to him that it was not his anus, it was his mouth, and that it was not the smells that were coming out, it was the thoughts that were coming out. And it became clear that these thoughts that were coming out of his mouth were coming from a part of himself that had been completely split off and denied. During the earlier part of his analysis it had taken the form of an extremely paranoid attitude towards me and my words, in that they were felt to be pushing bad thoughts and bad feelings into his mind and to be messing up his innocence and, as it were, his mental virginity. It was only after years of analysis that the splitting lessened sufficiently for him to begin to experience it as a somatic delusion instead of as paranoia.

The somatic delusion is a delusion about the body that comes from that kind of splitting-off of a very primitive bad part of the personality onto a particular organ, an organ over which the patient feels he has no control *vis-à-vis* external objects. In this case it was his anus that could not control the emission of flatus, although it was felt to be quite continent to faeces. The analysis of it gradually revealed it as part of his mind and of his mental functioning that had been in a sense somatized, that is, split off onto a portion of his body. This is rather different from the structure of hypochondriacal symptoms, and I mention it because from a differential diagnostic point of view it is very important to try to distinguish between those somatic disturbances that represent the functioning of bad parts of the self and those that represent the manifestations of relationships to internalized objects where this relationship has been damaged in one form or another. To make this differentiation more simple descriptively, the somatic delusions are more often delusions about malformation than about malfunctioning; for instance, in the case of this patient, it was very difficult to get information from him, but his conviction was that there was a defect in the structure of his sphincter, which enabled the gas to keep leaking out in some way. Earlier he had a delusion about his eyes—that he had little blocks of matter in each eye that kept him from seeing things clearly. This had been analysed and had turned out to be a somatic delusion having to do with a very bad part of himself that obstructed his vision whenever he tried to take any responsibility for damage done to any of his internal or external objects.

CASE MATERIAL
The unifying concept of hypochondria

Seven-year-old-girl

First session

A small, plump child, infantile in appearance, with a hypocritical façade of sweetness and docility. In the playroom, after the therapist introduced the situation by saying she might "use the toys in the box as (she) like(d)", the patient looked into the box and then stood rigidly in front of it and asked in a small voice if she could do sewing, and was then silent.

This child comes with a very strong pre-formed persecutory attitude and well-established defences of placation and hypocrisy towards persecutors.

Interpretation: She was waiting to do what the therapist wanted and afraid to do anything else.

Remained immobile, asking in an increasingly small but also more petulant voice what she should do.

The obvious inability to placate a person who makes no demands has an immediate shattering effect on her façade.

Interpretation: The invitation to "do as she pleased" made her feel afraid.

She moved, seemingly inadvertently giving the box a bang with her arm. She grew absolutely rigid with anxiety, white in the face, and turning to the therapist, said, "I feel sick". She eagerly agreed she wished to go to the lavatory, where instead of vomiting she urinated. Once more in the playroom, she returned to her post by the box.

Transference activity erupts from the depths. Her part-object relation to the box as a breast, which she had scooped out with her eyes on first entering and which has become very persecutory, is attacked and then attacks her in return, inside. It is of special interest that the need to expel, while at first felt as nausea, is subsequently affected by urination, showing how undifferentiated is her inner world in relation to the orifices of the body.

Interpretation: You felt sick after banging the box. You are afraid your sickness will come out in such banging if you use the box.

"Will you tell me what to do?" angrily but softly, rubbing her eyes as if crying.

The therapist has not given any relief because she has not taken up the splitting in the breast-transference. Consequently the split of idealized and persecutory breasts is experienced as a split between internal and external breast, followed by a withdrawal to an idealized internal breast.

Interpretation: She was afraid the therapist would think her bad (because of the banging) and now wanted her to feel that she was unhappy only.

The patient began rocking, her

posture hunching and drawing in, seeming both very small and very impenetrable, with her hunched back to the therapist.

Interpretation: Her withdrawal as a baby from the therapist felt to be offering her something very bad and dangerous in the box.

This brought no change to the situation.

Interpretation: She was turning her hard back to the therapist but protecting her front, as it was felt to contain her sickness, which she was afraid to let the therapist see, but would rather keep it inside or secretly be rid of it into the toilet.

The patient asked if she could go.

Interpretation: She wished to get away from the therapist as someone who was felt to accuse her of badness as the cause of the sickness.

The therapist has made no headway until she begins to recognize the split. The interpretation of hard and soft makes enough contact for the patient to feel some of the goodness to be also external. But she immediately splits it off again from the therapist and takes it back inside, as represented by including the chair in her rocking. It is significant that she wanted to go when she felt the split of the good and bad breast coming together as a result of the interpretation about protecting something in her tummy.

She moved now to a chair, which she included in her rocking.

Interpretation: She now felt there was something good in the room that she could hold onto, like holding onto a good Mummy to protect her against the therapist, whom she felt as a bad Mummy, accusing and

This is substantially correct and really saves the day, finally clarifying the split in the object, even though the nature and location of the objects are not clarified. The session ends with an improved contact and the

blaming. Indicated the end of the session.	"Sorry" can be seen as a request to come to try again.
Patient said, "I'll go now". Downstairs she seemed less persecuted and said in a small voice to the therapist, "Sorry".	

Summary

This child, entering with a pre-formed persecutory transference and prepared defences, finds herself plunged into a positive infantile reaction to the toy-box as a breast due to the therapist lack of demands and perhaps overly seductive phraseology in offering the box. A greedy scooping introjection takes place, followed by an attack on the damaged (emptied) breast to split it into idealized and persecutory—the latter being expelled into the therapist's toilet, meaning into her. This makes for a rigidly paranoid withdrawal, curling up with her idealized internal breast, turning her impervious back to the bad therapist-breast. But she is not completely impervious to interpretation, for the therapist's approach to the splitting brings movement to reintroject the good bit from the outside world.

Dynamic implications: This child has clearly made very little progress beyond the paranoid–schizoid position, with a strong oral fixation to the breast and a marked greedy drive to introject, split, and idealize. Her enuresis is revealed as a persecutory hypochondria, interchangeable with other methods of expulsion, as illustrated by the fact that her enuresis was temporarily replaced by aerophagia and belching during a period of several weeks after the initial referral to the clinic. A *potential cyclothyme with hypochondria*. However, despite the poor contact in much of this first session, she did respond to the therapist's efforts to understand and accept the negative transference, suggesting a reasonable drive towards integration. Problems seem to centre more on greed and envy than on separation or sensuous needs.

Therapeutic implications: Could probably be seen two or three times per week over a fairly prolonged time, working in an intense negative transference early on.

History: Mother only survivor of Nazi persecution in her family; an agitated, chaotic, and ineffectual person to whom patient is "*bête noire*". Father much like the patient, genial and hypocritical, seductive and self-indulgent. Breast-fed for ten days, sucked poorly, milk scanty. Took vigorously to the bottle, became fat and slow in development. Speech poor, always enuretic.

With such a background coupled with her initial negative feelings, one might wonder whether this child could be kept in treatment. This case is an example of the need to weigh up what was going on with the child herself rather than in the background.

5
Infantile autism

The category of early infantile autism was first described in the 1940s by two child psychiatrists, Leo Kanner and Barbara Betz, at John Hopkins Hospital at Baltimore, Maryland. It represents a very important achievement in descriptive child psychiatry. They made little or no attempt to formulate it dynamically, although Barbara Betz did later go on to describe what she called the "autistic barrier". The term "autism" was first used psychoanalytically in the early part of the century by Eugen Bleuler in describing "autistic thinking" in his attempt to apply Freud's findings to the psychopathology of schizophrenia. As he described autistic thinking, it corresponded very much to what Freud called the "primary process", in the mental processes of the unconscious and in dream formations. Eugen Bleuler made a very important distinction that had been rather obscured by other people who were outside psychoanalysis such as Levy-Bruhl, and I think Jung himself, who equated primary process with primitive thinking. Bleuler distinguished autistic thought processes as thought processes evolved from the primitive through the bifurcation into what Freud described as primary and secondary process. As the thought processes evolve and capacity for complex thought becomes more developed, the tendency to this bifurcation becomes more pronounced. Autistic thinking is dominated particularly by characteristics of the primary process such as the alogical forms of causality, ignoring of time sequence and its relation to causality, and above all the so-called concrete thinking in which words and thoughts are dealt with in exactly the same way as objects. Thoughts are equated exactly with the substances or the objects or the modes of action that they are meant to represent. From this point of view it might be considered quite legitimate to take over the term "autism" to describe a diagnostic category found in children.

The way in which this category was isolated was really a matter of pure medical clinical research. At a large child psychiatric clinic they began seeing over and over again and recognizing children with a certain similarity in clinical features in their history and in their family background. What these children presented was this: they were brought in as feeble-minded, mute, blind, or deaf. They were children who presented extreme chaos in their observable behaviour. Their relationship to people seemed to be completely undifferentiated from their relationship to inanimate objects. Their affects were unmodulated, fleeting, and expressed by unusual or stereotyped modes of behaviour. Aggression was very unusual and seemed mostly extremely manneristic and linked to some sort of extremely omnipotent conception of sounds and gestures. Their behaviour was extremely repetitive and somehow seemed inevitably to result in things being damaged in their surroundings and people being hurt, although they seldom seemed to make really concerted destructive attacks. Their behaviour towards people was quite identical to their behaviour towards objects; they would come and look in a person's car or a person's eye, just as they might look into a cup; they stumbled over people exactly as they stumbled over objects, climb on people as they climbed on chairs.

As for the apparent blindness or apparent deafness or seeming imbecility, there seemed to be no clear way of determining that they were not organically deficient in relation to those special senses.

In studying the family background, it was found that they were often first children or only children—though not always. One thing that stood out quite clearly was that they were almost exclusively children both of whose parents were educated and had professions. This was not a matter of selection of the population, for this clinic served the entire population of this community and saw a random sample of children. This impression was also linked to the appearance of these children, who generally presented rather fine features, were attractively built, and showed all the evidences, as it were, of good breeding, as you might say of race-horses or dogs. There was no resemblance to the mongoloid or the simple mental defectives. If you saw pictures of these children, contrasted to seeing them in action, they look like lovely, healthy children.

The reason I single this syndrome out to spend the whole lecture on is because it is a much more frequent clinical problem than is usually realized, and the prognosis is much better than the terrible clinical problem would suggest.

In discussing the dynamics of this illness, I would like to contrast it for you particularly with childhood schizophrenias or schizophrenia in general. I told you that schizophrenia is an illness that is, as Bion says, the consequence of a catastrophe, as contrasted to the psychoneuroses, which are the consequence of a tragedy. That is, when you unearth the pre-history of a neurosis, you find a tragedy that has not been coped with. When you unearth the history of a schizophrenia, you find a catastrophe, as with the unearthing of the city of Mohonjo-Daro in India, where you find a complete civilization that has been suddenly abandoned and allowed to fall to bits, or Carthage, where it was beset and absolutely sacked to the ground. Analysis of relatively healthy persons reveals something gradually abandoned and rebuilt over centuries, like Roman or Egyptian ruins—hence the catastrophic minute fragmentation of the acute schizophrenic process. The chronic schizophrenic process is an attempt at reconstruction in both the inner and the outer world, by putting these bits and pieces together in some way that gives a semblance to life. The external and internal objects relationships of the schizophrenic are carried on by multiple fragments of the ego, each fragment of which has been agglomerated from tiny ego bits; objects are correspondingly bizarre because they, too, have been agglomerated from bits of minutely fragmented objects. Thus the object relationships and the ego-structure of the schizophrenic is absolutely bizarre, completely different from anything that you see or that you can conceptualize in normal development.

In the autistic child, what you see is a terrible lack of integration. You see evidence that object-relations are dominated by omnipotence of sound and gestures and stereotyped modes of behaviour. But you do not see evidences of these really bizarre formations. In the motor sphere, for instance, when you see a schizophrenic child, you see something usually moving like some kind of badly put-together machine, but as if it were being manipulated like a puppet from outside. What you see in these children is extreme grace alternating with very unusual but still highly skilled performances.

Above all, one receives an entirely different impression from these children the moment one is able to break through what Barbara Betz has called the "autistic barrier" and make any contact with them. You get a feeling of great richness of inner emotionality, in contrast to the deadness of the schizophrenic. You get an impression of a latent capacity for an intense and passionate love, while with the schizophrenic you get the impression of ruthless, cold, mechanical destructiveness. On the other hand, making any kind of contact with these children is not something that happens immediately. In your first contact with them you find yourself being dealt with absolutely like the objects in the room; your eyes are practically never looked into. If they are looked into, it feels the same as a doctor using an ophthalmoscope looking at your eye instead of looking into you as a person and making any emotional contact. The first contact with these children seems extremely discouraging, in a way that is rather horrifying, and yet at the same time you get the feeling after a session or two of having become immensely important to the child—again something very different from what you feel with the schizophrenic. With the schizophrenic child you feel that when you have made good contact, something happens to make them extremely persecuted by you and hate you and want to get away from you, and your subsequent session is occupied with trying to restore some kind of contact. With these autistic children contact is really extraordinarily uniform in certain ways—that is, once they evolve a certain pattern of activity with yourself and the other objects in the room, it goes on with slight modification over and over and over again, from session to session.

I will mention, for instance, a little Negro autistic boy I treated, before I was a psychoanalyst, when I had only Melanie Klein's books to go by. I did not interpret a great deal to him. He was a Negro doctor's son, and his mother was a Negro nurse, and I treated him for about two years. And in just two years, seeing him three times a week he made the most extraordinary improvement. But the treatment process with him could not be contained inside the clinic and took place out in the garden, in all sorts of weather. During two years, this little mite of a thing absolutely annihilated that garden. There was not a concrete flagstone, there was not a shrub, there was nothing in that garden that was not in minute bits and pieces after those two years. Things were used against one another; each rock was used to smash the other rock and each bush used to pry out the other bush. I did not know enough at that time to interpret to him except his attacks on the mother's babies, which he eventually, when he began to speak, quite confirmed.

What these children require is somebody who can bear a great deal of projecting into, and what this boy was projecting into me (and my staff) was the anxiety that the whole world was being smashed. I had to bear the feeling that this garden was just the beginning; that it would invade the rest of the clinic first, and pretty soon my mind and my body would be completely annihilated by him. But it did not work out that way. The sadism and destructiveness tapered off, and as it tapered off, the manifestations of attachment to me and the beginnings of speech appeared. This was repeated in our clinic afterwards with three other autistic children and with other therapists, and I am quite convinced that these children are highly treatable, at least to a certain level.

This prognosis is linked to their capacity for bearing depressive feelings, the kind of depression that you only see when there is a very strong capacity for love. You know that in borderline cases and schizoid cases the smallest bit of depression is experienced in an extremely persecutory way. For instance, they never cry, and for months or years before they get their first tears they get itching in their eyes or they get conjunctivitis, or they accuse you of putting splinters of glass into their eyes, and they dream of blood coming out of their eyes and so on.

I describe this to you in order to go back to aetiology and to stress the suspicion that one aetiological factor has been a very primary failure in the capacity of the mothers of these children to accept the first projection of the cruel and destructive death instinct. The evidence for this can be found in their history, because these mothers have been almost uniformly deeply depressed inwardly, feeling cold and mechanical towards these children, for three or four months post-partum. This is almost a uniform finding. On the other hand, post-partum depression is a very common thing, and in most children with mothers with post-partum depression you do not see anything like this kind of clinical picture. I think that it links with the impression that these children are particularly sensitive by nature and have a very intense capacity for love, and that their object's inability to accept these projections of the death instinct causes them to recoil and to exert the most strenuous efforts to direct their projections away from the breast and away from the mother. Because of the inability to form this very primal relationship to the breast, which Klein describes, they seem to be unable to get into any kind of integrating process, and they seem to remain in a most unintegrated state as far as their ego is concerned. When I say that the mother cannot accept the first projection, I think that probably the way in which it is manifested is in the feeding behaviour, where these mothers are deeply depressed without any belief in what they have to offer their child emotionally, and they offer the breast or the bottle as a substitute. It seems to me that this breast must come to the child in the way one feels sometimes when one shakes hands with certain people who just give you their hand limply. The moment you have their hand in yours, you feel that there is nothing you can do with it that will not be experienced as aggressive. You cannot let go of it, because that is a rejection. You cannot hold on to it, because that is a seduction. You cannot shake it, because that is felt as competitive. Because of their sensitivity in response to the helplessness and fragility of the breast and mother, they just stop trying, not that they stop sucking, necessarily, but they stop utilizing the breast as an object into which to project their death instinct. The result is that they are left with great quantities of death instinct that works very strongly against any integrative drive within themselves. Also the inability to utilize the breast increases the zealous "dog in the manger" possessiveness.

To be able to experience and to bear projections from patients is, as far as ego strength is concerned, a primary requirement of a good psychotherapist and analyst—that is, to bear the tension, the anxieties, and the depression that the patient himself cannot bear and often for a very long time before the patient can take them back and begin to experience them. What seems to have gone wrong in the very earliest extra-uterine experience of these children is something that we really do know something about in psychoanalysis. This theory of Melanie Klein's has a tendency to remain unreal to most people, unless they study these children or schizophrenics. Here you can see that these initial projections into the breast and the splitting into good and bad breast are a life-saving procedure—life-saving in the sense of ego-saving. They enable then the introjection of objects containing big portions of the id, introjecting them as good and bad objects around which integration can then begin to take place as the result of the alliance with the good object and systematizing of defences against the bad object. This leads in the direction of the building-up of whole objects and the gradual taking-back of projections in the course of working through the depressive position.

I think that the genius of this theory of Klein's about the initial projection and splitting of the objects begins to become very real when you study these children in particular. What is the origin of object relations? The older, common-sense theory is that gratification leads the way to the object; Klein's is that it defends in the presence of an object that is willing to bear the child's projection of its death instinct without immediately shoving it back.

CASE MATERIAL
Early infantile autism

Six-and-three-quarter-year-old boy

THIRD TREATMENT SESSION

Mutters something like "Dad" on leaving mother, puts thumb in mouth, goes to door of garden, and bites the handle.

Interpretation: The thumb and the garden and the handle are the Mummy-parts he wants, and the person of the therapist is the Daddy-part he does not want.

Rushes around the room, shaking his fist at the floor, growling, and biting his thumb.

Interpretation: But the Mummy-room is full of babies that you are biting and chasing away out of the Mummy.

Therapist is interpreting a process in which the patient experiences the room as the inside of his object, which he proceeds to take absolute possession of by a number of omnipotent devices aimed primarily at innumerable babies, ignoring the therapist as the Daddy–penis. But clearly his attempt now to feed is not yet satisfactory, so that an attack on the penis and manic triumph over it ensues.

Makes noises like "wee–wee–wee", wandering about. Jumps onto therapist's chair, to couch, to basin, where he fills the mug, sips, and spits, fills it again and pours it out, biting the mug. Bites the table, sucks pencils, and then throws them away after biting bits, which he spits on floor, dancing about gleefully.

Interpretation: He is pretending not to be frightened of the room and of the therapist and

When the therapist interprets the manic triumph as a defence against persecutory anxiety to-his words, but when he feels he bites up the babies and penis of the Daddy inside this Mummy and spits out the bits, it becomes a Mummy breast full of frightening ka–ka faeces and wee–wee urine.

wards the breast, a bit of very elaborate hypocrisy seems to take place in the face of claustrophobic anxiety. The patient is triumphant again.

Comes and snuggles up to therapist, goes to the drawer and sucks the white horse and a car, drops them, looks out of window. Gives a shout of laughter and tries to run out of room.

Interpretation: He is using a trick to try to escape from this bad and frightening Mummy full of the ka–ka faeces.

He returns to the room, rushes to the couch, and begins to masturbate, lying on his tummy.

From now, on, the patient seems to be more outside the mother, experiencing the therapist as a part of him, along with the couch–genital and basin–breast. But his utilization of this fragmented object is purely for projection of bad bits from inside himself.

Interpretation: He is not so afraid of the Mummy now but hates the Mummy–therapist for giving the good milk to the Daddy and other babies.

Shakes fist at the floor, wanders round spitting. Goes back to couch after each journey—spits on the therapist.

Interpretation: He is spitting the broken-up bits of the breast from inside himself onto the Mummy therapist.

Sits quietly—fills mug at basin, drinks it. Fills it again and

When this is interpreted, he becomes able to drink from the mug–nipple, coming into strong positive contact with the therapist, but with a seductiveness that collapses when it is interpreted, being replaced by a pours it out. Loving towards therapist, kisses him.

Interpretation: He is offering to love the Mummy–breast–therapist if all the milk is kept only for him.

Gets plasticine, which he chews and spits out, big pieces at a time. Seems reluctant to leave.

greedy chewing-out of the breast and unwillingness to separate.

Dynamic implications: The therapist had no doubt that the patient was hearing and responding to interpretation, but, of course, the accuracy of the conceptualizing could be very little evaluated at the time. In looking back after 1½ years of treatment, it seems substantially correct. The implications are that this child is dominated by extremely repressive wishes and modes of relating to his objects by total projective identification; subject then to claustrophobic anxieties, dealt with by manic defences and omnipotent seductiveness. His object seems greatly disarticulated, leading to the suspicion that we are perhaps seeing only a small infantile bit of his total ego, dominated by intense possessive greed and jealousy towards the mother's body; unable to form a satisfactory introjective relationship, but very expert at expelling painful emotional content into his object. He is intensely object-seeking.

Therapeutic implications: There does not appear evidence of a schizophrenic process either of an acute or a chronic type, either in the child's demeanour, which is alert and object-seeking, or in his motor behaviour, which is well-integrated and does not betray evidences of identification with bizarre objects. While he appears to be tormented by myriad rivals, there is little evidence of persecutory anxieties overwhelming his manic defences. Prolonged analysis five or six times per week, combined with special schooling, and perhaps residential care.

History: Third child of professional people, born abroad and separated from mother, and weaned suddenly at five months when mother developed severe jaundice. In care of foreign nanny until age of one year, at which time he was walking and saying a few words. Grieved and regressed at her leaving, but not severe. Umbilical surgery at 25 months; next sibling at 32 months, both very traumatic. Recognized functioning at a defective level by three years, but *not* by parents. Psychotherapy abroad, one or two times per week until present analysis began, age 6¾.

Symptoms: Almost mute, rages, stereotypes, ineducable, unable to care for self at all, puts everything in mouth, destructive, unsocialized, nocturnal disturbances, masturbates openly.

6
Adolescence

It seems to me that in talking about adolescence it is useful to review two particular concepts. One is the general concept of the economic principle in metapsychology, and the other is the general concept of the latency period. The economic concept, you understand, embraces those particular aspects of conceptualizing the mental apparatus that view it as a very dynamic system in relative degrees of dynamic equilibrium. We conceive a structure really as structuralizing in our own thinking but these structures are not really fixed by any means. Mental structure changes, and the degree of the instability is, of course, a very important aspect of our evaluation of personality. The economic principle really covers something that can be thought of as pertaining to the energy concepts that Freud spoke of originally and that were tied up with his early libido theory.

These energy concepts, or what is sometimes called the hydro-static conception of the mental apparatus, view mental tensions as being something connected with the damming-up of energies or the damming-up of cathectic capacities, and so on. It is probably to a certain extent a wrong and misleading view of the mental apparatus. If you consider Klein's conceptualization, you will realize that in her emphasis on unconscious phantasy she is talking about something that has to do with the general problem on order versus disorder. That is, of phenomena that have to be described and conceptualized on a spectrum running from *order* to *chaos*. This is a more correct conception of the mental apparatus, which is, after all, a communication apparatus.

What this communication apparatus deals with is information, and it deals with information in terms of receiving it, storing it, sorting it, and distributing it. And it is not correct to think of the mental apparatus really as working on the basis of energy; it works on the basis of its capacity to deal with information coming to it from its various sources. This leads onto a better understanding of the concepts of stress where the mental apparatus is concerned, because we can understand that stress for that particular organ of the body has to do with its being flooded with more information than it can deal with, and that this is a conception that it is quite exclusive of *where* the information is coming from. It also does not include *why* it cannot deal with it. So if we take as a general conception that stress for the mental apparatus has to do with an imbalance between the information that is coming to it and the capacity to deal with it, we are closer to a better understanding of the economic principle in mental functioning.

We know the capacity of the mental apparatus to deal with the information has to do with the orderliness of the organization and the degree of structure that has been brought into the ego. We know from Klein's work, in particular, that the structure in the ego is absolutely dependent on and related to the nature of the internal object relationships and the stability as well as the intactness of the objects and the relationship to them. Klein has taught us that every time an object is split, the ego is also split and, conversely, that every time an object is integrated, a certain amount of integration goes on in the ego. With that as a background, if we take a look back at the latency period, we can get a little better idea of its nature as something that is not due to anything so wonderful that has gone on in the ego in the way of ordering itself, but, rather, that the latency period is one in which there has been an diminution of certain types of very disturbing information coming into the mental apparatus, particularly the disturbing information coming from the sexual organs and the sexual drives and the sexual instincts of the individual. This kind of information and the unconscious phantasies that are stimulated by it, we have reason to believe, are amongst the most difficult for the mental apparatus to deal with, because of the nature of the splitting described by Klein, splitting good and bad, splitting the good sexuality from the sadistic sexuality. This tends to confusion reactions in the ego. The moment that confusion reactions begin to develop, any communication engineer will tell you that the machine is in great danger, because there is a feed-back of muddle within it and it begins to get intoxicated by information coming from within itself. This is the kind of cyclical self-destruction that requires engineers to shut down IBM machines, for instance, or do what they call "clearing the machine". The same thing happens in the mental apparatus when it begins to develop a cycle of confusion reactions.

Viewing the latency period from the point of view of a period that is latent not so much from the point of view of the ego having achieved some marvellous passing of the Oedipus complex but a period of relative quiescence due to a sort of trough in the amount of stimulation and information that the central nervous system has to deal with particularly related to sexuality, we can predict that the latency period is not such a very stable structure. What the latency period achieves is not really a passing of the Oedipus complex so much as a by-passing of it, achieved by the splitting of internal from external, by a great deal of denial of psychic reality, by turning the infantile transference inward towards the internal objects and turning the more grown-up thoughts and feelings and interests outward, out of the home, to the school and environment, and by a certain separation from the stimulation of direct and intimate relationships to the parents as external objects. So the latency period is not really so much a passing of anything as it only achieves a certain temporary quiescence as a result preponderantly of a particular splitting that Freud discovered with the existence of repression; the splitting between internal and external is involved in the achievement of this repression.

Only a certain percentage of children achieve what can be called a reasonable latency period. We can measure the achievement of the latency period to a certain extent by the amount of masturbating the child does and that there are some children who do not achieve any control of their masturbation or any significant degree of separation between their internal and external object relationships. They continue quite relentlessly in their infantile preoccupation with their parents and with their parents' sexuality, both consciously and unconsciously. This intimate and continual interaction in relation to the outside parents perpetuates their activities during sleep and masturbation against their internal ones. Those children who do not achieve a latency period, who cannot achieve a latency period in spite of the physiological trough in the amount of sexual stimulation, are bound to be children who are absolutely knocked over by the upsurge of physiological stimulation on the one hand and the opening-up on the other hand of the new environmental areas that puberty and adolescence bring with them. Conversely, the ability to establish some sort of latency period signifies that there are mechanisms for achieving some control over their object relationships, i.e. some measure of separation and avoidance of stimulation from external objects by keeping away from them and avoiding stimulation from internal objects by obsessional control.

As far as understanding the approach to puberty and adolescence is concerned, we can generally classify children into those who really achieve something of a latency period and those who really do not, and we can with a considerable certainty feel that the children who cannot achieve a latency are in for a terrible time when adolescence and puberty really erupt and the increase of physiological and environmental stimulation occurs. You understand a great deal about the physiological stimulation. You also realize the change in the environment is very considerable when the child gets into puberty—not only a change in the opportunities open to the child for different kinds of object relationships because of the culture's change in attitude towards the child. There is also something else that occurs that is of extreme importance—that is, the size of the body and the capability of the body, and not only the capability for sexuality. The thing that I think is more important is the capability for aggression, for really successfully dangerous aggression against the self and against other people. Klein spoke of the degree to which children frequently commit partial suicide, "with as yet insufficient means", as she calls it, and she stressed that the very fact of having insufficient means is a tremendous reassurance to the child in regard to its destructive and self-destructive impulses. With the onset of adolescence and the great spurt of growth that occurs, the capacity for doing serious damage to people in the outside world and to their own bodies becomes very pressingly recognized or forced on their recognition.

With that in mind, I would like just briefly to describe a classification of three major types of adolescent reaction, because it is also a description of the three different kinds of approach to treatment of the adolescent. There is, first of all, the adolescent who has never been able to achieve a latency period, who uniformly hovers on the brink of a psychotic breakdown. These adolescents, if brought into treatment, make almost an immediate plunge into psychotic transference to the analyst that may either be in the form of immense idealization or in the form of tremendous persecution, but at an extremely primitive and infantile level. And from the very outset you get tremendously bizarre material and bizarre behaviour, and sometimes you see that the presence of the opportunity for treatment brings about such a deterioration in their defences or the stimulation of being alone with the therapist overwhelms them so much, that they really just fall into a breakdown and have to be hospitalized. So you have to be prepared with that kind of child that they go to pieces, and have to be hospitalized. I do not think that there is any reason to be frightened by them or to feel that you have necessarily driven them into a psychosis. The very fact of being with somebody who is taking an interest in them, or even being alone with another human body, is just too much for them.

In the relatively non-psychotic group, there are two fundamentally distinct ways of emerging, as it were, from the latency period. At one extreme are the children who seem to be completely dominated by their infantile phantasies of how they are going to have revenge on their parents for all the suffering of infancy as soon as they are grown up. Their adolescence is composed almost completely of group formation for the purpose of driving their parents into the grave. And I do not say it jokingly; it is absolutely so, that their group behaviour is dominated by a conception of their parents becoming old people; everything they do is intended to make them older, to make them envious of the youthfulness and vigour and sexuality and beauty of adolescence, to make them into old and miserable babies. And those are the adolescents whose energies are spent almost exclusively in group formation and group activities of a sexual and sadistic nature.

At the other extreme we have the type of adolescent that breaks down the splitting by which they had achieved something in the way of a latency period and something in the nature of a temporary peace or truce in their ambivalence to their parents. The result of the very sudden lessening of the splitting in these children is that their infantile curiosity and their envy floods back on them, in the form of ambition and a great thirst for knowledge and achievement. This way of experiencing adolescence does not very easily lead to group formation, but it does lead to the rather classical fluctuation of the manic-depressive type with periods of abandonment and elation, and periods of depression and asceticism.

The reason I have mentioned these two groups and have tried to clarify them is because they make for an entirely different approach to treatment, and they are both brought for entirely different reasons. The first type of adolescent is brought because the parents really cannot bear them and need something to be done, but generally feel that nothing can be done. They just cannot stand it any more and they bring the child for treatment, if they have still that much authority left. Naturally these children come feeling you to be one of the old fogies, no matter what your age or sex, and you become simply a representative of the parents. That is, the pre-formed transference to you is as a representative of this adult world on which they are busy wreaking their terrible infantile revenge.

The second group of adolescents, unless they develop florid symptomatology of an obviously psychogenic nature, generally are not recognized by parents as being in any great difficulty. Either they are not brought or, through their determination to get some kind of help because of their ambitiousness, somehow manage to be brought to treatment. This, of course, is a much more pleasant and easy type of child to approach because you can really settle into the general process similar to analysing an adult patient, whereas the technique of approach to the former group is a terrible problem because they do not want to give you any information, they tantalize you with the lack of information, and they are intent on making you feel little and helpless and stupid and of no use to anybody. And they succeed magnificently.

Before we go on to the clinical material, I want to mention one aspect of adolescence, which will help you to follow the material and to understand why the mechanism of projective identification and the related phenomena of augmented omnipotence and fleeting delusional identifications are such a very prominent part of adolescence. The question "who do you think you are?" is so very applicable to much of the typical posturing of this age group. The link is between the early phantasies of getting inside the parents' bodies, carried on in psychic reality in masturbation phantasies, play, and states of excitement in the small child, and the facts of the body changes in puberty—particularly the appearance of pubic hair, breast development, and beard. The image in the mirror becomes difficult to distinguish in the depths from the early projective experiences, the more so since the internal parents more closely resemble in youth and beauty the adolescent himself than the middle-aged parents of the external world. The consequence, of course, is a reinforcement of the already physiologically driven masturbation tendencies.

CASE MATERIAL
Adolescence

Sixteen-year-old girl

FIRST SESSION

Stocky but pleasant-looking, no make-up, slightly boyish demeanour. Invited to lie on couch, removes shoes and plunges down, curling up on	Both her behaviour and the material show clearly a plunging into the therapist as a good object so that the room becomes the inside of her body, while the

one side, looking at therapist. Also plunges into talk of her nightmares. On Friday she had dreamed that

. . . she was locked in a room and in danger of being crushed by a huge wooden beam, approaching her from behind. She had rushed to the window screaming

therapist inside the room becomes a part-object of mixed desire and suspicion. These dreams show the pre-formed anxiety connected with the expectation of her first analytic session.

and was awakened by her mother. Next she related a dream she *had not* told her mother, of *an underwater concrete tunnel, sealed at both ends.* She linked it to a television show, but she emphasized that her nightmares are not caused by external experiences.

Interpretation: The patient wants help with an internal situation and with a part of herself that is trapped and terrorized at night.

Yes, she wants to sleep like other girls do, so her work is not interfered with. During the day, if claustrophobic, she can overcome it by seeing a way out.

Interpretation: Awake, the frightened part can ally itself to a grown-up rational part of herself against the anxiety.

Yes, as in coming up in the lift from the waiting-room.

While this indicates good insight and drive for integration, note how ready she is to deal with her symptoms in a way that minimizes their intrusion rather than objecting to them as fundamentally irrational. This would indicate an intolerance to emotional pain and too great a readiness to placate persecutors rather than cleave to her good objects.

Interpretation: And in the room.

No, there is light from the window, though a big room would be better.

Interpretation: By looking at the therapist, she keeps her as a good mother and thus feels protected and not in need of finding an escape.

Even after the dream it is so vivid.

Interpretation: She feels that if she did not look at the therapist, the nightmare anxiety would return and compel her to run out of the room.

This material shows how the splitting and repression of infantile parts of the self and associated impulses and anxieties are being forced into her waking life by the adolescent upheaval.

No, she is looking to see if the therapist is listening to her.

Interpretation: She keeps the therapist as an attentive mother, lest she experience herself being crushed by a beam-father from behind. She's watching to see if the therapist has seen other cases like her own.

This interpretation touching on whole-object oedipal anxieties is not in touch with the material at the moment and produces a temporary impairment of trust and contact.

No, probably not.

Interpretation: She is afraid that the inexperienced mother-therapist will by overwhelmed by the nightmare part of the patient.

Well, she cannot see how just talking can help.

Because the anxiety about the father has not been clarified as part-object in nature and connected with the claustrophobic situation, a muddle results as the therapist tries to regain the contact, increasing the patient's suspicion of the sexual mother who inside is not safe because

Interpretation: She feels it would be better if she could get inside the therapist's mind to get what she wants.

of the intrusion of the beam–penis, as contrasted with the rope–tying mother, who both keeps the baby in and the penis out.

She can see how the therapist's thoughts could control a patient's fears, but she does not want anyone to understand her.

Interpretation: She feels when the therapist understands how attacking she is she will hate and crush her, like the beam.

No, she wants someone to be strong and control her.

Interpretation: Her need to watch the therapist reflects mainly her fear of being harmed.

She blushed easily with strangers. At a dance she saw a teddy–girl and did not like her. She trusts the therapist. For three years her mother has helped her with her nightmares by tying ropes across the windows so the patient would not throw herself out in her sleep.

Interpretation: She feels two therapist mothers to be here: a sexual teddy–girl mother, who is not shy with men or blushing, and a motherly, protective person. Indicates time is up.

Her contact is finally re-established by interpreting the split in the mother transference, even though it is not very clearly linked to the claustrophobic situation. The result is that the patient shows resistance to termination until the previous interpretation is clarified by the

Patient says she does not see how leaving now can help.

(makes no move to get up).

Interpretation: She feels a baby inside the mother who should not be pushed out until ready to survive, cured, independent.

addition of reference to the claustrophobic situation.

Yes, she knows it takes a long time. (Gets up.) She feels some relief already and thinks she has confidence in the therapist.

Metapsychological implications: This intelligent and well-motivated girl shows immediately the seriousness of her pathology, involving an infantile wish for the safety and irresponsibility of life inside the mother, complicated in her internal relationships by claustrophobic anxieties, which now not only involve her dream-life but are invading her waking life. That her heterosexuality is poorly established is evident. A potential severe *obsessive–compulsive–psychoneurotic*, with cyclothymic trends. Her assets for treatment are counterbalanced by a readiness to find clever compromises and placate her persecutors rather than to press on for the truth. However, the impression is of a few deep splits rather than a multiplicity of splitting or a strong tendency to projective identification.

Therapeutic implications: Would probably require four or five times/week treatment to maintain a dependent relationship and tolerate the separation anxieties once the claustrophobic situation had been overcome. Would need at least three or four years of analysis to make and secure major gains.

History: Three weeks premature. Breast-fed only for four weeks before mother developed breast–abscess and had to go to hospital, leaving patient with maternal grandmother, who ever after played a major role in her life, as the parents lived with the grandparents. Father in army service during her first four years, seeing her only once at age 2½. A crying, sensitive baby.

Severe nightmares in pre-school years. Relatively untroubled development once school adjustment began—sociable, athletic, excellent student, ambitious. Acute symptoms began about age 12—periods of inability to swallow, nightmares, sleepwalking, failure to establish normal menses, depressed and suicidal.

CASE MATERIAL
Adolescence

Fourteen-year-old girl

FIRST SESSION

Slim and attractively dressed, a mixture of depression and sulkiness. Sat, and after therapist introduced self and situation, patient spoke of her parents, saying she was coming for her troubles, but she thought it was a waste of time as she had no troubles, only some disagreement with parents about black stockings and high-heeled shoes. Father says the shoes are bad for her feet.

Immediately this youngster shows her paranoid solidarity with the delinquent group against the parents who are suspected of using their authority in a hypocritical way to hide their envy of youth and budding sexuality.

Interpretation: She feels her parents do not allow her to grow up and that the therapist will be in alliance with them in this respect.

This interpretation is correct but does not touch on the envy and hypocrisy of which she is suspected, stemming from her lack of sexuality (the mother who does not like black stockings) or her fear of sexuality (the father who keeps her in baby shoes).

She emphasized the other girls at school being allowed, then that she only likes either fine nylons or black ones, but her mother does not like black.

Interpretation: She feels the

treatment to single her out and set her apart from the other girls, feeling the therapist to be like the mother, imposing her own tastes and ideas onto the patient.

Smile, silence. Encouraged by the analyst, begins to speak about her swimming and doing badly in a recent time trial, but her father had discovered it was due to anaemia (smile). She wonders if she could see her local church spire from the therapist's window.

She indicates how identified and involved with her she feels the father to be, a bulwark of her denials of psychic reality and someone who wishes to be worshipped like a god.

Interpretation: She feels the therapist to be a stranger and the procedure unfamiliar, and she prefers her father's more familiar ways, such as the idea of anaemia, which can be cured with pills, instead of investigating her thoughts and feelings.

If such a relationship can be made with the therapist as a father. This has been taken up in substance by the therapist and earns her the first negative therapeutic reaction—i.e. a seduction into offering something and a slap in the face as her reward. But the material then shifts and the patient's bisexual muddle, her inability to do anything right because of the need to placate an envious and selfish internal mother, as well as her exhibitionisms in both male and female identification becomes evident.

Patient began looking for her coat while the therapist was still talking. When therapist inquired, said she was looking for a handkerchief but had not brought one. But when the therapist offered her a paper one, she refused it. Then turned to drawing and produced a girl, saying that it had started to be slacks but had "gone wrong" and been changed into a skirt. Next she drew a woman's face, saying it was connected with art class in school. They were supposed to draw an unusual face, African

perhaps, but it "went wrong". She then drew a stern-looking older woman, then a "boy and girl skating", and then "women shopping in the West End".

Interpretation: **She was showing the therapist how things go wrong inside her, how her boy and girl feelings get mixed up, how her wishes to be beautiful and have boyfriends are felt to be frustrated by a stern mother, who only buys expensive things for herself in the West End, with whom the therapist has become linked in her mind.**

This is correct but does not show the internal nature of the conflict, nor link the transference back to the envy aroused by the church-spire interpretation.

Dynamic implications: Here we see an adolescent involved in hateful revenge on the adult world for childhood deprivation, being projected into the external parents the overly severe, hypocritical, and selfish superego figures with which her latency period had been established. Heterosexuality seems poorly established, and her infantile ambivalent involvement with the father is still being acted out parallel to the adolescent rebellion. This implies quite deep splitting, as does the handkerchief episode, which shows a very intense and severely split-off envy towards the breast. Hypochondriacal trends are clearly strong and dealt with still by an alliance with an omnipotent penis (church spire) against the persecuting mother (stern-faced older woman). We see evidence primarily of structuring of part-object nature and relationships characteristic of the paranoid–schizoid position, with scarcely a note of warmth anywhere. A schizoid personality, mild, not likely to break down, barring trauma.

Therapeutic implications: A very difficult therapeutic problem due to schizoid flatness and paranoid solidarity with her adolescent group. Frequency of contact probably not so important—two or three times per week until anxieties really tapped. But a long-range undertaking if major gains to be arrived at.

History: Making parents' life miserable due to provocation, demands, tempers, and threats of delinquency. Irresponsible, accident-prone, neglects school work.

Only child of parents well on in life, professional man. Breast-fed for eight months, did well but weaning was a battle, holding solid foods in mouth for hours. Sucked a finger and rubbed nose with cotton-wool. Could not be alone, constipated periodically. Aggressive in nursery school but settled down in a girls' school after age 7. In plaster for three months at age 9, very good but disturbed sleep and bedtime rituals began. Analysis advised at 10½ but sent to boarding school, from which she ran away.

CHAPTER FOUR

A contribution to the metapsychology of cyclothymic states

(1963)

Detailed clinical examples from a 5½-year analysis illustrate the nature of internal objects that underlies the tendency to regress from obsessional organizations to hypomania. The basis of mania in unconscious phantasy expresses itself by a tendency to turn against good internal objects with oral greed—due to unintegrated primal envy—with the aim of violently removing a structure integral to the breast felt to be penis-like, co-extensive with the nipple, and a source of strength, creativity, and judgement in the mother. The breast-penis, because it is not retained after being stolen without becoming highly persecuting, is projected into father's penis, which becomes idealized and an object of greed at all levels and zones. The breast, now reduced to being a passive container, is open to further attacks, since love and admiration for it have greatly diminished.

A considerable body of knowledge has been built up on the metapsychology of cyclothymic states, in both the symptomatic (manic-depressive psychosis) and characterologic (cyclothymic character) forms, through the contributions of Freud, Abraham, Klein, Lewin, Helene Deutsch, Fenichel, and Schilder, to mention only a few of the major investigators who have taken a special interest in this area.

A review of their writing leaves little doubt that there is a substantial area of agreement, at least on the following points: (1) that mania and melancholia are intimately related metapsychologically; (2) that they are related to normal states of mourning and elation: (3) that some regression to narcissism is involved; (4) that they have a fixation point somewhere during the phase of transition from part- to whole-object relationships; and (5) that the fixation point represents difficulty at the developmental phase, centring upon inability to preserve a good object internally because of a tendency to denigrate it and triumph over it.

This paper aims at amplifying this knowledge by demonstrating the specific nature of the defect in the relationship to the good object that weakens the capacity for preservation and, associated with this, to demonstrate the nature of the periodic regression from the more integrated obsessional organization that the cyclothyme manifests. An attempt will also be made to show the link between these processes and the confusion and flux in the bisexuality that is so prominent in these patients. By demonstrating this particular clinical problem, it will be seen that a contribution is made to the broader theoretical problems of mood and hope as well.

The following order will be followed in the presentation: (1) outline of the psychoanalytic theory of manic-depressive states, with emphasis on the conception of mania in Klein's work, indicating the degree of agreement or disagreement with other major investigators; (2) description of the metapsychological contribution that this paper seeks to make; (3) demonstration of these concepts in action in a crucial phase of the analysis of a cyclothymic personality; (4) discussion of the implications of these findings for the broad theoretical problems of mood, hope, and differentiation of the bisexuality.

Present status of the theory of cyclothymia

In this brief review special stress will be laid on the vicissitudes of the internal object relationships. The foundations of our metapsychological interpretation of cyclothymia go back to Abraham's 1911 paper, amplified in 1924 following Freud's 1917 and 1921 papers. Already in these early times the inability of the cyclothyme to preserve his good object internally was recognized by both authors; the tendency to denigrate it and triumph over it, to expel it and reintroject it, to identify with it in its denigrated state as well as assailing it as an internal object—all these processes were observed by them both. The roles of oral and anal sadism, of regression to part-object relationships and to an increased narcissism, play a part in both conceptions. But Freud suggests more clearly that a fusion with the ego ideal in mania and identification with a denigrated superego in melancholia are the chief differentiating factors. Neither, however, clearly linked it with the Oedipus conflict. The nature of the process of "fusion" is not clarified by Freud, nor does his analysis indicate that the superego of melancholia and the ego-ideal of mania may be different objects within the same structural area of the mental apparatus.

These ambiguities are later resolved by Klein's theory of manic-depressive states, based as it is on a more detailed theory of the early superego, which she recognized as consisting of a multiplicity of part objects, good and bad, related to maternal and paternal introjects.

The early theories of Freud and Abraham also encompassed the relation between the character structure in obsessional states and cyclothymic states. Abraham in his early paper had already recognized that the remissions in manic-depressive states are characterized by the predominance of obsessional organization and defences in the object relationships. He emphasized the preservation of a relationship to a good internal object, recognizing that it was far from a happy and free relationship and far from a completely benign good object. Abraham saw the role of increased oral *sadism* as being a *consequence* of the regression into the cyclothymic state, and equated narcissism with the cannibalistic modes of introjection predominant in cyclothymia. In neither his nor Freud's work at that time is the *regression* seen as the *consequence* of anxiety due to sadistic attacks on the object, but rather, in keeping with libido theory, they view it as being due to a greed for new objects, carried out by cannibalistic means (narcissistic incorporation), which is not seen as necessarily sadistic.

This area of theory, the relationship of cyclothymia to obsessional states and the factors making for progression and regression between them, as well as the overall relationship to the developmental phases of infancy and childhood, has not been dealt with by other writers on mania and melancholia until the work of Klein (1935).

The connection of these problems with early infancy and particularly with the relation with the breast was stressed early by Rado (1928) and Helene Deutsch (1928), with special reference to the affects of elation and ecstasy, but the differentiation between an internal and an external breast was not made by these authors. Lewin (1932), on the other hand, links hypomania with sleep and his own theories of the "dream screen" and the "oral triad", but he speaks also of an identification with the parents in coitus. However, his material seems to show that the patient identified with a very bad, denigrated and rather lifeless coitus between internal parents. He also adds to the theory of mania the important role of denial, later confirmed by Helene Deutsch (1933). In Klein's work this mechanism achieved a deserved prominence and was clarified as to content, namely, the denial of psychic reality, i.e. of the existence or importance of the internal world and its objects.

Helene Deutsch was the first writer to bring oral envy into prominence in the theory of mania, although Lewin suggests that the identification with parental coitus has a basis in envy. This area, too, has been greatly elaborated in the work of Klein (1957) but not specifically linked back in detail by her to the earlier description of the processes of denigration of the primal good internal object, the breast, which precipitates the manic attack.

Klein's theory of the cyclothymic states is bound up with her conception of the transition in ego development from the paranoid–schizoid to the depressive position, characterized by the emergence of the whole-object relationship and love of a unique and irreplaceable object. With these changes there occurs an adaptation of the defences characterizing the early period, and their employment against persecutory anxiety. In the depressive position they are deployed in modified form against the spectrum of depressive anxieties. Thus splitting, projection, introjection, idealization, and omnipotent control find a new role in relation to the damaged and undamaged objects, internal and external. Added to these, to make up the full equipment of the manic defences, are denial of psychic reality and denigration of the object. She stresses the role of these manic defences in both the modulation and the preservation of normal development, as well as their excessive and destructive employment in pathological processes. This differentiation is primarily a quantitative one, depending on the balance between the loving and destructive forces and the degree to which envy and jealousy have been moderated in relation to a good object. But she states clearly that the basis for the fixation point for later cyclothymia is a qualitative one, founded on a *pathological* development at the onset of the depressive position, where Freud, and Abraham in particular, were more inclined to see a fixation to a normal but intensified phase of libidinal development.

Certain more recent work will be discussed after the clinical material has been presented.

Before passing on to the next section, it may be worthwhile to comment on the methodological problems that lie behind some of the disagreement among various investigators. The greatest areas of disagreement seem to centre about the nature of the anxiety situation being defended against and the specific mechanisms of the manic reaction. The impression is unmistakable, though not always clear in the clinical material cited, that either florid manic reactions have been briefly analysed (Katan, Schilder), or brief hypomanic states have been seen during the analyses of patients of varying diagnosis (Lewin,

Fenichel, Deutsch, Angel). The former situation is open to the suspicion that the efflorescence of the manic state has been seen, but not the manic reaction *in statu nascendi;* while in the latter, the workings of manic mechanisms over a wide spectrum of anxiety situations not specific to cyclothymia have been studied.

While the general conclusion of this paper has been drawn from a variety of clinical experiences, a single case will be demonstrated in detail. The diagnosis of cyclothymic personality will be documented both historically and by the nature of the transference process. Then in clinical material the specific process underlying the patient's repeated loss of the obsessional adjustment and regression back into hypomania will be demonstrated in the repeated progression and regression in the transference during a crucial period in the analysis.

The metapsychological contribution of this paper

It is sought here to extend the psychoanalytic theory of cyclothymia in one direction only, to clarify the nature of the internal object relationships that underlie the tendency to regress from the obsessional organization to the hypomanic situation. This latter state sets the stage for those further denigrating and expulsive attacks on the good internal object that may end, unless checked, in melancholia, may progress to paranoia, or may even give way to a full-blown acute schizophrenic catastrophe.

In the clinical material, the following thesis will be illustrated: the cyclothyme is characterized by a tendency, under psychological or physiological stress, to turn against his good internal object—fundamentally the breast of the internal mother—in his unconscious infantile relationships. This turning against the breast takes the characteristic form of an intensification of oral greed, which has the aim of violently removing a structure integral to the breast, felt to be penis-like, co-extensive with the nipple, and the source of strength, creativity, and judgement in the breast and mother. This breast-penis, because it cannot be retained after being stolen from the breast without becoming highly persecutory, is then projected into the father's penis, which thereby becomes enhanced and idealized, and an object of greed at all levels and zones. The breast, now reduced to the status of a passive container, is open to further attacks since love and admiration for it have been greatly diminished. This internal constellation is the basis of hypomania, the first step in regression from the obsessional organization.

The driving force in this attack on the breast is the unintegrated primal envy. The forces unleashing the envious attack may be various, at different times and in different patients. The character manifestations of this tendency are: (1) an instability in sexual identification and a confusion between masculine and feminine taking the form of an exaggeration of strong–active–masculine, and weak–passive–feminine; (2) pervasive pessimism about the value of life and the richness of its joys.

The restoration of the damaged internal breast can either be brought about by a good intercourse between the internal parents or by a good feed at the external breast (or a later transference representative, as, for instance, the analyst's mind). But these restoring processes are resisted because of the renewal of oedipal tensions and the pains of the depressive anxieties that accompany them.

The patient

At the outset of treatment, the patient presented herself as a small and slim, rather bow-legged and pigeon-toed woman, looking somewhat younger than her 35 years, tastelessly dressed, with a slightly mannish quality. This impression was enhanced by the lack of make-up, other than a little lipstick, and the short, straight boyish haircut. Her pleasant features were unexpressive of feeling, eyes always averted, posture rather angular and drawn inward. But her voice, with its soft European accent, suggested in its timbre both intelligence and a capacity for feeling, while a little gasping mode of showing assent, with its tic-like quality, gave the impression of continual inner anxiety.

At that time she was in the second three-month period of her third pregnancy, and was on leave of absence from her professional position, staying at home to care for her second child, a boy of 18 months. She had lost her first boy in infancy owing to asthma, probably cardiac in nature based on congenital heart defect. Her husband was described as very English and a good skilled worker, a rather passive man of whom she was fond but on whom she could not rely emotionally or financially. Their satisfactory standard of living was due largely to her good income and, in order to maintain it, she had to return to work once the new baby was weaned.

Her circumstances, she felt, were adequate to a happy life, but her illness made it a torment. She could not show affection for her son and was in constant dread of disturbing his mind with obsessional thoughts of his genital. She could not cook a meal without a fear that she had put something poisonous into it; could not go to sleep without hours of ritualistic checking of gas and water taps, doors, windows, and light switches. Her relationship to her husband was one in which he was felt as a burden, and even then their intercourse was managed by her to provide him with pleasure, for he was rather impotent, especially as to orgasm. Her own genital seemed greedy, and her orgasm came easily and was indistinguishable to her from a masturbatory climax. A depressed mood was always the sequel to coitus. She was a slave to her house, isolated from her neighbours, and she felt herself an unwanted foreigner, persecuted by the English weather and shopkeepers.

But her health was good, her body bursting with vigour, and her mind always active, planning and carrying out plans, despite the enveloping pessimism through which the world was seen as a true hell, or perhaps at best a purgatory. She secretly, with her own mixture of superstition and Christian dogma, looked forward to deliverance through death, and would often, in the midst of her rituals, ask God when her release would come.

Almost lifelong hay fever and eczema of hands and trunk added physical discomforts, which she experienced almost as a relief of the mental suffering. She could fight back by scratching the itch, rubbing the eyes, blowing the rebellious nose.

While she looked forward to the new baby and yearned for a little girl, she was terrified at the prospect of looking after it. The conviction that she had caused her first child to develop asthma because of her thoughts of his genital made her feel incapable of keeping her babies alive. She arranged for her mother to come from her native land to help for the first few months and for a nanny to take over after that, so that she could return to work after the weaning. She loved her work and was eager to return to it.

Her mental status at the initial interview gave no cause for alarm. She was oriented, presented a lucid history with insight into the mental nature of her symptomatology, gave no evidence of grossly impaired reality sense or of bizarre mental content or phenomena. She was clearly an intelligent woman and very well motivated for treatment.

History

The childhood of the patient, the sixth child of seven of a professional couple, was spent in a small city in northern Europe. The mother, who had been the eldest of her own large group of siblings, had been surrogate mother to the others from the age of 12, when her own mother had died. Subject to depressed periods as well as periods of intense extramural activity with women's organizations, she was nonetheless the stabilizing influence of the family. The father was a handsome and sociable person, vain of his status in the community and accustomed to pampering at home by wife and daughters. While he was too easily seduced by flattery and intemperate in his outbursts when thwarted or hurt, his goodness showed itself in a generosity that was apparently boundless, if not always judicious. But neither parent seems to have been deeply sensitive to emotional problems. Both maintained a mixture of superstition and Oxford Movement optimism in relation to the mysteries of life.

The household was a lively, well-ordered, and comfortable place, a favourite haunt of friends both of the children and the parents. The one son of the seven children, five years older than the patient, was an object of concern to parents and sisters alike owing to his passivity, artistic interests, and laziness. In contrast, the patient's many serious difficulties, primarily internal and secret, passed relatively unnoticed until adolescence.

There were no known complications in the pregnancy or delivery, except that the pregnancy was undesired and the mother was in a mild depressed state. Breast-feeding continued until close to one year, despite several complications. The first of these was extremely early teething, apparently of both upper and lower incisors, by three months. To complicate this, the infant developed severe whooping-cough with measles at three months and was given up for dead by the doctor. Devoted nursing by the mother, which included such measures as manual removal of pharyngeal secretions, alternate exposure of the child to heat and cold, and frequent suckling, brought recovery after a three-week period of acute illness, leaving the mother in a severely exhausted state and the child emaciated.

The birth having taken place in the winter months, this illness must have occurred in very early spring. All the next summer was spent by the parents building a summer cottage a few miles from town, taking the patient with them in her carrycot. This cottage subsequently became an object of great attachment for the patient.

Weaning from the breast before the end of the first year was preceded by the commencement of toilet training, with the use of paper suppository stimulation. The baby's response was in the direction of compliance, independence, ambition, and a turning from the mother towards an intense flirtation with the father, which seems to have had encouragement from both parents. Most of the first year had been spent in the parental bedroom.

The two years from the beginning of walking to the birth of the baby sister were ones of "bliss"; she was a great entertainer, pretty, flirtatious, greedy for the limelight. This hypomanic period was not disturbed on the surface by either the appearance for six months of a godchild for whom the mother cared following its mother's death, nor did the mother's pregnancy itself break through this elated period. Her relationships at that time were universally "good": that is, she was on good terms with mother, who was treated like a devoted and respected servant. Her life revolved around father, and already by the age of 2½ she was toddling down the hill from home carrying his lunch to him in a little basket, ushered across the street by his assistant, treated like visiting royalty by his office staff and clients, rewarded by him with a kiss and money to buy a banana at the fruit shop downstairs.

She was the darling of her sisters and brother. Even the next older by three years, the sweetest by nature of the family, doted on her. But for her demands to be thwarted was unbearable, felt as an affront, and dealt with by high-handedness—particularly by stealing without guilt—taking what was her due.

The birth of the baby sister shattered this little paradise, and the patient vividly remembers her despair and rage at finding her mother's bedroom door closed to her. Unfortunately the following year, while the patient struggled with bitterness, oscillating between tantrums and over-solicitude for the baby, family affairs turned for the worse and ushered in a prolonged period of marital conflict for the parents. Within a short period the father lost his savings and more in a maritime investment, the mother had a miscarriage, the home had to be sold and replaced by a smaller and less elegant one, servants were reduced in number, and in the midst of this the patient was sent away for a month to stay with a former maid and chauffeur.

It was from this separation, consciously felt as a banishment, that she returned to the family a chastened, neurotic, and depressed child. Thus by the age of four she manifested an unwholesome character distinguished by secrecy, an outward docility and helpfulness towards mother, mounting fastidiousness in her food habits, competitiveness with the older children, and preoccupation with her own, her mother's, and her baby sister's health.

During the next six years, family life was considerably disrupted by father being mildly alcoholic, inattentive to mother, and unreliable at work. The patient's character disturbance seemed to fall in with mother's needs, for she became the companion of mother's loneliness, often sharing the bed until father came home late at night, partly drunk. At school she was the same, with consequent mediocre accomplishment and a poverty of imagination. External reality seemed in many ways to coincide with internal reality, and thus, as we shall see, greatly strengthened certain defences.

But this picture of a joyless, obsessional little prig was done away with quite suddenly by a tonsillectomy at the age of 10. In its place appeared a very tomboyish exuberance, increased imaginativeness, and improved learning capacity, competitiveness in sport, and contempt for femininity. Again her father became the centre of her life. A dream from age 11 illustrating this renewed hypomanic state has always stood out in her memory. It illustrates the identification with the father, which replaced the earlier flirtation. In it

> . . . *she was standing proud and triumphant on a pile of dead bodies of thieves and murderers who had invaded her room.*

Skiing in the winter with father, fishing in the summer with father—everything revolved around gaining his attributes and his admiration. The onset of menses swept back into consciousness the sexual excitement in father's presence, spoiled her pleasure in his company, and brought the return of compulsive symptoms, now in the form of compulsive urination at night, and checking doors, switches, and taps. Depressive elements were intensified by mother having another miscarriage when the patient was aged 12. By 14 she had insomnia, was hypochondriacal about her internal genitalia and breasts, and was fearful lest she should grow a penis as a result of masturbation—an anxiety that became prominent later during her first pregnancy.

Thus as an adolescent she was shy and preoccupied with school work and her ambition to be a doctor or a dentist. But she was discouraged in this by her father because of her anxieties and hypochondria. After a brief period teaching in school before war began, she entered training for her profession. Her first love affair at age 19 led to intercourse with great pleasure but without orgasm. This relationship was rather sabotaged by the family, and its collapse ushered in a period of compulsive masturbation, feelings of persecution at the hands of her superiors at work, insomnia, fatigue, confusion, depression, and suicidal plans, from which she was saved only by her mother's unexpected arrival. (This type of acute illness was repeated at 22, when she was training again for a higher qualification in her profession, but was more hypochondriacal in structure and attributed by her to mercury poisoning. She rescued herself through a long holiday spent skiing.)

During the war and the Nazi occupation she worked away from home and gradually began to hold together an obsessional pattern, broken periodically by hypochondria, periods of social and sexual excesses, and periods of depression. When her father became terminally ill with carcinoma of the lung, she nursed him devotedly but without a feeling of love, for her ambivalence to him had been conscious all through the period of the war, thinking of him at one moment as secretly the leader of the underground and the next moment accusing him in her mind of being a coward and food hoarder.

His death brought in her most severe period of social and sexual excesses, this time with drinking, but she settled back into a more obsessional pattern, reinforced by the nature of her work. Hopes of marriage and children were more or less abandoned, until she met her husband after coming rather impulsively to work in England. He proved to be the first man with whom she found sexual satisfaction. A marked elation replaced her now chronic obsessional pattern as a result of the pregnancy that resulted from their premarital relations, and she then realized to what an extent she had abandoned all hope of ever having children. In her joy, she was relatively unconcerned about whether the father of the child would marry her, which he in fact was eager to do.

This brief respite from symptoms, a period of "bliss" covering the first six months of the pregnancy, was shattered abruptly thereafter with the appearance of the ruminative dread that she would harm her child by staring at it. She collapsed into a depressed and agitated state, at which time she was first referred by her general practitioner for analysis. This was in April 1952. By the time treatment could be offered 15 months later, she had lost the first baby at about 9 months of age and was again pregnant, living temporarily abroad, at home with her mother. She returned to England in a dreadful state of anxiety after the birth of this second little boy. Treatment was started five months later, in May 1955, at which time she was again pregnant, and urgently wanted to begin her treatment before the birth of the child.

The analytic process

The analytic process during the next six years can be divided with fair accuracy into six periods, the fourth of which is the focal point for this paper. The first period, covering the last months of her third pregnancy and the four months of her breast-feeding of the new baby, was characterized by idealization of the analysis.

Two transference patterns were reflected in the dreams and behaviour: one in which the analyst was an ideal mother and her husband a persecuting father; the other in which the analyst was a persecutory mother and her husband a father who offered her an ideal penis. These two patterns oscillated with each week-end, bill, and holiday.

The second period of analysis followed the collapse of her breast-feeding under the pressure both of anxieties about being harmed by a greedy and hostile baby and fears of harming it by feeding it bad milk and worse thoughts.

The year that followed was dominated by the gradual revelation of her ambivalence to the mother–analyst, defended against tooth and nail by acting out, which strikingly repeated the latency years in which she had been the companion of mother's unhappiness owing to father's drinking and indifference. This was tirelessly and secretly acted out by a slavish faithfulness to the drudgery of analysis and her job, accompanied by endless cleaning and decorating of her home. All disappointments or persecutory feelings towards the analyst–mother were experienced and acted out with shopkeepers and bus conductors.

The repeated analysis of the disruptions of this pattern caused by week-ends, holidays, bills, and other chance occurrences gradually brought a third and more obsessional structure into the transference, in which ambivalence to both parental figures was reflected, the bad relations being acted in the transference and the good ones with her home, work, children, and husband. The disappointments and disruptions during this period, which lasted for about a year, led more clearly to internal attacks, with hypochondriacal and depressive consequences on the one hand while on the other they were gradually more and more strongly defended against by a rigid control over the analyst–parents internally, reflected in a florid and migrating obsessional and compulsive symptomatology.

This third period finally gave way to a fourth, occupied with the analysis of her oral greed and envy, and dominated symptomatically by hypochondria gradually yielding more and more to periods of depression and periods of marked clinical improvement.

The fifth period, starting roughly in the spring of 1959, was occupied with a renewed working-over of her oedipal conflict, more now on the genital level and more clearly bisexual in its structure. This period was characterized by characterologic and symptomatic improvement, a deepening of her attachment to the analyst as a person, and the great lessening of her acting out, with consequent improvement in all her outside relationships. The sixth period, termination, is still in progress [1963].

To return now to the fourth period of the analysis.

By Christmas 1957, the strong maternal transference, dominated by oral greed and possessive jealousy, was recognized by the patient. The hypocrisy of the obsessional isolation of the internal mother and of its external counterpart in the begrudging attitudes towards the analyst with respect to money, week-ends, holidays, professional success, other patients, etc., was well understood. A strong contact with her own phallic masculinity kept coming through at times, but still too fraught with guilt to be long tolerated, usually promptly projected into her husband or her little boy. These insights were accompanied by acknowledgement of clinical improvement, particularly in relation to her ability to make contact with her children, her pleasure in her home and work, a lessening of her compulsions, and a decrease in her characteristic pessimism. Her relationship to her husband, however, was decidedly worse. The passing of this Christmas holiday of 1957 marked the beginning of the slow and repetitive process that I wish to emphasize in this paper as the central problem in the patient's analysis—namely, the restoration of the qualities of strength, judgement, and creativity to her internal mother and the reintegration of a part of her own personality containing the destructive oral envy towards the mother and her breast.

Signs of envy and a wish to steal or spoil appeared first in material and behaviour referable to the paternal transference. The oral nature of the greed was clarified. For instance, she reported that, after a refusal of coitus by her husband, she had angrily gone into the children's room to sleep, where she found herself getting into a rage with the analyst. Then she suddenly fell asleep and dreamed of *a man in a short night-shirt, but instead of a penis he had a stick of butter for a genital.* It could be established that her wish for coitus with her husband had derived partly from an infantile wish, split off from the transference, to steal by eating up with her mouth-genital this idealized butter-penis. But once she had it inside her, it changed to a persecuting urine-penis which forced her to urinate continually. This could be demonstrated in a dream in which

> ... *she passed a man holding a tray of dental instruments. Then one of them was in her hand and she instantly had the urge to urinate. But on the toilet her urine flowed endlessly.*

She clung to a particular claim as the bulwark against feelings of guilt about this greedy stealing from her internal object and its external manifestation in the transference of ingratitude, begrudging of payment, and indifference to the analyst's convenience or welfare. This claim was that the good things derived from the analysis were not for herself but for her home and children. This hypocrisy was acted out for months in which she flaunted with long sighs her joyless submission to the analysis, while she would happily run home afterward, reporting the following day the joys of staying up into the small hours decorating, sewing, planning treats for the children. If it occurred to her that these joys were in any way manifestations of improvement in her mental health, she promptly thanked God.

What seemed to be an impenetrable defence could only be broken through when I could show her that it was not from the father that this stealing occurred but from the mother. She dreamed that

> . . . *she was in a dingy, cheap cafe, with a new baby in a carrycot. She felt that God had miraculously given it to her and thanked him in silent prayer. But before her eyes the baby changed, first into twin babies and then into the twin breasts of a pretty young woman.*

Here I could show her that the analysis was felt as a gift for herself, but that the distortion consisted in confusing both the source and nature of the gift, representing it as a baby obtained from the idealized father (God) while the relationship to mother and breast was denigrated (the dingy, cheap cafe). But the dream goes on to acknowledge the recent recognition that she is the baby, and the gift is of an internal mother and her breast, which could only come from good feeds in the analysis from the analyst as a mother. The immediate reaction to this interpretation was an experience of pleasure, the expression of gratitude, and recollection of quiet talks with her mother over coffee in early adult life. But the next day a very violent negative therapeutic reaction ensued; she was in despair, and the analysis was worthless.

This pattern of negative therapeutic reaction to particularly fruitful, relieving, or enjoyable sessions became more and more the rule, and, parallel to it, with the passing of the summer holiday of 1957, the maternal transference pressed more and more to the fore. Her hypochondria now took the form of migratory pains, with associated phobia of cancer. Her former habit of taking abortifacient tablets prior to her menses returned, and with it a galaxy of fears for the safety of her children in the home. On the other hand she reported that she now spent more time and derived more pleasure from being with the children, feeding, playing, or teaching, and less time on the house itself, cleaning or decorating. The hypochondriacal symptoms now worsened every week-end, and the acting-out of these fears with her children representing the babies attacked inside the mother caused her to miss almost every Friday session for months.

I was gradually able to demonstrate to her how the neglect of the analysis during this acting-out worked in a circular fashion with the negative therapeutic reactions to cause the analytic mother externally to become damaged in the patient's mind and then neglected because of her loss of value; that this resulted in parallel changes in her internal situation; that she defended against her guilt through acting out her identification with this mother who was greedily eaten into (the hypochondria and cancer phobia), neglected (her now nearly complete sexual incompatibility with her husband), and enviously attacked, should she become pregnant (the taking of abortifacient tablets)—attacks that were too protean to be defended against (the galaxy of fears for the safety of the children inside the house).

But each painful contact with the guilt and feelings of worthlessness inherent in the process of reintegration of this infantile destructive greed was quickly recoiled from. The responsibility would be projected onto the internal father, then externalized to her husband, whom she was able, unfortunately, to provoke into tantrums and threats to murder the patient, the children, or himself. Bringing the situation back into the transference through interpretation would diminish the acting-out and bring improvement to the health and relationship of the internal parents. Then the obsessional defences would be invoked once more to prevent the coitus of these internal objects and would be acted out as various compulsive rituals of checking and obsessional suspicions about the sexual activities of the children, or her husband, or the husband with the children.

In turn, analysis of the transference and the internal situation underlying these symptomatic attitudes and activities would bring her relief, renewed contact with depressive feelings, renewed reparative efforts, and a new explosion of destructive envy. Typically, at this latter point she would dream of a happy, wealthy, attractive couple with one child. In a few days all would be a shambles in her dreams—a burnt-out ship, or a bombed quay-side with war orphans, or an Italian slum flat with an apathetic couple and a dead child.

A particular echelon of defence against the guilt about the attacks was discovered to be in the form of a secret accusation that the envy that motivated these attacks was in the first instance projected into her by the analyst. She dreamed of

> *... entering a little shop to order some whipped butter, but when the shopkeeper whipped it before her eyes, she*

> *angrily accused him of making it dirty. She demanded that he give it to her as heavy cream and she would whip it herself at home.*

It was possible to show her how she resisted any experience of admiration for the analyst's mind as a creative analytic breast, trying to force him to go along with the pretence that it was a passive organ that simply delivered its goods derived from books and teachers to whom the creativity was attributed (father) or that it delivered the raw materials, which she creatively whipped into shape in her mind.

To summarize briefly: by the time the 1958 summer break was nearing, the patient had reached a point where her envy, with its characteristic modes of operating both internally and externally in the transference, was well known to the patient and recognized as being directed towards the mother (and particularly the breast) as well as the father (and particularly the penis). But the admired and envied capacity for creativity still remained split between these two on the part-object level, with the qualities of wealth, generosity, and warmth delegated to the breast as a *container* and those of strength, endurance, and judgement allocated to the penis of the father as a *performer.* Although I had shown her evidence many times, she seemed unconvinced both consciously and in the depths that the obsessional control over and separation of her internal parents, and the consequent symptomatic eruptions of each week-end, were directed at preventing a coitus that was not only *hated* as the source of a rival baby who would push her out, but *feared* as an act that, by restoring the internal penis of the mother and breast and thus by restoring the full love and admiration, might also precipitate an all-out envious decimation of the good object, which would be irreparable (madness).

By the time the summer break arrived in 1958, the positive maternal attachment was so intense and the separation anxiety so great that a flight to her mother similar to one during the second summer break of the analysis took place, but with only temporary relief of her fears of some disaster overtaking the analyst while he was away. This flight was very different from the earlier one, which had been completely hypomanic in mood. The current journey was undertaken with considerable insight that she felt unable to bear six weeks without a mother-person. Much of the anxiety about the analyst's welfare and safety was at first split off onto her husband, who manifested a very suicidal attitude in fact about her going and was afraid she would not return to him. However, the anxieties could be brought back into the transference through interpretation. This resulted in a softening of her subtly provocative attitude towards her husband, so that she finally arranged for him to join her for the last two weeks of the holiday.

The work of the first two weeks in September 1958 illustrates in a rather condensed fashion the previous year's transference process, and at the same time encompasses the analytic formulation, which has formed a nodal point for the work since then—a point referred to in the analysis as the "Rocket-suction" dream.

On the first day, a *Tuesday*, she was clearly happy and relieved to be back in analysis, spoke at length about the positive and negative aspects of the trip to her mother, then related a dream from Monday night:

> *A man was presenting to a Customs official two white Israeli passports, each with a strange emblem on it.*

Her associations referred to the trouble in the Middle East. She had heard at home that her former boyfriend was working in the Middle East, but had had to send his wife and children home. In conversation with her mother she had brought up her old grievances about the sabotaging of her love affair. She had had a sleepless night over it but was pleased at how easily the bitterness towards her mother passed away.

I interpreted to her that the two white Israeli passports stood for the analytic mother's breasts, which the father part of the analyst was trusted to bring back safely to her from the dangerous outside world, a father whom the baby girl in her used to experience as the boyfriend who would one day be her husband but was now acknowledged as mother's husband. The bitterness at the relinquishment of this hope was now better balanced by the restored sweetness of her relation to the mother and her breasts. I further linked the strange insignia with the nipple, which was felt to be continuous with a penis inside the breast.

The following day she reported that to her surprise she had found herself walking down the alley in which she had met an exhibitionist some months previously. She believed she dreamed of having intercourse with her father or brother. At work she had a phantasy for the first time since the earliest months of analysis that it would be nice if her husband went away and she could have a love affair with the analyst. Her sister is believed to have a cancer of the breast, and she felt very hostilely scrutinized by this sister at times while at home, especially after she had made a comment on the patient's dark eyes. She herself made a silly comment one day to a sterile woman. Thinking to comfort the woman about her sterility, she had said that her own trouble was that she could not keep from getting pregnant.

I interpreted that in her masturbation-phantasy dream she had again removed the penis, the "strange" emblem on the Israeli passports, from the internal mother and attached it to the father's penis, with a resulting greedy desire to devour the penis on the one hand (the intercourse dream) and feelings of persecution on the other hand by this eaten-out mother and her breasts. She reported then in confirmation that that day she had phantasized an act of fellatio with a particular man she had known in her younger days. Seeing a picture of a baby resembling him had brought him to mind.

On the Thursday the material at first centred around a dream in which

> *. . . she discovered that her husband had been living with another woman for a year and was building for her a lovely cottage where only barren rocks had been before. The patient at first felt enraged and jealous, but this quickly passed, and she became concerned about the woman and whether her husband was being better to his new mate than he had been to herself.*

She associated to the cottage her parents had built when she was a baby and how they had taken her along, as she had heard, in her carrycot, in good weather.

This dream could be used to clarify for the patient the process of recovery from the consequences of Tuesday night's attack on the internal mother's breasts and consequent flight to a greedy attitude towards the penis in the paternal transference. Here she could see the acceptance of her baby position, on the couch as in the carrycot, admiring and appreciating the creative cooperation between the parents, fundamentally a reference to their coitus, to which she had been a witness in the parental bedroom. The cottage in the dream, like the cottage of her childhood, represented the restored breasts and thus the restored character of the mother, receptive and comforting, as compared to the hard and barren rock-breasts of the depressed mother, the cancer-eaten, accusing-eyed mother–sister of yesterday's association.

She then spoke of her eczema being worse that day; that she did not trust the new nanny with the children; and then, at great length and with strong feeling, of how she disapproved of mixing penicillin and sulpha in the same syringe, that it was potent but dangerous.

When I interpreted that she was feeling the analyst now to be a restored mother injecting into the baby parts of her this dangerous analytic milk, a mixed product of penis and breasts, which gets under her skin, irritates her, and might kill her, she replied that she felt afraid that the analysis would fail, that the analyst might be a "split personality". I interpreted that she had just split my head–breast again, separating the strength and creativity from the warmth and goodness, creating divided parents who were unable to help her to restore the splitting in herself.

The Friday session was spent largely in angry and frightened silence watching a storm outside, and on Monday she continued very resistant, but more sullen than angry. The analyst reviewed the material of the previous week. Towards the end of the session she softened somewhat and revealed two dreams from the week-end. One was of *a little boy's trousers in which the lining was worn out and torn*. The other was of *a girl's ski pants and two ski caps, one with the pom-pom hanging down and the other with it standing up*. Her associations were to her little boy's tantrums.

I reminded her here of the "dangerous mixture" that I was felt to be injecting into her on Thursday and the explosive mood, reflected in the thunderstorm of the Friday session with its angry silence. The dreams showed something in greater detail, namely that the bringing together of these restored internal parents put her also into contact with her infantile bisexuality. But when we examine the little-boy and little-girl reactions to the week-end, we find the storminess only in the little-boy part, with his trousers worn-out from masturbation, while the little-girl part enjoys the warmth and protection of the twin breasts (the two caps) and her identification with the sexual mother (girl's ski pants).

On the Tuesday she was in a very loving and appreciative mood, sleepy and lazy. She had dreamed of *a young mother carrying a baby.* But towards the end of the session she reported that her body felt like a stone, and she linked it with the druids, an "ancient sect worshipping nature"—as she understood it—and then to Stonehenge and the plans for restoring some of the triglyphs by raising the fallen stones onto the columns. I interpreted both the appreciation for being picked up by me as a mother who understood the nature of babies and the threat to crush me if I throw her down again in order to go to the Daddy, whose potency I was accused of worshipping.

This rather tenuous balance in the maternal transference persisted through part of Wednesday, but towards the end she became very persecuted, wishing to break off treatment, extremely concerned with her cancer fear, full of recriminations against her dead mother-in-law and anguish about her dead child. This reaction was not relieved by interpretation of content and its relation to the coming week-end. On the Thursday she did not appear until the very end of the session. She reported that while on her way to the session she had become so frightened by the idea that her children had stolen money from her purse, swallowed it, and were dying, that she had had to rush back home. She had then felt relieved, and wanted to call the analyst to explain, but, being unable to find his telephone number, had come along to explain to relieve his worry. I was unable to spend any time with her, nor did she press for any. This coming to me constituted an extraordinary act of consideration on her part and the first acknowledgement that I must surely worry about her when she was late or did not appear.

The following day, Friday, produced this very rich nodal material: The patient was twenty minutes late and talked at great length about the bad bus service, and especially about buses not stopping for her. The analyst interpreted the continuation of her fear of my sucked-out breast–brain, which she felt she had greedily destroyed and which she now feared would either desert her or offer her only a damaged and poisonous breast to suck, linking it with the previous day's acting-out. It was linked also with the sulpha–penicillin reaction of the previous Thursday and also with the events leading to the breaking-off of her breast-feeding of her little girl, especially her fear that one breast was watery and poisonous. She jumped up, rushed out of the room, and returned in two minutes, explaining that she had had to urinate. The analyst said that his interpretation had brought her into contact with the feeling of having damaged the breast by sucking the penis out of it. This stolen penis was just then felt to be inside the baby part of her and now became a bad penis that urinated continually inside her and forced her to urinate, as we had seen earlier when the details of her urinary compulsion had been worked out.

The patient then related the following dream:

> *She and her husband were on a motor scooter, she in front, but both had to tread on something to start it. It was a dangerous road, and he fell off. She noticed that instead of a wound he had a tumour growing on his head, with a white, fatty substance coming from it. She took him to the hospital for X-rays, but as soon as these were developed, she snatched them and ran away, thinking now she would find out the truth for herself. She then found herself with a doctor and nurse inside a little cottage, a nursing home. He said, "It is a myeloblast". The patient reacted to this with grief and pity, as if her husband would have only a few days to live. A nurse said, "The trouble is with the rocket suction", which the patient took as a reference to some trouble in the husband's urinary system or bowel. She then saw that the window was decorated for Christmas and said to the doctor, "What lovely weather; and only a year ago it was pouring with rain".*

Her associations went first to her own hypocrisy in the dream, recognizing that she was treating the creative myeloblast, which she knows very well to be the parent cell of the white blood cells, as if it were a cancer cell.

The analyst linked this for her with Thursday's acting out with her children, in which she dramatized her identification with the analyst-mother accused of deserting the baby parts of her, leaving them to die from poisonous breasts of the internal mother (swallowing the stolen money). It was clear that the trouble was with the stealing "rocket suction", not with the good internal objects with which she was left. These were meant to comfort and sustain ("What lovely weather") and would so do, if not attacked out of envy (wanting to find out the truth for herself).

By examining this dream in great detail, the whole panorama of greed and envy in relation to separation from the restored and harmoniously combined parents could be demonstrated as follows: At the outset the analysis is represented as something she and the analyst join in starting, but which she steers. The analyst is kept in the sexual husband-father role. The week-end is at first asserted to be an accidental separation and a trauma to the analyst and his head. But this supposed trauma to him is suddenly acknowledged as beneficial to his analytic productivity (producing a white, fatty substance). In renewed envy towards this head, which insists on being a breast, she snatches its innermost parts into her internal world (the X-rays she runs away with). But now even the internal breast (the cottage-hospital with the doctor-and-nurse staff) shows her the truth, that what she has stolen is a creative part of the breast (myeloblast) and that the trouble lies not with the intercourse (something wrong with the kidneys or bowel) but with her own envious greed (the rocket suction). Clearly this insight brings relief in the dream and a feeling of both greater confidence about the next holiday (Christmas) and a sense of accomplishment since the previous summer holiday, the destructive aspects of which had been represented most clearly in a dream of *a burning dirigible with bodies raining down from it* ("and only a year ago it was pouring with rain").

Review of crucial material

Let us now review the two weeks of analytic work. The patient had sought some refuge from her infantile separation anxieties in the transference during the summer break through a visit to her mother. She was pleased to find that she could bring out an old and virtually unmentioned grievance against her mother without lasting bitterness, but at the same time found that even this improved relation to her mother could not protect her from the infantile anxieties connected with her attachment in the transference to the analyst as both a mother and a father, i.e. linked to both internal parents.

The trust and expectation of renewed contact was reflected in the dream of the two Israeli passports, which filled the first session with relief and pleasure. But the first night-separation brought an attack on these returned breasts, with renewed idealization of the father's penis as an object of oral greed, while the internal breasts became damaged and persecutory. Consequently her external relation to the analyst as a mother passed through a persecutory period, which could be set right by interpretation. The satisfaction and gratitude for this restoration emerged clearly in the dream that night of *"the cottage-where-barren-rocks-had-been"*. In it there was manifest acceptance of her baby relationship to the two parents and acknowledgement of the reparative nature of the parental coitus.

Thus in three nights' dreaming and two days analytic work the first cycle of envious attacks on the internal mother's breasts and restoration of them by the good feed with the external mother was traversed in the transference.

But this was no sooner brought home to her—i.e. her dependence on the external analytic breasts—than the week-end loomed and the "penicillin–sulpha-mixture" episode commenced. Despite reasonably prompt and correct interpretation, this persisted throughout the Friday session and on Monday also, until near the session's end when she revealed bits of a dream. These helped to localize more satisfactorily the infantile rage coming from her little-boy (inverted) oedipal conflict, as seen in the dream of the *"worn-out lining"*. This bit of clarification closed the second cycle of attack and restoration, bringing the "*mother-and-baby*" dream and the happy Tuesday session, ending as it did with the "*Stonehenge*" material and its implicit acknowledgement of being both a grateful and burdensome babe-in-arms.

This instability of the good internal and external relationship to the breast led inevitably to the third and most violent, but also most fully documented, cycle of attack and restoration. Before the Wednesday session was ended, it had begun with the outbreak of depressive anguish and persecution intertwined, carrying through the acting-out with her children on the Thursday. The Friday session, with its "rocket-suction" dream, made the termination of this third cycle possible with a degree of clarity and conviction for the patient that has made the dream a nodal point for the working through of this problem.

Aftermath in the analysis: Period 5 and termination

At this point, I should like to restate the thesis of this paper—namely, that a particular form of stealing and denigrating attack, motivated by envious greed, undermines the stability of the internal relation to the breast and mother, forming a fundamental defect in those patients manifesting a cyclothymic type of disturbance.

I have up to this point demonstrated something of the revelation of this problem in the transference, its cyclical eruption under stress, and its restoration through the interpretive process. The working-through continued during the following year, giving way gradually by the spring of 1959 to a new period in the analysis, characterized by the strong emergence of genitality and related oedipal conflict, both direct and inverted. This development can be seen foreshadowed in the dreams of the "*little boy's trousers and the little girl's ski pants and caps*". As suggested there in the interpretive process, it was particularly the emergence with clarity of a vigorous masculine genitality, all too delicately balanced constitutionally with her femininity in this particular patient, which took the centre of the stage during the following year of work, ushering in the termination phase.

I wish to make this point clearly, since it is central in understanding the whole metapsychological significance of this problem. Prior to working through this central difficulty, not only was the patient's primal good object *poorly established*, but the differentiation between maleness and femaleness both of her objects and of parts of herself was likewise on ever-shifting ground. With the new and increasingly firm differentiation of the creativity of the inside of the breast (and consequently of the mother and her character), from that of the penis (and therefore the father and his character) a more clear-cut splitting and differentiation could take place between her own femaleness and maleness, starting in the depths with the infantile sexuality. This better splitting in the ego made integration possible, so that there could be a working-through of the positive and inverted oedipal conflicts, which had been a hopeless muddle in early life and in the first year of the analysis.

The aspects of clinical improvement that relate specifically to the working-through of this central problem have been difficult to separate from the overall lowering of anxiety levels and improvement of reality sense. But I would agree with the patient who feels that the most striking, and to her unexpected, benefit has been the relief of the deep pessimism and yearning for death, linked as it was all through her childhood to the nagging feeling of "not-belonging-in-the-family".

SUMMARY

The historical and psychoanalytic data from five-and-a-half years of analytic work are presented to document the diagnosis and illustrate the psychopathology of a patient in order to demonstrate the metapsychological thesis of this paper. The patient, with a cyclothymic heritage in both parents, with a constitutionally intense and delicately balanced bisexuality, traumatized in the first three months of life by a painful, near-fatal illness, had dealt with the loss of the breast at weaning by a flight to the father, which had a certain amount of reinforcement from the environment. This hypomanic state was based on the internal object relationships and defensive operations that are the central theme of this paper—that is, a denigration of the internal breast by an envious oral sadistic theft from it of a penis-like structure, felt as the core of its admired strength, creativity, and understanding, which was then projected onto the father's penis, thereby enhancing its admired qualities to an exalted degree, making it the object of oral and genital greed.

This fragile elation collapsed at the birth of the next child and was intensified into depression by the subsequent family turmoil and separation, leading to a premature step forward in development in the form of a latency period, too hastily established and excessively rigid and joyless in its obsessional quality. Her subsequent history was encompassed in a repeated progression and regression between this hypomanic organization and the obsessional, the latter characterized by an improvement in her internal objects, brought about either by an internal process (a good coitus between the internal parents) or an external relationship (involving a transference to the good breast, such as her mother's rescuing her from suicide, or a good skiing holiday). But progress beyond this obsessional organization, with its omnipotent control over internal objects, acted out early in relation to the parents during father's drinking period and later acted out in her professional activities, was not possible. Continual oscillation between these two organizations resulted.

I have also tried to show how the pervasive pessimism about the value and purpose of life, as well as the deep feeling of unworthiness ("not-belonging-in-the-family") that nagged at her in childhood, were manifestations of the basic insecurity of her relationship to her good internal object and the related fundamental defect in her reality sense on all levels, good–bad, inside–outside, male–female (Freud, 1925h).

Thus I have tried to demonstrate that the hypomanic organization, standing as it does as a first stage in regression from the obsessional organization and a jumping-off place for further regression into the manic-depressive psychosis or a more catastrophic fragmentation into schizophrenia, has as its good objects internally—not whole objects and not uninjured part-objects, but a damaged and denigrated breast and an idealized, exalted penis. The regression has taken place to a pathological state brought about by pathological mechanisms and not to a stage in normal ego-development. I have also shown that the tendency to regress to the hypomanic organization is due in great part to the unintegrated primal oral envy that tends to be set in motion by any internal or external stress. The analytic resolution of this tendency and preparation for development beyond an obsessional organization would therefore largely depend on the successful reintegration of split-off oral envy towards the breast.

DISCUSSION

There remains now only the task of reviewing briefly the history of the development of the psychoanalytic theory of obsessional and cyclothymic states and the transitional phenomena between them, in order to bring the contribution of this paper into historical context.

Abraham, in 1911, opening cyclothymic states to psychoanalytic investigation and treatment, discovered the link between this illness and obsessions, particularly the role of ambivalence towards a love object in both. Freud, in "Mourning and Melancholia" (1917e [1915]), showed how the melancholic loses his object owing to regression to narcissism, while the obsessional keeps his love-object relationship. He revealed the alteration both in ego structure (due to the lodging of the abandoned object within the ego) and the altered distribution of cathexes (due to a heightening of the sadism of the ego-ideal towards the ego identified with the abandoned object). With great clarity and detail he described the nature of the "ridiculing", "denigrating", and even "slaying" attacks by which the fixation of libidinal cathexis to this object, now in the ego, is loosened, both likening and contrasting this process with the work of mourning.

The fundamental formulation of mania was also offered, more tentatively, by Freud in this paper, namely the triumph over an object that had caused suffering and a limitation of freedom, through denigration of it and through the fusion of the ego with the ego-ideal. This was amplified in *Group Psychology* (1921c).

The whole theory of manic-depressive states and their relation to obsessional states was brought into relation to metapsychology and to the stages in libidinal development in Abraham's 1924 paper, "A Short Study of the Development of the Libido", where he added a clarification of how the object, by expulsion and reintrojection after it has been denigrated and equated with faeces, becomes lodged within the melancholic's ego, stressing particularly the move from whole-object to part-object relations involved in the total regression from obsessional to cyclothymic organization.

This, then, was the foundation upon which subsequent developments have been based, developments in which the work of Klein plays a unique role. By dissecting the superego in its deepest strata and tracing the multiplicity of internal objects found in the depths back to the earliest months and years of life, and by revealing the splitting processes within the ego in the depths and the complicated interrelationships among the internal objects and parts of the ego that underlie the general phenomenology of narcissism, she has laid the groundwork for a more detailed understanding of both these diseases we are discussing and the relation between them. In the chapter on obsessional states in *The Psycho-Analysis of Children* (1932a) and in the 1935 paper on manic-depressive illness, she brought together Freud's and Abraham's conclusions, along with Helene Deutsch's discovery of the role of denial in mania, into a coherent theory. The relationship to the breast of the internal mother was shown to be the foundation for the vicissitudes of mood, a conclusion with which Edith Jacobson, in her 1957 paper, seems in fundamental agreement, allowing for her special way of expressing things in terms of self- and object-representation. Klein added to Deutsch's findings about denial her own stress on the *denial of psychic reality* as central in the manic defences against both the depressive and paranoid anxieties that result from sadistic attacks in the good internal objects, especially the breast.

During the years after 1935, while Klein's findings were being integrated around her construct of paranoid–schizoid and depressive positions in ego development, other workers interested in the area of mania were struggling with the phenomena of hypomania. Angel, Deutsch, Lewin, and Fenichel seem all to have recognized the ubiquity of the problem itself, and the nature of many of its separate basic elements such as the role of oral greed and sadism in relation to the breast, the role of denial, of erotization, of identification with the primal scene, of idealization of the penis, of the part-object nature of the relationships. The thesis of this paper integrates these various elements by relating them to the oral sadism towards the inside of the breast and body of the mother (Klein, 1932).

In 1957, in *Envy and Gratitude*, Klein brought forward evidence of the central role of unintegrated (and thus unmodified) oral envy in undermining the security of the relationship to the good internal objects, primarily the breast. In the light of this discovery, it is necessary to re-evaluate her own and other workers' contributions to the metapsychology of obsessional and cyclothymic states and the transitional processes between them.

To a great extent this paper attempts to do this in the small area of the phenomenon of hypomania, both as an acute reaction and as a characterological structure. I have shown (1) the nature of the internal object relationships in hypomania, stressing (2) the central role of unintegrated oral envy towards the breast in producing the regression from the obsessional organization, differentiating this factor from (3) the more protean stresses, internal and external, which may release the envious attacks. I have also indicated and illustrated (4) the internal and external processes by which the obsessional organization can be recovered, emphasizing that (5) only by a process of integrating the oral envy can the way be cleared for progress beyond an obsessional state into the fully differentiated positive and inverted genital Oedipus complex.

CHAPTER FIVE

The differentiation of somatic delusions from hypochondria

(1963)

In this illustration of a metapsychological differentiation between hypochondriacal symptoms and somatic delusions, two cases are described in which the analysis of a somatic delusion consists of a process of reintegration of severely and widely split-off parts of the self, happening late in the analytic process.

Read at the Twenty-third International Psycho-Analytical Congress, Stockholm, July–August 1963.

INTRODUCTION

When Freud (1914c), in his paper "On Narcissism", suggested that hypochondriacal anxiety stood in relation to ego-libido as does neurotic anxiety to object libido, he had in mind the psychiatric syndrome of hypochondriasis and the hypochondria of schizophrenics. Since then, however, such anxiety has been referred to more contexts, broadly for two reasons: First, hypochondriacal elements have been recognized as playing a part in the clinical picture of the neuroses. Secondly, the deepening of psychoanalytic work has brought forth hypochondriacal phenomena as a ubiquitous and inevitable event in the transference.

The consequence of this development has been a broadening of the scope of the term and a corresponding loss of definition. "Hypochondriacal" has come to include clinical phenomena earlier described by such terms as "organ language", "somatization", "somatic delusion", and "psychosomatic". In a sense, this coalescence has been correct, for these various terms were used descriptively, not metapsychologically, and often inconsistently. Furthermore, the earlier sharp distinction between psychic and physical has been found to be unsatisfactory. Freud (1914c) suggested on the one hand that organ changes akin to those in the genital during excitement might occur in hypochondria to increase the erogenicity of the organ. He also suggested a continuity between hypochondriasis, neurasthenia, and anxiety neurosis that has been richly confirmed through the work of Melanie Klein on internal objects. She herself (Klein, 1935) first differentiated depressive and persecutory types of hypochondria, and later (1961), further broadened the term by including the hypochondriacal reaction to and elaboration of primarily organic diseases.

We have thus reached a point in the development of our theories and terminology where we use the term "hypochondriacal" to refer to any somatic accompaniment, representation, or component of mental life, be it represented as a rumination, a body sensation, a physiological change, or tissue (or organ) pathology. This confronts us with the task of refinement and differentiation along purely psychoanalytic (metapsychological) lines, leaving clinical differentiation to fall into place accordingly.

Rosenfeld (1958) made the first such contribution in his definitive paper on hypochondriasis. He made the following points: (a) hypochondriasis is produced by complicated identification with damaged internal objects; (b) the damage has been done through the use of projective identification; (c) this has been launched primarily out of oral envy; (d) since the projective identification and introjection produce a double basis of identification with the damaged object, a confusion of self and object is strongly maintained; (e) but the hypochondriacal state is clung to as a defence against integration of a part of the self that contains another type of confusional state, between depressive and persecutory anxieties.

While the aspect of hypochondriasis related to the part of the self that contains a severe confusional state is probably specific to the psychiatric disease proper and stands in close relation to the psychoses, the rest of Rosenfeld's description can be taken as a definition of the term "hypochondriacal" in its restricted sense.

The present paper attempts the next step in this work of differentiation—namely, to separate out, under the term "somatic delusion", another type of disturbance of the relation to the body. I will delineate it as best I can descriptively, but the emphasis is on its establishment as a metapsychological entity. The thesis is as follows: The somatic delusion is the physical and psychic expression of (a) a wide and deep split in the self, whereby (b) an expelled portion becomes represented by, and takes possession of, the function of a particular body part; (c) this part is then felt to take up a life completely of its own, totally ego-alien in orientation, and powerfully effective in its interference with all good internal and external relationships. It is my further suggestion that the experience of somatic delusion may be a ubiquitous phenomenon during the process in analysis of reintegration of any severely split-off part of the self. Lastly, the contention is that reintegration, which is brought about through sharing the good internal mother's breast with this split-off part both internally and in the analytic situation, produces a most extraordinary lessening of its malignant character, with resulting enrichment of the patient's total personality and enhancement of the stability and security of his internal world.

Clinical description

It is my impression from psychiatric work that the differentiation I shall apply to these two terms corresponds, in some degree, to the general trend in practice to use "hypochondriacal" for those symptoms concerned with the internal organs and "somatic" for all other morbid bodily preoccupations. It may also correspond to the distinction drawn by Bleuler (1916) between katathymic and depressive types of hypochondria, when he said that the "depressive delusion of disease postpones the worst for the future, while the katathymic hypochondria worries about the present".

The most striking contrast is in the area of social visibility. While the hypochondriacal symptom tends to be reported with a certain irritability and an expectation that its physical basis will neither be seen nor seriously searched for, the somatic delusion is shyly and suspiciously confessed under the pressure of delusion of reference, that everyone notices it but no one will bother to help with it.

Similarly distinctive is the history of the symptoms. The hypochondria is experienced as fluctuating, migratory, periodically responsive to ministration, a burden that holds the patient back from striding ahead in life, a condition with an onset that is often datable. The somatic delusion is relentlessly present, progressing from earlier dissemination towards unification to a particular part of the body, uniformly unresponsive to varied regimens, imprisoning by means of the social ostracism it is felt to cause, and vaguely lifelong in its origins. Even where the symptom centres on some recently acquired actual impairment such as acne, baldness, scarring, or loss of a limb, it will be found to be antedated by similar but more disseminated symptoms, though the eliciting of this information may be stubbornly resisted. The pitfall for a diagnostic physician, and for the patient's environment as a whole, lies in the countertransference aroused where a physical deformity of considerable proportions exists in fact. When the delusion is of smelling bad, of excessive sexual attractiveness or drive, lack or excess of intelligence, or concern about a negligible cosmetic defect, the irrational nature of the process is more readily recognized.

Presented thus baldly, the clinical differentiation between hypochondria and somatic delusions seems none too difficult—separate spheres with a certain amount of overlap, one might say, but the former concentrated on the inside of the body, its functioning, its sensations, the latter on the outside and its significance to other people. *I wish to stress that this is not a reliable rule by itself.* Psychoanalytic insight, with which this paper is largely concerned, must supplement descriptive clinical observation if accurate diagnostic differentiation is to take place.

Since the relation of psychiatry to psychoanalysis is very much like that of any macro- to micro-technique in medical science, what the one can recognize in its gross forms, the other soon finds to be more widespread in minute form and more recognizably related to normal structure and function. Thus it is with hypochondria—a disease entity in psychiatry but found by psychoanalysis to be an inevitable part of personality development and of the clinical phenomena of the psychoanalytic process. It may be the same in regard to somatic delusions. I intend to demonstrate the psychopathology of this type of symptom from a very severe borderline case, but will also mention a clinical example of its place in the analysis of a somewhat less ill patient.

But just as hypochondria may be hidden away from view by that habitual externalization of internal relationships which contributes so much to character pathology, so somatic delusion may also be hidden by the projective aspect of the splitting operation. In contrast to the character facets related to hypochondria which tend strongly to envelop the most intimate relationships, those aspects of character linked to somatic delusion prefer to find expression in attitudes and behaviour towards remote figures or groups. Thus they may contribute a very important, perhaps a central dynamism to the many variants of paranoia that, in forms of graded virulence, parade as political opinions, social prejudices, and aesthetic preferences. The sanctimonious preoccupation with justice is its hallmark, stridently demanding punishment for malefactors. It thus accounts for that peculiar form of envy, of the "bad ones who get away with murder". The loss of psychic reality attending the projective process always erases the recognition of the inevitable justice that prevails in internal relations.

Case material

The first material is from a young man in his early twenties, suffering from a mild schizophrenic reaction characterized by persecutory delusions, occasional frightening hallucinations, and marked hypochondriacal delusions concerning genitals, bowels, respiratory system, cardiac action, and visual apparatus. This condition had existed since a breakdown at age 13 and was superimposed on a severe schizoid personality characterized by paranoid trends, relative ineducability, social withdrawal alternating with hypomanic periods, severe dependence and ambivalence towards his mother, compulsive masturbation, and sadomasochistic perversions. His self-image was severely split, a beautiful, saintly, and brilliant self existing side by side with a horribly disfigured, vicious, degenerate, and stupid self.

The first three years of analysis were carried on with a punctilious superficial cooperation, behind which he maintained an attitude of mockery, pessimism, and contempt for the analyst and the analytic process. But in fact the rehabilitation of his internal objects went forward and caused the vanishing of much of his hypochondria, enabling him to hold a job and eventually begin to establish a proper career for himself, all much to his surprise. The result was a revival of hope and the beginning of respect and admiration, accompanied by a severe deterioration in his cooperation, or mock-cooperation: withholding of material and acting out began to alternate with passivity and indifference. In the material, the transference on a part-object level, involving a number of bits of his infantile self, could be clarified, when projective identification diminished and confusion between self and objects consequently lessened. But to his distress all parts of his self appeared to be grossly pathological in either greed, jealousy, envy, cruelty, incapacity for love, or intolerance to pain. No really good part of the self seemed able to come forward into a firm alliance with good objects. However, the core of his badness was soon located, and it is with this part of the patient that we are here concerned.

Although this "coldly destructive" (as he called it) aspect of the patient had declared itself in the first dream of the analysis, as *an escalator that he controlled and into which he dropped a little gold chain* (representing the analyst's words) *to be destroyed*, it never became available to analysis in the first 2½ years, being consistently kept split off into machines. But in the third year it quietly metamorphosed into a cat in the patient's dreams, then assumed corporeal form as a stray cat on his doorstep. This foundling became the object of great tenderness and solicitude owing to its damaged leg, but also came no closer to analytic scrutiny than to pass through the consulting-room en route to the veterinary surgeon. The patient acted out a claim that the cat was his damaged good object, and that he was being loving and reparative, while in fact dream after dream showed it to be a part of himself with whose baby-bird-killing he was in sympathy, whose promiscuity he relished, and with whose furtiveness he was in league to avoid analytic scrutiny.

When this acting out finally broke down under interpretation in the fourth year, the cat began to appear regularly in dreams again and to be experienced more as part of the self on a *physical* level. For instance, a dream of the cat *"almost dead with the cold"* awoke the patient shivering, only diminished by fixing himself a hot meal. When accusations that the analyst was "cold and unfeeling" appeared in the sessions, a subsequent dream showed the patient *feeding the cat frozen fish*—i.e. this part of himself was kept split off, in a sub-human form, and was given the analyst's words only after all warmth and concern had been removed from them.

Two and a half months later, another dream, one of extraordinary clarity, showed how mutual was this relation to the cat-part of himself. It provided a model of the transference situation at the analytic breast, showing how free this destructive cat-part was to intrude into the analytic feed, which was now acknowledged as warm, turning the nourishing interpretations into poisonous rubbish. It was the key for subsequent analytic work which eventually resolved the symptom, the focus of our inquiry here.

Some four weeks earlier, the Christmas break of two weeks intervening, the patient had revealed a long-withheld but recently more pressing symptom: the conviction that his anus was constantly incontinent of flatus, and that this required his keeping several feet away from other people to prevent their noticing. He felt it to be the basis of his social inhibitions, which were indeed still very severe. This revelation came as a result of analysing a dream in which the cat was *"letting himself die"*, a smug grin on his face, deriding the patient's despair and his pleadings. Despite interpretation, the patient acted this out in the consulting-room for some days, behaving in a supercilious and silly way, "passing jokes", and pouring forth pseudo-analysis in which the entire process and all my formulations were ridiculously distorted. When he dreamed that *"poisonous gas was being emitted by a left-wing newspaper"*, it became apparent that "letting himself die" meant exerting no control over sphincters, and that what emerged was mental flatus, the poisonous cynicism and contempt for life by which he projected despair and painful concern into the analyst from the couch, just as the cat had been seen to do to him, in the dream. He dreamed

> ... *he was eating at the table when the cat jumped up, uninvited but unimpeded, and, surmounting the plate, began to eat and defecate simultaneously. The patient, thinking to himself that the food seemed to pass so quickly through the cat that it could not be much altered in essentials, proceeded to eat the faeces.*

In the next two years of analysis, the cat further metamorphosed into human form in the patient's dreams. What had been the somatic delusion was replaced by the awareness of the "cat faeces" mental content, at first whispered to himself on the couch and later hurled at the analyst for sessions and even weeks at a time. In dreams this part gradually changed from a harmless layabout to a vicious tramp, then Adolf Eichmann at the crescendo of its intrusions in the consulting-room. It then slowly began to wane in its sadism, becoming in dreams the patient's brother or a "blue-eyed boy" against whom the patient's blazing jealousy was turned. We could then study in detail the way in which the part of himself that had become attached to the analytic breast resisted sharing it, wishing to keep other parts out, even though this would cause them to remain primitive and threatening.

* * *

The second case material I wish to present only briefly in order to illustrate the point that somatic delusions are manifestations of lack of integration of the self and that, as such, their significance for the patient and their prominence in the analytic work are phenomena of the latter phases of analysis. Hypochondria, on the other hand, being the consequence of double identification with objects damaged by projective identification, naturally tends to be prominent in analysis early on, when any question of reintegration of split-off parts of the self would still be unfeasible, owing to the inadequate establishment of the alliance of good objects and good parts of the self.

The patient, some of whose analysis was reported in my (Meltzer, 1963a) paper on cyclothymia, had, in a vague and only periodically distressing way, suffered since early childhood from the somatic delusion that her eyes were too black and that they frightened people. Off and on in the first few years of analysis, complaints about her eyes disturbing people entered into the material but without any great pressure. In the fifth year, as the split-off masculine genitality, which had at times been projected into father, brother, and other figures, began to be less widely split-off though still deeply alienated from the rest of the self, the complaints about her eyes became frequent and eventually became *the* central theme of analytic work. Gradually, concern about the *appearance* of her eyes was replaced by complaints of their *activity*: their uncontrollable tendency to stare, particularly at genitals, breasts, legs, buttocks. In dreams this was represented as the voyeuristic activities of a little boy, often her own little boy, or of her husband or brother. She also became increasingly fearful that she was fundamentally homosexual, that her masculinity was too strong and too delinquent.

This problem occupied the central place of the last two years of her analysis. Slowly, the complaints of uncontrollably *staring eyes* yielded to a less alienated state, uncontrollable *wishes to look*, then to an increased awareness of the mixture of envy and admiration with which she did in fact look at men and women—and, finally, at her analyst. Particularly as the envy became mitigated by admiration, her little-boy self became more acceptable to her, and her social isolation, which had been invoked as defence against these symptoms, was gradually discarded. The withdrawal of projection of this part produced a noticeable improvement in her relations to both her husband and son and a surprising relief of an inner loneliness that had been with her from the earliest times.

SUMMARY

I have presented material from the analyses of two patients, one severely schizoid and the other moderately cyclothymic, to illustrate the thesis of this paper—that a metapsychological differentiation can be made between hypochondriacal symptoms and what I have called "somatic delusions".

The first case shows how a split-off part of the patient's self, characterized by a ruthlessly destructive oral envy, had become located in his anus, producing the somatic delusion of incontinence of flatus as the conscious basis of social withdrawal. The process of reintegration of this part, through its metamorphoses from machine to cat to human form, has been traced.

The second case involves a delusion of having black and frightening eyes. It served primarily to illustrate how the analysis of a somatic delusion, being essentially a process of reintegration of a severely and widely split-off part of the self, is necessarily a late development in the analytic process. It cannot be accomplished until the reorganization of infantile relations to the primal good object (the internal mother's breast) has been firmly established.

DISCUSSION

In this very brief paper I have tried to present some of the psychiatric and psychoanalytic evidence for differentiating between "hypochondria" and what I have called "somatic delusions". Space has only permitted some demonstration of the relation of somatic delusions to problems of splitting and reintegration of the self; the entire problem of parallel developments in the internal objects has here been omitted. I have also not had space to discuss the connection between somatic delusion and thinking disorder, which I believe to be an intimate one, having special reference to the theories of alpha-function and beta-elements as developed by W. R. Bion (1962).

It might interest readers to review the first and second illnesses of the "Wolf Man", as described by Freud (1918b [1914]) and Brunswick (1928). The second illness, ushered in by a character change, was, I believe, preponderantly concerned with a somatic delusion about the nose and dealt with the problem of reintegration of an envious feminine infantile part of the personality. In contrast, the first illness had been obsessional and hypochondriacal, having broken out after contracting gonorrhoea. It involved gastrointestinal symptoms.

It is too early to make any statement concerning the differential relation of hypochondriasis and somatic delusions to psychosomatic diseases. Similarly, though my experience suggests that somatic delusion is the central dynamic in tic, stuttering, and strabismus, this remains to be verified.

CHAPTER SIX

The dual unconscious basis of materialism

(1965)

The Imago Group, to whom this paper was presented, consisted of people interested in applying psychoanalytic findings to other disciplines. They met regularly in the early 1960s, and among those attending were: Katherine Jones (Ernest Jones's wife), R. Money-Kyrle (psychoanalyst), Adrian Stokes (art critic), R. Wollheim (philosopher), the Holmes' (an LSE sociologist and his wife), and Ernst Gombrich (art critic and historian).

The author talks here about the concern with measurable possessions and how the extension of self-esteem through an identification with possession takes place through envy, delusional jealousy, projective identification and the defences used against them. He illustrates this by examining the social attitudes towards land tenure and the introduction of machinery to thirteenth-century rural England. Towards the end of the paper he refers to the "apocalyptic dread" feared in earlier centuries, as an inevitable consequence of the loss of a

---

Read to the Imago Group, 1965.

human relationship with the mother's body, which leads to the haunting dread of catastrophe: the death of the mother. When this paper was written in 1965, there were intimations of a "bomb" capable of apocalyptic destructiveness. This paper anticipates the writings stimulated by the danger of nuclear arms proliferation of the 1980s.

> The division of property has lessened the distance which separated the rich from the poor; but it would seem that the nearer they draw to each other, the greater is their mutual hatred, and the more vehement the envy and the dread with which they resist each other's claims to power.
>
> Alexis de Tocqueville, *Democracy in America* (Introduction)

As an organizing principle in social structure, materialism is characterized by allocating to inanimate objects a place of primary importance over human attributes in the stratification of society. I propose to illustrate some of the recent psychoanalytic discoveries about the role of unconscious envy in the forming of social attitudes by examining the attitudes found towards land tenure and the introduction of machinery in thirteenth-century rural England.

Only as recently as 1958, with the publication of Melanie Klein's seminal work *Envy and Gratitude*, has the role of envy as a destructive force in human object relations been fully

---

The historical data of this paper are primarily derived from the following books and papers: Clapham, 1949; Lipson, 1959; Power, 1924; Trevelyan, 1942. The psychoanalytic views referred to may be found in the following: Bion, 1961; Klein, 1946, 1957, 1961; Meltzer, 1963. For economic application of Kleinian theory, see Jaques, 1951; 1961. Political implications: Money-Kyrle, 1951; 1961.

appreciated. The ubiquity of envy has been hidden in two very secret modes of operation, namely *delusional jealousy* and *projective identification*, which at the same time both implement envy and are defences against it.

Delusional jealousy operates as follows: instead of envy of the human attributes of a good object (in the unconscious, primarily the mother and her breasts, genitals and mind, as well as the father in his many functions), a substitute emotion of sanctimonious concern about fair shares in the division of this object with actual or supposed rivals takes the centre of the stage. This can be seen beautifully illustrated in the material from Melanie Klein's *Narrative of a Child Analysis* (1961), where "Richard" represents his mother's body in drawings as an "empire" in which he, brother, father and mother herself are constantly vying for territories.

Projective identification, first described in "Notes on Some Schizoid Mechanisms" (1946), effects an appropriation of the qualities of the envied object by intrusion into and taking possession of its body and its functions. This is best set out in the paper "On Identification" (1955), in which Melanie Klein has used a novel, *Si J'Etais Vous* [If I Were You], by Julien Green, to illustrate the mechanism. It must be kept in mind that envy, as spoken of here, the hating and destructive counterpart of admiration, is held to be the most serious deterrent to love and gratitude and the most pernicious source of greed.

When externalized (away from their primary relation to internal objects), these two secret modes of operation of envy take the form of *concern about measurable possessions* (delusional jealousy) and the *extension of self-esteem through identification with possessions* (projective identification). Psychoanalytic experience has shown unequivocally that these processes deal with objects in the outside world as if they were the bodies of the parents. This of course is proverbial in the relation of women to their houses and men to their cars, for example.

It is my intention in this paper to suggest that these two forms of materialism—concern with measurable wealth and extension of self-esteem through identification with possessions since they possess an identical unconscious basis both in the manifesting of envy and in the defence against it, have, therefore, a mutual reinforcement, which precludes social stability. A society so structured can find no internal harmony and must break out in violence and live in the shadow of catastrophe. Why? As always, if we recognize the extent to which social behaviour of an irrational sort is an externalization of internal and essentially infantile modes of object relation, we must look for the answer in the world of psychic reality. In the psychoanalytic process, the resolution of problems of unconscious envy is absolutely prevented so long as delusional jealousy and projective identification are powerfully operative. Singly they are more easily dealt with, but in tandem they reinforce one another. As mentioned, projective identification functions through the agency of a split-off part of the self getting inside an envied object to take possession of its life-processes. Delusional jealousy visualizes creatures living inside the mother's body, protected from all the pain, stress, demands, and anxieties of the outside world. When these two mechanisms are functioning in tandem, the delusional jealousy also visualizes that these inside-babies of the mother are enjoying projective identification, i.e. the illusionary experience of *being* mother, as well as the paradisiacal state of *being inside* her. The delusional jealousy is thus reinforced. On the other hand, the phantasy behind the projective identification visualizes inside-babies who are *indulged* in identification, and the violence of the envy is thus *reinforced* by a sense of injustice.

From this it becomes apparent that when these two mechanisms are at work to distort the infantile envy of the parents' human attributes, the problem of envy becomes unavailable to the softening influence of love, admiration, gratitude. Instead, it hardens into a relentless holy war, of the outside- versus the inside-children, in which the mother's body is the battlefield.

To illustrate the workings of these mechanisms in social structure and to show its fundamental conservatism, I wish to describe the land tenure system in England of the thirteenth century, and to show how it resisted an industrial revolution in miniature resulting from the expansion of the wool trade.

The bulk of England, from Yorkshire to Somerset, is still seen to bear the marks, in its ridged meadows, of the feudal system of communal husbandry, which reached its apex in the thirteenth century during the long and relatively peaceful reigns of Henry III and Edward I. Ninety percent of the adult population tilled the soil, and most of them lived in villeinage at manorial villages owned by lords or monasteries. Wool was already England's major export, but the Staple (the marketing organization for overseas trade in wool and cloth) had not yet been established, the enclosure of land had not begun to dispossess farmers, nor was money yet sufficiently in circulation to replace the system of work and barter that dominated rural life.

The social structure of villages, and probably of boroughs as well, was so inflexibly stratified as to discourage struggle for social advancement. The church and military service gave some opportunity to the restless and disinherited, the latter group being very large, for among the villeins land tenure passed undivided, either by primogeniture, ultimogeniture, or paternal choice, leaving all the other children of a family dependent on the heir. Since villein holdings were generally 20 to 30 acres of "yardland" or "oxgang" and less for cotters, life was held down to subsistence level, not so much by the amount of time devoted to the lord's demesne but by the smallness of the holdings and the inefficiency of the methods of agriculture.

The freemen, of sokeman or franklin level, were economically better off, holding a "ploughland" (or "hide") of about 120 acres but customarily bound not to divide the holdings at death. It was similar, of course, with the aristocracy.

It is of special interest to note that the consequence of this inheritance of land-tenure was a socio-psychological isolation of the three major levels of land-occupiers from one another due to the completeness of structure within each level of the "haves" and the "have-nots" in regard to wealth, authority, and sexuality (for indeed marriage was virtually impossible for the disinherited without assistance from parent or heir).

What I am trying to portray is a community in which the different levels of society looked with little envy upward because of the hopelessness of mobility in the social scale and the availability of a suitable object of envy on the hearth (the heir) and in the next house. The heir was a suitable object for envy because of his privileged position and measurable wealth, which was often in fact transmitted before the parents' death, but also because *hope of succession* always existed through the agency of sterility or death. The villeins' peers were also suitable objects of envy because of the organization of land-tenure, the size of each holding being almost identical (although on some manors two different levels—householder and cotter—might exist), but especially because of the socio-economic structure of the community, so different in fact from the master–slave stereotype of the feudal system.

In the open-field system of agriculture, crops were rotated through two or three great fields, each of which was divided into plough lands of approximately 120 acres, in which each land-holding villein would be allocated a strip. The arable lands of the lord's demesne, of franklins and sokemen, if any, would be adjoining but separate. Here we see a system of land division that sanctified equality in defence against envy, for each villein had a strip of the good, bad, and indifferent fields. The consequence was an enforced community of labour and organization amounting almost to a corporate body, democratic in its decisions of economic significance as well as in legal disputes, since its own jury sitting in the lord's "hallmote" (court) gave judgement. Lands were ploughed, sown, and reaped in common, animals kept and slaughtered and fleeced in common, and disputes with the lord were communally undertaken, with community liability. But the tenancy to the lord and the obligations to day work, boon work, and other forms of rent were individual to the holder and to his household.

The community of villeins was strong in resistance to any alteration in the demands of the lord, however, for custom was sacred, and stability was the aim within each level of society.

In contrast to this community of agricultural effort, every villein household had sheep, produced wool, spun thread, and wove cloth for its own use and, where possible, a surplus for the market, one of the few avenues of access to coined money. The single hand-loom required no capitalist to supply it to the weaver, as did the more complicated looms of the sixteenth and seventeenth centuries when the wool trade was booming and England was becoming a country of huge sheep estates instead of manorial villages. The "fulling" to cleanse and shrink the cloth, the raising of the nap with teasles, sheering the nap, and dyeing were all household operations. The only "machine" ("machine"—containing its source of power, as distinct from "tool" or "mechanism") that the village possessed was the water- or wind-driven mill belonging to the lord and farmed out to the miller. The compulsion upon the villein to use the lord's mill was resented and evaded, and the miller was hated or at least distrusted. Grain was secretly milled by hand. The smith was not hated, the brewers were not hated—though they were no more honest. I will suggest that it was the *machine* that was hated. Further mechanization was resisted. For instance, the fulling of cloth consisted of pounding the loose weave in water and Fuller's earth to remove the grease and shrink it. This was an arduous and skill-less job done with bats, feet, fists, paddles, etc., which easily lent itself to mechanization. It was poorly paid and done by the lowest orders in the borough, where there were already organized small factories for cloth finishing. But when fulling mills were established with water-driven bats beating the cloth, their intrusion into *village* life was legally resisted time and time again by successful appeals to the King for over 150 years, well into the fifteenth century.

I would suggest that it was the machine that was hated because it seemed to produce wealth, and thus upset the very foundations of this feudal system in which only the land, with its beasts and men, were meant to produce wealth. The land was mensurable, equally divisible within each level, and yielded, because communally tilled, equally to its holders, varying only from year to year in response to the mysterious forces of nature, which were constantly solicited and placated through ceremony and superstition. The potency of precedent and custom held sway over reason, for the aim was stability—and, I am suggesting, communal defence against the deadly sin, according to the Christian tradition, of envy. But note that in this process fragmentation of the land took place into strips (approx. 30 feet by one furlong) for no conceivable reason other than in the interest of placating envy. It did not really succeed—within a single ploughland, some strips were closer to the sun, more on a level, more deeply top-soiled, less stony, sweeter, etc., etc., than others. But these realities were ignored, in favour of orienting the different ploughlands of the two or three great fields differently, even though this resulted in waste of land, difficulty of ploughing, etc. Still, men stole sheaves at harvest; they had to be forbidden to go into the fields at night; guards had to be set.

It seems to have been a stable enough system, overall, to serve for the movement from serfdom to freedom—that is to say, while the villein community, often acting in a corporate sense, sought to buy the freehold from the lord for money and yearly ground-rent. It coped with the great fluctuations in the labour market caused by the plagues; it fulfilled its commitments to send men for the king's armies when needed and to send its more ambitious sons into the church (in contrast to the aristocrats, who set up their most slothful ones with ecclesiastical livings). Its downfall was not due to the decay of feudal authority but, rather, to the growth of commerce.

If we turn now to examine this system in the light of psychoanalytic discovery, we see immediately that envy of human attributes has been replaced by envy of possessions and privileges, which really constitutes a delusional jealousy by nonholders of land-holding heirs. The earth itself was the external representation of the mother's body, of psychic reality (the internal world). Each level of society was both identically structured and decisively isolated from the others, so that this problem of materialistic delusional jealousy could be worked out within the separate levels. At each level it was further defended against by the means of land division and the other techniques mentioned, so that, in effect, the violence of conflict was enclosed within each household. Here, the drama of inside- and-outside children could be fully enacted in the relation of heir to disinherited.

To the stability—or, rather, rigidity—of this system the machine posed a most threatening concept, in that the exertion of human initiative might enable a man to rise above his fellows and his assigned station in life by means other than patronage. In this essentially agricultural society, the pre-scientific mystique of the generosity or niggardliness of mother earth still held sway, and she was more often placated in pagan than in Christian ways, secretly. The communal modes of work precluded concepts of initiative, knowledge, skill, courage, perseverance, etc., in respect to economic reward, though they must have manifested themselves in the political structure of the various levels of society. In a materialist society a man is easily forgiven his prestige, provided his purse be none the fatter; even fame is allowable, if he be poor enough—or, preferably, already dead.

So much for the workings in this system of the first modification of envy—namely, by delusional jealousy. Where and how is it reinforced by projective identification? As mentioned, the inheritance of land, meaning the entire holding other than a few movable possessions, passed on by a variety of modes, primogeniture, ultimogeniture, or, most frequently, paternal choice. Often, the transfer of possessions and authority occurred prior to the death of the parent, in exchange for an agreement of maintenance, in the manner of King Lear. In this age of sudden death, no man left his heir unnamed. Thus one child from early on had this extraordinary status, though not without some risk of loss through parental disfavour. In other words, in this concrete way there came to exist, on the hearth, a child who seemed to possess the wealth and privileges of the parent, bar expulsion from his intimate position. An inside-child! Can the blood-thirsty and hair-raising history of family relations that we know of royal houses be very different from life in a villein household? The records of the hallmote tell us little, for only extramural disputes came to its bar.

It is beyond the scope of this paper to investigate the implications of this new understanding for our own times in which conservatism parades as egalitarianism and materialism masquerades as progress. The work of Elliott Jaques (1951, 1961) has gone far to investigate it in regard to the "culture of the factory" and the basis of wage differentials in industry.

There is one parallel worth mentioning between the age described here and our modern dilemma. Where envy of the parents is easily defended against by the means described here, which involve the loss of human relation to the mother's body and its conversion into a battleground of greed, one consequence is inevitable—the "children" must suffer from a haunting dread of catastrophe—the death of the mother. We certainly have our sophisticated counterpart of the apocalyptic dreads of the earlier centuries, our "Bomb". Let us note, with appropriate anxiety, that such dread is neutralized by an insane yearning for ultimate equality in annihilation.

CHAPTER SEVEN

Return to the imperative: an ethical implication of psychoanalytic findings

(1965)

The author describes how "laws" of psychic reality with an ethical significance have to be differentiated from the "moral" implication of discoveries about the structure and function of the superego.

> But if the word "this" is to apply, as it should, to something that we directly experience, it cannot apply to the cat as an object in the outer world, but only to our own percept of a cat. Thus we must not say "this is a cat", but "this is a percept such as we associate with cat", or "this is a cat percept". This phase, in turn, can be replaced by "I am cat-perceptive. . . ."
>
> Bertrand Russell, "An Inquiry into Meaning and Truth", 1940

I start this paper with Lord Russell's statement for two reasons. First of all, it succinctly states that "egocentric particulars", as he calls such words as I, this, now, etc., are utilized to introduce statements about what Freud called, "The

---

Read to the Imago Group.

perception of psychic qualities", in his definition of the function of consciousness. The second reason is because of the interesting shifts from the subjunctive to the imperative mode of speech that take place as soon as he utilizes an egocentric particular himself. While it is "If the word this is . . . *it cannot* . . ." to begin with, suddenly we hear that "*we must not* . . .". Also note that it is "we" who "must" use egocentric particulars correctly, meaning that if *I* use them as statements of self-observation and you use them "intend(ing) to make a statement about something which is *not* merely a part of (your) own biography . . .", we will not understand one another.

What I will now suggest is that Bertrand Russell's unconscious shift from the subjunctive to the imperative mode of speech implies that these two modes have a specific differential reference to the external and internal worlds, respectively (you will understand that I am not talking about Lord Russell as a person nor citing him as an authority); further, that the specific relatedness of these two modes could be stated in the following way: *The ability of people to understand one another's communications varies directly with the extent to which they recognize that the accuracy of their perception of the outside world is dependent on their obedience to the laws of psychic reality.* Vide infra.

Progress in psychoanalysis since the earliest of Freud's work has moved steadily, in keeping with developments in other fields, such as philosophy, physics, engineering etc., to recognize that the problems of relationships between objects of whatever sort are more comprehensively understood in terms of communication than in terms of energy, and more accurately measured in terms of a gradient from chaos to order than in terms of closed systems of dynamic equilibria.

To the best of my knowledge, my use of the term *laws* of *psychic reality* is a new image in psychoanalysis, and I wish to make it clear that this is the central theme of this paper. I believe we are now in a position, thanks to the discoveries in metapsychology regarding the structure, mechanisms, development, and economy of the mental apparatus, to discern the existence of *laws* that imply an *ethical significance* distinct from the *moral implications* of the various discoveries about superego structure and function. The content of religious beliefs in all times and cultures is found to derive from the externalization of the various stages of superego development, but I suggest that whatever is inexorable in the quality of relationship between men and gods is an expression of the nature of these *laws* of *psychic reality*. This implies differentiating between the *omnipotence* of the gods and their *omniscience*, two qualities whose differing significance has not previously been clarified. Poor scholarship prevents me from documenting with any authority my impression that, while the *omnipotence* of the gods is, in all religions and mystiques, a quality open to all sorts of attenuation, placation, and appropriation by ritual practice, the *omniscience* of the gods is an unassailable quality.

I will now briefly state the psychoanalytic view of the mental apparatus (as seen in the light of that line of development leading from Freud and Abraham, through Melanie Klein, to the work by Bion and Rosenfeld on thinking).

1. By the *mental apparatus*, we mean to express a *concretization* of all those mental functions that undergo development through interaction with the environment as distinguished from other, largely more primitive functions, which are fixed by genetic mechanisms. While we cannot claim our knowledge to be so great that we can fix this boundary with any certainty *in fact*, we do so in theory, as expressed by the terms "*psychology*" and "*neurophysiology*".
2. *Internal objects and parts of the self:* This *mental apparatus* is experienced unconsciously as being composed of *internal objects* and *parts of the self* at varying levels of maturation, operating within and through the structures of the body. Internal objects and parts of the self are experienced as possessing a mental apparatus of their own (as are objects in the outside world), so that the geography of psychic reality is felt to be composed of an infinite series of compartments (objects inside of self, inside of objects, inside of self . . .). This series in the inner world is felt as being equivalent to the dimension of time in the outer world, stretching forward and backward, generation upon generation.

3. *Omnipotence and autoerotism:* *Omnipotence* is a quality of parts of the self that internal objects only obtain by projective identification. It is a psychic quality whose momentary generation stands in specific relation to the self-stimulation of *autoerotic activities*. It decays in any particular part of the self in the absence of autoerotism and can be controlled in any part of the self by any other parts of superior maturity.
4. *Maturity and capacity to think:* Maturity of parts of the self is felt to be measured by their capacity to think, which is strongly bound up with the capacity to utilize language to communicate.
5. *Thinking and primal good objects:* The *capacity to think* is a function of the relation to the primal good object in each part of the self. The nature of this primal good object extends from the primitive penis-in-the-breast part object to the combined-parent-figure whole object.
6. *Omniscience and primal objects:* The *primal good object* is experienced as *omniscient* regarding perception and comprehension of the truth. This quality is claimed as well by the *primal bad objects* and at times by bad parts of the self. While the primal good objects are experienced as parsimonious of their knowledge, willing only to assist parts of the self to think, primal bad objects are veritable cornucopias of thoughts asserting omniscience and aimed at preventing thinking (Bion).
7. *Maturation and integration:* *Maturation of the mental apparatus* involves a process of integration of parts of the self and objects by the gradual relinquishment of splitting processes, the surrender of omnipotence and acceptance of the pains of the depressive position in object relations, through the constant working of projection and introjection in relation to objects in the external and internal worlds.
8. *Consciousness:* In addition to this unconscious structure of the mental apparatus, there is *consciousness*—an "organ for the perception of psychic qualities" with a preferential relation to the organs of behaviour. Control of consciousness may be seized and held by any part of the self, which during its tenure is able to maintain control over gross behaviour, including speech.

As always, psychoanalysis seems to rediscover the obvious truths against which massive defences have been erected. The panorama of history shows how correct they are. The history of religion (genesis of the superego) shows the movement from multiplicity to unity and from persecuting to benevolent figures of deity. Social history (genesis of the self) shows the cyclic operation of splitting-and-idealization and integration. The development of the arts and sciences (thought and communication—the domain of consciousness) shows the ebb and flow of the employment of advancing knowledge for constructive and destructive purposes (knowledge vs. belief . . . Brecht puts into the mouth of Francis Bacon the pithy statement, "Man has too long believed too much and known too little".) Now there cannot be much doubt that the main vehicle of social integration operates through the capacity for thought of artists and scientists (a spurious dichotomy, in fact—more correctly artist–scientists). It remains, of course, for the social scientists to develop a method of getting inside the social system, as Freud discovered how to get inside an inter-personal system (the transference), before they will be able to influence the course of social evolution to any significant degree. The belief in the goodness and eventual value of knowledge laboriously acquired has characterized the artist-scientist of all ages, despite the apparent supremacy of power that has preyed on this creativity and put it to destructive use. Psychoanalysis shows clearly that the inexorable quality of "the fall" derives not from the knowledge itself, but from its mode of acquisition—Lilith to Eve to Adam (theft of the nipple–penis by oral sadistic attack under the aegis of envious omnipotence, simulating infantile pseudo-genitality).

To return now to the central theme of this paper—using the statement of Bertrand Russell, I have put forward the suggestion that the discoveries about the nature of the mental apparatus imply an imperative that amounts to an ethical principle. This, I suggest, can be discovered in a correct formulation of the *laws* of *psychic reality* and can be distinguished from the moral principles implied by the various levels of superego formation. My suggestion, further, is that these ethical principles take an imperative form, "*Unless* you do so-and-so, you will be *unable* to do this-and-that", as distinguished from moral principles of the subjunctive form, "If you fail to do so-and-so, this-and-that will (not) be done to (for) you."

The decay of belief in deity since the seventeenth century has been accompanied by a corresponding atrophy of morality in favour of the moral class-structure of humanism with a hierarchy of the form, "People at a higher level (of solicitude for their fellow creatures) are concerned about the moral development of those at a lower level, who respond to this concern with a variable mixture of admiration and envy". The morality of the nursery, with all its pitfalls and instability (see "Major Barbara")!!

What laws of psychic reality can be deduced from the picture of the mental apparatus that psychoanalytic discoveries enable us to form?

- *First Law of Psychic Reality:* experience of object-relations in the outside world is limited by the structure of internal object relations.
- *Second Law of Psychic Reality:* the balance of benevolence–malevolence of internal objects can only be improved by integration of split-off parts of the self (by movement within the gradient chaos . . . order).

It is, of course, no accident that these two laws have a certain correspondence to the first and second laws of thermodynamics. A proper student of semantics could, I feel sure, restate them in a more general form that would show the correspondence more clearly.

Of course, in ethics we are concerned primarily with principles governing human behaviour, but psychoanalysis shows that this cannot be limited to behaviour with external objects. In essence, the split between public and private behaviour is eliminated in a single stroke, for insofar as private behaviour affects the internal objects, we know it is bound to affect the experience of, and therefore the behaviour towards, external ones. In considering the processes of projection and introjection by which the ebb and flow of integration and disintegration are managed, we need to recognize that Melanie Klein's most surprising discovery, from the ethical point of view, is that the differentiation of good and bad, which starts with splitting-and-idealization in infantile development, gradually improves in its malevolence–benevolence balance *as integration proceeds*. This does not deny that high degrees of *organization* cannot take place in the mental apparatus under the sway of destructive objects and parts of the self, as in paranoia. But this is always based on *balancing* rather than integration and has no *element of strength* in its linkages, which are always in the nature of *control*, fraught with distrust and hatred. In comparison, the sphere of the primal good objects promotes integrative links of *cooperation*, assisted by trust and love. "Honour among thieves" has no application in psychic reality.

Bion's clarifications of the working of projection and introjection help us to understand the gradient of chaos–order that exists in a individual's life space from conception to death. It is clear that the child is surrounded by external objects of superior integration that provide a developmental gradient of ever-decreasing intensity as his own integration proceeds. The moment his integration outstrips that of his milieu, he is subject to a negative gradient. *Care in the selection of external objects* then becomes essential if further integration is to be achieved. Here the community of artist-scientists takes over where parents must leave off. Our schools, galleries, psychoanalytic consulting-rooms, concert halls, and libraries become the haunts, naturally, of those in search of further integration. The ethical implications are clear. Our relationship opportunities in the outside world, the mutual projection-introjection we accept with creatures and institutions, must be selected with a view and within a value system that stresses "their welfare"—i.e. that of our internal objects.

I will not here enter into any more detailed discussion of what constitutes "their welfare", but it is clear that the essential developmental step that makes such a consideration possible is, above all, the overcoming of the "denial of psychic reality" which plays such a large part in the structure of the latency period. Elliott Jaques' description of the "mid-life crisis" has clearly demonstrated that, following the period of early adult life when contact with psychic reality is kept active by the work of raising young children, most adults tend to lapse back in middle age into the mechanisms of the latency period, with all its impoverishment.

Now, all that I have written above, as I warned you, is a bit in the nature of an elliptical psychoanalytic (and therefore not very funny) type of joking. But I would not wish to turn away from this subject without acknowledging the serious side, on account of which I was originally asked to present this paper. The work of Melanie Klein has, like it or not, introduced, with the concepts of paranoid-schizoid and depressive positions, the element of *value* into the psychoanalytic system of thought—that is, into its previously relatively barren area of mental *economics*. Her discoveries about early superego formation and the role of projection and introjection, and later of projective identification, in this formation, have totally altered our concept of the role of the environment in the genesis of the mental apparatus . . . no, in personality development. The role of mental pain—of the two great ranges of mental pain, persecutory and depressive—has been clarified so that a concept of choice (free will) need no longer be attenuated by the recognition of the divisions in consciousness.

Therefore we are able to speak of *responsibility* without punitive intent and can conceive of children as being responsible for their mental processes while their errors may still be eminently forgivable due to immaturity. In fact, psychoanalytic work in problems of the depressive position teaches us unequivocally that forgiveness by objects, internal and external, is far more easily obtainable than self-forgiveness, which requires maturation. In other words, a parent can easily forgive his child, and an analyst his patient, but in order to forgive oneself a certainty that the crime will never be repeated must be attained. This achievement is the essence of that aspect of analysis which Freud named the "working through".

None of these discoveries undoes the great importance of Freud's and Abraham's discoveries of the biologically determined phases in the development of the libido, but are rather superimposed upon them. The implications are clear—we are born with minds in chaos, and every step towards order, and therefore towards structure, comes as a gift by the working of projection and introjection with objects in the outside world whose benevolence (maturity, really) enables them to contain projections of bad objects and bad parts of the self, while returning the good ones improved by splitting-and-idealization.

Only when such processes have been significantly established internally and structured as mature superego figures (the combined parent object) has the basis of independent integrity been established. However, the external objects that facilitate this process do not function effectively of themselves, but in relation to the degree to which they are allowed to function—a fiat represented by the mode of projecting and the readiness for introjecting that the individual brings to bear. We now, since *Envy and Gratitude* (Klein, 1957) can see that the play of envy, whether free or opposed from within, is the chief operative factor here. Virtually every paper by a member of the Klein group since the publication of this crucial book has dealt with the ways in which this balance of freedom and opposition operates, especially Bion's most recent works.

Now all of this, to my mind, establishes the *primacy of psychic reality* as the arbiter of human experience and lies at the basis of the contention, whose ethical implication is the subject of this paper—i.e. that absolute justice prevails in the realm of object relations, in all that may be correctly called the life of the mind. This does not mean the life-of-the-body, but only the experience-of-the-body. But justice is a concept that is irrelevant to biological processes below the level of mental, to the questions of physical attributes, to sensual pleasure and pain in themselves, to life and death of the biological organism. At the mental level death is, in psychic reality, merely the loss of time-of-life short of the complete cycle from conception to senescence. It can only appear catastrophic in relation to a delusion of potential immortality. Premature death is merely tragic. But so is failure of maturation, as we see it every day in our consulting-rooms, while the only true catastrophe is probably the self-destruction of the mental apparatus in schizophrenia.

Common sense, of course, says otherwise. It dwells on the surface. It sees chance operate in contempt of worthiness—it sees the ruthless rampant in their pride and the trampled whining in their assertion of innocence. It is deceived by sanctimony and dazzled by snobbery, of the poor (in heart) as of the rich (in power). Psychoanalysis sees below and finds the constant commerce in misery outside the depressive position, the degradation of rich and poor alike. And within the depressive position it finds the suffering of concern and responsibility. Bliss it finds nowhere, except in the infantile delusionally jealous phantasy of the life of the inside-babies. But Melanie Klein has shown us where the great difference in joy lies, that the transit from loneliness lies at the threshold between the two great positions and the shift in values requisite.

So we have made the circuit back to Bertrand Russell's "egocentric particulars" and the necessity for self-consciousness in the promotion of human communication. If we are to *talk with* one another, not merely in *the presence* of one another, we must both be "cat-perceptive".

CHAPTER EIGHT

An interruption technique for the analytic impasse

(1968)

This study of impasse and its differentiation from other resistances, based on the structure of the transference, suggests a technical device for dealing with impasse and appeals to the analyst's personal responsibility in relation to his internal objects. It underlines how this method demands courage and personal emotional involvement. This seems to be the first of a series of papers on the committed use of countertransference, born out of the description of the author's clinical work.

In my book, *The Psycho-analytical Process* (Meltzer, 1967a), I have described in some detail the structure of the "threshold of the depressive position" and the economic balance in relation to mental pain that forms the background for this most characteristic impasse of the psychoanalytic procedure. I have witnessed it during the past years of clinical work and supervision, and during the last six years I have experimented with several methods of dealing with the impasse. Finally, I have adopted one that seems humane, rational, and reasonably safe, and one that has proved on the whole surprisingly successful.

For the sake of clarity, I will lay this method out in the following format:

1. the differentiation of impasse from other intractable resistances;
2. the technique of interruption;
3. the rationale and dangers of the procedure.

Differentiation of impasse from other intractable resistances

The conservative nature of a resistance to the analytic procedure indicates that it contains potential intractability. We depend upon the setting for the modulation of anxiety and on interpretations for its gradual modification which erode and relieve resistance over a period of time. The scientific nature of the analyst's work will convince him that every resistance is potentially open to relief, and any intractability must be taken as an analytic failure, regardless of the personality defects in the patient—call them what you will—defective drive towards integration, inadequate cooperation, dishonesty, *folie à deux* with an external figure, overwhelming persecutory or depressive anxiety, inadequate drives, split-off psychosis, etc. This conviction, to my mind, forms the fundamental bulwark against countertransference acting against the patient and should, in all cases of intractability, be further strengthened by supervision with a colleague prior to a decision regarding termination, interruption, or partial interruption.

I will now describe in detail my experience of the impasse at the threshold of the depressive position. To begin with, I must report that I have never met it prior to the fourth year of a first analysis. On the other hand, I have had the experience in second or third analyses of finding that the pattern that had wrecked the previous procedure gradually took shape and crystallized anew within the first two years, or, rarely, that the impasse was so firmly and completely repeated from the beginning that a new analytic process did not really start at all.

Regarding the patient's adaptation outside analysis, this will have proceeded to a point of minimal mental pain in social adjustment, work accomplishment, and sexual relations. By this I do not mean that the patient will have become well-socialized, creative, nor potent, but only that the functions in these areas will have been sufficiently divested of infantile transference contamination to have assumed an unhampered, though as yet under-developed, adult functioning. The lack of development will be found to be based upon a very considerable preservation of ego-centricity, despite the fairly extensive erosion of infantile narcissistic organization that will have been accomplished. This ego-centricity can in turn be clearly related to failure of commitment to introjective identification with internal objects (more details of which are discussed in Meltzer, *Sexual States of Mind*, 1973). It is implicit in the aspirational quality of introjective identifications, in contrast to the immediacy of narcissistic, and especially projective, identification, that a considerable time-lag should exist between the establishment of a quality as an attribute of an internal object and its acceptance as an *obligatory intention* by the adult part of the self.

The general point about adaptation is that the patient is content, or relatively so, in his egocentricity and feels ready to stop analysis from the point of view of the conscious motives that first brought him to the couch. (I will not discuss in this paper the problem of impasse in the training analysis, which is a complicated situation requiring special elucidation in a different context from the present one). The analyst is therefore felt to be holding on to the patient for various reasons of his own and attempting to press him in a direction that is foreign to the patient's nature, aspirations, and "condition of servitude".

An extraordinary and powerful campaign therefore builds up over the period of impasse to terminate the analysis in an atmosphere of mutual idealization at an adult level in parallel with the leitmotif at various infantile levels. It is my suspicion—not undocumented—that this is the prevailing mode of termination among many analytic groups, and that resistance to these siren voices commits the analyst either to a war of attrition with his patient or to a more ordered method of utilizing the time factor, of which the present technique of interruption is one possibility. The only other method that has found any significant representation in the literature—namely that of sending the patient to another analyst—is, to my mind, an irrational one, or at least a haphazard one, unless specific limitations in the one analyst are known to be met by specific capabilities in the other. Such a procedure based on seniority does absolute violence to the concept of the psychoanalytic process.

This brings us to the description of the transference situation underlying the impasse at the threshold, and I must refer you in the first instance to the relevant chapter in my book, *The Psycho-analytical Process* (Meltzer, 1967a). Further experience now makes a somewhat more detailed clinical description possible. The fundamental splitting and idealization of the infantile structure and the internal objects will have been consummated and worked through, establishing the differentiation of good–bad beyond equivocation. In patients who are more ill, this will have taken many years of work and is very closely related to the relinquishment of massive projective identification as a preferred mode of defence. Therefore the core of omnipotence and narcissistic organization will have been abandoned, with the exception of those patients with a true addictive constellation, as I described in my paper on "Terror, Persecution and Dread" (Meltzer, 1968; also in *Sexual States of Mind*, 1973). This problem will only have been worked through after considerable travail on zonal confusions, and its resolution leads immediately to the threshold, though often by such gradual stages that the transition is obscure, as the addiction gives way, but the habitual participation in perversity—the use of drugs or misuse of money, for instance—is clung to as a defence against depressive pain.

Consequently the projective dependence upon objects, at root the toilet-breast, will have been firmly established and operative both in the transference and in relation to internal objects. Because of this latter function, holding during separations will be good, but separation anxiety will still be at a minimum because of the operation of manic mechanisms aimed at denial of the introjective dependence on the external analyst on the one hand and of obsessional mechanisms that vitiate the oedipal experience of the combined object on the other.

The adult insight into these infantile processes will have been extensively developed, as expressed particularly in the recognition of patterns of acting out and the understanding of the general configuration of dreams. But the patient will not have developed any creative insight, and independent analytic progress will not as yet be possible during the separations. My experience is very clear in this matter, that the first holiday break, usually a long summer holiday, which results in such progress marks the end of the impasse and has usually been preceded by an unusually stormy approach in which threats to abandon the analysis and accusations of various forms of countertransference possessiveness have been bruited.

But where the impasse persists, it will have come to be structured around the clamorous infantile demand for mutual idealization based on collusion with regard to one or more of the types of infantile confusion. Fundamentally it centres around a denial of the adult–infantile qualitative differentiation. In order to clarify this, I will describe briefly two of the configurations I have met in my own work.

An adolescent male formed in the fifth year of analysis an unconsummated sexual liaison with a fellow student, which paralleled completely his childhood relation to a sister. He systematically interfered with her relation to her parents, separated her from friends, prevented her from working, and gradually involved her in mutual masturbation. Dreams revealed that the internal parents (and the analytic ones, in the transference) were reduced to the "fat–foolish daddy" and the "flinching mummy", who envied but were incapable of controlling the children's sexuality. The actual parents had in fact divorced in his pubertal years, while the sister had a breakdown in adult life.

A woman in middle age whose parents were of different nationalities kept her objects severely separated internally on a geographical basis. After ten years of analysis, her partial projective identification with their impaired functioning was acted out by clinging to the analysis while longing for her native land and never being "at home". This corresponded to the unbending grievance of her early childhood, when the birth of the next sibling had coincided with the family moving to a new town, the patient being moved out of the parental bedroom, and her ceasing to be her father's "most beautiful girl in the world" because of her new sullenness. Her introjective relation was characterized not by an incapacity to take in, nor even to acknowledge the value of her introjection, but in a denial of the pleasure. This produced a relentless ingratitude, which was used to tyrannize over the mother and work out her possessiveness towards the breast.

These two examples illustrate the most clear-cut division in the structure of the impasse at the threshold between male and female patients. The former tend primarily towards an oedipal configuration by erotization of the breast and an insistence on a part-object relation to it as a "marriage" indistinguishable from a "little marriage" of the infantile bisexuality (cf. the young man and his sister). The women are driven more by possessive jealousy tinged with envy of the breast. This may utilize nipple–penis confusion (as a defence) and express itself as preoccupation with the father's penis in ways that appear to have the same oedipal configuration as that of the men. But deeper exploration seems always to reveal the drive towards mutual idealization by equation of breasts and testicles. Idealization of the faeces is thus reactivated in the woman patient; idealization of the semen (or, at its infantile level, of the golden urine) is invoked by the men.

It must be kept in mind that, although old and well-analysed confusions may be re-invoked *as* defences, one type of confusion does still exist unanalysed. It plays an important role in the oscillation between the strident demand for "freedom" from the analyst and behaviour aimed as settling into an interminable but unacknowledged dependence. This is the confusion between internal and external. Its poor delineation implies a defective comprehension of the primacy of psychic reality, even though—but this time in analysis—true denial of psychic reality is no longer ascendant.

It must also be remembered that the genital Oedipus complex at a whole-object level cannot really take shape in the transference until the threshold of the depressive position has been definitively breached. Consequently problems such as the integration of bisexuality, the integration of split-off envy or of a split-off psychotic part of the personality, are still in the analytic future.

Before closing this section, I must stress a technical aspect of the total problem. My experience is that this struggle on the threshold brings the analyst to grips with a highly sophisticated opponent, trained, as it were, in his own methods. Not only are infantile techniques of seduction and coercion highly organized to resist further advance, but a highly verbal adult structure is at their head, utilizing, or, rather, misusing analytic formulation and philosophic argument, ready to accuse the analyst of promulgating a Weltanschauung at the expense of analytic vigour.

In the face of this daunting opposition, the government of the analyst is frequently under pressure at a kind of "question time" when the rationale of his procedure will be minutely scrutinized. Information about the analyst's extra-analytic life, be it good, bad, or indifferent, will be seized upon to lend concreteness to the transference and prevent its further evolution. The difficulties this raises for patients in the analytic community are protean, but even the less unfavourably placed patient will have had years to collect a dossier of the films his analyst has seen, the books he reads, the newspapers he is acquainted with, the foreign languages he knows, his tastes in many areas, his family structure, and his general relation to psychoanalysis.

Intimidating as all of this may be and close as the patient's inferences may be to fact when the dossier is trotted out at question time, a position can be adopted, that his evidence is all of a second order and the inferences are at best of statistical significance. In the last resort, the analyst can even stand firm on the biological reality of his bisexuality.

In summary, it is this impasse at the threshold and this impasse only, for which I am proposing a technique, which I call "interruption". The more general technical problem of manipulating the factor of frequency and duration of analytic sessions must be dealt with at another time.

A technique of interruption

I would consider it unlikely for an impasse to be identified with any certainty, in the many facets of structure, economics, and dynamics, in less than a year of cessation of progress. It is necessary to stress the structural factor in defining progress—that is, the structure of infantile transference with regard to the divisions in the infantile self, the organization and quality of objects and their relationship, as well as the definition of the adult-part of the self. Economic factors are misleading because a certain gain due to economizing and consolidating of defences often takes place. The quality of cooperation cannot be taken as a guide, because it is usually excellent, descriptively speaking, while being defective in sincerity. Furthermore, evaluation of the patient's external adaptation is frequently paradoxical at this time, due to the working through into adult life of earlier gains of the analytic work. The patient will usually invoke items of this ilk in debate in the service of his unvoiced expectation of an interminable analysis. Despite the fact that this point will undoubtedly arouse great opposition in the patient—or reader—I must insist upon it as the keystone of the concept of impasse and the rationale of interruption. Anything other than structural criteria, clearly defined and dauntlessly held to, will lead to the prolongation of the impasse to the point of mutual exhaustion and render a technique of interruption feeble, if not completely unfeasible. I consider procrastination in the face of such evidence to be dangerous as well as wasteful.

The one note of special caution I would mention is of a genetic order. Where the impasse can be related clearly to a known historical event of the first two years of life, which could reasonably be considered as traumatic, in the strict sense of the term as used by Freud, and where the patient's impasse behaviour suggests underlying catastrophic anxiety, as described by Bion, I think that interruption should not be considered as an alternative to endless patience, even in the face of the danger of mutual exhaustion. I do not feel that the same reservation need be held in the case of evidence of a split-off psychosis, although at times the differentiation of these two can be very difficult indeed.

Having come to suspect an impasse at the threshold and having defined its structure, I strongly recommend that the evidence be reviewed with a colleague. Having decided that an interruption should be considered, I have in all cases taken at least a year to demonstrate the situation to the patient and explained to him the rationale of interruption bit by bit in relation to the clinical evidence. The structure of the impasse is seldom difficult to bring to the patient's attention with the help of dreams, the pattern of acting-out and acting-in, and the reconstruction, strengthened when possible by historical material from parents, regarding the period of infantile amnesia.

What is far more difficult is the demonstration of defects in the cooperation, since, as I have said, outside areas of acting-out and -in, it is often descriptively faultless. The inadequacy in sincerity is extremely evasive in its definable phenomenology. I have found a minute scrutiny of the patient's abuse of language to be the most fruitful approach, since by this time in analysis gross withholding of material is a rarity.

One can often show the patient that his subtle misuse of language reveals the continued existence of a system for evading responsibility for psychic reality by the employment of an echelon of negations similar to those mentioned by Freud in the joke about the bucket. What was it? Something like, "I never borrowed your bucket, and, besides, I returned it, and anyhow, it had a hole in it." The echelon of negations of responsibility for psychic reality runs something like, "I can't help it, and besides it's X's fault, and anyhow it's a good thing."

During all this time of preparation for interruption, the analyst's work must proceed with full vigour in the expectation that such a "last-resort" technique will prove to be unnecessary. But having at last decided upon it, the decision must be adhered to unless evidence appears which indicates that the structural evaluation upon which it was based had, in fact, been incorrect—not merely incomplete, but fundamentally incorrect.

My procedure has been to decide on the interruption shortly before a holiday and set a date, preferably at the next holiday. From that point I am willing to allow the patient to fix his own interruption arrangement regarding frequency of sessions, not exceeding once per week. I would view with some anxiety a patient's preference for an indefinite arrangement, such as sessions on request, and suspect that the structure of the transference would be likely to become scattered into other supporting figures of the environment if we met less frequently than once per month. I make it clear to my patients that this interruption in no way lessens my acceptance of analytic responsibility and that I stand ready to resume the analysis at any time, after at least one term's interruption, that evidence of relief of impasse becomes convincing.

I have learned, however, to be very cautious in "feeding back" the sessions and now do so only one at a time. My experience has been quite convincing that each returned session is followed by a negative therapeutic reaction and that a sudden resumption is taken unconsciously as an absolute recantation on the whole procedure.

Rationale and dangers of the technique

The fundamental structure of the impasse at the threshold is a rather simple one, and its economic nature stands out clearly. Indeed, one might say that it is essentially an economic rather than a dynamic or structural impasse, for the central problem is one concerned with the distribution of mental pain—distribution between self and objects, or among self, internal objects, and external objects.

It is important to stress the factor of distribution, for, when confronted with mental pain of a depressive sort in particular, the infantile structures are very prone to assume that the question, Hamlet-like, is to be or not to be in mental pain. Because the toilet-service of the internal or external object evokes very little admiration, the relief attained by the infantile structures is seldom accompanied by any strong experience of gratitude. There is a very decided resistance against coming to grips with the question of what it costs the object to serve in this way—far greater than the resistance to recognizing the sacrifice made by the feeding, introjective object. In the immediacy of the transference this takes the form of a very strong denial early on, and later a tenacious negation that the analyst feels mental pain on the patient's account. The horizontal splitting of the maternal object into below-the-waist toilet-mummy and above-the-waist breast-mummy is almost always split, externalized and acted-out with an external figure or an institution—a wife, friend, house, bank account, city, political party, native land, or mother earth. The breast-mummy appears in dreams as shapes, restaurants, corn-fields, mountains, homes, paintings, trees, caves, etc.

The bringing together of this split, with the differentiation of front-back, top-bottom, inside-outside—the three erotic areas of the mother's body—is the essential move in the breaching of the impasse and immediately joins the struggle of the genital Oedipus complex, for recognition of the unity of the maternal object and its burdens and sacrifices implies unequivocally the mother's dependence on the father and his genital. The economics of the depressive struggle rests very heavily on the recognition of the beauty as well as the goodness and generosity of the breast as part-object, or, one might say, the beauty of the breast becomes the symbolic representation of the goodness and generosity. Manic defences against recognition of the sacrifice and obsessional mechanisms aimed at quelling the pain of the Oedipus complex only begin to yield to concern for the object when its beauty is apprehended as deriving from the parental coitus and to remain refractory to restoration by manic reparation.

It is the confusion between internal and external objects in the transference that allows the analyst's health, vigour, and patience to be misused by the patient as the foundation for the denial of the cost to the object of serving the infantile structures. Interminable but unrecognized, dependence upon the analysis is taken as the logical *summum bonum*, and weaning is held to be unthinkable. The child, one might say, expects to be fed at the breast until its marriage-day. Until the constitution of the whole object brings into focus the psychic reality of the babies-inside-the mummy, and in the transference the reality of other people waiting for analysis somewhere in the world, the external reality of the preciousness of time and the psychic reality of the necessity for development can remain in abeyance.

The fundamental rationale of the technique of interruption is therefore one of quantitative deprivation without qualitative neglect. Its aim is to impose on the infantile structures, with the help of at least the acquiescence of the adult part, the necessity for longer periods of holding mental pain without expulsion and of containing damaged objects. One hopes by this experience to break through the infantile taking-for-granted of good objects and the adult impaired responsibility for psychic reality. A very similar move is sometimes accomplished at one stroke by an illness of the analyst, but one cannot consider this a technique. Furthermore, the balance at such times between depressive response by the patient and renewed denigration is perilously delicate.

In my experience so far this rationale seems strongly confirmed. A period of three to fifteen months has generally followed interruption during which the intensified use of the relatively infrequent sessions is accompanied by a sullen and complaining demeanour, a nagging reviewing of the material leading up to the interruption, and intensified threats to abandon the analysis, all with suicidal overtones. It is a time of great stress for analyst and patient alike, before the pattern of the impasse begins to yield—first the acting-out aspects, then the acting-in, and finally the impaired sincerity. However, the patients seldom agree, even with the most desirable outcome, that the interruption was absolutely necessary. They will grant, however, that an indeterminate period of precious time has probably been saved. One is forgiven for the aggression!

What can be said of the dangers of such a technique that does not apply generally to the dangers of analysis in its entirety? One can be careful regarding intellectual judgement by having supervision with a colleague before embarking on such a course. But the great hazard is in the countertransference, where every analyst no longer in analysis is alone with his internal situation. This area of responsibility cannot really be shared, and only conscientious self-analytic work can safeguard the procedure. Dreams about the patient should be very systematically analysed and one's emotionality during the sessions inspected with great care. As it is an uncompromising procedure, one must beware of any evidence of a sense of threat to one's self-esteem in the patient's arrested progress and therefore of the possibility of projective identification with the patient. Where the latter involves a hated part of the self, this is easily recognized, but where an idealized infantile part is involved, the feeling of tenderness, of admiration, of aspiration for the patient can more easily be confused with fondness and concern. My impression is that a very clear view of the adult relationship between analyst and patient and its distinction from the infantile transference–countertransference is the intellectual bulwark to this necessary emotional balance. To this end, the reconstruction of the patient's childhood, with special emphasis on the real qualities both of virtues and deficiencies of the real parents, is a great help. By this time in analysis most of the contamination of infantile memory by transference confusions between good and bad objects, between damaged and bad objects, and between parts of the self and objects has been relieved. A reliable reconstruction of the parental characters, their relationship, and the qualities of the patient at different epochs of childhood can be accomplished.

It seems to me that only at this point in an analysis, at the threshold of the depressive position, are we in a position to define with accuracy the crucial era of childhood or infancy which can reasonably be labelled "fixation point", in Freud's sense. It is of great importance to understand this with regard to ego-development, for it would be a mistake to think that all patients are like peas in a pod at the threshold. It is inevitable that the earlier in development the fixation point of the illness in the patient, the more primitive the ego will have remained. I have described in *The Psycho-analytical Process* (Meltzer, 1967a) the progress of sanity–health–maturity and would stress it again here. Basic sanity (by which I do not mean freedom from schizophrenia, which is a different problem, but of fundamental freedom from psychosis in the core of the self associated with the sense of identity) is the consequence of individuation from objects through the relinquishment of massive projective identification, while basic health is only acquired by penetration into the depressive position. Maturity, on the other hand, is an aspect of the adult part of the personality, which can only come gradually after commitment to introjective identification with internal objects and the acceptance of responsibility for psychic reality.

In our patients we meet a whole spectrum in relation to these three levels of development, both in depth and in breadth. Our neurotic patients usually have a part of the infantile self that is healthy, and there may even be a certain area of maturity in the adult structure outside the sexual area, while the psychosis is loculated and well split-off. Conversely, with our psychotic patients, who may have no adult structure at all, we find only a pseudo-mature infantile part and no penetration of the depressive position at all. Small wonder that the threshold is reached in such a wide diversity of analytic years and that the total personalities of the patients arrange themselves in such a broad spectrum as regards ego-strength, integration, and vitality at this point. By the time the threshold is breached in a neurotic, termination is in sight. With a psychotic or borderline patient, years of work towards integration still lie ahead. All of this emphasizes the point that the structure of the transference is the only reliable basis for distinguishing between an impasse at the threshold and other configurations of intractable resistance.

CHAPTER NINE

A note on analytic receptivity

(1968)

The role of visual perception of the patient's material at the expense of the verbal is delineated, and the importance is stressed of developing a sensitivity specific to the verbal expressions of the unconscious.

A wide experience of supervising other analysts and students has helped me to recognize in myself, in my own work, certain strengths and weaknesses in analytic receptivity, one of which, now that it has begun to improve a bit, I would like to describe.

Although certainly collateral senses such as smell or postural sense play some part in analytic communication, by far the most important are auditory and visual. I have an impression that analysts generally fall into two categories—verbal and visual—in regard to the material with which they work most easily. The writings of the two greatest analysts, Freud and Melanie Klein, suggest a strong divergence in their sensitivity in these areas, Freud being astonishingly sensitive to verbal nuance, while Melanie Klein seems to have had a primarily visual imagination, particularly well suited to work with children. This can most clearly be seen in the dream material from their writings, say in "Dora" (Freud, 1905 [1901]), as compared with *Envy and Gratitude* (Klein, 1957).

On the other hand, one suspects that the verbal representations of unconscious phantasies derive from far more mature levels of the mind than the pictorial ones—not that this in any way lessens their importance for the analytic work, since we must try to analyse whatever is presented to us. In fact, it would seem to signify a danger to the analysis if the analyst is too one-sided in his responsiveness, for certain defences, particularly those connected with mania, obsessional disorders, and paranoia, seem often to rest upon verbal linkages (or pseudo-linkages, such as in puns and jokes) or verbal confusions (homonymous or near homonymous). It seems certain from work with autistic children that the verbal relationship of the parents to one another has an immense "primal" significance for the infant and that the capacity to make words is one of the earliest objects of envy. Conversely, it can be utilized as the basis for a delusion of equality with adults, or even superiority to them, the moment the first word formation has been mastered.

To give an example, a young man of considerable literary gift and accomplishment has a vocabulary greater than my own in the area of aesthetics. It is noticeable that, as soon as feelings of inferiority begin to impinge upon him in the transference, he will use an exotic word, immediately becoming expansive in his material and patronizing in his tone.

Or, conversely, a man in the sixth year of his analysis, well into depressive conflict and coming to grips with his positive and inverted Oedipus complex, was disturbed at the end of certain sessions to find that, as he left the consulting-room, a conspiratorial smirk would break forth on his face. He could not look at me lest he find a similar expression on my face. Only gradually did we come to recognize that his material was full of anal *double entendres* and puns, which had the significance of passing flatus in public. When I had not paid sufficient attention to this aspect of the material, it had meant that there was a smell in the room, but no one mentioned it, because each person present (in this case he and myself, but in essence it meant the family gathering) suspected himself of having made the bad smell. This harked back to a long-standing denigration of his father and an old tweed jacket, which the patient thought of as the "shit jacket".

My impression of modern training in psychoanalysis—and certainly of my own—is that it tends to encourage and develop visual reception of material at the expense of the verbal because of the emphasis on comprehending the unconscious phantasies rather than the nuances of defence. Basically, I think it is a correct method, but is likely to leave a gap in the capabilities of young analysts unless they are gifted in a literary way themselves. This is bound to be particularly true for analysts not working in their mother tongue.

In my own work in recent years I have been fortunate to have four patients with high literary talents, at whose hands I have received a vigorous retraining in this area. But it is also my impression that increasing ease and certainty in the handling of the visual aspects of the communications (the "picture" of a patient's dream, for instance) have given me the opportunity to deploy greater attention to the verbal aspect. To give a recent example:

A young man of high intelligence and verbal skill is struggling with a deep-seated confusion of anus and vagina, which has undermined his differentiation between masculine, feminine, and anal homosexual activities. Two days before a holiday break, his son developed a high fever, and the patient was further distressed by a dream in which *they were swimming and the boy slipped beneath the surface and might have been drowned.* This dream had followed one involving the patient's last homosexual paramour.

It was clear from other material that the holiday threatened a return of homosexual acting out, and this meant to destroy his children by wasting his semen. The following night he dreamed:

> *Miss White said that Sir Henry's school would be fine for his son. So lively! The patient visited, but found it confusion.*

His associations went galloping off something like this (not verbatim): "Oh, Miss White is a research assistant with whom I have a very creative relationship—somehow we work well together, just pushing ideas back and forth, not expecting miracles—not expecting either one to shift his position—but somehow something comes out—something viable takes shape."

This surely sounds like some sort of coitus, but in what orifice, anus or vagina? The patient himself finds "Sir Henry's School" confusing, although it is deemed a "lively" place for his son. There is no such place in reality. However there was an ancestor of his wife called "Sir Harry". As we had known from previous material that the hairlessness of children's genitals has been claimed as aesthetically superior to the hairiness of adult ones during his proliferating childhood sexual play with a cousin his own age, we could assume that "Sir Harry's school" meant "Sir Hairy's school", or the vagina where the hairy ancestral penis presided over the womb teeming with life.

This sequence, in which "Miss White" represented both the analytic breast and his wife, corresponded to the facts—that his wife had first rescued him from despair about his sexuality by bearing him children and the analysis had rescued him from the longing for homosexuality by enabling him to distinguish the front-bottom (vagina) from the rear-bottom (anus).

In summary, I wish to stress my impression that sensitivity to the verbal aspects of patient's material is something that analysts are likely to need to teach themselves. From my own experience, I would suggest that the best tutor in this regard is a highly verbal and literarily gifted adult patient, especially an obsessional neurotic.

CHAPTER TEN

The relation of aims to methodology in the treatment of children

(1968)

The author postulates here that the aims in the treatment of children are identical to the analyst's interests and desires, while methodology is linked to the quality of internal objects. He remarks on the importance of aims—not goals—in the psychoanalytic process, and that the psychoanalytic method and technique are guided by internal objects and not by what is "right" and "wrong".

I want to attempt a purely psychoanalytic approach to a question that is not necessarily a psychoanalytic one by any means. Therefore I am going to start with two dreams from a patient, one dating from the beginning of the last year of his analysis, the other from the end of that year.

In the first dream the patient, a young doctor who was considering applying for analytic training,

---

Read to the Association of Child Psychotherapists, London, 1968.

> *. . . found himself wading into the sea following a tall man dressed in a sou'wester. In the distance there seemed to be a milk bottle, either floating or partly submerged. As the water became deeper and deeper, the patient felt panic that at any moment he might become unable to touch bottom and would be swept away by the current.*

One year later he dreamed that

> *Dr Ball, who seemed to be the new professor of another department, appeared unexpectedly in an informal visit to the patient's ward. He was immensely pleased but a bit nervous, as Dr Ball was a man he greatly admired for his integrity, devotion to his patients, and clinical experience—but in a field different from the patient's. The two nurses were a bit annoyed but greeted Dr Ball with respect—they were middle-aged, not sexually attractive but efficient and friendly.*

We have, then, two images: (1) patient, man in sou'wester, milk bottle; (2) patient, Dr Ball, two nurses. Panic in one, pleasure mixed with nervousness in the other. Let us leave them suspended as we turn to the problem of treating children. What is the sociological picture of the context in which the psychological treatment of children takes place? Who is concerned? What are the patterns of motivation, values, relationships, interests?

In the first place there is the child, whose motivations must be assumed to be dominated still by the repetition compulsion arising from his id and the pleasure–pain–reality principle regulating his ego's relationship to his id and external reality. Even as late as adolescence, we find little grasp of the relationship of past to future, and hence very little capacity for concern about the future. On the other hand, the more ill the child is, the more deeply enmeshed in the paranoid–schizoid position are his internal object relations and the greater his consequent incapacity for trust. In summary, we must say of the child that he brings very private motives, very personal or egocentric values, and a very short time-span of imagination into the situation.

His parents, on the other hand, bring a medley of motives, values, and concepts with them. Their good will towards the child is hampered to some extent by ambivalence, or contaminated by projective identification with him. Their readiness for sacrifice on his behalf is balanced against concern for the welfare of other children as well as against desires arising from their own life plans. Their personal sense of values is in conflict to some degree with those of the community and its agencies, as well as with those of their own parents, whether living or deceased. The time reference, so pressing to them, is also confusing, for concern with the past tends to deal with questions of guilt on their part, while the present concentrates on the child's happiness, and yet the future is dominated by concern for his social integration. In summary, one could say that parents bring a child, wanting him to be made happy, so that they will not feel guilty about the past, apprehensive of the future, ashamed before the community, or inferior towards their own parents. Tall order!

Community agencies—schools, courts, doctors, employers, etc.—these depersonalized actors in the situation operate on an entirely different system from the children or the parents, namely a statistical basis in which money and normality are the key concepts, normality meaning social invisibility as an individual to the agency involved; money meaning whether the expenditure on the individual is defensible in the face of hostile inquiry. In summary, community agencies require that the socially disruptive manifestations of the child are made inexpensively invisible within the milieu.

It is plain, then, that at the three different levels of participation in the operation that brings a child for treatment—child, parents, community agencies—three different systems of values pertain: the immediacy of the pleasure–pain–reality principle in the child; in the parents depressive concern about past upbringing and the child's future development, hedged by persecutory anxieties towards him and the milieu; statistical concepts and values regarding social order and welfare, including medical ethics, in the agencies of the community. To put it in an even more condensed way, the child wants relief, the parents reassurance, and the community control in relation to the current disturbance.

Clearly, in order to be entrusted with the situation, a therapist must meet all these requirements to some extent.

By providing a setting for the expression and experience of disturbance, we offer the child relief; by implying that the disturbance is treatable, we offer the parents reassurance; and by taking responsibility and gathering into our consulting-room the disturbance, we offer the community control. But this says nothing about the aims of the therapist, it merely declares his shop open for business. If we were shopkeepers, we need worry no more than to keep our customers happy. And this we must do, but as a precondition for being allowed to pursue our aims and utilize our methods.

So far nothing I have said suggests that the problem requires a lecture of this sort, unless it be for the purpose of giving me an opportunity to express my personal aims and the methods I pursue. In that case, I would be citing myself as typical or revealing myself as idiosyncratic, and in neither case could the discourse be of any interest. I could be typically medical, diagnosing illness and treating it. Soon, however, it would be revealed that we do not really know what the illnesses are, nor can we clearly detect who has them, let alone know how to treat them. Or I might be typically pedagogic in the area of the psychology of living, but it would soon be clear that I neither know what to teach, nor to whom. Or I could be typically sociological, helping people to adjust to their milieu, but it would soon be clear that I do not know what their milieu is, nor what adjusting to it means, beyond the most manifest forms of behaviour.

So I cannot lecture on how you should think about aims and methods of treatment, but must lift the subject to a higher level of abstraction and talk about how to think about thinking about aims and methods. So, let us return to our dreamer and his last year of analysis.

At the time of the first dream, after six years of analysis, his illness, mainly obsessional with hypochondriacal and psychosomatic features coupled with gross immaturity, was largely a thing of the past. He had a firm foot in the depressive position, his acknowledgement of psychic reality was good, and some considerable distance had been covered in the resolution of his direct and inverted Oedipus complex. What remained, in addition to the process of bringing the analysis to a close, was the residual immaturity manifest by a slight boyishness, dependence on the opinions and ideas of others and consequent slowness to take up responsibilities, though in fact he carried well the heavy ones thrust upon him. The boredom and lack of direction that had led him to analysis had been replaced by a rich participation in professional and family life, a wide intellectual interest, and a good capacity for pleasure at work and play. He was respected, liked, even loved—a good friend and an ethical opponent. But something was lacking, which undermined his stability and nipped creative imagination in the bud.

It could be seen, of course, that much room for development and integration at infantile levels still remained. His femininity was not fully integrated but still easily split off and projected. His destructive part, while seldom projected outward, was held inwardly in an unintegrated state, outside the sphere of the breast. But these, one could reasonably hope, would improve with time and self-analysis if the quality of his adult organization was right for fully assuming the burdens that had been carried by the analyst.

In fact something was wrong there which the first dream makes very clear. In the dream he is in a following-in-daddy's-footsteps relation to his good paternal object and following it to a *goal*—the milk bottle. We knew much about this figure in the sou'wester already, and its origins in a film he had seen as a boy, "Captains Courageous". We also knew that "touching bottom" meant anal masturbation and refuge in projective identification. We knew also that the milk bottle represented the acceptance of weaning as a goal. However, it took several sessions of associations and transference material to reveal that his fear of being "swept away" meant swept by a current of passionate interests of his *own*—in a word, by *aims*.

To recapitulate: so long as he was following-in-daddy's-footsteps and concerned with reaching goals, there remained both a timidity with regard to pursuit of his own interests and desires and an inability to commit himself to the abandonment of projective identification with the "daddy" at times of stress. His goal in life was to become a "real man, like daddy". The phallic quality of the masculinity implied in the figure in the sou'wester was clear from many items of association, in which courage in the face of danger was its overriding quality.

If we turn now to the dream of nine months later, a rather different spectacle is laid before us. The fact that a Dr Ball actually existed as admired, had recently become professor, etc., should not distract us from recognizing the testicular reference. The patient's relationship to this genital father was a more adult one, *under his aegis* but not *following in his footsteps.* Note the evidence of the patient's femininity—the two middle-aged nurses—being more integrated. Nothing in the dream suggests goals, only aims, of following his interests and doing his work under the inspiration of the principles of his internal objects—now a combined object—Dr Ball and his professorial chair.

Now, where does all this take us with regard to the problem of how to think about thinking about our aims and our methodology? Each worker in this field, largely due to chance events outside his control and to the working of the unconscious, which is beyond his comprehension, will have passed through various trainings, been impinged upon by various influences, been exposed to various clinical or laboratory experiences—all of which will have, to whatever extent the introjective process has been operative, made a contribution to the qualities of his internal objects—and thereby potentially to his character.

Freud writes, in "The Economic Problem of Masochism" (1924c):

> The course of childhood development leads to an ever-increasing detachment from parents, and their personal significance for the superego recedes into the background. To the imagos they leave behind there are then linked the influences of teachers and authorities, self-chosen models and publicly recognized heroes, whose figures need no longer be introjected by an ego which has become more resistant. The last figure in the series that began with the parents is the dark power of Destiny which only the fewest of us are able to look upon as impersonal [i.e.—death].

This point, that new qualities become linked to the imagos of the parents, but that the figures of the newer influences need not be introjected is of immense importance in understanding the modifications of the superego and why they are not incompatible with love for the original objects. It is because of this fact that one's internal objects can not only improve in quality but in scope, so that the aegis they raise in a person's inner world need never be incompatible with the interests and desires of the ego, as may easily happen in relation to external parents or mentors.

Recall that in the dream Dr Ball dropped in unexpectedly, informally, but that my patient was delighted to see him, though the two nurses were a bit nervous. This absence of superego anxiety—or, to give it a simpler name, secretiveness—is the hallmark to look for in thinking about one's aims and methods.

Where are we now? I seem to have decided that goals have no place in the treatment of children, only aims. But aims seem to turn out to be identical with one's interests and desires, or, in other words, one should be willing to continue a treatment so long as it holds one's interest and fulfils one's professional desires. And methodology turns out to mean anything that will pass muster with one's internal objects. For this reason the breach of technique, of one's own technique, is always accompanied by anxiety and guilt. And similarly yielding to external pressures in a way that imposes aims that are out of keeping with one's interests and desires is accompanied by anxiety and guilt.

What sort of field are we working in, then, where people must follow their own interests and desires and adhere to their own methods and techniques? Clearly a field of maximum individual responsibility and minimum demonstrability of results. In the face of this minimum demonstrability, we are all left with fingers crossed, hoping that at least something like natural selection and the *statistic of the generations* will give the answer to the historian, of who was right and who was wrong, what worked and what did not. In the meantime it does not really matter, for no one knows; we all only think, and work. We all must risk all, where the person who thinks he knows risks nothing. While there is a characterological gap between those who are equipped for this work and those who are not, one cannot even be sure of this about oneself. The other gaps of notation, technique, and theory are largely semantic and will eventually be bridged by the inevitable friendliness that arises from the realization of being "in the same boat"—and a solipsistic boat it is, in our case.

CHAPTER ELEVEN

Positive and negative forms

(1970)

In this study of spaces in the geography of the mind, the author questions whether they have formal qualities that are aesthetically meaningful apart from the meaning of the objects by which they are bounded. (Spaces are concretely conceptualized in unconscious phantasy in relation to time.) We must be reminded that this "architectural" paper originates around the time that Explorations in Autism *(1975) was written, where the pathological link between space and time comes under clinical and theoretical scrutiny. In this paper the author also proposes the creation of a Clinical Data Service to be made available to various professionals (aesthetes, philosophers, architects, etc.) willing to explore the Kleinian psychoanalytic view of their particular area of interest. This was to be a bulletin with papers written by psychoanalysts with special interests. This project did not become a viable proposition.*

This is primarily a methodological paper insofar as its aim is to set out a problem in aesthetics, mainly related to sculpture and architecture, in a form that may lend itself to psychoanalytic solution, at a certain level, and then by some illustrations to draw forth a methodology to which analysts could, individually and collectively, contribute towards its investigation.

Let me try to state the problem first in a way that opens it, or at least some aspects of it, to psychoanalytic inquiry. Do spaces have formal qualities that are meaningful aesthetically, apart from the meaning of the objects by which they are bounded? The title of the paper is meant to suggest the question, put in an other way: Can we investigate spaces as negative forms?

I can launch immediately into a psychoanalytic elaboration of the problem by laying out in extended form the term "space" as it is used in a technical sense, and for this purpose I would enumerate five potential spaces in the geography of the mind which may become actual, in the sense of the concreteness of psychic reality during personality development, healthy or pathological. Starting from inside out, I would list them as follows:

1. the space inside internal objects;
2. the space of internal reality;
3. the outside world;
4. the space inside external objects
   (a) possibly, though I have seen no convincing evidence of its existence, the space inside the internal objects of external objects—I will come back to this shortly;
5. the world of schizophrenia, beyond the boundaries of the emotional gravitation of the breast and its system.

To return to 4(a), my doubt is not about its potential existence, but about its actual existence in the system of object relations which we study in the consulting-room. But, from the point of view of the geography of phantasy, history is of this "Russian doll" configuration, or like the folk song of the "Old Woman who Swallowed a Fly" ("cider inside her inside"). This applies to both past and future, for just as the internal mother contains her mother containing her mother, etc., she also contains her babies containing their babies, etc. This I feel to be a very important point, for it reminds us that in moving from category to category of our roster of "spaces", we are also journeying in time, not in its chronometric sense, but in its categorical sense—past, present, future. Movement in phantasy among these categories, associated with the other phenomenology of projective identification, is also known to produce anomalies in the theory of time as a dimension of life space, the best-defined of which are circular time and oscillating time, as against the linear time of Space 3 relationships.

Now let us turn to some clinical examples, after which I can return to methodological considerations.

Example A

A girl of fourteen, whose analysis had carried her from early latency in the playroom to the flux of puberty on the couch, dreamed:

> *. . . five criminals were imprisoned in a flimsy slatted structure high in a tree, but each night they escaped and roamed abroad in the village. The she was one of them and they were in Regents Park, but it was in the time of Charles II.*

This dream relates to long-standing nocturnal masturbatory games and phantasies in which fingers were personified and engaged in various dramas in relation to the surface and orifices of her body. The spaces of interest are the slatted prison up in the tree and the round Regents Park.

Example B

A young married man whose wife was thought pregnant for the first time had the following dream: he dreamt that

... she was peeping into the window of an office building and could see a room with a purple stripe around the walls, decorated with small golden eagles. Leading in from the main entrance was a hundred-foot-tall passage called "Nelson's cabin".

The spaces of interest are the *eagles' room* (uterus) and *"Nelson's cabin", built to receive Nelson's column* (Nelson being in assonance with Meltzer), i.e. the vagina.

Example C

A married young woman who started her analysis after a one year interruption—her previous analysis gradually falling apart after the death of both her parents within a short period of time—dreamt

... she was one of two students who were running around to avoid being expelled from a building that looked like the Albert Hall or a Cathedral, and was filled with people sitting in rows of benches. From the top of a central structure a man was conducting what seemed to be a combination of religious ceremony and a stormy union meeting: the public shouted out their demands, and the man responded from the pulpit.

The space is the inside of the breast swarming with babies and presided over by the central penis–nipple. This compares with the structure of the Pantheon with its open dome and its central open space or with St. Peter's dome, with Michelangelo's canopy beneath it.

Example D

A young unmarried man in his third year of analysis had made noticeable progress regarding his confusional states, his periods of apathy and sexual immaturity, for which his motivation was set in motion; but he always found it discouraging at weekends and holidays when his dependence on the analytic breast gradually took the place of his usual delusional independence based on his intellectual superiority and his personal fortune. The patient was having a whole series of dreams in which the breasts were represented in an architectural way as domes, tents, windmills, etc. One week, on Wednesday and Friday, he had two dreams of this type, in which he showed his reluctance to give up his omnipotent intrusion into the breast.

WEDNESDAY: . . . *he was in the ring of a circus tent standing on a slatted structure which suddenly began to spiral up like an escalator carrying him towards an apex, very frightened of falling.*

FRIDAY: . . . *he was on the street outside a structure like those used for advertising posters in Paris. It seemed to be the Communist Party headquarters and a man was entering with his small son. When the door opened it looked very warm and snug inside and the patient realized how cold he was outside.*

On the THURSDAY he had brought a dream whose significance I did not comprehend until the Friday dream had suggested that the dreams of the three days could be arranged together spatially (Fig. 1). He had dreamed that

. . . *he was in a rectangular room, or rather its two ends bulged inward as a convexity. In the centre was a swimming pool, which looked black, he thought, until he noticed that there was no roof and only the night sky was above. The analyst's voice was then heard saying that it might seem lonely at first, but he would quite like it once he was accustomed to it.*

This dream seems to represent as a space the period of waiting with the memory of having been lifted to the breast and the prospect of its repetition—i.e.—the linear structure of past-present-future.

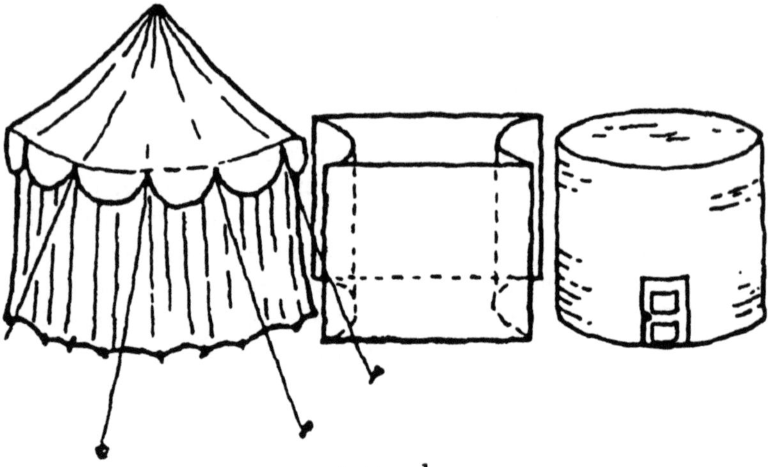

FIGURE 1

These examples are given in barest outline, merely to illustrate the categories of spaces and their relationship to the conceptualization of time as a dimension of life space which is represented so concretely in unconscious phantasy. Before we turn now to methodological considerations, I would like to give a further example from a different class of analytic data.

Example E

A student of architecture, the younger of two children, had been in analysis for some five years when, as part of his training programme, he was asked to design a nursery school. At that time his analysis was blanketed by an acting out with a girl-friend, which completely recapitulated the secret sexual relationship to an older sister during early childhood, in which they had dramatized their appropriation of sexuality from parents whose marriage was coming adrift in fact.

In keeping with the severe resistance that dominated his analysis, material referable to the project did not enter until it had been completed and rejected by his teachers

> as being more suitable for a prison than a nursery school. He had designed a single large, high room, surrounded by a catwalk onto which the front entrance opened at street level, and from which a ramp descended into the room, which opened upon an outdoor play area with a pool and surrounded by high, unadorned brick walls.
>
> In short, he had designed an interior for the mother's body in which babies were eaten, cast into the rectum and defecated into the toilet.

* * *

The methodological aspect of the paper falls into two sections: (1) the requirements for analytic research into aesthetic problems in this area, and (2) the formulation of problems for investigation.

Material of value in this area is almost exclusively derived from the analysis of adult patients and is of three sorts:

1. patients' description of the spaces in which they live in the outside world;
2. dreams;
3. spaces patients create in the course of creative work.

If accurate information is to be gathered regarding the formal aspects of these spaces, inquiry by the analyst is often necessary and must be carried on systematically as part of his technique, as retrospective inquiry is extremely unreliable.

The significance of specific spatial configurations can only be reliably defined by those that appear in series and not by isolated instances.

The significance must be derived from the transference and not from speculation. It is useless to define a space as "vagina", or "inside the breast", as these are mere notational terms and tell nothing about the individual meaning.

Only when spatial forms are identified in series in an individual and found to be akin in a series of cases can any statement useful to the aesthetician be made by the psychoanalytic investigator.

This last point brings us to the second section of the methodology, namely the formulation of the problem. Insofar as these are problems of aesthetics, we can assume that psychoanalysts are not likely to be in a position to formulate the problem at all. However, a student of aesthetics wishing to have a problem investigated could ask for it to be circulated to psychoanalysts for inquiry and await the results. To such research ends, a Clinical Data Service has been inaugurated among some 85 Kleinian analysts of 13 countries, to which you are invited to submit problems of applied psychoanalysis for collective probing.

CHAPTER TWELVE

Sincerity: a study in the atmosphere of human relations

(1971)

*This "chapter"—which was, in fact, written as a book in 1971—has remained unpublished until now. It presents a phenomenological conception of "sincerity" and links it with emotionality and states of mind. Using the text of three plays by Harold Pinter—"The Dwarfs", "The Birthday Party", and "The Homecoming"—as "clinical material", the author makes a systematic and detailed analysis and puts forward new, thought-provoking, ideas—as, for instance, the differentiation between insincerity and unsincerity in human relations. The notion of the claustrum is mentioned here in connection with "The Birthday Party", more than twenty years before the book on the subject (*The Claustrum*, 1992) appeared as a comprehensive investigation into claustrophobic phenomena and borderline patients.*

INTRODUCTION

Let us suppose that the human brain is the most complicated *thing* in the universe and that its existence has for some few millennia past made possible the emergence and evolution of the most complicated *phenomenon* in the universe, the human mind. Can we doubt that the essence of this phenomenon is emotion and that the great solipsistic loneliness of which all humans suffer rests in the impossibility of knowing—really feeling—some other human's emotions. For the bodily sensations we may achieve a sense of conviction by repeating, experimentally, the situation in which the other felt pain, saw redness, heard A-sharp. True, conviction is not *knowing*, but it will serve our needs. But how are we to repeat experimentally the situation in which A felt love, remorse, fear, humiliation so that B might experience conviction regarding the identity of his emotions? If lovers in the climax of their passion may later doubt each other, what hope is there of trust in less mutual areas of feeling?

We may safely leave those who confuse mind with brain to play with their electrical apparatus, their chemical determinations, their observation of human behaviour under controlled conditions, their ethological analogies. They can do little harm, but no good. Our only recourse is to description, endless description, through which the various symbolic forms expand and expand their various vocabularies, each new delineation serving also as a tool for further probing and dissection of the forms of life that we experience and share, in our fashion. And share them we do, each in his own fashion and with a certain degree of conviction, which, to my mind, measures the balance, fundamental to the personality, of optimism–pessimism that psychoanalysis discovers—and philosophy assumes—to have its roots in the blending of mentality of the mother–infant. If psychoanalysis were to lay claim to any methodological superiority to other methods of inquiry and description, of the arts, philosophy, theology, it would be only at this point, that Freud invented a method for recapitulating this blending so that two minds may work cooperatively (in the non-technical sense) to probe and describe themselves and each other. I hold it to be a great advance—potentially. As yet we are too clumsy, too ignorant, too bent on therapeutic preconceptions, too bound to social values to employ the method to its full potential.

In a sense, this volume is an acknowledgement of that fact. What the psychoanalyst can discover in his limited craftsmanship and virtuosity, and what in the increments of vocabulary he can evolve to describe, the emotionality of our life of the mind, he is still always lagging behind the artist, infuriating as that might seem. In the case of the discoveries that I wish to describe I have chosen Harold Pinter as the artist whose powers of penetration and poetic description go far beyond my own, as scientist or as poet. In my thoughts I link his work in two directions: psychologically with Freud's penetration of the dream and philosophically with Wittgenstein's penetration of the language-games. I will explain. I do not mean to imply that I think Pinter has been "influenced" by Freud and Wittgenstein. I mean that in his art he has pursued the "dream play" as a tradition that I trace, in my limited knowledge, from "The Tempest" through "The Spook Sonata" and "Heartbreak House" as a genre distinct from allegory. On the other hand he pursues a dissection of modern English usage that coincides with the "I'm in a muddle" preoccupation of much of "The Philosophical Investigations" with the double sense of "meaning"—that is, the meaning of language and the infinite shading of "meaning what we say".

I will state it as the main thesis of all that is to follow that these two aspects of "meaning" are bound up with one another and linked together by two different, but also intimately coupled, aspects of personality structure. I refer on the one hand to splitting processes in the self and to integration in the internal objects, foremost in the maternal figure. To put the problem in a more clinical frame, we are to be concerned with the difficulty that a person has to "know what he means" on the one hand, and to "mean what he means", on the other. Of these two problems, one might say that Freud was almost exclusively concerned with the former and its relation to repression, levels of consciousness, symptomatic acts, and amnesias. While he was too astute an observer to miss phenomena related to hypocrisy, lying, and insincerity, he had no conceptual framework for integrating these phenomena within the theoretical formulation of the transactions of the consulting-room. He could only note them as evidence of "resistance". Insofar as they appeared as manifestations of the transference, they could only be assigned a function, "transference resistance", and not a derivation.

It is largely for this reason, because he was mainly occupied with the gaps in people's awareness of their own mental functioning, rather than for an absence of the moralist in his makeup, that so little of an ethical position seems to be implicit, let alone explicit, in Freud's writing. Just as good a case could be made for his being a romantic, a stoic, a cynic, an iconoclast, a Mosaic father-figure, or what-have-you. But when Melanie Klein pursued the preoccupation with structure that Freud had expounded in the 1920s, value, and with it ethical implications, made its entrance into psychoanalytic theory—and practice. The differentiation of good and bad in objects and self, mitigated as it may be in its severity of judgement by the distinction she later reached between "good" and "idealized", left no doubt. Added to this, her description of the economic principles of the paranoid-schizoid and depressive positions pointed to an internal basis of moral values and ethical judgements that bore an unmistakable resemblance to the very theology that Freud had indicated as being illusory.

One consequence of these new developments is that the psychoanalyst now has some conceptual equipment with which to organize the wealth of observations, of patient and analyst alike, thrown up by the transference-countertransference process, bearing upon the two aspects of sincerity, of being able to know what one means and of being able to gauge to what extent one means this, or rather "these", meaning(s). One aspect, the more purely linguistic—semantic and syntactic—I have already tentatively explored elsewhere (*Explorations in Autism*, Meltzer et al., 1975). In the chapter dealing with the mutism of autistic children, I brought together evidence from the structure of dreams in neurotic and psychotic patients and linked it with the different types of language disturbance tending towards mutism in the autistic, schizophrenic, and manic-depressive illnesses. One conclusion drawn was that language structure is two-tiered, consisting of a deeper and essentially song-and-dance level of primitive vocalization for the communication of states of mind, upon which is superimposed a more purely verbal level of syntactic structure in which ambiguities are clarified for the sake of communicating information about the outside world. In this latter category we must include verbalization of the fruits of self-consciousness and of introspection (I take these to refer to different levels of abstraction) as aspects of the external world (thinking about oneself from the "outside", the analytic stance, as against reporting observations of what is going on in one's mind, the aim of free association).

One could make a compelling case for the influence of Freud's work upon the art of the first half of this century to the effect that it aroused artists to the task of widening self-consciousness (see A. Alvarez, 1971). An equally cogent plea could be entered for its influence on philosophy—I can hear more urgent denials now—namely, that Freud has set the task of precision of introspection. I am not inclined to this method of aggrandizement of Freud's achievement or to assign such a seminal role to psychoanalysis. Rather, I think we can see that socio-economic upheavals of our era have urgently demanded inquiry into mental functioning and human relations. But I will claim that the psychoanalytic process contains a methodological advantage that has been too little recognized, judging by the quality of people who are and are not attracted to its employment. I believe that what puts off many serious students is the reading of "early" Freud, where the excitement of the young, and ambitious, neurophysiologist-turned-psychologist produced a tendentious, not to say tautological, method of debate in search of "explanation". The "later" Freud and the best of his followers found a more patient and tentative logic, contenting themselves with "understanding" as a process of finding harmony and organization in what appeared to be the chaos and nonsense of dreams, symptoms, behaviour, and thought.

It is with this type of understanding that we are here concerned. There is no avoiding the implication that the volume contains one, but only one, level of understanding of the work of Harold Pinter. That level is again only one aspect, namely the psychopathological, of the content of these plays. I am not concerned with the formal, the literary, the aesthetic. And so this chapter cannot be reasonably taken as a contribution to literary or drama criticism. Perhaps most important of all—and here I must dissociate myself from a very bad aspect of psychoanalytic tradition—these pages have nothing whatever to do with the mental health of Harold Pinter, about whose personal life I know nothing, except that his wife is a splendid actress. I have never met him and am deeply in debt to him for the kindness of allowing me to exploit his work for scientific exposition.

I will not, however, deny that the material of this chapter could be of interest to students of literature and of Harold Pinter's work in particular. The processes of mind that his work so perfectly explores and illustrates are ubiquitous. Their study is part of the work of every deep-going psychoanalytic treatment, whether of relatively healthy, neurotic, or psychotic patients. But while this is primarily a technical chapter, directed to practising psychoanalysts and intended to direct their attention to the problems of sincerity in analyst and patient, the findings regarding this urgent problem of human relations cannot fail to interest every student of humanity—if they have any validity. Now, the question arises whether this method of exposition, which departs from the usual procedure of employing clinical data for exemplification, will strengthen or weaken the presentation of the theory. Why have I chosen it? Why have I not used the method elsewhere? In fact I have, in a chapter on "The Perverse Transference" in a book on *Sexual States of Mind* (Meltzer, 1973). I think it was not a successful experiment, on the whole. My reasons there were perhaps less valid, namely discretion. My reasons here are, I believe, far more cogent. Armed with Pinter's poetry and psychoanalytic theory, I hope to catch in a cross-fire those essentially emotional processes related to sincerity which my own clinical descriptions would never trap.

A few words need to be said about the general format of the chapter and of the way in which Harold Pinter's plays have been used. A general outline of a psychoanalytic theory of sincerity is first presented. This is followed by detailed analysis of three plays: "The Dwarfs", "The Birthday Party", and "The Homecoming". I am not sure at all that this is the chronological order of their creation, but it is certainly the correct order for our theoretical exposition. In using the plays I follow the Methuen editions, and all page numbers refer to them.* A general knowledge of the plays will not be sufficient for a satisfactory reading of this chapter. The play itself must be read prior to reading the section related to it, and the text must be followed along with the exposition by using page and line references. Without this discipline, the whole point of my use of Pinter's genius for the emotive employment of simple everyday English will be lost. At the end of each section, I summarize the analysis of the play's content and relate this to the theory of sincerity. Finally, the chapter closes with a resumé of the theory and some effort to investigate its implications for psychoanalytic practice—and perhaps for wider employment.

One further remark that must not be construed as an apology for sloth: this chapter will not be understandable without at least a general knowledge of psychoanalytic theory, and the work of Melanie Klein in particular. For the non-psychoanalytic reader, Hanna Segal's (1964) *Introduction to the Work of Melanie Klein* should be sufficient. I do not believe that a reading of any of my own previous works is essential for either the professional or lay reader.

1
A psychoanalytic theory of sincerity

One of the special virtues of the analytic situation lies in the extraordinary proving ground that it offers for the language of emotionality. The convergence of dream material,

*[Editor's note: "The Birthday Party" and "The Homecoming" in the currently available editions by Faber and Faber follow the page numbering of the early Methuen editions.]

emotional experience directly in the transference, and the process of recollection–reconstruction of past relations challenges both patient and analyst to find with precision the verbal forms that carry adequately the experience of understanding and being understood. Add to this the element of different age groups, foreign patients with varying command of English, and patients with widely divergent educational levels and severity of difficulty in communication due to psychopathology. Compounding this clinical field, the requirements of teaching in supervision offer a final testing place for precision, "bite", and refinement.

From this setting, the word "sincerity" has emerged as a uniquely valuable term in my experience, routing many alternatives such as honesty, truthfulness, integrity, frankness, openness, etc. Other considerations of a more scientific and historical vein have entered into my final choice, for I realize that a new technical term is to be erected to contain the meaning of a relatively unexplored, or at least not systematically explored, aspect of human relationships and communication. "Honesty", for instance, has a history of moralizing usage. "Truth" has been long and variously used in philosophical writings. "Integrity" carries too characterological an overtone. "Frankness" seems to imply an unpleasantly aggressive aspect of criticism. "Openness" has no bite into the emotions. "Sincerity" would appear to suffer none of these limitations and to be a lovely, musical, and poignant word, as virginal as one can find in our wordy culture. *The New (Oxford) English Dictionary* records the following:

Sincere

1. Not falsified or perverted in any way:
   a. of doctrine, etc.: genuine, pure
   b. true, veracious: correct, exact
   c. morally uncorrupted, uncontaminated
2. Pure, unmixed: free from any foreign element or ingredient
   a. of immaterial things
   b. of colours or substances
   c. (spec.) unadulterated: genuine

d. free from hurt, uninjured (obs.)

3. Containing no element of dissimulation or deception; not feigned or pretended; honest, straightforward

    a. of life, actions, etc.

    b. of persons, their character, etc.

To place ourselves on firm lexical ground, we should also note in passing the traditional use of the word in closing letters: "sincerely", or "sincerely yours". The only comment would be the coolness, formality, in contrast to the use of the word in common parlance, where, as I have said, it appears to be sparsely used for the very opposite reason, its emotional bite or grip.

However, a lexical stance needs perhaps to be supplemented by a philosophical one, before we proceed to the psychoanalytic heart of our inquiry. That is not to say that I wish to state any position or conviction of a philosophic kind, for that would require a formal command I do not claim. But, rather, the psychoanalytic foundation of this work has, to my mind, philosophic links and implications that it would be useful to state as part of the meaning that, I believe, the psychoanalytic understanding pours into the container of our word "sincere".

I take it that mental acts (Geach) necessarily involve concepts, and that concepts involve judgements, which do not necessarily relate to constant conjunctions of preconceptions with realizations involving emotional satisfaction (Bion) but may be false or unreal. Concepts, and judgements about them, relate simultaneously to perceptual modes ("seeing as"—Wittgenstein) and intentionality (Anscombe) through the various symbolic modes (Cassirer) in which unconscious phantasy (Freud, Melanie Klein) gives form to the essentially emotional (S. Langer) process. While intention always implies a plan of behaviour, intentions cannot be judged by behaviour as the necessary conditions of action may never arise, or may in fact be impossible of realization. However, actions, like the intentions that lie behind them, are subject to variations in the degree to which we "mean them" (Wittgenstein). It is this variable function of our ability to mean the implied intentionality of our concepts (feelings, thoughts) that is experienced as gradations of sincerity by self-consciousness. This aspect of another's state of mind is intuited accurately only by introjective identification (Meltzer) and produces variations in the emotion of trust. (I will distinguish the consequences of more narcissistic modes of identification as "variations in the emotion of dis-trust".) (The names in brackets are meant only to indicate some of the writers whose views are, I believe, in harmony with the implications of psychoanalytic experience.)

Having now planted our feet on the firmest ground of all, namely what amounts to a declaration of the primacy of psychic reality over external reality in the life of the mind, we may proceed. Psychoanalytic history starts with the famous "Anna O" of Breuer's section of the *Studies on Hysteria* (Freud, 1895d) where the true relation of analyst to patient is more correctly revealed than perhaps anywhere else in our literature. Respect, even awe, mark Breuer's attitude to the mind of this admirable young woman struggling with an illness that had overtaken her surrounding the terminal illness of her father. It is an account that bears reading and rereading, in order to be reminded of the scope, the range of mental functioning. I would call attention here particularly to three aspects of the record. First of all, the capacity of the mind for total recall under conditions of hypnosis is illustrated in a manner that would be unbelievable were it not for the absolute scientific integrity of the man who is reporting these facts. Second, the process of struggle and the mental pain attending it cannot fail to impress us. And, finally, "Anna" herself, after her recovery, raises the question with which we are concerning ourselves here—namely, to what extent did her illness involve a failure of sincerity. Where courage in the face of the transference failed Breuer, Freud's character, with its "Conquistador" ruthlessness (the former being Freud's own term for himself and the latter a word used by Jones to describe Melanie Klein's method—see his Introduction to her *Contributions to Psycho-Analysis, 1921–1945*) pressed on to create the method we use today. This type of courage, which Bion equates with the "hubris" of Oedipus in his determination to know the truth at all costs ("On Arrogance" in *Second Thoughts*, 1967), must eventually infuse any analytic process that is to penetrate into the depths of psychic life. Analyst and patient alike must determine to spare neither themselves nor one another in this pursuit. Small wonder such an undertaking is out of keeping with common sense, with its overriding query, "Is it worth it?" Not that psychoanalysis has cornered the market on this quality. I have expressed elsewhere (see Adrian Stokes' *Painting and the Inner World*, 1963, and "On Pornography" in *Sexual States of Mind*, Meltzer, 1973) the conviction that this kind of ruthless courage with self and audience is essential to the struggle that differentiates art from pornography.

I cite these three aspects of the record of "Anna O's" illness and recovery because I wish to establish a link between truth-function, identity, and the sense-of-identity as a component of the meaning I would like to pour into our word, "sincerity". Wittgenstein (1973) states the problem clearly:

> What does it mean to know *who* is in pain? It means, for example, to know which man in this room is in pain: for instance, that it is the one who is sitting over there, or the one who is standing in that corner, the tall one over there with the fair hair, and so on.—What am I getting at? At the fact that there is a great variety of criteria for personal *"identity"*.
>
> Now which of them determines my saying that '*I*' am in pain? None. [p. 404]

I think this is correct; that no criteria can be established for claiming, let alone for disclaiming, personal identity and the experiences attached to it. The best we can do is to claim a cognisance of our sense-of-identity, and this we soon discover to be a highly unstable, even at times wildly fluctuating entity. We must take identity as an ideal category, comprised of the sum-total of experiences, to which the actual sense-of-identity can only aspire as an asymptote. You will remember that I spoke of "Anna O" demonstrating "total recall" under hypnosis, the facts of which could, incidentally, be verified from her mother's diary, thus answering the "time-table" question raised by Wittgenstein (p. 265). But recall is not memory, as illustrated by the fact that the most certain thing about hypnosis is that it involves a temporary surrender of the sense-of-identity. Memory is a far more dynamic, conflicted process of momentary construction from elements available to self-consciousness. It is necessarily incomplete, usually inaccurate—a personality function. The fact that certain personalities manifest a selective ability to utilize total recall (so-called "photographic memory") does not in any way contradict this conception, but, rather, illustrates its divorce from understanding.

This link between memory and sense-of-identity is the key to the aspect of experience that, cumulatively, serves as the evidence against which we assess our intuitive judgement of the quality of sincerity as an aspect of the character of other people. If over time we find that a person disclaims facets of the identity that he manifested earlier—cannot remember having said "that", denies that he saw "such and such", has altered the wording of the reply he gave yesterday in retelling it today—such experiences sap our trust on the one hand and may arouse our distrust on the other. It is perhaps important here to remember that trust may be closely tied up with dependence and love at infantile levels and internally, but in more grown-up relationships in the outside world, predictability and thereby the stability rather than the goodness, strength, or skills of the other person determines our trust. It makes a witty remark, "You can always trust Frank to say the wrong thing", but it has this core of truth. Frank here is considered to be consistently gauche, the unconscious motivation being omitted from consideration. Distrust is quite a different phenomenon and absolutely tied to our assessment of the motives, conscious or unconscious, underlying the other person's behaviour. How subtle is the shading in our language between, "You can't trust George . . ." and "I do not trust George . . .", the former expressing lack of trust, the latter positive distrust, growing out of an intuition of aggressive or at least hurtful motives.

Consequently, our distrust is directed more towards "friends" whom we assess as hypocrites or liars than towards "enemies" whose interests conflict with our own; we may respect, even love them where the estimate of sincerity is high and the conflicting interests are held to be real, fundamental. The expression, "With friends like that, who needs enemies!" is a bit of wry Jewish humour relating to the metamorphosis of lack of trust into distrust. But this all relates, as I have said, to judgement based on cumulative experience. The more intuitive and subtle problem is the immediate one of confrontation in which we experience the state of mind of the other person emotionally through introjective unconscious processes. This brings us to the heart of the matter.

My contention is that people are poor judges of the sincerity of others in the face-to-face situation and hopelessly so in those indirect contacts such as through the post, over the telephone—in a sense, inversely with the distance in space and time. The fundamental reason for this seems to lie in the need to rely on the comfort of the interpersonal atmosphere that arises. On the face of it this would appear to be a very reliable indicator, until we realize that this comfort is a reflection of a matching process, akin to the technique of colorimetry in chemistry. Optimal comfort, a feeling of kinship, arises when the degree of sincerity matches. Perhaps "degree" is not a completely satisfactory word here, for I would wish to distinguish, to follow the chemical analogy, both colour and shade, both the quality and the quantity of the sincerity. This factor of matching sincerity seems to be the chief factor in people feeling "at home" with one another and is decisive, beyond sociocultural facets, in the process by which people "seek their own level." The mystique of "inspiring confidence", be it in bank manager, doctor, or confidence man, must depend on a personality factor of flexibility in the state of mind, sensitively adjusting the match in sincerity to the client, patient, or victim. One cannot take it as a virtue, and we will need, later on in our investigation, to probe the mechanisms by which this flexibility can be achieved.

It is to this differentiation of the quantitative from the qualitative factors underlying sincerity, both of immediate states of mind and of character, that we must now turn our attention. This will take us deep into the territory of the psychoanalytic theory of personality structure, for it is primarily from the structural point of view that I intend to organize both the exposition and the illustration of this concept. I realize that just as cogent a system could be constructed on dynamic or genetic grounds, but to my mind they neither lend themselves satisfactorily to demonstration, nor are they so sensitive as tools of inquiry in the consulting-room. Certainly every mechanism of defence produces a defect in the sincerity, every developmental problem that lies incompletely resolved in the unconscious hinders it. But I believe that the delineation along structural lines permits an easy and accurate extrapolation to dynamics and genetics, while the converse is not true.

Factors determining the quality of the sincerity

The James-Lang theory of emotion may seem a bit grotesque philosophically, but one can well understand how tempting it is to think that the bodily expressions of emotion *are* the emotions, and that what we perceive in ourselves, and in others, of these somatic concomitants is all there is to emotional life. While it places emotion in the position of by-product to mental processes rather than at the core of mental acts, there is a sense in which people treat their emotions in just this way out of self-doubt in respect of sincerity. It is not only the adolescent who ruminates on whether or not he would cry if his mother died, or fears that he will giggle at his uncle's funeral, have an erection on the dance floor, or tremble at his interview for a job. Such phenomena may be looked upon as betraying unwanted emotions, but they are also viewed as evidence that the dreaded poverty of emotion has not enveloped the person. Yet the trouble is that such somatic accompaniments are too equivocal. Crocodile tears pour as freely as those of grief, the hand trembles just as finely from excitement, the manic giggle is indistinguishable from the embarrassed one.

I think it would be correct to say, although I cannot document it, that the problem of sincerity has not been dealt with systematically because it has not been seen in a systematic light, but, rather, in an atomistic one. It has been assumed that sincerity was a quality inherent to the particular emotion and not a quality of the state of mind within whose framework the emotions were operative. Wittgenstein's category of "meaning it" sets us on our path towards making this distinction. And Melanie Klein's discovery of the operation of splitting processes directs us to the next question: "Who is meaning it?" We must return to our problem of the sense-of-identity as a personality function, having already distinguished it from identity as an ideal category.

Psychoanalysis would appear to have delineated three different types of inner experience that carry with them a sense-of-identity. The first of these belongs to the individual infantile parts of the personality and to the narcissistic organizations (as opposed to states of integration) that they may form with one another *vis-á-vis* internal and external objects. The second are forms of narcissistic identification, of which there must be many. However, only one, projective identification, has as yet been thoroughly investigated. Finally, there is the process of introjective identification from which the adult part of the personality arises and differentiates itself from the infantile structures. It is true that the sense-of-identity related to these three has a distinctive self-feeling, which marks them off subjectively from each other, just as it is true that the momentary sense-of-identity is likely to be compounded of elements derived from more than one of them. Let us deal with them separately.

The sense-of-identity of infantile structures

The mind develops through the dimension of time, and nothing of its experience is lost. The archaeological model of its stratification is not a satisfactory one because it implies loss of vitality of the structures upon whose immaturity more sophisticated ones are superimposed. They lose neither their vitality nor their potentiality for action, as is illustrated by the phenomena of dreaming on the one hand and regression on the other. What does in fact happen is a function of splitting and integration in the context of internalization, whereby relatively defined periods of development in the self gradually detach themselves through processes akin to mourning on the one hand or repression on the other, disengaging from external objects in favour of internal ones, from transactions in behaviour to ones in dreams. The metapsychological description of these periods by Freud, amplified and made more specific by Abraham ("A Short Study of the Development of the Libido", 1924) is only one possible method of definition. Behavioural ones are just as good. Social, logical, linguistic, or other systems of notation would do just as well and reach more or less similar delineations. The system that seems to find the most spontaneous and lucid expression in the work of analyst and patient is one that borrows the language and criteria of family and culture: the baby—youngest in the family; the child—already displaced by the next sibling but rather undifferentiated as to sex; the little boy and little girl—in the throes of pregenital and genital oedipal conflict; the schoolboy and schoolgirl; the boy and girl of puberty and early adolescence; the young man and woman of late adolescence, still family-bound. This stratification in depth is cleft, with greater or lesser clarity and stability, by the primal splitting-and-idealization of self and objects into bad and idealized parts or aspects at each level. It is this notation I will employ. In toto it describes, when placed in the context of internal objects, the internal world and its family-like organization—a very big family indeed, with a core of idealized parts clustered about idealized objects and a periphery of more or less alienated "relatives" and "strangers" composed of the split-off bad aspects of self and objects.

The clustering on the one hand and alienation of parts on the other that takes place in psychic reality is in constant interaction through the processes of projection and introjection with figures in the outside world. And these figures, with their various and changing qualities of character, play a part in the segregation, one might say, of various aspects of character or qualities of mind among the different infantile structures. In the clinical work it becomes noticeable that there is often a very unequal distribution of such qualities as intelligence, imagination, drive towards integration, tolerance of mental pain, capacity for love, dependent need, parasitic tendency, possessive jealousy, envy, tendency to action, to thought, to phantasy, talents, interests, capacity for pleasure, perversity, masochism, sensuality, etc. When alienation of a part by projection "fits" the external object, a special difficulty at re-introjecting the part tends to occur, which interferes with the process of disengagement and internalization. Much of the analytic work is taken up, in fact, with this task and is made possible only by the method of analysis of the transference. "Working through" is the process of its consummation.

Clearly every part of the infantile structure has an identity as a segment of our ideal category. But it is not useful to think of the sense-of-identity except in momentary terms with a cumulative or statistical implication. At any moment the sense-of-identity comprises the self-experience available to self-consciousness. It may be very narrow, derivative of a single infantile part and its history, but generally it has a certain stability related to the two types of linkages, narcissistic organization and integration in the sphere of good objects. While it is true that bad parts of the infantile structure generally play a leading role in the narcissistic organization, this is not necessarily the case. The most destructive parts may be severely alienated and isolated from other parts. It is also important to remember that when idealized parts rather than bad parts are alienated, particularly by projection into siblings, the sense-of-identity may become rigidly fixed in the most ill or bad part, as in the psychopathies. The other point to remember is that the clustering of idealized parts around good objects does not of itself produce integration of them. Indeed, oedipal conflict, jealousy of the baby-at-the-breast, resentment of parental tolerance towards the bad parts, and many other quasi-political motives tend to drive the various idealized parts into narcissistic organizations in which they become very vulnerable to a loss of splitting-and-idealization, renewed contact with destructive parts, and a return to confusion between good and bad.

Of course, description like this is bound to be heavy going, isolated as it is from clinical exemplification, but it is necessary to establish a theoretical home base to which we can refer once we begin our trek through Pinter country. The qualitative aspects of sincerity whose link to the component of the sense-of-identity bound up with the infantile structures is reflected in the dimension that we experience as "deep" versus "shallow" in other people's states of mind. It is connected with what is known technically as the acknowledgement or denial of psychic reality. The denial is primarily a denial of the existence of infantile structures and of the internal objects to which they are so closely bound. Most characteristically, it is manifested by more sophisticated infantile parts towards the less mature, but more essentially it is a turning away from cognisance of emotions and motives related to infantile life and psychic reality towards the external world, taking the appearance of things at a face value. Since infantile structures, unlike the adult self, are bound directly rather than indirectly (through identification) to the impulse life and its primitive emotionality, eschewing of psychic reality produces the matter-of-fact, reality-bound, calculating, and adaptive quality of character that we read as "shallow" for its lack of imagination, insensitivity to others' feelings, and materialism.

One further word before closing this section: the infantile parts are bound to chronology and cannot really escape "being their age", as it were. When a particular infantile part, or organization of them, seizes upon consciousness and dominates a person's behaviour, temporarily, say, the sense-of-identity is bound to be oppressed by the loneliness, however defiant, of the child-in-the-adult-world. The escape from this, with its sense of fraud and fear of humiliation, involves the area of the narcissistic identifications, which we are about discuss.

The sense-of-identity of narcissistic identifications

In passing over from those aspects of sense-of-identity that derive directly from infantile structures to narcissistic identifications, we pass from psychic reality to delusion; from real identity, be it ever so fragmentary, to delusions of identity. As I have said, there is evidence that many mechanisms operate in the sphere of narcissism in a way that carries facets of sense-of-identity, but of these only that mechanism described in 1946 by Melanie Klein and called by her "projective identification" has had any extensive or systematic investigation. My intention now is to describe the considerable knowledge we have in this area, in all its complexity, relating it back to what has been already described about the infantile structures and forward to the introjective identifications from which the adult structure of the self derives.

The motives that drive the employment of the mechanism of projective identification may have no specific aim of altering the sense-of-identity to escape from the infantile distress, and yet such an alteration is unavoidable, it seems. A part of the self cannot enter inside an object, either part of whole-object, without a degree of identification experience resulting. But it must be remembered that this experience is not one of altered or changed, but, rather, of *ex*changed identity. It is in this area of phenomenology that one can discern that an object's identity is a psychic category that stands apart from a mere summation of the object's qualities, however admired or envied, but relates more to its life history—perhaps even more to its future than to its past or present. One manifestation of this is to be found in the peculiar optimism, pomposity, and snobbish arrogance that characterizes states of projective identification. Clearly it is not merely the consortium of qualities of the object that are being worn like papal robes, but its life-history. A maniac Charles I will look forward to his beheading with the smug assurance of putting up a good show, of the eventual overthrow of the Protectorate, and of a joyous Restoration.

What appears stark and ludicrous in its blatant psychotic form has exactly the same quality of flavour in the processes of the daily lives of each of us to some extent. I doubt that anyone enters his home, slips into the driver's seat of his car, puts on his best suit, goes to the opera, puts on his spectacles, or gets into a hot bath without his state of mind and sense-of-identity being somewhat affected by processes of projective identification. A whole genre of comedy and humour rest upon this fact. The scene in Brecht's "Galileo", where the cardinal's attitudes alter as he is dressed in his vestments, one after the other, beautifully illustrates this.

Of course, one can enter a house or slip into a bath without doing any damage to these objects in the outside world, but the matter is quite different with respect to the entry by projective identification into either external or internal objects. Even where the natural orifices of an object are utilized, even where no resistance appears to be offered by the object in the unconscious phantasy, a certain damage is inflicted. Where the damage is not represented as concrete alteration of the anatomy of the object, a certain transformation, akin to deterioration, will be found to have taken place in its fabric, texture, atmosphere—or, of course, with whole-objects or part-objects still experienced as human, in its character, age, vitality. I say "experienced as" rather than "represented as" since I am not employing a theory of symbolism but, rather, the category of "seeing as" previously indicated in the Introduction. This is not a matter that can be entered upon here at any length, but it is important to indicate that this area of theory is different from the classical Freudian. By postulating a continuum of unconscious phantasy as the foundation of all mental acts, we establish psychic reality in a primary position. In consequence we are obliged to recognize that the objects we find in psychic reality are just as active in pouring meaning into external objects as vice versa. We therefore cannot say that a house in a dream represents "mother's body", any more than we can say that mother's body, in fact, in the outside world, is "seen as" a house that it has accrued this aspect of meaning—and, conversely, for a house in the outside world and mother's body in a dream. This implies that we are taking degrees of concreteness in meaning to relate to levels of abstraction (Carnap, Russell) and only, therefore, to have a rather statistical relation to primitiveness in mental functions. I think these matters will become clearer when we reach discussion of Pinter's poetic images and use of words, where we will find that fusion of emotive and cognitive employment that Empson has defined (*The Structure of Complex Words*, 1951).

To return, however, to the question of the damage done to objects by the omnipotent phantasy of projective identification, such damage always finds some degree of manifestation in the identificatory aspect and therefore in the sense-of-identity of the part or parts of the self involved. This is, of course, most clearly seen in the hypochondriacal phenomena and hypochondriacal ways of dealing with somatic disturbances.

Hypochondria is, in fact, a nice example to pause at, to recognize how poignant is Wittgenstein's question, "What does it mean to know *who* is in pain?" It illustrates quite perfectly the qualitative disturbance in sincerity induced when the sense-of-identity is at the moment tied up with parts that are in a state of projective identification. The irritating insincerity of the hypochondriac seems mysterious until we recognize that of course we are annoyed because the person is claiming concern that really by rights should be directed to his damaged object. This makes the major point of this section, so I will leave further consideration of the nature of the damage to objects for the later section on reparation processes.

The sense-of-identity of introjective identifications

I have written fairly extensively elsewhere (chapter 8 of Meltzer, *The Psycho-analytical Process*, 1967a, and chapter 11 of Meltzer, *Sexual States of Mind*, 1973) on the subject of introjective identification, to illustrate the way in which the superego-ideal is built up over the years, qualities of admired external figures being introjectively assimilated to the figures of the original objects of infancy. The character of the adult part of the personality is secondarily developed through identification with the internal objects that comprise the superego-ideal. Commitment to this identification rests upon the emotions of the depressive position, especially gratitude and the desire for worthiness. For this reason elements of the experience of sense-of-identity that relate to introjective identification have a prospective quality, an aspirational tone that is quite different from the immediate and delusional self-feeling produced by projective identification. Tentativeness, humility, self-doubt, and like nuances of emotion therefore attach to these aspects of the sense-of-identity and make up those shadings of a person's character that most deeply impress us as sincere. Paradoxically, or, perhaps better, pathetically, these same emotions induce in the person himself the highest degree of self-doubt regarding the very same issue, his own sincerity, as compared to this quality in his objects.

This brings us to the central complexity of this section. Inasmuch as the sense-of-identity of the adult part of the personality is built up by striving towards worthiness of the internal objects he loves and admires, the quality of sincerity in character is found to have a somewhat different derivation from the sincerity of momentary states of mind. There is a qualitative aspect of sincerity that has to do with richness of emotion. Clinical work strongly suggests that this aspect of the adult character is bound up with the richness of emotion characterizing the internal objects. It can be distinguished from other qualities such as their strength or goodness. It is different from their state of integration. It seems perhaps most coextensive with their beauty, which in turn seems related to capacity for compassion. If I were forced to state it in the most technical terms, I would say that this richness is linked with—perhaps identical to—the willingness to receive and contain projections of mental pain from the self. Would it be more correct to say, "capacity to introject the pain of parts of the self"? You can easily imagine that such an object, when entered by projective identification, would give rise to the moral masochism that strikes us as being at the very antipodes from sincerity.

But having now discussed the sense-of-identity in its three different sources, we are confronted with the fact that within each aspect—infantile, projective, and introjective—we have confronted a juxtaposition of parts of the self *vis-á-vis* internal objects. We must ask, "Are these different objects? Or are they different aspects of the same objects?" This immediately has the ring of theological mystery about it, and in fact we can do no better in seeking to understand this multiplicity in unity than to refer to the parallel of religion. Just as the history of comparative religion can serve as a useful paradigm for the development of internal objects in the individual psyche, so the coexistence of a multiplicity of religions in the world at any moment, each with its own unitary or multiple deities, can serve as a model for the situation in psychic reality. We must pass on to consider the relevance of the problem of integration of self and objects in relation to the phenomenon of sincerity.

Variable integration and momentary centre-of-gravity

Freud's conception of consciousness as an "organ for the perception of psychic qualities" has given us a proper vantage point from which to view the structure of the mind without being distracted by the differentiation between conscious and unconscious. From this point of view, any part of the self may seize control of this organ of consciousness and, by its possession, maintain temporary hegemony over behaviour, and thus over external communication. The part or organization of parts so established will dominate the sense-of-identity. I will refer to this link between consciousness and identity as the "centre of gravity" of the self, in order to speak of its alterations.

Two types of alteration beset the centre of gravity of the sense-of-identity, one being related to the existing state of integration and the other dependent upon changes in this state, either of regression or integration. Let us deal with them in that order.

We are able to discern, not only in the analytic consulting-room but in daily life, that people exhibit variations, one from the other and from time to time, in the stability of the configuration of personality characteristics that they exhibit in their dealings with the outside world. This instability, since it does not seem to imply a direction, either of development or of regression into illness, we take as an aspect of character linked to variations in maturity. We expect it in small children, are troubled by its manifestations in the latency period, resign ourselves to its unbridled state in adolescents, and tend to feel anger at it in grown-ups. But, by and large, we do not take it too seriously, since the very unpredictability that it implies informs us that the possibility of development still exists.

This dimension of instability lends a quantitative factor to our experience of a person's sincerity of character, but one that we tend to find forgivable, perhaps because of the child-like aspect of it and because of the hopefulness we attach to this element. Our judgement of people tends to be more harsh, or at least less tentative, when the stability is greater, when the centre of gravity seems fairly fixedly located in a particular part or organization. But truly a type of oscillation is discernible in everyone on close scrutiny, or better still within the specialized setting of psychoanalysis. This oscillation has for its own parameters the two poles of the personality, the ill and the healthy, the narcissistic organization and the integration in the sphere of good objects. The interaction of these two spheres is the storm centre of the conflict from which development or regression proceeds. It is the boundary area that the psychoanalytic setting is calculated to invite to expression as the transference. In that setting and with that method we are able to study in detail the ebb and flow of these processes as they unfold in the rhythmic and cyclical manner that I have described at length elsewhere (Meltzer, *The Psycho-analytical Process*, 1967a). The level of cooperation that a patient can bring to bear varies at different times in the session or in the week or term, and gradually improves as the analysis advances through the years. This cooperation gives a very quantifiable—or at least very comparable—item or indicator of sincerity to match with our intuition of the patient's state of mind. Of course, the measuring instrument in all of this is the analyst's mind and its own variable level of sincerity, fluctuating to some extent as it must with fatigue, from patient to patient, with different configurations of transference, under varying circumstances of stress derivative from his life outside the consulting-room.

As different parts of the self seize control and become the locus of this centre-of-gravity, as the predominant organization of the self oscillates between narcissistic organization and dependence upon good internal objects—in this shifting, kaleidoscopic scene we come to know and can bring the patient into acquaintance with the various parts of the personality and gain a view of their various internal objects, expressed as transference reactions. The experience, repeated again and again, leaves a strong impression of the unity of the objects and the diversity of the modes in which they are experienced by various parts of the self. But this unity, whose ultimate expression is the combined object of the parental coitus, must not be confused with integration. The integration of self and objects moves precisely in parallel, absolutely geared together, for the splitting processes cannot split one without the other, integration cannot take place in the self without a like alteration in the experience of the objects, no part can be alienated without a similar loss to the object.

I think that it must now be clearer why the archaeological model of psychic structure or the onion-simile are so unsuitable and must be replaced by a familial image, complicated and different from what any family could be, in fact, in the outside world, compounded as it is with an element akin to the distribution of theologies around the globe. What we are describing so far as regards internal objects relates to their state of integration. But there are two other factors that operate, one being the evolution of the objects and the other their intactness. This is a difficult subject, but one that lies at the very heart of the problems of health and illness.

The evolution of the objects, as they are experienced by each part of the self, is really an expression of the maturity of that part and the meaning that it is able to apprehend regarding the object. The gradient of meaning expresses itself in unconscious phantasy in the plastic image of the object proceeding from the most primitive inanimate conception to the most mature combined human object, with all the imaginable gradations between. Again I wish to stress that I am working in a framework of "seeing as" and not of symbolism. When we speak of splitting processes, we are referring to phantasies whereby the meaning of the object, and consequently its plastic image, is altered. Any splitting process will involve a loss in the richness of the meaning of the object, as the whole is greater than the sum of its parts. The most common expression of this is to be seen within the pregenital Oedipus complex—for instance, when the unified body of the mother is split into its significant component parts, each now represented in the unconscious phantasy as young girl. What is gained in multiplicity and sexual availability of these girls does not make up for what is lost in the womanliness and maternal capacities of the integrated whole-object mother.

But loss of meaning is a very different affair from damage by sadistic attack. It is the injurious attack upon the object, not the loss of integration and consequent loss of meaning, that sets regression in motion and produces illness. We have already spoken of one sort of damage, that caused by entry into the object to effect projective identification. We must now deal with the subject in a more unified way.

Masturbatory attack and regression of objects

Sadistic attacks upon objects have become known as "masturbatory attacks" for very good reason, tied up with function of omnipotence in unconscious phantasy. Again it is a subject that I have dealt with fairly extensively elsewhere (Meltzer, *Sexual States of Mind*, 1973) and will only summarize here. Omnipotence and omniscience have often been confused with one another in the literature of psychoanalysis, so we must set the latter aside clearly. It is a term referring to a certain poverty of imagination, closely connected with envy, which cannot conceive its own limitations of thought and knowledge. It therefore assumes that what it thinks or knows is the measure of all possible thought and knowledge. We are not at this point concerned with omniscience.

Omnipotence is a more difficult thing to conceptualize. First of all, its very existence rests upon a denial of impotence. That is fundamental. Where helplessness exists *vis-á-vis* objects in the outside world, omnipotence is likely to be generated in dealings with internal objects. So the second point is that it is a quality of the state of mind of parts of the self towards objects, and is not relevant to parts of the self towards one another in narcissistic organizations. It is worth noting here that both omniscience and omnipotence, which figure as qualities of mental function of infantile structures, derive from, and are modelled upon, one might say, identical aspects of idealized objects. The difference is this, however: these aspects do not figure as qualities of mental function of the objects, but only as categories in the meaning these objects have for the self. They are "seen as" containing all possible knowledge and all possible means of action.

In consequence of this category of meaning, and in the spirit of the dictum, "When you shoot at a king, you must kill him," attacks upon objects depend, for their Dutch courage, upon the generating of a sense of omnipotence. The third point relates to my use of the word "generate", by which I do not imply any model but only the abstract meaning "bring into existence". To say "create" would do too much honour and miss the fundamentally delusional quality of the "bringing into existence." If you can differentiate the function of mind, excitement, from the neurophysiological "excitation" on the one hand, and from the manic quality of pleasure that is so often associated with it in common parlance, you will end with a distillate almost identical with omnipotence as a self-feeling, an emotional tone. This is what is brought into existence in the masturbatory phantasy, invariably, I believe, with the aid of the masturbatory activity, hidden from view as it may be to consciousness. It is necessary therefore to widen our definition of masturbatory activity even wider than did Freud. We will say that it constitutes any activity practised upon the body with the intention of stirring the mind to certain emotional states. We do not limit ourselves to any pejorative sense, even though we may reserve a certain attitude of suspicion in general towards the whipping-up of emotion. There is no reason to limiting the "body" involved to that of the actor. People may just as well masturbate each other, of course. The crucial thing is the intent to stir emotion in the mind by stimulation (or deprivation of stimulation?) of the body. This gives us scope for the inclusion of all manner of physical and chemical stimuli, internal and external to the skin surface. But to keep it a useful category, we must limit ourselves to sensations and leave all communications aside. It could well be argued that separating the sting of the whip from its social meaning, the chemical effect of the alcohol from the meaning of whisky, creates an artificial distinction, that the mind does not perceive sensations but only meanings. I agree, the mind does not perceive sensations. This is the point about what is essentially masturbatory, that it is not intended for perception but to impinge directly upon the emotionality of the mental apparatus. Where this impingement stirs excitement, we have the necessary condition for the function of the omnipotence in unconscious phantasy. The scene is laid for the sadistic attack upon internal objects, or their representatives (transference) in the outside world.

On the face of it, the idea of sadistic attack does not seem to imply "damage" to an object but merely "pain". I think this is a mistake and grows out of a failure to distinguish between "punitive" and "sadistic" attacks. In the former the intention is to inflict sufficient pain to render forgiveness feasible under conditions where it is not a very robust virtue as yet. This can then be distinguished from "vengeful" attacks, which seem to straddle the categories, but do not really. Revenge has never really any intention of facilitating reconciliation, and its effects are surely intended to be lasting. This would seem to be the most crucial test of the distinction: "Is the attack intended to produce a lasting effect upon the object?" It is as operationally useful an indicator as we can find.

I know we are moving slowly, but this is, truly, somewhat new territory, and we must be careful not to build on the sand. What can we spell out in detail, then, about sadistic masturbatory attacks upon objects, external and subsequently internalized, and internal ones? How are we to distinguish between damaged objects and dis-integrated objects? You must remember that we are talking about something that is separate from, but appears in unconscious phantasy and its representations in dream and transference as superimposed upon, the spectrum of object-types that runs from the inanimate object to the combined human object. I can list five areas of change; there may be more that are not merely subtypes to these five: goodness, age, beauty, strength, contentment. Taken together as a chord or constellation, they comprise the object's parental sincerity. We must first examine them one by one, on the background of our contention that splitting, like integration, proceeds in parallel in the self and internal objects, and that regression is driven fundamentally by damage to the objects consequent to sadistic masturbatory attacks.

Five types of damage to internal objects

You will recall that I have used the historical example of the development of the concept of deity manifest in comparative religion, stretching from primitive animism to the most advanced forms of monotheism (none of which, I think, has achieved the combined object completely) to illustrate the integrative process of development of the internal objects. My point was that each step in integration is an advance to a new category of meaning, but that every category is a fundamental one in the development of the embracing human concept of parents and parental qualities. The house–tree–sun constellation so ubiquitous to young children's drawings is an example of primitive benevolent qualities, say of containment-protection–warmth—primitive, but undamaged, objects. The five qualities of the objects—goodness, age, beauty, strength, and contentment—are manifestly at their optimum within the limited meaning contained by such a representation. Alter it now to the stereotype of the haunted house on a stormy night, the tree denuded and tormented by the wind—broken panes, missing tiles, no smoke curling from the chimney, bats flying from the gaping doorway, and the promise of ghosts within!

My point is that the damaged object does not merely lose the qualities that make up its parental character, it replaces them by persecutory qualities. This is a fundamental difference from the loss of meaning that is consequent to the splitting processes. Every item of damage to the object has the significance of an infectious lesion, not in the bacteriological sense precisely but in the epidemiological one. The object is felt, to the extent of its damage, to have a malevolent impulse to inflict its lesion, to cure itself by projection, and not necessarily in revenge on its antagonist, but upon any available part of the self. From the paranoid-schizoid position it is seen as corrupted by a bit that is malevolent, old, ugly, functionless, and resentful. You will note that I have used "functionless" antonymically to "strong", as this seems to me more in keeping with clinical findings regarding damage, while weakness of objects seems to be more the consequence of splitting processes, rather than of sadistic attack.

Perhaps it would be as well to include here a reminder that we are not talking about the genesis of persecutors, but about the origin of persecutory qualities in idealized objects. These same qualities, seen from the depressive position, will set in motion the work of reparation, which we will soon discuss. However, it is true that when an idealized object is damaged, it may promote a resurgence of confusional anxiety in regard to the differentiation of good and bad in self and objects—the so-called "persecutory depression". This confusion is seldom severe, I think, under these circumstances, and certainly does not take its place in the structure of fixed psychopathology, as does the good-bad confusion induced either by defective splitting-and-idealization, as in borderline states, or by penetration of idealized objects by the projective identification of destructive parts of the infantile organization, as in paranoia.

The final item about sadistic masturbatory attacks upon objects which needs mentioning relates to the modes of sadism. This is such a thoroughly investigated and described area of psychoanalytic theory that we can content ourselves with the merest reminder. The Freudian categories of oral, anal, and urethral sadism have served quite adequately. Under "oral", we can generally locate the biting, cutting, tearing; under "anal", the smearing, poisoning, exploding, choking; under "urethral", the burning, drowning, and corrosive attacks. Many phantasies, of course, present us with compounds of these elemental modes of attack. The question of the object of the attack and the specific nature of the damage done is best left for discussion under the heading of the reparative processes.

Reparation: restitution, re-introjection, restoration

Time is not, in psychic reality, the necessarily linear, directional, and irreversible dimension that the physical sciences describe in the outside world. The idea of time is bound up with sequence, motion, distance, and ageing in a most complicated manner that lends itself very well to reversal, oscillation, circularity, discontinuity, and arrest. In its essence the idea of reparation is closely linked to these qualities of the idea of time. (Is it too confusing to talk of the "idea" of time in the unconscious as distinguished from our "concept" of the idea of time in, say, psychoanalytic theory?) The basic process is always a reversal of the destructive event that has preceded it, item for item. This is something that has been stressed, but in a way left in confusion, both by Freud and by Melanie Klein. I have attempted some clarification in previous publications, but one might say that further systematic exposition of this concept is the secondary theme of this present volume.

I feel certain that I am simplifying, rather than complicating, an area of confusion in terminology when I take time here to sort through the various items of vocabulary that are needed. I intend—but may not, of course, succeed—to define terms according to the most consistent and systematic usage they have had in the literature. *Reparation* seems to be used mainly as a broad term covering all aspects of the process in the mind, with its phantasy and behavioural accompaniments, whereby damaged objects are returned to their optimal state in form, function, and relationship—optimal, that is, with respect to the previous development. Reparation does not involve any progress in development, just as one would not reasonably expect to be able to play the piano after a broken arm has knitted, unless you were able to do so before. It proceeds by means of restoration, assisted when relevant by restitution and re-introjection. *Restoration* described that aspect which the internal objects perform for one another in the process of their coition. *Restitution* implies the self giving back those things, parts, possessions, or attributes stolen from the objects. And, finally, *re-introjection* means the self taking back those parts of its organization previously split off and projected into the objects. This last term is often used in a very confusing way in the literature where processes of externalization and re-internalization are not distinguished from projection and re-introjection.

Of these three aspects of the reparative process, it is of course the restoration that is the complex and, by and large, the mysterious one. It is an area in which psychic reality diverges most sharply and widely from common sense, and one can only describe the outlines we discover with a sort of astonishment, so utterly unexpected have they been. It will be far more excitingly presented in Pinter's plays than I can begin to do here, but in order to keep later descriptions in order, I will outline the events briefly. In short, damage to the father, which means especially to his genital, is repaired by the mother in a kind of coital babying in the alms-house and hospital of her genital. Damage to the mother is restored in a somewhat indirect way by the father through his intercourse with her, by supplying "internal penises" that serve her, and the "semen" she requires for her maternal functions. His most direct service is that of receptacle for the discharge of all the noxious substances that the children have put into her, either in attack or as part of their dependence upon her as "toilet-mummy". How silly and uninteresting it sounds in technical language! We can hurry on to the "clinical material" in a moment. It only remains to mention the fact that the overriding concern of the internal parents is with "all the mother's babies", those already born, comprising all parts of the self and of actual siblings, and the unborn, the internal mother's inside-babies.

These, then, are the structural aspects of damage from sadistic masturbatory attacks and processes of reparation, upon whose balance the fate of the personality hangs, both regarding development and health. The economics of the balance resides in the problem of the distribution of mental pain and the systems of values determining this distribution—either the paranoid–schizoid "Is it worth it?" or the depressive "Let it be at my expense!" Well, on to more poignant matters!

2
Commentary on Harold Pinter's "The Dwarfs"

We must start our "clinical" discussions with a bit of methodological agreement between author and reader, for this undertaking will either succeed or fail according to the cooperation that can be established through the printed page. The first requirement is that the reader must put this book away at this point and not return to it until he has read "The Dwarfs" at least once, preferably twice—it is 26 little pages—as it is the key to the two larger works, "The Birthday Party" (1951) and "The Homecoming" (1965).

First I am going to run through the play, describing its latent content, as if it were a dream, without any justification for the interpretation(s). This will require the reader to curb his irritation by assuming that it is all in good faith. It would probably be best if the reader were then to put this book aside for a day or two and re-read "The Dwarfs" in the light of the interpretation, before returning to the second part of the commentary.

This second part consists of discussion of the interpretation in the light of the theory of sincerity and its relation to personality structure. Throughout I will be referring to page and line (cf. 95/15 - page ninety-five, line fifteen) from the Methuen edition, *A Slight Ache and Other Plays* (1961).

Interpretation of "The Dwarfs"

From our point of view and interest, this play is a study in the organization of the infantile masculinity in its pregenital aspect (Len), struggling to free itself from narcissistic collusion with the destructive part (Pete) on the one hand and the sensual-parasitic baby-part (Mark) on the other. This struggle is hampered in several directions: first of all by the suffering during separation from the mother from which pain it takes refuge in projective identification (Len's house); second, by its attempt at manic independence (eating too much cheese); third, by its confusion about the reparative role of the father's penises inside the mother (dwarfs) and difficulty to distinguish the good penis from Pete's faecal penis (the German) and the sensual part in projective identification with the good penis (Mark in his new suit); and finally by its own competition with these inside-penises in manic reparation (work at Euston).

To turn now to the play itself, I wish to discuss very briefly the nature of the stage-set and then in outline the content of the seventeen scenes. After that we will be free to retrace, reorganize and analyse in detail.

The Setting

Although the stage might be divided four ways, front and rear, right and left, by scenery and lighting, the geography clearly implies the inside of the mother, either "seen-as" Len's house or as Mark's house, and the outside of her body, seen as "the road" or "by the river" or "in hospital". We will trace the significance of the setting as we follow in outline the progression of the scenes. (These are not indicated in the format of the play, but have been assigned by me for the present exposition.)

91/1 *Scene I*

Having already retreated into projective identifica-
91/9 tion (Mark's house) because sucking his thumb
(recorder) has ceased to comfort him, the baby (Len)
thinks there is sure to be milk where his friend
(Mark) lives, but finds only semen and penises (the
92/1-5 stiff pint and gherkin). He is confused about the
92/13 duration of his separation (two weeks—more than
two weeks) because he cannot tell the difference
between daddy's penis (gentleman) and a little boy
92/18 in projective identification with it (gentleman's gen-
tleman), although he suspects something perverse
92/28 (Portuguese toasting fork with monkey's head) in

the sexuality involved. In contrast, the baby's
thumb not only no longer comforts him but reminds
him of a broken nipple and increases his depressive
93/10 anxiety (shocking blasted cold), while his sensual
93/21 friend, whom he confuses with his daddy's penis
(bullock), seems to him to have devoured the whole
93/26 of mother's breast (loaf of bread), while his own
93/30 small capacity requires frequent feeds (five solid
square meals). In fact, his own life with mother is
94/6 divided into eating (finish what I'm doing—upstairs)
and defecating (cut a sandwich, etc.—downstairs)
which he tends to idealize. This idealization of his
faeces makes him vulnerable to the flattery (how's
work) of the destructive part (Pete), even though he
94/28 is rather suspicious of him (what are you doing with
95/4 your hand?) and his masturbatory practices (hand
of a homicidal maniac).

95/16 *Scene II*

Having recovered somewhat from the narcissistic
involvement, the baby is able to see the mother's
95/16 body as his possession once more (This is my table).
But being inside rapidly becomes claustrophobic
95/21–26 (octagon-octopus; ambush; centre of the cold), ac-
companied by an awareness of being inside a living
95/30 object that could die and entrap him (room moves;
dead halt). Yet it is a cosy refuge from his persecu-
96/5-7 tors (my kingdom; no hole in my side)—or would be,
were he not identified with a mother (hole) who does
not know the difference between daddy's good penis
(King) and the little boy in projective identification
96/9 with it (Mark in his new suit). The baby is dazzled
and drawn once more towards a narcissistic collu-
96/24 sion (gasps), until he realizes that this penis does
97/1 not know the difference between rectum (Earl's
Court) and vagina. He becomes fearful of being bug-
97/20 gered (no place for curiosities—Portuguese toasting
fork) as his projective identification does not pro-

duce true femininity (the natural behaviour of
97/30 rooms), any more than providing a reliable point of
97/32 view for perception (see the yellow lights). In fact, he
recognizes that his mental processes are deranged
98/6 (nutshell) by this attempt to identify himself with
98/9 the fountainhead of knowledge (criterion). He is in
danger of being drawn into a sado-masochistic per-
98/18 version (coal in your mouth—coal in my mouth) of
fellatio-coprophagia.

Scene III

The baby recoils from this sensuality by seeking an
98/23 alliance with the destructive part (I've got some
beigles) but immediately finds that it not only wants
98/28 to take possession of his good object, the breast (I'd
like a good table) but would detach the whole
mother from reality (boat—sail it down the river),
99/4 thus leading the baby towards madness (elastic).
When the baby resists his seduction, the destruc-
tive part suspects that an alliance of baby hunger
99/16 for knowledge (apprehension of experience) with
99/26 boyish sensuality (you knock around with Mark too
much) stands in his way, so he attacks this quality
99/34 of mind, on rather puritanical grounds (barren as a
bombed site). But feeling this to fail, he begins to
threaten the baby with destruction of the mother as
100/1 a hostage (Pete's dream). The baby is overwhelmed
100/9 with despair (whimper and groan); it is his own
nightmare.

Scene IV

But the touch of despair also brings the baby into
100/20 touch with the springs of hopefulness, the experi-
ence of the watchful and protective penises inside
the mother (the dwarfs), different from the daddy's

100/22 penis outside (they only work in cities), but part of
his transient experience of masculine identification
100/30 (into the gang—I won't stay with them long). Clearly
here is where his security lies, and yet he cannot
commit himself, out of fear of the possible death of
101/7 the mother (landslide).

Scene V

Alarm at possible depressive breakdown throws the
baby back upon its homosexuality, thinking the
101/11 penis stronger than the breast (mirror) but unable
to distinguish the true from bogus father (Mark).
Still he notices evidences of delusional identity (your
face—a farce) and decides that safety lies in playing
101/19 his seducer (Mark) off against his persecutor (Pete),
but with a certain regret at the loss of the erotic
102/14 excitement (fork drops), linking as it does with the
already established prohibition against masturba-
tion (don't touch it—Pete's homicidal hand). The loss
of erotism precipitates a wave of hopelessness, feel-
102/19 ing unattractive in mother's eyes (no one would
bother—I can't see the mirror side).

Scene VI

This hopelessness arouses his jealousy of the father
and his ability to win the mother's admiration by his
102/28 services (chucks the dregs), but now the work of the
penises is seen with ambivalence, attributing to
102/32 them the baby's greed (in time for the tuck), seeing
no substantial difference between these penises
103/4 (dwarfs) and little boys (Pete, Mark and Len).

Scene VII

This state brings the baby again within the sphere

of influence of the destructive part with its exciting
103/30 cynicism about the parental coitus (what's the sun
and moon but an efficient idea?), always coupled
with covert threats (nutcracker) of castration, etc.
The effect of the threat is to remind the baby of his
own sadistic attacks on the mother's inside babies
104/8 (tiny insect) and the harm that it has done to the
breast (dead bird).

Scene VIII

Thrown back upon the father's reparative penis in
the face of this renewed depressive anxiety, the
baby finds its ambivalence again too strong, now in
104/14 the form of manic reparative omnipotence (they've
left me to attend to the abode), projecting onto the
104/25 inside penises (dwarfs) all his own deficiencies (nod,
yawn, gobble, spew, don't know the difference) and
returning to the idealization, not of his faeces them-
105/5 selves (rats) but of his eating of them (rat steak) as a
form of manic reparation. The father is felt only as a
competitor who triumphs (victory dish) when the
baby's mania collapses (I fall).

Scene IX

This hostility to the father's reparative achieve-
ments drives the baby back towards sensuality
105/15 (Mark) to be rid of his jealousy (Holy plague). But to
his own surprise finds all the accusations he had
harboured against the father in his oedipal rivalry
105/22 had their origins with this part of the self (ventrilo-
quist's dummy, buying me, too big for me) and the
destructive part (Pete). The realization of the price of
105/34 narcissism (I've lost a kingdom) as a defence against
106/3 the pain of hearing the parental coitus (when
the world begins to bang), how it has led him to

masturbation (jig) and loss of identity through pro-
106/12 jection (retreat utterly), grows into a determination
106/22 to free himself of his addictive dependence (I do the
corner's will).

Scene X

Turning back to the reparative penises for inspira-
tion and strength, (they are not bothered),
particularly against castration anxiety (dip their
107/3 wicks—lick of flame), the baby begins to under-
stand that these penises, and by implication the
father in the outside world, the men, face dangers
and labours in the service of the mother and her
107/12 babies (community; hymn singing; progress; indus-
try).

Scene XI

The full contrast between daddies and big brothers
107/19 is now evident to the baby. He recognizes (Pete
107/29 walks by the river) the idle curiosity, sadism (slicing
gull) and wanton destructiveness (leave it, leave it).
He is afraid that, as one of mother's babies, he, too,
108/7 will be attacked (groan).

Scene XII

Driven by this fear back inside the mother and
108/13 idealization of his faeces (stale cheese), the baby
finds that this position is extremely vulnerable, not
only to the depressive situation of fouling the nest
108/16 (twenty-eight goes), but that the anal preoccupation
makes him very vulnerable to anal perversions
108/24 (German) and mania (in the pink).

Scene XIII

On the other hand, the smugness of the sensual
part (Mark) in its delusion of possessing the mother
109/8 entire (sits by the fire; wear a ring in utter security)
109/13 no change in the posture of the room must be con-
109/22 trasted with the life of daddy (wait; industrious;
watch). It is clear that this sensual part thinks it is
110/27 its own father (believe in God?) and therefore has no
111/10 real identity (who are you?); that identity cannot be
achieved, described, apprehended from the opin-
111/32 ions of others (sum of so many reflections). He is led
112/1 back to the mystery of the primal scene (I've seen
what happens), of the reparative penises that rid
the mother of filth (the scum is broken and sucked
112/5 back) and fill her with beauty (essence), and sees
clearly the contrast with his own weakness and the
112/12 harmful narcissism (you're both in the same boat).
Clearly the only thing to do is to break with the
destructive and the sensual parts by pitting them
112/13 against one another (Pete thinks you're a fool).

Scene XIV

112 The vanity of one and the violence of the other make
113 them natural enemies and just as natural allies.

Scene XV

The baby is now free to accept his dependence on
114/5 the mother and the breast (hospital), while recog-
nizing that it is not the same as being her husband
(like a king). The danger now lies in using his posi-
114/6 tion to project envy (Mark looks as though he's
caught a crab), which could lead to an attack on his
114/24 bottom when he's at the breast (driving the tank;
sitting on the bed).

Scene XVI

In fact, the baby's achievement of dependence on the mother is having the effect of encouraging the sensual aspect of the masculinity (Mark) to differen-
115/21 tiate between anus (up the garden) and vagina, to
115/31 disengage itself from perversity (infection).

Scene XVII

And now the baby, having come full circle, the reparation of its internal objects having been completed, must once more face the loneliness and conflict of
116/11 separation from the good objects (I'm left in the lurch). Only his recollection of the mystery of the reparation of his inner world will arm him against the resentment of the pain of loneliness, jealousy,
116/16 and envy of the parents (they seem to anticipate a rare dish, a choicer spread); that and the hope of
116/24 development. (There is a flower.)

Discussion

I have taken "The Dwarfs" first, although, as I have said, I do not necessarily assume it to be chronologically the earliest of the three plays that we are examining. On the contrary, it seems to form an exposition of the nodal struggle between narcissism and object relations based upon the delicate balance between paranoid–schizoid and depressive values, and as such it would be expected to lead in two directions, progressive and regressive. It is from this point of view that we will later scrutinize "The Birthday Party" and "The Homecoming"—the one showing the pathways to mental illness, the other pointing to the even more mysterious route taken by development.

Before proceeding, it is necessary to pull together the detailed analysis of "The Dwarfs" into a more didactic arrangement, to which we will be able to make systematic reference later on. The first point is that the play, taken in toto, illustrates the fundamental concept of the cyclical nature of the processes in the unconscious, to which I have devoted so much of the description of *The Psycho-analytical Process* (Meltzer, 1967a). It is interesting to note this element in Pinter's work and to relate it to the more revealed concern with the plight of the individual-in-the-culture for which he is more clearly recognized. One would like to compare it with the annoying pretentiousness of various philosophers and sociologists who have turned away from psychoanalysis with a certain manifest contempt, while borrowing its most central ideas for the purpose of carrying on a flirtation with generalization. Sartre's later work presents a striking example of this, where he writes off psychoanalysis as having "stood still" following a "spectacular beginning" (Sartre, *The Problem of Method*, 1963 [1960], p. 28), only to use its conceptualization of the cyclical interplay of progression and regression as an instrument to flagellate the Marxists—not for the purpose, mind you, of refuting the Marxist contempt for individuals and their psychology, but to prove himself the true and, one suspects, only disciple of Marx. It is the contortion of a man who thinks he loves a woman despite her bad treatment of him, never suspecting his own masochism. Correspondingly, when Sartre goes on to praise the unique view of the development of the individual-in-the-family and, by implication or extension, the family-in-the-culture, we are informed in the editor's footnote that of course he is not talking about Freud's psychoanalysis, but about Sartre's own Existential Psychoanalysis (p. 60).

What may seem a gratuitous attack is intended as a pre-emptive move against a possible misuse of analytic interpretation of the content of Pinter's art to demonstrate that it is preoccupied with the individual's internal conflicts and is not allegorical with regard to social issues. My own belief is that this is a totally meaningless distinction, a product of the same obsessional mentality that has wasted so much time on the non-existent "mind–body" problem, the "nature–nurture" problem, and similar either–or exercises.

Since we are going to move on in the later sections to examine the psychology of regression and development and the light that they throw on the problem of sincerity, we must take stock of the central position of fluctuating integration and oscillating narcissism and object relationship that is illustrated by "The Dwarfs". This central position is the jumping-off place for these two contrary movements in personality evolution and corresponds to what I have described at some length as the "threshold of the depressive position" in *The Psycho-analytical Process* (Meltzer, 1967a). The main point of this crucial organization, this watershed, this T-junction, is that the idealized infantile structures have begun to emerge from the blanketing confusions, of identity on the one hand, induced by the employment of projective identification, and of zones and modes of relationship, induced by masturbatory phantasy, so that they have begun to discern the difference between good and bad in action, as it were. The goodness of the parental objects is seen to express itself in aims, where it cannot be clearly delineated by mere description of behaviour, in contrast to the destructive parts of the self. What has not emerged as yet is any conviction of the *strength* of good objects *vis-à-vis* the destructive parts. The short-term view of winning-and-losing that the infantile mind is bound to take outside the depressive position leaves them with the conviction of the good objects inhabiting the "losing side", a stance not easily distinguished from masochism. Until the long-term aims of development are recognized, the readiness of the good objects to tolerate badness, their refusal to punish or deter with threats of punishment, their alacrity at accepting sacrifices to themselves—all this is mockingly presented as evidences of weakness, placation, delusion, or sentimentality by the propaganda coming from the destructive parts. Added to this, of course, is the confusion the infantile structures experience concerning internal and external reality, the role of chance, and the irreversibility of time and death. The powers of reparation that the internal objects manifest in the realm of psychic reality, and thereby of mental health, find only a very approximate and incomplete representation in the world of social relations and physical health. The infantile structures find this disillusioning, as they cannot grasp the idea of "a life-time" nor accept the inevitability and justice of death. Confronted with these aspects, their immediate response is of urgent greed and hatred of the "losing side".

"The Dwarfs" illustrates to perfection the process seen in analysis, whereby, part by part, the infantile structures free themselves from the domination of the destructive parts and ally themselves with the good objects when they reappear from the sequestered chamber of their reparative coitus, only to lose faith and hope once more as the mother tires, succumbs to attacks, and finally withdraws into seclusion. It is an endless process, in fact, as its end-point of total integration is not actually attainable. But when it proceeds, the inner world comes gradually to be dominated by the good objects and the principles of the depressive position. Melanie Klein has demonstrated in *Envy and Gratitude* (1957) that the destructive parts can at least be modified as to their virulence, even if they can never be fully integrated. A détente can be achieved in which their special qualities of perception can become available for creative employment. It has even been suggested that the violence can be enlisted in the service of defence, in the manner of a sublimation. I do not believe this. It confuses placation with integration, strength with cruelty. It compromises by taking a short-term view of a long-term problem.

3
Commentary on Harold Pinter's "The Birthday Party"

One would like to be able to say that our psychoanalytic knowledge of the regressive processes that lead to mental illness are derived from reconstruction rather than from direct observation. And to a large extent this is true. While it is probable that no schizophrenic illness has ever been completely cured by psychoanalytic treatment, experience of the analysis of patients who have had schizophrenic episodes, as well as clinical improvement in schizophrenic patients during analysis, does afford us a view of the recovery process, which makes a reconstruction of the original regressive movement feasible. But it is necessary to add to this happy roster also cases that have deteriorated during treatment and afforded a direct view. Psychoanalysis cannot honestly be presented as a method free from hazard.

I have selected Harold Pinter's "Birthday Party" as the "clinical material" to illustrate regression into mental illness, as it will be seen to include a fairly complete inventory of the factors and operations with which we are acquainted from analytic work. The central fact, as described earlier, is the pre-morbid organization of the personality at infantile levels outside the depressive position, still subject to a spectrum of confusions and still employing projective identification with internal objects as a refuge from mental pain and individual identity. Where this latter factor has been fixed for some period of time due to retreat from either traumatic experience or an overwhelmingly painful encounter with the pains of the developmental process, especially the oedipal conflict at genital or pregenital levels, the stage is set for an advance in the influence of the destructive parts over the other infantile structures. This they do in two ways: by undermining the prestige of the good objects, and—through the creation of confusion between good and bad, both descriptively and ethically—they attempt to present themselves as benevolent. By penetrating the claustrum to which an infantile part has retreated in its projective identification, the destructive parts gain dominance over this regressed part of the self and eventually lead it away to the unreal realm of the mind, the delusional system. This alienation takes the infantile structure beyond the sphere of attraction of the primal good objects, fundamentally the mother's breast, and is therefore a journey of the mind from which it cannot return by its own efforts, having lost not merely its bearings but its navigational instruments, so to say. It must await the rescue that never comes, as the process has left no Web of Ariadne for a rescuer to follow. Yet this seems an impossibility. Surely the difficulty is that we have not as yet learned to "read trail".

It can be seen that this regression to the delusional system has a striking resemblance to birth, and in fact is its negative, just as the "world" into which the infantile part emerges from the claustrum of the mother's body is the negative of the real external world in form and of the real internal world in ethos. It is the world behind the mirror of Cocteau's "Orpheus"; it is Milton's "City of Pandemonium", where Satan speaks:

> Thrones, Dominations, Princedoms, Vertues, Powers,
> For in possession such, not onely of right,
> I call ye and declare ye now, return'd
> Successful beyond hope, to lead ye forth
> Triumphant out of this infernal Pit
> Abominable, accurst, the house of woe,
> The Dungeon of our Tyrant: Now possess,
> as Lords, a spacious World, to our native Heaven
> Little inferior, by my adventure hard
> With peril great achiev'd. Long were to tell
> What I have don, what suffer'd, with what paine
> Voyag'd the unreal, vast, unbounded deep
> Of horrible confusion, over which
> By Sin and Death a broad way now is pav'd
> To expedite your glorious march;—
>
> [Milton, "Paradise Lost", Book X]

There is evidence from the structure of sexual perversions to suggest that the resemblance, inverted, to birth presented by a schizophrenic deterioration is neither fortuitous nor allegorical. It is possible that the most insidious function of envy commences at birth to exercise its spirit of negation by building up the delusional system *pari passu* with the evolution of psychic reality and the attendant image of the external world. It is perhaps always there, waiting to receive its tenants.

Two types of regressive loss of sincerity

Study of severe illness forces upon the analyst aspects of the realm of mental functions that may never have appeared in the course of his personal analysis and pose, therefore, a special stress to his mental health, but also, of course, a special opportunity to deepen his self-analysis. Where the content of the neurotic patient's communication oscillates, as the focus of analytic interest, with the transference behaviour of the acting-out and acting-in, the psychotic or borderline patient presents us, often from the outset, with the central problem of investigating this mode of communication, whether verbal or behavioural. We cannot escape the problem by seeking to establish, as if by contract, the meaning of the words or signs, but, rather, find ourselves enmeshed in an undergrowth of allusive vagueness, plural implication, and equivocal intention. The essence of this tangle is the inability of the patient either to say-what-he-means or to mean-what-he-says. I wish to examine them separately and suggest a structural basis which the "clinical material" of Pinter's "Birthday Party" will illustrate quite precisely.

Being unable to mean what one says

It would not appear that our ordinary language usage makes the distinction between defective sincerity and incomplete sincerity. But we must do so here, and I would beg permission to be allowed a rather simple, if unmusical, mode for expressing this by differentiating, say, "*un*sincere", as meaning defective in sincerity, from "*in*sincere", as indicating incomplete sincerity. In speaking of the alterations in communication associated with mental illness, I will therefore employ the former, reserving the latter for the description of the consequences of differing gradations of integration.

In the clinical situation with ill patients one becomes aware, as I say, of the impaired or defective sincerity that makes of communication an area of despair—Steinbeck's "flies conquering the flypaper". In the borderline patient, or in the neurotic with focal areas of psychotic difficulty, the problem can be circumscribed and subjected to systematic investigation, which, in my experience, reveals these two broad categories of interference, being unable to-mean-what-one-says and to-say-what-one-means.

The simpler of the two in structure seems to be the former, to "mean it". The clinical phenomenology of it is quite distinctive and can be well described, even if the patient may not "mean it" when he describes it. The emphasis of the patient's observations of his own functions rests upon the non-syntactic aspects—tone of voice, facial expression, gesture, posture, rhythm, pronunciation, speed, volume. Essentially the patient notices, if he will listen or, rather, adopt a position of self-observation, that what emerges from him as communicative behaviour is quite different from the internal formulation of his intention. He hears his voice hollow, as if from inside a diving bell. He notices an affectation of pronunciation or accent. She recognizes her gestures to be rather tight, her posture masculine. He notices that the self-image is contaminated by the film star he saw yesterday. The expectation of her companion is being catered for by her pretence of gaiety.

Before a patient has achieved a sufficient differentiation of adult from infantile levels of mental functioning to be able to adopt such a position of self-observation, a disquieting sense of being misunderstood or misconstrued tends to pervade their relationships. Often the complaints are bitter and long-standing—that people do not listen, that they are blinded by preconceptions, that they are only interested in appearances, insensitive to emotions, bound by custom, restricted by stereotypes. It is often clear that these complaints refer to adults and exempt children, or that they include all humans and exclude domestic animals, pertain to the "others" but not to "us", or concentrate themselves against a boss or a spouse. In the transference the complaints tend to be presented as a type of touchiness about being spoken to as a child, treated with insufficient respect, not taken seriously, seen as a "mere patient".

Investigation of the structure of the personality that underlies being unable-to-mean-what-one-says reveals a particular narcissistic structure of the following type, although it must not, of course be assumed, with any particular patient, that this organization is continual, nor even frequent, outside the analytic situation. One sees it in the analysis most clearly at times of pseudo-cooperation—that is, times when an infantile structure in projective identification with an internal object presents itself to the analyst as if it were the adult part of the patient. At such times, with certain more ill patients or ones with a psychotic focus, the phenomenology described makes its appearance and may be observed by the analyst and the adult self of the patient as well, if the latter can be mobilized from its inertia. Dreams make clear that the infantile structure that thinks it is grown up and is doing all the communicating stands in a relation to a destructive, cynical, and highly verbal infantile structure in the relation of a poor actor to his prompter in the wings. By accepting the formulation of thoughts and feelings as suggested by the prompter, the infantile part fails to notice that his intention, both as regards emotionality and intellectual conception, have been subjected to a gross, if subtle, distortion. He notices that he is, in fact, unable-to-mean-what-one-says. It is not insincerity, incompleteness of honesty, but unsincerity, dishonesty, that has resulted. He is not deceiving his audience but taking advantage of their trust, inferior subtlety, or ignorance of facts or language. The consequence is that his actual behaviour has a harshness and cruelty that goes far beyond his intention, which was merely to control or manipulate. In other words, while intending to be only insincere, he has found himself being unsincere, and therefore inclined to disavow any intention of producing the hurtful result that in fact eventuates.

Being unable to say what one means

The person who is unable-to-mean-what-he-says does not strike us as a tragic figure, but, rather, his continual assertion that he is mis-understood tends to irritate us by its irresponsibility. "But I didn't mean it that way" might elicit a more patient or sympathetic hearing if the old saying about "sticks and stones" were true. It is all quite different in our response to the person who cannot-say-what-he-means.

In its most florid form, catatonic mutism, this incapacity, perhaps rightly, strikes us as the ultimate catastrophe. Yet it would be wrong to take this ultimate form as the prototype, for its most frequent manifestation has a quality imbued with all the outward requirements—I am almost inclined to say "stigmata"—of social adaptation, at least in terms of the standards of the childhood milieu. Its abnormality is betrayed in its rigidity, which becomes so manifest when exposed to a different culture. Even its essential coldness, in the sense of unavailability to intimate relationships, is often well hidden in familiar surroundings. When the coldness emerges as a rebuff to an advance, it can be very similar to schizoid coldness.

In fact, many of its descriptive features are perilously similar to the flatness and colourlessness of the schizoid personality. One must look in the eyes to see that there is a prisoner in the tower. I remember a little girl who, at one point in the analysis, made a series of portraits of herself in which the deadness of one eye was sharply contrasted with the liveliness of the other. At that time she was still sitting always with her back to me in the playroom, giving only a cold and haughty glance on entry and exit from the sessions. Analytic progress made itself known by this inability-to-say becoming replaced by the inability-to-mean.

In the course of the work that brings about this transition—a work of tedious slowness, fraught with hopelessness on both sides—the structure of the incapacity becomes not only revealed but defiantly flaunted. The destructive infantile parts have captured the heterosexual infantile part within the claustrum of the internal mother's body and there hold it incommunicado. That it may also be held in thrall to perversions, addictions, paranoid preoccupations, etc. is not to the point here. The central fact is that all attempt at communication is met by the proverbial bad servant at the door, who always claims that his master is not at home, but that he will convey a message. In dreams such figures are naturally represented as porters, secretaries, interpreters, agents, solicitors, accountants, best friends, and older siblings. Could Kafka have had such a mother, perhaps?—a spine-chilling thought!

Interpretation of "The Birthday Party"

The three acts of the play take place inside a boarding house of a seaside town and involve three braces of characters: Meg and Petey, who are in in their sixties, Stanley and Lulu, in their thirties and twenties, respectively, and Goldberg and McCann, fifties and thirty. We will take the proceedings at the level at which Meg is the inside-breast and Petey the inside-penis of the mother inside of whom Stanley, the little-boy-part, has taken refuge from the disappointments of the outside world, only occasionally visited by Lulu, the little-girl-part, as his only link with the world outside the mother's body. It is this link that the destructive parts—the subtle Goldberg and the brutal McCann—must attack in order to render the little boy helpless against deportation to Monte, schizophrenia, the world of the delusional system.

Act I

9/7 The inside of the mother's body as presented is
poorly structured, particularly in regard to rectum/
vagina differentiation (kitchen hatch), and the part-
objects (Meg and Petey) display primitive and inad-
equate qualities, the penis being dependent, in poor
9/18 contact, eating faeces (corn-flakes), while the in-
9/23 side-breast is dull, concerned in its generosity only
to give pleasure. Their intercourse is feeble and
10/16 confused (up and down). This inside breast cannot
foster development in the baby because it knows
10/28 nothing of the outside world (light and dark), and
thinks of babies as possessions and part-objects
(much rather have a little boy). It is aware of the
11/5 little boy's withdrawal and masturbation (goes
through his socks, half the week in bed), but unable
11/33 to exert any influence or discipline. It displays all
12/12 the qualities of a little girl who confuses her bottom
with mummy's breasts (two pieces of fried bread).
We now hear that this Petey–penis has been unable
to protect his testicles from being intruded into in
12/31 projective identification (two men on the beach) and
that the destructive parts are to gain access to the
mother's body disguised, as it were, as parts of the
13/16 external father. This excites the inside-breast (on
the list), causing it to become confused about va-
13/29 gina and rectum again (the new show coming to the
Palace), wherein her confusion between baby and
14/8 penis is also revealed (straight show—Stanley play-
ing the piano). But she is aware of the real impo-
tence of the little boy (I tried to get him up then. But

14/15 he wouldn't, the little monkey), and resorts to trying
to excite him by taking the role of the erotized
14/19 outside-breast (goes upstairs, wild laughter, etc.).
The qualities of the little boy are now rapidly re-
15/12 vealed, his withdrawal from the cold outside world,
his sensual demands, his exploitation of the inside-
breast's jealousy of the outside-breast (smart hotels
16/8 on the front), insincerity (wonderful surprise) and
cruelty (bad wife). His arrogance of tenure (I'm your
17/23 visitor) is related to her erotic attachment to the
tongue, confused with penis (shouldn't say "succu-
18/4 lent" to a married woman). He has withdrawn into
the toilet-breast as his refuge (succulent old wash-
ing bag) from the depressive aspects of the outside
18/25 world (rubs eyes under glasses as he picks up the
newspaper). It is clear that the erotic enslavement
of the confused inside-breast has a high price for
the little boy, not only because of the faeces–food
and vagina–rectum confusions (muck, bloody, pig-
19/20 sty) but because of the paranoid anxiety of his
claustrum being inspected by the daddy–penis (he'd
19/12 report you) or invaded by the bad big-brothers (two
visitors), not clearly distinguished. (Who are they?)
21/7 This anxiety brings a rush of valuing his object
(where's my tea?) confronting the defence against
fear of loss through denigration; i.e. that no one else
would want it. The little boy tries to identify himself
with the daddy–penis (who exactly are you talking
22/12 to?) but quickly collapses, despite the inside-
breasts encouragement (you could play the piano
22/26 on the pier). He begins to lie and boast, and,
as the anxiety only increases, we get the first hint
of an incipient regression (Berlin to Athens to
23/8 whatsisname—i.e. Monte) to schizophrenia. The
claim of having been a success at the breast is
capped by the claim of once having had intercourse
23/19 with the vagina (concert at Lower Edmonton). The
tragedy of a catastrophic experience of weaning now
pours out in a heartbreaking way (they carved me
23/28 up—in winter, etc.) The inside-breast is sympa-

thetic but uncomprehending, inviting him to use her
as breast and toilet-mummy (rock cake—pay a visit).
24/9 The little boy proceeds to unload his paranoid anxi-
ety into her (They're coming in a van). This collapse
24/24 into dependence upon the maternal service brings
the little boy in touch with the little-girl part, which is
immediately revealed as plotting with the outside
breast to rescue the little boy from the claustrum
25/13 (Lulu whispering with Meg outside about the drum
for Stanley's Birthday Party). It is clear that this
improved integration of bisexuality immediately im-
proves the vitality of the little boy, partly because,
being identified with the outside-breast, the little girl
26/29 is insightful (You think I'm a liar, then?) The contrast
27/10 in orientation to the mother is clear (you're never
out—I'm always out). [Just as the opposite juxtaposi-
tion of the infantile bisexuality is made clear between
Julie and Jean in Strindberg's "Miss Julie".] The little
girl attempts to entice him out by offering to share
27/17 the breast (sandwiches) with him, but he would wish
27/24 her to go with him into the delusional system (No-
where–Whatsisname–Monte). His paranoid anxieties
are apparently the result of his choice of a particular
way of looking at things (glasses), connected with
28/2 distrust of the mother and intrusive voyeurism (Has
Meg had many guests?) This declaration of a plot to
rescue the little boy from his claustrum and return
him to the sphere of the good breast is now juxta-
posed to the entry into the mother's body through her
28/23 anus (back door), of the destructive parts disguised
as the daddy–genital (Goldberg with briefcase,
McCann with two suitcases) [Compare Pozo and
Lucky in Beckett's "Waiting for Godot"]. The maniac
and the paranoid qualities of the two immediately
29/5 declare themselves (Sure I'm sure. Are you going to
take a seat?) The avuncular homosexuality, omnis-
cience, fraudulence, obsessional undercurrent,
29/12 greed, and sentimentality are then paraded in total
self-idealization. [Compare Willy Loman in Arthur
Miller's "Death of a Salesman".] The manic lying is

almost unquestioningly credited by the dull and
30/12 brutal part in a way reminiscent of the relation of
the inside-breast to the little boy and in contrast to
his sister's incredulity. His only interest and skill is
31/1 in making things into faeces (do a job). But the
manic part is uneasy when, as flattery, he is re-
31/29 minded that he, too, fed at the mother's nipple (true
Christian), being inclined to think of himself as self-
made, based upon his "gift of the gab", with its
attendant facility for momentary projective identi-
32/9 fication with the father's penis (speaks in a quiet,
fluent, official tone). The first attack is almost im-
mediately launched, to poison the food supply with
33/9 spit (McCann being sent to the kitchen to gargle),
while the test of strength of the destructive parts
against sister and good objects is seductively ar-
35/4 ranged (birthday party). Clearly the rectum-vagina
(tulip) cannot distinguish semen from faeces
35/23 (McCann is the life and soul of any party). The act
draws to a close in a medley of emotion: the little
boy's panic at realizing that his expulsion from the
claustrum has been arranged by both his persecu-
tors and his good objects, that his hope of making
time stand still has ended: the inside-breast's
uncomprehending joy turned to bewilderment at
the evidence that she is unable to impart strength
38/25 (the drum instead of a piano).

Discussion

I wish to draw your attention to the similarity between the structure of this situation fashioned by Pinter and the situation in the analysis of borderline patients, addicts, and perverts, in whom it is almost always the case that the heterosexuality is particularly poorly established because of the withdrawal of that infantile part into massive projective identification. The essential step in the development of the analytic process involves just such a conspiracy of good objects to rescue the withdrawn part from its claustrum. Just such a duel of angels as the playwright has set his stage to portray must take place. It cannot be denied that the advent of the holiday breaks, illness of the analyst—any event in or around the analysis that undermines confidence in the strength of the good objects—can have disastrous results. It is vital that the process not be hurried, that the rehabilitation of the patient's internal objects from their debilitated state, as represented in the play by Meg and Petey, be allowed to take place before any challenge to the addiction or perversion is issued. In the play, one can see how the crisis is engineered by Goldberg, just as patients are prematurely pushed out of hospitals or home for questionable motives.

Act II

The theme of attack on information about the world outside the mother's body set's the scene for the
40/1 second act (McCann tearing the newspaper into strips). The brutal intimidation almost without resistance reduces the little boy to homosexual
41/17 passivity (whistling with McCann), but he is also
42/16 confused by the attractive faecal penis (picks up a strip—ever been anywhere near Maidenhead?) Clearly, he knows that this is a brother of his days
42/27 in the womb (born and brought up there). Frightened, the little boy's gibbering reveals his longing to be out of the claustrum and back at the breast
43/2 (home). He is effeminate, affected, and seductive to his persecutor, but in this state is more insightful about the parasitism that brought him to this dan-
43/7 ger (private income, everything delivered to the door). This failing, he begins to beg and lick-spittle
43/31 in the guise of feeble threats (you wouldn't think I was the sort of bloke to cause any trouble). Finally,
44/18 he is ready to betray his good objects (she's crazy),
45/17 even to claim he was never at the breast (never stepped outside the door at Basingstoke), but is very fond of the rectum (Ireland). But the manic
46/34 brother remembers the little boy at the breast (hot

milk) when he was already occupied with the moth-
46/9 er's bottom (down the canal with a girl). He begins to
torment the little boy with what he has lost in re-
48/10 treating into the mother's bottom (wake up with the
sun shining), while at the same time claiming that
49/2 he is the father and protector of the mother (get on
my breasts). In a paradoxical way, the little boy's
eagerness that it should be so causes him to behave
with a defiance clearly meant as taking advantage of
49/5 a good daddy. The result is disastrous, being in
50/2 danger of a vicious assault on body and mind (kick
the shit out of him—Goldberg's interrogation). In
this masterpiece of dialogue that follows Pinter has
recorded in minute detail the process by which
depressive feelings are converted into persecutory
guilt, driving the little boy into despair. Its tech-
nique clearly consists in the factual truth being
51/2 presented without compassion. Having intensified
the little boy's pain beyond his feeble endurance,
the cynical and manic big-brother deprives him of
the voyeuristic omniscience by means of which the
denigration of his good objects has always been
52/5 accomplished. Denuded of defence against mental
pain, the little boy can now be driven from confu-
sion to confusion, until he almost welcomes an
assault on his capacity to think and employ lan-
53/21 guage. Only the final assault on the little boy's belief
in the reality of his own existence, the last stop
(depersonalization) before the delusional system, is
55/23 resisted. This brings the little boy back in touch
56/5 with good objects once more. But it also brings back
56/17 his defences of voyeurism, which the big brother
57/2 takes advantage of to mount a display of seduction
59/10 and degradation of the inside-breast, followed by a
59/18 flatus attack on love itself, reducing it to ridiculous
sentimentality. Next the seduction of the little girl is
61/10 undertaken, appealing to her loneliness, her com-
petitiveness with the mother and sexual need. To
the stunned little boy there is now displayed the
62/19 complete breakdown of the differentiation of adults

64/27 and infantile sexuality. The final nightmare of an
66/17 orgiastic primal scene ensues, leading to the little
66/29 boy's withdrawal from reality. He is now destroying
68/10 everything that holds him to life—first the inside
68/26 breast, then the little-sister part. The little boy has
gone into the delusional system.

Discussion

No clinical material from analysis could, I think, reflect with greater accuracy and poetic revelation of emotion the systematic, step-by-step process by which the vulnerable and tenuous hold on life of a part of the personality that has taken refuge inside the mother's body can be loosened and ultimately destroyed during separation from good external objects. This "agony in the nursery", as I have called it after Thurber, follows, with quantitative variations, the order represented here. Brutality aggravates the claustrophobic anxiety to the point of readiness to betray good objects. The truth without compassion renders depressive pains indistinguishable from persecution. Cynicism attacks all differentiations, and finally that between good and bad, between adult and infantile. Ultimately capacity for thought and language is fragmented, and the part can be led helplessly away from life, into the delusional system, by means of the nightmare.

Act III

This masterful denouement is not germane to our
purpose here and will not be analysed. There are
just a few points that confirm earlier interpretation
that are worth mentioning. Goldberg's briefcase is
confirmed to represent the fetishistic object of per-
verse sexuality. The family relationship of Goldberg
72/19 and Stanley is asserted. The essential unity of cyni-
79/23 cism and brutality (Goldberg and McCann) is made
clear. Finally, the megalomaniacal position can be

seen as a defence against envy of the good object,
80/21 which produces a plethora of hypochondriacal anxi-
80/15 eties that must be constantly projected. It is a very
important feature of the presentation that the
source of evil, a mixture of person and place, Monty,
takes no direct role, but only acts through its lieu-
tenants, the destructive infantile parts of the
personality that are in thrall to it. Thus Goldberg
81/25, emits the same kind of wheeze-whine as the cata-
88/31 tonic Stanley.

Discussion

One feels that the marvellous structure and poetry of Pinter's work has laid everything out with such clarity that no more remains to be said. Perhaps we can draw attention to a few aspects and draw them together with the general theme of this chapter and the specific one of this section.

Stanley's mode of communication is an ill one and becomes more so as the play progresses to its climax in the second act. We find him unsincere in his relationship with both Meg and Lulu in the first act in a manner that is repeated in Goldberg's relation to the two of them in the second. The difference is that Stanley is an amateur and Goldberg a professional, one might say, at this dishonesty. But that difference in skill, which causes Stanley to fail and be dubbed a "washout" by Lulu, a term later repeated by Goldberg in his interrogation, does not really capture the essence. The real difference lies in the fact that Goldberg means it, and Stanley does not. The mobilization of little-girl excitement and masochism that satisfies Goldberg's greed and vanity causes Stanley anxiety and revulsion. By this device Pinter has made clear to us that Stanley is Goldberg's student, apprentice, ventriloquist's dummy—by implication at first, and more manifest as the passivity increases in Stanley later. The turning point, from dependence to submission to the bad-brother, is unmistakably marked. "She's crazy", Stanley says of Meg, meaning that she does not know his birthday because she is not his mother. By this abandonment of his birthright, he falls into despair.

It is a point of some interest to note that Pinter seems to be employing a concept of despair which reaches back for its formulation to the work of Kierkegaard (Goldberg's interrogation, 53/21, the possible and the necessary; see "The Sickness unto Death" Part First, III, A, b). It is my opinion that the formulations of this work (1849) reach precisely the understanding that psychoanalysis has reached a century later by a quite different route. Goldberg's travesty of Kierkegaard's method of argument is a useful illustration of the nature of the cynical attack on the capacity for abstraction and the ability to use language as notation for abstract thought.

A further problem arises with regard to the concept "liar", which is raised in Stanley's relation to Lulu and later manifests itself in Goldberg's confabulations and multiple nicknames—Nat, Simey, Benny. In clinical practice I think it is most useful to reserve the term "lie" for any statement—be it truth in fact, half truth, confabulation, or omission—that has the intention consciously to deceive, whether or not the motive for the deception is conscious. How to relate this concept to our present differentiation of insincere from unsincere seems puzzling. My own preference, from the sheer point of view of clinical usefulness, would be to consider the term "lie" as the particular conscious act subsumed under the more general category of disturbances of sincerity, in which the question of consciousness is of clinical but not of theoretical interest. "Liar", on the other hand, would not seem to be an acceptable technical term for describing a person, but only for characterizing a particular part of the total personality.

4
Commentary on Harold Pinter's "The Homecoming"

By taking "The Dwarfs" as our point of departure in this investigation of sincerity and its various disturbances, we hoped to establish a watershed point from which processes of regression and progression in development could be studied and described as the background functions underlying variations in sincerity. The first fruit of this scheme was a description of regressive events, with an emphasis on two particular disturbances of personality organization—massive projective identification and narcissistic organization of the self. We attempted to trace two, possibly *the* two, types of disorder of sincerity to the operation of these two mechanisms, deciding to refer to these as un-sincerity of the types unable-to-mean-what-one-says and unable-to-say-what-one-means, respectively. Harold Pinter's "The Birthday Party" served as our clinical material as through its illustration of these processes and by its links to "The Dwarfs" it demonstrated the regressive movement. Our investigations took us deep into the realm of mental illness and away from the ordinary, daily problems of human contact and communication, which we associate with the concept of sincerity and its fluctuations.

When we turn now from the disorders of sincerity to its variations of quality and degree, we first of all realize that we have turned our attention to the third category of the sources of the sense of identity of which we spoke in the first section—namely, the component derived from introjective identification with the good internal objects. You will recall that an attempt was made to distinguish between variations in sincerity coming from two directions, one a derivative of fluctuations in the qualities of the internal objects themselves, either of state of integration or of qualities integrated, the other dependent upon the degree to which the adult part of the self was committed to its identification and its implications for action in the outside world. In preparation for a detailed analysis of "The Homecoming", it is necessary to dissect these two determinants of the quality and degree of sincerity somewhat further.

Fluctuations in the quality of objects

When we grow up and begin to become self-conscious in the way that, it would appear, only the adult part of the personality can observe its own functioning in some degree of objectivity, one of the things that strike us most forcefully is the degree of calm, or perhaps blandness, with which we had accepted the world about us as "given," in the sense of "*donné*", in childhood. We come somehow to think that noticing the existence of the complexity of the world, and therefore to enter upon the possibility of being in awe or wonder, depended upon learning the names of things. Philosophers seem almost automatically to take this view. But I would suggest that the study of the inhibition of the epistemological instinct, which takes place universally with that change of organization that produces the infantile amnesia, raises precisely the opposite question from the philosopher's. We would not be impelled to ask why a child needs to know the names of the trees before he can notice their variety but, rather, how does he avoid noticing the variety until the diversity of names forces it upon him? We are prone to suspect that the institution of the infantile amnesia has carried away with it into the depths the infantile wonder, the aesthetic sense, the hunger of the mind, and in their place has set latency qualities of complacency, realism, and the greed for possessions.

The corollary of this misunderstanding of childhood would be the conception that children learn to speak by being taught words by their mothers. The truth is quite apparent to any observer, that they learn to speak by playing vocally, lalling, and that they sing prepositions long before they ever learn to speak words. In this lalling they are pushed by their awe of their parents to emulate their vocal intercourse as the quintessence of the primal scene. For it is the existence of understanding binding two minds into a new unity that catches at the imagination and sets it spinning and yearning. Between his parents, as between two mirrors, the child catches a glimpse of the past and future curving away from him in space after loculated space of mysterious moments in experience. Each mystery unlocked leads on to the next, whether in exploration of the past or adventuring into the future. Each observation raises a new question calling for a new observation. And in this way attention is deployed, now probing the present, now resting upon the past, now piercing the future, in rhythmic scansion, seeking the meaning-filled facts of the world.

This aspect of the primal scene, the parents' verbal communication by which in the child's view their minds seem to flow into one another and mingle as a new combined object, this aspect depicts only one of the many symbolic forms of creative activity which our art forms employ in their social or, rather, socialized coition. Where these art forms represent the creativity of the minds of the parents, which strike awe into the small child, other aspects of the world observed come to be assimilated to their bodies. It requires merely a twist of the mind's wrist to turn the theory of symbol formation on its head and come to the developmental view, which dictates that the child will explore the outside world with the template of its parents' bodies, finding each new object to have such meaning as this inner model can supply. This "seeing as" does not so much invest the outside world with meaning in the first instance, but, rather, gathers inward to the parental objects new forms, and thus new meanings, to enrich the conception of the combined object. From this enriched source the meaning can then flow secondarily to the external objects. Thus to see the flower "as" a female genital is the secondary discovery of the external object, flower. It is a scientific hypothesis that recognizes the flower as having a genital function. The primary discovery of the flower-like quality of the female genital is a poetic and creative function, which must serve as the background of intuition upon which scientific hypothesis may be formed. It is thus a mistake to think that the appearance of a mountain surmounted by a watchtower in a dream "symbolizes" the breast and nipple—has the "meaning of" breast and nipple. That does not state a meaning but simply denotes the object. Rather it is the mountain and watchtower that "expresses" the particular aspect of the manifold meanings of breast and nipple that this particular dream and dreamer have "in mind". We err in thinking that symbol translation reveals the meaning of the dream; rather, by translating the poetry of the dream image into the prose of abstraction, we lessen the richness and vitality of the image.

Thus in time the world is taken inside by the child's exploration and is assimilated at various levels of relationship to the bodies and minds of the parental figures. Thus mountain and watchtower would be a very infantile level of perception of breast and nipple, enriched by observations from childhood and beyond. This may seem a difficult conception to get one's mind around, but it really is little more than a statement of the ubiquity of the infantile transference. Our emotional relations with the world about have this infantile background of "seeing as" and the constant interplay of projection, introjection, and re-projection (or externalization) at infantile levels. All that we "know" of the world becomes assimilated to our internal objects through these transference interactions. For instance, the optimal integration of objects would locate all evil in "mummy's rectum", contained there and controlled by the mother's "internal penises" (Pinter's dwarfs) with the penis of the father in reserve, should anarchy threaten.

In fact, such integration of objects is probably never achieved, but the point is nonetheless worth emphasizing as an asymptote. Splitting and idealization of the objects is never fully reintegrated, with the result that one never fully overcomes the feeling, even if one has conquered the thought, that there are good and bad people in the world, rather than good and bad ideas. But this is not the only source of limitation in the quality of the objects. This structural limitation is augmented by the immaturity of the individual in terms of sheer experience of the world and limited grasp of what has already been experienced. Different aspects of the world catch the imagination at different ages, in keeping with the conflicts and strivings that are most active and the tendencies, interests, and talents that are most forceful in the particular person, and the penetration of perception that is available. The object-seeking hunger of the baby, which emerges so explosively once more in the adolescent, is just as actively seeking objects for assimilation by introjection as it is searching for objects to relate to in the outside world. The baby puts everything into its mouth to test its suitability for assimilation. The adolescent does the same with clothes, ideas, sexual partners, teachers, heroes—renewing the differentiation of good and bad, teetering on the edge in his choice of affiliation.

The astonishing metamorphosis of child into young adult at this time can be traced during analysis and be seen to relate to a very great extent to the enrichment of the qualities of the internal objects that result from this new or, rather, renewed hunger for objects. Nor is it only the human relationships that are sifted by the capacity for admiration and wonder, but the whole world. The internal objects seem fairly to reach out into the given world and probe its infinite variety for facets to add to their own adornment. The original figures of the parents and their qualities of mind become transfigured by this accretion so as to be fairly unrecognizable to the adolescent, with the result that a temporary, and sometimes permanent, sense of disappointment in the external parents ruptures all sense of mutual understanding, continuity, communication. But as a mating relationship takes shape and the stresses of preserving and extending a single union strip pretence to the nakedness beneath, so the objects become stripped, simplified, reduced in dazzle, and valued once more for their more enduring and deeper qualities. Mysteriously, external parents begin to improve once more, and a new respect and fondness supersedes the childish idealization that had been internally augmented and externally dismissed. Something of this process, so similar to a recovery from a mental illness, is represented, as we shall see, in "The Homecoming".

Interpretation of Harold Pinter's "The Homecoming"

We will be analysing the content of this play at a level corresponding to the threshold of the depressive position, in which the mother, Ruth–Jessie, returns to dominion over the inner world from which she had been expelled (death) by the subject's oedipal triumph. The intellectual part of the little boy (Teddy) had taken her away as wife from the split in the sexuality of both father (Max and Sam) and child (Lenny and Joey). This process is reversed in the course of the two acts of the play.

ACT I, Scene 1

7/2 The contrast between the phallic Lenny (pencil in
7/7 hand) and the impotent Max (carries a stick) accen-

tuates the fact that this part of the split father is
7/10 searching for an aspect of himself (scissors), which
7/5 he derived in the past from his own mother's breast
8/2 (sideboard) and its warmth (flannel vest). Clearly, in
8/15 being split into Max and Sam, the strength and
kind-heartedness were both diminished by becom-
ing separated from each other, bringing about also
a loss of continuity with his own father-and-son
8/18 past (MacGregor), as well as his capacity for sexual
9/2 love (fond of your mother). Instead, revulsion to-
9/6 wards the female genital (rotten stinking; bleeding)
9/12 and confusion with the faecal penis (lousy, filthy
father) earn only contempt from the phallic Lenny-
9/16 part, which recognizes that Max's words have be-
9/24 come flatus (Second Wind) but cannot feel the
nostalgia for the lost love of the mother (horses)
10/2 hidden in the bombast, in the covert reference to
10/7 coitus, birth, raising the children (held them;
calmed them; a trainer). The babies inside the
10/17 mother (colts and fillies) were the object of his coital
gift to her. This has all given way to impotence
11/17 (don't clout me) and muddle (dog cook; you bitch).
The Sam-part of the father is powerless in a quite
different way, the kind-heartedness and desire to
serve the mother turned to homosexual subservi-
11/21 ence (chauffeur; a Yankee at the Savoy) due to a
11/27 combination of loss of vitality (tired), confusions of a
11/31 zonal sort, anus–vagina (up the M4), male–female
12/21 (overpass and underpass), penis–faeces (box of ci-
12/32 gars), top–bottom (up at the Savoy—down to house
in Eaton Square) and need for praise (best he ever
had). The two parts of the father have regressed to
the relationship of jealous and rivalrous siblings
13/27 (they do get jealous); Sam idealizing his impotence (I
don't take liberties) while Max still denies his; Sam
14/2 is obsessional (a . . . b) while Max is disorganized;
Sam luxuriates in projective identification with a
14/5 powerful phallus (men of affairs in a Humber Super
Snipe), while Max is still boastful and rivalrous;
14/13 Sam is the eternal little brother (too young for the

First World War). He is the latency-boy waiting to
15/5 be rewarded by elevation to adult status (there's
still time) by the Big Brother he serves as if he were
15/18 a daddy but really despises (above all that). He is
still waiting for the breast to be brought back to
16/10 him (bride-apple) for the splitting which reduced
16/15 the lover-father to the Max-phallus, and Sam-heart
is indistinguishable emotionally from a weaning
(never get a bride like you had). At this moment of
recollection, the Max-Sam almost comes together in
16/24 the pain of mourning (Christ-Jessie). It is a suitable
moment for the entrance of the good-baby part of
the Lenny-Joey boy, who has never accepted his
17/1 weaning (hungry) or the loss of the mother involved
17/5 in the oedipal erotism (go and find yourself a
mother). Joey's need, Sam's helplessness, and
17/22 Lenny's mockery of the past (he used to like tucking
up his sons) sweep away the grief in impotent irrita-
bility, which is quickly projected onto the baby Joey
18/15 (you don't know how to defend or attack) and his
18/18 longing for the breast (go straight to the top—goes
up the stairs). The momentary rapprochement be-
19/5 tween Max and Sam breaks wide open, and the
conflict over Jessie can be seen to have been rooted
in an uncertain integration reaching back into
19/23 childhood (our mother's house—our father's house),
19/31 and part-object ambivalence (mother-mess, father-
cast-iron crap). The full extent of the lost intro-
20/2 jective identification is laid bare (Our father? I
remember him).

Scene 2

In this atmosphere of remembrance, the pseudo-
mature intellectual-boy Teddy and his mummy-
20/15 wife Ruth, with their part-object equipment (two
suitcases, the key in his hand) arrive during the
20/23 dream-life (they're asleep). Like Sam, the Ruth-
20/27 mother is tired of life with the little boy and resent-

21/6 ful of his self-idealization (it can't have moved).
Teddy clearly feels he has made time stand still for
the others by taking the mother away and is fright-
21/15 ened of their hostility (shall I go up?—like Joey
previously), for he clearly feels that he got the best
of the others in taking the sexual Ruth–mother
22/8 away (the wall), leaving the others with the lifeless
22/11 and undifferentiated house-mother (The structure
wasn't affected, you see. My mother was dead). But
22/16 in returning to triumph over them (just go to bed.
See them all in the morning) he is bringing about a
proximity of children and parents that he may not
22/24 be able to break up again (children missing us—
stay for a few days). So completely has he split the
23/5 sexual Ruth from the feeding Jesse–mother (I was
born here—I know) that he cannot comprehend her
23/24 self-containment (you don't have to go to bed). The
tide of strength and dependence is turning already
24/24 (But what am I going to do?), and we can see the
25/7 child with his mother (Why don't you go to bed?).

Scene 3

Left alone at night by mother, the split between the
Teddy–intellect and the phallic-Lenny parts comes
25/28 together in insomniac rumination (Can't sleep) con-
26/6 cerning the primal scene (something keeps waking
me up—a tick), in which their communication is
27/2 interfered with by differing points of view (Lenny
sleeping downstairs, Teddy upstairs) about time
28/10 and status (the clock).

Scene 4

For while Teddy has erotized and married the
27/11 breasts (suitcases), Lenny is preoccupied with
28/29 Ruth–genital (an aperitif?) and in exhibiting his

29/9 penis (clock—things that tick in the night, i.e. also
30/10 her clitoris). Denigration of Teddy (old Ted) and of
the relationship (sort of live with him over there) is
30/23 mixed with sexual innuendo (Venice: Venus, later
29/31 Greek Street; aperitif; aphrodisiac; the two glasses
of water) in caricature of Sam's technique with his
30/27 "man of affairs" (too young for the war) as a prelude
31/1 to physical contact (just a tickle). The mother's re-
buff brings out the threat of violence aimed at arous-
31/21 ing her masochism (clumped her one), but it is
coupled with the clear evidence of his confusion
31/17 between vagina and rectum (under the arch—falling
31/8 apart with pox) due to masturbation (playing about
the yardarm) while voyeuristically viewing the pri-
mal scene (men jibbing the boom out in the harbour)
in the parental bedroom, where he had been
31/24 brought by the kind-hearted daddy (chauffeur—
Sam) because of his night-terrors. The challenge to
32/6 his omniscience (How did you know she was dis-
eased?) brings increased respect for the mother
32/11 (newly-weds?), a desire to link himself with the intel-
lectual-Teddy-part (my favourite brother) and a
monologue, in contrast to the "playing with the
yardarm" one, filled with manic-reparative strivings
32/29 (snow-clearing, before cock-crow, the old lady and
her iron mangle) and a desire to clarify the con-
33/15 fusions such as vagina–rectum (front-room and
back-room) in competition with the father (brother-
33/23 in-law). This collapses in the face of his inferiority
33/35 (weighed half a ton) into a Sam-type pseudo-helpful-
ness (take this ashtray out of your way). A test of
strength ensues (give me the glass) in which the
34/13 Ruth–Jesse mother puts the Leonard-boy in his
35/9 place by reminding him how small he is (sit on my
35/1 lap, take a sip) and bringing out his jealousy (in love
with another man). The lady-under-the-arch and
35/22 the old-lady-with-the-mangle have come together to
control his violence and oedipal bombasts (shouts,
"Some kind of proposal?").

Scene 5

The presence of the Ruth–Jesse mother is making
itself felt even with the Max–father, whose irritabil-
36/8 ity now betrays concern for the children (You been
shouting at Joey? I think we got burglars here. I
36/14 think he's got a knife stuck in him), matched by
36/29 tenderness hidden in Lenny's oedipal cheek (the
night you got me—with Mum), and the brazen
37/9 flaunting of his masturbatory preoccupation with
37/14 the primal scene (ruminate singly and in groups).
37/23 Both are in pain and wildly projecting it (pop it to
you—spits at him).

Scene 6

Max in pain, in seeking to link his loneliness for the
38/10 mother (I hate this room) to someone, the Joey-
baby or the Sam–brother, for he is also guilty about
40/14 his violence (accuses Sam of spitting), stirred by the
39/23 contrast of present and past (room vs. kitchen,
Sam's behaviour in the kitchen). In a flurry of guilty
40/22 muddle he tries to idealize his violence (I commem-
orated his name in blood. I gave birth to three grown
men) while belittling the gentleness of the Sam part
40/26 as effeminate (you tit), confusing nipple and penis.
Into this comic atmosphere, the appearance of the
44/3 Ruth–mother (You a mother?) brings a gust of tear-
44/10 fulness (I didn't know) and spite (Teddy, why don't
we have a nice cuddle and kiss, eh?) towards her
44/8 (all yours, Ted?)

ACT II

Having brought the mother back to life and integration in the inner world, the process of reintegration of the Max–Sam father, combining strength and gentleness, can commence.

SCENE 1

Still split into Max and Sam, the Max-father, with
his spite and homosexuality, is prone to compete
45/13 with and bait the mother (first-rate cook). He resists
recognition of the resolved split in the Ruth–Jessie
45/21 mother (what would Jessie say) out of guilt for his
46/3 lack of heart (she had a heart; right, Sam?). This
46/13 builds into a spiral of self-justification (generous
man to her) for the split from the kind Sam-part
46/21 (what happened to that pouffe), which, when it
46/31 comes up against the goodness of the mother (knelt
down; like Christmas), collapses into a torrent of
47/14 abuse (bile come up in my mouth) at the slightest
46/33 challenge from the Ruth–mother (What happened),
touching on his identification with his own father
47/17 at part-object level (chopper and slab), projecting
his guilt for neglect onto the impotent Sam-part
47/26 (lazy idle bugger of a brother) for his passive anal
48/4 homosexual attitude (you'd bend over for half a
dollar). Having widened the split again (Sam goes
out), Max resumes the homosexual attitude towards
Teddy with flattery, along with patronization of the
Ruth–mother, out of renewed loneliness and guilt
49/16 (let bygones be bygones). It seems clear that the
split in the father and neglect of the mother dated
49/6 from the birth of Teddy (first-born), which had split
the mother and enthralled her sexuality to the baby
50/6 (I was different) at the breast as a virgin mother
49/22 (Doctor of Philosophy sitting down drinking). Her
guilt towards the father and the two younger
children has brought her back despite Teddy's
50/19 idealization (we've got everything). Their need of her
51/9 (children missing their mother) has freed her from
51/15 thralldom to Teddy's intelligence (Your cigar's gone
out). An immediate improvement in the intelligence
51/4 of the Joey–Lenny child results (hope to be full time;
logical incoherence in the central affirmations of
51/27 Christian theism?) from the improved integration
52/20 and humility (some people would envy your
certainty, wouldn't they, Joey?). The Ruth–Jessie

mother has re-established the primary significance
53/5 of non-verbal modes of communication (more sig-
nificant than the words) for emotionality, intimacy.
The barrenness of her romance with the Teddy–
53/13 Jesus baby is clear to her (it's all rock). Her love has
53/23 entered into Joey and linked Lenny to him (I'll come
with you).

Scene 2

This integration of the infantile masculinity, Joey–
Lenny, makes it possible for an adult masculinity to
54/13 begin to detach itself (your family here) from its
primary objects through the acknowledgement of
54/25 time (six hours behind us; six years ago in 53/11),
but not without struggle with its nostalgia for the
55/17 delight of mutual idealization (we can bathe till Oc-
tober). The mother, on the other hand, regrets her
failure of contact with other parts of the child, the
55/24 phallic-Lenny (nurse in the Italian campaign—[see
30/25]), for instance.

Scene 3

The opportunity to remedy this is immediately
seized, with the Ruth-mother showing her breasts
56/22 (shoes) to the Lenny-part to try to recover the hal-
57/1 cyon days (a model before I went away). But for him
the idealization is heavily freighted with anxiety and
57/4 depression (in a glass case) towards the nipple
57/7 (cloche of black veiling—i.e. *Clochemerle*). Really it
was only while the babies were still inside her
57/9 (model for the body) that she felt identified with an
57/16 idealized mother (place in the country) with bounte-
57/18 ous breasts (large white water tower) with a desire to
58/24 feed babies (Dancing. Lenny kisses Ruth). The reun-
58/22 ion of parents and baby (Max and Joey come in)
leaves the differentiated adult masculinity with only

58/21 a memory of a collapsed idealization (Teddy stands, with Ruth's coat). This is the metapsychological climax of the play, filled with tension of mixed emotion, erotized, on the verge of tears and laughter, as the tables are turned on the triumphant oedipal boy
59/20 (Joey lies heavily on Ruth, a "woman beneath you").
59/24 The mother has assumed control of her children, is
60/5 feeding them (rolls off the sofa—a tumbler), and
61/5 must be fed in turn by the father's testicles (rocks). The Teddy-boy has become the Teddy-man and realized the gap between adult and infantile sexual-
61/29 ity (operate on things and not in things). It is the precondition for introspection and self-observation
62/2 (to see: I can see what you do. It's the same as I do.
62/8 But you're lost in it.) and anguish.

Scene 4

This anguish is the result of the nostalgia for the mutual idealization of the oedipal romance, and so long as the Teddy-man clings to it, he is vulnerable
65/27 to the mockery of the parasitic Lenny-boy (we live a less rich life here than you do over there, etc.), but it can be seen that this nostalgia is based on the continued split in the father and the indulgence of
63/2 the tender-hearted Sam-part (always your mother's favourite). The honesty of the Joey-baby undercuts
69/9 it (sometimes you can be happy—and not go the whole hog) and sets the stage for the desexualization of the breast (without going any hog) and the reintegration of the father's potency and kindness. This occupies the denouement of the play, represented in such items as the mother being set up in Greek Street, the "death" of Sam, Max on his knees before her sobbing that he's not an old man, and finally Teddy going away but told by the mother not to be a "stranger", i.e. not to deny psychic reality. The curtain falls on a scene fairly indistinguishable from a Nativity, mixed with a Pietà.

Discussion

I have skimped the analysis of the last part of the play to allow the reader the fun of trying his hand, but also because it is not necessary to our discussion of sincerity. Taken *in toto*, it is a play about the recovery from the relative sterility of the latency period, intensified here by an oedipal success in establishing an intellectualized *folie á deux* between mother and child as one might see in an obsessional character disturbance. Despite this intensification, the general application of the play to the role of adolescence in the development of personality is very clear, for we are able to watch a process set out in great detail whereby the pseudo-adult Teddy, united with his enthralled Ruth–mother, must give way to the lonely and responsible adult–Teddy struggling not to be a "stranger" to his internal situation—that is, not to lapse back, settle down, lose contact with the internal sources of feeling and motivation towards the world.

The process that Pinter sets out matches in a most reassuring way that seen in the analytic consulting-room at the point of maximal conflict, which I have described as the "threshold of the depressive position". For this reason it can serve us in lieu of clinical material for examining the improvements in sincerity that accompany specific steps forward in integration of self and objects during this struggle. It is important to remember that this play, unlike "The Birthday Party", is a comedy and has no character to represent the destructive part of the personality, as Goldberg and McCann do. What we see of violence is all talk, bark without bite, and demonstrates relics of the influence of such destructiveness in the past, represented in references to the two World Wars. It is therefore a play full of hope and of hilarity as confusion after confusion is paraded and clarified. It is a combination of dream-play and comedy of manners, of mystery-play and farce. Of its richness, we are only, surely, teasing out a particular thread of interpretation for our own purposes of exposition.

I have emphasized in the interpretations this link of philosophy, theology, and dream-language in order to bring out the emotionality contained in the poetic use that Pinter makes of language. He juxtaposes the idiom of different age groups, different regions, and different classes for the purpose of delineating the barriers to communication. In our interpretive terms, it also brings out a certain aspect of splitting processes that is germane to the problem of variations in the quality of sincerity. Our best approach might be a fairly orderly one, of examining the defective sincerity of each character at the beginning of the play and the progress made during its course.

I want to start with the Joey–baby part of the child because of his being the least disturbed in this area to begin with and the first to make the change to utter frankness in declaring that you can be happy and not go the "whole hog", in fact, "no hog at all". Joey's impaired sincerity takes the form of boastfulness and consequent vulnerability to flattery and manipulation by Lenny. He seems all muscular, a greedy penis–tongue that is set into violent pre-genital Oedipal rage at the thought of anyone getting "the gravy" [70/2] other than himself. His recovery of the breast, the "two hours" upstairs with the Ruth–mother [69/19] moves him immediately from frustrated braggart to humble devotee. This can be taken as the essential move in his improved sincerity, to desire his dependence upon the breast to be known, which stands in contrast to Lenny's story of how Joey said to the "bird" in the car, "Yes you will. Never mind about the contraceptive protection" [68/27]. In his abandonment of the "whole hog" he wishes it to be understood that he is dependent upon the generosity of the breast.

The progress of the Lenny-part of the child is a more complicated matter, for his impaired sincerity is based upon phallic preoccupations and resentment of being a child who is "too young for the war". His rectification is a more step-wise affair, which starts with Ruth convincing him that femininity is based upon an admiring dependence of the woman upon the man's genital (the woman with the iron-mangle as a gift from her brother-in law [p. 32]) and not her masochistic submission to big-brother brutality (the woman under the arch and her proposition [p. 31]). This move towards acceptance of inferiority to the father moves Lenny closer to the Joey–baby, as shown later in his expectation of Joey going the "whole hog" with Ruth and the story of the two "birds" in the car [p. 68]. But Joey's move towards humility blocks this avenue and forces Lenny to attempt a projective identification with the Max-butcher penis in formulating the plan for setting Ruth up in "Greek Street" [p. 72], not reckoning on the possibility that she might not be "adaptable" [82/22]. In the final tableau, Lenny is left in silence, watching the father offer his love to the mother. His move towards sincerity is therefore one that takes him from phallic sadistic erotization of his relation to the mothers genital (under the arch) to a genital inferiority to the father's genital (men jibbing the boom out in the harbour [31/8]) with its reparative capacity, the snow-shovelling [32/11] so reminiscent of the activity of the "dwarfs". Acceptance of inferiority to his good object is then the particular quality of sincerity that the Lenny part achieves.

These accomplishments of the infantile masculinity form the background to the changes from pompous pseudo-man to adult masculinity in the Teddy-part, but before we can understand that fully, it is necessary to trace the changes in Max and Sam to form the Max–Sam–father who can offer his love to the mother-with-child. It seems clear that a honeymoon period of integration towards the Ruth–Jessie mother had existed despite the strain imposed by her vanity about her beauty (the model aspect) derivative from her girlish projective identification (the place in the country [p. 57]) with her own mother. But the birth of her first-born had swept her into a *folie á deux* with a very desexualized and messianic aspect of the child, which had made poor contact with other aspects of his masculinity. (We must remember that the child's femininity is not at all represented in the play, as, for instance, it is in "The Birthday Party" by Lulu—probably a direct take-over from Wedekind's heroine.) This loss of contact with her husband had split him into Max and Sam because of its link with his own oedipal period, epitomized in the play by what amounts to a recovery of an infantile amnesia, Sam's revelation that "MacGregor had Jessie in the back of my car" [79/10].

The recovery of integration of the Max–Sam father, in full introjective identification with his own MacGregor–father, who was both a driver [48/10] and a butcher [40/18] is consummated by this recollection of a primal scene, and the integration is represented in the "death" of Sam. In other words, the Lenny-part had achieved his capacity to tolerate inferiority partly through the realization that the Max–Sam father had once been a little boy in the same position with regard to his MacGregor–daddy. This is not the same as an identification but is, rather, in the nature of an understanding about the adult–child differentiation and its basis in the reality of time and development.

The same realization moves the Teddy part into introjective identification, and his pain-wracked speech [p. 61] reveals that he has come to understand the pain and sacrifice that the parents must bear in order to understand and help children by participating in their lives without being "lost in it". It makes clear that Teddy's move towards sincerity has taken him some distance from priggish arrogance, which prides itself on its benevolence when it is in fact triumphant, on its generosity when it is in fact contemptuous, on its courtesy when it is in fact aloof. All this changes to an awareness of responsibility for action based on understanding both internal and external reality (on things and in things [61/29]) to which he must gradually resign himself through recognition that his infantile oedipal triumph was merely a dream of cruelty and egotism. He must, like the father, find both heart and strength to offer a woman.

Here, then, in summary and outline, are the qualities of mind that progress towards greater sincerity during the course of Pinter's great play: boastfulness gives way to humility (Joey); sadism yields to a sense of inferiority (Lenny); sentimentality alters to passion (Sam); violence changes to strength (Max); vanity metamorphoses into tenderness (Ruth); and arrogance is replaced by a sense of responsibility (Teddy). Our problem is to comprehend the connection between these changes in the quality of social feeling and the processes of integration of self and objects.

5
Integration and sincerity

Now that our rather arid theoretical discussions have been brought to life by the magic of Pinter's art, it should be possible for us to retrace the ground in a more emotional way, investigating, as promised, the mysterious "atmosphere" that exists in human relationships. From childhood on we have again and again the opportunity to observe how quickly people find their "place" with one another and with groups. The resemblance of the processes to animal behaviour tempts the ethologist to generalizations that can only be explained by some sort of denial of psychic reality in him that will not recognize the subtlety and variety of human emotionality. But a similar lack of imagination must underlie the fairly ubiquitous tendency of human beings to sit in judgement upon one another, to think that they can "see"—to use Teddy's term—directly the meaning of behaviour without "balancing" and "allying" the two different aspects of experience, of "operating—on things—and in things". I suggest that the essence of the psychoanalytic method is just this, that the analyst must attempt to see what is happening in the relationship between himself and his patient by making both sets of observations, on and in, transference and countertransference, external and internal experience of the moment.

The consequent distinction may perhaps be expressed in our language by the nuance of difference between "sitting in judgement" and "having a judgement", the latter always implying primarily, "I notice that I tend to see him as . . .". When we "sit in judgement", we are only acting "on" the other person, and when we respond directly without judgement, we are only acting "in" the relationship. Teddy's behaviour until the end is entirely of this first variety, while Lenny's, for instance, is of the latter. In consequence, their dealings with one another, although carried on exclusively in words, have virtually no significance as communication but only as action upon one another's states of mind. One can see that a total failure of intimacy based upon mutual distrust results, which is very different from the failure of intimacy between Stanley and Lulu. That seems totally due to Stanley's unavailability as a result of withdrawal inside his object. One cannot, later on, speak of Stanley as "insincere", as he is not in the kind of contact that will permit him to say-what-he-means, later absolute mutism.

On the other hand, Goldberg and McCann achieve an intimacy that is not equalled in the three plays until Ruth's two hours upstairs with Joey. Their communication, the atmosphere of their relationship, is perhaps most beautifully illustrated in the sheer perversity of Goldberg asking McCann to blow in his mouth, "one for the road". Is it any wonder that pervert or, rather, perverse intimacy engenders an experience that negativism can call "love" and defy the world to prove otherwise. If we are to exploit the opportunity that art of the quality of Pinter's offers us for pouring emotional meaning into the containers of our psychoanalytic jargon, we must try to come to grips with this mystery of intimacy that breaches the solipsistic loneliness of individual mind and renders it tolerable.

Absolute isolation and relative intimacy

I want to use the word "intimacy" in a manner free from implication as to the quality, emotionally, of a relationship, but only having reference to the social distance. From this point of view, its limits, on a spectrum, would be isolation on the one hand and fusion on the other. In a certain sense these two limits, more like east and west than the ends of a spectrum, tend to meet at the antipodes, since fusion in one direction imposes isolation in all others. Stanley's fusion with Meg and Petey's house, or the Goldberg–McCann fusion, would be examples of this principle of narcissism, as regards narcissistic identifications as well as narcissistic organizations.

At these two narcissistic extremes, the quest for intimacy is seen to cease, represented as a place—Monte, i.e. hell or schizophrenia—or a person—Monte, i.e. Satan . . . or psychopathy? Between the two extremes lies a broad band of variations in intimacy and, I am suggesting, sincerity. In other words, I am trying to investigate this quality of social contact free of moral bias that would view it as a virtue. I wish to take it as a fact that can be observed in daily life, in the consulting-room, in others and in ourselves, in our external and in our internal relations. It is well to remember that our concern is with sincerity as a momentary phenomenon, the social contract of the instant. The characterological aspect, which can reasonably be endowed with a moral quality and considered a virtue, can be set aside temporarily.

This social contract of the moment is the focus of our interest. When Len says that someone is "driving a tank" [114/24] the image conveys quite completely that communication has ceased in favour of naked aggression. But it also implies that communication has ceased because one party has moved inside a part-object, the daddy's penis presumably, and that this disparity in the geography of phantasy, one inside and one outside an object, precludes understanding. I think this is correct—that for understanding to exist, direct contact is necessary. A meeting of the minds may exist between two parts of the self, for instance, so long as they are both inside the same object, regardless of the fact that so being may induce a most psychotic distortion of experience. If, on the contrary, as so often happens in the acting out of bisexual infantile phantasies, the two are inside different objects, then their contact is nullified regardless of the degree of intimacy and understanding between the objects they have invaded. This can be seem to be the case in the "dolls'-house" type of marriage, where a sort of continual honeymoon exists and love is wonderful—"I love me and you love me".

The first point, then, would be that contact, as a precondition to sincerity, requires geographic contiguity in terms of unconscious phantasy. This may be either within or without the sphere of good objects. For instance, Lenny's contrasting accounts of the "lady with the certain proposition" and the "lady with the iron mangle" represent encounters with part-objects, in this case the mother's anus-vagina, undifferentiated. The first is experienced as outside the sphere of a good object, "under the arch", while the second is within that sphere, "in the borough", a pun on "burrow!" "Under the arch" no contact occurs because of the confusion, that the object is within while Lenny is outside the sphere of the good breast, as Ruth shows when she punctures his omniscience with the question, "How did you know she was diseased?"

Our second condition for intimacy of contact, and therefore sincerity, would be that the two parties must inhabit the same emotive world, within or without the sphere of good objects. Until Scene XVI in "The Dwarfs", Mark inhabits the sphere of sensual perversity with Pete, and their contact is fairly intimate. By that point the baby, Len, having disengaged himself and being now committed to his good objects, feels the same loneliness that Teddy must face without becoming a "stranger". That is, he must accept differentiation from his good objects and, by exchanging dependence for identification, form the core for a new structure, the adult part of the personality.

In this regard it is important to note that intimate contact is often made through sallies outside the accustomed sphere. Bad parts of the self all too often invade the sphere of good objects, especially during times of separation or stress, to subvert and lead astray the infantile parts of the personality. Conversely, sallies for reclaiming the apostate or converting the heathen can be made beyond the sphere of good objects by good infantile parts or, more often, by the adult part of the personality. But it is a dangerous business for the self, best left to the good objects. It is perhaps quite central to our ideas of the "heroic" and our suspicion of the motives of flesh-and-blood "heroes". Yet there undoubtedly are heroes and saints. Freud was a hero. Was Rembrandt a saint?

These qualities, of hero and saint, are really applicable to the internal objects and characterize their activities in fostering development. Ruth's reclamation of the family consists largely of the impact of her saintliness, of the "tree of Jesse". The transference of such objects runs very powerfully at the threshold of the depressive position during analytic treatment, and an equally powerful current of megalomania can be stirred in the countertransference. Certainly the psychoanalytic method does not require either heroism or saintliness of the analyst, only a spirit of adventure.

In delineating two metapsychological conditions for intimacy, geographical contiguity, and identity of emotional world (it is possible that intimacy, for instance, could exist between two schizophrenic—schizophrenic what? parts of the personality? patients?—two schizophrenic systems of delusion), the groundwork is laid for investigating degrees of intimacy as social distance, internal and external, in order to see whether it is the sole determinant of sincerity of communication. There are a number of interesting moments in "The Homecoming" when one or another character seeks an alliance. For instance, the painful recollection of Jessie that Sam stirs in Max [16/20] in Scene I results in his pleading with Joey to go to the football match with him [38/27] in Scene 6, Act I. He is being driven by the pain of his loneliness and his guilt.

Or consider the situation that follows Lenny's reduction to infantile helplessness at Ruth's hands, when he approaches Max on the subject of his own conception, "the night you got me—with mum". His approach is driven also, like Max's to Joey, by pain, but it is heavily hedged by the impulse to project the pain. His sincerity is undercut and almost obscured in provocative cheek [36/29]. Consider the difference between Max saying to Teddy, "Why don't we have a nice cuddle and kiss, eh?" at the end of Act I and his pleading on his knees, "Kiss me" to Ruth at the end of Act II. In the former he is totally insincere, bent on spitefully wounding the Ruth–mother for her desertion of him in favour of the child. In the latter he is totally sincere, having become convinced that she "won't be—adaptable!" Contrast this with Teddy's speech, about how he can "see" [62/2]. He is in pain, but it is driving him away from his objects, and he has to be cautioned by Ruth, as he departs later, not to "be a stranger".

The point about these instances of variation in intimacy and sincerity is that, first of all, they all relate to pains connected with loving and are thereby essentially depressive in quality. The variations in sincerity cannot be accounted for quantitatively in respect of the intensity of the pain, but they can be seen to relate to the degree to which it is accepted.

What is true of these depressive pains can probably be taken as being true of emotionality and communication about it in general. The degree to which the emotion is accepted is a limiting factor to the degree to which it can be made understandable to someone else externally, or to another part of the self or object internally. This may help us, for instance, to understand why it is that small children and adolescents are far more capable of sincerity and intimacy than are latency children or their counterpart among the grown-ups, those "settled-down". In both small children and adolescents, a great flux is present regarding the sense of identity, so that the different infantile parts are repeatedly seizing the organ of consciousness, and thus of communication. The result, momentarily, is often urgent, direct, and sincere communication, both of emotion and concerning emotion. But since the part in control changes very rapidly, taken over a period of time the communication may seem so full of contradictions as to approximate hypocrisy.

The balanced committee-type organization of infantile structures seen in the latency child is quite different in its consequences. Because internal conflict is great and every decision must be a compromise internally if an obsessional stalemate is to be avoided, this so undercuts the possibility of emotionality being either fully experienced or accepted that a stilting of manner and expression results. Quite different from either being-unable-to-mean-what-one-says or to say-what-one-means, this aspect of insincerity could, rather, be called being-unable-to-mean-anything-in-particular. It is the bourgeois position, which, if it were to speak sincerely, would have to say, "I'm in favour of the winning side". But that, after all, *is* a sentiment. It can both be held with conviction and expressed with sincerity. It can be the basis of very great intimacy, as one sees in groups, religions, political parties. It looks just as hypocritical to the adolescent as he looks to it. Both create their own society of we-and-they intimacy and snobbery.

Sincerity as an aspect of character

The rather sad truth is that character is more of a concept than a fact. With the exception of the extraordinarily ill and the unusually healthy, the degree of instability in personality functioning is far too great in the real world to approximate the term employed in literature. In the consulting-room one sees the analysand-character, and the patient sees the analyst-character. The wife sees the husband, and the friend sees the friend. The rigidity imposed by severe illness creates a stable social character, and development towards integration aims at it.

But the great majority of people do evolve a healthy part of the personality, which can emerge to dominate activity and feeling in certain situations. Not surprisingly, as this structure, the adult part of the personality, arises through introjective identification with good objects, it is most in evidence in the bosom of the family, in parental functions. In consequence we find that the mother with her baby and the father with his small children display the highest degree of intimacy and sincerity of which the individual is capable. It is probably a somewhat rarer function between the parents, even in the passion of their sexual union, as this must require a further step in the integration of the internal objects into the combined whole-object of "being in love". The evolution traced in "The Homecoming" does not proceed this far, though it gives promise of doing so, of recovering that state of union represented in the image proclaimed by Sam, that "MacGregor had Jessie in the back seat of my cab as I drove them along" [79/10]—The Flight into Egypt. The evolution of the analytic process in the consulting-room also does not proceed this far, but we can, by an imaginative extrapolation, see its outline in our patients, and in ourselves.

6
Sincerity and social role

Up to this point I have rather parasitized Harold Pinter's genius for the purpose of presenting findings from the analytic consulting-room. In his representation of life, characters play their parts in a formal drama. I now wish to turn the process upside down and investigate the formal aspects of the drama of life as people live it with one another in the outside world. My purpose is to seek a bridge between the findings of psychoanalysis, which, by the very nature of the method, throw a specific light only upon those processes of the mind that make the individual unique, and those of the other human sciences—history, sociology, anthropology, etc.—that deal more with man as a social creature within his milieu.

But my purpose is not only a bridging one. By investigating the relation of sincerity, and thus of intimacy, to the concept of social role, I hope to bring to light another dimension of the central problem of this chapter—namely, the requirement for the successful implementation of the capacity for sincerity. Of course I am in a certain sense primarily interested in the transactions of the analytic consulting-room, but secondarily I hope to show that these disciplined circumstances can help us understand what goes on in less strictly prescribed and circumscribed occasions of human relations.

The material I wish to present, interestingly, centres upon the dream of a patient in which *she had to play a part in Wilde's "The Importance of Being Earnest"*. It demonstrates a very interesting thing indeed—namely, that knowing a social role and being able to play it with spontaneous sincerity have their roots in two very different aspects of psychic reality. It cannot escape anyone's notice that these two functions are relatively seldom combined successfully. Daily we meet people who know their social role—often many different ones—but play them with a lack of spontaneity and imagination. Similarly, in small children and adolescents we are accustomed to seeing spontaneity, imagination—and sincerity—amply displayed, but in a socially amorphous, confused, and confusing manner. How does the rarer combined function come about, and why is it in fact such a rarity?

Rather than following the usual procedure of exposition, stating thesis, then supposedly giving the evidence in support and finally a discussion, I wish to follow a procedure that is more honestly representative of psychoanalytic thought by presenting the description of a clinical experience for exploration.

This young woman had been forced to leave analysis in adolescence after about a year, when, despite her desire for help, she had been so persistently unable to speak that continuation seemed futile. When she returned to analysis a few years later, this difficulty did not present itself as an absolute obstacle but only as a continually threatening trend, which occupied part of every hour and always seemed in danger of spreading over the proceedings. Some progress seemed to take place in the revival of her oedipal conflict through the analysis of her narcissism, and, prior to a small holiday break, she was rather startled by the evidence of ill-will towards the analytic father indicative of wishing him dead. The following night she had a dream that took nearly half the session to report and seems full of implications regarding her tendency to mutism of a sort.

In order to do it justice, I wish to present it along with associated material—that is, along with the patient's immediate associations, aspects of earlier analytic material that are clearly linked, and the analyst's and patient's tentative interpretations. I will do this by dividing the page so that the reader may take the dream on its own to begin with in order to form his own impression before dealing with the associated material and interpretations.

Dream	*Associated material*
She was with her friend Di, and they were preparing to act in a play that was at their old school, though it seemed to be located in the West End. They had to put on their costumes, and hers, a taffeta gown to the ground, was wrinkled, and she was ironing it, though, she thought, it was silly to be so concerned as no one in the audience would be able to notice.	Her friend Di (Diana) seems often to enter when some reference to the death of her father or fear of other losses is in the material. The dress seems a pun on her feeling "too fat" to allow her legs to be seen by the analyst. She always wears trousers, although she thinks, rather than feels, that she is not too fat and that it is inconsequential to the analytic situation.
The play was "The Importance of Being Earnest" and was to start at 8:30, but it was already 8:25 and they were in her old flat in Hampstead. However, since Di did not seem concerned, she forgot about the matter, and they finally arrived at the theatre around 10:00 p.m.	The time of the patient's session is at 8:30, and she is almost always a few minutes late, contrary to conscious desire. Di seems here to represent a well-known figure in the analysis, of a good big sister who is a substitute for the mother but is often confused with her. What would be trust and dependence on the mother is rather caricatured in allowing this good big sister to do her thinking for her.
She became aware that she did not know her lines, partly because she had not learned them well and partly because she had not rehearsed them for several weeks. She thought she	We are promptly brought to the heart of the matter—that her lateness, her allowing her thinking to be done for her, her silence, her lack of earnestness in the analysis, all these are

must find a script to study, so she went upstairs. First she came to the dining hall of the school, which was closed, as a little boy prefect told her, so she passed on to the library, where another little boy prefect helped her to find what looked like a magazine but was in fact a script of the play. It was not really like her old school at all.

due to her not having learned how to play her part in a verbal way. This she must learn from the mother's breasts (dining-room and library) and nipples (little boy prefects). But clearly this is not a suitable representation for the nipples.

In the play she and another girl had to walk across the stage, then do a samba, then sit at a cafe table pretending to chat. The other girl, one from school to whom she had had no real relationship, had to stride boldly ahead of her onto the stage, and the patient thought to herself that, although it was a play, it was also true in life that this girl was more bold than herself. Similarly, when they sat at the cafe table, they really did chat, and it really was a quite amusing conversation and their laughter was quite genuine, although also part of the play.

This part corresponded to one in "Ring Around the Moon", which she had played at school in fact. The observations relate to the analytic situation and her gradual realization of the psychic reality of the transference. The samba she dances with the other girl shows the erotization of the relation to the mother, confused with the good big sister, connected with the dream of the previous day, which indicated a wish to stay with the mother and send the daddy away to his death. The genuineness of the laughter refers to her appreciation of the way in which a humorous mode of presentation of infantile conflict in the material seems to help her to feel less humiliated or threatened.

At the moment in the analysis, then, we seem to be dealing with a pregenital oedipal conflict in which possessiveness of the mother as a whole object appears to interfere with the relation to the breast and nipple as part-objects. This in itself seems a bit puzzling until we realize that what looks like a whole-object relation to the mother is probably heavily contaminated with projective identification of a more mature part of herself, bringing about a narcissistic confusion between mother and good-big-sister for the baby part. We have much evidence to suggest that such a closeness has in fact played an important part in her life for many reasons—absence of the mother due to her profession, threat of domination by a big bad sister against which she could not protect herself, and probably an element of chronic depression in the mother she sought manically to repair with sisterliness, and sexuality.

Perhaps it would be useful to pause at his point to see how far we have come in locating the problem that this material seems to have hidden within it. We have, first of all, a hidden pun about the taffeta dress and the patient feeling her legs too fat to reveal to the analyst. This appears to be the bridging point between language and dream image that carries with it the implication of not knowing how to play her part with earnestness. The willingness to use language in this playful way runs counter to a precise use of language for communication and appears to inform us that we are in contact with the problem that Wittgenstein (*Philosophical Investigations*) defined as the difference between "saying it" and "meaning it". In more accustomed psychoanalytic terms we would be inclined to say that the patient is playing with language as a toy in a form of action or behaviour that constitutes an acting-in the transference in preference to the employment of language as a tool in the work of communication and cooperation in the analysis.

The infantile counterpart of this transference behaviour is represented in the dream as her mode of participation in the play, where she has not learned her part. Only after she has done the work of learning—that is, learning to transform her action in the maternal transference from doing the samba with the bold girl to having a conversation at the cafe table—only then is she in a position to recognize the psychic reality, the earnestness, the emotional truthfulness of the interaction. This takes us back, then, to what seemed a meaningless complication in the dream—namely, the fact that the dining-room was closed, but the library was open. The full significance of this item seems clear now, for it declares that the dream is making reference to an important epoch in the baby's relationship to the mother when, in the process of weaning, it becomes necessary for the baby to transfer its concrete feeding relationship to the breast onto the mother's mind at a level of abstraction. In other words, we are confronted with the problem that must be quite crucial for the development of language, when the baby comes to recognize that it needs to feed its mind on the other mother's mind on the model of its earlier way of feeding its body on the mother's body—recently the breast, earlier the placenta.

We can now begin to see as well that the dream has a very complicated structural organization, in that the dining-room–library sequence and relation to the two little prefects stands in relation to the participation in the play as a internal situation does to an external one. It is necessary for the baby to learn from the breast of the internal mother how to put her state of mind into words in order that she may have an earnest relationship to the external mother and her mind. It is therefore of great importance that the current significance of the internal breast has shifted from the dining-room to library–breast. The implications that this relation to the library–breast is not as yet a satisfactory one seem hidden in the obscure items of the nipple being belittled as a little prefect and the breast being denigrated as a magazine. We cannot yet say the exact significance of these forms of attack.

We seem to have squeezed the dream very hard already, but perhaps we can still extract a few more drops of understanding from it if we go back to the item about her friend Di. As I have said, we already knew from recent material that we were dealing with a problem of separation from the mother in the transference confronting a short holiday break. The dream of the previous session had, as I have said, rather shocked the patient by its implication of sending the father to his death rather than allow the parents to go away together. The patient's willingness to be confused between mothers and big sisters certainly has, as one of its roots, the reluctance to have all her infantile dependence-eggs in the one basket, in view of the danger of the mother's dying. I suspect this to have its foundation in real maternal depression. But the big sister, albeit a good figure and related to the baby part of herself as a more mature part of the self, is not a figure who performs the necessary maternal function of fostering the baby's development.

This is represented in Di's casual attitude towards punctuality and, by implication, her willingness to do the patient's thinking for her.

May we therefore draw the implication that there is an important difference between Di doing the thinking and the library–breast supplying the magazine from which the patient can learn her part, the words she must speak in order to make her state of mind manifest verbally, as against behaviourally. Herein seems to lie the crux of the matter, that she cannot be earnest in her communication unless she knows the words. But what does it mean? Can one not act in earnest? Perhaps one can only act in earnest on another person's body, whereas to communicate in earnest to someone's mind one must speak . . . or sing, or paint a picture, or dance the samba alone.

But it is certainly clear that it is possible to speak without earnestness. Why is the patient silent when she cannot be earnest, instead of doing as others do in analysis, and as she undoubtedly does elsewhere, to use language as means of acting upon another person's mind in preference to communicating one's own state? The matter of the taffeta dress and of hiding her too-fat legs seems to imply that in the transference the alternative to honesty is secrecy, not deception at the moment. Perhaps it will change later in the analysis. But at the moment we are dealing with infantile problems where anxiety for the self and solicitous sparing of the object, the mother who might die, seem delicately balanced, while problems of hostility, envy, competition with the mother, etc. are in abeyance.

Somehow our inquiry seems unsatisfactory, disappointing. The dream gives every promise of hiding a precious insight, but so far what we have been able to extract seems a bit base metal, useful but neither beautiful not precious. The idea that "earnestness" or sincerity of communication requires "knowing one's part", and that this is dependent upon an internal relation to the "library–breast" at an infantile level, seems in a way no more than a tautology: "People of good character speak with sincerity", for we know that good character must have its foundation in the infantile relation to the breast. Still we must keep in mind that we are dealing with the problems of communication related to states of mind, not to the description of the external world—in a sense to the art rather than the science of communication, the part that cannot be subsumed under a mathematical exposition such as "information theory". The dream appears to pose a question that we have not come to grips with as yet: can a person mean-what-he-says if he does not himself know the meaning of it? If we accept that most communication of states of mind that employs language does not rely for its efficacy primarily on the syntactic and semantic aspects of the language but on a deeper, more primitive music, we might wish to say that the speaker does not himself "know" what he means but only "means it".

This is a very important problem in character structure as it is met with in analysis. Over and over again one finds that the person has a conception of himself that is compounded of his perception of other people's perception of him (i.e. identity as "the sum of so many reflections"—"The Dwarfs" [111/32]). In other words, we find that the patient has a severe limitation in his capacity for introspection and consequently, being unable to see inside himself to the essentials (or essences?) of his mental state, must try to see himself from the outside through the mirror of other people's minds. This is naturally a rather imprecise mode of operation: not only is the perception of other people's perception likely to be distorted by the processes of projective identification, but of course other people's perception is subject to constant manipulation by insincerity and dissimulation. In a way these two are very closely linked, for it is by deceptive forms of behaviour that we press ourselves into projective identification with external objects, just as the intrusion into internal objects is carried out by various forms of masturbatory activity and accompanying unconscious phantasy.

But in addition to the pitfalls and lack of precision of this method for the construction of an image of oneself, the method suffers a severe conceptual limitation. Although our conception of other people may be—no, certainly is—fundamentally based upon intuition of feelings and motives, our way of describing, or justifying of accounting for our opinion, not to say judgement, is descriptive in relation to behaviour—even fairly anecdotal. We are therefore inclined not to make manifest, or even truly to keep secret from a person those aspects of our intuition of his character that cannot be documented by observations of behaviour. In a sense it is only kindness and modesty to be sufficiently unsure of such intuition that you would be unwilling to make the opinion manifest, even though you would in all likelihood rely upon it to regulate your involvement with the other person. You might confide your intuition about the person to someone closer to you, but not to the person himself.

The result of this conceptual limitation is that our perception of other people's perception of us is more or less limited to behavioural categories and does not extend to motives and feelings. It leaves us in the lurch of making moral judgements about our own behaviour, having no access to the true interplay of the underlying good and evil. The point that I am trying to establish is that when a person is limited in the communication of his states of mind more or less to the employment of projective identificatory aspects of behaviour and language, he can rarely get back from other people a useful evacuation of his mental state, since its perception by the other person must rely almost wholly on intuition. I say "rarely" because clearly the function that an analyst tries to perform in the consulting-room, of describing his intuition of the patient's state of mind, is not a function that has been invented, patented, or held in monopoly by psychoanalysis.

Now if we go back to our patient's dream, it was clear that to "play her part", she had to go to the library. But on the stage she had not only to speak to the bold girl at the cafe table but to do a samba with her beforehand. It was clear in the dream that in fact her part, as written in the magazine, did not have an actual speech, but only a description of the situation at the cafe table. The two girls were meant to *simulate* a gay conversation, by mumbling "rhubarb, rhubarb" presumably in the ordinary stage manner. What surprised my patient so much in the dream was that they did in fact carry on an actual conversation, spontaneously and so wittily that their laughter was genuine.

Well, that seems to give the dream another squeeze. Clearly there is a distinction being made in the dream between what the audience sees of her relationship to the bold girl, which is described in the script of the play, the magazine in the library, and the surprising and spontaneous relationship, the witty conversation that the audience *cannot hear*. The audience is not meant to hear it, as the two girls at the cafe table are part of the stage setting and not central characters. The content of the witty conversation is personal to them and quite outside the formal structure of the play. Does it perhaps stand in relation to the structure of the play as the content of a patient's communication of mental states stands in relation to the formal structure of the psychoanalytic method? In a certain sense patient and analyst are playing their parts in a prescribed drama of psychoanalysis ("Ring round the Moon"?). If they play their parts well enough, there does indeed usually arise the spontaneous and earnest transference–countertransference process. They may act it out together as my patient and the bold girl did the samba, for you will recall that even at that point the patient was surprised that the way the other girl took the lead was true to life. Following Freud, most analysts consider this to be contrary to the basic method of psychoanalysis. But many analysts, in adapting this method to special circumstances such as psychotic patients, children, delinquents, etc., have allowed themselves greater liberty in this regard (Rosen, Winnicott, Sechehaye, for instance). Generally, the analyst does not wish to act in the countertransference but is prepared for the patient to act-in the transference, hoping subsequently to be able to enlist the patient's cooperation to investigate the acting-in.

Let us assume, then, for the sake of further exploration, that the silent but sincere samba followed by the witty conversation at the coffee table, seen but not heard by the audience, represent an aspect of the patient's experience of the analytic situation, taking place, like the play, at 8:30 in the evening. It does strongly suggest that the silence that had made her first attempt at analysis fail was now being relieved because the analyst was taking a bolder lead in bringing her to the breast in the transference. The suggestion that wittiness in the manner or style of interpretation played some part in this had already been suggested in a dream several months before. In that dream,

> *. . . she was surprised to see that a man was able to keep in contact with, and thereby control, the dinner-table behaviour of his rather mentally retarded son by couching his instructions amusingly.*

Let us catch our breath a moment. We seem to have turned over a spadeful of earth that is fairly wiggly with implications. We have come upon a impressive piece of evidence that the silence is a mode of relationship and not an absence of it. It is a loaded and not an empty silence—a Pinteresque silence, one might say. The silence of the playroom, belied by the immobilization imposed by the couch, one can see. It seems to imply that we must correct an idea that was expressed earlier that from the magazine-script of the library-breast the patient learned the words for playing-her-part, which is in fact a wordless part in the play itself, the formal structure of the analysis. The script only prescribed a witty conversation at the cafe table but did not make explicit the content of it. This had to come spontaneously and true to life from the patient and the bold-girl-mother, in contrast to the extra-analytic relationship to the Di-big-sister-part who did her thinking for her, and by doing so weakened her sense of urgency, the preciousness of the time. The script of the library-breast, therefore, only contained the idea of a witty conversation, not the conversation itself.

If we take it that the library represents an internal breast of the old-school-mother and the cafe table represents the external mind-breast of the analytic-mother, we are posed the problem of understanding the relationship between having access to the idea of a witty analytic conversation and the ability to carry on that conversation itself. Further, we are confronted with the problem of understanding the dream-thought of an analytic conversation, in which again we have no evidence that the actual words rather than an idea of the words was given, and the conversation about the dream that took place subsequently in the actual 8:30 session of the day after the dream. Three echelons of discourse have to be brought into their logical and structural relation to one another: the idea of a witty conversation, the dream representation of a witty conversation, and the actual analytic conversation about the dream, in lieu of the previously characteristic silence. The idea of speaking, the idea of language, language usage is juxtaposed to the idea of dancing the samba, dancing the samba in a dream, silence in a session. The alternative would appear to be lateness and not knowing her part in dream and analysis alike. While the bold-girl–analytic-mother makes the transition from dance to speech possible, the Di–big-sister part presides over the confusion by reassurance and doing her thinking for her—object-relation versus narcissistic organization.

DISCUSSION

We have burrowed into some very complex clinical material and thrown up quite a few ideas, linkages, implications. We must now try to summarize, bring together, and extract the significance of what we have discovered. The central problem was one of overcoming the tendency to silence that had wrecked the patient's first attempt at analysis and was linked, of course, to poor communication with other people generally. The exception to these difficulties in making her feelings, wishes, and intentions clear to others resided externally in a relationship to a friend, currently Di, which was modelled on the childhood closeness to her good older sister. The meeting of the minds in this type of relationship did not require language but existed *de facto* as like-mindedness in the face of the world. The internal counterpart, a gentle type of narcissism or narcissistic organization of baby-part and good-big-sister, dominated her states of mind and produced a type of shallow complacency, a lack of sense of urgency, and a tendency to slide imperceptibly away from intense emotional involvement, although highly emotional by temperament.

The dream suggests that this narcissistic organization has begun to be rivalled by an object relationship in the analysis. The quality of boldness, probably lacking in a somewhat obsessional and depressed mother, appears to have played a part in sweeping her to the breast in the infantile transference, while the quality of wit, or, rather, humour, again probably somewhat lacking in the mother, has facilitated acceptance of the communication-feed, the witty conversation. The dream, like the cine-frame that shows the hummingbird's wing, has caught for us a process that ordinarily occurs so rapidly that we find no representation of it in dreams. It demonstrates the structure of the personality that lies behind sincere human contact, how the idea of a certain relationship (the part in the script) is transformed into the configuration of relationship (seated with the bold girl at the cafe table simulating a witty conversation), which can then be filled with true-to-life content (the witty conversation itself). It was necessary for the patient to realize that she did not know her part, to be determined to learn it, and to seek out the library breast and prefect-nipple internally in order to equip herself. She could have funked any one of the operations and appeared on the stage without knowing her part, which she would have had to confabulate, or not appeared on the stage, confabulating an excuse or simply being defiant or indifferent to the others involved. I am pointing to the types of insincere relationships or non-relations that would have resulted from the patient not finding the script and learning her part, any one of which would ultimately have wrecked the analysis, as the first attempt had been wrecked.

Having equipped herself with knowledge of her part, she could then take part in the play in a way that enabled the bold girl to lead her, to her great surprise, into a mode of experience, the witty conversation, which she had only expected to simulate. This would appear to mean that she had expected only to play the part in life of being a patient in analysis, but had never expected that it would involve her in a personal experience of spontaneous thought and feeling. She expected that such experiences were only the province of her narcissism, as if to say that parents and children are never engaged in spontaneous emotional response to one another—they only, naturally, play the parts of parent and child with the feelings appropriate to those roles. If they do not know their parts, disruption of some kind results. On the other hand, one can see that in the narcissistic organization, represented by her close relation to Di, language is replaced by behaviour. Instead of discussing her feelings about her legs being too fat, she wears the taffeta dress to the ground. Nurturing dependence is replace by parasitic dependence. She lets Di do her thinking for her and loses her sense of the preciousness of time.

In the narcissistic organization language is used but is not employed for linguistic communication. Insofar as language is used as an instrument of relationship, and not merely for the transmission of information about the outside world, it is employed in a primitive way as a type of noise, chant, incantation, or song. In response to the patient making anxious noises while looking at the clock, Di, presumably, made "doesn't matter" incantations, which soothed the baby. In contrast to this, with the bold girl the formal category of "witty-conversation" that the patient expected to simulate became filled, to her surprise, with spontaneous content. I am pointing to the great complexity of machinery that lies behind the scenery when a spontaneous witty conversation takes place. Imagine the events again. You unexpectedly meet someone in the street; each person returns in his thoughts to his old school and finds the prefect who finds the magazine containing the script; each studies the script; the bolder of the two suggests that they take a seat at the nearby cafe; and to their great surprise a witty conversation ensues. What, as it were, are the odds against such an occurrence? How often does it in fact happen that one has an unexpected and surprising experience of intimate communication? Do you see what I mean about the hummingbird's wing?

Of course the matter is different in established relationships of intimacy. One is like an old trouper who knows his part backwards and could play it blind-drunk or in his sleep. How many such relationships does one develop in a lifetime? How often does the playing of parts fail to evolve spontaneity and feeling because neither boldly takes the lead, as they used to do in the early days, before they started to repeat themselves for lack of new thoughts, out of aversion to the stimulation and the vitality expense, or for fear of being hurt in the exchange. Hence the need for boldness if the old script is not to become jaded by repetition. But similarly the older person, while more established in his technique of playing the various parts in his repertoire of relationships than the younger one, has a relative aversion to new parts and new scripts. In contrast, the adolescent is hungry to experiment but cannot find a script. When he does so, he is like Bottom and wishes to play all the parts. The result is often the urge to intimate communication without a structure to inspire content. Verbal exchange deteriorates to an exchange of opinions or tastes and is finally abandoned in favour of action. The consequent plunging into sexuality as the only mode of intimate exchange constitutes a retreat from experience and thought, fostering the degradation into perversity to sustain flagging appetites.

When all this is recognized, when the blur of the humming-bird's wing is arrested and the complexity of its activity seen, one is left aghast at the temerity of the psychoanalytic method, which dares to throw two strangers together in the expectation of their having a thousand or so hours of intimate, spontaneous, emotional conversation, not to mention therapeutic benefit to patient and scientific or technical advance for the analyst. And the wonder of it is that they do eventually achieve a dialogue of endless interest, which must finally be relinquished by both of them, for the same reasons as it is necessary for the mother to wean her baby. Once the patient has made contact with an internal library-breast from which he can learn his part, it is only necessary for him to follow the formal structure of the analytic method of observing and reporting the observations on the content of his mind for an endlessly interesting conversation about the infantile transference to become possible.

Of course analysis has no monopoly on this method of discourse and dialogue. Very intimate relationships in which language plays a real part follow the same schema. What is required is that the partners know their parts, which are characterized by the idea of sharing the contents of their minds with one another without reservation. That is the part, according to the script, that the maternal breast makes available in its conceptualizing of love, without reservation. People of course cannot realize this ideal category of relationship, either in or out of analysis, and consequently their dialogues are inconsistent, disrupted, incomplete, equivocal. But the aegis of trust that the internal breast raises in psychic reality evokes an aspiration and a striving in friends and lovers towards unreserved communication. No symbolic form other than language can achieve it.

CONCLUSION

We have been digging about in this piece of clinical material from the analysis of a young woman who is struggling to free herself from a narcissistic organization of personality that has severely hampered the development of intimate relationships in the outside world outside the pattern of their narcissism. The dream and associated clinical phenomena have allowed us a glimpse of the complex processes that lie behind spontaneity and sincerity in the use of language for the communication of states of mind and the exploration of relationships. It has in particular given us a picture of the nature of the analytic work from which we can form a clearer understanding of its relationship to life, the qualities that make it "true to life" as the patient's dream expressed it.

In particular we have learned that such intimate discourse rests upon a two-tiered foundation, identification with the combined object of psychic reality and the realization of a suitable partner for conversation in the outside world. When two people come together who both know their parts in the same drama, such dialogue arises quite naturally and effortlessly. But as the case is usually one of unequal assurance in the matter, an extreme form of which is represented when an ill person comes to analysis, then it is necessary for the more confident to lead boldly on. In daily life this will often result in rebuffs—sometimes shy and sometimes cruel—if the other person does not in fact know their part in intimacy and openness. The boldness is required for just this reason, of the risk of pain involved for the one who makes the friendly advance.

You will notice that what was earlier simply left in the language of the dream as "learning one's part" has now been more theoretically described as identification with the combined object. I mean, of course, specifically introjective identification. How is this process reasonably equated with "learning one's part", and how does that differ from forms of narcissistic identification—by projection, in particular? I think that the dream gives a particularly cogent and precise representation of the peculiar quality of introjective identification and the way it enables the person to evolve his own identity with the help of his objects, rather than to lose his identity through becoming confused with the qualities of the object. The dream shows very clearly that the introjective identification with the breast as a combined object, prefect-nipple and library-breast provides the script of the social drama, the mode of relationship, but not its content. It is a container into which each person can pour his own unique ideas, phantasies, experiences. It is the craftsman's tools and materials and iconography, the musician's instruments, tonal scales, and notation. In a sense it is what history has prepared so that we need not start from scratch. It is the instrument of mental heredity as genes are the means of physical heredity. It makes it possible for the individual to recapitulate the social evolution of 50,000 years by the time he leaves adolescence, when he must choose between the adventure of going beyond his heredity or of seeking security in its earlier stages.

7
Conclusion

Writing a chapter of this sort is full of surprises, like an analysis, for, as the latter unfolds through the driving forces of development coming from the patient's unconscious, this work appears to have been driven by the force of the great art of Mr Pinter. Maurice Merleau Ponty says, "When I speak I discover what I think". In the minute scrutiny of Pinter's plays there not only emerged a thousand surprises of unexpected meanings, juxtapositions, and linkages in the works themselves, but a fresh ordering of my own thoughts and enrichment of my conceptions. It is necessary now, at the end, to take stock, to trace the journey made and assess its significance *as* an emotional and intellectual journey. What have I learned through this exercise that I did not know before, consciously, perhaps even unconsciously?

I am astonished at the minuteness of interpretive scrutiny to which these works have lent themselves, and I am set to wondering in two directions. In the first instance I am inclined to think that it suggests that the language of the dream is perhaps the *lingua franca* of emotionality and the key to aesthetics. If one could learn to look at dreams as works of art and at works of art as dreams, what enrichment in both directions might not result? But what would it mean, to look at a work of art as a dream, in the case of a fourteenth-century Madonna or a Bach cantata, where the iconography on the one hand or the formal structure on the other were rigidly prescribed and imposed upon the artist? In applying this method to Dostoievsky's "Gambler", the task was easy, as the content itself held the dream-drama. In Pinter's work it has been more complicated, involving both dramatic content and language usage. How would it work with a drama of prescribed content, such as Sophocles' "Oedipus Rex"? Was Melanie Klein's approach to the content of any interest to aesthetic problems?

I think not, in fact, nor am I at all sure that the present more complex approach to Pinter's work gets much closer to the heart of the artistry. But that is perhaps due, conversely, to the fact that we have not as yet learned to look at dreams as works of art. That is a technical problem that I hope to investigate another time. Here I am concerned to know what has, in fact, been done with these plays. Has it thrown light upon their beauty and enriched a reader's experience of them, or done violence to the art? I note an increase in my own wonder at Pinter's achievement and a corresponding strengthening of my conviction of creative inferiority. I feel a greater personal closeness to the characters, but, oddly, not to the author. Perhaps, even, I can note an increased feeling of distance to him, as if he were a figure of the past. What does it mean regarding my aesthetic experience?

The second line of inquiry growing out of my astonishment at the way in which the plays have yielded to interpretation revolves around the question of the implications for the validity of psychoanalytic theories. Would it make any difference if I were to discover that Mr Pinter has had an analysis, which in fact I have no reason to think he has? or has read the works of Freud and Melanie Klein? or those of St. Augustine? or the New or Old Testaments? or Heidegger? or had plagiarized the story from Plutarch? or that they were really written by his wife? or by his schizophrenic cousin?

I do not think that the answer to any of these questions would extinguish the impression that such harmony between art and theory bodes well for the truth content of the theories. But that statement relates to the established theories that have been employed in the enquiry. What of the extensions of theory that this chapter has undertaken? Does the artistic stature of the plays enhance the scientific stature of the new theories? Shall we apply the same roster of questions? Has Mr Pinter been analysed . . . his schizophrenic cousin? I note that I feel strengthened in my own conviction by the company of Pinter's characters and the examples I was able to cite. I find that having employed these plays with their powerful evocativeness has placed a strain upon my sense of conviction, which reporting transactions from the consulting-room did not do.

I do, therefore, in retrospect, think that the method of investigation, of testing upon works of art some of the subtle impressions regarding the emotional atmosphere of human relations drawn from the consulting-room and daily life—this unusual method has been a fruitful one. I feel more convinced that this particular aspect of atmosphere created by fluctuations in sincerity and its corollary, intimacy, throws a useful light on the processes by which understanding grows—or fails to grow—between people. I find my conception of sincerity, phenomenologically, sharpened for use in observation of myself and others. I feel a greater tolerance for failures of sincerity in others and particularly a sympathy for those caught in unsincerity. I can understand why sincerity is so powerfully attractive, for good and evil, in the eminent joyousness of the complete person and the charisma of the psychopath.

CHAPTER THIRTEEN

Towards an atelier system

(1971)

This article, written for circulation amongst the members of the British Psycho-Analytical Society, offers a critical view of the selection, training, and qualification of candidates at the Institute of Psycho-Analysis. It did not enhance the author's popularity with the psychoanalytic "establishment" that he suggested an organization to teach and learn psychoanalysis in a less authoritarian setting to function concurrently with the "official" training. These were felt in 1971 to be subversive ideas, and they aroused fears that the interest of psychoanalysts would be deflected away from the Society and from the established theories and doctrines.

Published in the *Scientific Bulletin of the British Psycho-Analytical Society*, 1971.

Some years of effort by the Curriculum Committee having now resulted in a new course of study for students and a new organization of teaching staff, the task has arisen for it of evaluation, feedback, development. Some of the difficulties in this area that have come under discussion throw into sharp relief the essential nature of the educational system we have, as a matter of course, perpetuated. It gives rise to some uneasiness and a need to reconsider the system itself. Insofar as these concerns with the microcosm of psychoanalysis, and thus with thought and opinion growing out of immediate experience and conflict, bear upon our understanding of the larger world, they can be considered of general interest. It is for this reason, I presume, that Dr Klauber invited me to write up some ideas I had expressed for distribution in the *Scientific Bulletin*.

These ideas relate closely to others of which I have written and spoken in the past and bear upon such interlocking considerations as the nature of psychoanalysis, the distinction between teaching and facilitating learning, the dynamics of the hierarchic structure now extant in psychoanalysis, and the relation of our movement to the community that it serves and inhabits. Under these four headings I discuss—or, rather, describe and evaluate—the system we now operate, defining its archaic and fallacious aspects in particular. I then describe one alternative system. At this point, a certain irritability might arise, to ask; "Why is it necessary to occupy ourselves with systems, generalities, abstractions? Do we not have a working system that, in the ordinary course of things, can be further improved bit by bit?" Indeed, in this mind the Curriculum Committee set blithely to work, once the course was a going concern, to deal with the problem of "feedback", assuming that information would lead to refinement and correction. But the complexity of the situation, the difficulty of defining the facts required, of eliciting them from students and teachers, the delicacy of the task of communication, criticism, the tendency for every discussion to take on the atmosphere of "present company excluded"—all these, and above all the appalling time-consumption involved, warn surely of an absolute slough of despond.

Still, the present system is the one towards which our medical background and its mediaeval tradition naturally inclines us. It is a pattern of education in which the teaching of theory and practice are separated, between amphitheatre and ward, as it were, based on the assumption that there exists a body of fact and nomenclature that must necessarily be mastered before the experience of the patient can either by apprehended or made communicable. But of course the very fact that we train lay people—and all know perfectly well that a degree in English literature would be a better preparation than one in medicine for life in the consulting-room—makes quite clear that we disbelieve our own tacit premise. The system's structure, with its emphasis on seniority, its assumption that research achievement implies tutorial ability, its paradoxical distinction between clinical practice and clinical research, its tenure of status without regard to fluctuations in capacity and migration of interests might very well suit a craft guild where standards really mean restraint of trade. Medicine generally has hardly risen above this level in its organization, but for the astonishing scientific advances of the past hundred years, which have given it such a factual monopoly of therapeutic capacity over its rivals: apothecaries, barbers, osteopaths, chiropractors, homeopaths, witches, and witch doctors. But psychoanalysis has no such monopoly to add status to an irrational and archaic organization. While we may think of ourselves as a medical subspeciality—and I am not at all sure that we do so, in all sincerity—the world generally probably either charitably includes us as an intellectual discipline or less kindly as a sect with a system of beliefs and an expensive method of convert creation.

The points that these considerations raise for debate are many. Do we have a defined body of information and nomenclature that can be taught? By what standard are we to judge the relation of the personal analysis to the learning of the method? Must we aim at a goal in the development of students of psychoanalysis, or can each person be allowed to find his own way and make his own use of its method and theories? Are standards possible to define and evaluate, or must we seek to construct a field of study on the model of a cross-country event, where natural obstacles facilitate self-evaluation and decision? Is a hierarchic structure of status, responsibility, and judgement necessary and realistic, or can people be allowed to select and pursue their interests in the matter of courses and teachers? Is it necessary or even desirable for the distinction between student and teacher to have a formal rather than a merely personal significance? As there is no possibility either of control over the title "psychoanalyst" or of monopoly of the method, is it not necessary to discard the hope of purity as a method of preservation of the psychoanalytic movement in favour of leadership by example?

What, after all, is the reality of a psychoanalyst's economic and social viability? He must have patients; he must have colleagues; if he wishes to teach, he must have students; if he has research findings, he needs an audience; if he is to develop, he needs a milieu of study; if he is to survive, he needs support and comfort. Is there today a real relationship between formal qualifications in our system and real viability? I think not. I feel that a marked disparity can be seen to exist between the formal structure and the real one, in which the former functions primarily as a mythology that impedes the free action and development of the real system based upon personal contact, private opinion, and public reputation. I am suggesting, of course, that there exists in fact the foundations of an atelier system bound within the constraint of a guild system, with the result that confusion is increased, unreal responsibilities are delegated, covert tyranny arises, and schismatic tendencies are fostered.

Of those four by-products of the dislocation between organization and function, it is the unreality of the responsibility for selection and judgement that is the most corrosive to all concerned. My own experience has demonstrated that this aspect is loathed by almost everyone, for it places the student in the position of defendant rather than aspirant, the teacher in the position of persecutor rather than colleague, the committee member in the vestments of an elite, and it sets the unnamed concept of heresy hanging heavy in the lovely corridors and rooms of Mansfield House.

What, then, is the atelier system that could be an alternative to what gives every promise of proliferating into a nightmare? I think we may conceive of it primarily as a place, much as a market is a market-place. Like Raphael's "School of Athens", one would like to think of a place where anyone with something to teach and anyone wanting to learn could have resort. It need offer no qualifications, process no applications, exercise no restrictions. It could stand completely outside the structure of a Society or a Clinic and perform a housekeeping function at minimal expense to all. Experienced people might wish to offer time as tutors or supervisors, give courses in areas that interest them, run seminars of various sorts, organize research or study groups. These could be advertised and applicants' names passed on for personal selection by teachers. The atelier might wish to undertake to collect a certifiable record of people's participation, with a view to supplying such factual information in the case of job application, society entrance, to prospective patients, etc. It might wish to perform a banking function with regard to fees; it can let its rooms, arrange social functions, study its own operations. It could do as much as its governing body aspired to and as little as their tolerance to impending chaos would allow. It is a system that need take no cognisance of the existence of the student's or teacher's personal analysis.

One final question before closing: is there any reason that an atelier of psychoanalysis and an institute of psychoanalysis should be mutually exclusive? Indeed, I think that there is every reason to believe that they would be mutually supporting, providing an alternative route for students, an outlet for teaching aspirations, a training and proving-ground for the Institute's program, and a facility available to the many who wish to study psychoanalysis but do not aspire to practice it.

CHAPTER FOURTEEN

Routine and inspired interpretations: their relation to the weaning process in analysis

(1973)

This clinical paper on the theory of technique explores the use of inspiration in the psychoanalytic method and was written as a further development of the book on The Psycho-analytical Process *(1967a). Like many of the author's papers on technique, this is a frank exposition of clinical work by the author, which provocatively deals with issues of countertransference, thinking, acting out, the function of the interpretative activity in analysis, and wild analysis.*

This paper is one of a series of essentially personal studies that have grown out of and are therefore an extension of the investigation of the nature of the psychoanalytic process that I reported in my book (1967a). In that work I left rather empty the description of the interpretive function of the analyst as one of his modes of participation in

Published in the *Scientific Bulletin of the British Psycho-Analytical Society*, 64 (1973).

the therapeutic relationship, as it was not central to the main theme. This centred on the process and its evolution seen as arising essentially in the unconscious of the patient. But it is probably true that any analysis that really taps the passions of the patient does the same for the analyst and promotes a development that can further his own self-analysis. Insofar as this is true, the main industrial hazard of this work lies in the danger of the transference–countertransference process taking a turn in the direction of perversion and thus becoming anti-therapeutic for both members of the undertaking.

The analyst's great safeguard against this lies in the method and its basic technique, any breach of which should serve as a warning bell that the countertransference requires special scrutiny. This subject was deeply investigated and reported in the 1950s, especially by members of the British Society. These studies dealt mainly with countertransference behaviour and emotion and thus extended in a more detailed way the concept of "wild analysis" described by Freud. These authors described, one might say, bits of wild analysis embedded in a matrix of correct procedure. But the difficult task of investigating the intrusion of the analyst's unanalysed psychopathology into his understanding of the phenomenology of the consulting-room is, perhaps necessarily, left untouched, since it entrenches itself unobtrusively in the guise of theoretical formulation, the hidden passions only emerging as the irrational heat of talmudic debate and society politics.

One reason for this vulnerability of analysts lies in the incompleteness of our methodology, which still leaves such vagueness in our formulation of technique that a great gap necessarily exists between what analysis can describe, what one thinks occurs, and what in fact takes place. Wilfred Bion has been revealing his own grapplings with this problem, perhaps most movingly in his book *Attention and Interpretation* (1970), and much of what I have to report seems to me to make an assault on the same citadel from a somewhat different direction. As Bion uses his extraordinary capacity for reverie to investigate his experience of analytic work, I wish to use my special interest in dreams. But in this instance I do not mean my own dreams but those of the patient, which hold up a mirror to the analyst.

Like our other categories of offspring, patients in states of projective or other types of narcissistic identification with the analyst hold up a fun-fair type of mirror, full of distortions and exaggerations no doubt, but revealing the truth in caricature. This becomes particularly germane to our present problem when the narcissistic identification is taking the form, early in an analysis, of premature attempts at self-analysis. I wish to use an instance of this sort and a dream that accompanied it to probe a particular problem concerning the interpretive work of the analyst.

This problem relates, as I say, to the interpretive activity of the analyst, as a personality function, and not primarily to the interpretation itself, although I hope to show that it has far-reaching consequences for the form as well as the content of the interpretation. I am going to employ a polarizing concept for investigating the range of analytic interpretive activity by assuming two extreme types: in one of these the analyst listens and observes the behaviour of the patient, which comes to assume a pattern or gestalt in his mind, to which he then applies certain aspects of his theoretical equipment in an explanatory way; at the other extreme the analyst, exposed to the activities of the patient, has an experience that is essentially personal, which he then uses, with the aid of his theoretical equipment, to explore the meaning of the relationship going on at that moment in his room. I am going to call these two extremes "routine" and "inspired" interpretations, respectively. I have chosen these two terms because of their implications of dullness on the one hand and megalomania on the other, as these are indeed the respective dangers of the two extreme poles of interpretive activity. The clinical instance I will present shows just this transition, from a routine to an inspired activity, along with its dangers.

The second part of the paper uses these understandings to investigate the significance of this differentiation between routine and inspired interpretation for the evolution of the psychoanalytic process, with special reference to the penetration of the depressive position, the formation of the combined object in psychic reality, the influence of the experience of this object on the weaning process—and the implication of all this for the patient's character and capacity for further development with the aid of self-analysis.

Clinical material

In the third year of analysis the evidence strongly suggested that this young man's rigid narcissistic organization, which had been built up from early in childhood around a very exclusive relationship to a cousin who later accompanied him through boarding school, was finally giving way a bit to the dominance of his object relations. The struggle against this had been manifested very strikingly in the transference during the previous year's work. Once the beauty of the internal mother had been restored from its earlier dilapidated state, she seemed, in her isolation, to begin to demand with increasing insistence a husband worthy of her, and no one but "daddy" would do. The patient's infantile search for alternative objects and relationships to satisfy her was externalized in an interesting obsessional investigation, which fell into three categories of preoccupation with the transference situation: the first was a search for a therapeutic method superior to psychoanalysis; the second for a man of greater stature than Freud; and the third for evidence of an analyst whose writings reflected superior comprehension to his own analyst's.

In all three instances his search foundered on the same rock—namely, the realization of his own limitations in knowledge and judgement. Unwillingly he gradually surrendered to the emotionality of the transference experience of being a child with the "best mummy and daddy in the world"—that is, best for him, because they were his own.

When he began to be gripped by this experience of being substantially without grievance to set against unworthiness and guilt related to neglect, delinquency, and perversity, a great urgency came upon him to dispel these incipient depressive pains before ever they were suffered from. This he attempted to do by a combination of sparing, premature independence and manic reparative achievement, both inside and outside the analytic situation. One of the consequences was a striking change in his cooperation. Previously he had been above reproach on the surface; he lay on the couch, presented his dreams and associations in a beautiful and free way, and waited politely for the analyst to "do his stuff". He was a good "client" and naturally felt it his prerogative to assess the quality of the goods, variously praising, criticizing gently, admonishing. But his other prerogative was to judge the limits of his privacy, and so long as this was not challenged as secrecy, all went smoothly—no sullen silences, no sense of grievance.

But now he was eager that there should be no secrecy or, rather, no cause for it, either in behaviour or in phantasy. In addition he showed a disposition to help with the interpretive work, and he was keen to finish the analysis as soon as possible to give some other sufferer a chance. From "seeming good" he now became a "really good" patient, the only trouble being that his motives were largely defensive with respect to depressive mental pain. If his analytic house had rising damp and he was eager to sell it, the reason was not to cheat some unsuspecting buyer but because he hated the cost of the repairs. He could live in a tent!

In this context, being an intelligent and sensitive man with a sense of the truth if not yet a love for it, he began to notice that there was somehow a difference between his own interpretations and those offered by the analyst. It was not so much that his were not "correct", if this term could be used for their being in basic agreement with the analyst's. In fact, he was a rather good observer and translator of behaviour and dream language into the theories with which he was now fairly familiar, though it was all a bit like school-boy Latin. But, after all, Freud himself had likened the first phase of dream analysis to translating Livy! He noticed that when he gave an interpretation himself, it seemed somehow to stop everything, to put a lid on it, like conversation-stoppers of the "just-human-nature" type. On the other hand, when the analyst interpreted, and often in a way that seemed no different in content to his own ideas about the material, it had a different effect. It took the lid off; it increased the excitement; it was tinged with pain.

The relevance of all this to the infantile transference was not clear at the time, except in its broad outlines: why was he inferior to mummy and daddy; why did his wee-wees not make babies and his buttocks not give milk? But the quality of his feelings of perplexity seemed rather mysterious. One Thursday he came complaining of having slept very badly. All night long he had felt an incipient diarrhoea, but on the toilet nothing came—a bit of flatus, a mushy stain. This he associated with an incident at age twelve, when he had soiled his pyjamas in the night and his somewhat harsh mother had been "incredibly understanding". But it also seemed to link in a puzzling way with an insistent recollection of his early student days in music composition, when he first discovered how virtually impossible it was to make up a melody "of one's own". In the night this had somehow turned into a ruminative attempt to hold together in his mind a certain note and one a semi-tone lower, but without success.

The patient agreed that the events of the night must be related to the transference and contain some re-experience of infantile suffering: of inability to control either his feelings (expressed in bodily terms, the incipient diarrhoea) or his objects (the inability to hold the two notes together in his mind), along with some recognition of creative incapacity, and thus inferiority (the inability to make a melody "of his own"). To the Friday session he brought the following dream:

> *He and the analyst seemed to be sharing a hotel room, which was overlooked by rooftops filled with people. At one point the analyst seemed to be squatting over the patient, saying something like, "In fact you have never actually seen my anus". The patient felt a mixture of intense emotions. On the one hand, he felt embarrassed that the people across the way would surely see this as a homosexual relationship. But even more acute was a feeling of triumph over the analyst, who was apparently quite unaware that behind him was a mirror, which enabled the patient to look directly between his buttocks. These appeared huge and muscular, like a Japanese wrestler's.*

The patient connected the dream with an important occurrence of puberty. His father had come into his bedroom early one morning and sat down on the bed, looking a bit amusedly at the patient's disarranged pyjamas, but after a few moments' silence he had left. At the time he had experienced this in the light of a common experience of tentative homosexual approaches made to him by older boys at boarding school. Later he had wondered if his father had wanted to broach the subject of masturbation but had lost his nerve. He also linked the dream with one-way screens used both for psychological research and for sexual perversions. His own interpretation was that he was accusing the analyst of having been triumphant over him the previous day; perhaps he was having his revenge by accusing the analyst of a type of showing off that revealed his anal homosexuality. But perhaps he was mistaken, as with his father. It was a week-end theme with which we were fairly familiar, and I could not add much to the interpretation. But I was disturbed by an insistent image that had arisen before my eyes as I had been listening to the dream—namely, of Velasquez' "Rokeby Venus", in which the goddess is visualized from behind, reclining and gazing into a mirror held up to her by an infant Cupid in which her face, looking rather thoughtful, is depicted.

Although this painting seemed irrelevant to the patient's dream, as he had never mentioned it, still it was a surprise to me, as I had not seen the picture for some years myself. But I had several reasons to pay attention to it: the patient is knowledgeable about art; the beauty of the mother's back was a prominent feature of his dream life and early recollections. I therefore asked him if he thought the dream could have anything to do with this famous painting and was relieved to be told that in fact it had been the subject of discussion at a dinner party a few nights ago. But how did this throw any light on the dream?

First of all, we could recognize the transpositions: the patient is in the position of the goddess, the analyst in that of Cupid, and the people on the rooftops see it as the painter. At this point it merely seems that the patient's dream has made a caricature of the painting in which he accuses Velasquez of being a pornographer and voyeur who does not even realize how he reveals his perversity. That is just the same as the patient's interpretation of the dream and probably quite right at some level. But if we follow this line, it is Cupid who is the main target of ridicule. What about the Japanese wrestler bit? They do not in fact wrestle naked but wear a very nappy-like loin-cloth. Is there here a revenge on the mummy who is "incredibly understanding" about the baby's dirty bottom? But in the painting Venus is supposed to be looking at herself. Why, then, is her face visualized in the mirror? Must she not in fact be looking at the painter with that shadowy, absorbed expression? Certainly not at Cupid's bottom! Rather, Cupid is facilitating the relationship of admiring and thoughtful contemplation between goddess–mummy and artist–daddy. The iconography of a Madonna-and-child shows through from its classical façade, and we are reminded of "Las Meninas" or of Vermeer's "Artist in His Studio".

A routine Friday session caught fire at this moment, and we plunged into a new area in the transference—namely, the patient's begrudging of his admiration to objects whose riches of admiration for one another were already too great for him to bear without overpowering envy. He was not going to be the loving Cupid boy who potentiated this admiration, but a dirty-bottomed mocker who attacked them and a sly little girl who intruded and spied upon their intimacy. In childish limitation of imagination the parents' pleasure in their creative combination to procreate and rear their children is seen as indistinguishable from the mutual-admiration conspiracy of two children admiring one another's urination and defecation! We could see more clearly now that the patient's self-analytic efforts were inadequate not merely due to inexperience but because of heavy contamination by infantile omnipotence in the service of defence against depressive anxieties. His pregenital bi-sexuality was trying to make poo-poo babies from his wee-wee and feed them with his mushy diarrhoea milk and keep all the admiration for himself. Or does the dream reveal a sharp insight into the analyst's megalomania and self-admiration regarding his artistic and creative way of doing psychoanalysis and writing papers about it? Or both? Can more precise formulation of methodology assist the analyst in his self-analytic efforts to answer such a question? Or must he wait somewhat helplessly for the proof-of-the-pudding in the future course and outcome of the work?

Explanation and exploration: pedagogy and comradeship

The medical tradition behind psychoanalysis has been very naturally conducive to an orientation of analyst towards patient that tends to confuse the therapeutic alliance with the transference–countertransference situation. While truly it is more like teacher to pupil than doctor to patient in many respects, still we are inclined to assume that we are helping the patient or analysand to traverse developmental territory familiar to us from our own personal experience, be it ever so idiosyncratic in its manifest content or particular permutation of emotions, phantasies, and defences. Consequently we are bound to acknowledge that we are limited by the boundaries of our self-knowledge. This Virgil-leading-Dante model seems to me, however, to be applicable to only one aspect of the interpretive work—namely, to whatever degree of contact and communication we are able to hold with the infantile structures of the patient's mind. In that sense every interpretation, insofar as it is explanatory of the infantile transference, is also a type of action-in-the-countertransference. At best this concretely parental activity may be nurturing to the mind, ready for sacrifice, tolerant and tender. In the face of resistance it cannot but feel to the patient quite the contrary—overbearing, paternalistic, intolerant, demanding.

Within this area of the interpretive work we are doing a task of introducing order, restoring linkages, unscrambling confusions, and finding a notation for anchoring the unconscious experience in consciousness for the purpose of memory. It is a great service and facilitates the evolution of the transference by reconstituting the conflicts that had been prevented from finding resolutions because of the excessive operation of mechanisms of defence that lessened the mental pain below the levels necessary for development. This is one way of formulating it and probably as good as another.

To this aspect of the interpretive work I have introduced the term "routine" in order to stress both its reliance on past experience and its danger of dullness. It is as much a part of the therapeutic alliance as is the patient's behaviour and verbalization that produces the material for analytic scrutiny, but insofar as the patient's behaviour of cooperation also always harbours the element of acting-in-the-transference, so does the analyst's explanatory communication harbour an element of acting-in-the-countertransference. When a "good" transference–countertransference is ascendant, the glow of family happiness fills the room, always tinged with mutual idealization. Such a glow would have arisen for a while in the session reported, had I given my agreement to the patient's interpretation, perhaps augmenting it with some reviewing and linking with earlier material and a bit of reconstructive comment on aspects of the patient's childhood relationships and development. It might have produced a happy Friday and a good return to the work on Monday. As it was, the patient went away quite stirred up and produced a dreadful week of what I hoped was negative therapeutic reaction.

Now, I can well imagine an analysis proceeding like this very well indeed, with the transference evolving and the patient being cured of his symptoms and even making some headway in his character development. I have no doubt that the problem that we penetrated—which changed the dream from what might have come to be called the "anus in the mirror" dream as a landmark of working through to the "Rokeby Venus" dream as a beachhead to new developments in the analysis—would have found its way into unmistakable expression in the patient's material sooner or later. What, then, is the advantage to psychoanalytic interpretation? Does it risk the stability and safety of the process merely in the hope of saving time?

If we were to say that the most desirable aim of an analysis was not only to accomplish what has been adumbrated above and equip the patient with the self-analytic means of preserving his gains but also to place him in possession of equipment to do a creative self-analysis by which he might continue his development after the termination of the formal analysis, what sort of basis in identification processes would this involve? Clearly it would require, in our theoretical terminology, an integration of his adult bi-sexuality in introjective identification with the combined object. What qualities in the work of the analyst would be necessary in order for him to carry the transference of this combined object sufficient to the establishment of it by introjection into the patient's internal world?

In order to answer this, I am going to ask you to join me for a moment in a phantasy in order to alter the model of the psychoanalytic procedure that I have called the Virgil-leading-Dante model. Since psychoanalysis cannot agree with the church in seeing an external and unified *inferno–purgatorio–paradiso* in which all humans participate after death but, rather, an individual one in which each person operates in his dream-life and unconscious phantasies during life, our model would be altered in this way. Virgil, having explored to some extent his own inner world, offers to help Dante do the same on the assumption that the corridors of these regions in each lie parallel, allow for communication, and are generally equivalent in their content though far from identical. Dante would, of course, be distrustful of the assumptions and of Virgil's reliability, while the latter would be frightened of the heavy responsibility. But the companionship would attract them. Each time, as they proceeded, Dante would describe his findings, and Virgil would reply with his understanding of the equivalent scene in his own corridor. At one point Dante says, "I have a Japanese wrestler bending over me, and I can see his anus in a mirror". Virgil is puzzled because he expected around that bend to meet his father sitting by his bedside, but, instead, he finds himself holding a mirror for his mother while his father paints her portrait. He did not even know his father could paint, nor had his mother ever seemed so dazzlingly lovely. He also feels confused about himself and has the insistent idea that his name is Leopold Bloom! Clearly he is lost. He has never been in this corridor before. But he is a bit reassured when his unseen companion answers to the name of Daedalus.

This is surely the type of experience that Freud was referring to when he wrote: "It remains for the future to decide whether there is more delirium in my theory than I should like to admit or whether there is more truth in Schreber's delusions than other people are prepared to believe." I think this must be the kind of experience that is an everyday occurrence with Bion, which he describes as the consequence of abandoning memory and desire. My own point of view tells me that it is the necessary state for being able to carry the transference of the combined object, of that type of internal companionship which promulgates an atmosphere of adventure in which comradeship develops between the adult part of the patient's personality and the analyst as creative scientist. This would deserve the name of therapeutic alliance, implying therapeutic possibilities for both parties to the adventure. Perhaps, when an analyst's training in the craftsmanship of psychoanalysis has ripened into virtuosity, these moments of potential adventure begin to arise quite naturally. By seizing them, he may foster in himself the tendency for moments such as Bion describes to arise again and again—moments of deep contact with his own combined object and the possibility of striving towards identification. But he probably risks everything, and few of us could do that very often. Still, perhaps being able to do it even on rare occasions may be enough to enable us to carry the transference of the patient's combined object, for, after all, we are never really required to be as good as the objects we are temporarily representing in the transference.

Discussion

Having now presented the two poles of interpretive activity, routine and inspired, the question must arise: are they really distinct from one another, or am I really only describing something that exists on a gradient involving more or less unconscious or intuitive contribution to the intellectual process of formulation? It will have been noticed that in my description of routine interpretive activity I said, "the analyst listens and observes the behaviour of the patient which *comes to assume* a pattern or gestalt in his mind. . . . " Is not this "comes to assume" an unconscious, intuitive, and therefore inspired process? No, it is not what I mean by inspired; I think it is generally agreed that psychoanalytic work cannot be done by the conscious intellect alone, but that any true understanding is based on intuition and not mere decipherment. I am probably trying to make the same distinction that Bion makes between knowledge and knowledge "about" something. He writes,

> The "act of faith" [which he is encouraging the analyst to achieve by the discipline of avoidance of memory and desire] has no association with memory or desire or sensation. It has a relation to thought analogous to the relation of

> prior knowledge to knowledge. . . . It does not by itself lead to knowledge "about" something, but knowledge "about" something may be the outcome of a defence against the consequences of an "act of faith". [Bion, 1970, p. 35]

To put it into my own words—and, of course, I am not in the least certain that it is at all similar to the "act of faith"—I mean by inspired interpretation a statement that has no explanatory significance ("Could this dream have anything to do with the 'Rokeby Venus'?") but involves the analyst in abandoning his pedagogic position *vis-à-vis* the infantile structures of the patient's personality in favour of one of comradeship with the adult part of the patient in an adventure that involves risking the whole analysis.

This risk to the analysis is shown very clearly in the dream, which, at one level, clearly accuses the analyst of a type of homosexual seduction through showing off his superior knowledge of sexuality ("In fact you have never actually seen my anus"). If this accusation were well founded, its natural implication would be that the analyst was about to lead the patient away from the sphere of his good objects into a perversion of the parent–child relation. In the psychoanalytic setting this would mean to abandon the basic method and aims of analysis for a wild "adventure" in the realm of mutual sexual excitation. What more likely form could this take than for the analyst to become inspired with new insights and to develop new techniques that would present themselves in his mind as scientific advances? In other, words, were an analyst to yield to his megalomania in this way and embody inspiration as a part of his own method in error, he would also be risking his mental health. The material I have presented is intended to emphasize this problem by leaving the question unresolved in the reader's mind.

Death of the breast

The paper thus far has been an addendum to Chapter VIII on "The Analytical Work" in *The Psycho-analytical Process* (Meltzer, 1967a). Because it is in a sense so idiosyncratic, because it is exemplified by a single complicated instance, and, above all, because it deals with matters on the fringe of the method where creativity tips over into megalomania and wild analysis, a further effort is required. This effort, if it is to succeed, must lend the matter in hand significance for the psychoanalytic method in general by demonstrating the relevance to the process of this particular mode of functioning by the analyst, which I have chosen to call "inspired" interpretation. In that sense, what is to follow is an addendum to Chapter V, on "The Weaning Process".

At the time of writing that section in 1965, the matter was still perhaps too close to the bone and my experience of carrying analysis to satisfactory termination too limited to speak with confidence. Seven years later [the time of writing this paper], I feel better able to fill with meaning the concept "death of the breast" which I could only indicate at that time. I wrote:

> The depressive situation, at bottom the death-of-the-breast, runs thread-like through all the material now. Attention to the analyst's physical and mental state, the urge to differentiate the person of the analyst in the outside world from the transference figures projected by psychic reality, and sensitivity to intrusion upon the psychoanalytic process from without, all become intensified, or may appear for the first time. [p. 47]

I have also described the increased preoccupation with the reproductive aspects of the parental sexuality and the expectation of the next baby, and how the struggle against possessive jealousy in this area is directly related to the struggle to integrate split-off parts of the infantile structure, especially the more destructive parts. I added,

> As yet we know relatively little, beyond what Melanie Klein has given us in *Envy and Gratitude* [1957], about this process in relation to the most split-off parts of all—namely, envious destructive parts, and, even more obscure, schizophrenic parts. One can, however, hardly imagine such advanced steps in integration being accomplished outside the setting of formal analysis to begin with, and without the greatest danger, of somatic disease in the first instance and schizophrenic episodes in the second.

If we may put these considerations to one side for a moment, I would now return to our concept of inspired interpretation and its relation to the establishment of the combined object in order to describe its special significance for the weaning process in psychoanalysis. In my experience the richness of combination of the parental couple in psychic reality with respect to beauty, goodness, strength, and creativity stands in direct relation to the richness of the comradeship that emerges in the therapeutic alliance and is thus a function of both partners' capacities to abandon themselves to the adventure of pushing beyond therapy for the patient's psychopathology into the unknown of character development for both. Were it not for the depressive problem of the "others" who are in need of treatment and its relation to the "next baby" in psychic reality, there might be no need, in fact, to bring an analysis to termination. But the weaning is required not merely desired, on this account. The objects must have their freedom, just as the self must be free to follow its own separate development under their aegis, and not merely to follow in their footsteps.

But in proportion to this richness the weaning takes on an agonizing quality for both partners, which I will now try to describe. The breast as part-object, which will die for the child internally and rise like the Phoenix from its ashes for the next baby, acts as prototype; it sets in motion a process of grief and anxiety that reawakens all those processes, past and expected, in relation to external figures, including the analyst and the patient himself. Where parent and other beloved persons have already died, this pain is acutely rekindled. But a combination of sparing tendencies to projective identification with the dying breast conspire to produce a current of death anxiety that may reach a crescendo at times in episodes of dying. These episodes have a sufficient hypochondriacal undertone to coopt the symptomatology of deceased loved ones.

Even when experience has deprived such events of any quality of surprise for the analyst, the anxiety and doubt that they engender for patient and analyst alike cannot be avoided. Because the richness of the experience has been a derivative of the abandonment of the pedagogic for the comradely relation in the adventure, a terrific current of mutual distrust as well as self-distrust seems to arise. The patient harbours suspicions that the analyst is mad, that he has seduced the analyst out of the path of proper conduct, that he has undermined his stability, that a surreptitious reversal of values has corrupted the work and turned it into a perversion on the model of his most pathological excursions, prior to the treatment. The analyst suspects that his judgement is disturbed, that he is killing the patient, that megalomania has crept into his work and separated him from his mentors and colleagues, that some serious deficiency in his own analysis is being relentlessly repeated, that psychoanalysis is, after all, just the tautological system of self-deception that its most virulent critics claim.

This buffeting by doubt and anxiety, which commences usually once a date for termination is broached, does in my experience continue for some time with lessening intensity up to termination and for some considerable time after.

To return now to the question of the integration of the most split-off parts and their attendant dangers, I am of the opinion that this process can never be completed. Aspects of envious destructiveness in the infantile levels of the mental structure that are bound directly to the id (unlike the adult part of the personality, which has only an indirect relation to impulse through introjective identificatory processes) are required to remain outside the sphere of good objects. Their virulence can never be very accurately assessed. The fear must always remain that, either by insidious means or as sudden eruptions, they will attack sanity and physical health.

It is precisely this fear of the split-off parts in patient and analyst alike that enters with such force to seed the pain of the weaning process with acute distrust. It is my contention that the richness of the analytic experience as a whole is bound up with the richness of the combined object that it assists to take shape, perhaps for the first time in the life of the particular patient. This paper offers as its main thesis that this richness has its source in the degree to which the pedagogic collaboration is replaced by an adventuresome comradeship at adult level. Since this requires an abandonment of the beaten track of routine interpretation at times, perhaps of the type Bion describes as the "Act of Faith" induced by the relinquishment of memory and desire, it is fraught with dread of incursion by the split-off parts. This becomes most acute in the period of working towards termination.

Discussion

The foregoing exposition has emphasized quite naturally the consequences and dangers of undertaking to make inspired interpretation a part of the method of work with a particular patient. I do not think that the opportunity for this mode of work arises with every patient, nor do I see it as a possibility with most patients until the analysis is well advanced. Clearly, therefore, I am talking about something that is different from Bion's attitude and method. I think that creativity as an individual characteristic is an extreme rarity and cannot be achieved by any specific discipline. But for people of lesser capabilities moments of inspiration do arise and, if seized and weathered with some courage, can lead on to other moments. In my own experience these moments arise particularly when the collaboration with the patient has reached a good level of trust and understanding, so that instances of comradeship can take place and the beaten track be abandoned for a bit. But the future buffeting of doubt and anxiety is quite severe, as I have explained.

What, then, are the consequences of retreat from these opportunities? I think that we fail the particular patients with whom such occasions arise and afford them a less rich experience, a diminished likelihood of being able to carry on the type of self-analytic work after the termination that can hold promise of further progress in integration. For the analyst the consequences must be a similar limitation in the development of his independence in psychoanalytic thought and method, curtailment of discovery, and reluctance to reveal his work to others.

CHAPTER FIFTEEN

Repression, forgetting, and unfaithfulness

(1974)

This clinical study of repression follows the vicissitudes of forgetfulness and unfaithfulness to love objects in the transference situation, when splitting and the use of projective identification have lessened in the threshold of the depressive position.

INTRODUCTION

The concept of repression winds its way throughout the entire length of Freud's work, beginning with the *Studies in Hysteria* (1895d) and ending with "Analysis Terminable and Interminable" (1937c). At first he considered it to be equivalent to the concept of defence, but later he differentiated between repression as a specific mechanism and defence as the wider category of defensive operations. In this process of

---

Published in the Scientific Bulletin of the British Psycho-Analytical Society, 1974.

subsuming repression under the wider category, the concept tended to get lost. Writing about it in the 1937 paper "Analysis Terminable and Interminable", Freud attempted to rescue it from being overwhelmed by the other mechanisms that were being described by various authors at the time. I do not wish here to trace in any detail the ways in which Freud struggled to give this important concept definitive form, the ways in which it was linked to the libido theory, later in a sense "sexualized" and linked to the conflicts between male and female and between active and passive, and, finally, linked to anxiety when Freud saw that anxiety was a motive force of repression and not a consequence of its activity. Instead, I want to turn attention to two more poetic statements of Freud's—one a very early statement in which he tried to find a model for the concept of the transference, and one thirty years later, when he tried to use the same model to describe the action of repression. I turn to these more poetic statements because I think that in them we find something of the clinician's vision, which is in the case of Freud something very different from the theoretician's conceptions.

In 1905 ("Fragment of an Analysis of a Case of Hysteria", 1905e [1901]), Freud writes:

> What are transferences? They are new editions or facsimiles of the impulses and phantasies which were aroused and made conscious during the process of analysis. But they have this peculiarity which is characteristic of their species—that they replace some earlier person by the person of the physician. To put it another way: a whole series of psychological experiences are reviewed, not as belonging to the past, but as applied to the person of the physician at the present moment. Some of these transferences have a content which differs from that of their model in no respect whatever except for substitution. These then, to keep to the same metaphor, are merely new impressions or reprints. Others are more ingeniously constructed. Their content has been subjected to a moderating influence—to sublimation as I call it. And they may even become conscious by cleverly taking advantage of some real peculiarity in the physician's person or circumstances,

> and attaching themselves to that. These then will no longer be new editions but revised editions. [p. 116]

I wish to draw attention to the "cleverness" that Freud cites as the foundation of these revised editions. By this he implies that the past has been made acceptable by some modification of its content. This tampering with the truth is emphasized again when Freud returns to this analogy 31 years later. He writes ("Analysis Terminable and Interminable", 1937c):

> It was from one of these mechanisms, repression, that the study of neurotic process took its whole start. There was never any doubt that repression was not the only procedure which the ego could employ for its purposes. Nevertheless a repression is something quite peculiar, and is more sharply differentiated from the other mechanisms than they are from one another. I should like to make this relation to the other mechanisms clear by an analogy, though I know that in these matters analogies never carry us very far. Let us imagine what might have happened to a book at a time when books were not printed in editions but were written out individually. Suppose that a book of this kind contained statements of a kind which in later times were regarded as undesirable, as for instance according to Robert Eisler (1929) the writings of Flavius Josephus must have contained passages about Jesus Christ which were offensive to later Christendom. At the present day the only defensive mechanism to which the official censorship could resort would be to confiscate and destroy every copy of the whole edition. At that time however various methods were used for making the book innocuous. One method would be for the offending passages to be thickly crossed through so that they were illegible. In that way the book could not be transcribed, and the next copyists of the book would produce a text which was unexceptionable but which had gaps in certain passages and so might be unintelligible in them. Another way, however, if the authorities were not satisfied with this but wished also to conceal any indication that the text had been mutilated, would be for them to proceed to distort the text. Single words would be left out or replaced by others and new sentences interpo-

> lated. Best of all the whole passage would be erased and a new one which said exactly the opposite set in its place. The next transcriber would then produce a text which would arouse no suspicion but was falsified. It no longer contained what the author wished to say. And it is highly probable that the corrections had not been made in the direction of truth. [p. 236]

If we attempt to amalgamate these two statements using the same analogy, one a statement about the transference and the other a statement about repressions, what we have as a result is something that can be envisaged as a series of relationships, each a transference relationship and each involving a clever distortion of the truth of this primary model. From this point of view the transference that we examine in the analytic situation would be seen as only the most recent transference event, and one that would present as its content evidences of this serial distortion of the primal relation that is being represented. The process of reconstruction of the infantile relationships would involve a whole series of revisions of bowdlerized history. For this reason, and for many others, of course, psychoanalysis has moved away from its early concern with reconstruction and is now inclined to view the transference as being primarily of interest because of its immediacy—that is, the immediate evidence of infantile relationships to internal objects being externalized onto the person of the analyst. Psychoanalysis is not alone in taking this view of history; there are historians who would also say that the writing of history is primarily an activity of the imagination working in the present and utilizing events of the past for investigating manifestations of the present. It is on the basis of this view of history and of the analytic process that I wish to discuss the mechanism of repression and to describe its operation in unconscious phantasy, very much in the way that Freud describes the activity of clever distortions of the truth, producing "revised editions" by means of omission and interpolation. I discuss it under four headings: (1) the content of the repressed; (2) the mechanism of repression; (3) the return of the repressed; (4) the economics of repression. In doing this, I try to relate the operation of the mechanism to the analytic process in its longitudinal aspect.

The content of the repressed

Clinical material No. 1

Shortly after a holiday break, and in expectation of a bill for the previous month, somewhat troubled by the realization that his improved income implied the necessity to raise the low fee he was paying to approximate to the analyst's regular fee, a patient dreamt the following:

> *He was upstairs in either the front or the back of a tram, and a gang entered to rob a safe that seemed to be there. . . . He felt he could either call for help and resist, or cooperate with them by allowing them to tie him up and knock him about a little. He decided on the latter course, thinking that perhaps he could get a share of the loot. Accordingly he allowed a tough fellow to knock him about and imprison him behind criss-cross aluminium bars (which reminded him of a piece of sculpture he had seen, called "Unknown Political Prisoner"). After the thieves had gone, he extricated himself and went down to tell the conductor, who said, "The devils!"—but showed no sympathy for the cut on the patient's cheek. At that moment he noticed a little Negro boy who was a favourite pupil of his, sitting with his father. But as he could not remember the child's name, he introduced himself to the father by saying: "I'm your child's teacher."*

He awoke at that moment and could not remember the child's name until he was relating the dream in his session some hours later.

We already knew this "gang" well from many dreams and knew its connection with the actual gang of semi-delinquents with whom the years of primary and secondary school had been spent. We knew how this "gang"-view of the world inspired in him an exploitative and insincere relation to the analyst as a member, or even leader, of a psychoanalytic "gang"; how it prevented his sexual relation with his wife from being tender, since he always had to be in a position of "getting a piece" to boast about internally; how it stamped on his character generally a shallow, opportunistic and fraudulent quality. An "unknown political prisoner", indeed!

What I wish to stress about the dream is the relation of the robbing of the safe and the loss from the patient's mind of the name of his favourite little boy pupil. The point is this: he allowed, and even connived in, the robbing of his good object—the breast, his analyst in regard to fees and cooperation—and as a result found himself identified with the robbed object in his own parental role towards his little pupil, empty-headed of the child's name. He is identified with an object that has lost its capacity to recognize a child as a unique individual, rather than merely "my pupil", "my child", "my patient"—in a possessive and egocentric sense. It is an old accusation from his childhood that his parents exploited him in this way, that his mother showed him off, his father boasted of his talents. Later work in the analysis strongly suggested that he had misconstrued the quality of their pride and affection.

Discussion

Repression is a mechanism of defence that creates gaps in the availability of experiences for conscious recollection and reconstruction. These gaps result from an unconscious phantasy in which something—either an object or its contents—is lost, strayed, or stolen. The clinical consequences are either primary, due to the altered internal situation, or secondary, due to identification processes. In that sense they appear to be symptomatic or characterological. In the first instance gaps in memory result; in the second, defective capacity for recollection. In the example given, both of these consequences are manifest in the patient after he had awakened from the dream. In the first instance the content of his object, the names of the children, had been stolen, as shown by the defective conductor–daddy only referring to the gang as "the devils" and ignoring the patient's cut cheek. The waking patient was then unable to remember either his little pupil's name or the name of the sculptor of the "Unknown Political Prisoner". But furthermore his identification with the defective object is manifested in the session by his attitude to his own inability to recollect these two names. In the dream he is content to cover the defect with

"I'm your little boy's teacher", and in the waking state to cover his defective relation to the sculptor with a vague reference to "The Tate" . . . "Zadkin, or somebody". He manifests unconcern about other people's individuality as an aspect of his character at this moment.

With regard to the primary defect of memory produced by an act of repression, the nature of the defect is distinctly different, depending on whether the lost, strayed, or stolen thing is an object or its content. Loss of an object produces a widespread and general amnesia for a whole *category of experiences* of the type represented by the relationship to that particular internal part- or whole-object; loss of an object's contents, on the other hand, produces only amnesia for specific events or facts.

The mechanism of repression

The circumstances of psychic structure that make repression possible are variable. The narcissistic organization shown in this dream is most frequent. Weakness, neglect, apathy, or stupidity on the part of good parts of the self, both adult and infantile, are in evidence towards the delinquent and destructive parts.

In my experiences, the stolen, strayed, or lost object or attribute is invariably hidden or buried in the faeces (note the little *Negro* boy), whence it is in danger of being lost by anal expulsion into the outside world. This is the link between repression and manic mechanism, with their characteristic denial of psychic reality, as described by Abraham ("Notes on Manic-Depressive Insanity", 1911) and later in greater detail by Melanie Klein ("A Contribution to The Psychogenesis of Manic-Depressive States", 1935). The dread of losing good objects in this way poses a depressive problem that is very clearly seen in patients who have lost a parent in early life and retain little or no conscious memory of the relationship or person.

Clinical material No. 2

The approach of the Christmas holidays at the end of the first year in the analysis of an adolescent student was complicated by his having early on entered an agreement for a package tour, along with some friends, which would take him away for three weeks, missing the first two weeks of analysis in the new term. The consequence had been a series of anxiety dreams related to his sexual behaviour and possessiveness of his widowed mother, but his mind was utterly closed to the reconsideration of his plans.

In the last week of the analysis before the holiday, he brought a dream:

> *There were some moths, and he wondered if they were British or had been bred abroad. They seemed either wax- or flesh-coloured, and he felt troubled by them in some way. But his professor said, "Don't worry. Put them in a capsule (You know, like they did with the Beatles records—a time capsule, Music of the 1960's) and bury them somewhere. Then forget about them. You can always dig them up later."*

He knew that the analyst, like his own parents, and he himself, in fact, had been "bred abroad" and could easily see that the moths referred to "MOTH–er" and to the butterfly on the lamp-shade of the consulting-room. He admired his professor but was suspicious of his being universally liked. He had studied the man's charm and had found it partly to consist of never hurting people's feelings by disagreeing or criticizing. He somehow always seemed to agree, even though he sometimes subtly altered the other person's meaning in restatement. The father, who died when the patient was in latency, was also very charming, but the patient had long associated his mother's affectionate appellation of "Hon", short for "Honey", to "HUN", the term used for the German in the First World War. He felt a similar suspicion towards the analyst as a father, while already clearly possessively attached to the analysis as a mothering situation. In his memory, the years prior to his father's death were relatively empty and the few recollections lacked vividness, markedly in contrast to the vibrant and full recall of the years immediately following.

After the dream was interpreted—a "beautiful interpretation", he said—the recollection of early separation from his mother flooded his associations in vivid detail. From the age of five, he had been sent to "camp", as was the custom in his parents' circle, for three weeks each summer up to the time of his father's death. These excursions had been a torment to him, of loneliness and anxiety, tantrums and weeping, until he learned to "forget about" his mother, probably under the tuition of an elder cousin.

Discussion

The dream shows with some brilliance the mechanism of this "forgetting". His internal mother was protectively encapsulated and buried in his faeces, under the direction of a destructive and tricky part—"cousin"—of himself, not yet clearly differentiated from the rival—"professor-HUN" father. The danger to the mother in this procedure is explicitly denied but revealed in the uncertainty between "wax" and "flesh" colour of the moths. The danger of loss is similarly denied in the assumption that "you can always dig them up later", but the injunction "forget about them" may also, after all, include forgetting that you buried them at all, or ever possessed them.

It is clear that the patient has been driven to act out an early anxiety situation with the aim of obviating separation anxiety in relation to the external object (mother–analyst) by repression of the relationship. The dream shows the dynamics of the repression and also the latent anxiety consequences that had been adumbrated in the earlier series of anxiety dreams. Again the narcissistic organization is evident (the bad cousin–professor) and shows how inadequate splitting-and-idealization (confusion between the father and the bad cousin part of the self) contributes to the strength of the defensive tendencies.

However, it is of interest to note how different is the "repressed" in the two cases mentioned, how much more primitive and pathological is the first instance than the second. There the primal good object is being robbed of its contents, with the result that the patient suffers a general defect in his mental capacities—i.e. to remember the names of his pupil–children, in identification with the damaged mother–breast. In the second case the object itself is being carefully buried-in-the-faeces with the consequent capacity for repression of the specific relationship, to be able to forget that particular object in the outside world, i.e. the analyst–mother, when he is on holiday.

The struggle set in motion by this piece of analytic work was particularly illuminating as the patient became distressingly aware of his reluctance to miss the two weeks of analysis but yet could not find the strength in himself to face the expected mockery from his friends in the event of his withdrawing from the group agreement.

The return of the repressed

In both cases events in psychic reality producing repression were set in motion by a *decision*. In both cases this decision involved a breach of fidelity to the good object, a retreat from depressive anxieties in a conflict situation. Although the ego of the first patient is clearly more primitive and the objects more partial, the events more subject to the use of projective identification (inside the tram) and the narcissism based on a more primitive form of sadism and aggression, both conflicts hang upon the balance of Ps↔D (Bion), between paranoid–schizoid and depressive value systems in the object relations. I am suggesting that indeed the mechanism of repression teeters upon the knife-edge of sparing-the-self vs. sparing-the-object mental pain, and thus it has already come a long way from the more abandonedly destructive schizoid mechanisms such as splitting processes and massive projective identification.

Recovery of lost objects, bits of objects, and contents of objects from the faeces is a depressive task, which must be performed for the self by good objects when the self rejects the mental pain of longing, guilt, remorse. This state of rejection is manifest in relation to gaps in the memory by dismissal of the problem. The recovery of lost dreams during an analytic session, either by effort on the patient's part out of concern for the work or spontaneously during the session as a result of the analyst's work, is the most common realization of this balanced situation.

Clinical material No. 3

A young woman, whose analysis had only recently broken through a severe impasse at the threshold of the depressive position, returned to the Monday session in a mood of aloofness, self-pity, evasion of responsibility, and abandonment to nymphomaniac phantasies, in all of which her disturbed little boy was the chief persecutor and fountainhead of her misery. The retreat into this state not only evaded the intense loneliness at infantile levels related to the weekend break, but also avoided the problem at an adult level, of continuing the education she had abandoned some years earlier for a hasty and early marriage. This problem related to her early betrayal of her parents by disappointing them at school, always showing promise with her unusual talents and intelligence, only to throw away each opportunity by indolence.

She dreamed on Saturday night that

> *. . . there was a dead girl who might have been murdered by the patient's little boy, and, to protect him, she was burying the body, covering it lightly with soil. The head, however, seemed separate from the body and was shaped like a ball. But then it seemed that there was a second body and that the crime consisted not in causing the deaths but in concealing the first one.*

During the weekend the boy had been annoying the cat by kicking his new ball at it. The patient had confiscated the ball and at first thrown it into the garden, but then, fearing it might deflate in the cold, she had hidden it in the house. In the morning, after the dream, she could not remember where she had hidden it. The body she connected with her brother-in-law's favourite calendar of a nude girl painted with gold, which he affectionately called "the finest brain in England". In fact, one of the patient's friends, the "finest brain" she knew, had been taken to hospital suddenly before the weekend.

After the dream and its related material had been interpreted, the patient acknowledged that, quite unlike weekends in the previous two months of the recent holiday, she had not thought of the analysis once during the separation and had felt reluctant to come to the session that day. As the warmth returned to the transference relationship during the session, she felt very weepy as thoughts turned to her father's early death.

The economics of repression and return

When the object has been buried in the faeces, its safety is always very precarious because of the danger of inadvertent anal expulsion. This is increased, of course, by the working of the repression, which induces forgetfulness of both the object itself and of the desire to preserve it for future recovery. To this source of insecurity there is added a manic trend towards expulsion of the object, in defence against the guilt coming from two sources—the unfaithfulness on the one hand, and the joylessness of the object's existence in the faeces on the other.

But one can see that a consortium of defensive tendencies of this type finds very little opposition unless the guilt is backed by an awareness of need for the object. If love were strong enough, the defences would never have been set in motion in the first place. But being a rather sophisticated defensive system mobilized by well-organized aspects of the infantile personality, it has an association with arrogance and ideas of independence that deny need for the object. Thus in the struggle from narcissistic organization towards object relations, progress in respect of the problem of repression as an aspect of character is only made when the process has gone some considerable distance and reached what I have described as the "threshold of the depressive position".

Clinical material No. 4

A middle-aged man who had undertaken analysis because of a lack of achievement in his business had come gradually to realize the pathological significance and compulsive structure of his promiscuity and unfaithfulness. Three years of work had shown the narcissistic organization, which consisted of an arrogant anal and phallic sadistic "Negro" aspect of the infantile structures who seduced and dominated the little-boy part, sometimes with threats but more often with promises of worldly gain and sensual gratification, a bit in the style of Mephistopheles with Faust. This representation derived its form from a period of homosexual submission in early puberty to an older Negro man, who used to take him to football games, a companionship earlier enjoyed with his deceased father.

During the third year of the analysis some gains had been made with regard to unfaithfulness to his wife and in resisting the opportunist trends in his behaviour. This advance was accompanied by dreams of mounting resistance to the influence of the "Negro". On the night before the last session prior to the Christmas break, he dreamed that

> *. . . he was cycling with a black briefcase under his arm, but it slipped out and seemed to become somehow attached to the back wheel, so that it was dragged along the ground. He went on, looking back occasionally to see that it was still there. Then he was going past the football stadium, and rowdy crowds were coming out. A Negro and another man began to molest him, and he fought back. At a pause in the fighting, however, he thought of a better course, since the violence had gone out of the conflict. He took an Atlas from the briefcase. This he showed to the two assailants, who were very interested in the maps.*

His association to the Atlas was "Charles Atlas", the strong man whose ads he had been so impressed by in his youth—"You can have a body like mine", or some such thing.

It was clear that the briefcase represented the faeces containing the dead father, who was only resurrected from his precarious position when the patient became aware of the need for an ego-ideal with whom to identify. It is of great interest that this identification was not of a projective sort, with the powerful body for the purpose of defeating his attackers, but an introjective one with the persuasive salesman aspect of the father, who was interested in helping boys develop their bodies and minds. Following the elucidation of the dream, the patient began to weep, mainly about his wife going to the States to visit her parents, occasions previously of secret satisfaction and promiscuous intentions for my patient. But he was also aware that he was unhappy about the break in the analysis. This was a very marked shift from his former manic flights from separation pain in the transference.

SUMMARY

We set out to rescue the concept of repression from an oblivion to which Freud's shift from libido theory, with its energetics model, to structural theory, with its emphasis on integration, seemed inevitably to consign it. In order to carry out this rescue, we attempted to show that the phenomenology of forgetfulness, particularly of a type that can be related directly to unfaithfulness to love objects, could best be understood in terms of the concept of repression when it was seen to act in a structural rather than in a cathectic manner. We tried to relate this point of view to the poetic analogies Freud had used, both early and late in his career, to describe the working of repression.

The main body of the paper consisted of four clinical examples by means of which we tried to exemplify a number of points: that repression comes into play in relation to the phenomenology of forgetfulness and unfaithfulness fairly late in the analytic process, at the threshold of the depressive position; that the mechanism operates through the unconscious phantasy of an object, whole or part, or its contents being lost, strayed, or stolen and buried in the faeces; that this carries a danger of inadvertent manic expulsion of the object; that a recovery of the lost object tends to depend upon the service of a good external object, unless the person can feel the need for recovery of the object to reinforce the impact of regret and guilt in moving the subject towards the depressive position.

Conclusions

By tracing Freud's use of a poetic image—the reprinting and revising of editions of books—from its early use describing the transference forward 32 years to its subsequent use to describe repression, I have attempted to create a background in his thought for a modern use of the term "repression" in the context of clinical work carried on with the structural framework of theory. What could only be thought of as a useful analogy in earlier days can now be given a certain concreteness in our mode of thought, even though our theory is no more than a model. The concrete object, the book, of Freud's analogy now becomes the concrete internal object, which is manipulated in psychic reality through the means of omnipotence generated in the narcissistic organization. In the first example, the manipulation appears to be exclusively contained within the dream of "sharing the loot", and only the consequences of this "cleverness" can be found in the patient's relations in the outside world, as manifest in forgetting the names of his pupils and in his characteristic indifference to the accuracy of his recollections. But in both the second and third examples, the cleverness has involved the acting-out part of the process, the holiday trip in the second example and the throwing out and hiding the ball in the third. In all three cases the attack is upon the maternal transference relationship, mainly at the part-object level of the breast, and represents a clever attempt to obviate the emotional cost of that object by seeking, by one means or other, to enjoy its benefits when it is present without suffering pain in separation. The fourth example is at a more whole-object level.

These four examples, by focusing on the momentary functioning of the mechanism of repression in the transference, demonstrate its operation in detail, so that one can appreciate that, while the wish to forget may be conscious, the mechanism of repression is totally unconscious, insofar as it consists of an infantile phantasy of violence and hiding the *corpus delicti* or its stolen or lost contents in the faeces. This distinction between the wish and the mechanism has been overlooked by critics of Freud's modes of thought, especially by philosophers (e.g. Wittgenstein, Hamlyn), who tend to accuse him of equivocation.

In closing this paper, I wish to make clear that I do not think that repression is the only, or even the main, mechanism operative in defects of memory. It is a relatively sophisticated mechanism, closely related to depressive conflicts, and it appears in analysis as an important factor in defensive operations in the transference only after more primitive mechanisms such as splitting and projective identification have been greatly lessened. I do not think that it accounts for the so-called "infantile amnesia".

CHAPTER SIXTEEN

Narcissistic foundation of the erotic transference

(1974)

This examination of the eroticized transference as an expression of a hidden focus of the narcissistic organization—which accounts for its intractable resistance—and which is usually accompanied by a compromised countertransference, includes an enlightening discussion on the technique for dealing with the erotic transference. Chapter seventeen, also written in 1974, discusses further the role of pregenital confusions in erotomania.

The concept of Oedipal conflict, even when taken at both part- and whole-object levels, coupled with powerful concepts such as zonal and geographical confusions, or recognized in terms of the powerful anxieties that drive the utilization of erotism as a defensive manoeuvre—this whole orchestration of the concept—does not seem adequate, in the sense of being able to cover the phenomenology at hand. My thesis is that the dynamic approach to the problem of erotization of the transference, and therefore the problem of a powerful type of resistance that lends itself too well to acting-out both in and out of the transference, does not adequately reveal the complexity of mental functioning, nor is interpretation along these lines successful in promoting working through.

In contrast, the structural consideration, especially that aspect of it which views narcissism and object relations from an organizational point of view and sees them deployed in constant conflict, like "armies in the night", their battles revealed by the flares of dreams, seems more satisfying intellectually and more potent in the consulting-room. The aim of this paper is to illustrate this thesis with clinical material and to undertake some discussion with reference to the analytic literature, Freud's "Dora" in particular.

Clinical material

A young woman, intelligent and attractive and probably gifted as an artist, came to analysis because of failure in her relations with men and a deteriorating relation to her professional field. An earlier attempt at analysis had been a failure, for she had found herself paralysed in thought and speech by the woman analyst's presence and ménage. After a somewhat difficult first year, fraught with silences and great difficulties in communication, it became apparent through her dreams that a very erotic transference was developing, which had its foundations in her early relation to a rather youthful and vivacious father. But her method of working in the analysis was so cyclical that this current of the transference did not appear to present any obstacle to progress for quite a long time. Interesting and important developments relevant to the organization of her personality, the distribution of parts of her infantile structure into her older sister and brother, her possessiveness of the mother, and her tendency to projective identification with the breast appeared to move steadily forward and seemed to promise relief of anxiety and release from inhibition in her daily life.

However, no such happy consequence materialized. On the contrary, her life seemed to become more constricted, her unhappiness to deepen, and her friendships to dry up. A tone of complaint and even accusation began to permeate her relationship to the analyst and the work, despite her evident interest and enjoyment. She did not think the analysis was fruitless. Far from it! Her complaint, unverbalized or only hinted at, was that the analysis was taking possession of her whole life. And, indeed, this seemed to be true. Although extremely attractive to men in the past, she had succeeded in denuding her life of boyfriends by means the analyst could not discern. Similarly, her relations to women her own age had fallen into a kind of disuse, and the several older women, for whom she either worked or with whom she studied, tended to be rather systematically provoked with complaints and criticisms. Evidence seemed quite convincing that she was in considerable distress, and making life a bit miserable, in addition, for the various people who were fond of her.

As this aspect of the transference moved into greater and greater domination of the proceedings, and fairly bid to push all else out of the way, the analytic sessions took on a new and fairly alarming complexion. Although there had always been sessions of relative silence and there had always been a tendency to vague and equivocal modes of expression and description, her communications now seemed rather divided. Either she was unusually forthright, complaining, and demanding, or her language became vague and allusive to the point of mystification. She cried a great deal in the sessions, claimed that her life outside the analysis was empty and unbearable, and generally left little doubt that nothing but marriage to the analyst–daddy could possibly keep her from suicide. Interpretation merely hurt her feelings, and the full weight of her impressive intelligence was brought to bear on the demolition of the differentiation of adult from infantile sexuality, of the infantile transference from the collaboration in the analytic work.

Finally accusations of wanton cruelty appeared, to the effect that the analyst enjoyed observing the effects of his powerful attraction for her, attraction that stemmed not from his body or even from his personality, but rather specifically from his voice. In fact, it could be made even more specific than that. It was the comforting quality of his voice that affected her directly, in her genitalia. No, she did not feel that it was an affected quality, she did not feel seduced or manipulated, but she could not deny the impression that the analyst's vanity was titillated by evidence of his power.

Into this atmosphere of mounting desperation—on both sides to be sure—the patient's continued, but faltering, capacity to recall her dreams entered like a cooling breeze in midsummer swelter. To a Monday session she brought the following:

> *She was walking with a middle-aged man along a beach that ran between the mud-flats of an estuary and a high embankment. She ran up this and to her surprise found that she could see a university town in the distance. It was much like Oxford, but the buildings were more like Italian cathedrals, with magnificent façades, their portals festooned with jewel-like rounded bobbles. The man came up behind her and, to her displeasure, put his hand between her thighs and felt her genitalia. He seemed to count to ten, and she thought perhaps she had some pimples there.*

She thought the man was quite like the analyst and that his being behind her and stimulating her genitalia resembled her recent complaints about his comforting voice. She had indeed recently had a spot or two on her face. She also thought that her annoyance in the dream was similar to her feelings about the analyst insisting on her describing the events she observed in her mind during the session, rather than allowing her to "talk about the things she wanted to", which generally meant topics that she had prepared before the session.

Interpretation of this dream linked it with many items of recent material, including evidence of anus–vagina confusion (mud-flats behind and cathedral portal in front), and of confusion of identity with mother due to projective identification (her own genitalia vs. the Cathedral portal). Emphasis was placed on the way in which this latter confusion caused her to misinterpret the analyst–father's examination of her masturbatory habits (often interpreted but never as yet acknowledged) as a sexual seduction, denying that it was indeed comforting for her secrecy to be penetrated. In the companion dream of the session:

> *She inadvertently hurt a woman's feelings by being critical of a third woman's red hair, not having noticed that her companion's was of the same colour.*

This referred to an event in which she had hurt a friend's feelings about her taste in clothes. The two dreams together show how obsessional mechanisms, of separating the parents and her relationship with them (into separate dreams), played a role in the difficulty of communication and the acting out with her women friends.

Once again the hoped-for relief of the patient's suffering and resistance was not forthcoming. If anything, a paradoxical worsening was evident, and feelings of humiliation were added to the existing list of mental pains. She became more complaining and hostile, but in the following two weeks she began to acknowledge and describe in some detail a manner of masturbation that had persisted from as far back in childhood as she could remember. Nonetheless the patient felt she was having a breakdown. It seemed unlikely, in view of the pace at which the material kept coming to clarify the transference.

On the Friday two weeks later, after a frantic Thursday of weeping and accusations, which was dealt with by an extensive review of the evidence of recent weeks, she brought the following dream:

> *Her friend Sonia was in an advanced state of pregnancy somewhere at the other end of a large room with her mother and brother. The patient was standing naked by a washbasin, and her older sister Louise was behind her masturbating her. On the adjacent wall was mounted a piece of paper in Louise's writing, telling something about a "dyed coney coat". Then she was at a drapery shop watching the pregnant Sonia, who was before a mirror holding against her body a length of emerald-green velvet with large white flowers, considering it for a wedding dress. The patient thought it lovely, and, when Sonia went awcy, she tried the material. But she realized that it did not really suit her.*

The patient connected the "coney" coat with one she had rather coveted recently, a "dyed striped coney", but she had not bought it because she generally thinks fur-coats are bourgeois.

The term "striped" was absent in the dream, and indeed she had felt in the dream that "something was missing". This was in fact the first time that Louise had appeared in a dream, and the analyst knew virtually nothing about this sister. The patient had never been close to her and now described her as a rather free, wilful, and wild creature. It became clear, as she talked, that in fact Louise had always been something of an ideal to her. In response to the analyst's direct question she admitted that "coney" probably meant "cunt", a "foul" word that she specially detests. Louise was very free in her use of strong language, a thing never encouraged by the parents.

It seems fairly unequivocal that looking at her own naked body in the dream, looking at Sonia's pregnant body, and looking at Sonia looking at herself in the mirror with the velvet material become condensed in the image of the patient looking at herself in the mirror draped with the velvet. Furthermore, the state of mind of envious voyeurism is clearly inspired by Louise masturbating the patient, which changes the lovely flowered-velvet genital into the striped coney "cunt", which is despised as "bourgeois"—that is, "married" rather than free and wild. It is of some importance that the analyst's couch is covered in emerald-green velvet with a white tissue spread on the pillow. In other words, the dream reveals how lying on the analyst's couch has had the significance of drawing her into a state of projective identification with the "mother full of babies" under the influence of a masturbatory excitement, stimulated, not by the analyst–father's voice, as claimed in the "Italian cathedral" dream, but of a "big sister" part of the patient's own infantile organization. The erotic transference resistance had been broken into by the revelation in the dream of a hidden area of narcissistic organization, which functioned as a collusion against parental standards.

DISCUSSION

Freud says, and it is usually taken to be true, that Dora broke off her analysis with him because he failed to analyse the erotic transference. Yet we have been analysing such transferences for many years now with scarcely greater success in many cases. I cannot, in this brief paper, review the literature on the subject, but clearly one hope after another regarding dynamics, genetics, countertransference, and clarification of anxiety has failed to produce a working solution for this knotty problem.

* * *

In this paper I have tried to illustrate the role of hidden narcissism in rendering the erotic transference so "sticky". The fact that it often fastens itself upon what Freud called the "peculiarities of the person of the analyst", by which he meant, not idiosyncrasies, but individual qualities, does indeed tend to arouse particular countertransference interference. However, these tend more to interfere with the analyst's capacity to investigate than to evoke the quality of the patient's resistance. In desperation the analyst may easily fall into a tacit encouragement of the patient's displacement of the erotic attachment into an acting out. This tends, inevitably, to render the analysis more, rather than less, difficult.

Instead of encouraging such a displacement, it is necessary for the analyst to struggle with the countertransference and meet the erotization directly. Insistence on the analytic method, on the fundamental infantile nature of the desires and feelings, and on the masturbatory origin of the excitement felt in the consulting-room, will usually, in my experience, bear the kind of fruit the clinical material illustrates. Even with patients who seem far from what one could reasonably call "narcissistic characters", a hidden focus of narcissistic organization will ultimately declare itself. From beneath the erotic transference the violence of Oedipal jealousy and the cruelty of wounded vanity will come into evidence.

CHAPTER SEVENTEEN

The role of pregenital confusions in erotomania

(1974)

A clinical example using mainly dream material illustrates how the narcissistic organization interferes with a proper differentiation between adult and infantile levels of functioning and with the ability to protect internal objects (mother's body and identity) from intrusive attacks through projective identification. Chapter sixteen provides further elucidation of the narcissistic organization and technique.

Clinical material

When Mrs R first came to analysis, she was disquieted mainly by evidences of an inexplicable coldness and brutality, which burst out at her children, a boy and girl, whose development seemed in many ways unsatisfactory. But in the course of a difficult analysis, and against great

Printed in the Scientific Bulletin of the British Psycho-Analytical Society, 1974.

resistance, the idealization of her husband and their marriage broke down and revealed a floridly perverse relationship in which she played the willing slave to his genius, obsessionality, and selfishness. As she gradually disengaged herself from this, the relationship became insupportable, and they agreed to stay together for the children's sake alone. Through this four-year period the analytic situation forged slowly ahead in the face of a strongly erotic transference and intense voyeurism, which gradually revealed an infantile situation of fusion with a parental couple related to sharing the parental bedroom during her breast-feeding period. This generated a strongly blissful state of mind, which resisted interpretation, but when it yielded on occasions, evidences appeared of a brutal wilfulness and independence of judgement covered by surface compliance. This attitude had indeed characterized her childhood following a period of stress during which a change of house, removal from the parental bedroom, weaning, toilet training, and the birth of a baby sister had followed hard upon the heels of one another.

As these transference configurations were worked through in the next year, Mrs R began to feel that the end of the analysis was in sight, and a tentative date was mooted. She then fell passionately in love with a man she had known but hardly noticed for many years, and she set about winding up her marriage in the expectation of consummating this new relationship once she was free. She now felt quite strong and independent, and a date of termination was set for the following summer. But no sooner was this agreed in principle than a distinct change became noticeable in her states of mind in and out of the analysis. Erotomania seemed to invade her new relationship, while a certain conspiratorial and brutal attitude began to spoil the orderly disengagement from her husband.

At the same time her relationship to the analyst became patronizing, doubt and even contempt invaded her feelings about the earlier analytic work, and she began to insist that she had to terminate forthwith for lack of money. When this was discounted as a motive, she agreed to continue on the grounds that the discussions with the analyst helped her to manage the relationship with her children in this critical and delicate period. At times her dominance seemed to threaten to destroy her new love relation, but for her lover's strength and patience.

During this period, in the face of contempt and coldness, a poverty of material and the constant threat of interruption, a particular formulation could nonetheless be constructed and tightened by each new piece of material. The formulation was to this effect: unlike her weaning in childhood, which had produced a splitting of a horizontal sort in which her relationship to the breast was relinquished in favour of a secret and perverse preoccupation with her faeces idealized variously as food, penis, and babies, she was now turning away from the breast to the father's penis and entering into a fierce competition for control and possession of that object, thus invoking a confusion between nipple-in-mouth and penis-in-vagina to obviate the experience of weaning and relinquishment. But Mrs R was adamant: she could now spare the analyst only two hours a week and would miss the first week after the Easter holiday to visit her lover.

She returned cold and aloof, but to our surprise a rich yield of material followed in the next two weeks, which broke into the acting out and brought things under control once more. The night after the first session she dreamed that

> *. . . She and her lover were invited to dinner by a a couple who were his best friends, but instead of eating they were embracing at the table. Then it seemed to have just been a dream that she awakened from to find herself in bed with her husband, and she felt repelled by his advances.*

She awoke in great distress but was relieved to realize it had all been a dream. She then returned to sleep, only to have an even more upsetting dream:

> *She and another woman were in rivalry for her lover, lying in bed on either side of him. She was horrified to see that both had dark erect penises in place of nipples.*
>
> [Mrs R associated this with the fact that her mother's nipples are in fact dark and had been erect on every occasion she could remember having seen them.]

This dream seemed to indicate the state of projective identification and confusion of identity in which the baby felt herself in rivalry with the mother for the father. It demonstrated the nipple–penis confusion involved in this erotization of the breast.

At the end of that session Mrs R said that she felt it unbearable to continue without payment and would prefer to stop. The analyst indicated that these dreams made him more willing to agree, but that his own preference was unequivocally on the side of trying to bring the analysis to a proper termination. The following session she brought a dream again:

> *She was warning her children to stay away from the hive of dormant bees that her cousin Doris* [who figured in the analysis as the friend who had taught her about sex and masturbation in puberty] *had given her, but the children paid no heed. The bees awoke, buzzing angrily, and the patient shouted to the children to run, and then awoke.*

This seemed an encouraging dream, an improved differentiation of adult from infantile levels and an awareness that infantile masturbation was related to rage at being disturbed and awakened from sleep by parental sexuality (referring to the dreams of the previous session).

Mrs R seemed shocked by the dream she brought to the next session, for it seemed so strongly to confirm the formulation of her brutal treatment of her husband and contempt for his penis. In the dream

> *. . . a dog was lying whimpering on the ground beside a bitch in heat, who finally allowed him to mount her. But his penis grew huge and human and then metamorphosed into an idiot boy covered with semen who came, to Mrs R's horror, to embrace her.*
>
> [Mrs R commented that she had always found her husband's semen very repulsive, but felt quite different with her lover.]

She began to understand the brutal aspect of the erotomania and its foundation in competition with the mother for control of the father's penis and how this linked with her former outbreaks of brutality to the children. A definite softening now appeared in the transference and brought the first renewed flush of trust and good feeling towards the analyst.

That night she dreamed that

> *. . . an American man was trying to persuade her to take part in an experiment at her mother's home, to which she finally agreed, but sceptically.*
>
> *It was to take place in the garage and involved wearing earphones. When she returned to the kitchen, Mrs R was shocked to see two prostitutes lying on the kitchen table, dressed but clearly awaiting coitus. She took her little girl aside and told her not to look.*

This dream seemed to suggest the following optimistic interpretation: the analyst–daddy (American man) was finally succeeding in persuading this little girl to try the experiment of living outside the confines of mother's body and identity (the garage) in order that her sleep might be in contact with her internal objects in an auditory way, as in analysis (the earphones) instead of being disturbed (Like the angry bees) by the sight of the parental intercourse (in bed with mummy and daddy and in competition with that "other" woman) externally. That only drives her into a narcissistic organization (with Doris, who teaches her about sex and masturbation) and interferes with her recognition of the difference between adult and infantile (herself and her daughter) and thus weakens the ability to understand and protect children from the brutality that is linked to erotomania (the bitch in heat).

CHAPTER EIGHTEEN

Adhesive identification

(1974)

In this lecture, the author traces Esther Bick's investigations and his own clinical findings with autistic patients, to describe a type of narcissistic identification that is different from projective identification and about which he had written at length in Explorations in Autism *(1975), which appeared soon afterwards. (See particularly chapter 9—on Dimensionality—of that book.)*

Psychoanalysis is such an essentially historical subject and method that it really does not make sense to talk about it in any way but historically, and, of course, we have to start with Freud. However, history is like the law: the law is what the courts do, and history is what historians say; and my history is different from your history and you must not

---

This is the transcript of an informal talk to the William Alanson White Psychoanalytic Society on 25 October 1974.

expect it necessarily to correspond. It is just my way of understanding psychoanalytic history. It is a very peculiar science that we have. I do not begin yet to understand how it works or develops, and why sometimes it does not develop and sometimes it seems to shoot ahead. You can see in Freud's way of working that while he thought himself an inductive scientist, he certainly did not work purely inductively at all—he worked deductively at times. The process of his development is interestingly documented. We have in the marvellous and somewhat horrific "Project for a Scientific Psychology" (Freud, 1950a [1887–1902]), a document that states with such clarity a mass of preconceptions that he had to gradually whittle away and get rid of in order to change from a neurophysiologist to the great phenomenological psychologist that he eventually became. I suppose all of us have to do that. We have from our education and development a massive preconception of models and theories and ideas that we gradually have to get rid of in order to free ourselves to receive new impressions and to think new thoughts and entertain new models. It seems to me an extraordinarily difficult process; it tends inevitably to grind to a halt. How is it that we get kicked forward? It seems to start mainly in our consulting-rooms; when we are in trouble and nothing good seems to be happening, we begin to think again, and what I am going to present here is an outgrowth of being in trouble, and trying to find new ways of thinking.

This process of "adhesive identification" that I am going to describe is something Esther Bick and I began working on in our own separate ways and talking about together back in the early 1960s after Melanie Klein's death. We were both terribly lonely, since the person who had been carrying the load was now gone. Somebody, everybody, had to pick up the bit of it that he could carry. During that time Esther Bick was working in various ways. First of all she introduced infant observation into the curriculum of the Tavistock Clinic training for child psychotherapists, and in the Institute of Psycho-Analysis. She was also treating some psychotic patients, children, and supervising the treatment of a large number of children. I remember there came a period when she kept saying to me, "Oh, I don't know how to talk about it, they are just like that" (sticking her hands together). "It is something different." I did not know what she was talking about for a long time. I myself at that time was doing my ordinary practice, which is a mixture of neurotic patients, training cases, one or two schizophrenic patients, a few children, and supervising a lot of work with children. I began to find things with autistic children that is also like something stuck together. Gradually we came to something that we think is new and interesting, but in order to understand it, one has to go back in history, and that is what I want to do now.

Identification processes seem to me to have a very funny place in Freud's writings. As phenomena, he seems to have been very brilliant in observing identification processes; even starting from the *Studies in Hysteria* (1895d) they are mentioned. "Elizabeth" was identified with her mother and her father. "Dora" was identified. The "Rat Man" was identified, and you hear this over and over again and mentioned as having something to do with imitation, something vaguely to do with character. Then he came to the *Leonardo* (1910c) paper. Although in many ways it is not a nice paper at all from the point of view of art history, it does seem to me to be an important paper from the point of view of psychoanalytic history, because it is really the first time that Freud tries to take a life as a whole thing and to try to understand it—a great move forward for him—to separate the pathology from a matrix of health and life processes. Health did not seem to interest him very much. He seems in his early writings to be more purely a psychopathologist and not to be interested in people, you might say. The *Leonardo* paper starts something different; there he speaks of identification processes in a meaningful way that is connected with the beginnings of a concept of narcissism, and he states that there is something that he would like to call narcissistic identifications. In his paper on the "Wolf Man" (1918b [1914]), also, Freud seems to recognize narcissistic identifications and to realize that they have something to do with identity, something to do with distortions of identity.

Then, suddenly, Freud begins to take an interest in the ideal ego and the ego ideal, and then finally the superego in the 1920s. The concept of identification comes to be used suddenly in a very different way. Using Ferenczi's term, he speaks of introjection into the ego and the establishment of a gradient within the ego by which a portion of it is separated off as the superego, and this he calls an identification. That is very puzzling, because what it seems to set up is an internal voice, an observing function, a part of the ego that now observes the ego, criticizes it. He seems quickly to forget the other ego ideal function—that is, of encouraging and supporting the ego in favour of the harsher, more restrictive and punitive aspects of it. Somehow this conceptual use of the term "identification" for the process by which the superego is established does not seem to fit with the phenomenological use of the term "identification" as it is used in the case histories in particular, whereas I think it has something to do with imitations and being like somebody else; the superego does not seem to be, as Freud sees it, part of the ego or to induce character manifestations. If you judge from the little paper on the anal character (1908b) or the one on "Some Character Types Met with in Psycho-Analytic Work" (1916d), Freud's idea of character still seems to be bound to the libido theory and the way in which libido is diverted, inhibited, sublimated, reacted against, and so on. His idea was that character is built up through the management of the vicissitudes of instinct. This problem has puzzled me greatly, and having taught it for many years, I have always tried to understand it. It seems to me that if you compare Freud's paper on *Mourning and Melancholia* (1917e [1915]) with Abraham's paper on melancholia and manic-depressive states, you can see that there is a very important difference in the kind of model they had in their minds. Freud in *Mourning and Melancholia* gets into a terrific muddle about who is abusing whom. Is the ego ideal abusing the ego? Is the ego abusing this object that has been taken inside? On the other hand, Abraham is quite clear about it and speaks about it in very concrete terms. He says that an object has been attacked internally and turned into faeces; it has then been defecated out and then compulsively reintrojected by a process that has the meaning of eating the faeces, and that this faecal object is then established internally. Freud could never have talked in this way, and for a very important reason. He could not get rid of the preconceptions of the neurophysiological sort on the one hand and the so-called hydrostatic model of instinct on the other in order to conceptualize the mind as a place, as a space. Nowhere in his writings is there a conceptualization of spaces. He comes a little closer to it in the Schreber case (Freud, 1911c [1910]), where he talks about the world destruction fantasy. He talks a little bit there about what world was destroyed—inner or outer—but then he hedges it in a very peculiar way and says that it was a world that had been built up through the precipitate of identifications. He uses the words "identifications" and "sublimations". I have never understood what he meant by that. He also hedges the problem, because you may remember that he speaks of this world as having fallen to pieces by the withdrawal of libido, as if a kind of magnet could draw the mortar out from between the bricks and the thing would just fall to pieces. But then, as a footnote, in which he quotes Heine's poem, he makes it quite clear that it has been smashed to pieces. It has not just crumbled from neglect or withdrawal of interest. It has been smashed to pieces.

I think one can see evidence that Freud had some sort of difficulty about allowing himself to shift to a model in which there was a conception of something very concrete—the inside of the mind as a place where things could really happen and not just be imagined. This term "imagined" is just not good enough to describe the events of the mind. It fudges the issue and does not account for the relentlessness and inevitability with which events follow one another, and particularly the inevitability with which attacks upon objects in this inner space, which damage these objects, produce psychopathological changes that really have to be painfully repaired and restored in order for the process of recovery to take place.

This is where Freud was and where he remained until the end of his life. In the 1920s, when Melanie Klein, who was studying with Abraham at the time, began to work with children, he almost immediately began to hear things from these children about spaces, and particularly about a very special space experienced in a very concrete way that was inside themselves, in their bodies, and in particular inside their mothers' bodies. This evidence had not really been unavailable to Freud, because if you read *Little Hans* (Freud, 1909b), you see that he talked about the same things. He talked about the time when little sister Hanna was inside the stork box, the stork box was inside the carriage, and the carriage was obviously his mother, and it was very closely connected with his fear of loaded wagons falling over, and the relationship of the horse to the wagon, and so on. Freud saw all that quite clearly, but *he did not take any interest in it.* He did not take any interest at all in Little Hans' proliferation of fantasy about the time before Hanna was born and the time before he was born, when he and Hanna were together in the stork box, and the things they did, and the things they ate, and the places they went, and so on. Freud sweeps all of that aside and attributes it to his pulling his father's leg and having revenge on him because of the stork story, as much as to say—I think, Freud says—something like, "if you expect me to believe the stork story, you've got to believe this rubbish". So he just sweeps it aside. That was the evidence that Melanie Klein did not sweep aside, and which put her on to this whole question of spaces—spaces inside the self, spaces inside objects, and a place where concrete things happened that had relentless and evident consequences and could be studied as part of the transference process. To me this is really a major move, and it was from the study of processes of phantasy related to these spaces that our concepts of the pregenital Oedipus complex and the concreteness of internal objects—the prelude to the genital Oedipus complex, part-object relationships, and so on—originate. All of the work she produced in the 1930s stemmed from this and was very controversial at that time. It took her until 1946 to make any headway at all with the problem of identification. It was in 1946 that she presented a paper called "Notes on Some Schizoid Mechanisms", in which she described splitting processes and projective identification. Under the term "projective identification" she described an omnipotent phantasy whereby, in combination with splitting processes, a part of the self can be split off and projected inside an object and by that means take possession of its body and its mentality and its identity. She described some of the consequences that arise from this confusion of identity, in particular claustrophobic anxieties and some of the severe persecutory anxieties related to claustrophobia.

The history of the so-called Kleinian group from 1946 on is by and large the history of the investigation of projective identification and splitting processes. The basic work done by

Melanie Klein on the pre-genital Oedipus complex and the technical development in child analysis are her original contributions. From 1946 on the people who worked with her really got their teeth into this, because it threw up a terrific snowstorm of phenomena and technical problems. It greatly widened the range of patients who could be approached through the psychoanalytic method. It encouraged people to apply the psychoanalytic method to more psychotic patients and schizophrenics without modifying the method. It gave them conceptual tools with which they could work, to explore phenomenology that they not only could not work with but could not even notice previously.

The point about projective identification is that it is the description of a process by which a narcissistic identification comes about—that is, a process of the omnipotent phantasy of splitting off and projecting a part of the self into an external or internal object. This process results in phenomena of identification with the object of an immediate and somewhat delusional sort, which is the identification aspect of projective identification. Then it throws up a spectrum of phenomena related to the projection itself, which is related to the emotional and phantasy experiences of the part of the self that is inside, leading into claustrophobic anxieties and related things like hypochondria, depersonalization states, confusion about time and space, and so on.

When I came on the scene in London in 1954, projective identification was used by the people in our group as synonymous with narcissistic identifications. We were comparing it with the processes of introjective identifications which Freud had described in relation to the genital Oedipus conflict and the establishment of the superego, and which Melanie Klein had moved to an earlier period in development by describing the introjection of the breast, both the good and bad breast, as part-objects. These internalized part-objects, preludes to the superego, she called superego, or precursors of the superego. This process of introjective identification was being understood as something very different from a narcissistic identification in that it was not something that happened in a moment—an object was set up internally through introjection, and this object, primarily through its ego-ideal functions, would promulgate in the ego—or really in the self, as she would speak of it—a thrust for development along certain lines, an aspiration to become like the object, worthy of it, all of which was part of what she described as the depressive position. At that time, we rather thought that the problem of narcissistic identifications was in a sense solved, conceptually speaking: that they were produced by projective identifications, and that was that. There was just the matter of exploring what began to look like an almost limitless field of phenomenology related to projective identification and its consequences. We got quite used to the term—it is not a very nice term, in the sense that it is not at all poetic—but it came easily off the tongue, and we found ourselves saying, "projective identification", "projective identification", and we got quite blasé about it and I think quite careless about it in a way. Of course we also began to notice that the interpretation along the lines of projective identification did not seem to carry any weight in certain situations. We were in trouble with certain kinds of patients and saw that something else was going on that certainly was connected with identification processes; it certainly was connected with narcissism, but it seemed to have quite a different phenomenology from what we had gathered together under the rubric of projective identification.

The first paper about it was finally produced by Esther Bick called the "The Function of the Skin in Early Object Relations" in 1968. There she described something connected with very early infantile development that she became aware of in her work with mothers and infants—something that had to do with states of catastrophic anxiety in certain infants whose mothers seemed somehow unable to contain them. When these infants became anxious, their mothers became anxious too, and then the infant became more anxious, and a spiral of anxiety tended to develop, which ended with the infant going into a state of some sort of quivering and a kind of disintegrated, disorganized state that was not screaming, nor a tantrum, just something that one would have to describe as disorganized. Esther Bick began to observe this phenomenon also in certain patients, generally patients who, on the whole, did not seem terribly ill, in candidates, in people who came because of problems like poor work accomplishment, unsatisfactory social lives, vague pathological complaints; in people who were somehow on the periphery of the analytic community and wanted to have an analysis and could not quite say why. She began to observe that these patients in their dream life and in their waking life were subject to states of temporary disintegration very much like the infants. Suddenly they just would not be able to do anything. They would have to sit down, and they would shake. It was not that they were anxious in the ordinary sense of an anxiety attack—they just felt muddled, paralysed, and confused and could not do anything. They just had to sit down or lie down until it went away. The material of the analysis at these times began to throw up images like a sack of potatoes that got wet and all the potatoes spilled out, or where the patient suddenly wet herself, or in which a patient's teeth fell out, or his arms fell off, or things like that, quite painlessly—which described disintegration processes of some sort, of something not held together, not contained. Bick began to notice that these people all had disturbances related to the skin or their experience of the skin—not so much dermatologic disorders as how they felt about the skin, that it was too thin, that it bruised easily, that it was easily lacerated, that it did not feel as if it had any strength to it, and so on. She discovered that this was a very pervasive kind of experience for these people: they were not properly held together by a good skin, but they had other ways of holding themselves together. In her paper on the skin, she describes some of these: Some of them held themselves together intellectually with their intelligent thinking and talking, with the "gift of the gab". They could hold themselves together with explanations, and they had explanations for everything. Bick felt she could observe situations in the infants who were disorganized showing that early verbalization had been encouraged, and they became children who were not prone to activity but to talking all the time; they turned into terrific chatterboxes. She observed in some adult patients that they seemed to hold themselves together muscularly: they did callisthenics, weight-lifting, and athletics, and their attitude towards life was a muscular one—that you did not think about a problem, you did it first and saw it happen, and if it did not work out you did it another way, but you moved your muscles. Esther Bick discovered that she could also trace processes in these infants where their mothers encouraged them to be rather aggressive little boxers and to attack the mother with their fists, laughing in an excited way. It was a way of overcoming these states of anxiety or disintegration, and she began to call these "secondary skin formations", or "substitute skin formations".

All the time she was describing this to me back in the 1960s, she was also going like this (hands together), and she said, "they are sticky, they stick". You feel in the analysis that this is a patient who does not intend ever to finish the analysis, that they are on to something good and they expect to be with you for the duration, plus six months. She also thought that these patients had some sort of difficulty about introjection and that they could not use projective identification very much, that their conception of their relationships was a very external one, that their values were very external and not generated by internal relationships, not based on internal principles, not based on observation of themselves, their own reactions, but, as it were, looking in the mirror of other people's eyes all the time, copying other people, imitating, fashion-conscious, preoccupied with manners and social forms and social status and things of that sort, not necessarily in an offensive way or even in a way that one would have noticed. In fact, many of them were "well-adjusted"—a hateful expression. They were well-adjusted people and people who would not ordinarily have come to analysis, had they not in most instances lived on the fringes of the analytic community where going into analysis was the thing to do. They most often came to analysis because some friend of theirs was in analysis.

Esther Bick had a vague feeling that there was something wrong with their identification processes: they somehow did not use introjection very well; they did not learn in a very experiential way from really having experiences but merely by imitating other people. Of course, our educational system is right up their alley, you might say, so that they were often educationally very successful—rote learners, imitators, unimaginative.

At this time, I was working with a group of child psychotherapists who were treating autistic children. I had worked with autistic children in the States, and I began supervising colleagues through the late 1950s and the 1960s; some eight or ten cases of autism that were being treated by psychoanalytic methods drifted into supervision with me. We finally set up a little group and began to study and review the material. We began to discover things about autistic children that began to ring a bell: in some way, these discoveries were connected also with phenomena that Esther Bick was observing. Without going into the whole business of autistic children, I would like to emphasize a few of the major things that we discovered and that impressed us very much.

First of all, what impressed us about these children was that when we looked back after several years of psychoanalytic treatment of a child, we felt we could divide the phenomenology that was manifest in the consulting-room into two categories. First, there was the category of purely autistic phenomena, which remained the same and never changed, consisting of an assortment of rather disparate items of behaviour with different objects in the room and involving in a simple way particular senses and very simple activities (a child might always, when he came into a room, go and suck the latch on the window, or go to smell the Plasticine, or go and lick the glass of the window: actions like that—very simple, very sensual). At first, of course, we had to assume that every item was meaningful and it must be related to every other item of behaviour; that all behaviour was strung together by a thread of meaning, and so on. These items did not change. They only shrank, as it were, from occupying nine-tenths of the session to begin with, to eventually occupying one-tenth of the session. They might even clear on Wednesday and only be present on Friday or Monday, before or after the weekend. Those seem to be the autistic items.

Then there was a second category of items that were more complicated; they were not repetitive. When you culled them out from the autistic matrix, you could string them together, and described to someone, they would sound like the ordinary play of a neurotic or psychotic child in the playroom that could be examined psychoanalytically and sometimes even understood a bit. So we felt we were seeing in this matrix of autistic phenomena something very simple, very meaningless, very sensual, very repetitive, and in a sense a flight from mental life. In this sea of meaninglessness there were little items of meaningful experience that gradually began to agglutinate, to fill up the Wednesdays, fill up the middle of the week or the middle of the term. These children turned out to have incredible intolerance to separation. We did not at first think of these two categories in terms of dimensionality of life-space; we thought of them in terms of "mental" and "non-mental", as if in the autistic phenomena we were seeing something equivalent to what you might see in a *petit mal* seizure or in the automatism of the comatose patient.

It was only after we studied in retrospect children who had been in treatment for three, four, five years that we began to think in terms of dimensionality and in terms of space, and of spaces and spatial relations, and with it, of course, the effect upon time relationships. What gradually emerged for us as we thought and talked about it was that outside the area of their autism, in what we came to think of as their post-autism, their post-autistic psychosis, these children functioned as if there really were no spaces, there were only surfaces, two dimensions. Things were not solid, only surfaces that they might lean up against or that they might feel, smell, touch, or get a sensation from. There were surfaces, and they leaned up against them; they leaned up against the analyst, they leaned up against the chest of drawers. They could not seem to crawl into places, like most children do. You would think they never had pockets—nothing ever went into their pockets. They did not seem to hold things well. Items just seemed to fall through them. They also gave the impression that they did not listen very well. You felt very strongly that your words went right through them. Their responses often seemed so delayed that you felt that all that had been left behind of what you had said was a kind of musical disturbance that they eventually reacted to or reacted against. Their relationships to inside and outside the playroom were very characteristic in that they seemed not really to distinguish between being inside and being outside. With one little boy it was quite typical that when he came into the playroom, he would rush to the window to see if there were any birds in the garden, and at first, if he saw any birds, he would be terrifically triumphant. We assumed this meant that he was inside and they were outside. But then in a moment it changed, and he felt very persecuted and began shaking his fist at them, and then he would run over to the analyst and look into his mouth or look into his ears, and it seemed fairly clear that a reversal had taken place. From being inside and the birds outside, it had suddenly reversed, and he was outside and they were inside—inside the analyst, inside the building, undistinguished by him. Another child, for instance, tended to draw pictures of houses, one on each side of the paper, and when you held it up to the light, you saw that the doors were superimposed—a kind of house where you open the front door and step out of the back door at the same time.

We came to understand that these children were having difficulty in conceptualizing or experiencing a space that could be closed. In a space that cannot be closed, there is just no space at all. Then we had the exciting experience of seeing some of them begin to close these orifices. One boy, for instance, went through a period in which he papered the walls of the playroom and papered the walls of his room at home, and then he began to draw pictures of maps, and these maps consisted mainly of the route between his home and the consulting-room. At first these pictures seemed to be of terrible things happening—absolute chaos, disorder, police cars that seemed to turn into criminals one minute, soldiers that turned into madmen the next, and so on. Gradually, over a period of months, stop-lights and little Royal Canadian mounted policemen began to appear in these drawings, and slowly order seemed to settle. Then he began to draw pictures of the inside of the clinic where he was being seen, in which there began to be rooms. There began to be doors, rooms began to have separate functions, and these pictures were very exciting, because they all looked like the insides of bodies. They did not look like the insides of buildings at all. So something could happen with these children that enabled them to take an object that was so open that getting inside it was impossible because you fell out and the inside was like a house without a roof, it rained inside as well as out, so you might as well stay out. They gradually began to close the orifices of their objects to make a space, and development—particularly language development—began to take place in them as it had not occurred before.

It was at that time that we began to think about dimensionality and of the autistic phenomena proper as a kind of mindlessness in which there was only a sort of tropism relationship, with direction. For instance, a child would come in and run right up to the window and suck on the latch or run between two doors, one door which he smelled and the other door which he licked. Then there was the two-dimensional surface relationship to objects in which there were no spaces and in which therefore identification processes could not take place and development did not seem to occur because they could neither use projective identification, which required a space to get into, nor introjective identification, which required a space that you could take something into. We did notice that these children had another kind of identification, something that we felt we could really call imitation. One could see it in their posture sometimes, one could hear it in their tone of voice. Suddenly out of a little mite of a boy a deep voice would come out, saying "bad boy". One could notice it in relation to their clothing: they would insist on items that were the same colour as the analyst had worn the day before. One could notice it in that it was difficult for them to take an interest in anything new: it was always the thing that had interested and attracted the attention of the analyst that would be repeated over and over again.

We began to see a link in what we were noticing with the autistic children and what Esther Bick was observing with her patients and with the infants. We began to think that we were now observing a new type of narcissistic identification, and that we could no longer think of projective identification as being synonymous with narcissistic identification but had to think of identification as a broader term in the sense that defence became a broader term and repression became subsumed under it. We had to think of narcissistic identification as the broader term, with projective identification subsumed under it, and we decided to call this new form of narcissistic identification *adhesive identification.* Some sort of identification process took place, which we thought was very closely connected with mimicry and very closely connected with the kind of shallowness and externalization of values that Esther Bick was observing in the patients that I have described to you. Time seemed not implied, as in four-dimensionality. In fact, a proper relation to time is a very sophisticated achievement. We began to observe that the two-dimensional patients had a very oscillating relationship to time, that it went in one direction and then it went back and then it went in another direction and went back, and it did not really move. When they came out of this and became more three-dimensional, concerned with spaces, they had a much more circular relationship with time, in which it went around and it really was cyclical. Day and night were different, but it always came back to the same spot. It did not get anywhere, and you did not really grow older; something grew bigger, something shrivelled up and died, but you really did not get older in any inevitable way. Ageing was a kind of accident due to poor planning, or negligence, or the aggression of other people. The progression to four-dimensionality, to an appreciation of time as a linear process and to a lifetime as a thing with a definable beginning and end came much later. Little Hans thought that he had always been in the stork box before he came out. That was a fairly sophisticated idea and had something to do with the achievement of what Melanie Klein had described as the depressive position—that is, a shift from egocentricity and preoccupation with one's own self, safety, and comfort to a primary concern with the welfare of one's objects. These processes connected with confusion about time, and attitudes towards time could now be noticed more in the phenomenology of the consulting-room and brought into the interpretive work. So we coined the term "adhesive identification", and the more we thought about it, the more we began to notice that it played a part in much of our patients' lives and in our own lives. This was particularly true in relation to values—the difficulty in establishing internal values, that is, an internal source of values. For instance, one noticed in people who were artistic and seemed to have good taste in art and to be very knowledgeable, that they often reported that they knew very well that there was something wrong because when they went to a gallery they always looked at the title and who painted it before they looked at the picture, because they wanted to know its value before they actually looked at it. This was, in a sense, a sort of prototype of their attitude towards the world. They really wanted to know the price of things, because they had no basis internally for establishing their own personal evaluation of it in terms of its meaningfulness to them. We discovered patches of shallowness present in everybody, patches in which emotionality was very attenuated—not in a sense of flatness, but as a kind of thinness, a kind of squeakiness of emotional response.

We think that in our own way of working we are beginning to open up a new area of phenomenology, we have a new conceptual tool with which we can pry things open and begin to see phenomena that we had not noticed before. Where it will lead and how it will enrich our work is a bit too soon to tell.

CHAPTER NINETEEN

Compulsive generosity

(1975)

This clinical paper describes a method of reconstruction of mental development by following the evolution of the infantile transference. It delineates a character structure borne out of a confusion between the mother's breasts and the little girl's buttocks as a solution to infantile anxieties which is symptomatically expressed as compulsive generosity. In the patient described, this character trait is formed around a single dominant unconscious infantile conflict.

The confusion, due to projective identification (Klein, 1955), between the mother's breasts and a little girl's buttocks (Meltzer, 1967a) can, under certain circumstances, become such a satisfactory solution to a multiplicity of infantile, and later, social anxieties that it may constitute the mainspring of character formation, the leading quality of which may be a charming, but compulsive, generosity. The economic problem of managing to be giving-to-others without completely depleting oneself tends, however, in such people, to promote a certain fragility in their adaptation, which may break down in various ways. In several patients, over a number of years, I have recognized this configuration to play a role in such diverse symptoms as depressive breakdown, anorexia, diarrhoea, manic or hypomanic reactions, examination anxiety, pseudo-nymphomania, suicidal rumination, and others. In this paper I wish to focus on the character structure and the means of its fragile maintenance. To this end I will try to describe the analytic experience with a young woman in the fourth year of whose analysis we came across most convincing evidence of the deep and lasting effect upon her of her mother having developed a transient breast abscess in the first month of feeding, which was incised and drained and left a small round scar.

Mrs G had been the beautiful child of a beautiful mother who had "the best legs in the village" and a magnificent head of hair, but the feeding of four children had ruined her breasts, which seemed to my patient quite totally collapsed compared to her own. She herself had been unable to breast-feed *her* children, to her great surprise, as she had looked forward to this experience with great expectation and confidence that had crumbled into overwhelming anxiety and doubt the moment her first baby was in her arms. Her own beauty was quite different from the *grande dame* type of her mother. She was a changeling, stolen-from-the-fairies type, who had charmed everyone from the earliest times. Except for a brief grizzly period around age four, she had been a cheerful, compliant, and sweetly disposed child whose growing-up had moved smoothly and successfully forward on all fronts, hiding quite completely from her parents a deep uncertainty, shyness, and despair. Her breakdown with anorexia, suicidal depression, and outbreaks of rage came as a complete surprise to the many people who loved and valued her, but not to herself. She knew quite well that there was a deeply false foundation to her character and that her achievements had been minimal compared to her potentialities, for she had never really been able to work or take herself seriously as wife, mother, dancer, artist, research scholar, or adult person-in-the-world.

This state had gone on for some considerable time before Mrs G came to analysis. The first year of the analysis, in which she would not agree to more than two sessions a week, was a nightmare for all concerned. Drinking, constant threats of suicide, retreats to bed, outbreaks of rage, flights from London, and bitter scepticism about the procedure constantly threatened a disruption of the effort. A minor car accident and loss of her license seemed to reassure her and produced a shift towards cooperation, which rewarded us with steady and rapid improvement to a position of vitality she had not known since university days. "Everyone" was pleased, and "everyone" knew about it, as, indeed, they could hardly help doing, for she entertained her family and droves of friends with a most amusing account of the comic person and method to which she was exposing herself. She gave dinner parties with masses of food, produced pictures and had an exhibition, took command of home and children as never before. Her dreams oscillated from catastrophe to persecution to dinner parties, and the beauty of nature filled her thoughts. Yet trees kept dying, dream-trees and waking-trees, and her associations were full of the breakdowns, suicides, divorces, and diseases of her current and former friends. Only her mother seemed to improve in health, disposition, sanity, and beauty, and to resume a place of affection in her life. Once more men were falling in love with her and were being tenderly assisted to relinquish their hopeless passions in favour of more suitable objects. The analyst, however, seemed to remain an amusing gnome, a Rumplestiltskin whose eventual persecutory demand would have to be evaded by some terminal device.

Up to this point, after two years of work, we knew nothing of the breast abscess. But it was fairly clear that the transference moved more and more at a part-object level in which I was the little-brother–penis–nipple, somehow making mother happy and taking from the patient's shoulders some sort of overwhelming burden of reparation to the damaged breasts (Klein & Riviere, 1936). Whenever I seemed to be demanding money, serious cooperation, or access to withheld material, I was allowed some modicum of substitute satisfaction looking at her languid body, rolling over on its side. When one day this occurred as she was saying "Help yourself", about something, it became clear that I also was being offered a smorgasbord, like her party guests. A bit of history now became clearer. It seemed that her mother had become depressed in the menopause, as the patient approached puberty, and, prior to some successful analytic treatment, had formed a near-delusional attitude to the patient. Mrs G's girlish beauty and purity of heart was to bring goodness to a wicked world of lusting men. She was to be the converse of Miss Haversham's foster child: to break men's hearts not destructively, but constructively.

Dream after dream in the third year of the analysis broke open this theme of the "smorgasbord bottom", the confusion of her own little-girl bottom with the mummy's breasts, and helped to demonstrate its origins in a masturbatory phantasy of projective identification (Meltzer, 1966). As this was closely worked through, her own neediness became apparent, and the compulsive generosity to others receded. The daddy began to appear in the transference, and her early love and admiration for her father and his doting love for her mother and the children replaced the denigration with which he had earlier been presented. He was, in fact, a man of some considerable achievement and stature, a willing consort to her queenly mother. The stage was now set, one can see in retrospect, for the main drama of the analysis—the problem of being able to take herself seriously as an adult-in-the-world and as a baby-at-the-breast in the transference and psychic reality.

In retrospect I would say that the breaking-into the compulsive generosity was brought about by what became known as her "levitation" dream, for it seemed to catch so perfectly both the mood and the mechanism. In a Monday session, which opened with some bitterness as she accused me of driving her over a precipice with my theories, like the swine in the Gospels, she related the following dream:

> *She was preparing for an exam at school in some panic until she finally found some torn-up notes. Then she was at lunch at a hundred-foot-long table in a tent, and when someone asked for the bread, she just levitated to six feet and floated down to the bottom of the table to fetch it. She did this twice, but when she sat down she had an uncontrollable urge to defecate and produced two pieces of faeces. She hid one, but an elegant young man noticed the other and told her it must be taken to the chemist to be analysed. The chemist said something that she felt indicated that she would never again be able to levitate.*

In the companion dream of that session

> *. . . the queen-mother was making a speech, but in the audience revolutionaries were hissing, despite a "gossamer" hair net that was dropped over them. She jerked her little brother out and scolded him for being such a swine.*
>
> [The patient thought this dream made some reference to her childhood habit of sucking her "pigtails." She recognized that "Gossamer" was the name of a contraceptive sheath.]

So it seemed—but, of course, further experience could not sustain it—that at a stroke the method of taking things lightly (levitation) gave way to swinishness, and *penis-on-the-brain* at the *queen-mother–breast*, en route to *seriousness-of-mind* about the joys and pains of relationship, work, and her development. The ease with which her beauty enabled her to intrude inside her beautiful mother (inside the tent) and go lightheartedly down to the bottom (of the table) to serve other people's needs (for bread) gave way painfully to the experience of her own infantile greed and envious ingratitude. It became clear that the erotization of the relationship to the nipple–penis was deeply felt to damage the breast, and in psychic reality did so. The pregenital Oedipus complex, with its struggle with the breast for possession of the nipple–penis, brought back the grizzliness of her fourth year, replete with accusations that I was ruining her life. Dream after dream brought scenes of love and sexual voluptuousness, interrupted by the appearance of her mother, of the analyst's wife, or of soiling herself. Only slowly did the persecutory depression give way to depressive pain as her strength began to mount. Periods of weeping and pain in the heart, dreams of being hopelessly in love with some tiny man or her baby brother, and a gnawing dissatisfaction with herself alternated with episodes of apathy and attempts to reconstitute the "levitation". Outside the analytic situation her life was in fact richer, more active, and more useful than before, and she felt her strength growing, her need for admiration and approval waning. But she could not yet feel grown-up or take herself seriously, although she had commenced some quite difficult work in addition to the full care of home and children.

By Christmas-time the infantile situation had come fully into the transference, and a train-wreck on the line that she knew I regularly took from Oxford quite shook her. She was suffering from menorrhagia but could hardly go to the doctor lest he discover cancer. It seemed to have been ushered in by a dream

> *. . . that she was in a panic because her cat had picked up a sparkler at the children's party and she was afraid it would burn her mouth.*
>
> [Actually, the cat was pregnant at the time.]

In another dream,

> *. . . she was in love with a tiny man, and they had to pass under a huge clock that was heaving and about to explode. But they rushed downhill into the mud and later heard a lecture on the archaeological finds of Pompeii.*

The patient now began to feel that the end of the analysis was in sight, but whether by happy termination or catastrophe she could not tell. Similarly, it was often unclear whether she or the cat were pregnant, and whether it was a baby, which she now painfully longed for, or the dreaded cancer. She had no conviction about the analysis curing or killing her, a martyr to my fanatical search for the truth. This uncertainty, and its foundation in a hypochondriacal projective identification (Rosenfeld, 1965) with the breast damaged by the baby's over-exciting the nipple–penis with her beauty, mouth, and touch, came out clearly in a dream and seemed to allay her pessimism. In the dream,

> *. . . she was visiting a huge atelier, where very interesting work of restoration of paintings was in progress. A girl offered to show her a Rembrandt, but in fact it seemed to be the figure of Adam from the Sistine Chapel, reclining and receiving the touch of life from God. In the dream she could not resist touching the head of the figure, and, to her horror, it began to turn, and spin, and finally fell off onto*

the ground spinning and shooting sparks like a Catherine-wheel.

[Catherine was the name of her cat. Associations led relentlessly to her clitoris and to the masturbation, which seems to have been held rigidly in abeyance, under her mother's prohibition, from the time of the grizzliness until the current period in analysis.]

This dream seemed to establish firmly the destructive omnipotence with which she erotized the relation to the nipple, so that her touch with finger, eye or tongue was felt to cause the breast to lose control, explode, ejaculate, be expelled from the Garden of Eden, etc. Her relations to men, especially to younger men who were prone to adore her, became clearer to her and could no longer be covered by the conception of generosity. The possibility of doing harm by arousing desires she could not or did not intend to gratify was clearer, not because she had any reason to think that she had in fact done harm, but because the omnipotence was revealed more openly. This seemed to put the seal on the levitation and to bring her closer to a serious view of herself in-the-world. However, while the step towards doing-no-harm was firmly taken, the identifications required and the motivation necessary to the implementation of desires to do-some-good in-the-world were still lacking. The experiences of the next four months, and the dreams with which the transference events were illustrated, seemed to both open up the possibility of the necessary identification with the breast as combined object and also to stir powerfully the depressive motivation.

During much of this time the patient varied between brief attempts to re-establish the levitation, periods of bitterness and scathing criticism of the analyst for having ruined her life, and longer and longer periods in which she felt broken-hearted but could hardly say what about. Sometimes she felt that she was married to the wrong man, at other times that her children were growing into monsters of deceit or perversity, or again that she was in love with the analyst, or psychoanalysis, or that she was dying of cancer. Dreams to illustrate these moods were juxtaposed to ones in which the theme of the volcano–breast, or the fishing-boat–breast dumping tons of fish on her, or the trestle-table–breast where she was pursued by the lascivious teacher—this theme of breast and nipple was worked over and over. As her resistance to the erotization of the nipple increased, so also there arose a certain surrender to the dependence of being the baby and to the pain of remorse when she felt she damaged the breast. For instance, she dreamed that

> *. . . she was going from one pub named "The Swan" to another of the same name in pursuit of a young man, until she realized that a bomb was about to fall. Instead of running for cover like the others, she remained, resigning herself to death, for the pub was so beautiful, with a minstrel gallery, just the kind of house she would love to live in.*

However, the patient also felt urgently that she must bring her analysis to an end, noticing now so many people about her who seemed to need analysis. Her dreams, in contrast, bristled with new-baby jealousy and resentment of being hurried through exams, having to make way for her younger brother, etc. The anomalous situation arose in which she was accusing the analyst of pushing her out but bravely resigned to go, while he was a bit desperately showing her evidence that she was not yet ready to stop. This disparity between her feelings and thoughts in the situation seemed to come to some resolution in a rather lovely dream and put an end to her urgency to terminate. In the dream,

> *. . . she had gone to visit her old ballet teacher, as if for the last time, and on the way home she stopped in at a house that was being renovated. The work seemed to be done by a rather fat Polish couple and their equally fat daughter. The latter kept looking so lovingly towards her and kept pressing on her as a gift her identification papers, Polish recipes, and the like, until in some annoyance the patient asked her own mother (who now seemed present) what to do about it, as she had never met the girl before. But her mother insisted that the girl had been in love with her for a year and that she had encouraged it and must now accept this gift of love.*

This was felt to imply that the processes of internalization of the maternal transference and the acceptance of the burden of introjective identification were now commencing. In the dream her mother had laughed and said that the patient would now have to do her own dirty work. This was taken to mean her own analytic work. An approach to termination could now be made with greater confidence and the patient no longer felt in a hurry to make way for the next "baby". Most important of all, she felt that some foundation had now been laid for her metamorphosis from the ballet-girl with the help-yourself smorgasbord bottom into a worker, the daughter of workers, identified with the full feeding breast with the nipple-penis (Pole) giving it strength. With certainty it can be said that she has caught a glimpse of a new vision of herself and her life. Whether she will be able to work it through will lie with the "quantitative factors", as Freud was so fond of calling them—the imponderables of the future that constantly remind us that nothing in human mental life can be predicted, as nothing was ever inevitable.

DISCUSSION

The method of reconstruction of mental development by a process that, since it depends so largely on the evolution of the infantile transference, must necessarily tap mainly the pathological configurations in the personality, led Freud to a view of character that was at once pessimistic and morbid. It was pessimistic because it tended to emphasize negative motivation, as in the famous image of the beleaguered ego trying to serve or placate three masters: *Id*, *Superego*, and *Outside Reality* (Freud, 1923b). It was morbid because it favoured a view of character tied to the vicissitudes of the libido. This seemed to imply that by means of reaction formation, sublimation, and inhibition, mainly, the social character was built up. Thus health, as opposed to illness, depended largely on the employment of these tricks for remaining free of symptoms of mental illness. Only very late in his life, in the papers on *Fetishism* (1927e) and "Splitting of the Ego" (1940e [1938]) did Freud suggest an alternative, namely that a healthy ego might coexist side by side with an ill one, which might be kept under relative repression. Freud did not, however, suggest any particular structure for this healthy part of the ego. This may be due to the fact that his view of identification processes had remained somewhat confused. As early as the "Wolf Man" (1918b [1914]) and *Leonardo* (1910c), he had been able to distinguish between narcissistic identifications and those, later connected with Ferenczi's (1926) concept of "introjection" and the resolution of the Oedipus complex, which gave rise to the "gradient in the ego", the definitive superego.

However, in the years following the first formulation of the ego-ideal—in "Mourning and Melancholia" (1917e [1915]) and *Group Psychology* (1921c)—a rather strange and relentless metamorphosis seems to have taken place in Freud's mind, whereby the helpful, nurturing, encouraging, and educative aspects of the introjected parents, who were the "heirs of the Oedipus complex", the complete bisexual complex, quite disappeared. Instead, the new instinct theory formulated in *Beyond the Pleasure Principle* (1920g) posed so compelling a problem of "neutralization", "fusion", and "defusion", that the limelight was quite snatched away from sexuality and the libido. The superego met with in obsessional and melancholic states was taken as the prototype, so that it seemed quite natural that the effort of development should involve essentially a struggle by the ego to gain its freedom from the harshness of the superego.

In this way the "introjection", which gave rise to the definitive superego, was seen to eventuate not in identification processes that modified the ego, but in identification only in the sense of creating the "gradient", the formation of the superego. Thus no contribution to character was envisaged so long as the ego-ideal aspects of these internalized figures were ignored or forgotten.

In contrast to this classical method of research with adult patients and the construction or reconstruction of the infantile neurosis, work with children threw an entirely different light on developmental processes. This is not only true of Melanie Klein's findings; it is inherent in the altered situation in the analysis.

A child analyst finds himself observing a developing young person in whose life the analysis is only one of many influences playing upon the continual flux of his internal and external relations. Where an analysis is carried on across the borders, one might say, from infancy to latency or latency to puberty, the analyst is bound to be impressed by the huge changes in character and their relation to the alterations in structure and organization of the personality that are instituted by these developmental moves. In this way it seems quite natural that the analyst of children should come to take a view of character that binds it more to structure and to the waxing and waning of identification processes, both introjective and narcissistic, rather than to mechanisms of defence against anxiety and problems of distribution, fusion, defusion, etc. of life and death instincts. Truly, of course, these processes, which determine structure, particularly the interplay of the narcissistic organizations with the object relations, are implemented by the dynamisms and are affected by the economics of instincts and anxieties, whether one thinks of them in terms of "signal" functions or economic "positions". But the view of development, the "forward" view of child analysis, has a rather inherent difference from the "retrospective" or reconstructive view attained from the treatment of adult patients.

It may seem tedious, and even tangential, to labour these points in this paper, but they are quite central to my reason for choosing for presentation this subject—the character trait of "compulsive generosity". I hope that the clinical material has clearly delineated (it cannot, of course, "prove" anything) that this young woman's character had been formed around a single dominant unconscious infantile conflict. The traumatic influence of her mother's abscess of the breast, which in all descriptive psychiatric respects would seem to have been trivial in its consequences, is revealed by the evolution of the transference to have been quite central to her development. A psychotic focus, formed around the depressive anxieties engendered by her erotization of the relation to the nipple juxtaposed to the event of the breast abscess, was apparently reactivated at puberty by the event of her mother's menopausal depression and once again activated by the difficulties in breast-feeding her first child.

The consequence of the first reactivation of the conflict seems to have been the crystallization of her character, while the second reactivation not only broke down this character somewhat but set in train a psychotic depressive reaction with dipsomania, anorexia nervosa, and suicidal ruminations and attempts. I think it is probably accurate to say that in the years intervening between these two crises, as in the years between her "grizzliness" and puberty, the patient had seemed healthy to everyone but herself. It is perhaps a tribute to her excellent constitution that this successful adaptation did not satisfy her. We cannot therefore consider her as an example of Freud's "splitting of the ego" but must conclude that she was indeed, characterologically ill.

The question that remains is an economic one: *how was the patient able to maintain this defensive structure so "successfully" for fifteen years, and why did it break down?* I find it rather mysterious and prefer to leave it open for discussion. The only contribution I can make towards it is based on my experience of the patient's personality—namely, that as a child her beauty, charm, and innately tender disposition made her quite irresistible to adults. Yet one cannot suppose that in her adult life such qualities could satisfy the needs of her newborn infant, who would require quite different attributes in its mother.

CHAPTER TWENTY

The role of narcissistic organization in the communication difficulties of the schizophrenic

(1975)

A clinical description of three schizophrenic patients and their difficulties of verbalization and vocalization. The case study shows how a part of the personality lives in a delusional system, while in all cases the language link to the good object is loosened or attacked.

The operational description of narcissism that served Freud so well in dealing with neurotic disorders and relating them to a topographic model with its quantitative approach to economics as formulated in the libido theory quite fell to the ground when confronted with more primitive and psychotic functions. Narcissistic identifications, masochism, hypochondria, melancholia—these and many other clinical phenomena called for a more flexible model, more concrete in its structural dimension and more qualitative in its approach to the economics of the mind.

Those who have followed the way opened up by Melanie Klein tend to hold the view that she accomplished both of these moves in her later work. By describing splitting processes and projective identification in her 1946 paper, she gave new concreteness to Freud's structural theory and set it on a background of values rather than quantities through relating structural development to the paranoid–schizoid and depressive positions in object relations. This introduction of value into the economic area of metapsychology brought psychoanalysis into its rightful historic continuity with philosophy, psychology, and theology and removed it from a spurious position as handmaiden to psychiatry. It also called the psychoanalyst back to the central problems of emotion and mental pain, and of the meaning of things, removing the jigsaw-puzzle atmosphere of investigating the past (Freud's archaeology model) and replacing it by the immediacy and passions of the transference as the central object of exploration.

It is this structural and organizational meaning of the term "narcissistic" with which this paper is concerned. I want to describe my experience with three schizophrenic patients whom I was fortunate enough to have in analysis for five years or more, with a view to the conceptualization of a basis for asking the questions "Who is talking, is thinking?" and "To whom is this language, this thought directed?" I wish therefore to call before you a view of the unconscious as structured by various infantile parts of the self and their internal objects dwelling in a space whose dimensions are emotional rather than geometric, and whose laws are those of psychic reality (the content of which is still largely unknown to us) rather than of the external world (whose exploration has been carried far by the physical and biological sciences). From this point of view being with a disturbed person is much like beginning to read a Chekov play for the first time. On the stage it is quite all right, even though you do not know the names, because the actors present so many visual clues by which they may be distinguished. But when reading, it takes a long time to assemble the patterns of character and language by which these strangely named people can be differentiated without constantly turning back to the Dramatis Personae.

Case 1: Charles

When Charles finally came into analysis with me, at his own request, he was thirty-one; he had been having schizophrenic breakdowns since the age of fifteen and had been a patient in analysis or mental hospital against his will for much of the intervening time. I had, in fact, seen him first for a five-week trial treatment when his then analyst had to be away and a change of therapists was under consideration. At that time he had been virtually mute, standing facing away from me, straining to emit a few words, but with little success. I had interpreted quite a lot, very tentatively, with the result that he happily returned to his previous analyst and insisted on continuing with him.

So I was surprised by his request to return to analysis with me some eight years later, and after the death of his analyst—though Charles had, in fact, interrupted that analysis four years before, after his most severe breakdown. At that time he had thought his analyst was God, and he was hallucinated and deluded. His delusions were essentially two-fold: one was that he had stolen two shillings for which crime his father was to be sent to jail, and the only means of saving him—so the voice of his friend, "We Three", told him—was to go down to the railway line where another patient was waiting for him to throw himself under a train (which he very nearly did). The other delusion was somatic: that wires had been run from his rectum to his brain, and it was by this means that his thoughts and actions were being controlled by "We Three".

By the time he came to analysis with me, he was neither in the catatonic bind of his first visits nor the acutely excited and hallucinated delusional state of the breakdown. He was a bit dishevelled, slouching along, evasive of glance, muttering of speech, and fragmented in thought. He coughed, squirmed about on the couch, kicked his feet, and muttered to himself, with occasional explosive mid-sentence communications that quickly were interrupted by "I don't know". Nonetheless he earnestly participated in the analysis and improved very rapidly during the first three years, once he, or we, had weathered a near-breakdown before the first summer-holiday break. In fact his apparent improvement far outstripped his structural change, for although he became able to work, resumed his schooling, became more socialized, and improved his family relations, as soon as tender feelings and depressive pains began to assail him in the transference situation he beat a hasty retreat. It was during the next two years that we learned most about the structure of his narcissistic organization.

What we learned can be described fairly briefly. He had a friend, formerly known as "We Three" (my echo, my shadow, and me, as in the song), who lived in his rectum, which was like a cave in the basement or back-garden of his mother's house (and therefore also his mother's rectum), from which vantage point he was able to maintain an anus-eye view of the world, seeing everyone's faults, errors, hypocrisy, perversity, dishonesty, greed, lust, etc. Together with his friend, Charles could sally forth into the world to throw contempt at everyone, much as he and his friends had sallied from their cave to throw mud at passers-by as a boy. And this was, in fact, the nature of his relation to the outside world and to the analysis during this period. Getting girls, at which he was a dismal failure despite his good looks (even prostitutes refused him), was the main preoccupation, and recognizing the hidden traits of latent homosexuality that proliferated behind the façade of manliness in his analyst, teachers, bosses, and work-mates was the main sport. He did not hallucinate the voices of "We Three", they just conversed in his mind. But he did hallucinate other people, especially women in pubs, calling him a "drip" when they were not filled with desire by his extraordinary "attractiveness".

During these two years the struggle for his loyalty was joined in the analytic situation, as I tried to demonstrate to him the difference in his view of the world when he was in collusion with "We Three" from the times—only moments—when he was in a trusting or admiring relation to his good internal parents in the transference. It was the world of Mack-the-knife, of parasitism, prostitution, and violence, in which meeting of the minds was irrelevant and the communication of states of mind impossible. There was neither the apparatus for sending nor an audience to receive. And when the analyst, as representative of the world of "meeting of the minds", attempted to break in with communication, his words were attacked with missiles of mockery, punning, caricature; they were fragmented, rearranged to alter the sense, the logic twisted and the historic facts changed. It was an impressive performance that now filled the sessions with linguistic virtuosity and the music of the House of Commons or the Law Courts, where before there had been only mumble, whisper, blurted fragments of sentences, and the music of a one-string instrument. If such dubious progress continued, we might hope to have cured his schizophrenia and replaced it with talented psychopathy.

Case 2: Philippa

After three years of hospital treatment for depression, Philippa had awakened from a dream with a full-blown schizophrenic delusional system. It was too elaborate to describe in detail here, but it can be summarized as follows: this 16-year-old fat girl, intelligent and rather gifted verbally, had now become the captive of a rich man who had bought her for five pounds from her parents as the subject of a huge research project on schizophrenia. For this purpose she was confined to a movie set, where nothing was real—not the air, the scenery, nor the people—only she herself. As everything was being followed by carefully concealed television cameras, Philippa's every utterance and gesture was studied, theatrical, controlled. However, as it seemed that this control was exerted over her by the rich man and not by herself, she felt no personal responsibility for her behaviour. Her relation to the analyst, on the other hand, once treatment was begun, stood in marked contrast to this dream, being one of omnipotent control over his words and actions, despite the fact that it soon appeared that she had discovered that the rich man had the same name as the analyst. It seemed necessary for the analyst to restrain his behaviour, especially changes in posture or facial expression, for such irrelevant acts resulted in outbreaks of hilarious triumph over him. With flawless logic she explained: "You can't seem to control yourself, Dr Meltzer. However, as there are only two of us here, I must be controlling you."

Although these manic outbreaks initially followed upon extraneous movements of the analyst (such as crossing a leg or scratching an itch), they gradually spread to his analytic activity itself. The effect was intimidating indeed, such that an inner struggle to overcome an inertia and the tendency to remain silent became apparent. But perseverance in the interpretive function seemed gradually to produce a most undesirable effect on the patient, both from the therapeutic and from the scientific point of view. As the analyst persisted in talking, the patient tended to lapse into mime; then it could also be seen that she appeared to look at him less and less, until this was reduced to an initial glance at the beginning of the session, after which she directed her attention out of the window. From the behaviour of her eyes, which now commenced a most complicated and bizarre system of blinking and staring that lasted for months, it was possible to construe that she was using her eyes as a camera in the initial moments of the session and as a projector the remaining time.

When it was finally interpreted to Philippa that she was making a photo of the analyst, which she then projected outside the analytic setting in order to recover an object of more docile quality, an astonishing confirmation broke the silence of her negativism: "Pictures are just as good as people." Three years of analysis had produced a marked shift in the patient's delusion, though it can hardly be claimed as a therapeutic triumph; from being the only real thing, the actress in the delusional setting, Philippa had metamorphosed into the director, cameraman, and camera, all fused together. One might say that she had shifted from a paranoid to a catatonic delusional system; instead of being controlled by the rich Dr Meltzer, she was now in control of the picture of him. In the process of this, her need to vocalize her thoughts dried up, and her conversations could be conducted in mime. Obviously pictures cannot hear, they can only see; but they are nonetheless "just as good as people".

The point of this material is to clarify the role of the actual vocalization of language. One must not take it for granted. The usual distinction between inner and outer speech does not really cover the possibilities, for one can see that Philippa's mimed conversations were "outer", and still silent; she would have to be described as mute in the analytic situation, not merely silent. Philippa shows a process—the achievement of an object, but a delusional one, which had qualities that made vocalization redundant for the purpose of understanding. But it must not be thought that such qualities are possessed only by delusional objects; the omnipotent aspect of projective identification probably always has some of this aspect in it—namely, that the state of mind, and the image or dream image in which it is embedded, can be implanted intact in the object's mind. The child must in some way apprehend the necessity of vocalization, and most young children demonstrate only a partial appreciation of this—with their mothers, in particular.

In our third example, however, we are going to move in the other direction, to examine the role of mental content, and how (as Bion, 1965, puts it) it must consist of elements suitable for communication, and not merely for evacuation.

Case 3: Jonathan

When Jonathan came to analysis, he had already been in a catatonic state of increasing depth for five years, which he had drifted into relentlessly during several years of mounting confusion, paranoid anxieties, and outbreaks of rage commencing in puberty. By the age of 20 he looked more like a dishevelled child of twelve or a sad little clown, or even a rag-doll at times. His verbal responses were almost limited to a tic-like "dunno, dunno" or "yeh, yeh", except at moments of rage, when he ran about slamming doors and shouting "Get off my back" or "Stop fucking me". Occasionally he angrily insisted, apropos of nothing in particular, "I'm going to do as I please". His voice was without music, unrhythmic, mechanical. He wet and soiled constantly, masturbated, tore off his clothes, giggled and smirked, and was unable to look at people's faces, especially into the eyes. In some sessions he was completely motionless, sitting with clothes wrongly worn—shoeless or with slippers on the wrong feet, flies open and shirt-tail out, hands far up his sleeves. He generally seemed exhausted, though he slept long and deeply.

I cannot describe the full content of the first five years of his analysis, but I wish here to concentrate on the language aspect. As contact was established, the tic-like "dunno, dunno" was replaced by occasional runs of words that seemed to refer to dreams and, more rarely, to television song or film titles. Later he attempted to recite the full lyrics, so that it was apparent that the content had meaning in terms of the psychoanalytic transference. Very occasionally a fragment of memory, utterly unlocated in the time or geography of his life experience, broke through; but inevitably it trailed off into inaudibility and was replaced by "dunno, dunno, dunno". As these fragments began to be assembled by the analyst into a history, elements such as the fixing of his age at 18—the time of his entrance to the hospital—gradually budged in the patient's recognized view of his life; and this was accompanied by his resuming his own identity in lieu of the adopted name of "Boris". The impression was unmistakable that he had begun at times to be able to return from the "nowhere" of his delusional system to the time–space-identity world of psychic and external reality; somehow the absolute despair (in the Kierkegaardian sense) of his illness had given way to hope, and separation reactions now began to be very severe.

By the fourth year of the analysis, he was able to relate an occasional dream, or a garbled memory, or to describe a recent event at the hospital or at the home of a couple he regularly visited. By the fifth year he was collecting words with abstract meanings, could experience puzzlement about the meaning of other people's behaviour or of his own proliferating compulsions, which involved peculiar modes of locomotion, counting, and repetition of words two or four times. But his use of language for the purpose of communication was greatly opposed from within, so that his speech was frequently broken into by his hands being put into his mouth, or picking at his lips, by having to giggle and scratch his bottom, or jump up to go and "have a wash". The degree of his enslavement to an internal persecutor could be fairly judged by the distance his hand was withdrawn up into his shirt-sleeve.

This lengthy description of a process of partial recovery from a schizophrenic catastrophe is intended to illustrate a certain thesis about language development and about mutism in the catatonic patient. The illness has involved such a destruction of the internal objects, the basis of identity, that it has carried to destruction with it the capacity to have thoughts and thus the foundations of speech, both in its vocal and its verbal aspects. In Jonathan's slow movement towards recovery of his mental structure and functions, one can discern a slow-motion recapitulation of these two dimensions of the process of evolution of speech, albeit with great distortion and pain.

The first dimension, verbalization, is illustrated by the way in which Jonathan was able to introject a speaking—or, rather, a singing—object and could repeat with remarkable accuracy the lyrics of a song, at first mechanically but gradually with increasing rhythm and tonal modulation. It was easily recognizable that the content of these songs bore a reference to recent interpretations concerning the evolution of the qualities and relationship of his internal objects and their transference significance, drawn from the analytic inference of his dreams, reports of events and memories, and his behaviour in the sessions.

The second dimension, of vocalization, corresponding to the small child's lalling or playing with language, was represented in a rather tormented form in his repetition of words and his building or rebuilding of a vocabulary for the expression of his own thoughts and experiences, all of which could be seen to lend substance to a growing sense of identity.

* * *

In the paper on mutism (1974) and Chapter VII of *Explorations in Autism* (1975), cases two and three were discussed from the point of view of a psychoanalytic theory of language development with the aim of understanding why autistic children are mute or, put in the Wittgensteinian sense, why speech is not part of their "natural history". Here, along with case one, Charles, I have another, less ambitious and more clinical, aim in view.

What I should like to be able to do is to evoke for you the particular quality of the experience that I think is particularly focused on language in the psychoanalytic treatment of the schizophrenic patient. In my view, the part of the personality that has become schizophrenic is that part which has so far departed into the realm of narcissism (in a spatial:emotional sense) as to be beyond the "gravitational" attraction of good objects and therefore of beauty, truth, and goodness. This realm beyond the pale is "nowhere" and has purely negative characteristics. It is a world reached along the path of negativism passing through the perversions en route. It is Bion's world of "$-K$", where K stands for knowledge, beyond the world of L and H (love and hate) (Bion, 1970). This part of the personality suffers from absolute loneliness, and, while it despairs of finding its way back or of being rescued, it lives in hope of capturing at least one other part of the personality to keep it company in its isolation from everything real.

In Philippa we meet that part of the personality that is living in the delusional system; with Jonathan, we contact and to some extent rescue a part that was on the brink of such departure; Charles, on the other hand, demonstrates a considerable return from the brink of being launched into space, the space beneath the wheels of the train. It may seem strange to say that Jonathan was only "on the brink" when he was clearly so very dilapidated. But the point is that he was in a state comparable to the "world-destruction" phase of Schreber's illness, from the debris of which the delusional system, a "world not more grand but at least one in which he could live", may be constructed. I found no evidence that Jonathan had a delusional system.

The point that I am making is that the language link to good objects has been severely loosened in all three cases, and the evidence suggests that this is not merely a consequence of some pathological process but lies somehow at the very heart of the regressive movement. The further worsening of Philippa's illness and the moves towards recovery in Jonathan and Charles all imply that the capacity to communicate states of mind to an object with parental qualities (mainly those for containing confusion and distress and the projected parts of the personality that have become unbearably painful) has been attacked. Philippa herself takes on the role of attacker of communication and demonstrates one very ingenious method. Charles's friend, "We Three", does the same and eventually enters into a proper "duel of angels" for the mind of the baby–Charles in the transference. Jonathan, on the other hand, seems to have lost both his vocabulary for expressing thoughts and his apparatus (Bion's alpha-process) for elaborating thoughts suitable for thinking, and not merely for evacuation.

and thus suitable for transformation into language (Bion, 1965).

The clinical implications of this approach to the psychoanalytic treatment of schizophrenia are apparent. In this illness we are dealing with something like the burning of the Reichstag, the seizing of the newspapers, the control of radio and television. Tyrannical thought control under the leadership of the most enviously destructive aspect of the personality is being launched and has already gone some distance by the time a patient reaches the consulting-room. The containment of the illness, and even possibly some degree of recovery from it, can be hoped for if the avenues of communication of states of mind can be kept open. The investigation of the actual processes of communication, therefore, takes precedence over any other aspect of the phenomenology of the consulting-room. We must operate often like an underground newspaper and cannot expect our readers to do so openly. We must expect, rather, that the patient will openly join in the ridicule and mockery, gradually moving quietly to the sidelines to watch the struggle between truth and cynicism.

CHAPTER TWENTY-ONE

Temperature and distance as technical dimensions of interpretation

(1976)

This technical paper, based on a description and conceptualization of his own technique, provides a model for dealing with changes of emotionality and splits in the analytic session, by creating a working atmosphere through the dynamic use of the interpretative function and the countertransference. This paper invites others to examine their own development of "linguistic ingenuity" and to differentiate areas of ingenuity within the "basic technical principles" from acting-in-the-countertransference. This paper, together with the author's 1973 paper on "Routine and Inspired Interpretations" makes an important contribution to the theory of psychoanalytic technique. It also encourages a self-critical observation and analysis of the interaction between patient and analyst as a form of self-supervision of unedited clinical material.*

Paper read at the European Psycho-Analytical Federation Conference in Aix-en-Provence, 1976.

*Chapter fourteen, this volume.

The task of supervising others helps one to notice things about one's own clinical work that would otherwise have escaped attention. While this is true about the content of comprehension of material, it seems even more true of technique. Our so-called teaching of technique is a peculiar and ill-defined area—a mixture of basic technical principles, of technical ingenuity within this basic method, of stylistic elements, and even of inconsequential idiosyncrasy. In this paper I wish to try to separate out this area of the *limits of technical ingenuity within the bounds of fundamental method* in order to pay attention to a particular aspect of it—namely, *ingenuity of verbal expression.*

Before launching into the body of this enquiry, it is necessary to define the boundaries of this area of technique as distinguished from the other three. The basic technical principles I employ are those derived from Freud and Melanie Klein, modified by my own view of the method as process (see Meltzer, 1967a). In this view the analyst's task is to create a setting in which a systematic evolution of a transference process may evolve, be monitored, and be assisted by interpretation. The distinction from Freud's method of investigation of the transference as resistance and in the service of reconstruction is clearly defined. Thus *interpretation proper* as a metapsychological statement (with genetic, dynamic, structural, and economic aspects of the transference defined) can be distinguished from more *general interpretive exploration* of the patient's material, which is intended to facilitate its emergence.

This basic method lends itself to rich variation by ingenuity and can be distinguished fairly clearly from technical experimentation. Similarly, the area of ingenuity can be distinguished from those elements of style that are emanations of the analyst's personality, in the social sense. These stylistic modulations, insofar as they are observed by the analyst himself, are presumably allowed to continue because he deems them of no special significance for the work in hand, and he would therefore not consider them valuable for formulation and communication to students. They are, however, just the elements in his way of working that will be mirrored and perhaps caricatured by his own analysands insofar as their identification processes remain narcissistic.

Finally, by an "area of inconsequential idiosyncrasy" I mean to distinguish that area of an analyst's behaviour with a patient that is dictated by his adaptation to the peculiarities that are not part of the psychopathology of the patient. These might include assisting a handicapped patient, special politeness to women, simplification of language for foreigners, etc.

To return now to the area of "technical ingenuity" within the limits of basic technique, I wish to define it more precisely in terms of its internal structure and its significance for the method, and then to go on to examine the particular segment of it that is the main subject of this paper: temperature and distance as dimensions of verbal ingenuity. Some years ago I became aware through my work with children and with very ill adult patients that I felt very restricted by concepts of timing on the one hand and of Melanie Klein's precept of seeking out the deepest anxieties implied in the immediate material on the other hand. I was aware that this latter applied mainly to her method for what she called "establishing the analytic situation", but it was also, in my opinion, characteristic of her approach in general. Both these approaches, and perhaps the possibility of their being mutually exclusive, were felt to be restraints upon spontaneity of communication and eventually of thought. The former carried a bad conscience towards the patient of reserve bordering on secrecy and invited omniscience in the analyst. The latter was felt to hamper free exploration of the material and gave a tone of explanation to the proceedings that belied this more uncertain and exploratory monitoring of a process in the patient. I felt that it encouraged an element of passivity in the patient's dependence, and an unrealistic responsibility for control in the analyst.

In contrast, I found that I wished to find ways of expressing my peregrinating thought in order to share it with the patient, but without leading him, without causing alarm, erotic excitement, or confusion. Insofar as the aim was to encourage enrichment of the material in order for unconscious intuitive processes in patient and analyst alike to function more widely, this was felt to be a useful preparation for the patient's introjection into his internal objects of analytic qualities of mind in view of the hope of his becoming capable of self-analysis in the future, when rectified personality structure would make this a real possibility.

I also noticed that this wish was finding implementation in a linguistic differentiation between a language of uncertain rumination for expressing exploratory thought (interpretive activity) and one of commitment for presenting metapsychological statements (interpretation proper). When I examined this development in my technique more closely, I could see that I was employing verbal techniques for achieving these aims that might reasonably be called modulations of temperature and distance. I will try to define and illustrate this.

Elsewhere (Meltzer, 1975) I have spelled out the view of language derived from the work of various grammarians and philosophers, which sees language moving on two levels, deep and superficial. The deep and more primitive roots (Wittgenstein, Langer) are essentially musical and function originally—in both the historic and developmental sense—for the communication of states of mind by the mechanism of projective identification (Bion). Upon this foundation there has gradually been built (and the child rapidly constructs) the lexical level for the conveying of information about the outside world. Finally, the poetic function finds the metaphoric means of describing the inner world through the forms of the external world. It is through the modulation of the interplay of these three levels that the means can be found for controlling the atmosphere of communication, the dimensions of which I wish to describe as temperature and distance.

If one imagines that the speaking voice could be modulated through its entire range musically, this would provide a spectrum stretching from monotone to full operatic splendour. In practice, of course, we neither can nor wish to do this but operate within a segment of this spectrum. Its elements would be the ordinary ones of music: tone, rhythm, key, volume, and timbre. By modulating these musical elements, we can control the emotionality of the voice and thus what I mean by the temperature of our communication. This, in turn, has an impact on the emotional atmosphere of the consulting-room and the reverberation between patient and analyst, variously heightening or damping this atmosphere.

But the distance between the analyst and patient can also be modified from moment to moment. An awareness of splitting processes in the patient makes this possible, especially if we take note of the language differences between various parts of his personality when they present themselves directly at times of acting-in-the-transference. We can by this means utilize rather different language as a directional advice, each different from the other in vocabulary, imagery drawn from the patient's speech and dreams, level of education, degrees of vulgarity or refinement, etc. In addition to this directional device for addressing different parts of the patient's personality at different times, we can also modify the distance by not addressing the part concerned in our formulation at all, but, rather, talking about that part to another, or by ruminating aloud in the presence of the patient, leaving it to his choice to listen or ignore.

Having now briefly described these two dimensions of technique in communication which are felt to lend themselves to ingenuity of modulation, it should be possible to make some more general statement about the principles that seem to guide the modulation itself, and then to illustrate this with some clinical material. Since the purpose of this modulating ingenuity is to free the analyst to share his thoughts with the patient without distorting the analytic process in its origins in the patient (that is, neither to lead nor to provoke, stimulate, confuse, etc.) and since the speed with which things happen in the consulting-room is too great for preconceived experimentation without serious loss of spontaneity and rapport, what I am going to describe is hindsight. It is an evaluation of the virtuosity, whether for good or ill, which I realize I have been evolving over the years and can now recognize as an established aspect of my technique. Of course these are the survivors of countless pieces of ingenuity, many of which have failed and needed to be guarded against in subsequent work. Naturally, I do not put these forward for others to adopt but, rather, as a guide to help others to examine their own development of linguistic ingenuity. I think I can claim that the whole area is fairly free of methodological or theoretical preconception, but, of course, being based to such a degree on hindsight, the attempts at generalization are open to wide error. But from my own point of view my interest in presenting such a paper for discussion is to elicit my colleagues' help to evaluate the crucial question: *do such ingenious devices, indeed, stay within the framework of basic technical method? In other words, where does ingenuity end and acting-in-the-countertransference begin?* I am, of course, claiming that I want my freedom in order to enrich the process and not for its own sake; to increase my pleasure in the work, etc. But we know well from Freud the serious limitations and distortions that the unconscious countertransference can introduce, and that this manifests itself in the analyst, as does the transference in the patient, through difficulty in interposing thought between impulse and action. Freud's advice of the "blank-screen" demeanour and other technical restrictions had as one aim the minimizing of the danger of "wild analysis". This was a bit of do-as-I-say-and-not-as-I-do advice to the young, but strictures are in themselves unsuccessful, as morality is in other areas of life. The matter is too complicated to be settled by simple means. Not only, say, can acting be hidden in "blank-screen" demeanour, but the patient can easily take it as characteristic rather than formal or technical.

If, then, the methodological problem exists and cannot be side-stepped by rules of conduct, if we wish to free the analyst for the sake of enriching the communication *qua* communication, if we wish to accomplish this while still avoiding the pitfall of opening a Pandora's Box of acting-in-the-countertransference, then we must examine and formulate and evaluate what we actually find ourselves doing to see if guiding principles can be formulated in lieu of constricting rules of conduct.

On close examination of my own technique, I think I can discern the operation of the following principles for the modulation of temperature and distance:

1. In the realm of the emotional music of the voice, it is my impression that I tend towards the centre, you might say. That is, if we envisage this emotional spectrum and the segment of it in which people actually operate, my contribu-

tion at any moment seems to function to bring the atmosphere back to the mean, generally damping ardour and infusing vitality into languor. I notice that I tend to talk a bit more loudly than the whisperer and more softly than the shouter, less minor-key than the depressed and less major-key than the manic, more slowly than the galloper and faster than the tarrier, with less vibrato than the passionate, etc. Perhaps everyone does this, naturally, automatically. But in fact I think not, for I know from myself and supervisees how easy it is to be swept on or retarded by the atmosphere created by patients who are powerful projectors, how tempting it is to simulate empathy by mimicry. I believe that major difficulties in the analysis can result from the patient experiencing that evidence of his success in omnipotently controlling the analyst.

2. With regard to the dimensions of distance, I have described two aspects—variations in the object of the communication and variations of the direction. Perhaps I could categorize these more fully before trying to adduce general principles:
   a. The object may be either the adult part of the patient's personality or one or more infantile structures or a more generalized class of object of which some part of the patient is a member (men, children, babies, etc.), and these may be referred to in the past, present, or future.
   b. The direction of the communication may be described as direct to a particular part, indirect (to some part about another part), or directionless (simply put out into the room as an uncertain rumination that might possibly interest the patient or some part of him, though this seems unlikely at the moment).

I notice that I tend to modify these aspects of direction and object to regulate distance according to whether what I have to say seems likely to increase or diminish the pain in the patient's awareness at the moment. I am, of course, assuming that the pain is there and that the patient may or may not be suffering from it at the moment (Bion). In general, interpretations referable to persecutory anxiety are likely to diminish the pain, and those referable to depressive anxiety to increase the suffering at the moment. Therefore, I seem to be more likely to address an interpretation of persecutory anxiety directly to the part in pain and more likely to talk to the adult part about a part that is suffering from depressive anxiety. Likewise, I notice that when problems of cooperation and responsibility are at issue, I seem to talk to the adult part about himself. The question of direction seems to be handled mainly linguistically, through differential vocabulary, partly derived from the patient's account of the parental language of his particular childhood, or cultural in origin where this information is lacking (mummy and daddy, pooh-pooh and wee-wee talk). I am willing to use the patient's own degree of vulgarity (fuck, shit, etc.) when addressing that part, to talk in simple language to the child in him, and at his maximum level of linguistic sophistication to the adult (or perhaps above, where his educational level is lower than his cultural aspirations).

I think I can go no further in exploring my own technique until presentation of some clinical material makes this possible. The best thing to do would be to present an example of successful modulation and also of an unsuccessful one. But as space is limited and what I consider "successful" will certainly be open to contrary construction, I will restrict myself to a single session. It is not verbatim, of course, but was constructed in the evening from an outline made in ten minutes immediately after the session. I will try to identify the modulatory linguistic shifts and to categorize them.

Clinical material

Mr G is a man of thirty, a sociologist doing research, and he comes to analysis partly for professional reasons. I see him four times per week, and he is approaching the end of his second year of treatment, hovering between breaking off the analysis as a fraud and becoming deeply devoted to it as the means of releasing him from being a "sod", a "selfish bastard". He had spent most of the previous session complaining about his mother. She is never pleased with him because she cannot boast of his achievements with confidence, as other mothers seem always to top her boasts of his status, income, or achievements. I had interpreted mainly that he seemed to accuse me of being such an analytic mother, using a carrot-and-stick technique. He had responded by complaining that no one he knows who has had an analysis seems to him particularly admirable, although, of course, he has never met anyone treated by me. But I seem to him to be always implying that my other patients are so much better, etc.

At the end of the session, after I had reminded him of an earlier Isaac-formulation, of how he wished to be the favourite by placing his life in my hands trustingly, even though he thought that I and psychoanalysis might be madly destructive, he left scowling and did not take his briefcase. It was only after he had left the house that I realized this, and, knowing that he was in need of it, I took it out to him as he was turning his car. He had come twenty minutes late to the session through oversleeping, and I had gone three minutes overtime and might have gone further, had he not looked at his watch.

The following session he came on time, entering with an aggressive look, and he launched immediately into a diatribe for about ten minutes. The substance of it was that I was always trying to make him feel inferior and guilty by my behaviour, so that it would seem that he was unfriendly while I was above reproach in my psychoanalytic decorum, so carefully thought out and meticulously applied. But it was clear yesterday, when I had handed him his case, that I was annoyed, because I did not say "welcome" to his "thank you" nor smiled to his smile. At first he had felt grateful and guilty for inconveniencing me, until he had recognized the truth of my annoyance.

ANALYST: That is, until you had courageously fought off these bad feelings that I was so ruthlessly projecting into you *[ironic, with a slight laugh] [to the little boy, lightly]*.

PATIENT: *[laughing against his will]* Yes, it's true. I'm not going to be bullied by you. That is exactly what happened.

ANALYST: It can only be an account of your experience and seems to have been retrospectively modified. Even so, you would not challenge the possibility of error in observation and judgement. For instance, the child in you may not have noticed that I had nodded in reply to your thanks; perhaps there was a smile in my eyes if not on my lips, just as you had not noticed when I held the briefcase up but continued to turn your car *[serious, to the adult]*.

PATIENT: I did notice you holding it up and was pleased. I thought it was a normal, friendly greeting, like "Hi, Joe", but I didn't realize it was my case. And that's why I was so shocked by your unfriendly behaviour when I opened the window and said, "Thank you".

ANALYST: Perhaps what was shocked and disappointed was the desire in the little boy for me to set aside my analytic technique as a sign of favouritism, to be the good mummy and daddy who never cause him the pain of jealousy of other good children *[slightly teasing to the adult about the child, as shift towards baby-talk]*.

PATIENT: Anyone would feel offended by such behaviour *[trying to whip up anger again, but not very successfully]*. The whole world says "Hello" and "Good-bye" except you. Why can't you say "welcome" instead of just nodding? You are the unfriendly and out-of-step one *[warming to his task]*. You hide it behind a façade of technical behaviour but in fact you treat your patients with contempt and try to make them feel inferior as a way of driving them to accept your theories and values *[with triumphant finality]*.

ANALYST: These values suggest that if you oversleep, if you leave your case behind, if you accept the benefits of analysis, you might feel some valuable guilt or unworthiness to spur your development. But if you do not distinguish between the valuable pains aroused by the goodness of your objects from the pains of persecution by your enemies, then it follows that anyone who causes you pain is an enemy *[to the infantile structures generally, serious and a bit severe]*.

PATIENT: *[smiling but sarcastic]* Then you'll like the dream I had last night and interpret it as confirmation, but I see it as a vindication of my courageous and pugnacious attitude to life. You remember I told you that my old boss was coming to lecture, and I had invited him to stay with us and was arranging a dinner-party for him. Well, David phoned to say he didn't need to trouble us to put him up as he had friends at Stanton St John.

ANALYST: *[dubious]* But that sounds fairly uncivilized *[a bit teasing, to the adult]*.

PATIENT: Yes, I realized it as I said it. That isn't really how it happened; I didn't contact him directly. He may not have known of our invitation until he'd already accepted the other. He's not a rude or ungrateful person, though he can be thoughtless and egocentric. I did feel hurt, but perhaps without good reason. My touchiness. Anyhow, in the dream *I had gone into a bar, and someone just punched me on the nose. Well, I think he did—something hurt me, I think on the nose. So I put on boxing gloves and so did he, and we fought, and every punch I threw hit him in the face, and every one he threw missed me. But he didn't seem to get damaged somehow, and when David passed I commented on this to him. But then I noticed that instead of getting damaged, the other bloke seemed to get smaller and smaller, until it was clear that by continuing to fight I was just being a bully. So I suggested we stop, and anyhow I was no longer angry.*

ANALYST: If every time mummy offers you her nipple you think she is flaunting the big penis she got from daddy during the last holiday, you are likely to feel justified in biting that nipple–penis. Only if mummy can bear this aggression without really striking back do things gradually assume their correct proportions. Then you can see it is a friendly little nipple, like the smile in her eyes *[gently and softly, to the baby]*.

[Silence for three minutes.]

PATIENT: Well, there's nothing more to say *[depressed]*.

ANALYST: Ever? *[laughing] [lightly, to the baby]*.

PATIENT: *[laughing]* You win again, I suppose.

ANALYST: But isn't that just the issue? Are we in a fight where someone wins and someone loses, or can we shift to another vertex where either we both win or we both lose, because our individual developments are at issue, not social triumph and superiority? *[serious, to the adult]*.

[Silence for three minutes.]

PATIENT: *[petulantly]* But my mother is like that, and she must have been that way all my life, since I was born, so it isn't surprising if I'm unfriendly and suspicious and view the world as a place of competition and ruthless fighting. So I'm not to blame *[ends weakly, trailing off]*.

ANALYST: But this material also suggests another possibility, that a baby who is still incontinent, as you were about over-sleeping and leaving your case, may be unable to accept the kindness from the breast because, when it is in pain about the loss of control, feels little and humiliated, it experiences the pain as being put into it by a breast that uses the nipple to remind the baby of the daddy's big and continent penis. Your mother today does not relate herself to the baby in you, as I can do in the analysis, so perhaps her behaviour with you does not give a picture of her motherliness but of some level of girlish vanity. If you can begin to recognize different levels in yourself, you may also begin to recognize them in others as well *[persuasive, to adult and baby simultaneously]*.

* * *

This clinical material should now permit me to refine a bit the ideas put forward in the earlier sections. The method of psychoanalysis that Freud designed and developed is one, I firmly believe, of great beauty and humanity. Furthermore, it seems to me to combine a scientific means of making observations about a psychological situation to which precise modes of thought may then be applied for the sake of combining the single periods of observation into a longitudinal study. This can be raised to a high level of abstraction so that varied experiences may be combined to allow for valid generalization. But even more than this, it is a method that gives scope to both analyst and patient for creative artistic activity. One of the areas for this is that of technique—generally speaking, in the sensitive and tactful application of the basic principles. It also, I am claiming, can allow for an adventuresome exploration of the limits to which ingenuity can extend and render flexible and potent these basic principles, thus allowing patient and analyst to create between them a highly unique interaction that goes beyond mere practice and borders on art.

In the heat of the moment in the consulting-room or playroom we have little time to make systematic observations of our technical functioning. But as experience grows and facility gives way to virtuosity as a manifestation of growth in our own personalities, a retrospective observation of the technical area becomes possible in repose. Naturally, it is wide open to falsification, error probably increasing directly with the square of the distance in time from the session, but this is surely open to serial refinement of observation and thought. The questions in my mind upon which I would value discussion centre on two issues: (1) Is the matter of this paper indeed worthy of being considered technical, or are these merely matters of style? and (2) what sort of criteria could be used for deciding whether we have crossed the border from the area of ingenuity within basic principles into the boundless infinite of acting-in-the-countertransference?

Finally, of course, there is the question whether such a paper is of interest to one's colleagues or is essentially private. This is important, for it will also determine what we try to teach our students. If it is essentially private and essentially stylistic, I submit that it should not be taught, for it cannot be learned but only identified with. This carries the danger of narcissistic identifications in a supervisory situation where there is no means of either detecting or correcting the tendency, as one may hope to do with candidates in analysis. But that this is an area of private interest and concern, I am certain; for though we do gradually become skilful in doing what we know, our activity is of such a complex nature that we can only claim to know a little about what we do.

CHAPTER TWENTY-TWO

A psychoanalytic model of the child-in-the-family-in-the-community

with Martha Harris

(1976)

This report was commissioned by the Organisation of Economic and Cultural Development (OECD) of the United Nations and was written in partnership with Martha Harris. It has not been published before in English, although it has been in its French, Italian, and Spanish translations. The model it describes is meant to provide guidelines for rationalizing the observation of human behaviour and mental states for the diagnosis of relationships of the child in the family in the community, and for therapeutic uses. This model is borne out of the creative application of psychoanalytic thinking to family processes, and it has specific applications regarding the educational functions of the family.

Published in Spanish in: *Familia y Comunidad* (Buenos Aires: Spatia Editorial, 1990).

1
Introduction to the study

Theoretical background

Models are not theories but are organizations of theories for use. The model described in Section 2 derives its theoretical background from the work of, mainly, Freud, Karl Abraham, Melanie Klein, Wilfred Bion, Roger Money-Kyrle, and Donald Meltzer. It is intended to be used as a framework of reference for the construction of social-psychological research into the educational function of the family in our culture and for the interpretation of the findings of this research.

Concept of metapsychology as six-dimensional

For our purpose it is necessary to employ a multi-dimensional model to fit an extended concept of metapsychology. It needs to embrace the six dimensions from which mental life may be considered—namely, the structural, dynamic, economic, genetic, geographic, and epistemologic. The model should be able to encompass these six dimensions from the point of view of the individual, of the family, and of the community. It should also, by defining the forces that mediate flux within and between these three spheres provide a means of systematic description—not explanation—of the movements of growth or regression.

For the purpose of exposition, and perhaps later of use, a graphic representation of the total situation is to be employed which undertakes this six-dimensional task. Its components will be separately described and their interactions subsequently traced. In the course of doing so, we will attempt a brief description of the background theories, the first requirement being an elucidation of the six dimensions themselves.

Role of mental pain

The central phenomenon in all psychoanalytic conceptions is that of mental pain, which may generally be divided into three categories: persecutory, confusional, and depressive. The first refers to pains involving threat to the self, the second implies threat to the capacity to think and function, and the third indicates threat to love objects.

Study of mental pain requires not only definition of its quality and reference, but also of its distribution and source. Because mental pain can be distributed in both the external and the internal world, it is necessary in the clinical situation to ask, "Whose pain is this?" Pains may be passed serially within any social grouping, and modifications of quality and intensity, consequent to this serial passage must be clarified.

1. The structural dimension: the self

Mental pains, generally called *anxiety* (persecutory, confusional, or depressive), are dealt with, at least from birth onwards, through relations with objects, initially with the mothering person experienced first at a part-object level as a breast or its representation, a presence that feeds, comforts, nurtures, or frustrates. The consequence of these interactions is that mental pain becomes bound in the grown-up structure of the personality. This structure, the *self*, is at first far from unified in its functions or its body reference or image, but it gradually organizes around an internalized object that has the meaning experienced in the nurturing situation. It therefore tends to be experienced in phantasy as breast-and-nipple (*partial object*) and later as mother-and-father, the *combined object*.

These internal objects are idealized insofar as the pain-provoking aspects of them, particularly the frustrating, disappearing, keeping-waiting aspects, tend to be held in a split-off position, as if they were quite distinct from the gratifying ones. This has the effect of inducing a certain degree of splitting in the self into idealized and bad—or destructive—parts, the latter reacting with violence and envy to frustration.

Since the functional aspect of the personality, the self, has both instinctual endowments (id) and developmental capacities (ego), the splits that occur during development distribute the instinctual endowment unevenly, so that often very valuable inclinations (talents?) rest under the domination of the destructive part of the personality and are not available for constructive use and development within the sphere of the good objects and sentiments of love and gratitude.

This is noticeably so with intellectual capacities, verbal gifts, and sexual vitality. Where the latter is marked, a severe impoverishment of sexuality in the sphere of loving relations may develop, which favours the organization of perverse sexuality, anti-social attitudes, addictive tendencies, and mental illness.

It is possible that along with the structuralizing of the personality as just outlined, a parallel development takes place, which evolves an alternate "world" on the basis of negativism and envy, the delusional system of the schizophrenic part of the personality. Its prominence in the whole structure, its access to consciousness, and its indirect influences on development vary, of course, from individual to individual from time to time (being most pressing at times of great stress and flux, such as adolescence), but they will be assumed for the purpose of this model to be ubiquitous.

2. *The dynamic dimension: mechanisms for dealing with pain*

These processes of development which *bind* mental pain in the form of structure are further amplified by mental mechanisms aimed variously at modulating, modifying, or evading mental pain.

The *modulation* is accomplished primarily by thought leading to understanding and actions that may successfully modify or adapt to the external world or internalize new qualities into the internal object that comfort or strengthen the personality. *Modification* of anxieties is achieved through *omnipotent phantasy* of various sorts called the *mechanisms of defence*, but many of these same defences may be employed in a more violent way to *evade* mental pain through its distribution either in the internal world or in the external. These three processes, taken together, constitute the dynamic dimension of personality functioning.

While omnipotent phantasies are limitless, they are usually described or categorized for convenience under such headings as introjection, projective identification, obsessional mechanisms, manic mechanisms, confusional mechanisms, and acting out, any one of which may have the effect of instituting repression or loss of insight.

3. *The economic dimension*

The overall consequence of the operation of these means of dealing with mental pain constitutes the dimension of the economics of the mind and may by considered to follow one or other of three principles. The most primitive of these is a *compulsion to repeat* previous patterns of behaviour, unmodified by the experience of its consequences. The second, more evolved, is a "pleasure principle" to minimize mental pain, and it is subject to modification by experience of the consequences in the outside world. The third principle relates not so much to behaviour and its results but to the meaning of relationships and is called the *paranoid-schizoid* and *depressive positions* (slightly modified by Bion and abbreviated $Ps \leftrightarrow D$).

These are value systems and, respectively, emphasize the safety and comfort of the self versus the welfare of the love object (especially, in the depressive position, the internal object).

4. *The genetic dimension*

Freud's fourth dimension of personality is the *genetic* one, which views the personality as the resultant of summation of its life experience, where these experiences have left their mark either as structural modifications, altered dynamic tendencies, shifts in economic principles, or memories. But two addenda to Freud's metapsychology must be entertained in order to make our model capable of fulfilling the functions for which it is intended.

5. *The geographic dimension*

A fifth dimension must take into account the *geography of phantasy* and its consequent view of the world. The life-space of the individual is experienced to be taking place in at least four different spaces delimited by the body boundary: namely, an internal world containing infantile parts of the self and internal objects, an outside world which the self inhabits and where it encounters external objects, and further, the internal space (or world) of internal objects and, finally, of external objects. Added to this list, one must suspect the existence in phantasy of the "nowhere" of the delusional system.

6. *The epistemological dimension*

The sixth, and for the purposes of this model in research on educational functions the most important, is the *epistemological* dimension. It is a dimension of metapsychology inherent in the later work of Wilfred Bion and the amplified model of the mind that he has superimposed on Freud's model as implicitly modified by Melanie Klein. It enables us to distinguish various categories of learning, to define the mental state underlying them, and to trace their consequences for personality development. Because they are so crucial to our later exposition, we will describe them at some length. They may be named learning from experience, from projective identification, from adhesive identification, from scavenging, from delusion. All contrast with *learning about*.

* * *

Learning from experience. Learning from experience, as described by Bion (1965), involves participation in an emotional experience in such a way that a modification of the personality takes place. The person "becomes" something that he was not before—say, a "walker" in the case of a small child, or a "doctor" in the case of an adult. Internal qualification of this sort may be contrasted with the varieties of external qualification bestowed by social structures.

* * *

Learning by projective identification. In contrast, learning by projective identification involves an omnipotent phantasy of entry into, and taking over, the mental qualities and capabilities of another person. Because the conception of the other person is limited and since the projection imbues him with the qualities of the subject, the result is something of a caricature. Where the projective identification is with an internal object, qualities of omniscience and judgemental attitudes predominate.

* * *

Learning by adhesive identification. On the other hand, learning by adhesive identification, which involves a deeply unconscious phantasy of sticking on to the surface of the object, the resulting identification picks out only the social appearance and thus takes on the attributes of a somewhat mindless imitation of appearance and behaviour. It is characterized by instability, tending to collapse easily under stress and to be fickle, easily shifting to new objects of immediate interest or attachment.

* * *

Learning by scavenging. This is typified by the envious part of the personality, which cannot ask for help nor accept it with gratitude. It tends to view all skill and knowledge as essentially secret and magical in its control of nature and people. It watches and listens for items "thrown away", as it were, where no "please" or "thank you" need enter in, and therefore tends to feel triumphant over the stupidity of others for giving away the formula.

* * *

Delusional learning. Of an entirely different order, delusional learning consists in believing that whatever is revealed in nature or by man is essentially worthless and that only the hidden and therefore occult is of value. It sees evidence in the nuances while neglecting the apparent and constructs a world that is essentially anti-nature.

* * *

All five of these forms of learning are essentially autonomous in their inception and express either the thirst for knowledge and understanding, or its converse—intrusive curiosity. By contrast, *learning about* the world has its source in the motives of the teacher.

* * *

Learning about the world. Its methods are essentially those of animal training—stick-and-carrot, dependent for their success on coopting greed, timidity, docility, or competitiveness of the subject. Its achievements effect no deep modification of the person but, rather, decorate his social persona for purposes of adaptation to the demands of the environment, and they have little connection with ultimate goals or ethical principles.

* * *

Of these six forms of learning only the first, learning from experience, requires a shift in values in keeping with the move from the paranoid–schizoid to the depressive position. It is heavily dependent on the assistance and guidance of benevolent objects (either internal or external) with whom it can share the burden of the anxiety (confusional or persecutory) attending the impact of a new idea. The advent of the depressive feeling resulting from the changed view of self and world inherent in such learning is accompanied by feelings of gratitude and privileged indebtedness to the mentor.

2
The model

This graphic representation of "life-space" (K. Lewin) is intended to give a visual image of the life situation of the individual-in-the-family-in-the-community (see Figure 2). The longitudinal axis is life-time, the *genetic dimension*, while the cross-section represents the situation of the moment of study, (*structure*), the present, ever shifting but held in suspense for the sake of exposition. Flux is represented by two different forms of movement, centrifugal and perimetric. The *dynamic* and *geographic* dimensions are shown by movement to and from the centre, and clockwise or anti-clockwise movement demonstrates the *economic* and *epistemological* dimensions. The six concentric rings of the circle indicate the total structure of personality functioning at its various levels in the individual and in the social organizations to which he relates. We plan to discuss each of these constituents of the model in a general way and then to examine in detail the finer structure of each.

The structural dimension

Temperament

The innate disposition of the individual is hardly definable by means of the psychoanalytic method of research but tends to be thought of as comprised of two categories, one being a set of innate preconceptions that await experiences that approximate to them so that they may grow into conceptions and concepts (Bion, Money-Kyrle), and the second a set of innate balanced inclinations, which may be strongly bound to the general physiology and may thus vary in life according to shifts in the physiological state.

They may be described, for instance, by various dualities such as active–passive, masculine–feminine, violent–placid, reflective–outgoing, slow–fast. They may be thought to declare themselves in some degree at birth and immediately thereafter, or even to some extent in pre-natal activity, but these estimates are rendered uncertain by the unanswered—perhaps

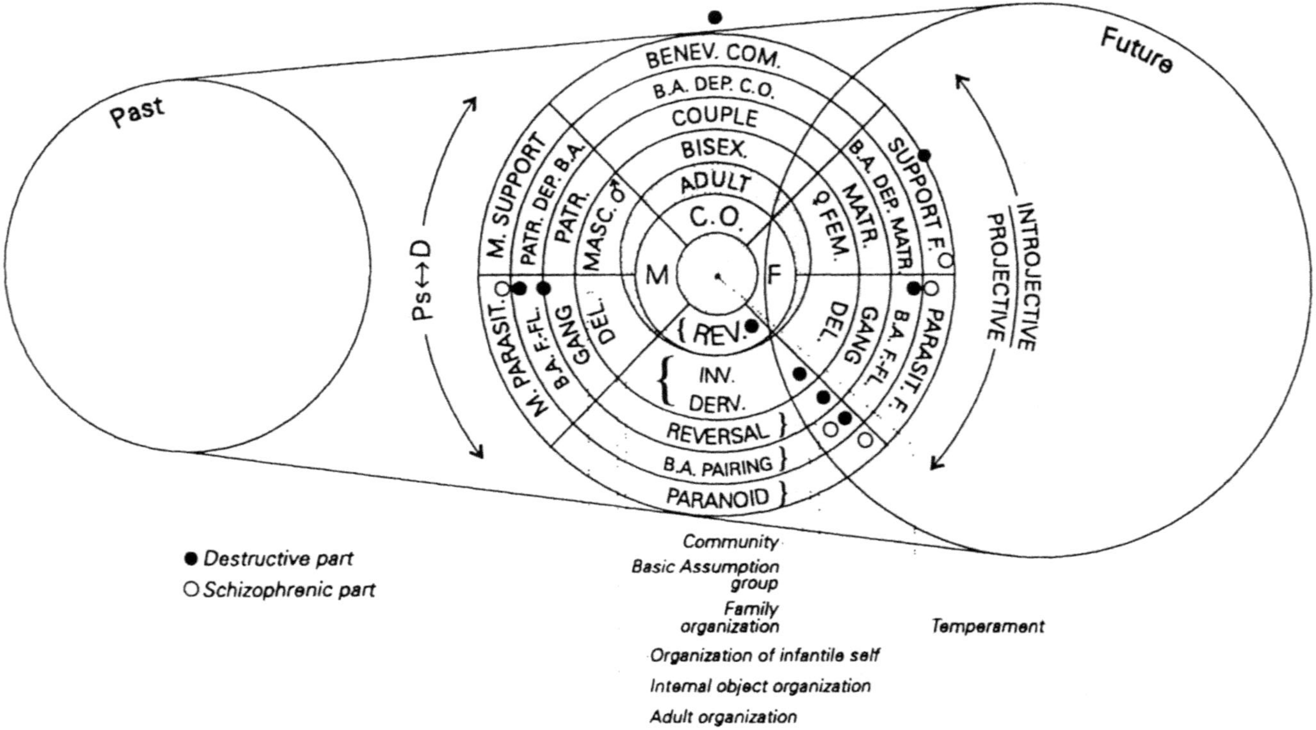

FIGURE 2. *Cross-sectional model of the* INDIVIDUAL-*in-the-*FAMILY-*in-the-*COMMUNITY

unanswerable—question: "When does life-experience begin?" Given its imponderable aspect, the cautious observer will be reluctant to assign great significance to it on the basis of history of infantile development. The danger is that it may be used as a waste-basket for explaining away, and for thus obscuring the extent of our ignorance. It corresponds to Freud's concept of the id insofar as he meant "instinct" but not insofar as he meant "mental representation of bodily states". The concept of "self" is taken to be the functional, if not the most poetic, theoretical unit of structure in the mind and is seen to comprise both ego and id aspects in respect of both functions and representations of bodily states, the latter being subsumed under the general perceptual functions of the self.

So the temperament may be viewed as innate equipment, standing in relation to the self as the natural resources of a country stand in relation to the human community—or, perhaps, a more accurate analogy would be, as the total physical environment, given by nature and history, stands in relation to the new generation. This gathers together the physiological–anatomical equipment and the mental inheritance.

Internal object organization

This level of structure moves towards stability with time and may be taken as the basis of *mood*. The internal objects fluctuate in various ways that lend themselves to fairly minute and precise study through the dreams of adults and the play of children.

The parameters of variation are along lines of integration (partial or whole objects), degree of relatedness (separated or combined objects), beauty, goodness, truthfulness, dependability, strength, attentiveness, intelligence, and emotional richness, and on a spectrum from harsh to gentle with respect to the ethical aegis they evoke in the mind (conscience). They may be damaged from cruel attacks from infantile parts of the personality, but they can repair one another, even restore one another to life, given the proper emotional climate (depressive anxiety). Sexuality, reproduction, and the nurturing of the mother's internal and external babies are their overwhelming preoccupation.

They may be identified with, in various ways, by parts of the self, one form, *introjective identification*, giving rise to the adult part of the personality. But they may also be invaded, taken over, corrupted by the destructive part of the personality. In its most malignant form this produces the sadistic superego (Freud) or the "super"-ego (Bion).

The view taken here is that "learning from experience" (Bion) occurs where a new idea is assimilated by the internal combined object, which then helps the self to master it and the emotional upheaval that attends its advent (Meltzer).

The adult organization

While infantile structures are in direct contact with the physiological state and the needs arising there, the adult structure of the personality is only indirectly related, in much the same way as parents were concerned with the physiological state of the infant and child.

The direct relation of the adult structure is to the internal objects with whom it is identified in an aspirational sense, as to teachers or mentors. This relation may be externalized in the form of an adult transference, as in religious belief, or to inspiring figures in the outside world, current or historic.

Its degree of integration of masculine and feminine attributes of mind is directly dependent on the state of integration of the internal objects, identification with the combined object being a precondition for creative mental functioning. The parental ethic of work and responsibility for the world and its children, human, animal, or vegetable, is its central preoccupation and the source of its joy. Its capacity for loving companionship in sexuality generates the family, while its capacity for friendly cooperation makes the work-group (Bion) possible. It begins to form early in childhood.

The infantile organization

In its simplified form, the infantile organization may be thought of as consisting of the boy–girl, baby, destructive, and schizophrenic parts of the personality. But these basic parts are subject to defensive splitting processes and may be multiplied or confused. Furthermore, the distribution of capabilities may be very unequal amongst the parts with respect to such qualities as intelligence, strength, and the other qualities mentioned under temperament.

But it is the distribution of strength—meaning essentially tolerance to mental pain—and intelligence—particularly imaginativeness and speed, with special reference to verbal facility—that determines their dominance in the organization at infantile levels.

The *destructive part* is always in competition with the good objects for the leadership and naturally makes capital of every separation situation to establish its hegemony, exploiting all the techniques of propaganda, seduction, and threat to dominate the other infantile parts. It is the liar, the bully, the cynic, the corrupter. It exploits the jealousy, intolerance to mental pain, and ignorance of the other parts to impose its authority, claiming omniscience (the know-it-all) and omnipotence (the capacity to achieve its ends by the power of its wish, without regard to the techniques of implementation).

It is deeply opposed to examining the meaning of things and is therefore inclined to insist that only external objets exist (denial of psychic reality) and that things are only what they seem. People may, therefore, be taken as the summation of their observable behaviour. It therefore promotes transference relations—that is, the externalization of relations to the internal parents—to inadequate objects that it can discredit, collecting dossiers and insisting that the future may be foretold as a direct extrapolation of the past. Its tendency is to form the *delinquent gang* from its infantile cohort, but given sufficient success it becomes grandiose and establishes the *basic assumption group* (Bion).

The family organization

Considering that each member of a family group, limited and extended, may be thought of in terms of the personality core just described, it is clear that a number of different principles of organization may operate to produce very different milieux for growth and education of its members. From the point of view of this model it is necessary to put to one side the nominal structure of families in order to describe their real psychosocial arrangement, both with respect to roles (titular) and functions (actual). Taking each member as a human being, unfettered by the preconceptions on stereotype, it is possible in studying a family group to recognize the actual organization of functions and to notice its interaction with the preservation of titular roles.

We are differentiating only four levels of family organization: (1) the *parental family*; (2) the *matriarch–patriarchy*; (3) the *gang*; and (4) the *reverse* or *negative family*. Under conditions that will be discussed later, the family may lose its sophistication and become more primitive or tribal, both internally and *vis-à-vis* the community, showing the characteristics of one of the three basic assumption groups (BaDep, BaF–Fl, BaP) (Bion).

Basic assumption organization

Following Bion, we are taking the view that the more primitive form of organization, characterized by the sharing of an unconscious primal myth and implemented by communication through projective identification (action and non-lexical level of language), can be seen to be present, although not always active or obvious. Its unanimity of mind and speed of action stand in marked contrast to the progressive importance of thought and judgement as more sophisticated organization forms, accompanied by increased reluctance to act before adequate communication and conference has taken place.

Community organization

This model limits itself to the consideration of four different orientations of the community and the individual-in-the-family towards one another, each being an outgrowth of selection and interaction. We take it that selection is in all but the most extreme cases of political tyranny the prime operative factor in both directions. By and large, we would view the impetus as arising in the family towards the community, but this may be reversed where prejudice is strong.

Again following Bion's (1970) use of the terms, we will call these orientations *commensal*, *symbiotic*, *parasitic*, and *paranoid*, assuming that in each case, selection, evocation, and provocation being what they are, the relationship of family to community will be found to be mutual.

Destructive and schizophrenic parts

It will have been noted that a dot and a circle have been used in the model to indicate the position of the destructive and schizophrenic parts of the personality with respect to the different types of organization of self, family, and community. The clarification of these placements will have to be left for the more detailed discussion.

The genetic dimension

While the concept of genetic dimension is part of the equipment of the psychologist and social scientist, seeking to understand present structures and organizations in terms of their history, it must also take into account the attitudes towards time of the subjects of study. The scientist may take a sophisticated view that time is linear; or even a super-sophisticated view that it is relative; but far more primitive attitudes towards it may dominate aspects of individual, family, and community life. *Timelessness*, *oscillating time*, or *circular time* may be the operative concepts and have a far-reaching significance. Insofar as time and change are strongly interrelated ideas, the attitude towards one influences that towards the other and makes an impact on values and thus on actions.

* * *

Timelessness tends to promote sensuality and the pleasure principle into a dominant position in values, favouring a mindless acquiescence in the compulsion to repeat that disregards prior evidence of consequences.

* * *

Oscillating time favours attitudes of apathy, for it sees the world as being controlled by overwhelming inanimate (or anthropomorphized) forces and structures of perfect resilience. As day follows night, every action has an equal and opposite reaction. Nothing therefore can or need be done to alter anything. Infancy and senility are simply square one, to and from which the individual rebounds from the climacteric to be reincarnated as the next generation is named for the deceased.

* * *

Circular time. The concept of *circular time* generates attitudes of cynicism. "*Plus ça change, plus c'est la même chose!*" Life is a treadmill, a merry-go-round, a cabaret. "Dust we are, to dust returneth" (was not written of the soul). Forms may change, but the substance of the human condition remains the same. There is neither good nor evil (but thinking makes it so), and one may therefore stand on the sidelines, enjoying the fruitless struggles and passions of the unwise.

* * *

Linear time. He who sees time as *linear* adventures in the infinite, always leaving behind what has been strenuously won. He knows that the meaning of the world must be created by bringing imagination to bear on facts. So he must travel and observe, whether in the inner or outer world, to enjoy a too brief life-space, inheritor of a beautiful estate that must be left even more beautiful.

The dynamic dimension

The primary aim of the dynamic operations of the personality is the modification of mental pain within the limits required for the apprehension of emotional experiences. The level at which different individuals can operate is widely variable and further subject to the momentary state of body and mind.

From the point of view that takes *unconscious phantasy* as the initial move in thought and emotion, the modulation of mental pain proceeds by the manipulation in phantasy of the meaning of the experience, creating dream-thoughts through the narrative arrangement of symbolic representations. When a particular dream-thought becomes established as part of the vertex (Bion) or view of the world, it takes on the significance of myth and may find congruence with the myths of other individuals, groups, or communities as the basis of social bonds.

This bonding creates a security system in the outside world that rivals the relationship to internal objects as a bulwark against catastrophic anxiety (Bion). But the two security systems have different significance. Social bonding is in its essential nature conservative, even where the aims of the group seem to be quite radical. This is due to its fundamental resistance to new ideas that would require a re-ordering of the view of the world inherent in the commonly held mythology (expressed as history, philosophy, economic or political theory, theology, or aesthetics), whether formalized or not.

The security system based on dependence at infantile levels and identification at the adult level with loved internal objects can risk everything in the outside world because its internal home is assailable only by destructive activity of the self. Incipient catastrophic anxiety due to the advent of new ideas may be immediately bound at infantile levels in the dependent relation to the parental figures, in much the way that a devout person is resistant to catastrophe so long as his belief remains unassailed (see Kierkegaard's examination of the myth of Abraham and Isaac in *Fear and Trembling*).

Similarly, the dynamic means of modulating anxiety may go too far and become a process of modification or evasion of pain, operating in the first instance internally but which may be externalized and put into action in the outside world. This is the essential meaning of *transference* processes, which are ubiquitous in the realm of intimate relationships.

No adult relationship escapes contamination at times of stress, no casual, or contractual, or group relation is immune to misuse from the externalization of internal relations. The skill with which people manipulate others to play roles in the drama of their phantasy life is exceeded only by the eagerness with which people enlist to play the parts prescribed. Charismatic quality is not always flamboyant as in the impresario, but may move quietly behind the scenes like a puppeteer. Accordingly, the technical concept in psychoanalysis of *countertransference* may also be applied usefully outside the consulting-room to indicate times when a person loses his insight into the nature of an emotional situation and is carried away by the drama whose author and director he may not always be able to locate.

The essential techniques for modulating pain are phantasy, thought, verbal thought, and communication, where thought is taken, in Freud's sense, to be trial action, and verbal thought is its description internally in preparation for communication with others. Verbal thought is probably closely bound to consciousness, if this faculty is viewed in a Platonic sense suggested by Freud as "an organ for the perception of psychic qualities". It is very largely an adult function when employed for communication, for this utilizes the lexical level mainly, the musical level colouring the lexical with the emotionality intended.

But language may also be used at more infantile levels as a form of action, where the lexical level takes on the form of cliché largely, while the musical level projects a state of mind into the audience, either to manipulate their states or to use them as a receptacle for unwanted aspects of the speaker (projective identification of a split-off part of the personality). A person may not have the internal equipment to modulate his mental pain and must then seek an essentially transference relation to some external person to perform the functions (the most primitive being the representation of the situation in dream-thought, called by Bion alpha-function and likened by him to the service of maternal reverie for the distressed infant).

Insofar as modulation is desired, the aim is to discover the truth of the meaning and the significance of the emotional experience and of any new idea that may be inherent. This is the food of the mind, essential to its growth and development.

But modification or evasion of the pain may be sought, and this generates the lies that are the poison of the mind, seeking to demonstrate that nothing important has happened that requires any re-ordering of the concept of self or the world. In its most dangerous form it builds a world of its own of which it is the centre, the delusional system.

All the so-called mechanisms of defence are lies, known to be false but adopted as the basis of values, attitudes, judgements, and actions in a manner that is essentially cynical—that is, they are adopted on a delinquent basis as being true because they cannot be proved to be false, although known to be such.

In the unconscious their most primitive form is the acceptance of false symbols to represent the emotional situation; but more sophisticated forms of lying distort history (memory), and introduce false logic, semantic ambiguities, spurious generalizations, counterfeit emotions.

When these techniques operate in the unconscious phantasies and dream-life, they generate omnipotent phantasies whose categorization has already been mentioned: splitting, projective and adhesive identifications, obsessional mechanisms of omnipotent control of objects, and manic mechanisms of denial of psychic reality. One consequence, and the first noted by Freud, is repression or distortion of memory either in the form of incompleteness (amnesias) or falsification (paramnesias).

Where thought fails to discover the truth, confusions of various sorts may be said to reign. These confusions may be grouped under various headings for the purposes of discussion in accordance with the differentiations that have failed to be made: good–bad, male–female, internal–external, inside–outside, confusions of zonal references of emotion and impulse, adult–infantile, real–unreal (delusional), sleeping–waking, temporal confusions, confusions of identity.

But these confusions are also generated by the lies that defend against—that is, modify or evade—mental pain. Our discussion of the other three dimensions will be largely concerned with these confusions. But we wish to emphasize here the overall distinction between confusions that exist because of the impingement of new emotional experiences and those confusions that have been generated and tenaciously held for their defensive value.

From this dynamic dimension it appears that people are driven into their various social combinations and organizations in two general ways: by their need for companionship in the search for truth to modulate their mental pain, and by the search for allies or victims in the quest for modification or evasion of it.

In a sense it is the success of the former in smaller combinations that moves men to attempt larger social arrangements suited to the larger tasks of adaptation to the environment or the alteration of it. On the other hand, it is the failure in smaller combinations that drives them into gangs and basic assumption groupings.

The balance between the two tendencies lies in the realm of emotional values, which we will discuss at greater length under the economic dimension. But it will make a clearer exposition if we lead on from the previous discussion of the variety of confusions to elaborate the concept of the geography of phantasy.

The geographic dimension

Man's emotional experiences fall into several great categories according to the nature of the space where they are felt to take place. These spaces, earlier described as four and possibly five in number, are discovered to have qualities and laws that differ so significantly that life within them could be thought of as belonging to different worlds.

The *external world* is essentially the world of nature, ruled by the laws of physics, chemistry, biology—and chance. It is a world without meaning, but full of form and movement and qualities that may be apprehended by the senses. Upon this is superimposed the works and personality of man, making their impact wherever they go on the mineral, vegetable, and animal environment, imprinting it with meaning.

This meaning is manifested mainly formally and always with some degree of equivocation, or at least ambiguity. A hammer may strike the head of a person instead of a nail, a table may become "invisible" by being turned upside down, a desert may be seen "as" beautiful.

From this world of forms and sensual qualities man borrows the means of giving meaning its representations in his internal world, from whence he deploys it once more. He therefore elliptically tends to treat the world outside as if it had in itself meaning and significance and is disappointed when it will not conform to the ethical principles he harbours.

The *internal world* is inhabited by the infantile structures of the personality and the internalized objects, occupying a space that is mental but represented as physical within the boundaries of the skin. Where this boundary is felt to be fragile, permeable, or incomplete, due to laceration, patent orifices, or transparency, the differentiation of internal and external is so impaired that a stable internal family cannot be built, and identity must be built up by more primitive means, using omnipotent phantasies of projection or adhesion to external people (as in autism, "as-if" personality, many borderline states, and perhaps some forms of psychopathy).

When the bonding is adequate, the internal world becomes the stage upon which the dramas of unconscious phantasy and dream generate the meaning that is the material upon which thought can operate. It is in the course of these dramas that the impact of new emotional experiences is moulded into the history of the individual, enabling him to *become*. He may, if he tolerates the impact and works over the meaning in dream and phantasy sufficiently so as to discern its significance for his image of himself and the world, become a different person tomorrow from the one he was yesterday—different, but not necessarily better. Or he may stay the same, or return (regress) to previous states of organization.

Thus the internal world *is* the world that imagination builds, but it is a real world insofar as it is built upon truth, intangible but real in its dominion over man's view of the outside world. Its state determines, or really *is*, his state-of-mind. But there are two other spaces that he may, totally or partially or from time to time, inhabit: *inside his internal or external objects.*

The *world inside objects*, based as it is on the assumption that others must, like oneself, have an internal world, is conceived in unconscious phantasy as vulnerable to penetration by omnipotent phantasies of stealth, violence, or compliance. While it is a space that is felt to give access to the other person's mental life and qualities, it is also potentially a trap. Claustrophobic and agoraphobic anxieties surround its entrances and exits, while the delusion of fusion with the other's personality generates qualities of mind or, rather, ideas of qualities of mind felt to be possessed by the other.

Since the attraction of the world inside another generally comes from seeing it as a refuge or a place of enviable status and capability, the states of mind induced by phantasies of projective identification tend towards either withdrawal or grandiosity. The delusion of clarity of insight is one such and that of omniscience another. This omniscience is of a particular quality, a type of poverty of imagination—like the Oxford don who is reputed to have said, "What I don't know isn't knowledge".

Because the most common object of such intrusion is the internal mother, and because her body tends to be divided into three great regions, three realms of emotionality of near-theological significance can be seen to emerge distinct from one another: (1) heaven of bliss inside the breasts; (2) a garden of sexuality and reproduction in her genitals; and (3) a most attractive hell of perversity and sado-masochism in her rectum.

It seems apparent from clinical experience that people living in different worlds cannot communicate but they often, Pinteresque fashion, carry on their non-communication unawares. One task of the analyst is to find his way into the world inhabited by his patient, but this is just as true of parent or teacher. A person or part of the personality trapped inside an object can usually be helped and enticed out because the pressures of claustrophobic anxiety usually outweigh the miseries or envy from which he had fled, given at least one person interested enough to seek him out in his claustrum.

The same is probably not true of the part of the personality caught in the *delusional system*, the schizophrenic part proper. It is difficult to say from the present state of psychoanalytic research whether this part is ever recoverable, for it generally seems that the transference with which the analyst works emanates from infantile structures that are teetering on the edge of that plunge into delusion.

The part or parts held in the delusional system (Freud's great exposition of the "Schreber case" is the prototype) operate upon such altered premises, employ language in so idiosyncratic a way, experience emotions that are so off-key and bound to bodily sensations, use perception according to such abstruse laws of evidence, and fashion a logic so wilful that communication with same parts of the personality or other same creatures is impossible. Above all considerations, schizophrenic parts seem to have passed beyond the gravitational pull of the good internal objects; psychological astronauts adrift in a lifeless universe.

The economic dimension

The three economic principles to describe (again, not explain) the movement to and fro in mental organization—namely, *the repetition compulsion, pleasure–reality principle, and the paranoid–schizoid and depressive positions*—intend to mark the movement from mindlessness through quantitative considerations with respect to the economics of mental pain.

* * *

Repetition compulsion. The primitive repetition compulsion is seen as the basis of learning by training, where obedience, or perhaps more accurately conditioning, is induced by repetition reinforced by reward and punishment.

* * *

Pleasure–reality principle enlists the power of understanding in the interest of adaptation. While it is not subject to the crudeness of stick-and-carrot, it does thrive in an atmosphere of promised satisfaction and approval. It is ideal as the basis of acquiring information and skills at the "learning about" level, which does not alter the self-image or the image of the world and therefore involves no great emotional upheaval. But it also fails to promote growth. It easily gives way, in a harsh atmosphere or where the operation of envy is too great, to more autonomous forms of learning already mentioned—namely, learning by projective identification, by scavenging, by mimicry (adhesive identification), or by delusion.

Under the pleasure–reality principle judgement operates on the basis of quantification, and therefore the interest tends to be drawn to those considerations in the outside world that lend themselves most willingly to this form of representation. Money, time (and therefore age), and frequency (of sexual intercourse, for instance) are its most cherished parameters. Its dominion lies outside the realm of intimate relations, serving reasonably well for casual, contractual, or basic assumption grouping. The reason for this lies in its attitude towards emotionality, for which it has no use beyond its pleasure–pain aspects.

* * *

Paranoid–schizoid and depressive positions. The movement between *paranoid–schizoid* and *depressive positions* (Ps↔D) appears to have its inceptions around the third month of post-natal life (Klein) and to remain as the economic focus of the struggle between love and hate in intimate relationships. Since emotionality is the heart of the matter and is recognized as the carrier of the meaning bound in the relationship, quantitative judgements are overridden by qualitative ones, and therefore by judgements of value. The two value systems implicit, while descriptively in clear opposition to one another—namely, self-interest versus the welfare of the love object—are in practice overlapping, in fact. The persecutory pains of the one (persecution, dread, terror, paranoid fear, confusion, etc.) overlap the pains of the other (sympathy, remorse, regret, loneliness, grief, etc.) in an area that may be described as persecutory depression (mainly guilt and isolation).

Since emotionality is the heart of the matter, and since it is, or seems to be, a transferable phenomenon, the crucial question mediating the movement between the two positions is always, "Who shall have the pain?" This may be spoken of as the problem of containment and follows a law analogous to that of the conservation of energy.

From the point of view of psychic reality, mental pain is an ultimate item, irreducible to further fractions and indestructible. It must be reckoned with. Its toleration is co-extensive with the bearing of responsibility, which makes of it the chief item in relationships that may be classified on a spectrum ranging from service to parasitism.

From this viewpoint the essence of service is the sharing of someone else's pain with a view to lowering it within the limits of their toleration, while going beyond this limit produces indulgence and overprotection. At the other end of the spectrum the off-loading of mental pain, whether into a willing or unwilling host, shades from dependence into parasitism, depending on the degree of ruthlessness employed. The means of its transportation and distribution are described by the dynamic dimension.

We will now take the view that *containment* of mental pain is the central concept for examining the educational functions of the family under this model.

The epistemological dimension

It becomes necessary at this point to clarify the philosophic position implicit in all that has gone before in order to make a more minute examination of the model, wherein we hope to demonstrate the means by which it may be put to use. We do not mean to insist on either the verity or the utility of this philosophic position but merely to clarify its relation to the model, that is its utility for this particular point of view.

In keeping with the general point of view of psychoanalysis, with its emphasis on the primary position of psychic reality for the generating of meaning and the overriding importance of intentionality in generating value, a concept of knowledge would need to be divided into two great categories: knowledge directed towards understanding the world, and knowledge directed towards controlling the world. It would be amiss to equate these with art and science, for we would then have to talk about the art of science and the science of art. Nor can we distinguish them as contemplative and active, for action follows from the one as surely as planning characterizes the other. We will adhere to a motivational definition, recognizing that this is only observable to the person himself, never directly to another.

The second stone in our philosophic foundation is the idea that all knowledge must derive from thinking and cannot be given, as for instance items of a dream may be given without being represented in the dream content. Furthermore, thinking can only operate upon observations of fact, be they facts of the external or of the internal world.

The facts of the external world are knowable only by their secondary qualities as they impinge upon our senses in the context of emotional experience. The ability to think about these facts of an emotional experience requires that the emotionality, especially the pain, be contained. This pain is essentially the "cloud of unknowing", the "negative capability", related to uncertainty.

We will take the position that few people are thinkers, but that many are learners capable of teaching. Our theory of knowledge is, therefore, a trickle-down theory, starting with the rare genius or prophet. But as there are good geniuses there are also evil ones, the inventors of the great lies and the technologists of misrepresentation (*"Dulce et decorum est pro patria mori"*, for instance, as promulgated by a Hitler).

We have, therefore, ranged the epistemological dimension alongside the economic one to emphasize the parallelism between *introjection, depressive position,* and *learning from experience* (truth), as against *projection,* the *paranoid–schizoid position,* and *propaganda* (lies).

The other forms of learning and training we have mentioned may take place outside the emotional context of an intimate relationship and therefore outside the essentially hedonistic or conditioned dominance of the paranoid–schizoid and depressive positions.

But the influence of Ps↔D may be felt as a subsidiary force, as with children at school who do not form a transference relation to their teachers, yet their performance at school may be heavily influenced by their relationship to parents at home as well as to their internal objects. For this to be so, they must carry some identification with the family, internal or external, with them into the community to function as representatives of the family group. One might think this was always the case, but the study of children so often indicates a gross disparity between their states of mind in and out of the home, and in fact experience in schools and child-guidance clinics seems to reveal how often the child in the community is a stranger to the parents.

3
The community

The previous sections have centred attention to a large extent on a psychoanalytic view of the individual and his conception of the world as the theoretical background of the model we are constructing. Since it is a model intended for use outside the analytic consulting-room (it is probably the model used implicitly *inside* it), it is necessary that the general structure of community and family be investigated in some detail insofar as these finer structures relate to this model.

This is not to undertake a new theory of social structures nor particularly to embrace an old one, but, rather, to trace the implications of the psychoanalytic view of the individual for the understanding of these social structures.

As our discussion thus far has had a rather centrifugal movement in relation to the model, moving outwards from temperament to community, it may be useful now to work centripetally. This may correct the impression that all movement on the model has its inception from the centre—that is, from the individual's temperament, operating through his internal situation, shaping his character and its impingement on the family, thus influencing his adjustment to the community.

The opposite influence is equally important—that is, the character of the community influencing the structure of the family and thus contributing formative influences for the shaping of the characters of its members. But it must be kept in mind that our model deals with the structure of the community *only* insofar as it has an influence on, or reacts to the family within the special confines of its impact on the development and education of the children.

It will be seen that the structure of the model implies a certain continuity from the centre outward—a basic four-part division at each level or organization, augmented by a subdivision within each as dominated by one sex or the other (see Fig. 2, p. 396). Each division of the community ring denotes a particular emotional and attitudinal *aspect* of the community with which the family *qua* family or as individual representatives of the family are interacting. It must also be remembered that we are trying to represent the situation in which the individuals are not behaving as individuals but, rather, are fulfilling a role, as they comprehend it, in a social organization. But since the comprehension or interpretation of the role is held to be self-evident ("I am a soldier. I was only obeying orders"), the responsibility for the action of the member is felt to devolve upon the organization, unless its hierarchy specifically repudiates it by punishing or expelling the perpetrator. Can an organization *feel* responsible, or only *act as if*? We will take it that depressive anxieties and the sense of responsibility vary inversely with the size (perhaps with the square of the size) of the organization.

Therefore, in our description of the community level we are dealing with the overall situation in which individual people are behaving towards one another contractually within the bounds of their understanding of the social contract, each fulfilling a social role held by him to be self-evident in the contract ("I know my rights") and in its implementation ("what would you have done?"). This situation of contractual relationships is open to modification where the contact is repeated, or its shallowness may be resisted by the person who resents this mindless and unfeeling mechanization. But generally it may be said that most people do not notice the alteration (for instance, the great scene in Brecht's "Galileo", in which the astronomer is seeking the support of his good friend the cardinal during the process of his being dressed to conduct High Mass).

In keeping with the central psychoanalytic orientation of the model we have named these different aspects of the community as follows:

1. the benevolent community of the combined object (Benev. Com. C. O.);
2. the supportive maternal community (M. Support.);
3. the supportive paternal community (F. Support.);
4. the maternal parasitic community (M. Parasit.);
5. the paternal parasitic community (F. Parasit.);
6. the paranoid community (Paranoid.).

We must now undertake to discuss each aspect in some detail, including their attitude to the destructive and schizophrenic aspects of their members.

The benevolent community of the combined object

We will take it that every community organizes itself around a myth of itself that in one form or another expresses the idea that a happy combination of a mother and father are presiding benevolently over the welfare of its children: king and queen, executive and legislature, capitalist and entrepreneur, the party and the politburo, owner and manager, church and Pope, etc.

While it is a caricature and in a sense a travesty of the family, for the emotionality is sentimental when not frankly hypocritical, the community under this myth is certainly able to behave in a parental fashion with regard to such descriptive qualities as generosity, forgiveness, tolerance, patience, wisdom, justice.

But it is all *as if* and therefore has very little perseverance under stress or disappointment. The myth of benevolence fades, and the community shifts its attitude and behaviour. This shift does not require any change in the contract but merely a change in the interpretation of the contract. And this need not—perhaps must not—be acknowledged.

Certainly the community must not acknowledge that any of its members reside outside the sphere of its benevolence. But this is easily done by altering the definition of member (for instance "Jew" – "vermin"), implemented by liquidation, exile, sequestration, ghetto formation, or denial of existence (the tramp, for instance).

The benevolent community treats the destructive and schizophrenic aspects of the personality of its members as if they were in fact members of some paranoid community who had wandered or slipped across its borders. The obstinate obtrusiveness of such a part of a member's personality can have a paralysing and schismatic effect (see, for instance, Melville's wonderful story *Bartleby*, or the impact of James Wait in Conrad's *Nigger of the Narcissus*), or may seize the leadership and alter the community itself into a paranoid one (see Bion's *Experiences in Groups*).

In keeping with its central historical myth, the benevolent community behaves as if it were the fountain-head of all order and creativity, the powers for which it delegates down the line to its subsidiary levels of organization and ultimately to the individuals it has invested as its surrogates. Whether it is the humblest worker or the most celebrated artist or scientist, the community presumes to take the credit for any accomplishment of value, enabling all members to participate in the central myth that progress is always being made, although everything is already perfect, if only the ungrateful and naughty children would but behave themselves (see Bion's myth of the scientists and the liars in *Attention and Interpretation*).

We wish to stress that we are discussing the mythic organization of the community corresponding to the principles of basic assumption group formation, which we will discuss at greater length in Section 4.

Outside this mythic area, which embraces generally the political organization of the community, there exists, of course, an entirely different area: the housekeeping, work-group area, in which individuals do their assigned and accepted tasks with their learned skills as individuals *vis-à-vis* other individuals, as adult to adult, taking their own decisions, carrying their own responsibilities, making their own mistakes. But the two co-exist. You get oil or vinegar depending on which cork you pull, the individual or group psychology cork.

The maternal and paternal supportive communities

This myth of combined, harmonious parental deity does not bear up as well under the stress of deprivation or disappointment as it can under that of physical illness. The latter tends to mobilize, while the former strains the sense of benevolence, for deprivation and disappointment suggest by their nature that someone is to blame. Either the maternal bosomy richness and generosity of the community has failed, or the paternal strength and courage has given way. In either case, a division in the image of the sexes takes place. Courageous and vital women are being abandoned by their shiftless, drunken, or stupidly promiscuous husbands and left to care for the begotten but unwanted children, or devoted, hard-working husbands are burdened by sluttish and unfaithful wives, who neglect or abandon the children.

The community responds, confronted with evidence of such states, with conviction. Husbandly solicitude rushes to fill the need of the disappointed woman, and wifely tenderness warms the betrayed man. The community *is* the mother or *is* the father, while the disappointing spouse is reduced in rank to one of the children. The one-parent family may be treated as a non-existent problem, like the virginity of nuns, all wearing their rings of marriage to the community. Irresponsibility passes unnoticed, covered by the myth of community responsibility, until the patience of the officials who implement the myth wears thin in the face of escalating greed, parasitism, depression, and disorder.

The maternal and paternal parasitic community

So long as the mythology is held on both sides, the family and the community, the drama of their interaction slides fairly relentlessly into parasitism. But parasitism, having such a sado-masochistic foundation, is a highly reversible system of relationship. It is not always easy to see who is exploiting whom, and certainly the various participants tend to disagree wildly on this issue.

The guardians of the community resources feel that a ruthless attack is being made by the unjust to empty the cornucopia meant for the just and worthy. The indigent feel that their rights are being invaded insidiously with a view to their eventual enslavement. Mutual paranoia is not far away as all concern for the realities of the situation gives way to litigiousness.

Each side projects into the other the destructive element of the personality of its members. In the supportive community this was recognized as existing but outside, although having a bad influence on the delinquent member of the parental couple. Now it is a matter of fight, flight, or knuckle under.

The paranoid community

As distrust mounts between family and community, evil enters the drama. It is no longer the system that is inadequate, faulty, or mistakenly interpreted; it is no longer a matter of breakdown of the marriage; evil has invaded the situation and is corrupting what should be a paradise of harmony and plenty. Perhaps even a mad genius has usurped the power of the kindly genius of the combined parents.

In any event, revolutionary change is required, if not to replace an insidiously corrupted system, then to rout out the usurpers of parental power, whether in the family or the community. A new mating of beauty and strength must usher in a new era. Youth will find the way where corrupted age has failed. Sanity must triumph over madness, good over evil. The family may behave as if it had to take flight into Egypt to bear the new Messiah, while the community behaves as if an invasion from Mars might commence at any moment.

* * *

We must emphasize again that all these tendencies are actively present in the community and may easily be tapped by any family which has entered into a basic assumption state of organization.

4
The basic assumption level of family organization

There can be little doubt that a community, whether it be a nation, a business firm, a ship on the high seas, or a photographic club, has a wide-ranging capacity for organization. In general, Bion has divided these manifold capabilities into two large categories: the *work group* and the *basic assumption group.*

While time, thought, and communication in close cooperation is required to establish the former, the basic assumption (B.A.) group may spring up in a moment whenever two or more people are present. It may have absent members who are just as important as those present, and its mode of functioning is by unconscious common consent in the myth that is its basic assumption.

Bion has described three of these: *B.A. dependence, B.A. fight–flight,* and *B.A. pairing,* and we will follow his lead here, while placing upon these categories and their interaction with one another certain constructions of our own.

For instance, we will suggest that the three B.A. groups have a natural sequential relation to one another, as suggested by the arrangement in the model [see Figure 2, p. 396].

This sequence could be described by the following narrative myth: in the beginning, all the needs of the group were fulfilled through the wisdom of the leaders (parents), so that the natural envy and enmity of the surrounding group (tribe) was held in check. But as they grew old and more retiring, disagreement among the younger aspirants to the succession produced conflicting policies: some of fight, some of flight. The result was that on the death of the leaders the group broke into two, one sector remaining to fight, and the other fleeing in search of more peaceful neighbours. While the former was gradually decimated or assimilated, the latter waited for the birth of a new leader, who in due course appeared. He fulfilled by his wisdom, etc., all the needs of the group, having first, by his fighting spirit, established and stabilized their relations with the new neighbours.

We will take this myth as paradigmatic of the movement in a family at the basic assumption level of organization *vis-à-vis* the community of its neighbours and surrounding social and political structures.

In other words, we will presume that a family may at any moment shift from a level of organization of individuals (*family*, *gang*, or *reversed family*: see Section 5) having multilateral relations into a level of organization dominated by a unanimously held, but usually unconscious, historic myth of its origins. This is characterized by an ability to organize momentarily on the basis of an homogenous shared state of mind generated by mutual projective identification. Although the titular family roles may remain unchanged, the distribution of functions undergoes a drastic alteration, which has less resemblance to a family than to a primitive tribe. We will examine them now in greater detail.

Basic assumption group: dependence

Whether the leader is in the form of the combined parents, of one or other parent, or of a child, relative, lodger, neighbour, or absent member, the function of leadership falls naturally into the hands of the most quietly grandiose member of the group. The function of the leader is to represent (not, by any means, to perform), the functions of thought, planning, and carrying responsibility.

While one would expect this to devolve upon the person with the highest verbal gifts, in fact golden silence more easily passes for wisdom.

The leader of the B.A. dependence (B.A. Dep) group generates towards the surrounding community an attitude expectant of benevolence, generosity, peace, and goodwill. Evil is not denied but placed at some distance—say, Russia or Mars.

Where one of the two sexes is dominant, this dominance is assumed to inhere in the benevolent community as well.

The mythology of the group then includes indications of historic inferiority, inadequacy, and unreliability, though not necessarily viciousness, of the recessive sex. Family history, mixed with the social, economic, and political history of the community, plays a large role in the justification of policy and attitude. The non-conformist or scapegoat may be an important member and binding force.

Basic assumption group: fight–flight

The leadership of this group tends to fall to the most violent, regardless of age or sex or titular family role. Violence, mistaken for strength and conviction, generates an attitude of ruthless greed towards the surrounding community, whether in the service of "seeing justice done" and "getting our rights", or for the purpose of scavenging supplies in preparation for flight to a new neighbourhood.

Time is felt to be pressing—too pressing to allow for thought. Action is the essential thing, for the world is too imponderable to be approached in any way but by trial and error. Alliances with other embattled families may be sought, but a general pessimism of the "can't beat the city hall" type urges flight, comforted by some degree of scorched earth policy.

If the vitality for flight is inadequate or the community fails to respond with persecutory colouring, the fight may settle into a war of attrition: the cold war of parasitizing and wasting the community's resources through litigious perseverance. But this leads to decimation of the group as the young slip away to more exciting possibilities.

Basic assumption group: pairing

The world surrounding the B.A. group becomes progressively more alien and persecuting when the ethos of the group (as represented in its conscious or, more often, unconscious mythology) moves from dependence through fight–flight to pairing. The pairing group is leaderless but lives in expectation of the arrival of the new leader, either in the form of an actual baby or of some facsimile or representation of a baby.

It might be a new (old) idea, or a place, or an undertaking like a business, but whatever its galvanizing focus, it has the meaning of a nuptial chamber where a saviour is to be brought into existence. For this reason sex, or at least the atmosphere of sexual passion, pervades the thoughts and attitudes. Making-love in a near manufacturing sense makes "love" into a vendable or at least transmittable, commodity, its central activity. It may be highly represented, as in "natural" farming, free of chemicals and the noise and odour of machinery ("the cut worm forgives the plough"—Blake, *The Marriage of Heaven and Hell*), or nudism, a new Christian sect, or a family business—or just the procreation of a genius.

Having fled the Sodom and Gomorrah of so-called civilization, the family feels every hand potentially against them, so that geographic isolation as well as emotional isolation from the community is desired. They feel spied upon, they resent laws that compel them to send their children to be corrupted in the ordinary schools, they use money as little as possible except by way of business, aiming self-sufficiency—or, rather, they aim at preserving a delusion of self-sufficiency by not noticing the benefits of a technological civilization of which they avail themselves, nor, for that matter, the absence of the genocidal tribal warfare that does pervade stone-age cultures.

Ignorance of history enables them to equate goodness with primitiveness, while ignorance of natural sciences allows for a similar equation of natural and kindly. No degree of isolation dispels the paranoid idea of being the centre of vast unfriendly curiosity.

There is almost always a text with Testamentary significance, occidental or oriental, scientific or mythical, that serves as the word of the prophet of the coming of the New Jerusalem. If the messianic dream does not give adequate promise of immanent realization, the children drift away unless held by tyranny, but they may be replaced by recruits from among the disaffected in search of a group. When thus amplified, the pairing group can become dangerously antisocial in its sanctimony, or in preparation for resuming the fight–flight stance in order to force its way back into or even take over the community.

It is not possible to say much about the forces within a family that facilitate the shift to B.A. organization. We would suggest that two factors must come into play at the same time—namely, an impasse in some problem of family organization, which we study in Section 5, and the charismatic impact of a member whose vitality is matched by severe confusion between dream (myth), and external reality, someone to whom the past and future are far more alive and real than the present moment. Such an individual is able to galvanize a spirit of living *in* the past or *for* the future that caricatures selflessness, love, and the overcoming of egocentricity.

States of B.A. organization in a family may be momentary or they may be continuous. Probably they are continuous but hang in abeyance when less primitive principles of organization are dominant.

Bion has made the brilliant suggestion, which clinical experience strongly reinforces, that psychosomatic disturbance has a closer relation to the B.A. function when it is in abeyance rather than when it is being put into action. This has a particular import for the B.A. pairing group, with its religious atmosphere, since religion and curing tend to go hand in hand.

For this reason it seems understandable that as the B.A. fight–flight group settles into the war of attrition and parasitism, in lieu of flight, its pressure on the community should become more and more focused on the health of its members. The responsibility of the community for curing them, which becomes fairly indistinguishable from making them happy, since unhappiness makes them ill, heads the list of litigious clamourings.

On the other hand, the B.A. flight group, which has fled into isolation and is busy with its pairing mythology, defiantly and competitively declares its independence of the medical pretensions of the community and places its faith in more spiritual or magical means. These consist of essentially negative techniques for avoiding the sinfulness that ushers in the diseases generally speaking seen as social ills.

We do not wish to give the impression that B.A. functions are to be equated with madness, for this would be to confuse primitive and psychotic. However, it is true that the psychotic individual may far more easily achieve a position of leadership at the B.A. level than at the family level because the capacity for reality testing loses its significance, being replaced as a guideline by the mythology of the B.A.

5
The family organization

This section is probably the heart of the model. In it we are at some pains to define roles and functions. There is special reference to the educational functions, relating them backwards to the B.A. level and to the community, and forwards to problems of individual development which have already been introduced in the discussion of dimensions.

It will be seen from the graphic representation of the model that we have traced *six categories of family organization*, in keeping with the *six types of personality organization of individual members*.

Before we enter into the detailed description of these six, it would be useful to define our classification of the roles and functions, stressing that these are not sociological divisions but extrapolations of psychoanalytic researches into the internal structure of the personality as described by Melanie Klein and her co-workers. These would belong to Row C—dream-thought and myth—as defined by Bion in the Grid (*Elements of Psycho-Analysis*, 1963), one of the genetic levels of thought in his model of the apparatus of thought.

Roles and functions in family life

We have stressed in the introductory section that the central concept of this model is the *problem of containment and distri-*

bution of the mental pains connected with growth and development of the members of the family-in-the-community. It can be taken as a tenet of the psychoanalytic view that there is no development without pain and, conversely, that any regression in the personality involves the remobilization of the mental pain bound in the structuring of the personality in previous periods of growth.

Consequently, a primary dynamic and economic classification, which applies equally to all members of the family (at times also, by anthropomorphic extension, to pets, the home, the family fortunes), is referred to as "*growing*", "*stabilized*", and "*regressing*". This is to be understood to have a direct relation to the level of mental pain tolerated by the individual and whether it is adequate, critical, or inadequate for growth. We try to give these categories some phenomenological firmness later on in the discussion.

The *titular roles* we consider are classical—that is, the parents, the baby, the pre-school children, the school children, the members of the adolescent community, grandparents and members of the extended family.

But the functions with which we are overridingly concerned may not have any resemblance to those implied by the titular roles. We will name these functions as follows: *generating love, promulgating hate, promoting hope, sowing despair, containing depressive pain, emanating persecutory anxiety, creating confusion, thinking.*

Any one of these functions may be implemented by actions or communications, open or covert, by truth or by lies—that is, by actions or statements whose meaning is known to be false.

At any one moment, these functions tend to be delegated to the individual members, bringing them into functional conflict with their opposite number. Where individuals are at the moment attaching themselves to someone else to perform a function for them, we will speak of functional dependence. Functions may be assumed by the individual or may be imposed upon him by other members. Functions may be in abeyance, being carried out by no one, thus forming a focus of chaos with implicit catastrophic anxiety.

* * *

It must be remembered that we are not intending to present a concept of the ideal and its variations. We are attempting a highly dynamic model, which assumes some degree of flux as a constant factor in the life processes of individuals, families, and communities. Therefore the following descriptions of organization must be taken in two senses: as the description of a momentary state, and as a general tendency.

The couple family

At the moment when the family is presided over by a couple (not necessarily the actual parents), this combination will be seen to carry between them the functions of generating love, promoting hope, containing depressive pain, and thinking.

The other members will be dependent upon them for these functions and thus for the modulation of their mental pain to a level consonant with growth. This will place them in conflict with any member promulgating hate, sowing despair, emanating persecution, or creating confusion; in the interest of protecting the members who are dependent upon them for their modulating functions.

The capacity of the couple to perform these functions will be felt to require their periodic withdrawal into privacy, which is supposed to be sexual and mysterious. The times when they are obliged to be apart produces a hovering Sword of Damocles atmosphere, while their conjunction arouses a constant expectation of the new baby member of the family. The history of their courtship is of mythological interest to the dependent members, giving form to their hopes for the future [Fig. 2, p. 396].

The four introjective *functions* of the couple—generating love, promoting hope, containing pain, and thinking—are not felt to subdivide into masculine and feminine aspects but, rather, to be arranged in a more linear way, with the maternal person taking the brunt of the children's projections and the father being the end of the line for these mental waste products (Harry Truman's "the buck stops here").

All the catastrophic anxiety of the dependent members tends to centre on the mother, regardless of the intensity of love that may be felt for the father and the depressive anxieties that may accompany it. Therefore any evidence of debility in the mother tends to be blamed on the father's possible or suspected inadequacies.

On the other hand, debility in the father is taken as evidence that the system is being overloaded with hate and projected persecution, and encourages polarization among the dependent members with scape-goating tendency.

The growth of all members of the family, as evidenced by carefully monitored and frequently discussed indicators of physical, social, intellectual, and emotional development, is necessary to maintain the sense of security, which is intrinsic to the family and is felt to be utterly independent of the community, despite the overall optimistic and benevolent view taken of the natural and social milieu. Thus the family is felt to be mobile potentially, even though it may be tenderly attached to the home or landscape or community of friends and neighbours. If opportunity glows on the horizon, a pioneer atmosphere begins to scintillate, akin in feeling to the times when the mother is pregnant.

The overall relation to the community is felt to proceed through the individual members moving about, at school, at work, shopping, etc., as representatives of the family. Their individual identities (first name) are secondary in their significance to their family identity (surname), not as an indicator of status but as a burden of responsibility. It is not so much a matter of, "What will the neighbours think?" as of "letting the side down" in the matter of contributing to the general ethos of the community.

The great vulnerability of the couple family resides in the unique identity of each individual, for the death of a child seems to be the one unbearable stress (Wordsworth's "We Are Seven"). Even a miscarriage or a stillbirth can have a shattering effect upon the joyousness and commence a deterioration in ethos, relationships, cohesiveness, from which recovery may seem impossible. It has a more devastating effect than, say, the impact of a defective child, the development of a schizophrenic illness in a child, or the delinquency or defection of a member.

The matriarchal family

Where the mothering person (generally, but not necessarily, a woman) seems to arrogate to herself all the introjective functions, the difficulty may lie in the inadequacy, absence, or debility of the fathering one, or it may reflect the force and vitality of the woman. Where this force has a hostile anti-masculine flavour, the matriarchal shades into the girl-gang family of delinquent type. But in some cases the mothering person combines in herself such bisexual attributes of character and outlook, skills and strength, that the matriarchy shades into the couple family in its ethos.

In the aspects of the community where the matriarchal family is traditional (the Jamaican immigrant population, for instance), the paternal function is fulfilled in a split way, by a combination of avuncular and grandfatherly figures. Where the father is absent through death or from necessity for some period, his presence as an absent object may fulfil the necessary function in spirit, while the actual psychological services are distributed among intrinsic or extrinsic male figures.

But often the community is looked to for this function and these services. This is particularly true of the matriarchal family, which has been constructed around the strength and anti-masculine aspects of the mothering person.

It is this configuration in particular that most easily slips into the B.A-dependent relation to the community, not in a hostile, parasitic way, but taking for granted the benevolence and generosity of the community, particularly of male figures in authority.

Bank managers, social workers, ministers, doctors, and solicitors are naturally looked to for services and are preferably brought into some degree of avuncular intimacy with the family group. The education of the children and their health supplies the motivation and justification for any degree of financial, moral, or intellectual support, and since the mothering person often, in her vitality and optimism, makes an attractive figure, this support is readily proffered. The possibility of sexual entanglements is never far off but is generally denied unless marriage seems feasible, even if unlikely.

The atmosphere in the home tends to rest upon discipline through guilt, and the standards are different from the growth-indicator one of the couple family. In the matriarchal family the standards are more likely to be moralistic, aiming at adaptation to the supposed standards of the community. "What will the neighbours think?" is therefore more important, and in a persecutory way, as if the moral status of the mother were in question for unaccountable reasons. This is most pressing where the mother is divorced or the children are illegitimate.

Unlike the outcome one would expect in the couple family, serious maladjustment of an anti-social, psychotic, or defective sort cannot easily be contained by a matriarchal family structure. Children who come into these categories tend more easily to be farmed out to childless relatives or grandparents or placed in care in the community.

It is unusual for the matriarchal figure to be able to carry all four of the *introjective functions of generating love, promoting hope, containing depression, and thinking.* One or more of these tends to be placed out, as it were.

For instance, a good baby may be treated as the generator of love; a particularly clever child may be the thinker; a cheerful one as the generator of hope; or an obsessional one the reservoir of depressive feelings. Since these surrogates for parental part-functions are more able to represent, than actually to perform, the function, the basic instability of the situation declares itself whenever these functions are strained. The move into B.A. dependence or regression to a more narcissistic pseudo-family organization ensues.

The patriarchal family

A very different atmosphere is found where the paternal figure is very dominant, in particular if the mother has become incapacitated for psychological reasons—for example, alcoholic or depressed—or because of diagnosed physical illness, generally presumed to be post-partum in origin.

A soft type of paternalism may resemble the matriarchal family, and again where strong bisexuality in character exists may approximate to the couple family even when the mother is one of the dependent figures.

But where the patriarchy is imposed by the father's aggressive and often somewhat grandiose character, and particularly where the mother has defected, a stern discipline rules both boys and girls, often supplemented by father's unmarried sister or ageing mother. A bullying and punitively scathing type of tongue-lashing may follow upon the actual beating of younger children, and the relics of religiosity are brought in to shore up the authority of the father.

A feudal system arises, with economic control at its centre, from which the adolescents are quick to escape, being "ungrateful" to their father. But girls may be held in masochistic quasi-sexual submission well into their twenties; partly to protect younger children from the father's harshness, and partly for unconscious erotic attachment to the father, characteristically followed by equally unsuitable marriages.

The relation of the patriarchal family to the community is one of proud independence and of unacknowledged dependence, for the father is unlikely to notice how much nurturing his children seek and get from neighbours, teachers, club leaders, etc. Denigration of the female is unmistakable, tenderness is held to be soft or weak, and lying is the worst crime, for it threatens to plunge the family into a paranoid atmosphere. But the goodness of the father in terms of dependability, selflessness, and unequivocal devotion to the children may save the atmosphere from dourness.

The father may be able to carry some of the *introjective functions*, particularly those of promoting hope, of containing depression, or of thinking, if he is an educated man. But the more common pattern would seem to be that the generating of love becomes a grandparental function and binds the children very closely to these figures—the maternal ones, in particular—when the mother has died. The function of thinking may pass at an early age to the most forward child at school if the father is of low educational level.

The containment of delinquent or even of psychotic or defective children is much better than in the matriarchal family, aid being sought from relatives or the community only when the best interests of the child seems to demand it.

The prospect of the father's remarrying, where this is a possibility, is held to be remote on the basis of his presumed "seriousness", implying a desexualized state based on disillusionment. Only if the children are numerous and still very young does the figure of a housekeeper appear, gradually metamorphosing into wife in name, but not really in acknowledged function.

The patriarchal family is far more unstable in certain respects than the matriarchal one because of the ease with which the tyrannical aspect can escalate into gang-formation on the one hand, or the quasi-religious aspect slip into B.A.-dependent organization of a particularly delicately balanced sort.

Illness in the father can bring sudden disorganization, at which point the unacknowledged dependence on the benevolence of the community becomes apparent. If the father's wage-earning capacity is thereby threatened, disintegration and dispersal may result, the children going to relatives or into care. Family reorganization after such a breakdown is far more difficult than in the matriarchy, because once the authority behind the discipline is broken, it is difficult to reconstitute.

The gang family

Both matriarchy and patriarchy tend easily to slip into the more narcissistic state of gang-formation if the dominant person's character is delicately balanced between maturity and pseudo-maturity.

But the more characteristic configuration arises when either one or both parental figures are strongly impelled by negative identifications. This is to be found in people who have established an early independence from parents whom they considered inadequate, bad, or misguided in their methods of child-rearing.

Since policies built upon the foundation of criticism of the grandparents have largely negative implications, positive policies tend to be constructed intellectually rather than on the basis of feeling for the children or understanding and sensitivity to their feelings or anxieties.

An underlying determination to be right, to demonstrate their superiority and thereby justify their earlier rebellion promulgates a certain urgency to make the children conform to expectations, whether these be of "goodness", "independence", or accomplishment.

In this atmosphere the *introjective functions tend to be simulated rather than performed*, so that titular roles and their dramatization replace the genuine functions. Feelings of love are replaced by seductiveness, cuddling, and indulgence. Hopefulness is simulated by manic cheerfulness, thereby denying the quantities of depressive feeling; while thinking is replaced by slogans, cliché, dogma, catechism, often at a shallow level dealing with posture, dress, deportment, cleanliness, accent, the status of friends' families, and other forms of snobbery.

Rebellion or failure to meet the requirements tends to bring sharp rejection and recourse to punishment or exclusion. Since the gang family is matriarchal or patriarchal (Amazonian and Titan might be better terms), it is not inclined to acknowledge its dependence on the community but adopts a delinquent and scavenging attitude towards the facilities and services that are potentially available.

Its tendency to metamorphose at a moment's notice into a B.A. fight–flight group is forestalled by the excitement of the delinquent system. The evasion of feelings of guilt by projecting all responsibility for exercising ethical judgement places the gang in a field of high tension and attention. Bold and clever exploitation in the loopholes of either the benevolent social services or the potentially punitive legal system places a premium on the capacity to lie.

Since this, in turn, depends on some considerable recognition of the truth, leadership of the family gang can easily pass from parental hands to those of the clever child who functions as prime minister to the ruling parent. Thus a high premium can be placed on gift-of-the-gab, especially insofar as it includes a facility for misrepresenting the truth, either in terms of historical facts or logical operations.

The aggressive attitude towards the community tends to find its most unassailable position in defence of debilitated members of the family, particularly if this is due to physical illness, accidental injury, or mental deficiency. Righteous indignation in defence of the weak against the strong serves as a banner for endless raids on community resources.

The gang family, by virtue of its ambiguous relation to the community—at once defiant and yet seeking acceptance, greedy and at the same time scornfully proud—imposes a very confusing task on its members *vis-à-vis* the educational facilities available. Its members are forestalled from forming a dependent and trusting relation to teachers and yet are expected to make sufficient progress to substantiate the ethos of the home environment and its avowed principles of child-rearing and social organization.

Defiance of authority and scholastic accomplishment are unlikely partners until a firm foundation of learning skills has been established. This can seldom be expected before late adolescence, because of lack of skill early on and lack of discipline later. Consequently, low accomplishment or very unbalanced school achievement seems to be the rule.

Where it is possible to rationalize away the responsibility, the situation is then used as a further pretext for raids on the community's facilities for special schooling. The strong tendency to *folie-à-deux* relationships of parents and children predisposes to school refusal and school phobia.

The reversed family

A hostile caricature of family life may arise when one or both parental figures are either psychotic or dominated by sexual perversity or criminal tendencies. The reversal of values sets the family group in a defiant relationship to the community and its values, in an isolating way that tends to be obscured by its mobility.

Since its members are seldom skilled, their economy is precarious, with a clear tendency to be illegal. The relation to neighbours is therefore clearly predatory and provocative, where it is not frankly collusive with similar families. It tends easily to acquire new members from migratory figures and gravitates towards gainful activities in the entertainment, second-hand goods, criminal, prostitute, or corrupt political areas.

Gambling, drinking, promiscuity, drug-taking, sexual perversions, incest, and assault are part of the atmosphere of family life.

The *introjective functions, and therefore thinking and planning, are almost absent.* Consequently, action tends to be unrestrained, with the result that the mental pain (almost entirely persecutory) tends to circulate in the intra-familial pecking order and eventually to be evacuated into the community by predatory actions.

The tyrannical order strongly promotes projective forms of identification with the stronger figures, although the measure of strength is not always physical. It may reside in intelligence operating to promote confusion, aggravate rivalries, promulgate distrust, or foster irrational persecutory anxieties.

In consequence, the titular roles in the family tend to be a travesty, while the functions migrate in a haphazard way. The tendency to chaos plays an important role in the reversed family's strong tendency to move into B.A. pairing, especially if the community reacts against its predatory or defiant attitude or actions. It can quickly tighten, become a kind of guerrilla band, and take to the road.

This, added to its general peregrinating tendency, adds to the likelihood of the children being maladjusted at school and unintegrated into any community or organization of neighbourhood children.

Such a description may seem to suggest a class implication, and in a sociological sense this may be true, but ethnically it is not. The characteristics of speech, mannerism, attitudes, interests, and habits, the educational level of the parents, the existence of private wealth and property, all these are extremely variable and might place such families in any class from decayed aristocracy to non-traditional gypsy.

We think it correct to say that bizarre beliefs, superstitions, and delusions, along with the tendency to sexual perversity, arson, and semi-accidental suicide are always close at hand. The flirtation with satanic religious sects and practices may be constant and can suddenly gel into a B.A. group with religious pretensions, caricaturing hopefulness that relieves the atmosphere of general despair hidden behind paranoid anger.

6
The personality organization of the individual

Having now operated our model both centrifugally in the early sections dealing with general considerations, the general structure of the model, and the dimensions of mental functioning, and then centripetally with respect to the levels of organization of mental life of the child-in-the-family-in-the-community, we come back to the psychoanalytic view of the mental life of the individual *qua* individual—namely, that which is private to himself, essentially internal, and unknowable to anyone except himself.

Our task in this section must be particularly to examine the forces within the individual personality that favour social engagement of various sorts, whether it be in the service of growth and development, of defence against mental pain, or of destructive attacks upon the growth and development of others.

We will take it that these are the three major categories of social engagement with which our model is expected to cope.

The first category corresponds essentially to the relationship with objects that assists in the *modulation* of the mental pursuant to growth; the defensive use of social relations embraces the area described as *modification* or *evasion* of mental pain; while destructive attacks on the growth and development of others may include the more violent forms of *evasion* (for instance where a good part of the self has been projected into a younger sibling whose ability to grow is then interfered with), or certain primitive forms of violence (some vandalism, for instance), which appear to be simply expressions of infantile omnipotence and are fairly meaningless.

In thus focusing this section we mean explicitly to exclude from it any systematic attempt at classification of individual psychopathology. That is a task with a different orientation from the present work. Our concern is with *structures and forces* and not with clinical manifestations at any of the three levels of mental life that our model is meant to serve for the purposes of coherent description.

It is hoped that the model is general enough to lend itself to the correlation of phenomenological descriptions of varying disciplines of thought and methods of observation. We will therefore attempt a description of the seven types of organization of the *momentary state of mind* of the individual, neglecting completely the question of chronological age of the individual.

The seven, as indicated in the model, comprise: *the adult, the bi-sexual, masculine, feminine, masculine–delinquent, feminine–delinquent,* and *inverted (or perverted)* states of mind. For each, the central organization and the peripheral role of the *destructive* and *schizophrenic parts* is indicated, along with their characteristic relation to internal and external objects and different levels of social organization. In a sense this is a repetition of what has gone before, but pulled together in a different way.

The adult state of mind

Whether it is well integrated in its bisexuality because of identification with a combined internal object (good parents working together to protect and nurture all the children) or weighted on the masculine or feminine side because of some degree of separation and imbalance in the qualities of the internal object, this aspect or state of mind is clearly characterized by a sense of purpose.

It tends to have aims rather than goals, and these aims have an ethical quality that is promulgated by the internal objects. The struggle for worthiness of these objects dominates its relation to external objects, whether peers, superiors, dependents, or enemies. On the other hand, obedience to moral precepts, insofar as these prescribe and proscribe behaviour, is totally alien, since this undermines the sense of responsibility based on decisions reached through conflict of a purely internal nature.

This part of the personality or this state of mind cannot, therefore, be obedient, but it may agree to take orders up to a point; it cannot ignore an unpleasant observation, though it may easily forgive the person observed; it does not forget, though it may dismiss the past as no longer relevant.

It tends to view every activity as a form of work meant to be useful to those dependent upon it or to meet the expectations of its transference figures (mentors, teachers, parents).

Its love-life is closely bound to a shared view of the world, side by side *vis-à-vis* the world and face-to-face in private sharing of the internal world of objects.

This level of relationship is no respecter of age and may arise among peers or across a great expanse of age. When children's relationship with parents is freed (momentarily, or for longer periods, or eventually) of infantile transference, this kind of loving intimacy results.

Although it is strongly inclined to rest upon its aesthetic reactions, thus equating goodness and beauty and truth, it is always on the alert for the worm in the apple, knowing well the liar and cheat in itself.

A person in this state of mind is a good member for the work group but digs in his heels when B.A. group mentality begins to arise. He may be easily stigmatized by the B.A. group as "uncooperative" at best and as the "enemy" when grandiosity or aggression take over; he may be seen as "indecisive" because of his uncertainty, "weak" because of the tendency to see things from multiple points of view, "placatory" because of easy forgiveness, and "disloyal" because of his dismissal of the precedents of the past. The family does not command any special claim on his sense of identity, for this is essentially internal in origin.

But when the basis of the adult state of mind is less bisexual, the mentality of the other sex tends to be somewhat incomprehensible, even mysterious. The need for a love object of the opposite sex is then rooted in a deep sense of loneliness and a tragic inclination that may undermine *joie de vivre*, making it difficult to find a love object with equivalent needs for exclusive intimacy. The boundary between adult state and pseudo-maturity (based upon an infantile part of the self in narcissistic identification with an internal object) can then become blurred.

In more extreme forms this difficulty in sharing family and group ethos can become indistinguishable from a delinquent narcissistic organization, seen with particular frequency in the unstable states of adolescents.

The adult part or state of mind, which remains open to learning from experience, steadily grows in strength with the passage of time, becoming more "at home in the world". Since its security is built internally, it is able to tolerate extremes of environmental shift, peace and war, happiness and tragedy, health and illness. Since it fears neither the love nor the hate of others, it tends to command the respect of individuals and the hatred of groups (Bion).

Probably its greatest weakness is its difficulty in accepting the random factors operative in the outside world. It can therefore be plummeted into despair by senseless aggression or tragic fate operative against its love objects. This promotes a certain tendency to withdrawal that may manifest itself outwardly as asceticism or inwardly within the personality in a certain abdication from participation in active social life and external relationships, leaving the business of living in the world to be managed by the infantile structures.

Although the adult structure begins to form very early (evidences of it can certainly be seen in babies), it probably does not come fully into its own until it has experienced a bereavement, especially the death of a parent, for this brings home then the sense of being "responsible for the world" as its estate.

The infantile states of mind

It is necessary to discuss the qualities of this level of mentality in a general way before entering upon our *six categories* [see Fig. 2, p. 396].

The most central concept related to infantile states that differentiates them from the adult state of mind is their very close relation to the body with its sensations and urges or impulses. Sensuality and action are therefore their most characteristic modes of experience and participation in the world; whereas observation, emotionality, and thought, all of which require some degree of inhibition of action for their full experience, enter secondarily, usually either by training or by identification.

The relationship of infantile structures, and therefore of states of mind, to the outside world is only imperfectly differentiated from the internal world situation where the geography of the mother's body is the overwhelming focus of interest and desire. For this reason the infantile states tend very strongly to be dominated by greed and to lend themselves easily to erotization.

The overriding sense of being children in *competition* for limited supplies stands in sharp contrast with the adult's awareness of infinite possibilities open to thought and creativity. This lends a certain concreteness and quantitative trend to the infantile modes of thought and thus favours a moral or anti-moral outlook, where justice is not viewed as natural consequence but as judgement that, at best, can be egalitarian.

Since its distinction between internal and external world is uncertain at best, random factors and meaningless events are unknown, determinism being its natural philosophy. So deity always exists in some form: parental, familial, in the community, or the skies.

But if justice exists, the possibility of escaping justice must also exist, whether by stealth or indulgence. Thus a great pressure to delinquency results from the summation of competitiveness in the exciting game of evading justice.

For infantile states, the problems of pleasure and pain in the moment tend to take precedence over future aims or goals, but may be overturned to an astonishing degree by fixation to some imagined goal—living in some dream of the future or nostalgic idealization of the past that precludes experiencing the present.

On the other hand, aims with direction dictated by principle tend to have far less hold. Opportunism is the natural way for infantile structures or organizations to operate. They seek to avoid pain, but only under the influence of great pessimism does this retreat become a principle of life, (the so-called Nirvana principle), because the positive pleasures of sensuality and successful action (successful being equated with triumph) are so delicious.

These various factors of greed, pleasure in competitive triumph, and sensuality combine to create a great thirst for information and skills, which finds an outlet in games and is quite different from the adult states' need of knowledge and capability.

Infantile epistemophilia, being at its root directed towards the mother's body, is satisfied to learn about it but does not need to understand. It is easily contented to learn the name and acquire the use of an object in the outside world but does not easily undertake its maintenance, which requires understanding. For this reason it is given to collecting, as function of both its quantitative bent and its relatively shallow interest.

As the love and hate aspects of the infantile state are bound to sensuality rather than to aesthetics, it naturally seeks possession of objects, which it tends to exhaust and to exchange. Thus it is not inclined to relinquish an object until its desire is spent. Only when depressive feelings are strongly to the fore does it manage to relinquish an object of desire in the external world and make a move towards internalization, thus setting the stage for an advance in the qualities of the adult structure. Since this is equivalent to containing a part of itself in distress, the ability to make this move, equivalent to abandoning the hope of modifying the pain or evading it, is central to its capacity to grow and develop.

The result is a near-constant need for monitoring and supervision by the internal parents, by external figures, and eventually by the adult part of the self in order that this movement may occur in a relatively smooth way. Even so, even under the best of circumstances, the infantile rebellion against pain makes for a cyclical mode of progression—two forward and one back, or, in terms of our model, rather circumferential. This strong tendency to cycling depends upon the individual's capacity for love of the parental figures to recover from the evasion of pain at their expense (Bion's Ps↔D).

Bearing in mind these general characteristics of the infantile states, we should be able to delineate the six distinct organizations of the infantile level in a manner that lends them easily to application for phenomenological descriptions of various sorts.

The structure of the model is designed to indicate a natural continuity between individual personality, family organization, and integration in the community when the titular parents are the actual carriers of the parental functions. This should lend itself to a ready recognition of discontinuities for the purpose of recognizing the level of impingement of the disorder in relationships, whether of individual to family, individual to community, family to community, or conversely, of community to family or individual, or family to its individual members. But more of this later on. At this point we wish only to remind the reader that the graphic model is meant for use and not merely for exposition.

* * *

The bisexual infantile state of mind. This state is characterized by dependence, obedience, and cooperation with the parental figures in their presence and competitive independence in their absence. When it manifests itself in either the one or two-parent grown-ups of the family, the relation of obedience, dependence, and cooperation is manifested towards the grandparents or the community and generates something of the "doll's house" type of family structure, where the emphasis is strongly placed on the amenities of the home and the "good" integration in the community at a descriptive and therefore "moral" level.

The same pattern continues with the children in this state of mind, "the keeping up with the Joneses" aspect applying to competition with the parents as well as competitive attitudes towards neighbours when the parents are in their "doll's house" state.

Coupling between the children, often with overt, but more usually covert, sexual content, is the rule, but the odd-man-out or the only child may manage both roles. Children of the same sex may couple with equal facility, but, because of the anxiety about homosexuality both in themselves and parents, this coupling is more fraught and easily deteriorates to a more tyrannical relationship. The uncoupled child in the family may, when in this state, form a strong coupled relation of a "married" sort to a relative or neighbourhood child; but again, as with the coupling of children of the same sex, anxiety about the sexual behaviour is more acute and tends to produce a secretive, unstable relationship.

It is important to keep in mind that the morality involved, deriving so much from external rather than internal objects, may be out of step, even outrageously so, with the mores of the community. Incidents arising out of this confrontation are probably very conducive to the sudden galvanizing of the B.A. fight–flight state in the family.

Similarly, because the children in this state of mind are strongly held in a state of *projective* identification with the external parents, their interests and activities tend to be in harmony with those of the immediate community to the same degree as those of the parents. Dislocation may occur if, as the children grow older, their educational and social skills begin to exceed those of the parents. One can see this in immigrant groups whose aspirations for the children are that they should be "good"—i.e. not delinquent (as among Jamaicans in the United Kingdom.)—rather than "successful" (as amongst Indians or middle-European Jews). Again where the sub-community holds very different mores and customs from the larger community (as, for instance, the Sicilians in the United States), the well-integrated child-in-the-family may be grossly delinquent *vis-à-vis* the larger community.

Where the "doll's house" state exists between parental figures, a state of co-existence with coupling in the children is the rule, dependent upon turning a blind eye. This tends towards a confusion between secrecy and privacy in a manner that blurs the boundary between truth and lies. "What they don't know does not hurt them" can become a fiat for self-indulgence, leading eventually to explosive confrontations, especially with adolescent children, when the sexual competition between children and parents can have shattering consequences on both sides. Actions incestuous in their implications and often in their form force premature departure of the children from the home.

* * *

The masculine infantile state of mind. Where the internal objects are not tolerated in a combined state (which is generally the case in the latency period), an exaggerated sexual quality appears in the character. When this is masculine, it is generally reinforced by family attitudes for the boys and is well tolerated for the girls (in contrast to feminine characteristics for the boys, for instance, which cannot be easily distinguished from effeminacy and homosexual trends).

Whereas unbalanced masculinity in the adult state is conducive to an awe of femininity, in the infantile masculine state this is replaced by contempt. The concept of masculine is so tied up with a part-object concept of the penis rather than the genital (penis and testicles) that ideas of potency tend to be equated with physical prowess, endurance, stoicism, and daring, all conducive to extreme competitiveness. This blurs the demarcation between possessive and protective jealousy and gives way easily to confusion between courageous defence and aggressive violence, towards love objects and rivals alike.

Acquisition of skills becomes far more interesting than learning about the world; information being prized in proportion to its technological application. Since the image of the body is very easily amplified by equipment, interest in weapons and machines predominates. This may seem as comic in small children but can arouse great anxiety in the family or community as puberty approaches.

The titular father in this state can be a great stimulus to such development in his boys, though a menacing possessor of the women and harsh and punitive to his small competitors. But usually they find their hero among more mythical figures, against which background fathers tend to be found wanting or even quite desexualized. Possessiveness of boys towards sisters lends itself mainly to protecting them and controlling their relations with other boys, but may easily degenerate to a more sexual and tyrannical level.

Identification with the family as a militant group, based often on family mythology, also easily galvanizes B.A. fight–flight movements in the family if this masculinity is seen as violent by the community. And generally the distinction between "naughty" and "bad" is shakily established, both inside and outside the family.

Where the surname can be held to carry any distinction of an hereditary sort, even if the actual lineage is obscure, it may be carried as a banner, or conversely as a chip-on-the-shoulder if it has any disreputable connections. Thus family and tribe tend to shade into one another as concepts.

Since the *destructive infantile part* is less widely split off in this state of mind than in the bisexual, it is likely to present itself in the guise of the opposite sex—Delilah or Circe.

unmanning or turning men into swine. Thus, while femininity may be despised, its powers of attraction are also feared. Even more than money, as seen by the bisexual part, the lure of Lilith, working through Eve, is felt as the root of all evil. In contrast, the masculine enemy can be trusted to be what he appears, can be respected and admired.

Nonetheless, its sexual inclination is polygamous but far from reproductive. As with Achilles and Agamemnon, poaching is the one sure way of turning comrades into enemies. It is naturally superstitious, its god being Mars and its devil something like Lamia or La Belle Dame sans Merci. But it is capable of falling in love, especially in a masochistic way in the manner of the Romantic Agony. This is the area in which its capacity for depressive anxiety is weakened both by its tendency to persecutory depression and its masochism.

* * *

The feminine infantile state of mind. Girlishness, almost from infancy on, can be seen to embrace vanity about physical beauty, either of the whole or part of the body, in a manner that betrays a projective identification with the breast of the mother as an object of irresistible attraction: to babies, children, men, women, animals, the gods.

Since beautiful children generally, but little girls especially, are treated in almost all cultures with extraordinary deference, the omnipotence finds little opposition from experience except from the random factors in the outside world. Less beautiful children, boys or girls in whom the femininity is dominant, must invest this power in some part: the face, hair, buttocks, eyes—or mind.

Its greed for babies shades into the more sadistic greed for slaves characteristic of the delinquent state of mind, with its Amazonian colouring. But the purely feminine is more inclined to stoop to conquer with softness, pseudo-dependence, and rationalization of greed in the service of the babies, real or imagined, present or prospective. Essentially monogamous in its inclination, it seems more a consort than a mate and would really prefer the companionship of some other girl-with-babies lest its children be disturbed by the sexual privileges of the consort.

When economically feasible, grown-up girls are likely to get rid of their husbands once the desired number of children has been achieved. Husbandly functions are freely delegated to anyone who is willing: sons, brothers, uncles, the family doctor, social worker, solicitor, the butcher, the baker, etc. But the feminine infantile mind's flirtatiousness belies chastity, eventuating in a coterie of good men and boys as "friends".

But boys and men in whom femininity is dominant have a difficult adaptation in most cultures, unlike the Hellenic. Where it is attached to beauty of whole or part, it almost inevitably attracts homosexual seduction, but when attached to the mind, it may find the means of being "one of the girls" in both companionship and occupation. Its happiest fulfilment probably comes when finding the complementary love and companionship of a masculine woman.

Because the willingness to receive from others is hallowed as tribute and homage, the feminine state of mind can slip imperceptibly into being predatory and parasitic, using money as beauty fades, guilt when devotion fails. Its natural religion would be ranged somewhere between being the Virgin Mary and Rider Haggard's *She*. Thus the fading bloom of youth is as dreaded as its advent was impatiently awaited. This may be modified by the hope of "vintage" charm.

The distancing of the destructive part of the personality is probably more dependent upon success than is the case with the masculine state of mind. Frustration gives way easily to bitterness regarding the unfairness of fate when beauty is inadequate, or the injustice of the social order where femininity is not in itself obviously valued (as in Moslem cultures or American Indians). Then the Cassandra aspect of the femininity may show itself with its pessimism, or a more witch-like and perverse sexuality may ensue.

In any case, the lure of the delusional system is far stronger than for the masculine state, which is probably more inclined to mania than to deluded psychosis until its paranoid tendencies are tapped.

The delusional tendency of the feminine state leads very directly into the B.A. pairing group formation, which is probably not far away with every pregnancy. Correspondingly, the lioness with her cubs can mobilize the B.A. fight–flight any time a child is menaced by the community.

Since the body and the home or nest become easily confused due to the state of confusion of identity with the internal or external mother (projective), intrusion by vermin, human or otherwise, is the feminine infantile mind's nightmare; while inadequate space for the endless supplies and equipment pursuant to its matriarchal occupation is its preoccupation. Its persecutory anxieties cluster about bad penises of one sort or another, while its nemesis is the death of a child, a blow from which it feels it can never recover, since it has the meaning of punishment for greed and overweening ambition. It is strongly inclined to feel that only other girl-women can understand this dread, thus forming a barrier of relentless grievance against the consort. Its possessiveness of the children is justified by this grievance, escalating into the typical "all men want is sex" attitude.

Because of the pseudo-maturity consequent to the projective identification, the feminine infantile state feels very close to children and tends to over-protect, indulge, and enter into *folie à deux* with respect to anxieties. "I was just the same as a child" is meant to imply "and see how fine I am now". Difficulty in acknowledging that anything is wrong with the children's mental health (implying an indictment of its mothering) is exceeded only by a readiness to see physical illness and to demand the best of medical care from the community. The greatest sin it can commit would be neglect, so every bodily function of the children must be monitored.

The girl-gang state of mind

Since the preservation of the split that differentiates the good from the bad infantile parts of the personality requires constant monitoring by internal parental objects or their transference representatives in the outside world, lapse in attentiveness or separation tends to collapse this distinction.

In fact, the destructive part of the personality tends then to make its bid for the leadership of the children, characteristically presenting itself as the big-brother or -sister figure.

Competitiveness with good objects may have taken the form in the girlish state of being a better-mummy-than-mummy, but in the girl-gang state something more drastic and durable than competition is at hand.

In fact, the destructive part of the personality is in a state of deadly enmity towards the parental good objects, and desires to overthrow entirely their power in the mind. But this rebellion is not in the interest of establishing evil as good. Its aim is to remove all parental prohibitions that interfere with the gratification of infantile sensuality and greed in the name of egalitarianism.

In many ways the girl-gang bears a greater grudge against the father for his hypocrisy about sex than against the mother for monopolization. This contributes to its anti-masculine, Amazonian quality. Freedom from maternal restrictions, revenge on the father, and tormenting of the brothers is its ethos. The myth of feminine inferiority is vigorously denied, and yet its remnants seem affirmed by this very vigour. The trouble seems to lie in the lingering awe of physical strength, fear, and excitement towards the big penis and consequent masochistic trends. But guile and strength, patience and ambiguity, and, above all, allure, are more powerful weapons. Men are viewed as all boys to be easily degraded and rendered impotent.

So the girl-gang tends to build a pseudo-family of colluding females and emasculated boys. It easily slips into the feminist B.A. fight–flight state, full of righteous indignation, proselytising, collecting dossiers of its historic grievances. Cleanliness and discipline are necessary bulwarks against defection by its members into masochistic submission and seduction of transference daddy-figures. But frustration of its predatory aims may drive it into fury and breakdown of the manic-depressive sort, Medea-like. Its characteristic hey-day is puberty, but it has a quieter and more unobtrusive peak in later life, in matriarchal grandmothers.

"The boys" state of mind

Probably most of history—at least political and economic history—could be written in terms of the organized manifestation of this state of mind. Although the "great" movements of history move at the B.A. level, the day-to-day operation of politics and business, sex and entertainment tend to be operated by "the boys".

The school playground would serve as well as the House of Commons as a venue for its sociological study. Bullying and patronage are its modes of operation, and the plundering of the riches of the mother (mother-earth and her daughters) is its aim. Unable to think, it is a great exploiter of the thoughts of others for purposes to which those thoughts would never have been aimed. Since its great enemy is the family it pretends always to be its great friend and protector, building super-families ruled by god-fathers.

Since it finds, by its masculine standards, that women are manifestly inferior, clearly they must be protected—that is, used as men wish and relegated to service when they cease to be desirable. Unconsciously this state has no doubt that (as the Greeks, even the most brilliant, believed) men beget children, and women merely serve them. So children are naturally both possessions and extensions of the self into infinity, one's actual immortality.

This dynastic inclination is probably more conducive to B.A. groupings than is even the madness of war. It need not ponder whether might is right, since what matters is winning. Losers are either weaklings or fools, and the great fools are the self-imposed "losers" like mummy and daddy, who make endless sacrifices for ungrateful children.

But somehow their attraction keeps decimating its war-like ranks. These defections are incomprehensible to it, since it works upon quantitative criteria that are so self-evident, while the parents seem to operate so unscientifically, by premises that are so vague they are unstateable, let alone provable.

Bafflement at this failure to win enduring admiration leads to escalation of self-congratulation and can slip over into grandiose delusion with its paranoid undercurrent. Thus the *schizophrenic part of the personality* is not far away when this state of mind is "successful" in the outside world and can use this to consolidate its dominance in the personality organization of the individual. Money, power, and fame so undermine trust in other people's interest, kindness, or cooperation that the leader of the boys' gang becomes fairly relentlessly drawn into isolation, clinging to one favourite lieutenant after another, always in fear of the palace revolution.

The inverted or perverted state of mind

Where the intelligence has been disproportionately captured by the *destructive part* of the personality, and/or where its strength has been further augmented by a collusive relationship with a destructive aspect of a titular parent or powerful grown-up figure in the outside world, a state of mind can be established in which values are inverted.

The equivalent of a satanic religion tends to arise in the individual, and the slip into perversity in the sexual area, sado-masochism in the social, and delusion in the spiritual rests in delicate balance with the psychopathic manoeuvre. While the satanic aspect always tries to build its pandemonium in competition with the good objects, the psychopath is content to attack the links of trust that hold the more shaky of the parents' children to their sphere of goodness and truth.

The demagogue and the renegade are both liars, one employing his charisma to organize the rebelliousness of the children, the other using his theatrical talent to disappoint and disillusion them into states of despair and guilt. The grandiosity of one, which would rather rule in hell than serve in heaven, is only the converse of the other—the paranoid and the projector of paranoia.

Where the grandiosity of the pseudo-mature "better-mummy-girl" or "better-daddy-boy" may settle into a B.A. pairing group whose ethos is "those who are not against me are with me", the B.A. tendency of the inverted state is clearly paranoid: "those who are not with me are against me."

It may form a family that is in a criminal relation to its community, but its preference is clearly tribal. It tends to invade every organization with the purpose of perverting its ethos and its aims, cynically disguising tyranny in the most flamboyant rags, whether in uniforms or in slogans.

Elitism, exclusiveness, indolence, and unbridled sensuality are the temptations with which it seduces the children from the austere (seen as joyless) responsibility-for-world promulgated by the good objects. The world it builds always falls apart because of the undercurrent of distrust among its adherents and the gnawing guilt of those seduced by it. Since its nightmare is the slave revolt, its policy is eventually genocidal—and self-destructive. Its contempt for life is ultimately suicidal.

7
The uses of the model

As already mentioned, this model is meant for use. But being a first attempt at a comprehensive psychoanalytic model, it is bound to require *modification with use*. In addition, it should lend itself to infinite amplification, subdivision, and elaboration.

The different categories of use for which it has been designed specifically, not so much as a manual as for the purpose of illustrating possibilities, are divided generally into methodological, diagnostic, and therapeutic uses.

Methodological uses

Since the overriding aim in creating the model was to provide an instrument for the rationalization of observations of human behaviour and mental states from different points of view and by different methods, workers interested in a particular area should be able to locate their problem within its definitions, so that they can see what other areas of study and what other methods could contribute findings that would both assist them and be enlightened by the results of their research.

By pinpointing the problem within the dimensions of the model, they should be assisted in judging the relevance of the methods they wish to employ to the nature of the problem.

It should aid workers particularly in research design to avoid tautological or elliptical procedures, to distinguish between observation and interpretation, and to find a language of description as free from preconception as possible, or at least to define the area of preconception. It should impose a rigour on thought that will help workers distinguish between correlations that suggest a link and the kind of data that enables description of the link itself.

Above all, it should help workers to notice the problems they encounter so that useful research questions can be asked. In other words it is hoped that the model will facilitate the movement between deductive and inductive modes of thought, upon which fruitful research in the human sciences seem to depend.

Diagnostic uses of the model

Since the model is a kind of flow-sheet of the possible relationships of the "*child in the family in the community*", it should make possible a graphic representation of the actual structures and processes of interaction discovered on investigation.

Its genetic dimension allows for the correlation of serial observations, while the cross-sectional profile of different members of a system of relationships should allow for the location of continuities and discontinuities in a most revealing way.

It is in itself a nosological system, but it has been constructed on a basis that should not render it exclusive of other systems but, rather, able to embrace them within its overall structure.

Take, for example, the syndrome type of medical classification used in psychiatry: many of its categories would find immediate placement within the model, while the difficulty in placing others would serve to define the areas of uncertainty about their structure to which research needs to be applied.

Since the model allows for the definition of casual and contractual areas of relationship and interaction as well as for the intimate and internal, it could embrace all levels of social and anthropological classification. Although it is called a model of the "child in the family in the community", it could just as well be called a model of the "community of families and their children", or of the "family and its children in the community". It should lend itself to studies of change and migration as well as to those of stability and stagnation at all three levels. It should assist ordinary workers to describe processes at a level of complexity with the scope and precision if not with the poetry that only a Tolstoy or George Eliot could undertake in the past.

Therapeutic uses

Because it has both cross-sectional and longitudinal dimensions, the model should be of use in tracing the development of patients in various forms of treatment, and in following the interaction of people closely related who are simultaneously in therapies of different sorts.

It should enable therapists to distinguish between the developmental accomplishments of the individual, the impact of the therapy itself, and the impact of other helpful or harmful relationships and events in a person's life.

It could conceivably provide an instrument for the comparison of different methods of therapy applied to different problems, in a manner that could facilitate a more rational prescription of therapeutic techniques and a more economic use of community resources.

The specific use of the model with regard to the educational functions of the family

Although this is intended to be a model and not a theory, it has a theoretical background—one that is intended to be descriptive rather than explanatory and based on experiences of living in general, and of the psychoanalytic consulting-room in particular. While it makes room, as it were, for all possible philosophies, it cannot hide the value system and world view that it favours, if only by virtue of the twelve-o'clock position of this cross-section.

But, of course, life is not simply occupied solely with the climb towards perfection, with mystical union with the godhead, or experience of the pure Platonic forms. Education cannot concern itself only with the character, but must also transmit skills, information, social habits, attitudes, values. It cannot content itself with facilitating the acquisition of internal qualifications: it must also bestow, or withhold, external ones.

No system of education can avoid entirely being, as well as *being experienced as*, tyrannical. By bestowing and withholding, it must seem to reward and punish, to create an elite and disinherited classes, to perpetuate whatever degree of exploitation already exists. Above all, the accumulation and institutionalization of knowledge creates a conservative bulwark that resists, if not from hostility, then from sheer inertia, any really new ideas.

Since new ideas are easily confused with experimental actions, the latter may thrive as a stimulation of radical movement. An area for fraudulence and corruption then increases when the official system's rigidity has created a considerable class of refusees. Thus the problem of distinguishing the revolutionary expression of a new idea from the rebellion of the disgruntled who cannot master the old idea is all a part of the educational system, which, like any organism, must either grow or wither.

To employ this model with regard to the special problem of the *educational functions of the family* is, we suggest, to use it to view *the family as an educational institution*.

The model embraces *seven types of learning, six types of families, six plus one (the schizophrenic) states of mind* in the individual, the *three types of the B.A. groups* where learning is replaced by action, and *six types of orientation* that the community *may seem to manifest* towards families and their members. It represents the *six dimensions of mental* functioning from which these different levels of interaction and structure are fashioned, all in dynamic flux.

Of course, one does not really need to have a high-speed camera in order to believe that hummingbirds have wings. We do all know that life is lived from moment to moment, but the great difficulty is to think about it. In order to do so, we must take a hint from the cine-camera and content ourselves with individual static pictures (the cross-sections) serially arranged in order to avoid the vertigo induced by contemplating the scintillations of life with the naked eye.

The static cross-sectional image marks a trend, while its perseverance denotes a fixation, which is equivalent to cessation of development and impending regression. By using the model in this way, we can achieve a genuine *process view*.

This process view has built into it something that will be noticed if you look at the model in a three-dimensional way, which is really a *four-dimensional view of life*. You will notice the implication that movement from left to right in time is almost surely a *spiral mode of progression*.

This carries an implication that may be made clear by an image. If you are training a young horse on the long rein in a field where he can see his companions, he will walk very nicely to command on the arc of the circle nearest to them but will break into a trot or canter on the most distant arc. Perhaps the art of pedagogy could be compared to this, in terms of our model: to so arrange the geography of the emotional situation that the individual will hurry through the more disturbed and anti-social arc of the process and linger at its more convivial aspect.

We may view our task as model-makers ended here. We must take responsibility for its architectonics and aesthetics, but the engineering must come from those who wish to implement it.

CHAPTER TWENTY-THREE

Impressions concerning adolescent confusional states

(1977)

This brief paper was written after a series of consultations with adolescents, and given to the Editor, who was at the time concerned with diagnostic and technical problems related to adolescent psychotic states. In these notes the author makes a diagnostic differentiation between manic-depressive states and the failure of second-skin formation and alpha functioning.

Crucial transitional moments in adolescence, especially those that seem to formalize hoped-for access to adult status and privilege, appear to have a marked effect on some youngsters, far more frequently in boys than in girls, in my experience. The types of events are mainly successes in exams, some form of notoriety or recognition, first sexual successes, especially if the partner is felt to be very high in social status, unexpected acquisition of money, a car. Or, in a paradoxical way, injuries that have social status (in sport or dangerous events) may have the same impact. In any event, the emphasis seems to be on the social visibility of some event and during elevation in social status.

The impact appears to present relatively unnoticed because happiness and elation are not easily distinguished, but in retrospect or on second time around or when grossly exaggerated, they can be seen to be marked by grandiosity, triumph, and spite, which are by no means in keeping with gratification of hopes. The triumph over peers very thinly disguises contempt for the parents or at least for the older generation in general as compared to the venerated heroes of the past. Dress, mannerisms, and associations often reveal these figures to be objects of projective identification, and they seem to represent the part-object prehistory of the oedipal whole-object figures, in that sense out of proportion, gigantic, godlike. The messianic atmosphere is never very far away, and loss of time-sense is very noticeable. When the state is not too extreme, the youngster may continue to function very well, sometimes exceptionally well when temporary overcoming of shyness, inhibition, and self-effacement is involved. Also, the ready flow of manic ideation and language may show up their latent intelligence to great advantage.

But it is a pretty self-terminating process because of the fragility of relation to reality. Often very minor checks to plans can tumble the state, and what happens then is of the greatest interest to understand, because the whole process looks so much like depressive illness that it is likely to be treated as such. Freud's description of the "radiance" and the "shadow" of the object are more apposite than Abraham's and Melanie Klein's formulations, which apply to mania and depressive illness proper. Indeed, the transition emphasizes the nature of the narcissistic identification involved to be far more in the nature of "adhesive" than "projective" identification, and where it collapses, it presents a state far more like Esther Bick's formulations about failure of skin-containment than collapse into identification with a debilitated object. In fact, my impression of these states is that they represent something in-between the sloughing-off of a skin acquired by projective identification (on a part-object level) and a failure of "second-skin" functioning. In any event, the adolescent in this state appears to be without a skin or with one so naked to the wind as to require shielding from stimuli of any sort. The very confusing clinical picture so resembles the retardation and withdrawal of depressive illness that only very close attention to the thought processes—or, rather, the near-absence of thought capacity—reveals the difference. Here I think Bion's formulation about failure of an alpha-function is extremely useful and clarifies the nature of the confusional state, for it is essentially one of being unable to think and therefore to act. The youngsters will tend to withdraw into bed, not so much into a world of phantasy as in pursuit of dreamless sleep. The resemblance to battle-fatigue is striking.

It seems to me that the implications of this way of understanding the clinical picture are fairly apparent—namely, that containment and shielding, both in the nursing as well as in the analytic situation, are the prime requirements. The analyst in addition probably has to take on the ego-function of thinking, spending his time not in seeking new material but, rather, in reviewing and bringing order into the previous events and material of the analysis.

CHAPTER TWENTY-FOUR

A note on introjective processes

(1978)

This clinical paper—the last one read to the British Psycho-Analytical Society—was published in its Scientific Bulletin. The author postulates here that the moment in which introjection becomes possible is when an object can be given its freedom to come and go at will and how the moment of "closure" sets in motion the depressive struggle towards introjective identification.

In *Explorations in Autism* (1975) some evidence was adduced from the psychoanalytic treatment of autistic children that suggested a stage in the evolution of the personality prior to the formation of the concepts of internal and external spaces. On this basis a fairly extensive discussion of two-, three- and four-dimensional worlds was entered into, during which it was suggested that time as an aspect of reality

Presented to the British Psycho-Analytical Society on 18 October 1978. Published in the *Scientific Bulletin 1978*. No. 9, of the British Psycho-Analytical Society.

was similarly imperfectly apprehended as oscillating, circular, and linear time, respectively. In *The Psycho-analytical Process* (Meltzer, 1967a) it had been suggested that one major mode of operation of the therapeutic method was to allow for new qualities to be introjected into the internal objects, thus enhancing them with analytic capability as the necessary equipment for self-analysis. Evidence of this enhancement, therefore, could be used as an indicator of a patient's readiness to terminate.

In this paper I wish to bring together these two findings, regarding time-dimensionality on the one hand and introjection of objects and their qualities on the other, in order to try to make some headway in exploring what seems to me to be the most important and most mysterious concept in psychoanalysis—introjection. How does it operate, and what does it mean? What is the difference between recalling an event or person and having introjected a person or event so that they exist "in the mind" alive and independent of one's self and will? Freud's description of the establishment of a "gradient" in the ego whereby the superego became established as a separate structure of the personality was made more concrete and intelligible by Melanie Klein's description of internal space and the concreteness of internalized objects. But she was no more able than Freud had been, with his ideas of cannibalistic introjection, to find any means of describing the process by which experience of an external object is internalized.

It will be recalled that from very early on Freud spoke of neurotics as "suffering from recollections". The transference and the repetition compulsion gave theoretical body to this idea. But it could be said with equal cogency that neurotics suffer from expectations. Their tendency to live in the future shows itself to consist of a hope of finding again lost objects and happiness and also shows clearly that recollections and expectations can be indistinguishable. What is perhaps more significant is that neurotics *do not live in the moment*. I wish to present some clinical material that will give some substance to this assertion and serve as food for thought about the nature of introjection.

A wealthy business-man, who had come to analysis because of the progressive deterioration of his third marriage, eventually found himself facing the termination of treatment without ever having come to grips with certain problems. Some of these problems had been acted out in a fairly relentless way, such as his taking holidays during the analytic term to pursue his favourite sport of deer-stalking. Others had been mentioned only in passing and had never seemed to come into the forefront of the material. The fact that he had never been able to learn to swim, or had a tendency to mild migraine, were examples of this. In fact his analysis, which lasted for five-and-a-half years, had at first been restricted by him to two sessions a week and later to three, but never more, on the grounds of the requirements of his business, the opposition of his wife, and—frankly—his fear of becoming dependent in some paralysing way.

In fact, by the time the material began to suggest that termination was in sight, the patient felt that the analysis had transformed his life in the most important ways for which he had sought help: his cold aloofness had melted; his pessimism and ennui had given way to zestful interest in work and family; the nature of his work had changed into very constructive channels; and his sexual capability had greatly improved. This had been brought about in a reasonably contained way in the transference analysis assisted by very close cooperation, a rich dream life, and a consistently positive transference substrate. But the analytic situation cost him a lot of pain in climbing down from an accustomed position of aristocratic superiority to join the human race. Awareness of his loneliness and appreciation of the suffering of others had greatly softened his demeanour and brought much improvement to his relationships.

One day he announced that he had learned to swim, on his own, in the swimming-pool he had had built unbeknownst to me. Another deer-stalking holiday was in the offing, but he was hesitating, feeling it a bit disrespectful to the analyst. And perhaps some of his zest for the shooting was cooling. Once, recently, he had failed because his safety-catch was on, and another time he was laughed at by companions because he had not even loaded his rifle. To the Friday session prior to a weekend of sport, he brought a dream. In it

> *. . . he was at the Game Fair with some companions and went to put himself down for the clay-pigeon shooting, but when his turn came he realized he had left his gun with his*

> *friends and went to seek them. On the way he was passed by an apparition moving at speed, a broomstick with skirt and white kerchief. Two women in a booth were heard to say, one to the other: "Look up quick, or you will miss Mr A"* [my patient].

The dream yielded very little to investigation. The voodoo-like broomstick woman was clearly a nasty representation of his wife (and mother) when pre-occupied and taking no notice of him in her flurry of activity. Like many recent dreams, this one, too, suggested that his relentless opposition to mother having more babies (blood sports) was giving way to the wish for siblings but only so long as he felt he was not himself neglected by her. This showed itself in the transference with regard to other patients, in the loss of zest for shooting, and in a greater interest in his children. But we could make nothing of the two women in the booth, except for some connection to his mother and nanny. Yes, what they said ("look up quick or you'll miss . . .") seemed to be connected with the clay-pigeon shooting, but this seemed to lead nowhere.

Mr A returned from the weekend stalking celebrating an almost "perfect" stake and shot, but his celebration sounded hollow and troubled. He had a worse migraine than for many years, accompanied by very distinct visual effects and nausea. The scintillating scotoma had started as a pin-point at the fovea and spread gradually as a circle, to disappear in his peripheral field. Two days later he had the worst migraine since his finals at university during an evening out with his wife and her wealthy boss, but it disappeared when the three were joined by several couples of lively younger people. The previous night he had dreamed that

> *. . . he had three brothers* [in fact he has one younger sister], *who were to share in a property left to them. The others each inherited a farm, but he was left a park-land.*

After the evening with his wife's boss, he dreamed

> *. . . he had forgotten to take the wine bottle when he left the dining-room. The others said he was no longer drinking as much whisky, and the wine-bottle was big enough for all to share.*

Yes, he had stopped drinking whisky. He always thought of it as his father's drink. At the weekend he had seen "Soldier Blue", a film about a man who sells guns to the Indians but whether out of greed and treachery or out of sympathy for the Indians was not clear. No, he would not be pleased if the deer acquired firearms, but he could imagine that stalking Japanese in Burma might have been the ultimate in blood-sports. Perhaps he had dreamed of three Greek soldiers in their traditional skirt-and-stocking uniform, except that the stockings were blue rather than white.

From the point of view of the analysis, the material was quite convincing evidence of Mr A's struggle to allow father his place (the whisky) to share the mother with siblings (the property, the wine). In fact, clearly the siblings could relieve the stress of the Oedipal triangle (the young guests at the dinner party). Killing the deer seems to have caused him pain and guilt connected with treachery to the parents and hostility to their children. In that context, the triangular situation at dinner, the analysis, and final exams at university become indistinguishable.

On that basis, one may say that the migraine seems to be both a somatic manifestation in lieu of mental pain and a rejection of any attempt to see the truth (see Roger Money-Kyrle's paper, "A Note on Migraine", 1963). But what can we say about the broomstick woman, the two women in the booth with their "Look up quick", and the pattern of the scintillating scotoma? This is what interests me about this material. What has gone before is clinical psychoanalytic thinking, convincing or not. What is to follow is speculation. Imagine first that you are driving through the Mont Blanc Tunnel, and the end of it appears first as a spot of light, which grows gradually into a bright circle and suddenly passes you by as you emerge into the sunshine. Now imagine that you are a baby who sees your mother enter the room, your eyes riveted to the slight bulge of her nipple in her blouse, and she moves towards you only to seem to rush past and out of sight. Now change what one woman in the booth says to the other from: "Look up quick, or you'll miss Mr A" to a slightly teasing breast, saying: "Look up quick or you'll miss Mr A".

My patient was the first-born of well-to-do-parents; his mother was a pretty, sociable, and vivacious girl-woman, while his nanny (much the same age) was plainer, calmer. What I am trying to find is a concept of the moment as not merely fleeting but teasingly, disappointingly so. A moment full of promise, too quickly past to be fulfilling. Could Mr A not swim because his pessimism could not believe in the existence of a buoyant object inside himself? Is the "perfect shot" the moment when the bullet has left the gun but not yet struck the deer? Mr A's companion, in fact, has taken to hunting with a camera rather than a gun, and he may do the same. "Forever wilt thou love and she be fair."

I wish now to pass on to consider the moment and those qualities and circumstances that affect a situation, causing it to hang precariously. Will it result in satisfaction with internalization (introjection), fragmentation with evacuation (projection), or imprisonment with suspended animation (omnipotent control)? In doing so, I wish occasionally to quote short passages from Keats' "Ode on a Grecian Urn", because they seem to cast what Bion calls a "beam of darkness" that illuminates the processes I am labouring less successfully to capture in language.

Bion's work, stretching from *Experiences in Groups* (1961) to the trilogy *A Memoir of the Future* (1975–1981), rests upon the conception of the "emotional experience" as the ultimate unit of mental data upon which the apparatus of thought (alpha-function, Ps↔D, and container–contained) operate to produce thoughts and develop them to higher levels of sophistication, abstraction, and complexity (*The Grid*, 1989) usable for thinking. He has stressed that the precondition for the apprehension of the emotional experience is the temporary suspension of "memory and desire"—that is, of those representations of the past and the future because they interfere with the experience of the moment of the present. I wish to examine the foregoing clinical material to see if we can learn from it what are the factors that prevent Mr A from "looking up quick" and cause him to "miss" introjecting his good object (deer–dear). What determines whether he seizes the moment with his gun, his camera, or his living eye?

Clearly, Mr A is confronted in the analytic termination with a problem of renunciation, and his headway towards it is indicated by such things as leaving on his safety-catch, forgetting to load his rifle, leaving his gun with his dream-friends. He is facing the end of his analysis and is trying to renounce the holidays of stalking that have marked his rebellion against the dependence of the analytic situation. But if he does not take violent possession of the beauty of his object so that it becomes a trophy in his gun-room, he must face mental pain, which at this point manifests itself as the physical pain of the migraine, associated as it seems to be with being compared by mummy with daddy (his final exams at university, dinner with his wife and her boss). This pain tends to make him blind to the beauty of his object (the scotomata) but replaces that dear object with a voodoo-figure, witch-like, flitting past him in her pre-occupation with other children. In childhood he had split his object between his buoyant mother and his "still unravished bride of quietness", his nanny. That is, he had sacrificed the beauty of the relationship with the breast for a more prolonged and sensual, possessive, and exclusive one with his nanny. In fact, his relationship with his mother had been cool, though not unloving, as long as he could remember—quite different from his sister's feeling for her. So the sensuality had also to be relinquished as well as the possessiveness.

> *. . . therefore, ye soft pipes, play on:*
> *Not to the sensual ear, but, more endeared,*
> *Pipe to the spirit ditties of no tone.*

The point that I am trying to make is that the "memory" that needed to be put aside embraced the split between his mother and nanny, while the "desire" he needed to eschew was for sensual satisfaction and exclusive possession of his object. This movement was now represented in the analytic transference as the problem of relinquishing the analysis, despite the disappointment that it had not settled many problems he had hoped it might resolve. More immediately, he was in conflict about the abandonment of his mid-term holidays as a token of respect and acceptance of the dependence on the buoyancy of its object. The infantile hostility to siblings represented in his proclivity for blood sports had been reduced to its representation as clay-pigeons rather than partridge, grouse, and pheasant. His recovery from the migraine attack when other young people arrived at the dinner party confirmed the significance of his greater interest in his children and friendly feeling for the analyst's other patients. The movement of relinquishment was still hedged by a feeling of being the "exception", as seen in the dream of the three farms and the park-land legacy, but he now felt rather ashamed of these pretentions. Two weeks later he dreamed that

> *. . . he entered a train in the first class but made his way forward until he was standing in the baggage car just behind the engine. When it came to a stop with a bump, both he and the engineer were surprised to see that the terminus looked like a bombed-out building.*

He thought that perhaps the analysis had won the war, and it was now up to him to win the peace.

In Keats' terms, I am suggesting that the moment of experience, as a "still unravished bride of quietness", must be allowed to bear upon it the mysterious signs of "that wild ecstasy" and to pass on in its buoyancy to disappear into the past without hindrance, in order to leave behind in the mind an object of beauty and truth. Keats' poem could be taken as a prototype of the action of the mechanisms of thought that Bion has formulated, raising the experience of the momentary view of the Grecian Urn through serial transformations to shape a poem that "pipes to the spirit". Mr A's material, like the poem, chronicles the pains that need to be borne to accomplish this relinquishment. (There can be little doubt of the formative role in the shaping of the poet of his struggle to encompass the experience of the early loss of his buoyant mother.) The gun as the instrument of possession and the camera as the instrument for making time stand still must both be put aside. The pain involved is essentially the pain of separation and thus of grief, to

> *tease us out of thought*
> *as does eternity. . . .*

Thus the coming and going of the mother's breast, which stays only a moment to fill the baby and must be allowed to go its way, is also the prototype of the emotional experience, which satisfies only insofar as the object can be allowed its freedom. The meaning and significance of the experience can only be apprehended if this precondition is established, so that the moment may be "recollected in tranquillity" (Wordsworth).

Our inquiry has now lead us to conceptualize the "moment" of experience and, following Bion, to define it as something that has been loosened from its connections with past and future by means of yielding to the object its freedom to have been elsewhere and to again disappear thence. This moment, which must be given some firmness of conception to free it also from the tyranny of time as a dimension of external reality, would involve, as the "moment of force" in physics, both intensity and duration, as well as structure. The "moment of experience"—or, rather, in keeping with Bion's exposition, the "moment of emotional experience"—would be seen as the unit of data upon which the apparatus for thinking operates. The transference experience of Mr A is repeating the events of infancy where the "moment" would be the breast-feed, beset with the problems of accepting the object "coming from afar" and relinquishing it to disappear once again. The implication of the material is clearly indicative of difficulty with this acceptance and relinquishment. The moment is crushed between these two problems and produces no "satisfaction".

Now this seems to be leading us to a very different idea of satisfaction from that inherent in Freud's neurophysiological model, but also very much at variance with Melanie Klein's idea of a "good experience". It would seem to imply that "sufficient unto the day" is *both* the good *and* evil thereof. This I think is absolutely Bionic in its philosophic implication. An experience is "satisfying", by this definition, insofar as it produces an "emotional experience" that can be utilized for thinking. And I am suggesting that this satisfaction, of having something to think about, whether pleasurable or painful, is the essential precondition for introjection. This leads us back to Melanie Klein's great contribution to our understanding of the economics of mental functioning, the paranoid-schizoid and depressive positions, which Wilfred Bion, by adding the item of "selected fact", has amplified and condensed to form the concept Ps↔D. It is clear from the history of our patients that they have often been broken in their development by bad, painful experiences—weaning, birth of the next sibling, the primal scene, death of a love object. But it is equally apparent from the histories of great men—Keats, for example—that they have been "made" by the acceptance and assimilation of these same events. Equally, we see patients who have been "broken" by good experiences, where they have inflamed megalomania, or, conversely, stirred intolerable feelings of gratitude and indebtedness. Freud's "character types met within analysis" could be seen to fall into this category.

To return to Mr A, it could be said that he came to analysis for just this general reason, that despite the conditions for happiness being richly present in his life, he could get no satisfaction, whether from his marriage, children, work, friends, interests, pastimes. That is not to say that there were no pleasures in his life, but that they did not "add up to anything". He felt—rightly, I think—that he had remained essentially the same in his character since he was a small boy, at least since the birth of his sister and probably, he thought, before. Interestingly the most satisfying experiences of his life had been on the stage, in amateur dramatic groups. These, he felt, had allowed him for a moment to escape from being himself, bound to non-development, and afforded at least a glimpse of what being a different kind of person could be like. One could perhaps say that the gun and the camera represented his experiential approach to life, which always seemed to be passing him by, a world of objects always bound, like the broomstick woman, from somewhere else to somewhere else and never abiding with him. The by now traditional psychoanalytic view, best stated by Winnicott in his conception of the "good enough mother", would need, by the ideas presented here, to be set aside in favour of a more responsibility-laden construct of the individual, building his personality by "learning from (both good and bad) experience"—"becoming O", in Bion's poetry. His differentiation between "learning from experience" and "learning about" things would be given a more general application and substance, as in his memorable example of "becoming a walker" being so different from "learning about walking". Mr A long knew "about" swimming, but it awaited a certain development in his internal relations for him to "become a swimmer".

What, then, can we say about the duration of the moment of experience? May it last a second, or years? How does one "become a psychoanalyst", for example? Does the moment have a point of closure that transforms the individual so that he will never again be the same person as he was before?

The burden of this paper can now be restated as follows: when an object can be given its freedom to come and go as it will, the moment of experience of relationship with that object can be introjected. This produces modification in the qualities and capabilities of the internal object to which it is most congruent (see Chapter VIII of *The Psycho-analytical Process*, Meltzer, 1967a) which can serve as the model for striving and aspiration, and thus of identification, for the self. The closure of the moment marks this introjection and sets in motion the depressive struggle towards identification. This latter may be either positive in the case of good experience or negative in the case of bad ones. But negative identifications cannot further constructive activity in the same sense as the prohibitive aspects of superego. This is, however, a subject for another paper.

CHAPTER TWENTY-FIVE

"The diameter of the circle" in Wilfred Bion's work

(1980)

This paper is based on an observation of Bion at work, both with groups and in his writings between 1967 and 1978. Suggested complementary reading to this paper are The Kleinian Development, Part III: *"The Clinical Significance of the Work of Bion" (1978), and "Three Lectures on W. R. Bion's The Memoir of the Future"*.*

> I know the argument is circular. I am depending on the length of the diameter.
>
> Bion, 1963, *Elements of Psycho-Analysis*

I remember feeling rather furious when I first met this statement, but my conviction of Bion's seriousness and earnestness rose to defend him and pressed me to think about this seeming throw-away remark. Subsequent seminars

---

Published in the *Scientific Bulletin, 1980*, of the British Psycho-Analytical Society.

*This volume, chapter thirty.

with him in the last year of his life gave me an opportunity that I had not enjoyed before to study his method of operation under pressure of the group, both of its admiration and its latent hostility, so reminiscent of the "experienced officer who is afraid neither of the hatred nor of the love of his troops" (*Experiences in Groups*, Bion, 1961).

What I observed is worth recording, I think. When confronted with a direct question, Bion's tactics seemed military indeed. He seemed to start off in a direction quite contrary to that of the question, as if in retreat from the aggressive intent, then made a wide sweep, ending by taking the enemy, not even on its flank, but from the rear. During this excursion he would make little sallies at the question, trying one vertex after another, until one of them found a rather soft spot in the armour of the language in which the question had been phrased. But I also noted times at which I lost the thread of his excursion and was left indignant, having more than half forgotten the question, even when it was one of my own. During the course of those excursions that I did succeed in following, I thought that I could discern a certain sequence to his probings. He seemed often first to tap the wording to see if the vocabulary of the question rang true or seemed soft at the centre. Then he probed it for preconceptions, leading qualities, various penumbra of meaning from common parlance. Then often came a kind of brutal thumping of its presumption that an answer existed as the "*malheur de la question*". And, finally, he attacked it as a problem related to the central question of the meaning of psychoanalysis as a thing-in-itself. Because of this method, certain phrases central to his modes of thought, certain analogies and metaphors turned up again and again, giving a superficial impression of repetitiveness, cliché, covert confusion, or even boredom. But that was the impression when one had lost the thread of the excursion. When one was able to hold on to the thread, the performance was rather dazzling, though not always immediately illuminating.

Now that is a rather military model of Bion's mentality, and one to which the three volumes of the *Memoir of the Future* lend considerable credence. But one can also discern the voyager in mental space–time convinced that the world of the mind is four-dimensional and infinite. Recklessly he surges on, depending on the centre of gravity of his fundamental sanity holding him in orbit so that he can risk sailing westward to Cathay and thence safely home. So I am suggesting that the diameter of his circle was a measure of his confidence in his sanity, which allowed him to abandon himself with such startling freedom to the capacity of his mind for imaginative conjecture.

With this preamble as backdrop, I would like to examine in a general way the four volumes that comprise the strictly literary output of the last twelve years of his life, 1967–1978—that is, his last two years in London and the eleven-year period in California. It would be reasonable to say that the real creative strain, which produced *Learning from Experience* (1962), *Elements of Psycho-Analysis* (1963), and *Transformations* (1965), was behind him, and in a certain sense their content was dismissed. The flirtation with mathematics as a language of precision had not worked out; the belief in the refinement of interpretation as an instrument analogous to the surgeon's scalpel that could be honed to a fine linguistic edge had also faded. But the disappointment in the limited capabilities of psychoanalysts gave way to an ever stronger conviction of the beauty and power of the psychoanalytic method and the possibility of its growth. This brought him to a clear recognition of the similarity of psychoanalytic history and theological history, where the qualities of the clergy and the organization of the Church could be seen to have strangled or crushed the creative power of the theological ideas. He had only to return to his own ideas in *Experiences in Groups* (1961) to shift from a mathematical vertex and mode of exposition to a theological one in order to describe his social and internal experiences as a thinker who had been found by new ideas.

The writing of *Attention and Interpretation* (1970) seems to have brought him to a caesura in his life, and with it a need to change his environment from the aqueous medium of London, where he was threatened with being "loaded with honours and sunk without a trace", to the gaseous atmosphere of California, where he would need to fight for his professional life. (This is all my fantasy, of course, and need have no resemblance to the reality of Bion, a licence he would readily extend. I am, after all, writing literary criticism and not history.) Out of this struggle came this strange trilogy with its paradoxical title. In Volume 2 of *Memoir*—"The Past Presented"—we note the following bit of dialogue:

P.A.: . . . One of the war aims of the Allies was "open Covenants openly arrived at".

ROBIN: Since these Covenants have become so openly arrived at, lying has achieved a new dimension.

P.A.: Its quality has improved too. The expert liar, as contrasted with the amateur or untrained liar, is at a premium.

ROLAND [*with ill-concealed hostility*]: Have you found the demand for your services much increased?

P.A.: No; there has always been a high demand for my services.

ROBIN: Fifty minutes a session, five times a week—

ROLAND: —for ever!

P.A.: That is about it, but the demand changes.

ROLAND: Can you give me an idea how?

P.A.: At first people used to think I was just a simple obvious fool—

ROBIN: —and then they thought you were a bigger fool than you looked. Aren't you?

P.A.: I am usually aware of hostility and contempt. If it is obvious, it requires—as now—no interpretation, because you and I are both aware of it. Interpretation would be redundant. But in the old days—were you going to say "the *good* old days"? No? Then we can proceed. In the good old days men and women used to lie freely and elegantly; there was gradually built up an Empire of hypocrisy. Although the "British Empire" seemed to contract, the Empire of the mind did not. I am no poet, but I succumbed to the temptation to compose a patriotic anthem, almost a New World Symphony, using the theme—borrowed, of course, without acknowledgement—"My Mind to Me a Kingdom Is."

ROLAND: How very apposite. Just right for a psycho-analyst.

P.A.: Alas, no.

ROLAND and ROBIN: Really? How was that?

P.A.: His Satanic Jargonieur took offence; on some pretence that psycho-analytic jargon was being eroded by eruptions of clarity. I was compelled to seek asylum in fiction. Disguised as fiction, the truth occasionally slipped through.

With this hint in mind, we would do well to approach the *Memoir* as a fictionalized outline, to borrow Freud's optimistic term, of Bion's ideas, and at the same time a kind of answer to the complaint that he never gave enough clinical exemplification of his thought to make his poetry recognizably related to experiences in the consulting-room. As dream-life and waking life, past, present, and future time swirl together, so do body and mind through these three volumes, while the lack of unity of the mind finds its representation in the central characters of the dialogue. A peculiarly timeless literary melange results—Socratic, Shavian, Beckett-like, filled with literary and historic references, puns often too personal to be understood by the reader, and obscenities too childlike to fulfil the promise of "writing a pornographic novel", which had initiated the project.

The general flow of the three volumes seems to be something like this: When the mind is stripped of its external-world supporting social structure of language, manners, occupations, and rituals, it becomes aware of the great difficulty of harmonizing that aspect of the personality which is turned outwards (usually awake) and that which is turned inwards (frequently asleep). These two worlds brought into confrontation display the inadequacy of language, especially for the communication of emotional states, which in turn reveals the poverty of our knowledge when compared, on the one hand, to our pretensions and, on the other, to the immensity of time–space ("The Dream", Volume 1). We can then see our dependence on the great thinkers (artists–scientists) who have performed the alpha-functions and transformations that have given some measure of coherence to our chaotic experiences. Into this world-picture, psychoanalysis has entered as a stripling, using a new method that is as old as religion and art but less pretentious than the science of Bacon that seeks to explain, less authoritarian than the Church, which seeks to guide, more poorly implemented than the arts, which have developed their craft for several millennia ("The Past Presented", Volume 2). Psychoanalysis discovers that gods exist as necessary structures of the human mind, but also that a body exists, which thinks. This body, which imposes its powerful soma-psychotic experiences, with their emotional spectrum ranging from in-love-ness to terror, becomes separated from the mind (we are more accustomed to notice) in daily life and in analysis, perhaps at the "caesura" of birth. Thus the psychosomatic experiences of casual, contractual, and intimate relations are only occasionally penetrated by the soma-psychotic experiences of the body at points of great passion, when we meet the beauty and ugliness of truth and lies, of representation and misrepresentation, of good and evil; in ourselves. Psychoanalysis should help analyst and analysand to notice this conjunction of psycho-somatic and soma-psychotic and mend the split induced, perhaps, by the caesura. This is where wisdom lies ("The Dawn of Oblivion", Volume 3).

So the wide excursion that started with the "Experiences in Groups" comes full circle in this dialogue of Bion's experience of the group composing himself. But perhaps the circle started with the second caesura in his life, when he crawled out of a burning tank in 1918.

I think that the quality that distinguished Wilfred Bion, and which marks his passing from us with such serious consequences for psychoanalysis—perhaps for the world—was his capacity to tolerate caesura after caesura, to weather what he called "catastrophic change"—an event of unpredictable sequelae. "Break-down, break-up, break-out, break-through?" He was prepared, rooted in "negative capability", to wait and see. Bion's last years, like Milton's years of blindness, embody the great dictum. But perhaps it needs amending. "They serve us best who bear to stand and wait". For Bion, "bearing" would not mean merely surviving, but bringing to bear the strenuous work of creative thought—imaginative conjecture and its attendant train.

CHAPTER TWENTY-SIX

The relation of splitting of attention to splitting of self and objects

(1981)

This clinical case describes the claustrum as the place inside the internal mother and differentiates "interest" and "attention" as mental functions that can be deployed to the internal objects.

Although the delineation of splitting-and-idealization as an essential step in early development found its place in Melanie Klein's theories of development quite soon in her researches, it was only with the 1946 paper, "Notes on Some Schizoid Mechanisms", that the wide variety of splitting processes, normal and pathological, came under systematic scrutiny. The use of splitting processes in the sense of constructive differentiation as against their use for breaking links in the service of defence found repeated expression in the literature of the 1950s and 1960s. But Wilfred Bion's description of processes of attention and their relation to thinking in *Attention and Interpretation* (1970) marked the beginning of a new dimension of investigation of the modes of operation of splitting processes. Those who had followed Melanie Klein's way of thinking—her implicit model of the mind, that is—assumed that splitting processes operated by unconscious phantasy, implemented by omnipotence, effecting concrete alterations in the structure of self and objects in psychic reality. Bion's extension of Kleinian mechanisms to an arena of operation on mental functions as well as mental structures revealed a new level of phenomenology in the consulting-room.

This paper is intended merely as an illustration of how these two levels of splitting processes can operate in parallel and potentiate one another's impact on mental states. The exposition will be confined to a single piece of rather intricate clinical material, for which a considerable amount of background in the psychoanalytic process is required to consolidate the credibility of the interpretation being put forward.

A young man of twenty-one entered analysis two-and-one-half years following his failure to achieve satisfactory-enough results in his A-level exams to obtain a place at Oxford. Six months of depressed indolence had followed this disappointment, the therapy for which was a working visit to his godparents in another country. There he had seemed to fare well for the first half-year, living in their house and working in their factory, until he was asked to move out for a month to make room for some of their married children to come visiting. This had initiated a quietly delusional state, with severe anxiety of being "thrown away" accompanied by a frantic increase in his diligence and almost complete cessation of eating. Padding his clothing and seclusiveness succeeded in hiding his deteriorating state, until he was so emaciated and weak that he could hardly stand. Six months after his physical recovery, he started analysis, and had completed the first year at the time of this material. His illness proved to be a long-standing confusional state based on massive projective identification, which, prior to the eruption of severe anxiety, had mainly shown itself in his character structure. He was an unusual boy, rather babyish-looking thanks to a large head and puppy fat. Very high intelligence had enabled him to excel effortlessly at school through docility to his persecutors, but he was fairly unsocialized, cynically critical and dissatisfied, and without genuine interests of his own. For instance, an extraordinary competence in music, both instrumental and theoretical, had been achieved purely on the basis of feeling that he had been designated the musical genius of the five variously talented children of distinguished parents.

The patient's confusional state (a "geographical psychosis", which I have described in some detail elsewhere) manifested itself in his picture of the world in which he lived—or was, rather, imprisoned. It characteristically consisted of three different areas with differing characteristics: his room, an erotic masturbation chamber; his place of work, a slave-labour camp; and the consulting-room, a place of light and air, looking out on a happy and free world that he could not reach. These three areas, corresponding in meaning to the internal mother's vagina, rectum, and head-breast, respectively, were connected by the city of Oxford with its tortuous alleys filled with hostile university students through which he had to cycle with eyes on the ground (the mother's intestine), snatching a bit of food from a small shop en route. His relation to food as stolen bits of faeces was the main focus of the analytic work in the first six months and seemed to eventuate in his emergence from the claustrum.

The consequent change in his state of mind was fairly dramatic. A frantic hunger of the mind replaced the furtive hunger for food, but he soon discovered that the analysis alone did not satisfy this craving. Ambition and competitiveness, particularly with his older brother and his distinguished father, and with his analyst and the male patients who preceded and followed him at his sessions, began to obsess him. He began reading literature and psychoanalytic literature as well, but soon discovered that his capacity for concentration was greatly interfered with. His attention would be drawn away to ruminations of a mathematical sort, or phantasies in which he was carrying on a scathing commentary on a football game, or on the commentator who was reporting a football game, or on himself for commenting on the commentator's comments on the game. This began to invade the analytic situation as well, so that he would fall silent or break off listening during interpretive work by the analyst. Furthermore, his dreams, which had been so illuminating to the work, dried up, and his plans for resuming his education came to a standstill.

In this context a breakthrough occurred, which was set in motion by an intrusion on the analytic process. A seminar given weekly by the analyst in the local child-guidance clinic had been moved to a new hospital, where the patient worked as supplies clerk. The knowledge that the analyst was in the hospital on Tuesday afternoons, and actually seeing him enter on one occasion, disturbed the patient in ways that quite surprised him, for the eruption of jealousy of the people who attended the seminar was unmistakable. In the third week of this intrusive change in routine, dreams broke through and revealed the nature of the transference situation on the very eve of his twenty-second birthday.

To the fourth session of the week, he brought the following dream, very pleased to be able to do so:

> *There were three buildings arranged on three sides of a square. One was a very dilapidated warehouse, with one broken window and a broken glass canopy over its front door, from which a ramp descended. The second was the canteen of the old hospital, filled with people, and the third was long and narrow, like a Nissan hut or a train, and he was in it seated at a table, as in an inter-city train. From the window of the warehouse, which now seemed to be a maternity hospital, a huge object resembling a furniture castor was thrown. It rolled down the ramp, seemed to threaten to invade the canteen, but finally collapsed like a spent top in front of the train-building. Then two youths appeared from the warehouse–maternity hospital, the smaller one looking a typical "middle-class swat", and four or five men in hospital porter's coats came out to surround him. But to the delight of the people in the canteen, the boy of perhaps eight or ten years hit one and knocked him out. But they were less pleased when he commenced kicking him with his "Doc Marten" boots* [a type of heavy work shoe worn by aggressive youths, but similar to the ones recently worn by the patient to replace the tattered suede shoes of the early months of the analysis]. *Furthermore, the boy kept taunting the fallen porter, saying, "Do you like that, Andrew?" and "How does that feel, Andrew?" Then the train-building where the patient was seated began to move over the countryside, which seemed diagrammatic, with*

> *rather toy-like farms and houses. At one house they passed, he could see the boy's mother on the telephone to the porter's mother, defending her boy on the grounds that he had been provoked.*

The patient immediately recognized that the "Doc Marten" boots referred to the analyst's initials, and it was suggested that this kicking represented an aggressive use of interpretation. He agreed that he had been doing this in fact in his mind lately, replacing his old vocabulary of contempt with a new one derived from psychoanalese. It also reminded him of the time at age sixteen when he had actually struck his father and in fact knocked him out. But he could think of no one named Andrew. It was suggested that it might be a pun, the four or five porters being the *hand* that *drew* him out of the mother's body, first of all at his birth, whose anniversary was approaching, and in the analysis. Perhaps this was the thanks the father–doctor gets for bringing the baby out of its dilapidated womb into a world, where it has to "swat" in order to develop. But it seemed that some differentiation between that baby and an adult observing and thinking part of his mind now existed, a part that was eager for development, perhaps another pun on *training*. Was the boy who had never had any interests of his own beginning to form an ambition to train as a psychoanalyst? The patient confessed that this was in his mind, and that he had recently found himself watching how the analyst operated. The analyst further suggested that this castor-like object looked like the placenta, but this did not seem to enlighten anything. But the patient added that he had recently been looking at a book about childbirth in which it was mentioned that animals eat the placenta and perhaps human mothers should do likewise.

This brought to a close that day's investigation. Its harvest had been a bit of a surprise to both of us, revealing so clearly the area of infantile resentment over being drawn forth from a world of slavery and seclusiveness into one of work and development, a "provocation" in regard to which the mother was felt to be in sympathy with the baby. But perhaps most interesting to the analyst was the evidence of the "Doc Marten" boots, with their implication of wishing to learn the father's skills in order to use them against him aggressively, to "draw forth" from the symbolic representations their meaning and forge them into weapons for control, tyranny, revenge. It was in line with this aspect that the dream of Friday did not come as so complete a surprise.

> The patient started the Friday session in fact in a state of somewhat sullen inhibition of thought, but after two minutes he suddenly remembered the dream from the night before, which he had awakened from at about four in the morning and then returned to sleep. In this dream it seemed that. . . *he and another man had been ordered to decapitate two people. The one that fell to him was a small boy who seemed quite resigned to the event, which was to take place in the mud of an unmade-up alley, his head resting on the edge of one of the ruts. But that seemed not to be satisfactory, so the scene shifted to a small corridor down which he wheeled the boy on a strange trolley to a room with a window looking out on playing-fields. There he took his curved Turkish sword to do the job, but, feeling unwilling, he kept missing the neck. And as he did so, the boy seemed to gain some resistance to being beheaded and began to avoid the stroke as well. Eventually a Negro "dressed as a doctor" entered and put an end to the game by lowering a bar (like the bar which ends the game in slot-machine snooker tables by preventing the balls from rolling down into the tray). But he also pointed out the window for the patient to notice what was going on there. In fact he realized at that point that he had been partly watching all the time he was "beheading" the boy and had seen the following process: on one field there was a football-game and on the other a cricket-match. Because a girl had joined the football game, most of the boys had left in protest to go to queue for bowling in the cricket.*

The dream seemed all too clear to both analyst and patient to require much association. It told the story of how he renders himself mindless by watching phantasy football and cricket games and carrying on a subsidiary game of commentary and anti-commentary. Why the analyst should be represented as a Negro was puzzling, but it was clear that the hand that had drawn him forth from his claustrum had also lowered the bar on his ruminative mindlessness. But it was not clear who had ordered this beheading, nor why its implementation was so docilely effected by both executioner and victim alike. Some hint came when the question was raised about the "curved Turkish sword". The patient reported that at the moment of telling the dream he had been unable to think of the word "scimitar". It is a car model that he much admires, but he remembers that when he first saw the analyst's Volvo SE he had thought it superior and that all Scimitar owners would now be buying the Volvo instead, although it was clearly a copy. In fact, the Reliant Scimitar used to be a four-door saloon until they copied the Volvo and changed it into a sports estate car, when it achieved its present popularity.

So there would seem to be a hidden link between the two dreams, distinguishing between ambition that grows out of envy and that which springs from admiration and gratitude. The little boy whose mother excuses his aggressive behaviour in knocking out his father on the grounds that he was provoked, has used the "Doc Marten" interpretations as the patient has used the scimitar interpretations, for aggressive splitting processes, in the first instance on his object, splitting the one finger-porter from the others of the hand that drew him forth, in the second instance on his own mind, to destroy his capacity for observation and thought.

But notice also that what has been split is his attention, for while he is attending to the beheading, he is also watching the transactions on the playing-fields, just as the patient reports that while listening to the analyst's interpretations he has also been watching his method of operation as the first step in his psychoanalytic training. It is of some interest that the landscape of the first dream may have a reference, with its neat toy-like fields, farms, and houses to the waiting-room of the analytic suite. This room is equipped also to be used as a playroom for child therapy and has a linoleum floor marked in squares of tiles; on one occasion there was a plastic bowl of toys left by mistake on the table.

Material as rich as this lends itself clearly to almost endless investigation, but for the purpose of this brief paper it seems best to concentrate on the obtrusive item of the parallel processes of splitting self and object and splitting of attention. It raises the provocative question of the nature of *interest*. It is a very major aspect of this patient's character disorder that he has never been able to form *his own* interests but has, out of the sort of docility exemplified in the beheading-dream, pursued the activities he felt bid to by his persecutors, mainly internal but confused with his father as an external autocrat (which, in fact, I think he probably is not). It is not clear whether we should take *interest* merely to signify that which is the object of attention or rather to take *attention* to be that state that manifests interest. Perhaps we would do best to think of it both ways in different circumstances: of attention and interest being mental functions that can be deployed to objects; but also of objects having qualities whose apprehension can attract interest and attention. Where the thirst for knowledge is strong, the mind must surely actively seek objects to which it can fruitfully deploy its interest and attention, while weak or inhibited epistemophilic instinct would wait in relative passivity to have its interest and attention attracted or aroused. In either case, the nature of the objects of interest and attention would differ, depending on whether the mind is in a state corresponding to the paranoid-schizoid or the depressive position, dangerous objects in the former and beautiful objects in the latter being most charismatic. But the material here presented suggest a third and clinically important category of objects to which attention may be deployed—uninteresting objects, represented here by the transactions on the playing fields.

CHAPTER TWENTY-SEVEN

Ego ideal functions and the psychoanalytic process

with Mauro Mancia

(1981)

This clinical material, based on three dreams, demonstrates two important phenomena at the threshold of the depressive position: how the withdrawal of projective identification in the threshold allows the harsh superego to give place to the emergence of ego-ideal functions, and how a growing dependence in the transference allows the emergence of depressive feelings with massive alterations of internal values and the view of the world.

The aim of this work is to present and discuss some clinical material demonstrating some transformations in the relationship of the internal objects to one another and to parts of the self in psychic reality. These changes, induced by the psychoanalytic process in a highly narcissistic personality, illustrate the progress from superego functions by these objects towards ego ideal status.

It would be useful to outline some aspects of the ego ideal before the presentation of clinical material. Freud (1914c) introduced the ego ideal concept in "On Narcissism: An Introduction" and connected it with narcissism. Subsequently this was absorbed by the formulation of superego and correlated with the evolution of the Oedipus complex (Freud, 1923b). The concepts of ego ideal and superego underwent different elaborations by several subsequent authors. Some—for instance, Jacobson (1946, 1964), Hartmann and Loewenstein (1962), and Laufer (1964)—maintained the fusion between the two concepts, while others—Jones (1927), Bibring (1964), Nunberg (1932), A. Reich (1954), Kramer (1958), Lampl de Groot (1962), Deutsch (1964), and Murray (1964)—suggest that ego ideal and superego must be kept apart, both on a theoretical and on a clinical level. Still other authors, such as Grunberger (1973) and Chasseguet-Smirgel (1973), seem to maintain that the ego ideal is opposed to the superego and is capable of transforming a non-destructive libidinal energy to assist maturative functions with respect to the ego.

Melanie Klein's early contribution was concerned with the formation of the superego, which she traced to a period much earlier than Freud had done (Klein, 1928). In her writing Klein did not, however, pay any special attention to the term "ego ideal" and its relation with the term "superego". Even so, in discussing Freud's concepts of ego ideal, Klein (1955) admits that "there are some features of the ego ideal which have not been fully taken over in his superego concept. My description of the ideal self which Fabian is trying to regain comes, I think, much closer to Freud's original views about the ego ideal than to his views about the superego" (p. 173). This would seem to confuse, as did Freud, the formulation of "ideal ego" and "ego ideal". Klein (1942) considered that the ego ideal derives its qualities from the endowment of parental figures, especially those of a protective nature, on which the child's well-being and development actually depend. Moreover, in her book on Richard's analysis, Klein (1961) points out that the idealized good object functions as the source of love and confidence and therefore is fundamental in the transference. She felt that the most important therapeutic transformations are realized through the breast during the psychoanalytic work.

For Rosenfeld (1962), the ego ideal describes the aspect of the superego that derives from identification with the idealized objects, while a concept of superego ideal was introduced by one of us (Meltzer, 1967a, 1973) to indicate a structural relationship between the ego ideal and the superego functions, where these two terms need not be used synonymously, but can differentiate functions of the internal objects in a dialectic relationship: "superego" indicates prohibitive and inhibitive functions, while "ego ideal" would indicate protective, nurturing and encouraging functions (Meltzer, 1967):

> If the sequence of events in the natural history of the psychoanalytic process is as faithful a recapitulation of early development as I am suggesting, we can see that the progress from superego to ego ideal is first and foremost a consequence of the surrendering of omnipotence by the infantile parts of the self. . . . The evolution from superego to ego ideal functions is promoted by the interpretation and the crucial step in this direction is the threshold of the depressive position.

According to Bion (1962), envy is the feeling that opposes this evolution and prevents mental development and growth. He has identified a part of the personality that projects envy by presenting itself—to quote Bion—as "morally superior" to other structures of the self, thereby simulating superego functions. He has called this "super"-ego.

* * *

The patient, whom I shall call L, is very intelligent, successful, in his early forties, now in his third year of analysis. His complaints were that he had serious difficulties with his wife—sexual impotence, compulsive masturbation, and uncontrolled outbursts of rage with aggressive behaviour. The difficulties sometimes extended as well to his children and collaborators. Masturbation was practised through rubbing the penis on the mattress without ever touching it with the hands. The masturbatory phantasies mostly concerned rather deteriorated childish prostitutes whose genitals he would examine and caress. L lives with a wife, who seems to accept passively his attacks and sexual indifference, which have now lasted for many years. He has two sons conceived by using the penis like an artificial insemination syringe inserted in the wife's vagina at the moment of an ejaculation prepared by masturbatory phantasies and activities.

L's background is as follows: He is the first of three children of quite rich upper-middle-class parents. He has a younger brother and sister, with whom he does not, at present, maintain any relationship. His father, a successful industrialist, is said to be a simple, cold man who offended L by selling the house where he had spent the best years of his childhood, and to which he was very attached. The sale of the house had the effect of an unhealable narcissistic wound to the patient and stimulated in him a deep hatred for his father about which, however, he also felt guilty. His mother is described as a fat woman, easily angered, violent, and intolerant with regard to the patient's needs, quick to punish him, as a child, for frequent enuretic episodes.

L's childhood history is characterized by solitude and a difficult relationship with his parents, particularly the mother, from whom he isolated himself in the garden, where he indulged in intense masturbatory phantasies and practices. His scholastic life was characterized by difficulty in attention and understanding—a kind of psychic deafness, which has also persisted in his work and characterizes some of his resistance to analytic work. The patient is a very strict practising Catholic.

His most recent history is dominated by an arrogant, presumptuous, intolerant, aggressive attitude with regard to his wife, children, and closest collaborators. The arrogance and aggressiveness often extend to his clients and people he comes across in his work.

In these two years of analysis, L's attitude from the first session seemed characterized by cynicism, irony, and contempt for analytic work. He refused every possibility to work constructively in analysis, to think or to understand, for fear that analysis might change his life, weaken his religious faith, modify the relationship with his wife, alter the family equilibrium, modify his prestige at work.

His relationship with the analyst seemed at first to be dominated by the overwhelming narcissism of his personality from which destructive attacks on the analyst–analysand couple derived. The more he felt understood and urged to understand his infantile feelings of envy and intolerance to frustration, the greater the attack. This attack seemed to be directed towards the analyst–analysand adult cooperation as a parent couple—

especially on the father, who is envied for power, money, and the penis that gratifies the mother by giving her another child without asking the child-L's permission. The mother is envied for her creativity and the good things she has and is hated for the punishment she might inflict on the little masturbator and enuretic.

In the transference, going out to urinate quickly became a feature of great importance. During the session using the analyst's toilet took on the significance of a continual acting in. It interrupted his communications, the analyst's interpretations, diverting the flow of feelings during the session, hindering work. Evidence suggested its significance in phantasy was that of a destructive attack on the maternal breast. This behaviour was, perhaps, also aimed at projecting into the analyst feelings of irritation, uselessness, and impotence. Going to urinate was also repeated during every night and contributed to insomnia. Sleep would then only be induced by masturbation, often preceded in the evening by the intake of a large quantity of food. Rather than encouraging sleep, the food brought on intense headache and insomnia, for which he felt the need to take various pills.

Separations during the weekends and vacations did not at first have impact consciously, but the eating of large quantities of food, masturbation, and outbursts of rage against his wife and children resulted instead. Moreover, confusion increased during the weekends.

It soon became clear that L was a highly narcissistic personality, who was using projective identifications into his wife, children, collaborators, clients, and friends. But the repeated acts of splitting and projective identification also transformed the patient's mind into a perforated structure that could hold nothing; everything was forgotten, so that the analysis appeared to him to be a hopeless operation. The narcissistic attacks on the link continually threatened to interrupt the analysis by destroying all work done. In a dramatic dream during this period, L *was a famous delinquent whose body was full of holes through which plasma, transfused from an old and deteriorated woman, leaked away*. The dream represented well the feelings dominating the analysis during this period. The analyst was transformed into a poor, deteriorated old mother capable of giving plasma, which he could not contain for survival. A similar situation existed in L's sexuality. This area was so completely dominated by masturbatory phantasies and practices that the act of penetrating his wife's vagina resulted in the immediate disappearance of any erection and disinterest in further sexual activity.

We would like now to present some dreams and associations brought by the patient at the end of the second year of analysis on the occasion of separation for the summer vacation. This phase of his analysis represented a very important moment, since it marked the start of a transformation in his internalized parent-figures and a modification of their functions. The transformation of the internalized objects can be specifically demonstrated by three dreams the patient brought just before, and soon after, the summer vacation.

Dream before vacation:

> *There is a puppy wanting to feed from a bigger dog, a Doberman, which, however, has no breast. It is reduced to an arid, infiltrating tumour. In the dream a little mouse emerges from the earth. . . . It starts to play with the puppy, but I start to pour beer, lots of beer, over them, from my view point overhead, dividing and drowning them.*

The patient associated to the dream:

> "It is a period in which I am busy giving to everybody, with nothing in return. . . . Client S . . . Client V . . . they all cost me, and nobody pays. . . . I do not think that the dream has anything to do with you here, rather the reality situation outside . . . now I am sorry that I have related it to you . . . it is better not to understand . . . it occurs to me that the beer may be the sperm of my masturbation, which attacks every relationship . . . but it is also manipulation, which divides the others and manoeuvres them. . . . I do not give good things but an appearance of good things . . . in reality I destroy, attack, manipulate. . . . I treat everybody that way—my clients, my wife, my children."

This dream, which we shall call the *beer dream*, related on the return from a long weekend, a month before the beginning of the summer vacation, had been preceded by a series of sessions dominated by frequent exits to urinate and by provocation through ironic questions. Envious attacks on the analyst's position as a university professor were frequent, leading L to consider applying for a Professorship in his own field—which would, incidentally, have obliged him to spend two weeks a month away from home and from analysis.

In the *beer dream* a dependent part of L is represented as the puppy who wants to feed from the analyst–Doberman, but the envy of the "superior" part sees the analytic breast merely as an arid and infiltrating tumour. This not only prevents the puppy's growth, but also represents an attack on the growth of other children, who thus have no possibility of feeding. The mouse that emerges from the earth is the little brother who emerges from the womb, stimulating jealousy. The arrogant and omnipotent child pours a great quantity of beer (urine and sperm) over them, thus killing and drowning the little brother together with the dependent-puppy part of the self.

It seems clear that urination and masturbation are an attack on the mother's breast and the analytic possibility of mental nourishment for L or other patients. The omnipotent envious attack on the analyst's breast represents also the competitiveness, wishing to appear to be generous but without genuine sacrifice. As a result, he actually treats his wife, children, and closest collaborators very badly, while pretending to be helpful.

It might be interesting at this point to quote from Klein's *The Psycho-Analysis of Children* (1932a).

> As far as can be seen, the sadistic tendency most closely allied to oral sadism is urethral sadism. Observations have confirmed that children's phantasies of flooding and destroying by means of enormous quantities of urine in terms of soaking, drowning, burning and poisoning are a sadistic reaction to their having been deprived of fluid by their mother and are ultimately directed against her breast. I should like in this connection to point out the great importance, hitherto little recognized, of urethral sadism in the development of the child. Phantasies, familiar to analysts, of flooding and destroying things by means of great quantities of urine, and the more generally known

> connection between playing with fire and bed-wetting, are merely the more visible and less repressed signs of the sadistic impulses which are attached to the function of urinating. In analysing both children and adults I have constantly come across phantasies in which urine was imagined as a burning, corroding and poisoning liquid and as a secret and insidious poison. These urethral-sadistic phantasies have a fundamental share in giving the penis the unconscious significance of an instrument of cruelty and in bringing about disturbances of sexual potency in the male. In a number of instances I have found that bed-wetting was caused by phantasies of this kind. [pp. 128–129]

We should like now to relate two other dreams the patient had a few days after the resumption of analysis after the summer vacation. The first of these dreams was preceded by associations on feeling guilty for having accepted a contract involving large amounts of money and prestige while neglecting more serious work already undertaken. He then associates the impossibility of declaring everything to the tax-man, a feeling of guilt for having manipulated dates, and worries, induced by his father, that the company employing him, thanks to its great economic and political power, might in reality devise a way of blackmailing him. Halfway through the session he produced a dream, full of anxiety, a real nightmare:

> *I am in Naples, in a tree-lined avenue. Parallel cords attached to the tops of the trees are being handled by a man on one side of the avenue. People are hanging from the cords. One of them is a big fat man, like a swelling marionette and there is a danger of his bursting . . . a terrible anxiety . . . then a child prostitute appears below . . . like in the book by Garcia Marquez, "One Hundred Years of Solitude".*

> The associations were as follows:

> "In the book the child could have been ten, and hundreds of men laid her, stretched out on the bed; she was dependent on them, waiting for them to come, her back covered in sores from lying under men who used her. . . . I have problems with my work which I do not enjoy,

> professional choices are always conditioned by the need to earn money. . . . The fat marionette in the dream is me . . . last night I ate so much soup that I could not digest it; I had a whisky, various pills to aid the digestion, but in vain, I could not sleep . . . then I masturbated. . . . Everything can depend on dependence . . . I am frightened of being accused of being a Fascist . . . I felt like the police who killed a woman's husband and defended them in my thoughts . . . it occurs to me that at the hospital of M there is a psychiatrist who authorized all the women to interrupt pregnancy in the name of ideology . . . "

This dream, which we shall call the *Naples dream*, reveals the patient's internalized parent figures at this moment of the psychoanalytic process. It shows projective identification with both figures in the parental coitus, manipulated by an omnipotent part of the self. The swelling marionette father and child prostitute destroy one another in mutual dependence. It must be remembered that L's masturbatory phantasies already concerned deteriorated, childlike prostitutes. The little girl of the dream is a combination of little girl and mother damaged by his attacks on her breast. The need for prestigious clients who can guarantee a high income, like over-eating, represents the greedy and omnipotent desire to have all the analyst's breast to himself, without leaving any milk for anyone else. Dependence on the breast triggers the attack on the analyst transformed into a marionette showman, a psychiatrist–manipulator conditioned by his own ideology to abort the mother. From the dream it appears that the patient may accept the dependence only to guarantee him the satisfaction of his desire to be the pompous, swelling marionette–father, way above the others, or the possibility of continuing his masturbatory attack on the mother's womb and breast.

Despite implicit defence mechanisms, the *Naples dream* seems to represent some progress in respect to the *beer dream*. There is in fact an allusion to the acceptance, even if conditional, of dependence and fear that his omnipotence could fail (the anxiety in the dream connected with the fear that the swelling marionette could burst). The emergence in the dream of guilt for the attack on the mother's breast and womb implies a possible attempt, even if embryonic, to reduce the splitting.

L introduced the third dream in the Thursday session, three days after the *Naples dream:*

> *There was a man, dressed in a phosphorescent yellow overall, like the road-sweeper's, standing near a dustbin which he was looking in, as if he was part of the dustbin.*

The dream had been preceded by a typical evening for the patient—eating "like a pig", streams of urine, insomnia, sleeping tablets, masturbation, and finally sleep. The associations to the dream were as follows:

> "Today there was a meeting I enjoyed. . . . I enjoyed working, it was a good conference. . . . M is old and deaf. . . . For a moment today I forgot that I had to come here. . . . I met R, a megalomaniac, psychotic, who only likes princesses . . . it is as if he were obliged to boast, it irritates me. . . . I think about how great old M is . . . now I understand that everything that is useless should be thrown in the dustbin . . . as the Bible says: blessed are the poor. . . . I wonder whether psychoanalysis teaches for better or for worse, but by being authentic the true significance of what we are doing here should emerge. . . . Today I have been really happy at my work and did not even have the usual economic worries."

The analyst here made a short intervention, tending to suggest his present identification with M representing a road-sweeper–internal father of the dream who is great, although deaf (L often repeated in the session that he had cotton-wool in his ears) and is obliged to clean the road (vagina) and empty the dustbin (rectum) of the mother, while the mad and megalomaniac part of himself is split off and projected into R. The patient exclaimed:

> "breast . . . vagina . . . dependence . . . all the things I tend not to feel or understand and which I forget . . . of course, the masturbation is an attack . . . one of my sons does not want to continue his analysis any more, he has not any symptoms. . . . besides the other son is different, he stammers. . . . I too have symptoms: I cannot make love to my wife and I cannot work . . . but today I am happy, I

have managed to work and hope to be able to make love too . . ."

This *road-sweeper dream* seems to represent further progress in respect to the second one. It shows the patient's effort to come into contact with his unconscious world, for his acceptance of the "psychotic" dimension of his destructive narcissism seems clear.

The stages in the rehabilitation of this patient's internal objects can be clearly seen in the three dreams, reaching a point at the threshold of the depressive position. The paternal line of development (beer–urinating patient–father; marionette–father; road-sweeper–father) proceeds mainly through the withdrawal of a projective identification and is thus accompanied by evolution of the infantile–masculine part of the self (omnipotent producer of urine–beer → swelling marionette → rubbish-producer) and the emergence of an introjective identification.

Similarly, the internal mother and infantile–feminine self undergo a clarification by withdrawal of projective identification (bitch-with-tumour-breast → trees and child-prostitute → roads-and-dustbins) (paralleled by infiltrating tumour → prostitute-girl → rubbish producer).

The most advanced position at the time of the third dream can be represented as shown in Figure 3.

It is clear that the omnipotence both of the self and therefore of objects is in process of diminution; a theoretical problem of a chicken-and-egg sort remains: does withdrawal from projective identification lessen the omnipotence, or does the analytic experience, by lessening omnipotence, force the withdrawal

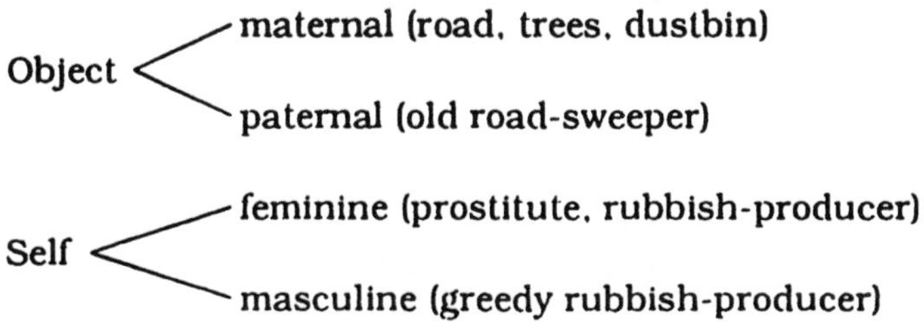

FIGURE 3

from projective identification? The omnipotence becomes replaced by begrudgingness as the current expression of envy, directed mainly at the paternal figure—old, deaf, and poor, his coition restricted to clearing up the road (vagina) and emptying the rubbish-bin (rectum) of the mother. Nonetheless, such a paternal object can serve as a focus of gratifying identification for the patient's work and some concerned paternal relation to his children: an ego ideal function.

This phase of work with the patient L has mainly dealt with his projective relation to his objects, since his introjective relations, even by the time of the *road-sweeper dream*, are still fairly rudimentary. But within this limited field upon which his symptomatic and some characterological pathology has been founded, the therapeutic accomplishment reveals a process of withdrawal of projective identification with internal objects. It can be seen that one consequence is a shift in their functions from superego prohibitions, by punitive threat (mother's handling of his enuresis) or deprivation (father selling the family home) towards ego ideal attributes. Where the mother has the significance of a world where children can develop and the father represents the forces of reparation for the damage incurred by the greedy little rubbish-producers, an ideal for aspiration and (introjective) identification begins to form before our wondering eyes.

SUMMARY

This paper has been centred around an aspect of the problem of the harshness of the superego, which derives from the internal object being altered by projective identifications from infantile structures. Under these circumstances not only do the internal objects lose their ego ideal functions, but they also suffer a structural and ethical deterioration.

Clinical material from a highly narcissistic but very intelligent and talented man in his forties demonstrates the process by which these internal objects have been rehabilitated through the experience of the analytic transference over the period of the first three years of his analysis. Three crucial dreams surrounding a holiday break have been selected to show the nucleus of the process of withdrawal of projective identifications from both the maternal and paternal figures and the consequent changes in their qualities and functions. In very clear terms the emergence of ego ideal functions, of support, comfort, and encouragement can be seen to take their place along with the superego functions of these objects, tending towards a fusion in the combined object of breast-and-nipple, in both their receptive-containing (toilet-breast) aspects as well as the nurturing (feeding breast) one.

The material demonstrates clearly how the growing acceptance of dependence in the transference, with its attendant lessening of omnipotence, allowed for the emergence of depressive feelings and a massive alteration in values and view-of-the-world. In this sense the paper is a contribution to the phenomenology of the threshold of the depressive position.

CHAPTER TWENTY-EIGHT

Does Money-Kyrle's concept of misconception have any unique descriptive power?

(1981)

Written after R. Money-Kyrle's death in July 1980, this paper deals with aspects of emotional sympathy and alienation between individuals and demonstrates in a clinical example the use of "misconception"—an idea developed by Money-Kyrle in his 1968 paper on "Cognitive Development"—as a new conceptual tool. This paper has two endings, the second of which was included in the publication of the paper in the Scientific Bulletin *of the British Psycho-Analytical Society, as an appreciation of Money-Kyrle's contribution to psychoanalysis.*

With his extraordinary capacity to go directly to the heart of the matter, Roger Money-Kyrle has described the three epochs of psychoanalytic development—his own and the science's—with these references to the concept of mental illness.

Published in the *Scientific Bulletin 1981*, No. 8, of the British Psycho-Analytical Society.

1. 1896–1930: "Mental illness is the result of sexual inhibitions."
2. 1930–1960 "Mental illness is the result of unconscious moral conflict."
3. 1960 to the present "The patient, whether clinically ill or not, suffers from unconscious misconceptions and delusions."

He goes on with his characteristic modesty to explain that he is hoping to outline a theory of "cognitive development" that merely aspires to fashion "two hooks to hang a lot of existing theories on". In this paper I wish to examine the possibility that the theory of "misconception" may be a new idea with considerable descriptive power that other psychoanalytic theories do not possess. He explains (Money-Kyrle, 1968):

> The two hooks relate to the two mental tasks any new-born animal has to perform if it is to survive: the acquisition of a few, I believe innately pre-determined, concepts (or class notions), and, what is not innately pre-determined, the location of their members in a space–time system. [p. 691]

In the pages that follow in that brilliant paper, Money-Kyrle (1968) examines "concept building" and "system building" from a point of view based on Bion's work on thinking but resting on a foundation of Melanie Klein's schizoid mechanisms and Freud's "Formulations on the Two Principles of Mental Functioning" (Freud, 1911b):

> What actually seems to happen is that, while part of the developing personality does learn to understand the facts of life, suffers the pains of an Oedipus complex, discards it from guilt, becomes reconciled to the parental relation, internalizes it and achieves maturity, other parts remain ignorant and retarded. [p. 693]

The ways in which a part (or whole) of the personality may become "cognitively retarded" are investigated both in terms of the necessity for individual concepts to proceed from concrete to ideographic to conscious verbal representation and for systems of concepts of both external and internal world to evolve. "From the beginning, the capacity to retain a latent memory of the external world system seems to depend on a capacity to internalize the base, at first in a very concrete way" (1968, p. 695). This base, Money-Kyrle suggests, "appears not to be normally the body-ego, but something to which the body-ego orients itself as its 'home'." This "home" must, in the beginning, be the nipple as the "0 of the co-ordinate geometry" of the mind.

But this "home", the "0" of the coordinate geometry of the mind, can be lost in several ways.

> I am not concerned at the moment with the ways in which the good base can turn "bad" by the infant projecting his own aggression into it so that it is misrecognized as bad. Apart from this the orientation to the good base can be lost in at least three ways: the baby can get into it by total projective identification, either out of envy or as an escape from a persecuting outer world; he can get orientated to the wrong base, in the sense that it is not the one he really needs; or he can become confused in his orientation because his base is confused with a part of his own body. [1968, p. 695]

Money-Kyrle acknowledges that the "wrong base" and the "confused base" are not easily distinguished and, furthermore, that the processes that lead to them are obscure. This paper will now try to explore this obscure area and, as stated, to examine whether this concept is merely "a hook to hang existing theories on" or a new theory with a new descriptive power. I am going to suggest that it is a new theory that opens the way to the exploration of processes of mother–baby (and thus of analyst–analysand) interaction that lie beyond the descriptive power of our existing theories, including Bion's "grid" and his putative "negative grid". The jumping-off place for this examination resides in Money-Kyrle's own postscript to the paper on "Cognitive Development" written in 1977 (Money-Kyrle, 1978) where he examines the implications of Bion's concept of maternal reverie. In the course of examining the beautiful dream of the motherly woman who gave the patient a bag to put in the box so that it would not spill out the prickly pine-needles, Money-Kyrle writes: "And if I am right, this is what happens in normal development: the infant finds a breast to cry into, and in turn gets back from it his distress in a detoxicated form which is capable of being stored and recalled, if necessary, as an element of thought." He suspected in this patient a maternal failure of reverie due to depression.

Existing theories seem to go some considerable distance to enable us to describe the "normal" course of development and the interaction of pathological aspects of the developing child *vis-à-vis* its intimate surroundings, both in its normal (or, better, "optimal") and "inadequate" aspects. But this is only taking into consideration the intentional aspects of the behaviour of figures in the environment. It is like describing a painting only in its iconographic aspects, without reference to the mysterious compositional qualities wherein its unique impact on the viewer reside. Similarly, our powers of describing the analytic situation tend to be limited to descriptions of the content—emotional and fantasy—of the transference and countertransference. May this be the mere "iconography" of the analytic situation, throwing very little light on the development of the treatment situation and its overall impact on the lives of analyst and analysand? In a paper read to the European Psychoanalytical Association in 1976 (see chapter twenty-one, this volume), I attempted an exploration of some of the more "compositional" aspects of the analytic situation in an attempt to extend the scope of our observation of our functioning in the consulting-room, thinking that a wider range of self-observation by the analyst could also increase his technical mastery of his behaviour in keeping with the individual patient's needs. In that paper two particular "dimensions" of interaction, interpersonal "temperature" and "distance", were examined. In the material I am about to present in order to examine the utility of the concept "misconception", the dimension of "relative speed" of mental functioning and behaviour between mother and baby (analyst and analysand) will be considered.

Clinical material

An intelligent and educated young man in his thirties found himself by the end of the fourth year of his analysis confronting both the prospect of marriage and the ending of the analysis with equal misgivings. Although the urgent symptoms and instability that had driven him to analysis were overcome, he was far from pleased with his character, particularly from a point of view that seemed to him to involve cowardliness about commitments and responsibility. But this seemed secondary to an impairment in the passion with which his desires and interests were pursued due to an indecisive, at times even vicious, capacity for criticism of self as well as others. It seemed from the very rich material of the analysis to be a fairly ordinary problem of a narcissistic area, with a destructively envious part attacking his good relationships and undermining his heterosexuality, his capacity for creative work, and his ability to enjoy the rich opportunities of his life.

A series of dreams at this stage threw additional light on the situation. On the Friday he had been in something of a state of collapse and felt that the analysis was rushing him towards termination and marriage. This mood was somewhat continued on the Monday because of a letter from his younger sister, and on the Tuesday because of a related one from his mother. The sister's letter announced that she was coming from South Africa to London to continue her studies and hoped to live with him until she could get settled. He knew that it was another of her ill-considered schemes which would end up as a parasitic dependence on him and the parents, but "how could he refuse?" His mother's letter mentioned the matter only *en passant*, from which it was clear to the analyst that the sister was attempting to involve her brother in an arrangement that would later be presented to the parents as a *fait accompli* when their financial support was required.

Only on the Wednesday did we hear his dreams for the weekend:

> *a wine-bottle with a corkscrew emerging from the cork, as if the bottle were the handle of the corkscrew.*

The patient indicates that he does not drink much, not because he does not like the taste—in fact, he does—but he generally dislikes being even slightly intoxicated. He then reports a further dream from the weekend:

> *The patient and his fiancée were intending to cross a river to a house on the other bank, but having gone directly towards it through the town, a route that led them past a*

> *pornography shop, which momentarily distracted him, they found that there was no bridge. It was necessary to go the long way round, up-stream.*

He is in despair at ever being able to love, his critical faculties interfere so. He and his fiancée are approaching the anniversary of their first meeting, which led to such a rapid evolution of intimacy, but it went wrong. Now for some months they have had to withdraw from their sexual relationship because it had been invaded by pornographic phantasies. Clearly there is a structural problem in his love relationship, an interference represented by the pornography shop. But the difficulty with which the dream is occupied is the *route* for crossing the river, whether it represents marriage, maturity, the end of the analysis, or the completion of his first major research work. His own tendency is to go directly to the goal and not to survey the landscape for the most suitable or feasible route. Or was it his fiancée who took them too rapidly to bed, the analyst who is in too much of a hurry to finish, his mentor who is urging him to get into print, his sister who is thrusting herself upon him ("And how can I refuse?")? It seems clear that had they taken the more circumspect route in the dream, they would not have passed the pornography shop, for the bridge was outside the town. What is it about his mother that leads her to mention his sister's plan only in passing, though the context in the letter suggests to the analyst that she is hurt and foresees the consequences? What is the meaning of the patient's dislike of the heady impact of wine, and how is this related to the strange screw-cork of the dream?

Let us compose a Bion–Money-Kyrle-type myth about a baby to see if it helps us with these questions. There is a strongly bisexual baby whose little-girl part is very thrusting and whose boy part is very passive, coupled to the breast-mother who cannot resist the demands of her children, even though she can foresee the difficulties that too prompt gratification may precipitate. The eyes of this little girl see the nipple–penis and want urgently to marry it, but the baby is not hungry. The little boy, in approaching the breast, is disturbed by its erotic charms and therefore sees the nipple in an alarming way as a mouth-opener, rather than experiencing his tongue (as he would if hungry) as a breast-opener that has to pull on the nipple–cork to get the intoxicating milk. His experiences of the breast are repeatedly disturbed by pornographic images of the parental intercourse, and he develops a certain aversion to these experiences.

This was the line of tentative exploration in the Wednesday session, along with some attempt to relate it to the analytic situation—namely, that somebody seems to be in a hurry to finish the analysis, although it does not appear to be either the patient or the analyst. At the next session he brought the following dream:

> *There seemed to be a professional meeting, but it was also a dinner party that he had been planning. One of the participants said to him that the last meeting had been a bad one and perhaps the next ought to be at his house, the name of which seemed to be "Dugger Austeads".*

In fact, my patient felt that he had rather spoiled the last meeting by talking too much and too assertively. The meetings are usually held at the house of a senior colleague, who serves wine, and people, especially the host, tend to get a bit drunk. There was, in fact, to be a meeting that evening. He was reminded, by the man in the dream, of a fellow student years earlier who had invited him to dinner and attempted a homosexual seduction—a man named Douglas—and those two elements seemed linked by the easy infant-school confusion of "b" and "d". But the "dug" also referred to "Romeo and Juliet", when the old nurse reminisces about weaning Juliet by putting wormwood on her dugs. The "*aus*" is German for "out". It seemed possible that in the dream the patient was being invited to the home of people who had been driven out of their minds by weaning, leading to an attempted homosexual seduction:

> "Do not get drunk on the beauty of women; all they want is to parasitize you like your sister and to drive you out of your mind by leaving you full of unsatisfied erotic desires."

It seems that this line of interpretation is a cogent one, but it is not my intention to plead its special powers over some other line of interpretation. Rather, I want to use it to explore the utility, the special descriptive power of the concept "misconception". The "crossing-the-river" dream lends itself to an interesting exploration in an ordinary Kleinian way. The "screw-cork" dream might be explored by concepts of projective identification, the baby projecting its aggressive tongue into the nipple. But would the two dreams then find any creative conjunction with one another? What would such an interpretation make of the implication that it was the *route* that was wrong, not the goal? Why is it implied that the weaning is brought about by some factor that spoils the baby's pleasure, by something wooden and worm-like penetrating his mouth?

Clearly his sexual relation to his fiancée had had to be suspended because he developed a distaste for the act if not for her body. The implication of the "Dugger Austead" dream is that he can be tempted away because the last meeting was spoiled, not by the intoxication of the wine, but by his own aggressive and assertive behaviour.

We know, in fact, that it has long been his contention that his much loved mother has spoiled her children, including himself, by the endless devotion to their happiness. All the children seem to the patient to be weak, rather self-indulgent, prone to self-idealization, and guiltless parasites of their parents.

I would not think it unreasonable to state the patient's residual psychopathology as an "inability to enjoy his happiness". It seems to me, and the patient would fully agree, that all the necessary conditions for happiness are present in his life now. But in a certain way, while he is no longer miserable, anxious, and frustrated, he is also no more happy than he ever was. Does a concept of a primal misconception of the nipple help us to describe this enigma?

Discussion

Perhaps it has been the experience of listening to mother–baby observation seminars in the last few years that has so impressed upon me the inadequacy of the psychoanalytic model, even in its most sophisticated form, to describe the nuances and complexities of that primal relationship, the experiences of which undoubtedly shape the foundations of character. And since it is character with which we eventually find ourselves confronted in the consulting-room (the character of the patient interacting with the character of the analyst), we probably must find some way of noticing and describing these processes. I say first of all "noticing", and yet it is difficult to be sure which comes first, for Goethe's dictum, *"Was man weiss, man sieht"*, is probably generally the truth: we do not see it until we know it, and we do not know it until we know that we know it, that is, can describe it.

If I give credence to the evidence from my patient that marriage and termination of analysis somehow confront him with a similar dilemma—namely, that it is not possible for him to cross this river which divides him from happiness by the direct route that he is accustomed to take—I must ask myself what the route by the bridge upstream actually means in terms of the psychoanalytic method. In what way has the route that brought his love relationship with his fiancée to a sexual stand-still and which threatens to bring the analysis to a like impasse operated? Or has it already done so without my noticing it? An answer to this question is perhaps suggested by a rather puzzling aspect of the "Dugger Austeads" dream which I have not yet mentioned. In the beginning of the dream

> *. . . his fiancée was about to read aloud from one of the patient's diaries, which was standing open on top of a stereo speaker. This reading aloud did not seem to be an intrusion on his privacy, nor otherwise offensive; her performance was then interrupted by his colleague taking him aside to invite the next meeting to Dugger Austeads.*

Diary-keeping has a long history in his life, having, with minor breaks, been a generally systematic activity since almost the age of sixteen. The diaries have varied in their content but have been mainly log-books, only rarely recording thoughts, emotional experiences, or conflicts. He has tried to keep his own account of the analysis, initially as part of his diary, more recently as a separate notebook. He now explained that keeping this record was impelled by his interest in psychoanalysis itself, realizing that his own analysis would be the only clinical material available to him from first-hand experience for use in any later attempt to study and think about analysis. So the reading from his diary in the dream had perhaps a resemblance to the reading of the minutes at a formal meeting. In fact, the patient, from my experience, has a splendid memory. But of course he knows that the human faculty does not operate like a computer and is therefore not a record, a log, of facts.

My patient's fiancée would seem in the dream to be functioning as the secretary to himself as the "speaker", who had talked too much and too vehemently at the "bad" meeting. It is this relationship that the attempted seduction to "Dugger Austeads" interrupts, analogous to the impact of the pornography shop, judging from the association to the ancient attempted homosexual seduction. This implies that his having acted like a bad chairman at the meeting was analogous to having made a bee-line to his goal instead of going round about to the bridge upstream. So perhaps some of the difficulty lies in his baby–boy part thinking that the breast-feed is a dinner party that he is giving or a meeting that he is chairing. Perhaps the intrusiveness of his sister is the natural sequel to a long history of his having been a better-daddy-than-daddy to her. My patient would certainly agree to this formulation, nor would he claim that his fiancée had rushed him to bed. Does this, then, throw some light on the "screw-cork" dream? Does a baby who is offered the breast when he is not yet hungry enough to be quite desperate for it quite naturally form the misconception that the nipple has come to open his mouth so that gurgles and saliva may issue forth for mummy's delight? One is certainly reminded of the nearly universal habit of cheerful babies to blow bubbles and put their finger in mummy's mouth, a great—perhaps the first—joke. And does a baby with an over solicitous-for-his-happiness mother take this all too seriously, not seeing the joke?

Let us now go back to a dream from the same night as the short-cut dream, which the patient related only at the end of that week, when time was too short for its exploration.

> *A woman was soliciting for charity on the street and seemed to be offering carriages for sale at a ridiculously low price to raise money (like an Oxfam shop). A beautiful one in dark wood with brass fittings was £3 and a plain one painted white was £2. He bought them immediately and only later began to worry how he would store them.*

> *Clearly they would need to be dismantled. Would he be able to do that without damaging them?*

His only association to this dream was to the last dream of Shirley Hoxter's child "Piffie" in *Explorations in Autism* (1975) which he had read a few months earlier. In it a shelter is preserved from destruction by a tidal wave because it falls into a dismantled state that can readily be reassembled. It would not seem too great a leap of imagination to suppose that this charitable woman is the mother, that her carrying the baby is part of the qualities of the breasts, and that we are dealing with a baby who cannot clearly distinguish between being the donor and the recipient of her charity.

Twenty-odd years of diary-keeping must present the patient with a (potential) transportation problem. His diaries and his collections of books related to his profession constitute the main body of his possessions and form impediments which raise serious doubts about their value in his life. But may not the two carriages, the beautiful one in dark wood with brass fittings and the plain one painted white, represent two different ways of preserving his relation to the breast, and thus to the analysis—one being his living memory and the other his log or diary? In true optimism, it might be suggested that the problem of the misconception of the breast and nipple has come to light in the analytic situation, as in the patient's life generally (fiancée, writing, relationship to his family), because it is in fact beginning to be rectified. Seen in this hopeful light, one could join together the "screw-cork", the "river-crossing", the "Dugger Austeads", and the "two-carriages" dreams into a single narrative, which would go something like this:

> "All my life I had thought that my mouth was a fountainhead of goodness and wisdom which people, starting with my mother, were constantly seeking to open by various devices, and that I could not refuse them. Resentment of this plundering of my mind made it necessary, I thought, to keep my memories carefully dismantled and stored away, while at the same time making me very cautious towards people who took any special interest in me. But now I am beginning to see that

> I have perhaps been the recipient of charity and that a precious object that can itself carry my memories, thoughts, and ideas has been bestowed upon me at very little cost to myself. Perhaps I jumped to a wrong conclusion years ago and did not realize what a long way round it would be before I would be able to bestow in charity a like precious object to anyone."

There is an amusing addendum to this story of the screw-cork, which not only strengthens the interpretation but also demonstrates how insight (by which one means the ability to penetrate and to comprehend the unconscious with the organ of consciousness) and dreams converge during the analytic process. Some days after the material examined above, or precisely one week after reporting the screw-cork dream and nine days after having dreamt it, a surprising event occurred. During a moment in which the analyst was examining another dream that seemed to bring out clearly the confusion between guest and host, between recipient and donor, the patient interrupted to report an image that had flashed through his mind. He had experienced seeing a corkscrew "worming" its way through the glass of the consulting-room window in front of him, moving forward in the plane of the window pane without shattering or cracking the glass, as it would do in the yielding material of a cork.

If we compare this image with the screw-cork, does it perhaps represent a rectification of the misconception? One could see it as a representation of his baby–tongue (the worm, as distinct from the worm-wood nipple) slowly progressing in its clarity of understanding (the window) despite the pain (pane), drawing the interpretative milk from this talkative analyst.

Just to review briefly: material has been presented to substantiate the claim that Money-Kyrle's concept of misconceptions puts a descriptive tool in our hands which enables us to examine the developmental processes in a new dimension. This new dimension lies outside the range of description utilizing existing concepts of personality development, with special reference to the immensely complex and subtle interaction between mother and baby. It has been suggested that problems of "fit", one might say, or congruence in mental functioning in such dimensions as temperature, distance, and speed could now be examined insofar as they play a role in the process that Bion has drawn our attention to, innate preconceptions mating with adequate realizations. An example has been adduced that suggests a "misfit" between mother and baby, probably also between patient and analyst, conducive to a primal misconception of the relationship of nipple to mouth, and thereby of interpretation to patient's material.

* * *

[Editor's note: What follows is the ending of the original paper.]

Finally, there is a second postscript that may lend strength to the argument put forward here. Following the work that has been outlined above, the patient seemed to feel that this formulation had had a profound effect upon him, somehow increasing his hopefulness and diminishing his sense of always being overburdened. The dependence in the transference was also more keenly felt, and the prospect of termination loomed in a rather dreadful way. The material seemed to work away quite systematically at the problem of vulnerability to humiliation, his feelings of fraudulence, and his ambiguous sexual identity. Self-analytic capacity began to come through quite strongly, to his surprise, as was illustrated most clearly some three months after the "screw-cork" dream. To a Wednesday session he brought the following dream:

> *There seemed to be a rather strange bicycle-like contraption—extremely shiny, almost radiant, with extremely high handlebars, but most strange was the driving apparatus. Instead of the usual arrangement of chain and cogged pulleys, there was a belt of soft material, like a fan-belt, and grooved pulleys. But the really extraordinary feature was that it was attached to the front rather than the rear wheel, and the axle was spirally grooved, like a screw. The result was that as the pulley turned, it also oscillated in and out on the axle.*

The patient thought that this was somehow a representation of the baby sucking at the breast with a soft, toothless mouth, and represented an improvement in his relationship to the analysis—that is, that he could take in the interpretations in a less critical and supervisory way. I agreed and suggested that the "fan-belt" might be a play on words, having to do with admiration for the analytic breast. At that point the patient remembered that the handle-bars were like those on the cycle of the wife of a friend of his, a woman named Felicity. That seemed to clinch the argument—a "felicity"-cycle, a representation of happiness and good fortune. It seemed also of some importance that in the dream this soft fan-belt and pulley apparatus was attached to the front-side and not the backside of the cycle-mummy.

* * *

Perhaps even a third postscript to the clinical material might be permitted. Approximately three months later, when the tentative date for termination had already been set, the patient found himself keenly desiring to come to a greater understanding of psychoanalytic theories and modes of thought in the hope of making a more firm rapprochement between his own field of work and psychology or philosophy of mind. In this context, feeling very worried that this was yet another move to intrude into the parental relationship and usurp "daddy's" functions, he dreamed:

> *There seemed to be a separation in the university library between the books of his own field, which were on the ground floor, and the psychology section, which was on the first floor. They seemed to be connected by a spiral staircase, but he felt uncertain whether it was for the use of students or only for the staff of the library.*

It is the formal element, the spiral, to which I would draw attention. It seems to be a very evocative representation in the patient's unconscious of what Bion would call the "link". We cannot avoid being struck by its connection with the "double helix", but also with the aesthetic aspect of such a form. The contrast now before us of this form in its aggressive and penetrating aspect as the original "screw-cork" and its evolution from "worm" to "felicity cycle" to "spiral staircase" seems to me to be impressive.

Discussion

The task now remains to investigate the implications of Money-Kyrle's concept of misconception in order to discover why it seems to me to break new ground, or at least to widen the emotional–ethical scope of our investigations of human mentality, development, and relationships. A brief historical survey would appear to be in order at this point—a personal one, to be sure, and therefore not one with which all analysts would agree.

It appears to me that, despite his expressed wish to avoid putting forward a theory of the mind that embraced a particular "*Weltanschauung*", Freud was unable to avoid it. The overall picture of the human condition inherent in his theories, both the early "topographic" and the later "structural", is of a mechanical apparatus seeking equilibrium, battered by stimuli from within and without, the "three masters" described most explicitly in *The Ego and the Id* (Freud, 1923b). Both "death theory" and "Nirvana Principle" make it clear that "pleasure" is negative in its significance, the release from the "unpleasure" of "accretions of stimuli". While the manifestations of the problem of adaptation may seem to be full of meaning, the problem itself is seen as essentially mechanical, and therefore meaningless.

Melanie Klein's determination to follow the lead of the children whose phantasies she observed—namely, to treat the "internal world" as a "fact" as concrete in its meaning for the mind as were the "facts" of the physical world for the body—brought her ideas into the philosophical areas of Platonism, where meaning was to be seen as a creation of the mind. This evocation of an internal world as a theatre for the generating of meaning increased the complexity of the phenomena that could be discerned in the consulting-room by multiplying the number of "worlds" that could be brought into view by the transference. The transformation of the concept of narcissism from a directional aspect of the libido into a structural and organizational one referable to infantile structures brought in its wake a renewed optimism as regards both therapy and prophylaxis. Childhood development might be seen as biologically programmed, as Freud saw it, but the programming took on a new hopefulness so long as it took place within a benign environment. The family became a kind of hot-house in which baby plants might grow and blossom, be gradually "hardened off", and enter the raw atmosphere of the culture with great survival capacity, once the good internal objects were secured within the depressive position.

But this early optimism did not long survive the bold excursions into the psychoanalytic treatment of the more severe disorders. The outcome was the theory of envy and a revival of the concept of the negative therapeutic reaction. The canker had entered the rose, the snake into the garden, and with this it was revealed that a puritanical conception had, indeed, lurked behind this early benign vision, that the struggle between good and evil in the soul of man was, after all, the final arbiter. Bion's work did nothing to dispel this harsh view by its dissection of thinking, evoking the conflict between truth and lies as the phenomenology of the conflict between love and hate, life and death, truth and falsehood, the food or poison of the mind. The "foul fiend" still lurked in the underbrush.

I would suggest that such a view has lost what the Renaissance rediscovered: namely, the Hellenic view of tragedy, of the human condition overwhelmed by forces of which it is not only ignorant, but essentially innocent. This is not to be confused with the ample tragic aspect of Freud's view, which, however, seems rather to embrace the Romantic Agony of the individual versus the group, essentially external. I would wish to suggest that Money-Kyrle's concept of misconception opens the way for investigation of factors of innocent misunderstanding between people based upon discontinuity in their conceptual frame of reference, the "O" of their mental analytic geometry.

I realize, of course, that a paper of this sort cannot be convincing in its clinical demonstration for the very reason that what it is attempting to evoke is essentially negative, the absence of intentionality as a factor in interpersonal conflict and developmental distortion. But while it cannot convince, it can suggest. It can suggest that innocent, unintentional misunderstandings based on primal misconceptions growing out of early developmental experience can seriously distort the entire structure of "cognitive development". While the importance of this for clinical therapeutic work may not be very great—that would remain to be seen—its importance for the psychoanalytic attitude may be extensive. I would suggest that by merely allowing this concept to enter into our framework of thought, we soften the harsh and puritanical aspects of theory that can enter in such a judgemental way into our work. Perhaps by increasing our awareness of the complexity and the ineffable aspects of our work, it can help us to distance ourselves even further from the vice of explanation, contenting ourselves with description and partial comprehension.

* * *

[Editor's note: What follows is a second ending to the paper, as it was published in the *Scientific Bulletin* of the British Psycho-Analytical Society.]

The question will arise: "What is the importance of this increment to our descriptive tools?" The material presented in this paper suggests to me that it opens up areas of developmental processes hitherto inaccessible to description. Psychoanalytic theories of development have always emphasized the impact of the environment upon the constitutional tendencies of the individual child. To this viewpoint of Freud's there was added by Melanie Klein the viewpoint that took account of the schizoid mechanisms of splitting and projective identification. This introduced the problem of confusion: confusions of value, of geography, of identity, and of zones and modes of interaction between self and object. Bion has added the dimension of disturbances in thought processes, and the constant conflict between the desire to discover the truth and the tendency to employ the capacity for fabricating lies in order to evade the pain connected with the truth. I wish to suggest that Money-Kyrle's concept of misconception introduces a dimension in developmental factors, and thus a viewpoint about development that goes outside the realm of conflict about meaning. It makes an approach to the aspects of emotional sympathy and alienation between individuals that is surely at its root emotional but for which we have virtually no accepted descriptive language. Vague words like "congenial", "*simpatico*", "*gemütlich*", "*agréable*" do not go very far to explore the content or basis of empathic bonding in human relationships.

Perhaps the special charm of this concept is its non-judgemental quality. My personal experience of Roger Money-Kyrle over the years is deeply connected with this special quality. His method of work in the consulting-room, his technique of teaching in supervision as well as the atmosphere of his written works all bear witness to the sort of humility that recoiled from sitting in judgement on his fellow men. While he had a deep sense of the role of evil in conflict with good in regard to internal processes, he was nonetheless convinced that the huge proportion of people wished to live in peace and amity with one another. And he was convinced that they would do so some day when the many misunderstandings that divide them against one another—parents against children, husbands against wives, ethnic and political groups against one other—were clarified. It was his firm belief that psychoanalysis, arm in arm with philosophy and the social sciences, art, and literature, would eventually succeed in this task. Nor was it simply an expression of a sanguine disposition. It arose from his experience of life, in peace and in war, and was continually strengthened by his experience in the analytic consulting-room.

CHAPTER TWENTY-NINE

Models of dependence

(1981)

This short paper deals with the Bionic notion of the "work group" in a family structure and its relation to the development of dependency in the transference in psychoanalysis. It shows how, in moments of crisis, the basic assumption organization asserts itself in a family group—a theme already touched upon in the 1976 paper, "A Psychoanalytic Model of the Child-in-the-Family-in-the-Community".*

I had recently moved Dr M's already extremely early morning session back another twenty minutes, so that he could get home in time to look after the children while his wife went to her consulting-room to see a new patient who could come at no other time. Thus a chain of accommodation had been set up from myself to Dr M, to his children, to his wife, to her patient. Dr M knew my home circumstances and under-

*Chapter twenty-two, this volume.

stood that I might oversleep, in which case I preferred that he ring the front-door bell and wait for me to appear, rather than to follow his own bent of allowing me to "sleep on", since this had already proved to contain such a degree of patronizing-poor-old-daddy that the analysis had stagnated for weeks thereafter. I had forgot to mention, however, that the Meltzer–Harris bell was non-functional, and he should therefore ring the Harris–Williams one.

At his first session of the week he rang the Meltzer-Harris bell and I did not appear. So he returned home after some twenty minutes and rang me towards the end of his session time "to make sure everything was all right". The following session he was unusually punctual and, after my apology, he asked again for reassurance that "everything was all right" and then described the events of the previous morning. Two patterns of anxiety emerged clearly: one was that I was carrying too heavy a load of responsibility and that it might either exhaust me or affect me in some psychosomatic way. An image emerged as of the strong man in the acrobatic team at the circus on whose shoulders the other five members of the team are poised. Second was the anxiety about the children. What if he should be delayed by traffic going home? Should his wife wait for his arrival, or was it all right for her to go to her consulting-room, which was in a house just two doors away? But that did leave the children alone in the house, although probably only for a few minutes, and in all likelihood still asleep. But what if they awoke and found neither mummy nor daddy at home? Might it be a shattering experience? Even the controlled and informed circumstances of the previous session had been quite shaking to him, a sane adult. And anyhow, it was illegal to leave small children unattended.

And so it appeared that he was the second member of the acrobatic team standing on the strong man's shoulder and doing his juggling act, in danger of dropping and shattering his plates. His wife, in turn, had a second predicament. It had been somewhat difficult to find a training case in their part of North London, and she felt it was quite urgent that she finish her training, since the expenses of it were running them into debt. Anyhow, the patient seemed rather exacting and perhaps not well motivated to come five times per week. She had to balance the welfare of the children against these factors in her training, relying on her husband to keep the children safe while she balanced the Training Committee and the patient. So the other members of the acrobatic team came into view: the wife on Dr M's shoulders supporting a rigid beam called a "Training", on either end of which were balanced a Training Committee and a patient, neither of great stability in the act. I was seen as in danger of being crushed, the children of being shattered, and the patient or Training Committee of being lost for lack of motivation or investment in the success of the act.

After I had summarized his ruminations and described his three models of dependence as "supporting", "juggling", and "balancing", his associations turned towards his father, full of admiration for his vitality and the breadth of his interests despite his advanced age. He had known Jung. Well, at least he had met him. Probably not an equally memorable event for Jung as for his father. Had the analyst ever known Jung? Or Freud? His father had dabbled with the I-Ching cards. He does enjoy his father's company and is puzzled that he does not arrange to spend more time with him.

I suggested that this failure to use the opportunity had something to do with denying his father's advanced age on the grounds of his vitality and retirement, that he was no longer the strong man in an acrobatic act, taking the strain. He then spoke of his mother's equal vitality and interests: CND, feminism, race relations; but without the same tone of admiration he had bestowed on father. I commented that his mother and father did not seem to him to belong to the same acrobatic team, and he could not imagine himself ever having been able to stand on both their shoulders, since they were so far apart. That might make a far more stable situation, though, of course, not so spectacular for circus purposes.

The anxieties implicit in this model of dependence and of family structure are self-evident: the strong man overestimates his strength; the plate–children are too fragile; the training case and Committee are too little motivated in regard to the success of the act; and even if the burden were to be shared between the mother and father, they would have to be so close in their interests and attitudes to enable the children to span their relationship—i.e. to resolve their oedipal conflicts by virtue of lack of conflict because mummy and daddy are identical in their meaning and functions.

But is not the basic model unsatisfactory in a fundamental way? It pictures the family structure as a hierarchic one, standing on its head—as it were, an upside-down pyramid. It is a basic assumption group, dependence. You might say that its basic assumption could be stated as: the law of gravity must be overcome if the family is to present a spectacular act to the watching world. Notice also that in this model the roles and functions are rigidly determined and cannot be altered once assumed without dismantling the entire arrangement (catastrophic change).

The purpose of this exposition shows, in a rather caricatured manner, the way in which, at a moment of crisis (in this case, a trivial one) a family group can dissolve into a basic assumption group. It requires no catastrophic change to move in that direction, just the hoop-la of the acrobats, and all members leap into their primitive, tribal positions in the hierarchy. And even the movement back, as it occurs in the moment-to-moment life of a well-organized family, engenders no great anxiety—perhaps just a certain sheepishness towards one another for the moment of automatic obedience and tyrannical command. In Dr M's case it is almost only at the phantasy level that the regression occurs, and sanity will prevail in action as the sense of proportion is regained. But what is it that is regained with this sense of proportion? What constitutes a family structure in the work group sense?

Bion (*Experiences in Groups*, 1961) has defined the work group quite precisely. First of all there must be a task, and the task must be a real one, not delusional. We will come back to this point later. Second, there must be available among the members of the group the skills and knowledge adequate to the realization of the task. Third, there must be a space and resources sufficient for the task. Fourth, there must be a table of organization in which roles and functions are realistically distributed according to knowledge, skill, and experience. Fifth, there must be a means of communication that is communally agreed and comprehended by the members, at least to the degree consonant with their roles and functions. The task of the family is evident—the raising of children. The more expanded form of this statement might be: to provide a place where children can grow in body and mind towards the capacity to survive and continue their development outside and independent of the family.

Not so simple or evident is the question of roles and functions, since the former are conventional and fixed by the culture from the ritual and ceremonial points of view. But the distribution of functions is more idiosyncratic, variable from family to family, from time to time, and from era to era in a particular family's evolution. A psychoanalytic view would immediately divide functions into those related to the setting and those concerned with relationships within the task as work group. Under the general category of setting there could be said to be two general areas, providing the housekeeping, while under the heading of relationships there are two areas, government and culture. Governing functions can be ordinarily grouped under executive, legislative, and judicial functions, where it is understood that legislative includes the establishment of values as well as organization, while executive functions would include foreign relations to the community and neighbours.

The functions of creating and maintaining the culture of the family are more difficult to define. I would be inclined to name the functions within his area as generating love, promoting hope, modulating pain, and stimulating interests. But such a list does not take into account the necessity of conflict and the role of devil's disciple, which is so essential for the development of children and the richness of the family culture. Thus the sowing of despair, stirring up hatred and rivalry, poisoning the atmosphere with cynicism (Bion's negative L, H, and K links) are important functions but hopefully never a fixed role.

Superimposed upon this organizational schema, the dynamic of flexibility seems essential. While roles may remain relatively fixed, it seems important that the functions operate with a certain degree of mobility amongst the members. For this to occur, it seems necessary for the principle of prerogative and privilege to be abandoned. This means that functions, either governmental or cultural, may fall to the most capable member available at the moment of crisis. And it is probably essential that a fluidity of governmental principles should be allowed, depending on the nature of the crisis, ranging from democracy to oligarchy to benevolent despotism at moments of emergency.

All of the above may sound like a prescription for the ideal family, but it is intended actually to be a description of how families do actually operate in the moments when all is well. Observations of family life, most poignantly of our own families, shows how unstable the organization in fact is, unless rigidified by the hierarchic structure of the basic assumption group of dependence, pairing, or fight–flight. I have used the word "crisis" in a purely qualitative way, to indicate any situation outside routine for which decision and action are required. Thus the crisis in the M-family is trivial, but it illustrates how, at the moment of crisis, the tendency to basic assumption organization asserts itself and must be recovered through observation and thought, while temporizing with action.

CHAPTER THIRTY

Three lectures on W. R. Bion's *A Memoir of the Future*

with Meg Harris Williams

(1985)

These three lectures were part of a series on the work of W. R. Bion, given in conjunction with Meg Harris Williams, in Oxford in 1982. This very detailed study and interpretation of the text of the three books that constitute the text of this volume—"The Dream", "The Past Presented", and "The Dawn of Oblivion"—are seen in the context of Bion's work and biography.

1
The dream of reversible perspective

When Wilfred Bion left England to take up a semi-retirement in California at the age of seventy, he left behind students and colleagues stunned by his loss—the more so that it seemed a desertion and an accusation, that we were the ones who threatened to "load him with honours and sink him without a trace", that we were the container squeezing the life out of the mystic and his ideas. Egocentricity and downright need of his moral and intellectual support prevented consideration of his needs and certainly obscured any idea that this move could have anything but destructive consequences, for himself as well as for the colleagues and society he left behind.

As the ensuing years brought news of conflicts within the psychoanalytic community in Los Angeles and the slim volumes of the *Memoir* began to appear in their shoddy and error-ridden Brazilian edition (1975, 1977), along with the equally unattractive and inaccurate so-called "lectures" (1973–1974) in Brazil, it seemed that perhaps Dr Bion had not left us but, rather, had been kidnapped and was being tortured or degraded, or perhaps was just becoming senile. I remember my first visit to him in California, where, sitting with him in the garden, I was equally thrilled to experience my first earthquake and the realization of how alive, alert, and seriously disposed he was towards his recent writing. But by that time I had managed to forgive him for the departure that, in my view, opened the way to such serious loss of organization and purpose amongst his colleagues at home, while seeming to bear little fruit abroad. I suspect that this forgiveness has not been universal, prejudicing many against serious reading, and necessarily re-reading, of the *Memoir*. Hence the necessity also of these lectures, which Meg Harris Williams and I have undertaken, to give the trilogy a thoughtful evaluation as regards its scientific and literary merit. Perhaps it has only been the publication recently of the autobiography of his childhood and experiences in World War I, *The Long Weekend* (Bion, 1982), that has made this possible by its revelation not only of his character, so enigmatic in its extreme privacy, but also of many of the obscure references to his experiences that are sprinkled throughout the *Memoir*.

The outcome of this intensified study, from the scientific point of view, has been a growing conviction of the closing of the wide circle of the work of thirty years which began with the papers on *Experiences in Groups* (Bion, 1961). Undoubtedly the central theme of the trilogy is the dismembering of the universal preconception of the unity of the mind, replacing it by a vision of individual mental development, which reproduces in condensed form the mental history of the species, in the true spirit of the dictum that ontogeny reproduces phylogeny. This

*Revised and corrected editions of both *A Memoir of the Future* and *Brazilian Lectures* were published as single volumes by Karnac Books in 1990.

historic model had long been the central metaphor by means of which Bion had leaped o'er the mind–body problem in supposing that the brain had evolved a mind by a simple, in a sense self-evident, preconception and that it functioned like a gastrointestinal system with regard to its natural food, sense data. This preconception, the primal analogy or original metaphor (replacing original sin, perhaps) assumed that sense data were taken in, chewed over, digested; that waste products were excreted. But, most important of all, that something was retained that could be used to construct a mind. But what of the plan for this construction? Do we end up, as always, with a cosmic preconception in the mind of God upon which image man's mind has built itself?

In the *Memoir* Dr Bion has addressed himself to these questions, which, though seldom named or acknowledged, have bound psychoanalytic thought to its prehistory in theology and philosophy, and in the trilogy we have his answer, which should appear as we examine the books one by one. But before we address ourselves to "The Dream", it is necessary to raise some questions about the form that Bion has chosen for his exposition, this Shavian, Socratic semi-novel, semi-drama. Throughout his later work, at least from *Elements of Psycho-Analysis* (Bion, 1963) onwards, and made explicit in the caustic *Second Thoughts* (Bion, 1982) about his own earlier papers, he has apologized for and regretted the inadequacy of language for the precise formulation of thoughts that reach beyond the sensual for their formal structure. He has often pleaded that, even given his own literary inadequacies, the fault lies in language itself, a fault that only art can overcome. Evocativeness must raise communication to the second power in order that the truth of the vision being transmitted should be made available without attenuation. His own earlier attempts at using quasi-mathematical formulations or speaking from a quasi-religious vertex had not, in his opinion, succeeded. His "Satanic Jargonieur" had foiled such attempts, as Bion was only too aware from seeing the ease with which his own language could be mobilized, made so attractive by its idiosyncrasy, while its freight of unique thought lay jettisoned.

I would suggest that a certain despair that his thought also, like the person, might be "sunk without a trace" necessitated this attempt at a unique art-form, the success of which I must leave to a better-qualified person to evaluate. But its impact upon myself as an individual, without claiming to interpret Dr Bion apostolically, must make up the substance of these lectures. They must say, "Look, I have squeezed this fruit through my little wine-press, and see, a potable vintage has resulted. Do thou likewise." In fact, I am sure, from many personal contacts with Bion, that he never wished to implant his thought in other people's heads. His vision of the air, like Prospero's island's air, being full of thoughts seeking thinkers places the artist–scientist (for they were never separated in his mind) in a position of using his special receptiveness and gifts for making public his experiences as an intermediary for others to catch the thoughts that are in the wind at the moment.

In "The Dream" there are 44 chapters, bearing only the page number at their head. I think it is necessary to take them one at a time, and I will number them in sequence. The main characters are essentially four in number: Roland and Alice, owners of English Farm, Rosemary, who was Alice's maid before the Invasion, and Robin, friend and neighbour, long hopelessly in love with Alice. The forces that have "pacified" England are represented by Man, with his holster containing either an automatic or a chocolate bar (though not the chocolate cream of Shaw's "Chocolate Soldier" but a powerful weapon of conquest). Tom, the man of all work, a kind of Caliban figure, is juxtaposed to "imaginary characters"—Holmes, his brother Mycroft, and Watson. And the dialogue becomes gradually dominated by a couple named, obscurely, Bion and Myself, presumably, as with Mycroft, a "brother". The scenario *in toto*, as the prologue tells us, is Bion's dream, "something about reversed perspective", like getting "down to the arse and looking up at the mouth full of teeth, tonsils and tongue", but it is also "a fictitious account of a psychoanalysis including an artificially constructed dream". But clearly he hopes to breathe as much life into his characters as Shakespeare did into Falstaff. This prologue must be our safety belt for the wild ride ahead.

Chapters 1 and 2 introduce us to the invasion of Roland's and Alice's comfortable way of life and show their inability to imagine the total change that is about to envelop them. The sexual implications of reversing the master–servant relationship are hinted at, and there is some indication also that the sacredness of private property (including sexual chattels) is to disappear. Chapter 3 makes it explicit that boredom is to be replaced by "flaming dread" and shows us Rosemary reversing her servant relationship to Alice by her powerful sexual attractiveness and vitality. The reversal of the master–mistress relation to Roland is then only a short step away, as is the "invasion", which will appropriate all the personal property of "Mr and Mrs Trubshaw, deceased".

By this time, had the author not been Dr Bion, we would have successfully thrown off the perverse fascination of this not very well written first novel, wondering how it had ever been accepted for publication. But as the author *is* Dr Bion, we are caught in a feeling of horror about the "invasion" of that Augustan mind. Chapter 4 offers us no relief as the sexual reversal is completed by Rosemary's engineering Alice's rape by Tom, the scene of which the following morning reminds Roland of his mother in her coffin. Ah, our interest is aroused—perhaps Dr Bion really is the author! In Chapter 5 this image is augmented by the memory of having "once seen a pregnant child stare at him with feral eyes and suddenly disappear". The names of Puckeridge and Munden tell us we are in the territory of Bion's school-days, when the harshness of school life and the pain of separation from his family in India was relieved in the holidays by visits to the families of friends. "Flaming dread" is destroying Roland's capacity for feeling for Alice, or women in general, and in his urge to run we are reminded of that terrible run against the Classic master's favourite at school, where the young Bion ran as if his life indeed depended on overcoming feelings of jealousy.

In Chapter 6 we find that Alice's capacity for thought and feeling have also suffered a loss, which seems to be related to the loss of her ownership of the clothes and the privacy of nakedness. Vulnerability for the women is contrasted in Chapter 7 to the men's preoccupation with food as Roland finds his friend Robin, also in hiding now, ready to kill for it ("Board and lodging, peace and . . . till you had to come"). We are now introduced to Man, the intelligent, cultured, and urbane representative of the invading forces, a truly Shavian

Mephistopheles. Somehow the impact of his words becomes equated with the "heavy bullets" that smash into their hiding-place, for they are now the objects of "target practice". Here ends the resemblance of the book to a third-rate imitation of 1984.

Chapter 8, the "who are you?" passage, introduces us to the primal power of the beauty of the woman's, the mother's, body, which "lifts the veil" and gives not "sight" but "insight", the price of which is for "the balance of the mind to be disturbed", condemning the person "to live imprisoned in everlasting sanity", blind to the prophets and artists, making of the mind a death-pit of benumbed senses and imagination, robbed of the creative capacity. And from this blindness, which hastens away from the impact of the beauty to premature concepts, comes strife, the serpent, the lie that hides the ignorance of the truth. It is from this dilemma, the ability to use thought as a defence against the impact of the beauty of truth, that Bion wishes to establish the method of reversible perspective, to whose exposition much of the rest of the book is dedicated. In place of strife and conflict, with its deep commitment to dualism, competition, heroism, victory, he wishes to establish a new value system, whose foundation is concern for growth and development. Anticipatory moral judgements must be replaced by "waiting" to see the outcome, for retrospective, historical judgements to take place. This declaration of the terrifying power of beauty and truth is set in the context of Rosemary's contempt for masculine values.

These masculine values are traced, in Chapter 9, to masturbatory practices and their connection with deceit, with Roland and Robin (under fire as target practice) like two boys in a boarding-school dormitory, "wiggling" away from the nightmare of loneliness with the devil "at their service". The implication seems to be that all worship is at root man's worship of his own cleverness in escaping from the truth—"and in some worshipped that part of themselves which they thought enabled them to make tools, the tools that make tools. . . ." Rosemary evokes the devil of clitoral masturbation in her hatred of female subjection, not merely to masculine brute strength but to the male inventions of the language of lying, the language of "Our Father", the Arf-arfer of Bion's childhood terrors and confusion. Thus Chapter 10 passes on to Roland's sleepy-talk exposition of Plato's cave and Jesus' use of the parable, opposed by the liars and "noumena-robbers", exemplified in Chapter 11 by Robin's pun-riddled sleep-talk, the opposition of paranoid–schizoid and depressive positions, with their differing types of questioning:

P.S.: Are reminiscences and premonitions the same thing?

D.P.: How does a person know of blushing so invisible, etc.

Paranoid–schizoid orientation seeks to destroy the manifest facts of observation while depressive orientation seeks new facts by ever more refined means through Leonardo-like imagination. The triumph of paranoid–schizoid attacks on thought are then epitomized in Captain Bion's drunken clang-associations of the tiny Chapter 12. We are certainly taken "down to the arse" for the reverse perspective of Robin's concern with "room and board", and language is the first casualty of this tank warfare. The overall impression is that under the vertex of terror the mind is bombarded with sensa and emotionality, which overwhelms its capacity for thought, and an outpouring of beta-screen clears the machine of its "accretions of stimuli".

Having now stated the case for viewing the social organization in which we are now accustomed to live as a universal conspiracy to hide from ourselves the depths of our ignorance and confusion, a situation easily revealed by simply turning the world upside-down in this "Pacification" of England, the character Myself steps into view for the first time in Chapter 13 to state the case for reversible perspective and binocular vision as new ways to avoid the "unbalancing of the mind" by catastrophic change. "The revelatory instrument could be employed by the object scrutinized to look at the scrutineer in the other sense [direction]". The task is then for different institutions of the mind to enter into this mutual scrutinizing, paranoid–schizoid and depressive, alpha and beta functions, memory and desire, to people mental space with a new kind of psychology, akin to the revolution in mathematics by the invention of negative numbers or non-Euclidean geometry. We are concerned to move from measurement of quantity to description of quality. "But in the domain that concerns us" (Chapter 14), "there is nothing that lends itself to the exercise of discrimination. . . . Sooner or later we reach a point where there is nothing to be done except . . . wait."

The required "revelatory instrument" that lends itself to reversible perspective is the analogy, the basis of symbol formation. It is this instrument that psychoanalysis, like poetry, art, and parable, utilize to make "visible" the invisible or "infra- and ultra-sensual". Rosemary's memory of the terror of hearing her prostitute mother being beaten up, Roland's memory of the terror of being pinned down by shell-fire—the rat in the corner when "you couldn't even be brave"—all lend themselves to resolution: "But thanks to reversed perspective, I could cower in the corner where the angle of wall protected me." The angle of the wall appears to be the capacity "to run away", the realization of choice, that one need not obey the past, in the form of one's upbringing, in the form of one's culture. Chapters 15 and 16 portray this in the interweaving of sleep and waking, past and present, real and imaginary, in the life memories of Roland, Alice, and Rosemary struggling against the dread of a cruel god enshrined in religion, morality, and cliché language. Thus the "angle of the wall", that infinitesimal moment between past and future, is the moment of choice, which is made available by the function of analogy, for it makes the person available to the "thought without a thinker", the new thought, such as the thought, "I can run away", which would be unthinkable to "brave" Captain Bion, but not to the fevered and drunk Bion who ordered his men to abandon their tank before it suffered its inevitable direct hit when sent out idiotically in a 10:30 a.m. attack.

Juxtaposed to this capacity for thought in the face of terror, Bion asserts, is the human tendency to worship, based on the assumption of dualities: two separate objects, good and evil, conscious and unconscious, pain and pleasure, beautiful and ugly. But in Chapter 17 he proposes values based on "the element of growth". But unfortunately there is a "lack of any simple framework of co-ordinates by which growth could be perceived or measured" in the course of life experience, because "the normal activity of growth does not betray itself unless it becomes significant through some secondary attribute . . ." that is satisfactory for the body but not for the mind. Manifestations of education "in his best Oxbridge manner" do not signify growth, as Rosemary demonstrates by tracing her lineage to Eve, Lilith, Helen of Troy, just as Tom's lineage can be traced to Cain. *Has* there been any growth of the mind? Is it all pretence and pretentiousness?

The answer in Chapter 18 is a grim one as Adolf Tyrannosaurus and Albert Stegosaurus pit attack against defence in their mutual resistance to thought and feeling. The joke is too grim, in the light of the all too recent facts of the baths at Auschwitz. But it is Bion's opinion that at the level of political organization there has been no growth, that the group is still in the service of mindlessness, gratification of animal needs, escape from terror, and enjoyment of gratuitous cruelty. And with this implicit assertion the character of the book changes, ushered in by Roland's and then Bion's soliloquies on the question of order in nature and its reality. What is the evidence, what are the observations, upon which this idea is based—or is it a preconception, a prejudice, defending us from the unbearable idea that the cosmos is meaningless, and concepts of beginning and end have only a psychic reality? Part of the trouble lies, he thinks, with notational systems and the false sense of reality they convey, of concreteness far exceeding their conventional basis.

From Chapter 20 onward the book is all dialogue, clearly Dr Bion's internal dialogue debating the problem of meaning and reality, illustrating the use of reversed perspective in making the mind available to receive new thoughts. The fraternal gatherings of the various aspects of Bion's personality (it is clear that Alice is Bion's sister from their mentioning earlier how her little brother had been frightened in the night in India by the roaring of the tiger that had lost its mate) meet in various combinations and will eventually, in "The Dawn of Oblivion", mould themselves into a standing committee. But first the Sherlock–Mycroft brothers assert their fictitious reality in confrontation with the Bion–Myself brothers. The debate begins with the establishment, in Chapter 21 of the thesis that, taking consciousness as an organ for the perception of psychic qualities, as Freud suggested, we might make use of it in a very sensitive way by persevering in introspection rather than squandering its capabilities by anchoring it to the sensual perception of external reality. But to do this, we would need to overcome our dread of operating without the rules, the laws of nature, which man has imposed on the meaningless, constant conjunctions of the cosmos. Through reversal of perspective, which employs imagination in a way quite different from the multiplication of vertices for reality testing, the organ of consciousness "functions as a receptor so sensitive that no machine can replace it".

Arrayed in a phalanx against any such attempt at sensitive introspection as a means of coming to understand the mind are all the forces of the group with its meaningless rituals (the Cup Final sequence of Chapter 23) and the social rituals of obtaining security and sensual satisfaction despite the dread of intimacy with another human being (Chapter 22). Alice's account of her reversal from fear to happiness on hearing that it was "only" Gerald, not Roland, who had been killed matches Rosemary's reminder of the loss of feeling on the battlefield (the man spinning round with his guts hanging out), or his bitterness about class differences in sexual matters. Clearly the problem is to preserve sensitivity in the face of mental pain when confronted by the group's continual pressure to abandon both feeling and thought for mindlessness.

The group, however, is not only external, but internal as well. In a long soliloquy in Chapter 24 Myself declares his defence of privacy, and, indeed, his solipsistic loneliness and disgust with the way in which exploration of the mind has remained on the surface of things, evading by every means penetration to the heart of the terror (psychoanalysis itself is just a stripe on the coat of the tiger; ultimately it may meet "the Tiger–the Thing Itself–O"). The bitter disappointment seems to be the discovery that even experiences of combat and tragic loss have not enabled him to come to grips with the deep terror of Arf–Arfer, the Tiger in the night, the coldness that invaded even his mother's lap when he was a small boy. Somehow the action of the dread has been to keep the different parts of the personality separated from one another, incommunicado. How can this organ of consciousness and introspection bring them together? In this context it is clearer that Alice's and Rosemary's bitterness about their relationships with men represents female parts of the personality that have never been properly "known", perhaps through fear of group stigma to a homosexual (Chapter 25).

Here, I would say, in Chapter 26 we see clearly the mainspring of Bion's purpose in writing these books, namely his disappointment with the thought of the past ("Any moral system so far invented cannot solve the problem—") and a full turning to art–science and its "priesthood" for the means. But also to entertainment, which Plato so distrusted ("If there were such a thing as a mental digestive system I could say that the mental diet of entertaining fictitious characters has contributed greatly to my mental health."—Chapter 27). Somehow this entertainment, as contrasted with the manic chaos of the Cup Final, effects a bringing together of the opposites of good and bad, ugly and beautiful, past and future, animate and inanimate, the Priests of Ur and the Tomb Robbers (Chapter 28). But it must be free of censorship, represented by Man and the word "only" and the question of the artist's responsibility for his brain-children, but not for the use others make of them. The little Boy's story of the dogs and jackal (Chapter 29) corresponds to censorship and the way in which unanimity of voice, mistaken for harmony, is achieved. Here the artist–scientist–mystic become united conceptually.

Now (Chapter 30) Myself and Bion set to work to forge this instrument of reversed perspective for studying the "unknown", MIND—analogous to sending a human animal to the moon instead of a machine. The need is to find ways of turning the repeated experience of quantity into a description of quality. For instance, the contrast and similarity between Myself's loss of love (Chapter 31) because the girl accepted it as tribute to her qualities and Bion's loss of the capacity for love as a result of the experiences at Ypres illustrate a difference in the quality of loss—loss of an object and loss of a capacity. Both are contrasted with "seeming callous" about Rosemary's account of a young mother dying in childbirth (as Bion's first wife had done), because he was viewing it from the reversed perspective of the child becoming a "frightful wreck" like Old Woman, the Indian beggar (Chapter 32). These explorations of loss of feeling bring an episode of rage at the unfeeling War artist, Tonks, and a deserved dressing down by Man for Bion's clinging to the adolescent vanity about his decoration for bravery, which has also been his private shame, linked as it is to loss of feeling. This, too, is an example of exploration by reversal of perspective (Chapter 33) and leads into the oral primal scene of the skull-crushing and brain-sucking by which Man shows Bion the essence of the depression reimposed upon him by the experience of tank warfare, that analogue of Staurian mentality from which he is attempting to escape, like the chick from its shell (Chapter 34). "The Omnipotent opposes the extension of the human ability to have intercourse"—that is, to bring container and contained together in creative thought.

This experience of self-loathing and horror seem to bring Bion, Myself, Man, and Alice into richer communication, talking the same language (Chapter 35). It is the language that has done away with God and Laws in favour of "constant conjunctions", which may be experienced by the reversible perspective produced by the workings of projection and introjection (reversal of the function of the sense organs) that enable meaning to be seen, with consequent feelings that must be accepted. This breaking-down of a rigid differentiation between thought and action, dreaming and waking life, hinges on the full acceptance of responsibility for the meaning one experiences, which, however, may be evaded by blaming one's culture or upbringing.

The possibilities of discussion rather than inter-action even become extended to Rosemary now (Chapter 37). Bion's extension of psychoanalytic theory by "supposing that not only does the individual harbour omnipotent phantasies of destruction and dispersal, but that there is an omnipotent being or force that destroys the whole object and disperses the fragments widely". This extension of "the field of play" of the "game" of psychoanalysis brings into view the necessity of the function, belief as the "action-generator" of the mind, equivalent to the "ferocity with which children sometimes play games". But it is to be defined by its "necessary conditions". You don't reject any formulation though you are not in a position to confirm it. "Time" may confirm it or not. A tenable working hypothesis, then, not a conviction; does Man have a chocolate bar or an automatic in his holster? At this point they all act as if they believed he had an automatic. Drawn together by this belief, the seven of them—Bion, Myself, Roland, Alice, Rosemary, Robin, and Man—are beginning to share an experience where Rosemary can recognize that she is "becoming" different even if she does not and may never "understand" the "it" that is bringing this about. But there is some suspicion that it is connected with becoming "able to love" (Chapter 38).

Now we are obliged to move on to explore the ways in which the capacity for thought may be interfered with by an equally precise misuse of language, illustrated by the debate about the ownership of the famous painting, or its ownership of the people (Chapter 39). The obscurity of language attempting to describe the ultra- and infra-sensual is contrasted with a "trick" language that could precisely obscure already formulated thoughts. The search for the techniques for precise obscurantism is, however, mounted in the service of learning how to detect its functioning to prevent one from knowing one's own thoughts and meanings (Chapter 40). Again the contrast between multiplication of vertices for reality testing—in this case what Bion calls the sequential and spatial views, one giving penetration and the other spread—distinguishes this from reversed perspective as a device for making the infra- and ultra-sensual aspects of experience "visible". Again we note progress towards integration, as Bion and Myself become almost indistinguishable.

But the problem of adaptation between container and contained, between masculine and feminine aspects of the personality, remains to be achieved if the result is to be "stable" (Chapter 41). This brings us back to the impact of feminine beauty and Bion's retreat to psychoanalytic questioning when Rosemary threatens to kiss him, for it might be a "Judas kiss" (Chapter 41). But Rosemary and Man go off for coffee, and Roland and Alice come back together (Chapter 42). They are moved to action by belief in the necessity of action, leaving Myself and Bion puzzling over the question of intuition and its combination with negative capability as a basis for pursuing the truth without recourse to experimental action. And so we are left at the end of this first volume (Chapter 44) with the problem defined—that of investigating the individual as a "group" with only the tools of analogy, reversible perspectives, multiplication of vertices, and negative capability as our equipment. But certainly the weathering of the disintegrative effect of the catastrophic change wrought by the "pacification of England" has brought about a change in O.

2
The past presented (what's the date? does it matter?)

In this second volume of the trilogy of *A Memoir of the Future* (Bion, 1975–1981), the general method of exposition, and thereby of investigation is followed: the reversible perspectives of waking–dreaming and the multiplication of vertices by the different characters enable thought to penetrate without recourse to experimental action by sharpening observation through binocular vision. Again, as in Section I, I shall examine the content chapter by chapter.

But it might be helpful to state the overall plan in advance in order that the swirling debates may be followed in an organized way. In general, the book is composed of two types of meetings: the waking meeting in Roland's and Alice's home and the dream-meetings allowed by Man in the kitchen of the former property of "Mr and Mrs Trubshaw, deceased", where Rosemary presides through her power over Man, her "hooks in his eyes". The latter meetings culminate in the "wedding of Man and Rosemary, following the "shooting" of Roland, and it is to this illustration of the growth potential of catastrophic change in the mind that our attention will mainly be drawn.

Chapters 1 to 3 present the debates in Alice's salon, among her guests Paul, the Priest, Robin, the farmer, Edmund, the mathematician, Doctor, the local practitioner, and P.A., the psychoanalyst. In Chapter 1 the debate opens up the problem of language for communication and for action, the "touché" of the New Yorker cartoon. The central problem of "two minds meeting" finds a means of investigation in the transference–countertransference situation in analysis but is, in reality, a ubiquitous phenomenon, as is illustrated in the cut and thrust of the debate ("The line cutting the circle"). It is soon revealed that each member of the debate is imprisoned in the preconceptions of his own life history, group identifications, and education, which invest words with idiosyncratic meaning. Perhaps the aesthetic sense would provide a Lingua Franca to enhance understanding of one another. The debate is friendly and civilized on the surface, until mental pains are stirred. Then tempers flare, as when Alice mockingly suggests to P.A. that his own analysis should have cured him of the "irrational" guilt towards a dying comrade in the war. "They hang across the gaping wound of my mind. . . ." Religion versus science, male versus female, the group affiliations declare themselves despite the friendly intentions. What is needed is an intuition that will lead to a concept that could do for their conflicting languages what algebraic coordinates did for Euclidean geometry to enlarge the container of meaning. The great artists and writers of the past, creators of the "classic", have been able to perform this function because "What they said with one meaning turned out to have, like a many-faceted diamond, a fresh, fiery brilliance of truth the "generators" did not know because it hadn't happened". But since great books require "great readers" in order to "focus the mind as a prelude to action", there is "something to be said for 'learning it by heart'", so that the mind may function without recourse to memory, as with walking. If we could add to this guidance the acceptance of the "facts we 'sense' as well as those available to our senses we might be able to 'think things through'" and "do something about it" without having to resort to actions. In order to pay attention to what our bodies "think" we would need the courage to resist the "closure", and "thus far and no further" that our timidity requires. It is in the hope that in the night a dream with its "roughness between the smooth polished consciousness of daylight" might allow an "idea to lodge". It is in this hope that the book then turns to the dream once more, the "pacification" of England in which the former skivvy Rosemary now holds her salon with an assortment of characters, some real and some even more than real—the "figments of imagination".

The first slip into dreaming (Chapter 4) is Roland's encounter with Du, a pun on "do", who claims to be his alienated aspect, the "not-I", unrecognized since they left the "protection of the womb". This figure will, in the third volume, "Dawn of Oblivion", turn into the "pre-natals" of the "somapsychotic" system, the final version of what began as the "protomental apparatus" in the *Experiences in Groups* (Bion, 1961). This little chapter, and the character Du, who never appears again, seem to be the hub of the whole process that Bion is attempting to illustrate: in order to be able to progress beyond the non-sense and mindlessness of the group mentality, it is necessary to integrate the alienated prenatal parts of the personality; these, barred from the system of symbol formation (alpha function etc.), remain bound to the body and the autonomic nervous system. Thus Du claims that it was he, "drowned in adrenal stimulation", that enabled Roland to "have the sense to lie flat on the ground" when he was being sniped at at Berles aux Bois. But he also claims to have been at the root of "one small boy's" ability to see Prince, an old cart-horse, as "a magnificent Shire". But it is also clear from the choice of the German "du" and the occasional outbreak of violence ("Do you want your teeth smashed in?") that the alienated violence, split off when leaving the "protection of the womb", would become, if integrated, the basis of the genuine courage and fighting spirit that the young Bion of *The Long Weekend* (1982) so yearned for and never believed he possessed despite his decoration.

ROLAND: I used to envy you. I thought, "How wonderful to be decorated for bravery, to be a rugger blue, to be . . ."

P.A.: So did I. I used to wonder why it didn't work. Each success left me further from my goal, further into the icy wastes, till I couldn't even recognize a character which had once seemed to be someone I could respect. But my Distinguished . . .

ROLAND: I didn't know you had any distinctions.

P.A.: I hadn't; only the insignia. I never rid myself of the fear that the shell which all could recognize was all that was left.

So we are carried into a more precise formulation: that if we could experience our fear at a level of mental life where we could think about it, we would be able to mobilize our violence in the form of fighting spirit in defence of the love objects apprehended by our aesthetic sense, one of these love objects being ourselves, "a character which had once seemed to be someone I could respect."

That such "terrible nights" are the result of being "too imaginative" is brought out in Chapter 5, in another meeting in Alice's salon, where P.A. and Paul continue the debate in which religious feelings and religious institutions are distinguished. Religious sentiments, like sex, must be "properly" deployed, which is defined (for all time, as it were) as "in a manner which is capable of development rather than decay". This mating of science and religion is revealed to have a connection with Bion's parents' yearning for religious experience: "Sometimes a light surprises a Christian when he sings", which his father sadly admits never having experienced. It would seem that the proper deployment of religious sentiment in that mad war of the Padres, the Government, and the Generals was Quentin's shell-shock, his breakdown into "sanity" analogous to Bion's fevered and confused abandonment of his tank, by which his and his men's lives were saved. In Chapter 6 the ghosts of dead comrades debate this, and P.A. again encounters his great shame, the heartlessness towards mortally wounded men: "Why can't I cough, Sir?", "Because—blast you—your thoracic wall has been blown off!"

From Chapter 7 to Chapter 19 the pulse of the Dream Meetings takes over, culminating in the "marriage" (Blake's "Marriage of Heaven and Hell"). The general pattern of the interaction moves from various groupings to assorted couplings, with interspersed soliloquies. The central groups are: Man and Rosemary; the "pacifying" force; the members of Alice's salon; the "figments of imagination", mainly Holmes, Watson, and Moriarty. The couplings in which the individuals are attempting to free themselves from group identity in order to make contact, are: Rosemary and Man; P.A. and Priest; Rosemary and Alice; Roland and Robin. The depth of the gulf of incomprehension between men and women is an underlying theme. (Page 41, Robin: "No woman will understand that life cannot be the same for a man who has been fighting. Page 68, Alice: ". . . but I do say that a woman's world is a far more sombre one"—referring to childbirth and maternal death, i.e.

the death of the first Mrs Bion—"than that discerned by the man".)

The first meeting of Rosemary's salon in the kitchen leaves no doubt that the central character from now on is to be this child of the moral whore—"What a woman!" as Holmes declares. With her knife-edge sense of psychic reality she cuts through everyone's humbug and pretence, except her own pretence of not being frightened. P.A. is forced to admit that, for all his talk about "facts" and "knowledge", he, like Priest, functions mainly on a system of "beliefs" called "theories", "when there are no facts available". The attack on psychoanalysis as an institution enables P.A. to disengage himself somewhat from his group identity and recognize its constructing influence. "His Satanic Jargonieur took offence [at his theme, "My Mind to Me a Kingdom Is"]; on some pretext that psychoanalytic jargon was being eroded by eruption of clarity. I was compelled to seek asylum in fiction. Disguised as fiction the truth occasionally slipped through."

The atmosphere of the Meetings is thick with mutual hostility and suspicion: everyone hates P.A.'s smug pedantry, Rosemary's arrogance, Priest's cynicism, and Holmes and Co.'s demand for recognition as real. Murder is in the air, or perhaps "self-murder". Catastrophic anxiety scintillates as the cut and thrust of the conversation becomes more and more cruel. "Some emotional storm" is disturbing everyone. It appears to be the sexual relationship between Rosemary and Man, sado-masochistic in parallel with Alice's erotic submission, although Man's seems to be more fetishistic, directed towards her "well-shod foot". Basic assumption mentality and appropriate grouping are predominant, P.A. and Priest with their respective hardly distinguishable dependent organizations, Rosemary and Man as the focus of the pairing group, while Roland and Robin hover between Fight and Flight.

Two soliloquies now reveal some of the forces that unite, or at least link, the three types of basic assumption groups. Rosemary's reminiscences of her childhood reveal the longing for the return of her dependence on her mother and its tendency to transfer to Alice when she is cold and lonely despite her triumphant pairing with Man. Priest ruminates about his history through the ages, always on the side of the "winning religion". His suspicion has been aroused that Psychoanalysis may be the newest winning religion, so naturally he cogitates on the wisdom of joining it. "Is the psycho-analyst any more than a tomb robber about to stage a grand 'resurrection' with a Vatican in which another vicar is to display his effulgence?" The implication seems to be that the old dependent group disintegrates (English Farm and the suicide of Robin's cowman) and is replaced by the fight–flight grouping (the Pacification of England), which gives rise to Pairing (Rosemary and Man) whose offspring the church (P.A. or Priest or both) will be ready to hail as the new dependency figure (the new vicar displaying his effulgence).

The Weekly Meetings continue, but the atmosphere has changed. Rosemary's epistemophilic instinct and her hard sense of reality begin to preside over discussions that become more truthful, as one after another Priest and P.A. confess their helplessness to alter the course of human events. Priest, in his belief in God, has had to change his vestments through the ages to stay on the winning side to survive. P.A. has to wait weeks and years to grasp the "gist" of a patient's state of mind in order to be able to make an interpretation that may illuminate the patient's mental state, only again to be helpless to influence whether this insight is to be well or badly used. However, this emergence of individuality from the dependent and pairing members leaves the fight–flight advocates in an even more murderous state. Rosemary turns into Clytemnestra in Robin's dream, warning him of the fierceness of women in defence of their children (the expected new vicar).

This rapprochement between Rosemary, P.A., Priest, and Man as individuals, respecting one another's experiences and viewpoints (and powers), brings back into view the philosopher's "excluded middle", which Bion does not wish to exclude. Rather it is, for him, the only tenable position for the artist–scientist–mystic.

PRIEST: But don't you think that when you have demonstrated all the multitudes of "false gods", there may yet be discernible "God" who is not false?

P.A.: Certainly. I have no difficulty in accepting that such a possibility could exist. But as far as my limited capacity enables me to achieve the truth, I have not experienced the reality of which you speak. I remember my mother asking my father if he had ever experienced what a poet said—"Sometimes a light surprises a Christian while he sings" and his reply, after a moment of thought, that he had not. I remember the sudden onset of tropical night, the lamp-lit room, and the frighteningly solemn and incomprehensible conversation. Why were they so sad? Experience has not answered.

Clearly being "uncertain", "not knowing", "negative capability" are positive states of mind and not merely the absence of certainty, states of confusion, or indecision. As such, they are the bastion of the individual's resistance to the seductive comfort of the group and its certainty, derived by logic (including the exclusion of the middle) from its basic assumption, unmodified by experience.

The Meetings begin to take on the appearance of a work group with the exception of the fight–flight contingent, which repeatedly poisons the atmosphere with sarcasm and suspicion.

P.A.: We have the opportunity to mobilize the impressions of several people, not just one; to bring to bear several different powers of discrimination to assess what information our senses glean.

ROBIN: Assuming, of course, that the judgement of the individual is not vitiated by the presence of the rest of the group. In that case, the combined wisdom of the group could be less than that of the individual members composing it.

P.A.: Unless the experience of the group promotes growth of the health and strength of the individuals. Perhaps these group meetings might have that developmental force.

It begins to seem more and more inevitable that in order for "something to be born" of this work group someone—namely, Roland—will have to be eliminated. He and Robin are plotting the destruction of the work group either by killing Man and Rosemary or by sabotaging the discussion by badgering.

But the shooting of Roland by Man, with Rosemary's permission, comes in the context of information that Alice is pregnant (presumably from Tom's rape of her). It seems more than hinted at that Rosemary covets the baby, for her dominance over Man by his fetishism does not give promise of the kind of pairing that would be fruitful of the new messiah. In her nightmare she meets the schoolboy who so wounded her vanity by being afraid to be seen with her by his friends. But she also meets the apparition who likens her position to that of Hagar, mother of Ishmael the outcast, whose pride at conceiving, when the aged Sarah could not, was later dashed by the birth of Isaac. Rosemary's grievances are falling away as her thirst for knowledge and her aesthetic sense begin to stir more tender sentiments. ("That boy made me laugh, etc." "Perhaps I've been too hard on Alice.")

It is in this atmosphere of impending birth, represented in Rosemary by "needing a doctor", by Priest in his dream of "an explosion of vast, tremendous and majestic proportion," by Tom in his difficulty with Curly the cow, that the marriage of Man and Rosemary is approached. The debate between P.A. and Priest has become a process of jockeying for position in relation to Rosemary ("he's busy getting a pedestal for me to get onto or a servile function to perform"), as if both were vying to be official tutor to the expected messianic baby.

The "wedding" in Chapter 19 turns into a riot in which persons, ghosts of persons, and figments of imagination mill about in defiance of Man's New Order, condemning him to "live by the fruits of his victory". The unexcluded middle between being and not-being, between beginning and end, life and death, is "the Kingdom of God within you" (religious vertex), "man's inner world" (P.A. vertex), or "All change at Purgatory". It is the mental counterpart of the womb, where a "foetal idea can kill itself or be killed" or grow and "break out of its shell". It is the place where the "shock" of new experiences is felt, whether it is Man's first experience of killing or Rosemary's of dancing, since "our senses are so dulled or rudimentary that great changes are un-observed. A foetus is not likely to know it is growing". Despite Robin's desire "to live in peace and quiet and run my farm", he has been shocked when "a farm worker desired to blow his brains out and did so". Roland and Alice's conventional life has been shocked by the impact of their maid Rosemary's powerful sexual attraction and mental toughness. But, most of all, the daytime meetings at Alice's salon, with P.A., Paul, and Edmund, have shocked them all by the recognition of the timidity of their modes of thought, the powerful hostility underlying their civility to one another, and the degree to which their individual imprisonment in the past so rigidifies their language that they can hardly understand one another.

This is the daytime experience that is being worked over in the dream of the "Pacification of England". Each member, each of whom represents an aspect of Bion's mind, is held within a rigid container constructed at a crucial developmental period, a container whose objective was "so far and no further". From the autobiography we can recognize many of the events—the Tiger Hunt, the Rhodes' farm, fears of being expelled from school, feelings of cowardice, which the experiences of war only confirmed, despite his decorations, the death of his first wife in childbirth. The second volume of the *Memoir* has brought us this far, to a moving, tumultuous picture of the inner world of dreams under pressure of catastrophic change, uncertain whether the "foetal idea" is going to grow, kill itself, or be killed.

3
Discrimination or oblivion? How to choose?

The third volume of *A Memoir of the Future* (1975–1981), which is also rather paradoxically entitled, "The Dawn of Oblivion" in the overriding spirit of reversible perspective does not lend itself to such consecutive examination, as did the first two volumes. The main reason is that it lacks their dramatic plan. The first four chapters consist of a fanciful attempt to describe in dialogue the personality in terms of its developmental history from conception to death. Each era of development expresses its particular critical problem and its grievances against the other parts of this stratified personality for their lack of interest, sympathy, communication. In its midst is the "otter hunt", in which the fundamental division in our personality, psycho:soma, is also represented by the caesura or barrier to communication and understanding between humans and other animals. To resolve these failures of integration, the "committee" is set up—a "talking shop", a "parliament" of the personality on the model of psychoanalysis, to try to "do something" by avoiding action and concentrating on the problems of language and discrimination. This "committee", the work group, is the "foetal idea", and its task is to try to allow the "meaning to get through the barrier" between mind and body. (SOMA: "If you had any respect for my feelings and what I feel, you wouldn't be in this mess.")

This problem of non-communication between the pre-natal and post-natal parts of the personality, this barrier, the "Caesura of Birth", is being put forward by Bion as the source of our lack of discrimination and tendency to make "wrong choices", such as war. The trouble lies on both sides of the barrier. On the post-natal side, there is the problem of education, aimed by the parents at conformity rather than development. Anxiety for the child's survival outside the family induces them to represent the institutions of their culture, despite their rigidity and inhumanity. (P.A.: "All Institutes are dead and therefore conform, like all inanimate objects, to laws and bye-laws which are comprehensible within the limits of human understanding. However, as they are composed of people and individuals who are liable to develop the Institution begins to yield to pressure.")

But on the pre-natal side the difficulty comes from a tendency to reject the stimulation that makes the experience that could eventually be thought about. One danger is of failing to make the transition from invertebrate to vertebrate mentality:

> EM-MATURE: I may borrow a case or sheath as an exo-skeleton temporarily, but—
>
> TERM: No, don't! If you borrow an exo-skeleton you will never get out of it. I swallowed an erection and now it is part of ME. Its my endo-skeleton. I am an erection. I am independent.)

We cannot ignore the possibility of non-Mendelian inheritance of ideas based on the foetus' experiences in the womb, from which it may wish to take refuge in such a "case" or "sheath". And conversely:

> ALICE: The bloom on the cheeks of men and women can show that the pair in love are suffused by a reality which cannot be gainsaid.
>
> BION: . . . Could not the blush on the bridal cheeks be communicated by a corresponding blush on the walls of the uterus, and vice versa? . . . The child might inherit a passionate love which seemingly could only be acquired.

Hence, when the "committee" is formed, it is faced immediately with very considerable problems of communication. Nor do the hundred pages that follow give very convincing evidence of much progress. When age 75 complains that the personality parts never go to sleep all at once and at other times create a "perfect Bedlam", P.A. remains hopeful that "it might some day be possible for them all to be awake and carry on a fairly disciplined debate". This does not seem to happen, although gradually P.A. becomes the dominant figure, and something of a seminar results into which "Bion" becomes introduced when tempers flare over the question, raised by P.A., "Why didn't Bion go on with groups?" It is Alice who quietens these contending "English fools". In fact, it is Alice, and to a lesser extent Rosemary, who consistently bring in the theme of love and its many falsifications. The male figures, as in "The Past Presented" continue to be occupied with courage/cowardice (Roland and Robin), heaven/hell (P.A. and Priest).

In fact, it gradually comes across that the women are much less motivated by fears than are the men—by social anxieties or the fear of death, like Roland and Robin, or by preoccupations with immortality related to the fear of death. It is Alice's constant introduction of the feminine primarily maternal vertex that directs the tone of the discussion. It is reinforced by the maternal vertex, as presented by Rosemary's reminiscences of her mother's (the "moral" whore) protective and nurturing attitudes. The implied promise of Volume II, that a messianic idea was to be born, is carried out both by the formation of the committee and its striving for "disciplined debate" in lieu of action, and also by the subject matter of the debate. Gradually, the figment of imagination, the hypothetical foetus, this conjectural object becomes more and more real. And so the foetal idea, the idea of a foetus and every new idea *as* a foetus, become equated with one another. There is certainly in this some feeling that the conceptual caesura between mind and body and the linguistic caesura by which it is entrapped are being eroded by imagination:

> P.A.: In real life problems present themselves in a form which is not susceptible to solution theoretically; you have to act or refrain from acting. These discussions are important not in themselves, but because they promote readiness. Psycho-analysis is a kind of action that is a *prelude* to action.

Answers are not being sought, not only because they are "the misfortune of the question", but on the "general principle (that) the personality must be stimulated so that curiosity is aroused but not satisfied: If desire is too early satisfied there is a loss of mental vigour" (page 95). It is, after all, the restoration and preservation of this mental vigour that is the secret of development:

> P.A.: The so-called *laws* of logic were a prescription for Chaos. They left no living space at all for vitality.

Bion's plea in favour of imaginative conjectures, coupled with repetition of observations, "however compulsively repetitive they seemed to be, until a pattern became discernible in the chaos of chance", is aimed at opening our minds as scientists to the meaningfulness of phenomena that are ordinarily dismissed as "visual or auditory hallucinations, or chemically generated feelings of pugnacity or fear born of the adrenals—as if that made them unworthy of attention".

> P.A.: I know (men and women) have minds as well as bodies.
>
> SOMITE THIRTY: Somitically speaking, I know a lot that I cannot make clear to you, but that is factual enough to me. I have to borrow articulate speech from Soma.
>
> SOMA: My difficulty exactly. I cannot make anything clear

> to Psyche unless I borrow a bellyache or headache or respiratory distress from somitic vocabulary for any of these post-natal structures. I *believe* in mind and personality [i.e. rather than *know* them] as there is no evidence whatever for anything but body. And when I manage to make anyone aware of a bellyache, the probability is that they immediately drag in a "cure".

Bion suggests that one of the ways in which this "articulate speech" makes contact with the bellyache, etc., is through language not ordinarily acceptable for communication of information: "Phantasies sometimes burst through into articulate words when the individual is 'off his guard'—":

> P.A.: Sometimes the "acceptable convention" has to stretch, alter, to accommodate the thing that "breaks through"; sometimes the "conventionally acceptable" crushes the "outbreaking impulse". Usually it is a compromise between the two. Just now Alice allowed her ears and lips to be degraded by "bloody cunt" and "fucking bastard"; the rest of us have had to allow ourselves to be limited by being polite.

This way of playing fast and loose with language, with wit, obscenity, endless punning, splitting, and recombining words, is part of the method that the individuals of the "committee" use to try to "get through" to one another. ". . . archaic terms hide or disguise or preserve some powerful germ of vital development in a way that is not true of "bloody vagina".

But the central problem is one of willingness to know ourselves even though "we find [page 58] that merely trying to know who 'I' am involves an intolerable amount of discovery. . . ."

> P.A.: It seems to me we need to develop a capacity to use a screen, a resistance, a caesura, as Picasso could use a plate of glass. Look on *this* and see a delineation of psycho-somatic disorder, look on *this* side and see a soma-psychosis.

* * *

There can be little doubt that reading *A Memoir of the Future*, especially when combined with *The Long Weekend*, enables the reader to "know" Bion in a way that even considerable professional and social contact during his lifetime had not afforded. Considering what an extremely private and reserved, not to say shy, person he was, the degree of honest revelation of his person in these books, whatever their artistic or literary value may be, confers an extraordinary privilege on the reader. As a person who has been helped and inspired by his work for many years, it is not possible for me to imagine in a clear way how this trilogy would impose itself on a person not so oriented to Bion. The general reaction to them has been one of shocked rejection. "He was a great man, but he had no experience of writing fiction", a well-known literary critic is reported to have said, declining to review the books. He was very old; he was not well; he was disappointed by his experience in California; his isolation denied him the modulating influence of his former colleagues—all these remarks have been heard uttered as an excuse for not reading, or not reading carefully, and certainly for not re-reading, the *Memoir*. Re-reading is essential. While not claiming for it a place next to Tolstoy's *War and Peace*, as Henry Reed did for Melanie Klein's *Narrative of a Child Analysis* (1961), I would urge that it cannot be appreciated without this effort. I would certainly say the same for every great book I have ever read. It may not be—probably as a literary experiment it is not—a great book. But that it is a great contribution to the vast circle of Dr Bion's thought and closes the gestalt of this thought on a ringing note, this I will claim.

But it must be recognized that what Wilfred Bion has left us in the body of his work is, largely, a massive "imaginative conjecture" whose clinical reality, however firmly based it may have been in his own experience of life in and out of the consulting-room, each of us must discover for himself. I can claim that much of what has gone before the *Memoir* has already found substantial use, and therefore validity, in my own experience of psychoanalysis. Such massive profit cannot be accepted without the indebtedness to take fully seriously the implications of the *Memoir*, fanciful as they may seem. They are fanciful, but not outrageous, not bizarre, certainly not suggestive of conceptual confusion of the senile brain, nor are they delusionally organized. The most useful way to bring this short series of lectures on the *Memoir* to an end would seem to be to give a brief description of the full circle of Bion's thought about the development and workings of the human personality, including some discussion of the difficulties involved in studying these phenomena by the psychoanalytic method.

During its sojourn in the uterus, the human foetus begins to receive sensations of pressure, gravitational orientation, acceleration, sound, dim light changes, taste and smell from the amniotic fluid, as well as proprioceptive sensations from its own body. These may be pleasurable, but when they are painful, they generate emotional experiences about which the foetus is unable to think. Then it may retreat from these pains by withdrawal of attention within the confines of its foetal membranes, the walls of the uterus, or its own skin, in an invertebrate way. Or it may seek to take in some comforting substance from the placenta, or to swallow the amniotic fluid, or to find something like a finger or toe to suck, establishing thereby an internal alliance, a feeling of internal strength, an endo-skeletal mentality. The maternal state of mind may contribute to this choice of alternatives, as may, in particular, the intrusion, within the foetus' space, of the father's penis. But one way or another a certain mental disposition has already been established by "non-Mendelian" means prior to the "Caesura" of birth. Reaching out for helpful objects or retreating within his own skin by means of the deployment of his attention will determine within the early hour and days after birth the extent to which the beginnings of personality formation (the "protomental apparatus", the "soma-psychotic level", the "prenatal parts" of the personality) will be split off and kept separate from the structures of personality that subsequently develop.

The degree of severity of this splitting has very important consequences, both in terms of overall mental vitality and in terms of sensibility to the non-sensuous, purely emotional, impact of the environment. But it will also determine the degree to which the developing personality is able to be in touch with bodily processes and their potential meaning, as expressions of need or desire, of pleasure or pain, of fear or expectation. Since the infant is dependent upon the mother for assistance, through her capacity for reverie and the experiences of maternal care, especially feeding, for the inception of his capacity for symbol formation, dream thought, and the creation of meaning for the chaos of sensations and intuitions by which he is bombarded, limitations on his self-perception are a serious loss. They would correspondingly limit his capacity to communicate to the mother the kind of mental state of which she could help him to "make sense".

Correspondingly, from the very beginning the child's mental life is divided within the areas for which communication with a mothering person, subsequently internalized, enable him to dream and think, and other areas that remain unsymbolized. The potential experiences of these unsymbolized areas (protomental, etc.), remain at a level of raw *sensa* and *intuita* (beta elements), which cannot be thought about or stored as memory but must be evacuated in some manner. These evacuations characteristically take the form of hallucinations of a primitive sort, delusional notions, also very primitive, somatic sensations or malfunctions, or behaviour of a mindless sort. Among the possible mindless types of behaviour the least obtrusive is group or herd behaviour (basic assumption mentality).

Because these split-off prenatal aspects of the personality have no means of representing themselves through the media of dreams and phantasy, they are not available for transformation into other symbolic forms such as language or music or graphic arts. They are constantly trying to utilize alpha-function, but the pain and anxiety they engender result in their being turned back (alpha-function in reverse) with the production of mental phenomena (beta elements, with traces of ego and superego), which are the stuff of which hallucinations (organized) and delusions (also organized) and eventually delusional systems are made. If these processes of aborted thought could be assisted, integration of the prenatal aspects of vitality and sensibility could be reintegrated with the symbolic, thought-full area of the personality, thus also diminishing the pressure towards somatic, delusional, and hallucinatory expression.

But the great outlet of prenatal phenomena is through our un-thinking conformity, born of training and habit, to the standards of behaviour of our culture, class, group, or, at times, family. Many of these habits are beneficial (brushing one's teeth) and time-saving (routines undeterred by decision), but many involve us in tacit, or sometimes active, collusion with group processes of a primitive, destructive sort (war, prejudice, overeating, smoking, etc.) The tensions of anxiety encountered when attempting to replace these areas of compliance with observation, thought, judgement, and decision gives some indication of the internal problem. For just as the symbolic area has developed under the nurturing of family love (L, H, and K), privation and intolerance to mental pain has fostered another internal system of pseudo-symbol formation and pseudo-thought (minus L, minus H, minus K), which not only favours the preservation of the split between pre- and postnatal, between mind and body, but is continually striving to extend its hegemony. The anti-rational and the irrational aspects of the personality thus tend to come together, perhaps particularly in the form of political and religious fanaticism, and their close relatives, sexual perversion and psychopathy.

The task facing psychoanalysts, if they are to extend the range of the method they employ, is to carry it beyond the limits for which it has already been strongly equipped, namely to strengthen the integration of the healthy parts of the personality in the sphere of good internal objects. Although this method can succeed in limiting the inroads of irrationality into the object relations, internal and external, of the individual, it probably does very little to diminish the underlying irrational, primitive, and ill parts of the personality. Thus, as experience shows, it probably does very little to diminish the analysed person's liability to psycho-somatic illness, nor does it do much to enhance his capacity to function as a thoughtful individual in groups.

The extension of the range of the method is probably not so much dependent upon any amplification of theory as it is on an intensification of technique. This intensification involves the analyst in a greater abandonment to the emotional experience of the session from moment to moment, without the comforting and protective use of either recollections of past events in the analysis and the patient's history (memory) or striving towards formulated goals of therapy (desire). By this means, and by concentrating his attention on his observations (internal and external) and waiting for a pattern to make itself manifest, he may begin to "hear" the prenatals, in his own body, dreams, hallucinations, delusional ideas. By assisting these proto-mental phenomena to find symbolic form by his own (maternal) reverie, he may both perform a function and assist in the internalization of an augmented function of understanding.

CHAPTER THIRTY-ONE

The psychoanalytic process: twenty years on, the setting of the analytic encounter and the gathering of the transference

(1986)

In this lecture, originally given in Paris, the author gives account of the development of his ideas on the issues raised in his The Psycho-analytical Process *(1967a).*

In order to examine the changes in my views—twenty years of psychoanalytic practice, supervision and teaching having passed since publishing *The Psycho-analytical Process* (Meltzer, 1967a)—and since I have not, I confess, read the book for many years, I undertook first of all to give a series of conferences, all of which were improvised and recorded, revising one by one the subjects of each chapter. I then began to examine the validity of these spontaneous presentations. It might be useful to say that, in general, my views on the fundamental nature of psychoanalytic practice and the nature of the

Translated from *Journal de la Psychanalyse de l'Enfant* by Daniel Hahn.

psychoanalytic process have not changed. Many things of some interest could be added, however, and a certain change of emphasis may be noted. In this paper I will simply recall the outline of the contents of the original book, in order to focus primarily on the additions and modifications. As it is available in English, French, Italian, Spanish, and Portuguese, I will suppose the reader to be familiar with it.

In my opinion, the therapeutic method of psychoanalysis is based on the patient's capacity to experience a transference relationship, and to tolerate if not actively to participate in his analyst's description and investigation of this transference relationship. The therapeutic benefit for the patient is found in the evolution of the transference, an evolution that depends above all on the meeting of the transference with a congruent countertransference, which the patient can recognize and use towards a goal of comprehension rather than action. My experience as a young analyst, and the subsequent continuation of that experience during 35 years of practice and of teaching young analysts, have convinced me that the precision of understanding, and therefore of interpretation, is not the crucial factor that brings about the evolution of the transference, but one of the quantitative factors in the economy in which development can take place. By establishing a distinction between "modulation" and "modification" of anxiety, I basically tended to attribute "modification" to the analyst's process of interpretation, a point of view to which I no longer subscribe. I would now consider the correct description of the functions of interpretation in terms of richness, clarity, and economy, rather than in terms of the evolution of the transference. The "modification" of anxiety seems, rather, to depend on the actual evolution of the configuration of the transference.

Bearing in mind this fundamental change in perspective, we can now move on to the examination of the setting of the analytic work and of its first impact, which I called "the gathering of the transference". Although the original text was written primarily for analysts dealing with children, for whom the movement of the analytic process seemed to emerge most clearly, I did not entirely realize at that point, when a large proportion of analytic work with children was being conducted in private practices, the existence of certain difficulties peculiar to institutional work in child-guidance clinics, hospitals, schools, and day centres. During these last 20 years, when the decline in the training of child analysts in psychoanalytic institutes was paralleled by the growth of child psychotherapy as a profession, first in this country and then across the whole of western Europe, a large proportion of analytic work has become institutionally based. The tradition of "teamwork", the need to communicate with colleagues, the difficulty of avoiding the bombardment of information concerning the child's life outside the consulting-room, the intrusion of secretaries for the purpose of communication, the need to produce reports, and the limitations on the frequency of sessions all hinder the establishment of the intimacy and isolation that are essential to the analytic process. For adolescents and older patients, an institutional setting creates yet another problem—that of the transference *vis-à-vis* the institution itself, of which the therapist tends to be considered no more than a representative, controlled by the hierarchy, whether this be real or imaginary.

Nevertheless, laying aside these problems, which apply only to institutional work, the dominant themes of the text still hold intimacy, regularity, simplicity. However, the original description of the setting now seems much more rigid and restricted than my current practice. For example, I now prefer to begin analysis gradually, with two or three sessions per week, and to increase this number when the need becomes clear both to the patient and to myself. My long experience of sessions at different times of the day—an experience due to the fact that I practise in two locations (London and Oxford)—has made it absolutely clear to me that arranging each session at the same time of day is preferable. I always prefer a rather small room, bare of any objects that may prove distracting, but I consider this a question of style. I find it convenient to give the patient sight of a window, whether or not this means that people will come into his field of vision. I always prefer my armchair to be behind and to the side of the patient, so that I can see his face in profile. I still prefer to have neither a telephone nor a clock in the room. I am absolutely convinced that an analyst who works at his own home places a useless burden on his patients, a burden of feelings of exclusion, curiosity, and confusion. With very sick patients it may even become a crucial element in their tolerating the analytic situation. On the other hand, I am much more willing to change the time of a session to accommodate a patient, unless past experience has shown such an arrangement to have a negative therapeutic effect. On the whole, I do suggest that young therapists work in a context that is fairly rigorous.

As for choosing patients, I have lost all faith in the possibility of doing so intelligently, apart from cases of psychotic patients who lack a clear means of support in their environment. The information that comes out of a psychiatric evaluation provides very little scope for predicting the probability of the patient's benefiting from the analysis. In general, I find it better to refer to someone else patients who come to me for an evaluation or a consultation. When I deal with the logistic arrangements of someone who has been sent to me for treatment, I find it better to leave the matter of fees until the end, but if it is dealt with, the analyst should be prepared to accept whatever the patient feels himself able to pay. I generally ask the patient to calculate the figure on a forty-week-per-year basis, and to divide the weekly total by the number of sessions we agree to start with. This happens in cases when the patient has neither enough money nor the possibility of his parents' support. If a patient happens to pay below the analyst's usual fee, this means that the analyst is subsidizing him and must be careful, during the course of the analysis, to ensure that the situation is realistic and is neither indulgent nor the object of deceit. Dealing with the question of fees in this way makes it possible to separate the matters of finance and the frequency of sessions. It goes without saying that the analyst should not subsidize his patient's immorality.

There is another reason for dealing in this logistic way with a patient referred to us: it eliminates any possible hint of selection, and thus reduces the atmosphere of mutual idealization, which, as far as the preformed transference is concerned, can lead to a serious inhibition of the incipient analytic process. It is probably better to set a date for the analysis to begin, rather than letting the initial logistic session become an analytic one. Information about holiday dates should be provided at that point, as should the analyst's policies on changing times and payment for missed sessions. However, I tend to keep for the first session of analysis the explanation of the use, the advantage, and the *raison d'être* of the couch, the basic principles of the analytic method that the analyst hopes to communicate to the patient, and the instructions concerning what is considered the fundamental rule (report whatever you observe is going on in your mind or body), as well as explaining the importance of dreams.

I much prefer to make it clear that beginning analysis is an experimental process, to "work together for a term at the very least, in order to determine whether we can put the analytic process into practice"; in this way, the patient is also given some room for manoeuvre, in case he might not like his analyst's method or style of work and communication. This is also necessary, because the fact that many people come to analysis uninformed feeds the general impression that being in analysis gives *carte blanche* for dishonest or sexual acting out.

Of course, all these matters of logistics and style are negligible when compared with the most important factor, which consists in the analyst's state of mind and the atmosphere he is capable of creating and maintaining in his consulting-room. To draw up a comprehensive list of the qualities needed for maintaining the psychoanalytic attitude would seem superfluous. These are, simply, parental qualities, with the emphasis on kindness, patience, and unintrusiveness. The analyst can only be sure of maintaining the private aspect of other areas of intimate relationships of the patient if he follows the material without ever seeking to direct it. If freedom of investigation is a concession the patient must make to his analyst, this freedom must be limited to the patient's material and must not be used to satisfy the analyst's curiosity. Above all, the analyst must have absolute conviction that therapeutic effectiveness stems from the analytic method and the patient's tendency to development, and not on some curative power of the analyst. It is equally important for the analyst to remember that his mind and character are exposed to his patient no less than the patient's are to his analyst. In order to support the transference during the long period of time necessary for an analysis, the analyst must, to a certain extent, deserve the interest, and even the love, that surrounds him; as for the hatred and suspicion, he deserves them only as a result of the inequality of a dependent relationship.

The establishing of such a setting—or of what Melanie Klein called "the analytic situation"—gives rise to a certain movement and a certain disruption in relationships that the patient has established in the world outside his analysis. This usually reaches a certain intensity, when a disturbance becomes noticeable in the patient's internal world. This change in external object relations results in the gradual freeing of infantile components that contaminate the more mature aspects of the relationship. This is as true for children and adolescents as it is for adults, but of these three types of patient progress is generally much slower in adolescents. The adolescent's infantile transference to his parents and to the adult community is generally maintained in a state of suspended animation, due to the excessive splitting and projective identification with the adolescent community, their attitudes, their groupings, and their goals.

As this infantile transference is freed, bit by bit, it "comes home" on its own, so to speak, like Little Bo-Peep's sheep, attracted by the atmosphere of the consulting-room, and visibly affected by the suffering resulting from the interruption of the usual rhythm of sessions during weekends and holidays. It is this return "home" that I call "the gathering of the transference", in an intransitive sense, as one might speak of "the gathering of the clans in Scotland". As this infantile transference gradually begins to appear in the material in the form of bits of "acting in" or "acting out", of memories or dreams, their recognition and investigation sets in motion the analytic process.

CHAPTER THIRTY-TWO

Concerning the distinction between conflicts of desire and paradoxes of thought

(1987)

The author concerns himself with the aesthetic experience and postulates that conflict (between love and hate) is to emotional disorders what paradoxes are to thought disorders, when there is an impingement of –K on K.

It was with obvious relish that Freud listed himself, along with Copernicus and Darwin, among those thinkers who have contributed to the shattering of man's elitist conception of his nature and of his place in the universe. Taken in that sense, that these figures have attacked and destroyed old misconceptions, their unpopularity, for which Freud was attempting to account, seems quite intelligible. But it misses the central issue, which Wilfred Bion has focused attention upon, of the unpopularity of the new idea that they introduced. If we accept this focus, we are likely to realize that these thinkers did not shatter old ideas but revealed the emptiness that had been covered over by confabulation, as in the story of the Emperor's New Clothes.

This type of conceptual emptiness is always with us, clothed, if not with expressed confabulation, then with tacit assumptions so unvoiced that it is difficult to discover them. They belong to the basic assumptions that Bion suggested were the point of origins of group behaviour—tacit basic assumptions from which actions could be derived by simple logical operations without recourse to the arduous and anxious business of observation, thought, judgement, and decision.

The work of psychoanalysts, following the lead of Freud and Abraham, in the first half century of this science worked with the tacit assumption of the unity of the mind and the logical conclusion that the illnesses as well as the follies of men were to be understood, as Socrates would have agreed, on the basis of the economics of mental pleasure and pain, modified, or, rather, disguised by recognition of external reality. At the end of his life Freud saw that this was not true, that the mind can split itself, and Melanie Klein's 1946 paper on schizoid mechanisms put this into a conceptual form that could be used in the consulting-room. To some extent the simplicity of the Socratic assumption that a man, given the choice, would always choose the good was brought into question, both in the form of the hypothesis of a death instinct, but more pregnantly by the recognition of the issue of confusion of identity in masochism and depressive states.

But it remained to Bion to reveal the emptiness of the assumption that the mind thinks, that it is a thinking machine that naturally functions, albeit with some differential of acuity and complexity, given that the neuroanatomical apparatus is intact and the general bodily physiology is in an homeostatic condition. That this new revelation of conceptual nakedness threatens to swamp us with complex and frightening realizations about ourselves and our fellow creatures is not so much evidenced by positive signs of catastrophic anxiety as it is in keeping with Bion's prediction, by his being "loaded with honours and sunk without a trace"—that is, a trace of his "imaginative conjectures".

There is no doubt about it, Bion's ideas have revealed a new continent of the mind, previously thought to be the brain, and a dense jungle filled with primitive creatures it surely begins to show itself to be. Of course we are now very blasé about the "unconscious" of dreams and infantile sexuality and violence that so alarmed our Edwardian forbears. A late evening of television bears ample witness to this. But if you watch carefully, you will see that it is not merely sexuality, perversity, violence, and delusion that is being depicted for entertainment; there is something else, which the finer artists like Pinter or Beckett have caught the scent of on the wind. It has been hard enough for human beings to shed the concept of God, to allow for meaningless, random factors to play a role in the lives of men; but now to acknowledge that man himself can behave in meaningless, senseless ways is more than we can bear. The denial of the problem, in true keeping with the negative grid and –K, has invented a pseudo-anxiety: what if there are super-intelligent creatures on other planets? what if computers and automata become more intelligent than man?

Perhaps it should not surprise us that the philosophers, who have been so behindhand in acknowledging and understanding the area of emotions and their place in our lives, have been in the forefront in recognizing this problem. But, characteristically, they have done so in so sterilized and hypothetical a way that its impact has hardly even been felt as the proverbial whiff of grapeshot. Nevertheless, it is to them that we must look for help with this problem, for its linguistic presentation has been very intelligently explored. The exploration of language is of such major importance not because other symbolic forms are unimpaired by the invasion of meaninglessness, but because it is in the transformations of a verbal sort that the problem can be most accurately identified and dissected. It is particularly with those aspects of language which relate to different levels of abstraction that the philosophers, Russell in particular, have made such progress. Also with the concept of the paradox and its essential senselessness, based as it is on a confusion of levels of abstraction (meta-languages), we find the most fruitful analogy to the problems met with in the consulting-room.

That is to say, what conflict of love and hate (ambivalence) is for emotional disorders, paradox is for the thought disorders. In paradox, we meet the impingement of –K on K, the thirst and quest for knowledge. It is important to realize that emotion plays as major a role here, as it does in the area of infantile conflicts of ambivalence, but they are modalities of emotion that we are unaccustomed to observe or to pay attention to when patients can name them. And yet we experience them ourselves in the course of our work, and they play a part in the countertransference. On the positive side, I would name the emotion "the thrill of understanding", the "Eureka" of Demosthenes, the "Now I can go on" of Wittgenstein. And I would say that the response is essentially aesthetic, that understanding and "seeing the beauty" are indistinguishable. What desire is to the emotional links of L and H, valuing is to the K link, devoid of possessiveness. In fact, quite to the contrary, the aesthetic experience in the K link carries with it a very powerful impulse to share the apprehension of beauty with at least one other mind. For this reason, the emotionality of the K link has the same generative power with respect to the work group as L and H have to the formation of the family. When the K link arises within the parental couple linked by L and H, their relationship to the children takes on a new observatory and thoughtful quality, which makes the family into a work group and protects it from its tendency, under stress, to revert either to a gang or basic assumption organization.

But on the negative side of emotions, the attacks by the negative grid on the capacity for thought and understanding undermine the sense of value. The paradoxical juxtapositions that it furnishes, by subverting meaning, sense, significance, produce a type of despair and loss of interest that is quite different from the despair that comes from relinquishing hope of possessing the love object, the Kierkegaardian or Hamlet either–or type of despair.

CHAPTER THIRTY-THREE

Concerning the stupidity of evil

(1988)

A recapitulation of the formulation of the aesthetic conflict and a reformulation of the concept of envy, which is described as an urge to interfere with the object's capacity for passionate experiences.

"He hath a daily beauty in his life/That makes me ugly", says Iago of Cassio (Shakespeare's "Othello", Act V, Scene 1). Iago is not referring to Desdemona or Bianca. The "daily beauty" is an inner beauty of innocence and good will, which he also discerns in Othello and exploits to his destruction. In a recent study (Meltzer, 1988) I explored the conflict incited by the beauty of the world, and its primal representation—the breast and face of the feeding mother. This conflict, aroused by the impact of the manifest external forms and the ambiguous internal mental state (feelings, intentions, attitudes) of the object of attachment, may be thought of as activated in the new-born, arousing passionate emotions, of love, of hate, of a yearning to know the inside of the object, its "heart of mystery".

This formulation would appear to be an inevitable extrapolation of the model of the mind developed in that line of research leading from Freud through Abraham to Melanie Klein and Bion. Building upon Freud's four-part metapsychology, Klein added a fifth dimension, the geographic, by defining the concreteness of psychic reality as a psychic space, a world different in its laws and qualities from the external world. This was amplified in the 1946 paper on schizoid mechanisms by the implication of still another world inside objects, their internal world. Penetration into this private world, through the omnipotent phantasy of projective identification, was gradually revealed by the researches of the following 40 years to be a major factor in the structuring of psychopathology.

Bion's famous pre-psychoanalytic work on groups brought a rapprochement between the psychology of the individual and of social organizations, which later developed into his amplification of the model of the mind. He recognized that personality is structured with both an outer exoskeleton for adaptation to the casual and contractual relations of daily life, operating by signs, and the interior endoskeleton of emotional relationships and meaning, operating through symbol formation. His theory of thinking relates to the latter, mentality proper, while he considered the former, the exoskeletal structures, to be a protomental apparatus. The mental apparatus grows through the digestion of emotional events, learning from experience. The protomental apparatus evolves by training processes. The most important emotional experiences that contribute to the development of the mind are those of a passionate quality, in which love, hatred, and the thirst for the truth are held in integration and not split onto separate objects.

Clinical experience, particularly with young psychotic children, has suggested the theory of aesthetic conflict as a primal developmental event. The painful state of uncertainty about the congruence of the external form of objects (the beauty of the world) and the enigmatic interior qualities is defended against by splitting the passionate response. This is effected in the spirit of revulsion from emotion itself, anti-emotion (Bion's –L, H, and K). Under this theory of emotion, which sees emotion confronted by anti-emotion rather than love confronted by hatred, Melanie Klein's formulation on envy finds a new base. I would formulate primal envy not as the breast-that-feeds-itself, for instance, but as an urge to interfere with the object's capacity for passionate experience, and thus with the relationship to truth. Bion has suggested that *The Grid* (1989) for describing the processes by which emotional experiences are digested into true thoughts may be paralleled by a negative Grid for the construction of lies.

But whereas truthful thought is imaginative and constructs symbols by which dream thought can be evolved and transformed, into language and other symbolic forms (Cassirer), a negative grid would operate by means of the simple techniques of mimicry and negation. The categories of anti-emotion, –L (Puritanism), anti-hate (hypocrisy), and anti-knowledge (philistinism) can be seen thus to be essentially stupid in their operation.

Insofar as individuals have sacrificed their capacity for passionate response to the beauty of the world, they are prey to the envy of others who seem to have "a daily beauty in their lives", an inner beauty. But here again stupidity mistakes outward form for inner beauty and sees "secrets of success" instead of a "heart of mystery".

CHAPTER THIRTY-FOUR

Narcissism and violence in adolescents

(1989)

The replacement of the family for a political structure and the blunting of aesthetic sensibilities generates violence in adolescence.

The second post-war generation has now reached adolescence, and the present adolescent community is the first to have been raised in the atmosphere of the sexual revolution following the turbulence of 1968. The changes in values and behaviour help us to separate out the cultural from the intrinsic factors in the adolescent state of mind. Gone is the Romantic Agony of the nineteenth century, but also gone is the tendency to fall in love. Instead of the expectation that love will lead to sexual intimacy, today's young people expect that the sexual activity will ripen into love. The earlier predatory pubertal gang sexual behaviour, in which the boys boasted to their fellows of the conquests and the girls flaunted their capacity to attract and frustrate the boys, has given way to a more athletic mental-hygiene approach with mutual seduction. The brutality of "fucking" has yielded to the triviality of "bonking". In its openness it has replaced the secrecy of masturbation.

Unfortunately, the young people who come to analysis are largely those who stand outside the active adolescent community for reasons of psychopathology. They yield us information about their incapacities but very little insight into the essential nature of the adolescent state of mind. This we have to gather at the other end of the analytic population, the people who cannot emerge from the adolescent community, its values, behaviour, and state of mind. They comprise primarily the upwardly mobile "yuppie" who comes for training, the ambisexual who cannot shake off his perversion, the woman who operated on the basis of negative identification with her mother in her attempt to raise her children. They have an adequately adjusted social carapace and yield themselves to the infantile transference with difficulty. But from them we reap a rich insight into the state of mind beyond which they have been unable to progress, despite evident success in their progress up the social ladder. They have been well adjusted indeed to the adolescent community, and its charms still hold them.

The picture of adolescent life-style that slowly emerges is one in which the concept of family has been replaced by a political structure of benevolent patriarchal or matriarchal quasi-democracy and socialism, in which the ideal of justice through understanding has been replaced by egalitarianism between grown-ups and children. The essence of this political system is the denial of the development of judgement through experience. As a consequence, systematic self-effacement by the grown-ups is aimed at dispelling any sense in the children that the parents are in possession of mysterious knowledge and powers, and therefore suitable objects of transference from the figures of psychic reality. Common sense and the capacity to argue for the fulfilment of desires is valued and encouraged in the children, with consequent stifling of imagination and emotionality, tenderness, and dependence.

This political concept of family life, which forms the conceptual background of both their adolescent rebellion and their later attempts to form their own family, has hidden in it a complete confusion between private and secret. This is central to the denial of psychic reality. Having thus cut themselves off from the infantile level of dependence on internal objects, which stand accused of elitism, tyranny, and mystification, they are thrown into a slavish dependence upon the company of their fellows, in which a homogeneity of opinion and attitude provides a snugness that substitutes for an internally generated sense of security—that is, a feeling of readiness to face the consequences of their individual judgement and decisions. The upshot of this dependence upon their fellows is a value system in which success is the ultimate arbiter and values become cynically relative to the culture. This is nowhere clearer than in the loss of aesthetic sense and its replacement by fashion. It must be stressed that this is not only evidenced as a rebellion against or criticism of their original families in particular, but against the culture of which their parents were exemplary. It carries, therefore, the banner of revolution rather than of rebellion. The sanctimony is daunting. Just how this politicizing of family life and values and the blunting of aesthetic sensibilities generates violence requires a considerable exposition.

REFERENCES

Abraham, K. (1911). Notes on the Psycho-Analytic Investigation and Treatment of Manic-Depressive Insanity and Allied Conditions. In: *Selected Papers*. London: Hogarth Press, 1973. [Reprinted London: Karnac Books, 1979.]

Abraham, K. (1924). A Short Study of the Development of the Libido, Viewed in the Light of Mental Disorders. In: *Selected Papers*. London: Hogarth Press, 1973. [Reprinted London: Karnac Books, 1979.]

Ackerman, N. (1953). Psychopathology of Childhood. In: P. N. Hoch & J. Zubin, *Child and Family Psychotherapy: Problems of Correlation*. New York/London: Grune & Stratton.

Alvarez, A. (1971). *The Savage God*. Weidenfeld & Nicolson.

Angel, A. (1934). Einige Bemerkungen über den Optimismus. *Int. Z. für Psychoanal.*, *20*: 191–199.

Betz, B. (1947). A Study of Tactics for Reaching the Autistic Barrier in the Psychotherapy of the Schizophrenic Personality. *Am. J. Psychiatry*, *104*: 267.

Bibring, G. (1964). Some Considerations Regarding the Ego Ideal in the Psychoanalytic Process. *Journal of the American Psychoanalytic Association*, *12*: 517–521.

Bick, E. (1968). The Function of the Skin in Early Object Relations. *International Journal of Psycho-Analysis, 49* (2, 3): 484–486.

Bion, W. R. (1961). *Experiences in Groups and Other Papers.* London: Tavistock.

Bion, W. R. (1962). *Learning from Experience.* London: Heinemann. [Reprinted London: Karnac Books, 1984.].

Bion, W. R. (1963). *Elements of Psycho-Analysis.* London: Heinemann. [Reprinted London: Karnac Books, 1984.]

Bion, W. R. (1965). *Transformations: Change from Learning to Growth.* London: Heinemann. [Reprinted London: Karnac Books, 1984.]

Bion, W. R. (1967). *Second Thoughts.* London: Heinemann. [Reprinted London: Karnac Books, 1984.]

Bion, W. R. (1970). *Attention and Interpretation.* London: Tavistock. [Reprinted London: Karnac Books, 1984.]

Bion, W. R. (1973). *Brazilian Lectures, Vol. 1.* Rio de Janeiro: Imago Editore. [Also in *Brazilian Lectures.* London: Karnac Books, 1990.]

Bion, W. R. (1974). *Brazilian Lectures, Vol. 2.* Rio de Janeiro: Imago Editore. [Also in *Brazilian Lectures.* London: Karnac Books, 1990.]

Bion, W. R. (1975). *The Dream (A Memoir of the Future, Vol. 1).* Rio de Janeiro, Brazil: Imago Editora. [Also in: *A Memoir of the Future.* London: Karnac Books, 1990.]

Bion, W. R. (1975–81). *A Memoir of the Future.* London: Karnac Books, 1990.

Bion, W. R. (1977). *The Past Presented (A Memoir of the Future, Vol. 2).* Rio de Janeiro, Brazil: Imago Editora. [Also in: *A Memoir of the Future.* London: Karnac Books, 1990.]

Bion, W. R. (1979). *The Dawn of Oblivion (A Memoir of the Future, Vol. 3).* Strathclyde, Perthshire: Clunie Press. [Also in: *A Memoir of the Future.* London: Karnac Books, 1990.]

Bion, W. R. (1982). *The Long Weekend—1897–1919.* Oxford: Fleetwood Press.

Bion, W. R. (1989). *Two Papers: The Grid and Caesura.* London: Karnac Books.

Bleuler, E. (1916). *A Textbook of Psychiatry.* London: Allen & Unwin, 1923.

Brunswick, R. M. (1928). A Supplement to Freud's "History of an Infantile Neurosis". *International Journal of Psycho-Analysis*, *9*: 439–476.

Chasseguet-Smirgel, G. (1973). L'ideal du moi. *Revue Française de Psychanalyse*, *37*: 709–929.

Clapham, J. H. (1949). *A Concise Economic History of Great Britain*. Cambridge: Cambridge University Press.

Despert, L. (1951). Some Considerations Relating to the Genesis of Autistic Behavior in Children. *Am. J. Orthopsych.*, *21*: 335.

Deutsch, H. (1928). On Contentment, Happiness and Ecstasy. *Psychoanal. Rev.*, *15*: 90

Deutsch, H. (1930). Melancholic and Depressive States. In: *Psycho-Analysis of the Neuroses*. London: Hogarth Press, 1932.

Deutsch, H. (1933). Psychologie der manisch-depressiven Zustände insbesondere der chronischen Hypomanie. *Int. Z. fur Psychoanal.*, *19*: 358–371.

Deutsch, H. (1964). Some Clinical Considerations of the Ego Ideal. *Journal of the American Psychoanalytic Association*, *12*: 512–516.

Eisler, R. (1929). *The Messiah Jesus and John the Baptist* (translated by A. H. Krappe). London, 1931.

Empson, W. (1951). *The Structure of Complex Words*. London: Chatto & Windus.

Erikson, E. H. (1950). *Childhood and Society*. New York: Norton.

Fenichel, O. (1934). Defence against Anxiety, Particularly by Libidinization. *Collected Papers, 1*. London: Routledge & Kegan Paul, 1954.

Fenichel, O. (1939). The Counterphobic Attitude. *Int. J. Psycho-Anal.*, *20*: 263–275. [Also in: *Collected Papers, 2*. London: Routledge & Kegan Paul, 1955.]

Fenichel, O. (1939). Trophy and Triumph. In: *Collected Papers, 2*. London: Routledge & Kegan Paul, 1955.

Ferenczi, S. (1926). *Final Contributions to Psycho-analysis*. London: Hogarth Press, 1950. [Reprinted London: Karnac Books, 1980.]

Freud, S. (1895d) [with Breuer, J.]. *Studies on Hysteria*. *S.E.*, *2*.

Freud, S. (1905e [1901]). Fragment of an Analysis of a Case of Hysteria. *S.E.*, *7*.

Freud, S. (1908b). Character and Anal Erotism. *S.E.*, *9*.

Freud, S. (1909b). Analysis of a Phobia in a Five-Year-Old Boy. *S.E., 10.*

Freud, S. (1910c). *Leonardo da Vinci and a Memory of His Childhood, S.E., 11.*

Freud, S. (1911b). Formulations on the Two Principles of Mental Functioning. *S.E., 12.*

Freud, S. (1911c [1910]). Psycho-Analytic Notes on an Autobiographical Account of a Case of Paranoia. *S.E., 12.*

Freud, S. (1914c). On Narcissism: An Introduction. *S.E., 14.*

Freud, S. (1916d). Some Character-Types Met with in Psycho-Analytic Work. *S.E., 14.*

Freud, S. (1917e [1915]). Mourning and Melancholia. *S.E., 14.*

Freud, S. (1918b [1914]). From the History of an Infantile Neurosis. *S.E., 17.*

Freud, S. (1920g). *Beyond the Pleasure Principle. S.E., 18.*

Freud, S. (1921c). *Group Psychology and the Analysis of the Ego. S.E., 18.*

Freud, S. (1923b). *The Ego and the Id. S.E.,* 19.

Freud, S. (1924c). The Economic Problem of Masochism. *S.E., 19.*

Freud, S. (1925h). Negation. *S.E., 19.*

Freud, S. (1927e). Fetishism. *S.E., 21.*

Freud, S. (1933a). *New Introductory Lectures on Psycho-Analysis. S.E., 22.*

Freud, S. (1937c). Analysis Terminable and Interminable. *S.E., 23.*

Freud, S. (1940e [1938]). Splitting of the Ego in the Process of Defence. *S.E., 23.*

Freud, S. (1950a [1887–1902]). Project for a Scientific Psychology. *S.E., 1.*

Glover, E. (1933). A Psycho-analytic Approach to the Classification of Mental Disorders. *International Journal of Psycho-Analysis, 14* (1): 110–111.

Grunberger, B. (1973). Ideal du Moi et Surmoi precoce. *Revue Française de Psychanalyse, 37*: 959–967.

Hartmann, H., & Loewenstein, R. M. (1962). Notes on the Superego. *Psychoanalytic Study of the Child,* 17: 42–81.

Hoch, P. N. & Zubin, J. (1954). *Child and Family Psychotherapy: Problems of Correlation.* New York/London: Grune & Stratton.

Isaacs, S. (1952). The Nature and Function of Phantasy. In: M. Klein, P. Heimann, S. Isaacs, & J. Riviere, *Developments in*

Psycho-Analysis (J. Riviere, Ed.) (pp. 67–121). London: Hogarth Press, 1952. [Reprinted London: Karnac Books, 1989.]

Jacobson, E. (1946). The effect of disappointment on ego and superego formation in normal and depressive development. *Psychoanalytic Review*, 33: 129–147.

Jacobson, E. (1957). Normal and Pathological Moods: Their Nature and Functions. *Psychoanalytic Study of the Child, 12*. New York: International Universities Press.

Jacobson, E. (1964). *The Self and the Object World*. New York: International Universities Press.

Jaques, E. (1951). *The Changing Culture of a Factory*. London: Tavistock.

Jaques, E. (1961). *Equitable Payment*. London: Heinemann.

Jones, E. (1927). La conception du Surmoi. *Revue Française de Psychanalyse, 1*: 324–336.

Jones, E. (1948). Introduction. In: M. Klein, *Contributions to Psycho-Analysis, 1921–1945*. London: Hogarth Press.

Kanner, L. (1948). *Textbook of Child Psychiatry*. Oxford: Blackwell.

Kanner, L. (1949). Mental Deficiency. *Am. J. Psychiatry, 105*: 526.

Katan, M. (1940). Die Rolle des Wortes in der Schizophrenie und Manie. *Int. Z. Psychoanal., 25*. Abstract: *Psychoanal. Rev.* (1945), *32*: 138–173.

Klein, M. (1928). Early stages of the Oedipus Conflict. In: *Love, Guilt and Reparation and Other Works* (pp. 186–198). London: Hogarth Press, 1975. [Reprinted London: Karnac Books, 1992.]

Klein, M. (1932a). *The Psycho-Analysis of Children*. London: Hogarth Press.

Klein, M. (1932b). The Relations between Obsessional Neurosis and the Early Stages of the Superego. In: *The Psycho-Analysis of Children*. London: Hogarth Press, 1932.

Klein, M. (1935). A Contribution to the Psychogenesis of Manic-Depressive States. In: *Love, Guilt and Reparation and Other Works* (pp. 262–289). London: Hogarth Press, 1975. [Reprinted London: Karnac Books, 1992.]

Klein, M. (1940). Mourning and Its Relation to Manic-Depressive States. In: *Love, Guilt and Reparation and Other Works* (pp. 344–370). London: Hogarth Press, 1975. [Reprinted London: Karnac Books, 1992.]

Klein, M. (1942). Some Psychological Considerations: A Comment. In: *Envy and Gratitude and Other Works* (pp. 320–323). London: Hogarth Press, 1975. [Reprinted London: Karnac Books, 1993.]

Klein, M. (1946). Notes on Some Schizoid Mechanisms. *International Journal of Psychoanalysis, 27*: 99-110. Also in: *Envy and Gratitude and Other Works* (pp. 1–24). London: Hogarth Press, 1975. [Reprinted London: Karnac Books, 1993.]

Klein, M. (1948). *Contributions to Psycho-Analysis, 1921–1945.* London: Hogarth Press.

Klein, M. (1955). *Developments in Psycho-analysis.* London: Hogarth Press. [Reprinted London: Karnac Books, 1989.]

Klein, M. (1955). On Identification. In: *Envy and Gratitude and Other Works* (pp. 141–175). London: Hogarth Press, 1975. [Reprinted London: Karnac Books, 1993.]

Klein, M. (1957). Envy and Gratitude. In: *Envy and Gratitude and Other Works* (pp. 176–235). London: Hogarth Press; 1975. [Reprinted London: Karnac Books, 1993.]

Klein, M. (1958). On the Development of Mental Functioning. *International Journal of Psycho-Analysis, 39:* 84–90. [Also in: *Envy and Gratitude and Other Works* (pp. 236–246). London, Hogarth Press, 1975. Reprinted London: Karnac Books, 1993.]

Klein, M. (1961). *Narrative of a Child Analysis. Writings, IV:* London: Hogarth Press, 1975.

Klein, M. (1975). *Envy and Gratitude and Other Works.* London: Hogarth Press. [Reprinted London: Karnac Books, 1993.]

Klein, M., & Riviere, J. (1936). *Love, Hate and Reparation.* London: Hogarth Press.

Kramer, P. (1958). Note on One of the Preoedipal Roots of the Superego. *Journal of the American Psychoanalytic Association, 6*: 38–46.

Lampl De Groot, J. (1962). Ego Ideal and Superego. In: *The Development of the Mind.* New York: International Universities Press, 1965.

Laufer, M. (1964). Ego Ideal and Pseudo Ego Ideal in Adolescence. *Psychoanalytic Study of the Child, 19*: 196–221.

Lewin, B. (1932). The Analysis and Structure of a Transient Hypomania. *Psychoanal. Quart., 1*: 43–58.

Lewin, B. (1935). *A Dynamic Theory of Personality*. New York: McGraw-Hill.

Lewin, B. (1937). A Type of Neurotic Hypomanic Reaction. *Arch. Neurol. Psychiat.*, *37*.

Lewin, B. (1941). Comments on Hypomanic and Related States. *Psychoanal. Rev.*, *28*: 86–91.

Lewin, B. (1949). Mania and Sleep. *Psychoanal. Quart.*, *18*: 419–433 [Also in: *The Psychoanalysis of Elation*. New York: Norton, 1950.]

Lewin, B. (1950) *The Psychoanalysis of Elation*. New York: Norton.

Lewin, K. (1935). *A Dynamic Theory of Personality*. New York: McGraw-Hill.

Lipson, E. (1959). *The Economic History of England* (12th ed.). London: Adam & Charles Black.

Meltzer, D. (1963a). A Contribution to the Metapsychology of Cyclothymic States. *International Journal of Psycho-Analysis*, *44*, 83–96.

Meltzer, D. (1963b). Concerning the Social Basis of Art: A Dialogue with Donald Meltzer. In: A. Stokes, *Painting and the Inner World*. London: Tavistock.

Meltzer, D. (1964). The Differentiation of Somatic Delusions from Hypochondria. *International Journal of Psycho-Analysis*, *45*, 246–250.

Meltzer, D. (1966). The Relation of Anal Masturbation to Projective Identification. *International Journal of Psycho-Analysis*, *47*, 335. [Also in: E. B. Spillius (Ed.), *Melanie Klein Today*, *Vol. 1*. London: Routledge, 1988.]

Meltzer, D. (1967a) *The Psycho-analytical Process*. London: Heinemann. [Reprinted Strathclyde, Perthshire: Clunie Press, 1979.]

Meltzer, D. (1967b). Identification and Socialisation in Adolescents. *Contemporary Psycho-Analysis*, *3* (2): 96–103. [Also in: E. B. Spillius (Ed.), *Melanie Klein Today*, *Vol. 1*. London: Routledge, 1988.]

Meltzer, D. (1968). Terror, Persecution and Dread. *International Journal of Psycho-Analysis*, *49*, 396–400. [Also in: *Sexual States of Mind* (pp. 99–106). Strathclyde, Perthshire: Clunie Press, 1973; and in: E. B. Spillius (Ed.), *Melanie Klein Today*, *Vol. 1* (pp. 230–238). London: Routledge.]

Meltzer, D. (1973). *Sexual States of Mind.* Strathclyde, Perthshire: Clunie Press.

Meltzer, D. (1974). Mutism in Infantile Autism, Schizophrenia and Manic-Depressive States: The Correlation of Clinical Psychopathology and Linguistics. *International Journal of Psycho-Analysis, 55,* 397–404. [Also in: Meltzer et al., *Explorations in Autism.* Strathclyde, Perthshire: Clunie Press, 1975.]

Meltzer, D. (1977). Preface. In: D. Meltzer & E. O'Shaugnessy (Eds.), *The Collected Papers of Roger Money-Kyrle.* Strathclyde, Perthshire: Clunie Press, 1978.

Meltzer, D. (1978). *The Kleinian Development.* Strathclyde, Perthshire: Clunie Press.

Meltzer, D. (1984). *Dream Life: A Re-examination of Psychoanalytic Theory and Technique.* Strathclyde, Perthshire: Clunie Press.

Meltzer, D. (1986). *Studies in Extended Metapsychology.* Strathclyde, Perthshire: Clunie Press.

Meltzer, D. (1988). *The Apprehension of Beauty.* Strathclyde, Perthshire: Clunie Press.

Meltzer, D. (1992). *The Claustrum: An Investigation of Claustrophobic Phenomena.* Strathclyde, Perthshire: Clunie Press.

Meltzer, D., Bremner, J., Hoxter, S., Wedell, D., & Wittenberg, I. (1975). *Explorations in Autism.* Strathclyde, Perthshire: Clunie Press.

Money-Kyrle, R. M. (1951). *Psycho-Analysis and Politics.* London: Duckworth.

Money-Kyrle, R. M. (1961). *Man's Picture of His World.* London: Duckworth.

Money-Kyrle, R. M. (1963). A Note on Migraine. *International Journal of Psycho-Analysis, 44,* 490–492. [Also in: *The Collected Papers of Roger Money-Kyrle* (pp. 361–365). Strathclyde, Perthshire: Clunie Press, 1978.]

Money-Kyrle, R. M. (1968). Cognitive Development. *International Journal of Psycho-Analysis, 49, 691–698.* [Also in: *The Collected Papers of Roger Money-Kyrle* (pp. 416–433). Strathclyde, Perthshire: Clunie Press, 1978].

Money-Kyrle, R. M. (1978). *The Collected Papers of Roger Money-Kyrle.* D. Meltzer & E. O'Shaugnessy (Eds.). Strathclyde, Perthshire: Clunie Press.

Murray, J. (1964). Narcissism and the Ego-Ideal. *Journal of the American Psychoanalytic Association, 12*: 477–511.

Nunberg, H. (1932). *Principes de Psychanalyse*. Paris: Presses Universitaires de France.

Pinter, H. (1959). *The Birthday Party*. London: Methuen, 1961. [Reprinted London: Faber & Faber, 1991.]

Pinter, H. (1961). The Dwarfs. In: *A Slight Ache and Other Plays*. London: Methuen.

Pinter, H. (1965). The Homecoming. In: *A Slight Ache and Other Plays*. London: Methuen. [Reprinted London: Faber & Faber, 1991.]

Pinter, H. (1961). *A Slight Ache and Other Plays*. London: Methuen.

Power, E. (1924). *Medieval People* (10th ed.). London: Methuen, 1963.

Putnam, M. (1948). Case Study of a Two and a Half Year Old. Round Table. *Am. J. Orthopsych., 18*, 1–30.

Rado, S. (1928). The Problem of Melancholia. *International Journal of Psycho-Analysis, 9*: 420–438.

Rank, B. (1949). Adaptation of the Psychoanalytic Technique for the Treatment of Young Children with Atypical Development. *Am. J. Orthopsych., 19:* 130.

Reich, A. (1954). Early Identifications as Archaic Elements in the Superego. *Journal of the American Psychoanalytic Association, 2*: 218–238.

Ribble, M. (1951). Some Considerations Relating to the Genesis of Autistic Behavior in Children: Dicussion. *Am. J. Orthopsych., 21*: 347.

Rosenfeld, H. (1958). Some Observations on the Psychopathology of Hypochondriacal States. *International Journal of Psycho-Analysis, 39, 121–124.*

Rosenfeld, H. (1962). The Superego and the Ego-Ideal. *International Journal of Psychoanalysis, 43*: 258–263. [Also in: *Psychotic States*. London: Hogarth Press, 1965. Reprinted London: Karnac Books, 1982.]

Rosenfeld, H. (1965). *Psychotic States*. London: Hogarth Press. [Reprinted London: Karnac Books, 1982.]

Russell, B. (1940). *An Inquiry into Meaning and Truth*. London: Allen & Unwin.

Sartre, J.-P. (1963 [1960]). *The Problem of Method.* New York: Knopf.

Schilder, P. (1933). Notes on Psychogenic Depression and Melancholia. *Psychoanal. Rev., 20*: 10–18.

Schilder, P. (1938). The Psychological Effects of Benzedrene Sulfate. *J. Nerv. Ment. Dis., 87*: 10–18.

Schilder, P. (1942). *Mind: Perception and Thought in Their Constructive Aspects.* New York: Columbia University Press.

Schilder, P. (1950). *The Image and Appearance of the Human Body.* New York: International Universities Press.

Segal, H. (1964). *Introduction to the Work of Melanie Klein.* London: Hogarth Press. [Reprinted London: Karnac Books, 1988].

Stokes, A. (1973). On Pornography. In: D. Meltzer, *Sexual States of Mind.* Strathclyde: Clunie Press.

Stokes, A. (1963). *Painting and the Inner World.* London: Tavistock.

Sullivan, H. S. (1953). *The Interpersonal Theory of Psychiatry.* New York: W. W. Norton.

Sullivan, H. S. (1963). *Conceptions of Modern Psychiatry.* New York: Norton.

Trevelyan, G. M. (1942). *English Social History.* London: Longman, Green.

Wiener, N. (1948). *Cybernetics.* New York: Wiley.

Wittgenstein, L. A. P. (1973). *Philosophical Investigations.* Oxford: Blackwell.

CHRONOLOGICAL LIST
OF BOOKS WRITTEN BY DONALD MELTZER

1967 *The Psycho-analytical Process*. London: Heinemann. Clunie Press.

1973 *Sexual States of Mind*. Clunie Press.

1975 (with J. Bremner, S. Hoxter, D. Wedell, & I. Wittenberg) *Explorations in Autism: A Psychoanalytic Study*. Clunie Press.

1978 *The Kleinian Development*. Clunie Press.

1981 *La comprensione della bellezza e altri saggi di psicoanalisi*. Loescher Editore.

1984 *Dream Life: A Re-examination of Psychoanalytic Theory and Technique*. Clunie Press.

1986 *Studies in Extended Metapsychology: A Clinical Application of Bion's Ideas*. Clunie Press.

1988 (with Meg Harris Williams) *The Apprehension of Beauty: The Role of Aesthetic Conflict in Development, Art and Violence*. Clunie Press.

1992 *The Claustrum: An Investigation of Claustrophobic Phenomena*. Clunie Press.

INDEX